FOUR REIGNS
(SI PHAENDIN)

FOUR REIGNS

(SI PHAENDIN)

by

KUKRIT PRAMOJ

ENGLISH VERSION

by

TULACHANDRA

Silkworm Books

สี่แผ่นดิน โดย หม่อมราชวงศ์คึกฤทธิ์ ปราโมช

© 1953 by M.R. Kukrit Pramoj
English translation © 1981 by Chancham Bunnag

ISBN 978-984-7100-66-2

This edition first published in 1998 by

Silkworm Books
6 Sukkasem Road, T. Suthep
Chiang Mai 50200, Thailand.
www.silkwormbooks.com
E-mail: info@silkwormbooks.com

Cover design by Trasvin Jittidejarak
Cover graphic by Woraphong Yuhun
Set in 10.5 pt. Garamond by Silk Type

Printed in Thailand by O.S. Printing House, Bangkok.

10 9 8 7

PREFACE

There comes a time in a man's life when he feels the urge to set down in writing the modes and mores of a disappearing age, of which he was a part, however small. I had this urge when I sat down to write this book in Thai over thirty years ago.

It was merely an urge with no inspiration, no forethought and no plot in mind. Phloi, the so-called heroine of the story, just left home to enter the Grand Palace. This was a natural act for a young girl of her position at that time. The reason for her departure was also natural: her mother was disillusioned with her father and could no longer live with him as happily as she wished. After Phloi had been placed in the palace, the recording of events and the way of life of that once magical place began. It came naturally day by day, because I wrote the story day by day, just enough to fill the columns allotted to me in the Siam Rath newspaper.

Other characters were brought into the tale because it was natural that they should be there, and before long they seemed to dictate to me what they wanted to say and do. This book is one of the easiest novels that I have ever written, since it is a novel of a life that my ancestors and myself have lived rather fully. It is a Thai novel pure and simple and the Thai readers understand every statement and nuance and seem to feel that they are sharing anew the life that is past and gone.

The problem is how to translate it. How to make foreign readers understand the book in the way Thai readers do. One way is to translate it literally and fill it with footnotes and appendices as has been done in the translation in other languages. By doing it this way the book becomes a text and not a novel, thereby losing all the affection and care that had been put into it while it was being written.

This translation by Tulachandra seems to be the perfect solution to the problem stated above. She has somehow brought out the Thai mentality of this book clearly, to be understood, to be appreciated and I hope to be cherished by our foreign friends.

I wish to express here my profound admiration and gratitude to Tulachandra for her ingenuity and hard work.

It is my sincere hope that those friends of Thailand who do not read Thai will, after reading this book, gain a little more understanding toward us.

KUKRIT PRAMOJ

Bangkok
April 1981

PRONUNCIATION GUIDE

The Thai words in this volume are romanised according to the Royal Institute system, except in two or three cases where identical spellings were altered slightly to avoid confusion. A few of the Thai Buddhist terms are romanised using the generally accepted spellings, as are some names of historical people and places.

Below is an approximate pronunciation guide. In several cases, a single English letter is used to represent more than one sound.

CONSONANTS

Initial position:		Final position:	
K	SKIN	K	WEEK
KH	KIN	P	CAP
P	SPIN	T	HIT
PH	PIN	NG	SING
T	STILL		
TH	TILL		
CH	JAR; or CHIN		
NG	SING		
R	trilled "r" sound		

All other consonants are pronounced as in English.

VOWELS

A	ACROSS, FATHER
E	HEN, DAY
I	BIT, BEE
O	HOPE, SNOW; or SAUCE, SONG
U	BOOK, SHOE; or this "u" sound said with a wide smile

AE	HAT
OE	FUR (without "r" sound)
IA	INDIA
UA	JOSHUA; or OE + A (as in FUR and ACROSS)
AI	ICE
AO	OUT
UI	COOING
OI	COIN
IU	FEW
EO	LAY OVER
OEI	OE + I (as in FUR and BEE)
UAI	UA + I (as in JOSHUA and BEE)
AEO	AE + O (as in HAT and HOPE)
IEO	IA + O (as in INDIA and HOPE, similar to CLEOPATRA)

RAMA V

ONE

THEIR ferryboat was turning into the river Chao Phraya when Phloi's mother said to her, "Pay attention to what I'm saying, Phloi. When the time comes for you to take a husband, make sure you find one with a single heart. Keep away from the great lover who must have many wives about him, or you will suffer like your mother." A short pause followed before the advice was concluded. "And you must never become any man's minor wife. Never. Do you hear?"

Phloi heard and, duty done, peered out from under the awning at life on the Chao Phraya. There were boats, floats, houses and people—and sky and flowing water, like on their *khlong*, Khlong Bang Luang, which they had left behind only moments ago. And yet, how different! So much more of everything out here on the river—boats, houses, people, water. Everything larger, merrier, moving brightly along in every direction, looking, sounding, smelling altogether new. A born-and-bred *khlong* child having her first taste of the open river, Phloi took it all in and was more excited than she could say. Stealing a glance at Mother, she said nothing. This was the first time Phloi had travelled so far from home. Her mother had told her they were never going back there, never set foot on the old landing again, that they had left it forever, unto death.

Their home on Khlong Bang Luang had a brick and iron fence running the length of the grounds on the *khlong* side. There was a pavilion at the landing, then a spacious courtyard to cross to the big house where Phloi's father, His Excellency the Chao Khun, resided. This brick mansion was considered highly stylish by Bangkok's fashionable citizens during these years in the mid-1880s and 90s, during the long reign of Rama V, His Majesty King Chulalongkorn Phra Buddha Chao Luang the Great. From the courtyard one climbed either of the twin staircases that merged into a platform, from whence rose another flight of steps up to the veranda with its green ceramic balusters. Set back off the veranda, which shielded them on all sides from direct contact with the heat and glare of the sun, were the three large rooms of His Excellency's suite, and that smaller one where the urns containing the ashes of his ancestors stood on symmetrically arranged tiers of mother-of-pearl inlaid altars. Phloi was particularly afraid of this room and, given a choice, would rather not go too near it. Not that she had to very often; she did not live in the big house, but in one of the several wooden houses to be found among the trees and footpaths farther back in the compound. Nevertheless now and again she had to make her way past its closed, silent door, and she had never been able to do this without feeling shivery and having her heart beat faster. Over the last few years, there had been those few times she was summoned inside by Chao Khun Father to pay homage to Chao Khun Great-grandfather and other forbears, to light candles and incense sticks and prostrate herself before the altars. This experience—the fact that she had been face to face, so to speak, with the contents of the room—had not served to temper her fear of it in any way, except to give that fear a more definite shape and flavour.

When he was at home, Chao Khun Father's favourite area of relaxed living was the back veranda. Here, sitting cross-legged or reclining on the rug amid the cluttered splendour of tea trays, silver bowls, cheroot boxes and betel nut paraphernalia, he could be seen having a leisurely meal, being massaged by a servant, or receiving relatives and friends. Phloi had gone up there that morning—alone, dispatched by Mother—to take her leave of him. In years to come, whenever she thought of her father, Phloi would invariably fetch up from her memory this picture of him seated before her that day in 1892. She would recall the exact shade and pattern of the *phalai* cloth he was wearing, and just as vividly how his eyes had scanned her face as if he were learning its features by heart. He didn't speak to her during the entire leave-taking. Not one word from him either of greeting, of dismissal, or forbidding her departure. Nothing but those memorable eyes—and a slight nod of the revered head to suggest the meeting was at an end.

In that year 1892, or 2435 of the Buddhist Era, Phloi at the age of ten was still being asked those rather rhetorical questions grownups like to put to children: "What is your father's name? And your mother's?" In reply she would nicely recite her father's name and title, "Phraya Phiphit, etc., etc.," or less formally, "Chao Khun Phiphit." Her mother's name, Chaem, coming immediately after this, tended to sound somewhat abrupt. Her mother was His Excellency's Wife Number One, but not his Khunying, which would have been her title had she been his officially wedded wife. The Khunying, as a matter of fact, still existed, but she was no longer a member of their household and Phloi had never met her. She had gone back to her family estate up-country before Phloi had come into the world, leaving in the care of her husband their three children—Khun Un, Khun Chit and Khun Choei.

Phloi once asked her mother why these three had "Khun" in front of their names, why they were not addressed "Mae" this and "Pho" that—"Mae" for girls and "Pho" for boys—like the other children including herself and her elder brother Phoem. Mother had replied with a laugh, "Because they are Khunying's children and the rest of you have lesser wives for mothers, that's why. Be thankful they call you Mae Phloi and Pho Phoem, and not the lowly *Ee* Phloi and *Ai* Phoem!" Khun Un, the eldest of the three Khuns, was then a young woman of nineteen, but to Phloi she was a formidable grand lady who lived in the big house, towards whom one must behave with extra caution and respect. The Chao Khun had given her the responsibility of over-seeing his domestic affairs and had placed in her keeping the keys to the chests and cabinets containing his silver and gold. She regarded it as part of the natural order that she should serve him as deputy and confidante and have more power to wield than any of his wives.

She could do very little, however, when it came to managing her younger brother Khun Chit, who was sixteen and a dandy with slicked-down hair, blotchy skin covered with perfumed powder, each temple modishly adorned with a circular bit of medicated plaster designed as a headache cure for modishly delicate young men of that era. At home, Khun Chit passed the time lounging or strolling about the landing pavilion leering at pretty girls in the passing boats, but more often waiting for an opportunity to slip into town with some of his father's young attendants. Once, after Khun Chit and his escorts had vanished for days, they returned only to receive a whipping by the Chao Khun in the empty courtyard, before a delighted out-of-sight audience stationed here and there behind tree trunks and flower bushes. The culprits were on their knees, each with his wrists tied up, emitting screams heard up and down the *khlong*.

Then there was another time when Khun Chit became very ill after yet another forbidden trip across the river. No whipping that time, but he was kept in bed for weeks on end, thin and haggard as a ghost. Old retainers who knew about these things brewed pots of dark herbal liquid for him to take, and his younger sister Khun Choei, who was Phloi's close and constant friend, told her in a gleefully solemn whisper, "Khun Chit has Women's Disease. This is a secret. If you tell anyone I shall be very angry."

But Phloi was good at guarding secrets. She would never divulge the name of Khun Chit's ailment. Neither would she tell Mother that Brother Phoem had been to visit him. Mother was wont to beat Phoem with one or more of her slender sticks upon finding out he had once again disobeyed her and gone consorting with Khun Half Brother the Bad.

Mother was frank with Khunying's younger children. She liked Khun Choei, despised Khun Chit, and let them know it. With Khun Un she wore an expressionless mask and spoke in crisply enunciated phrases, taking infinite care to adorn each phrase with the very polite ending of "*chao kha,*" the ending demanded of her inferior status. But sometimes when alone with Phloi, her defences would break down, her mask dissolving into real tears, polite phrases into heartfelt protests at the injustice of it all. It was becoming unbearable to have to defer to Khun Un at all times, in all things. The daughter had become the absolute ruler of the house while she, the old wife, had been reduced to nothing, entitled to only one right, the right to go on living from day to day, the right not denied any poor girl who had sold herself into the household. And was it not Khun Un who had so cunningly brought about the promotion of one of her trusty maids, Waeo, to the position of a minor wife of the Chao Khun? Mother admitted she had been mad with jealousy at the time, had wanted to run away then and there, but Phloi being still such a tiny tot she couldn't bring herself to do it.

There were days when the tension between Khun Un and her mother filled Phloi with apprehension, made her dread the mere thought of having to go near either of them. The Chao Khun himself was not unaffected by this highly charged atmosphere produced by Eldest Daughter and Wife Number One. He would keep very much to himself when it descended on the house, staying on neutral grounds as it were, sometimes even to the extent of forgoing the pleasure of being with his younger children in the courtyard, to watch them play in the soft light of the late afternoon. For Phloi his absence had a damping effect on their games. Chao Khun Father was at his jolliest on these occasions, shouting encouragement to them all to run faster, letting them make as much noise as they wanted, and himself laughing louder than any of them. Phloi had the impression that his jolliness was reserved for them, his small children. He usually frowned in Khun Chit's company— but then, of late he and Khun Chit had been avoiding each other. He was amiable with Khun Un, of course, but in a serious fashion, as one important grownup to another. He was very considerate regarding her wishes and always took care not to impose his own.

All their short simple names—Un, Chit and the rest—had been given them by the Chao Khun himself. Unlike some of his acquaintances, he had not asked a higher-ranking personage or a venerated abbot to do the honour, and unlike others had not chosen to confer upon his children multi-syllabic names comprising words of Sanskrit or Pali origin and often strung together to be read like a rhyme. Phloi heard him say to Mother one day that such names were for the royals, and commoners who tried to imitate them were only inviting the lice of ill luck onto their foolish heads. In any case, these imitators never failed to distinguish themselves in absurdity. He then sang out the names invented by a prominent neighbour of theirs for four of his children: "Phenphisamai" (Beloved Moon-light), "Saisukontharot" (Bright and Fragrant), "Sotsamran-chit" (Bouyant Happy Mind), and "Sanitsaneha" (Bind with Affection). He made them sound quite ridiculous and Mother had laughed heartily. Phloi did not laugh because her mind was on something else. She wanted to question Father on those lice of ill luck now that he had mentioned them. These lice were famous. She had been told by various people that if you dared to compare yourself with the royals, or boasted of your connection with them, or joked about them, then—beware—you'd get those lice on your head. She had heard remarks such as: "Trying to raise yourself to royal heights, are you? Lice on your head for sure!" Even so, one or two things still puzzled her, and when the laughter was over and the funny names died away Phloi respectfully put forward her questions: Do these lice then come from the royals themselves? She, Phloi, once got lice in her hair from playing with Chup the slave-girl. Are these the same kind as royal lice? This was greeted with another burst of laughter, mixed with some alarm on Mother's part, but with no reply from either parent.

Laughter had been scarce these past few weeks. Her father had been keeping more aloof, her mother looking more grim, and Khun Un acting more pleased with herself than ever. The whole house knew that His Excellency was about to be presented with another minor wife, that this lucky person was none other than Yuan, the prettiest among Khun Un's own current crop of maids, and that it was Khun Un herself doing the presenting. It occurred to Phloi, watching her elders, that this time something terrible might happen.

And on the preceding night, it did. Mother had marched off from their quarters early in the evening, gone up to the big house to see Chao Khun Father, and Phloi had fallen asleep after hours of waiting for her. Waking up with a start, she saw Mother lighting a lamp and a sleepy Phoem standing about.

"You are coming with me, Phloi," Mother said. "Since it's quite clear that he doesn't want me under his care and protection any more, I must go. Let the course of karma take me where it will. Better than to stay and be trampled on like a bonded slave . . . But you have to stay, Phoem. His Excellency refuses to let you come with us. 'Phoem's a son,' he says, 'and must remain with Father.' You'll be on your own from now on, so mind how you behave your-self. Be a dutiful son to him, show him your reverence and gratitude, and don't ever think that because you're a son of His Excellency you can do as you please. And, don't forget that his eldest daughter will always insist on treating you like a serving boy . . . But I'll not leave you here to be bullied, Phloi. It's not as if we're rootless people without a shelter to turn to. I'm taking you to the palace. I'll beg Sadet to accept you into her entourage."

Mother had started her speech in fiercely bitter tones but at the end she was weeping helplessly, and Phoem, a now wide-awake Phoem, was sobbing and imploring not to be left behind. Phloi was too bewildered to cry. The word *sadet* had caught her ear and for a while she clung to it. She understood what it meant. Sadet was the princess in the palace, related to Mother even if distantly (but one mustn't talk about it on account of those mysterious lice), in whose service Mother had been for many years and where she had been planning to place Phloi some day. And Chao Khun Father had expressed his approval. "Girls get good training in the palace," he had said, though without forgetting to add, "but let's keep her with us a few more years. I like having my little ones round me. They grow up all too quickly."

So we're going to Sadet in the palace, Phloi thought. But this glimpse of the future soon got lost in the present confusion. She wished to say something to Mother and Phoem, to tell them not to cry so hard, but the words got all tangled and she could only stare dumbly at them.

At last, taking Phoem into her arms, rocking and soothing him, Mother was able to calm down both herself and her son. The maid Phit was sent for; the business of packing got under way. Phloi dozed off again, but was woken before dawn to be washed, dressed, have her topknot combed out and retwined, and instructed to go and wait quietly outside on the balcony. She had not been there long when she heard Khun Choei's voice softly calling from below.

"Come down, Mae Phloi. Don't make any noise!" After glancing back at the room, Phloi tiptoed down the steps to meet her half sister and friend. Khun Choei grabbed her wrist and held it tight.

"So it's true you're leaving! Khun Un said so but I didn't want to believe it."

Phloi swallowed, nodding her head. Large drops of tears coursed down Khun Choei's cheeks.

"But who am I going to play with when you're gone?" she demanded. "You won't forget me? Promise you won't forget me."

Phloi half nodded, half shook her head. Khun Choei handed over a small package. "Some sweets for you, Mae Phloi. Some *chan-ap* I stole from Khun Un."

Phloi accepted the gift with another nod. Her throat was aching, her eyes so blurred she could hardly make out Khun Choei's face. Then Mother's voice came floating down asking where she was. Her wrist was still in Khun Choei's clasp. Phloi shook it free and fled upstairs clutching the package to her heart.

Three wooden chests, ready to be hauled away, stood near the door glaring at her as she entered the room. Two of them—black with a gold design in the shapes of swans and dragons—belonged to Mother; the other one, painted red, was hers. Grouped together on the far side of the room was an assortment of things that would remain with Phoem—bowls and cups and such like. The floor looked bare because the mat and the mattress had been rolled up and pushed against the wall. The mosquito net, too, had been taken down. She would never sleep in this room again, it was plain to see. Suddenly the unshed tears came streaming down and there was nothing she could do to stop them. She felt Mother's hands stroking her head and back, heard her voice talking about her great love for her, about the package—asking where it came from, about what fun it would be living in the palace; and she went on crying until the tears drained away of their own accord.

Presently Mother said, "Time for us to be off. You go up to the big house, Phloi, prostrate yourself at your father's feet and take your leave. I'll be waiting at the landing."

Dry-eyed, burdened with the new experience of separation and loss, Phloi took her time coming away from her wooden home on stilts, from the floorboard, walls and stairs, and the holes, gaps and creaky parts that had figured in the pattern of her daily life. (To drop custard-apple seeds through a gap in the floor, for instance, gave an altogether different sensation from getting rid of them by using a spittoon or tossing them over the railings of the balcony.) Then, along the clearing on the way to the big house, it was the old trees that kept holding her back. Here was the old cork tree. Only yesterday she and Khun Choei were playing Let's-Cook-Rice-and-Curry under its shade. It was the ideal spot for the game. When the tree was in bloom, they always gathered its flowers off the ground to take to Mother, who put them in the mixture for Father's cheroots. Father's cheroots—Phloi wondered with some concern who would be doing them in her mother's absence. Who would be boiling the honey, the pineapple juice and the *cha-em* juice—even the best Muang Song tobacco could not do without them, Mother always said. And what about the pressing and cutting of banana leaves, and of course the actual rolling . . .

Reluctantly she left the uncertain fate of Father's cheroots with the cork tree and continued on her way. Past the night-flowering jasmine bush—its red-stemmed flowers provided a dye for Mother's bodice cloths. Past the *khieo kratae*—its tiny white blooms were often threaded by Mother into garlands for Phloi's topknot. Past the most magnificent, the best-tasting mango tree in all of Khlong Bang Luang! These and other old friends bade her farewell as Phloi made her way to the back veranda, and to that unforgettable wordless audience with Chao Khun Father. They had looked at each other at first. But it would have taken more boldness than Phloi possessed not to flinch under the scrutiny of those eyes—and not to escape from it by shifting hers to her own fingers, which were busily tracing a minute section of lines and circles on the edge of the rug.

Not a word. But as Phloi was to recall to herself afterwards, he did clear his throat a few times. And then, with no one there to prompt her, she herself had had to chose the appropriate moment for making obeisance. She joined her palms together and bent forward, bringing head and hands down on the rug; then, straightening up, she saw the barely noticeable nod and prepared to crawl away.

At that point the silence was broken, not by Father, but by Khun Un's voice calling out sharp and shrill from her room.

"Phloi! Come in here!"

It was like being pounced upon from behind, and punishing enough without the ordeal of confronting the owner's voice. She looked inquiringly, hopefully, at her father, but the answer in his eyes told her she had no choice in the matter.

She entered Khun Un's room—also referred to by those in the know as "the room where the silver and gold are kept"—on her hands and knees, making as little noise as possible, making every effort not to do the least provocative thing. Khun Un was seated on the floor flanked by her tea set, her betel-nut set, and her keys. Phloi went to sit before her. The early morning sun was shining but the room was murky as always. Khun Un kept it that way on purpose, being very proud of her fair skin and finicky about protecting it from the sun. Lacking in light, the room made up for it by enveloping one in a cloud of lovely scents, mostly emanating from Khun Un's person and garments. It was a Wednesday and she was wearing a green *phanung* with a deep orange bodice cloth on top, a most correct colour combination for Wednesday wear, in accordance with custom as well as the dictates of fashion. Not a hair on her head was out of place, and every small hair on her forehead had been plucked so as to accentuate its outline. Correctness, neatness, immaculateness—Khun Un's appearance proclaimed these qualities.

She fixed her eyes on Phloi while neatly applying wax on her lips out of a small ivory box. Putting the box away she began to speak in that piercingly malicious tone familiar to all her victims. The short monologue—for Phloi did not once open her mouth—went as follows:

"Leaving this house, are you? . . . Going with that mother of yours? . . . Just don't change your mind and come back, understand? We can't have people coming and going as they please, especially people who set themselves up so high and mighty. To come crawling back wouldn't be such a high and mighty thing to do, would it? Go then! Get out! Tigers and crocodiles can never be nurtured in a house. Go—and good riddance!"

Phloi went, naturally more eager to go now rather than sad to be leaving. At the landing pavilion, Phoem, with his arms hugging a post, was crying quietly. Looking pale and weary but determined, Mother whispered a final word in his ear before getting Phloi and herself into the boat. The maid Phit, already on board with their possessions, chatted with the boatman as if nothing out of the ordinary had happened, though she did enjoin him, as they set off from the landing, to bear in mind the importance of the journey and be most careful how he worked his oar.

The tide was low at this hour so that, looking back at her birthplace from the moving boat, all Phloi could see at first was the lower half of the landing—some steps and the moss-coated posts rising from the water. It was not until the boat had passed beyond the compound that the whole scene came into view—the whole of the pavilion with Phoem still crying in the same position, the fence, the trees, and at last the yellow corrugated tile roof of Father's big house shimmering among the treetops. Phloi looked at it until it vanished from sight, replaced by other people's houses, landings, orchards, shops, in an ever-changing procession, all vanishing in their turn. The *khlong* and its banks grew more congested, noisier and livelier the nearer they approached its mouth. From a passing boat someone called out to Mother, "Going to Bangkok, Mae Chaem?" and from another, "Where are you going so early?" Their boat went on and Mother was spared such further questions as: "Have some business in Bangkok?" or "Taking a pleasure trip?"

And then, it seemed that almost immediately after having borne them to the river, the *khlong* itself had disappeared to become one with the sunny horizon, and Phloi found herself discovering an entirely bright new world on the Chao Phraya. Mother had been talking—about minor wives and other serious matters; Phloi heard her voice but kept missing the actual words. Her head was in a whirl.

In her short life she had never known such a morning, such a miserable morning, a chaotic morning, a thrilling morning, all mixed up together and stranger than a dream. She had remained silent partly out of respect for her mother's sorrows, but now, as their boat drew near the other side, she could no longer refrain from imparting some of her excitement.

"Oh look, Mother! Look at those spires! What's that place, Mother?"

Mother gave her first smile since leaving home. "That's where we're going. That's the Grand Palace."

"Oh-ho!" Phloi had imagined Sadet's dwelling as somewhat bigger than her father's big house, had not expected anything remotely resembling this glittering skyful of roofs and spires. "The Grand Palace belongs to Sadet?" She asked for confirmation.

This time she made her mother laugh out loud. "How Sadet will be amused when I tell her! No, little one, it belongs to His Majesty the King. Our Sadet lives in a palace inside the Grand Palace, sepa-rated from the king's halls by an inner wall. She lives in the Inner Court, where men are not allowed. Don't lean too far out, Phloi! You want to fall in?"

"Look at that houseboat—you see it, Phit? Is it a royal houseboat, Mother?"

"Yes. Sit still, Phloi."

"Will we be in the palace soon?"

"Quite soon. We'll walk from Tha Phra landing to Sri Sudawong Gate."

"Are you going to stay with me in the palace, Mother?"

"Ye-es. Then I must find some way to earn a living. But let's not talk about it now. We'll see, daughter." And before Phloi could brood over the reply she turned to address the maid. "When we get to Tha Phra, will you hire someone to bring our things later in the morning? Don't carry too much with you, like a woman just come from the farm."

"Never," said Phit knowingly. "I was with you in the palace many years. I haven't forgotten how they stared at strangers in the Inner Court. I'll show them we're no strangers!"

She certainly did not act like a stranger when they disembarked at Tha Phra, but went about getting things done in her confident manner and in no time at all was able to usher her mistresses from the landing, escort them up the road and across it onto the grass terrace bordering the palace wall. A short walk brought them to a high open gate crowded with people moving in and out.

"Follow me and don't get stepped on," Mother said as she went in, and when they had entered the courtyard, she added, "You're now inside the Grand Palace wall, Phloi." The courtyard, paved with stone, looked to Phloi so huge as to be unbelievable. At least Khun Choei would never believe her if she told her how huge it was. It must be a hundred times or more the size of the one at home. She gaped at the beautiful tall buildings and planned to ask Mother about them when she had a chance; and she also would like to know why there were so many people, and where they came from. They were milling about, strolling, hurrying somewhere, or sitting and standing in chattering groups. There were also countless vendors among them, with portable basket-stores, surrounded by bargaining customers. The air was filled with the sound of talk and laughter, and Phloi was reminded of Mother's repeated assurance: "What fun—living in the palace."

Her eyes came upon a structure. It was the inner wall. It stretched to the left and right of an enormous gate, which stood ajar and appeared to be the most crowded spot of all. They were heading for the gate with Mother leading the way, and Phloi could see that the people thronging about it were all female, whereas the groups nearer the outer wall included men and boys as well. Their progress towards the gate was halted now and again as Mother ran into acquaintances from the old days. Most of these greeted her with pleasure, some with a great show of respect, bowing low in a diffi-dent manner while joining their hands in a *wai*. There were also a few with whom Mother exchanged long looks of recognition absolutely devoid of friendliness.

"Hard for some species to die out, isn't it?" she remarked after one of these exchanges.

"I should say so!" agreed Phit readily, spitting out betel juice by way of emphasis.

On they went, part of the stream flowing towards the interior. Phloi had caught sight of a beribboned blouse flashing by and was gazing after it when Mother turned round and said to her, "By the way, don't step on the threshold of the gate. It's forbidden. Step clear over it. Remember now." Having said it she was off again, briskly picking her way through the crowd, while behind her Phloi was slowing down in reaction to the warning.

A lightly given warning, but one which had a distinctly ominous ring to Phloi's sensitive ear. "Remember now . . . It's forbidden . . ." This could only mean *Danger Ahead!* She could sense it and started to tremble in anticipation. What if she should stumble? Or have cramps in her legs, which were already growing weak? If she failed, would she be put in the king's prison? What would the penalty be? Not to have her head cut off, surely . . .

The threshold loomed nearer and nearer—a wooden bulk lying solidly across from one end of the gate to the other. It had gold leaves on it, and joss sticks burning at its sides. It had masses of faces swarming about it and watching her every movement. She realized now it was not a threshold but a many-headed monster waiting to devour wayward children. It was baring its fangs, and hissing its threat: "Don't you dare step on me!"

"Hurry up," Phit was prodding her. "Look, your mother's gone in."

Mother had safely crossed the barrier and was standing at a distance from the gate, in conversation with some old friends. Phloi was compelled to make a do-or-die decision in order not to lose her permanently. Thus, taking long desperate strides she reached the gate and lifted her foot. It landed on the threshold followed by the other foot. For a dazed second she stood looking down at these feet, then plunged off and broke into a run.

Shouts and shrieks rose up behind her like pursuing phantoms. "Stop! Stop! AT ONCE !" Terror drove her onwards. A hand shot out blocking her flight. Phloi struggled but in vain.

"What's the matter?" Mother's voice was asking. It was Mother's arm holding her. What a relief!

"What's the matter?" repeated Mother. "What are you running from?" Then she understood—the shouting and the guilt written so plainly on Phloi's face having provided sufficient information. She understood and gave Phloi a loving hug, laughing all the while. She laughed till she cried, and her friends were laughing with her. Phloi could not quite share their mirth, but took it as a good sign—an indication of the mild nature of her crime.

"All right," Mother said, "let's go back and see the sergeant—she's the one calling us. You see her? She and the others round her are *khlon*s—guards of the Inner Court. Now all you have to do is make obeisance to the threshold and ask for forgiveness. Nothing to be afraid of."

Nevertheless she had another warning to convey, which she did by dropping her voice to a discreet murmur. "One thing you must remember living here—don't get into a fight with the *khlon*s. They can give you such a lashing with their tongues alone." Taking Phloi's hand she led her back to the group of women seated near the gate.

"Well, Mae Chaem," said one of the women, the most senior of them all. "So this is your daughter. Quite new to the palace, isn't she?"

Mother nodded, all smiles and politeness. "I'm placing her under Sadet's protection, Khun Sergeant. Please help look after her." Under more auspicious circumstances Phloi would have been intrigued by the sight of this middle-aged woman with the striped insignia on the sleeves of her blouse, vigorously chewing betel and rubbing her teeth with a brown ball of tobacco and looking most impressive among her subordinates, who were also in uniform. As it happened she merely longed to disappear underneath the earth and hide from them all, not only the *khlon*s but all the passersby who had stopped to inquire about the commotion and were now watching the spectacle which was herself—watching, laughing, and waiting for the finale to take place.

"Be quick about it, Phloi," Mother said matter-of-factly. More laughter from the crowd.

Feeling hot and cold and covered with sweat, Phloi inched forward somehow, went down on her knees to place her joined hands and head on the threshold in a reverent gesture called a *krap*. She had done the same this morning at her father's feet. The spectators roared with appreciation. But at least it was over and she had not died of shame.

In the next instant she was together again with Mother, and seconds later walking unharmed between her and Phit away from the inner gate towards the inner parts of the Inner Court.

Mother and Phit were reminiscing as they went along. They were also announcing for Phloi's benefit one name after another—names of buildings, gardens, pavilions, people—until Phloi began to despair of ever remembering them all.

"That pavilion over there, that's the theatre . . . the pond is called Orathai . . . and here's the *khlons*' quarters!" At the sound of this name Phloi nearly flew off again. Nothing fearful came to pass however. The *khlons* here were off duty after all and, more important to her peace of mind, still ignorant of the incident at the gate. Some were engaged in familiar homely tasks like washing clothes while others were not doing anything in particular except enjoying their own inactivity. Those who had known Mother cheerily shouted questions and greetings, and were pleased to learn the purpose of her visit. One promised to keep an eye on Phloi and keep her under control. Another said that that would be impossible if the daughter took after the mother. Everybody laughed at this while Phloi tried to picture to herself Mother as a little girl running about in the palace, outnumbered by the *khlons* but able to overcome them.

"WHERE are we now? What's this place—what is it called?"

Phloi was nudging her mother, asking questions and looking round at the same time. They had arrived at a square with narrow streets stretching away in several directions and were now walking down one of them past a very long two-storey building divided up into rooms of equal size—a very long building and a very crowded one, both inside and out. In one room a couple of girls were embroidering. In another, a woman was having a nap. In the third Phloi had glimpses of some vegetable-peelers and fruit-eaters. On the street there were stalls and benches displaying many things for sale—useful things, delicious things, pretty things. Some sold and others bought. Some came out of the building and others went in. Everyone, it seemed to Phloi, was making some sort of noise. Chatting, laughing, shouting, whispering.

Buzz, buzz, buzz. More friends for Mother to exchange greetings with, and it was not until they had turned another corner that Phloi got her reply. "That's Teng Row."

"And who lives in Teng Row, Mother?"

"Oh, let's see. Khun Attendants live there, Khun Supervisors, Khun Officers of the Kitchen, Khun Upper-Residence Maids. Lots of people live in Teng Row."

"This Grand Palace is a big place, Mother," Phloi said, rather proud of having discovered a fact almost all by herself. "It is a big city, Mother," she added. Though she had never known one, she was fairly sure that a city could not be any larger, or have more guards, or more roads and buildings, than this place. She would get lost if left to herself. The thought was alarming, and it made her feel all the more secure that she had Mother to hold her hand and Phit to direct her from the rear.

After a few more turnings, through narrow flagged streets lined with buildings of various dimensions and styles, the travellers from Khlong Bang Luang reached their destination. Here was Sadet's palace at last. In contrast with Teng Row, there was not a soul in sight. The stucco mansion sat serenely before them, large and square yet conveying a pleasing effect of lightness. There were garland mouldings above the doors and windows for Phloi to gaze at and like, and the marble steps looking so cool and inviting that she was a little surprised at the absence of loungers. Perhaps lounging here was not permitted. They went up, but did not go into the drawing room, which had slim elegant chairs and tables, and glass-fronted cabinets. Entering the hall next to it, they walked noiselessly past the foot of a wide gleaming staircase, out another door and down a corridor to where Khun Sai's domain was located.

Khun Sai was Sadet's housekeeper, her chief attendant. "My greatest debt of gratitude," Mother had told Phloi more than once, "I owe Sadet. And after her, Khun Sai." From Mother's nostalgic accounts of her palace days, Phloi was well acquainted with Khun Sai's manifold merits such as her devotion to Sadet, her kindness to friends and subordinates, her exceptional skill at any number of handicrafts and, not least, her fun-loving nature—her being a *sanuk* sort besides a good one. Now Phloi would meet her in person for the first time, but it felt more like going to call on an aunt one has known all one's life. In fact, Mother had taught her to say "Khun Aunt Sai" since as far back as she could remember.

They dropped to their knees at the open door and went in. As was to be expected, Mother's unannounced visit after all these years brought forth from the good lady cries of disbelief, surprise and much delight. Pushing away some of the trays and baskets surrounding her—she was in the middle of her morning betel preparations—Khun Sai made room on the shiny teak floor and drew Mother and Phloi close to her, affectionately patting their heads and backs and firing questions at them. Beaming from ear to ear at the happy scene, Phit paid her respects and took off for a reunion of her own somewhere in the kitchen quarters. Khun Sai had a plump figure, a youthful unlined face, a sprinkling of grey in her hair, and was as comfortable to be with as Phloi's instincts had predicted. She was also a sympathetic and patient listener. She consoled Mother as though she were a child, lending her support without siding with her against anyone, and then, noticing Phloi's rapt admiration of the jars of sweets and savouries arrayed on the shelves nearby, she suddenly asked if they had had their morning rice.

Mother's reply made her exclaim, "What! You haven't eaten anything? Oh, Mae Chaem, you ought to know better! No need to starve the child when fighting with the husband. Here, Phloi, have some of this while I go and tell them to bring you a proper meal."

Hungry as she was, Phloi hesitated, nonetheless, after inspecting the shrimps in the bowl Khun Sai had placed before her.

"Sugared shrimps," Mother explained. "A palace delicacy."

Phloi put one in her mouth and regretted it immediately. The sweetness was of the most intense, stabbing kind. She was amazed to see Mother munching away with no apparent discomfort. No, no more for her, she said, shaking her head and making a wry face.

Khun Sai returned with two serving girls trailing behind, carrying in the rice and side dishes all of which, to Phloi's relief, looked reassuringly familiar. "Delicious food!" said Mother. "Umm, catfish roe salad!"

But Khun Sai had a complaint. "If you had let me know beforehand, I would have ordered really special things, and you'd be having your favourite dishes instead of these leftovers."

Mother laughed at this, saying, "Ah, this is the reason I came back— to have you spoiling and pampering me again."

While they ate, Khun Sai bustled about the room. She went to a cabinet and brought out a gold stem tray. From another she fetched some candles and incense sticks. Then she called out to Mae Phaad, her number one girl, to bring fresh flowers and banana leaves.

"Now what are you doing, Khun?" Mother asked. "What's all this for?"

"Phloi's presentation, of course."

"But, Khun . . ." Mother began doubtfully. "Must we have the ceremony? After all Phloi's only my daughter, and since Sadet already knows me as her loyal maid . . ."

Khun Sai cut her short. "Really Mae Chaem! When will you grow up? How could you say Phloi's *only* your daughter? She's got a father, too, who's a Phraya and one of the Clan Across the River. If Phloi is not correctly presented, you and I—yes, I'd be dragged into it, too— we'll never hear the end of it from her relatives. And what's so difficult about presenting her this way? Look," she made an expansive gesture, "I've got everything here, plenty of candles, joss sticks . . ." It was her turn to be interrupted.

"Listen to your Khun Aunt, Phloi," Mother said with a chuckle. "She's telling us how rich she is and everything here belongs to her."

"The tray does belong to me," Khun Sai protested laughingly. "As to the candles and joss sticks—well, everybody knows they've been presented to Sadet by all sorts of people on all sorts of occasions. They're turned over to me and it's my duty to put them to good use, isn't that right? Well, that means some of them must find their way back to her now and again."

They laughed together as Phloi went on eating with the concentration and relish of the truly hungry. Now visitors began to flock into Khun

Sai's room, more old friends of Mother's who had heard the news. Soon there was hardly any space left on the floor. For a few minutes Phloi was the centre of their attention, the object of their amiable if disjointed questioning, the recipient of their embraces. She felt very shy and preferred it when, almost entirely forgetting her existence, they clustered round Mother, allowing her to watch them unobserved. They were even more well-groomed and sweet-smelling than Khun Un, these lively talkative women apparently without a care in the world. And after a while her mother became one of them, just as gay and light-hearted, her eyes sparkling as she laughed and regaled them with one amusing retort after another. She had slipped back easily into her former Inner Court self, and Phloi was glad, having been accustomed these past months to seeing her either in an angry mood, or looking dejected, or staring into space, indifferent to everything that went on round her.

Then it was time for the audience. Khun Sai had finished the intricate banana-leaf *krathong* she had been making and someone had come by the door with the information that Her Royal Highness was now in the veranda room and about to be served breakfast. The friends dispersed. The flowers were placed in the *krathong*, which along with the incense and candles were then arranged on the stem tray to be carried by Phloi.

"It's good to have an audience now," Khun Sai remarked to Mother. "It will give her an appetite, to listen to your chatter."

Along the corridor and up the gleaming stairs in the hall, the two women spoke in low tones and conducted themselves no longer in an easy-going manner, but became markedly deliberate and subdued. Phloi noticed this while she herself was growing more and more nervously afraid. From above came a hum of conversation interspersed with soft laughter. The climb seemed very long, but they did gain the top of the stairs eventually, and with no mishap. Their appearance caused the hum to cease temporarily, and in the brief silence that ensued Khun Sai crawled forward a little way, then veered to one side, leaving Phloi and her mother to go on by themselves. After another yard or two Mother stopped and prostrated herself in a *krap*. Phloi followed her example, after depositing the tray on the floor with a mild sense of triumph, for it was no easy task to proceed on hands and knees with such an object in hand.

Their heads were still bowed low when Phloi heard Sadet's clear, resonant voice for the first time. "Who's that? Isn't that Chaem?"

Mother sat up in order to execute another *krap*. Phloi did the same, and kept her eyes glued to the floor. "What's this? Am I going to get one *krap* for every question? Well, how are you, Chaem? How long has it been since I last saw you—how many years? Sometimes I thought you must have died."

"Today I've brought my daughter to present to Your Highness," said Mother.

"So the little girl is your daughter. It seems only yesterday that the mother was a little girl herself. I brought her up, then she disappeared. Now she's brought me a daughter to bring up in her place. So simple, except that I shall have to start all over again!"

Tinkling laughs rang out from here and there in the veranda room. With her eyes remaining fixed on the floor Phloi was wondering how many women there were in audience. The voice continued, "It was too peaceful for you in here, wasn't it, Chaem? You wanted to be a wife—a minor one at that. What's happened now? Did he throw you out, or did you walk out?"

"I left him, Your Highness," Mother replied. "But then he didn't try to stop me leaving."

Another ripple of friendly merriment, while the voice went on good-humouredly, "Same old Chaem, never at a loss for an answer. And what's the daughter's name? How old is she?"

Mother supplied the answer; and the voice said: "Do raise your head, Phloi, and let me see what you look like. Don't hide your face like a slow loris."

Phloi raised her head, though not before Mother had given her a little push, and saw Sadet smiling at her. Some phrases of Mother's sprang to her mind at that instant. "My refuge," Mother had called her. "Sadet is my refuge, my bo tree spreading its cool protecting shade." Seated on a green carpet, on a red silk cushion with triangular back,

Sadet was dressed in a *phalai* and *sabai* like most of her attendants. Phloi thought she had never seen anyone look so radiant in a *phalai* and *sabai*. No wonder Mother had been a happy child under her protection. "Present your incense and candles," Mother said to her in a whisper, and aloud to Sadet, "She is very shy, Your Highness. She has never been out anywhere until today."

Picking up the tray, Phloi went forward with it to the edge of the carpet, stopped short of it, and lowered her head as far down as it would go. Sadet had to come to her aid. "Come closer, Phloi... That's better ... Oh, look, you haven't opened the flower *krathong*. Lift the cover ... Now hand me the tray. Don't be shy. There!"

After accepting the tray from Phloi and laying it by her side, Sadet gave a small sigh. "Poor little thing," she said. "So young and helpless. You mustn't be terrified of me, Phloi. I'm not the demon Yaksa or the devil Mara, you know." She paused, smiling, gave Phloi a long attentive look, and pronounced her a pretty child, whose fair complexion was worthy of a Phraya's daughter, a statement which, needless to say, made Phloi very happy, especially as she had never heard anyone call her pretty before. Sweet, at best, but never pretty.

Turning her attention from daughter to mother, Sadet asked, "And now what will you do, Chaem, wait here till he sends for you?"

"I'm never going back, Your Highness. I've suffered enough."

"You and many others. I don't know what to say. You all rush outside telling yourself now you'll be free to live a glorious life as Than Phuyings, Khunyings, and what not. Instead you suffer, and return to complain to me. Later on you might patch it up with your husband and call me an interfering old fool. That's why I take care not to get myself involved in your quarrels."

"'Never mingle in husband-wife affairs,' as the old saying goes, Your Highness." This comment was contributed by Khun Sai in an aptly didactic tone of voice.

Sadet laughed. "How wise and experienced you sound, Sai! As if you had a husband of your own." At the word "husband" Khun Sai cried out and tried to defend herself, but ended up laughing like everybody else.

When the silver food tray was brought in, Phloi, at a sign from Mother, withdrew from the carpet to sit near her. Looking at the tray and what it contained, she could not help but marvel at the small portion of each side dish and the mere handful of rice in the dainty bowl. The whole thing was not much bigger than a ritual offering to the spirit of the Lord Buddha! As she ate, Sadet chatted with Mother. Or rather it was Mother who did most of the talking while Sadet ate. Phloi had never seen anyone eat so unhurriedly, so casually, as though food were something incidental. She decided that she had never witnessed a more gracious meal, but was also afraid that Sadet would soon be hungry again, as she herself would certainly be.

After the meal Sadet said to Khun Sai, "There'll be monks chanting in the Throne Hall this afternoon. Will you find out if Sadet of the Upper Palace would like to come with me?"

A woman seated behind Phloi spoke up. "Mae Malai is here from the Upper Palace, Your Highness." Whereupon Mae Malai's voice was heard delivering what in fact was the answer to Her Highness's question. The sense of the message was clear enough, but Phloi was so struck by its phrasing that she forgot herself and turned to stare at the speaker. She had had some lessons in the royal language from her mother, and knew that the word *sadet* had several functions: it was not only a noun and pronoun for royals, but served as the royal verbs "to come" and "to go." But mother had never hinted that it could be used seven times in rapid succession in a single sentence. "Sadet would like to know if Sadet will *sadet* to the Throne Hall this afternoon and if Sadet intends to *sadet*, then Sadet would like to *sadet* with her." This was the message spoken by Mae Malai. Phloi's astonishment on hearing it did not escape Sadet's notice.

"That's court talk, Phloi," she said, with a smile that was at once amused and encouraging. "Now let's hear you say this to Malai: 'Sadet wishes to let Sadet know that Sadet plans to *sadet* and will be very happy if Sadet will *sadet* with her.'"

Phloi did not dare laugh, let alone attempt to repeat the tongue-twisting sentence. Trying to suppress her smile, which threatened to broaden into a grin, she bent her head floorwards and said nothing.

TWO

SADET had gone to the Throne Hall. It was quiet throughout her palace that afternoon. It was quiet and peaceful in Khun Sai's room where Phloi was helping its owner re-pleat a pile of bodice cloths brought in by the laundry maid and Mother was taking a well-earned nap on the floor beside them. Into this peace and quiet there came a girl of Phloi's age whose face—a nice face, Phloi thought—was grimy with dust and sweat, and crowned with an untidy wobbling topknot. On seeing Phloi the girl raised her eyebrows, making them fly up much higher than in a normal questioning glance. It made Phloi want to smile. Just then Khun Sai looked up and spoke to the girl in severe tones: "So there you are, Mae Choi, Mae Gadabout! Come and sit still for a change and tell me where you have been all this time. I want to know why you were not in attendance this morning. And I think it's time you had a few strokes of the twig . . . And don't try to look innocent. You can't fool me! Now where have you been? Speak up!"

"I went to Teng Row, Khun Aunt," replied Choi carelessly.

"Where in Teng Row?"

"Khun Lamai's rooms."

"Which Lamai?"

"Khun Officer Lamai."

"Why did you go there?"

"To play with Mae Lamun, Khun Lamai's sister."

"And then?"

"Then we went to Auntie Khian's room."

"Ah! Looking for food, I suppose."

"She gave us delicious sausages and *nampla*"

"Oh she did, did she? And after that?"

"We went to see Khun Dame Klip."

"My word! What on earth for?"

"She has some lovely dolls—courtier dolls, you know. We wanted to look at them, so we went."

"Is that so!" said Khun Sai, bringing a swift hand smack down on Choi's thigh to signify that the interrogation was over and that she had had her fill of the blithe answers. The girl burst into tears, moaning loudly as if in great pain, and just as suddenly resumed her composure when Khun Sai said, "Stop it or you'll get a real beating."

"You two had better get acquainted," Khun Sai went on. "This Mae Choi here is my own niece, Phloi—daughter of my own brother, I'm sorry to say. It's a waste of rice bringing her up . . . And this is Phloi. She has come to live here. That person stretched out like a sleeping Ravna is her mother."

"I'm awake now," mumbled Mother.

"Her name is Mae Chaem. Call her Aunt Chaem. She and I have known each other since long before you were born. Now you must not lead Phloi into mischief, you understand? She's a nice polite girl, not a handful like yourself." To Phloi, she added with some weariness, "She's more than a handful, Phloi, as you can see."

Phloi had seen it already. She had been watching the other girl with increasing admiration. Shy, obedient, anything but a handful herself, she was inclined to look up to girls like Choi and her dear Khun Choei back home. Fearless spirits both of them. Thinking of Khun Choei she gave Choi a friendly smile and did not take it amiss when the latter, in a quick, deft movement unnoticed by either aunt or mother, poked her in the leg and stuck out a long pink tongue at her. It was the sort of thing Khun Choei might have done in a similar encounter.

Choi now addressed herself to her aunt. "I saw Khun Saiyut at Khun Lamai's," she said with an air of a mature woman long past her tongue-sticking days. "She would like to know when you're going to decide about the box."

"Oh the box!" her aunt sighed. "Well, you can tell your Khun Saiyut that I'm not a rich woman and do not have the means to chew betel out of a thirty to forty *chang* box." A *chang* was eighty baht, and forty *chang* was a sum large enough to pay for a mansion in those days.

"But it's only ten *chang*, Khun Aunt," said Choi. "She'll accept ten *chang*. That's what she says."

"And I say it's none of your business! You're too young to know about these things."

The conversation had aroused Mother's interest. Sitting up, she asked who this Khun Saiyut could be who had such a costly betel-nut box in her possession, and why she should want to dispose of it.

"Surely you remember her," said Khun Sai. "She's a relative of your husband's. The rich Saiyut who never let us forget how rich she was, how well born, how smart. Poor soul, she's not at all smart nowadays, or rich. Far from it." Sadly Khun Sai shook her head, then her expression changed as a reminiscent smile came into it. "Do you remember, Mae Chaem, the time she brought bread to the palace—when none of us had ever set eyes on a loaf of bread before? And the story about her father importing ice for the first time from Singapore, and when it arrived he ordered one of his serving boys to try it first. The boy had the shock of his life—couldn't spit it out fast enough, and nearly shattered the roof with his screaming and hollering that his tongue was so cold it was falling out. Remember the story?"

Mother laughed. "How could I forget? We told and retold it for weeks. But what about Khun Saiyut and this betel box? What's the story?"

"It's an old story and not a happy one," Khun Sai said. "It began after her tonsure ceremony, a very grand affair of course. She went round saying now she's old enough to carry a betel box but her father was not giving her one because he knew she had karmic merit and was destined to become a Chao Chom with a royal box of her own. That's why he sent her to live in the Inner Court in the first place. 'My father looks forward to having royal highnesses as grandchildren,' she used to say."

"Oh, no!" Mother cried, scandalized yet laughing at the same time.

"I remember those words as distinctly as if they were spoken the day before yesterday," Khun Sai assured her. "I warned her not to say such things or even think them. One must guard against being cocksure about anticipating royal wishes. But she believed in her glorious destiny. Her heart was set on becoming a Chao Chom. Then, when it was plain she was never going to get her wish, she went away for a time, and returned to the palace armed with this box—a gold one with diamonds set in a mesh pattern in the middle of the lid, and a snake in tiny first-rate emeralds coiled on the mesh—she was born in the year of the little snake. To anyone who would listen she said a royal box was so common and she much preferred using her own! And how she would hate to be a Chao Chom and risk sharing the lot of those who rose briefly only to fall and have nothing left but to crouch in the Yellow Room all their lives. Her favourite phrase at that period was 'Oh, how I pity those Yellow-Room Chao Choms.' Well, not long after this she went away to marry some man, who, after her father died, squandered all her money. And now she's back here trying to sell what's left of her jewellery. I sincerely hope she finds a buyer for her high-class box."

Khun Sai paused, then gave a rueful smile, "I should look ridiculous carrying it, really, apart from the fact that I was not born in the year of the little snake but the year of the tiger!"

Phloi had been an attentive listener to Khun Sai's recounting of this Inner Court anecdote. Now she made a mental note to seek Mother's explanation on certain obscure details when she had a chance. What had those Chao Choms done, for instance, to be doomed to all that crouching in the Yellow Room? And where was this room situated— in a prison? Did every woman with merit and glorious destiny become a Chao Chom? This was the title of a minor wife of the king. That much she understood but not very much else. She glanced at Choi, who was rearranging for her own amuse-ment the contents of Khun Sai's betel tray, and had not been listening to the story, obviously because she had heard it before and understood everything.

"It's strange how I haven't thought of Khun Saiyut for years and years," Mother was saying. "I remember her haughty ways all right, but even so I can't help feeling sorry for her. To come down in the world from such a height is bad fate for anyone."

Khun Sai nodded. "That's how I feel. I wish I could help her. But there's not very much a person in my humble station can do for her. There are some who can—among those who used to flatter her and egg her on in her days of plenty, but I'm afraid most of them have dropped her, or are about to.

"All is impermanence," Khun Sai concluded. Mother said she could not agree with her more.

It was not long after she had heard the story of the luckless betel box that Phloi became acutely conscious of that daily need of her body which the excitement of the day had caused to be neglected or suppressed for so many long hours. At home she would have gone to her room to sit on the pot, which would afterwards be taken away by the maid Phit to empty into the *khlong*. She had no idea where or how this call of nature was met in the Inner Court. To her whispered question Mother said aloud, "Oh, my little one, I forgot all about it! . . . Look here, Mae Choi, will you please take Phloi to the tunnel?"

What tunnel? Phloi would have liked to ask, but there was no time. In a flash, Choi was outside the door and beckoning at her to follow.

Once they were out on the street, Choi suggested helpfully, "We can run if you want to go real badly." Phloi assured her it had not reached that stage. She called her Mae Choi, which seemed to infuriate the other.

"Don't you call me Mae Choi!" It sounded like a threat. But when Phloi meekly changed the address to Khun Choi, she was further reprimanded. "Silly girl! Nobody calls me Khun except Mae Phaad, Aunt Sai's servant. Just call me Choi, without trimmings. That's what I meant."

Phloi then inquired about the tunnel. But Choi grew impatient. "You'll see for yourself when we get there. Don't ask too many questions. And hurry up. I don't want you to let go and have to do it in the street and shame us all."

The tunnel was a long way off. Barely stopping to exchange greetings with Choi's friends along the way, they hurried down streets and alleys, past Teng Row, past the Sri Sudawong Gate—and the threshold Phloi had paid homage to this morning—and finally arrived at what indeed looked like a tunnel jutting out from a section of the inner wall.

They stepped in, and Phloi's heart sank at what she saw.

"I can't do it here, Choi," she said. "I can't with so many people."

"Nonsense," was Choi's sensible retort. "If they can, so can you. Come, I'll keep you company."

The wooden platform stretching away before them on either side of the tunnel was partitioned into small open-topped, breast-high cubicles, thus allowing their occupants as well as those moving along the passage—newcomers and those on the way out—to converse easily with one another. And converse they did, some sounding as if they had come here only with this purpose in mind. This gave the place a friendly, convivial atmosphere which Phloi, absorbed as she was in her own embarrassment, did not fail to appreciate. She only wished she could behave as naturally as the rest of them, and felt much encouraged when Choi admitted that she too, on *her* first day, had found the tunnel too crowded.

The sun was setting when they re-emerged. The sky was a lovely riot of changing colours that would soon fade into twilight. The trip back took them once again past the enormous inner gate, in time to witness it being closed, bolted, locked, and chained with a great deal of banging and clanking by a contingent of energetic-looking *khlon*s. "Now no one can get in or out," Choi said im-pressively. "The gate will not be opened again until morning. No matter what happens." These remarks, combined with the awesome sight of the locked gate, sent a shudder through Phloi. True, at her home by the *khlong* she herself had never had occasion to go outside the compound after dark, but there were always comings and goings in and out of the gate at the back, and up and down the landing pavilion on the *khlong* side, often until late at night. At home she had never had this sinking feeling of being shut away, cut off, except when left alone inside a locked room by Mother as a form of punishment.

Choi had more information to impart. "We must get back before dark, because we haven't brought a candle. If you wander in the dark without carrying a light, you get arrested by the *khlon*s." Then she gave the same sort of advice offered by Mother earlier in the day: "You want to watch these *khlon*s, Phloi. They are fierce." As if I didn't know it already, Phloi thought.

They made it safely back before nightfall and were instructed by Khun Sai to go on straightaway to the courtyard in the back. This was a large square ground paved with flagstones like the streets everywhere in the Grand Palace—stones which, Choi had told her during their recent outing, had been brought over the ocean in big junks all the way from China. Looking round her, Phloi saw that the yard was surrounded on three sides by the verandas of the ground floor and on the fourth by a lower wall which had a small gate in it. In the gathering dusk she could make out the neat rows of pots and jars along the border on the veranda sides—pots of flowering shrubs alternating with jars containing lotuses; and against the wall a neat row of orange jasmine alternating with ixora bushes; and at the far end of the wall, Mother sitting with a friend under a big mimusops tree where stood many water jars—dragon jars like the ones at their Khlong Bang Luang home. And when Mother bathed her, scooping up water from one of the jars and giving her a thorough scrub the way she had always done, Phloi reflected that some things in the palace were not too different from home after all. Mother also helped bathe Choi, and while doing so commended her for having brought Phloi back promptly, without dawdling, and promised her a nice reward for responsible behaviour.

Back in Khun Sai's room, having dressed Phloi and finished her own toilet with a far greater care than was her custom, Mother took out from her black-and-gold chest many sets of *phalai*s and bodice cloths—most of which Phloi had never seen her wear, laid them out on the floor and launched into a lengthy discourse with hardly any pause for breath.

"You're now a palace girl, Phloi. It's time you knew what to put on for each day of the week. Look at this. Now either of these combinations is right for Monday—the yellow *phalai* with the light blue top or the pigeon blue *phalai* with the top in *champa* red. For Tuesday, this lime pink or this *maprang*-pit purple, topped by *sok*-leaf green, you see? Or, if you prefer a green *phalai*, then your top should be in pale purple. Where am I now? Oh, yes, Wednesday. Both bean colour and iron colour are correct for your Wednesday *phalai*, to be worn with *champa* orange. And this is for Thursday: green *phalai* with bird's-blood red, or orange *phalai* topped by pale green. For Friday it's dark blue with yellow on top, and for Saturday the *phalai* in *maprang*-pit purple with the cloth in *sok*-leaf green. Dark purple is also acceptable for Saturday—lovely shade, isn't it?—and oh so hard to find. By the way, you also wear dark purple when in mourning, but the bodice cloth must be in beige. For Sunday, you may dress as on Thursday if you wish or you may choose a lichee red or a pig's-blood red *phalai*, with the top in *sok*-leaf green. All right? You must learn those combinations and not dress like a clumsy peasant. You don't want people to say it's a pity your mother's from the palace but hasn't taught you anything."

"My dear Mae Chaem!" Khun Sai remarked at the end of the lecture. "Of course you haven't taught her anything, But that's no reason why she should be made to learn it all in one lesson. She'll pick it up soon enough, don't you worry."

No sooner had the clothes been put away than visitors started to drop in for another get-together with their old friend Mae Chaem. Before long Phloi began to lose interest in their grown-up chatter and at a signal from Choi followed her out into the yard, taking with her the sweets Khun Choei had thrust into her hand at dawn. The dawn of this very same day, it struck Phloi looking at the rather crumpled package, but how long ago it seemed.

They sat down near the back gate—to go out after dark without permission would be sure to earn her some twig-strokes from Khun Aunt, Choi said. They ate the sweets—the crunchy *chan-ap* pilfered from Khun Un's overflowing cupboard—and watched the lights coming on in the rooms off the veranda. What was Khun Choei doing now, Phloi wondered, and Chao Khun Father, and Elder Brother Phoem? She had a sudden intense longing for them, and for her mother, wanting to run to her, to feel safe and secure in her nearness. But at the moment her mother seemed to belong to her happy laughing friends rather than to her lonely daughter.

"Do you miss your home very much?" asked Choi.

When no answer was forthcoming, Choi understood and went on.

"You are much braver than I ever was, Phloi. I cried nonstop for three days when I first came, and refused to eat rice—I ate other things, though. Khun Aunt nearly sent me home. It was her idea, my coming to live in the palace. She said I was turning into a boy because I ran about with my elder brother all day long. My only brother—his name is Nueng. She said my character needed correct-ing. So here I am.

"Khun Aunt is really very kind even though she scolds me all the time. Did you hear her, Phloi, when she said it was a waste of rice bringing me up? She's said it before, many times. Grownups say funny things when they're not pleased with us. You know, Phloi, I'm going to stop Khun Aunt from saying it again. You wait and see.

"Are you afraid of ghosts, Phloi?"

At last she won a response. Phloi was nodding her head, trembling a little.

"Do you see that tree over there? It's haunted. A woman hanged herself there."

"What's that big palace, Choi?" Phloi suddenly asked. She loved listening to a ghost story as much as anybody, but not while sharing a vast shadowy courtyard with only one other living person. The question, however, did not entirely stem from her desire to change the subject. For even to a girl on the verge of tears, wanting to go home, scared at the thought of haunted trees, it was still the prettiest sight—the top floor of the big palace outlined against the blue evening sky beyond the wall, with noble spires rising into the heavens behind it, and the lights gaily twinkling in its countless doors and windows.

After telling her that Phra Chao Yu Hua, that is, the king, and Somdet, the queen, lived up there, Choi waved her arm about pointing to various parts of the royal residence, in and out of view, giving the name of each and telling Phloi she had never been there herself. "Not yet," she said hopefully. Heavenly Garden, Emerald House, Thi Bon, Phra Tamnak—these were some of the names Phloi heard that first night she came to the palace. "Heavenly Garden," she repeated after Choi, feeling glad that their beloved Phra Chao Yu Hua, whom she had never seen, should have this place, which must be as inviting as its name, high up there near the stars.

When it was time to go back inside for their evening rice, Choi said somewhat mysteriously, "You go in, Phloi. I have to get some-thing first. It won't take long."

She entered the room only a few moments after the meal had started, carrying a *krathong* of boiled rice and wearing a sorrowful expression on her face.

"Why the rice?" inquired her astonished aunt. "There is enough rice here for everybody."

"You said it was a waste of rice bringing me up, so I bought some with my own money. I'll just take a bit of your curry." She glanced at the other dishes before continuing, "and your fish, and a few prawns, if I may," and having said it, proceeded to suit action to words.

Seeing one of their stock phrases thus literally acted upon and stripped of its moralizing intent, the grownups went into fits of laughter, while Choi went on munching imperturbably.

Phloi was smiling. She was proud of her new friend, and content to be close to her mother again, sharing with her the food that had been planned and cooked especially for them.

The smile did not last long. Her first dinner in the Palace, after such a promising start, quickly collapsed into a nightmare of a meal, into visions of loneliness and starvation. Happiness is indeed a fragile thing, and that time it was shattered by Khun Sai's hospitable question, "And you will stay with us a long time, won't you, Mae Chaem?" and Mother replying in her commonsensical voice, "I don't know, Khun. It's hard to explain. Life is good within these walls, everything so comfortable. But having lived outside for so many years I find it, well, a little stifling, you know. I guess I'm spoiled. And, what's more important, I'll have to start earning a living pretty soon—my money is not going to last forever. What I have in mind is to go to Chachoengsao and open a shop selling this and that. I've got some cousins there and they've invited me to go and stay with them."

Then she added, speaking as though her daughter were not sitting there by her side, "I'll be grateful if you'll take good care of Phloi for me. I'll come to visit her as often as I can."

"You stay here with me, Phloi," said Khun Sai gently. "I'll look after you like my own niece—in fact, you're going to be much easier to look after than that urchin. You'll have many friends to play with. You're still a little girl, so it will be more play than work for you, isn't that nice? And you're going to become a great favourite of Sadet, I'm sure, like your mother before you. Don't look so sad, Phloi. Let me tell you about Sadet. She is the kindest patroness, the most generous protector you could hope to find. She also has the most penetrating eyes that can see right inside your head and heart. She likes her girls to talk to her, to be frank and open with her, but watch out, never let her friendly ways turn your head and make you insolent or conceited. That will never do. And don't be frightened away when she scolds you. She does it out of love. She is loving-kindness itself when you deserve it."

"Sometimes even when you don't," Mother joined in. "I will never forget how angry she was when I asked her permission to go and live with Chao Khun—Chao Khun who already had his official wife and children. She was dead set against it—and with good reason, the way things have turned out. Yet in the end she didn't let me go empty-handed but gave me a present of ten *chang*. By the way, Khun, I've made a few more *chang* out of that sum, by lending it out and collecting interest. It's going to be with this money—with Sadet's gift—that I'll be able to start a new life. You're not eating anything, Phloi."

Blinking unseeingly at her plate of rice, Phloi tried to swallow a mouthful. It went down, but felt dry as uncooked flour in her parched throat.

Later, after the two women had gone upstairs for the evening audience with Sadet, Choi brought out her large collection of dolls and their miniature accessories—houses, pots, stoves and whatnot. It was a laudable though vain attempt on her part to cheer up a friend; she gave it up after a while, which left only the maid Phit, a noisy doll-enthusiast despite her age, to play with them until it was time to unroll the mattresses and put up the mosquito nets.

Late that night, in answer to Phloi's questions, Mother held her closer and said, "Yes, sweetheart, I really must move on. But no matter where I go, no matter what I do, I love you most of all. You must remember that. And whatever happens to me, I do so want you to have a good life."

Mother's warm loving arms, rather than her words, comforted Phloi and soon lulled her, in spite of her fears of a motherless existence, into a deep unbroken sleep lasting till sunrise.

THREE

THESE fears came to occupy less and less space in Phloi's mind as days went by without Mother so much as mentioning again the word "leaving." Besides, each passing day had been eventful enough, pleasantly exciting enough, to keep her from unduly moping about the future. To begin with, she had a reading lesson in the morning, with Khun Sai conducting the class of two—Choi being the other pupil, the one who often burst into tears on getting rapped on the knuckles for making mistakes. Choi's copy of the primer had red smudges all over it from tears dropping on the stick-half of a burnt-out joss stick which was painted red and used as an instrument to point at words by children learning to read in those days. In this class, the girls were acquiring not only the art of reading but a sense of gratitude towards knowledge itself and towards those who handed it to them, and at the end of every lesson, with joined palms and bowed head, they performed their gesture of thanks and reverence to the textbook and the teacher.

Then there were the myriad activities having to do with the preparation of food or betel nuts, or the care of clothes, or the making of sachets and scented water. Phloi had become Khun Sai's little assistant-apprentice at these tasks, had even once or twice tried her unskilled hand at rolling *phlu* leaves in the elegant manner of the palace. These heart-shaped leaves, which had red lime spread on them and were chewed with betel nuts, were fashioned by Khun Sai's deft fingers into long tapering things so attractive in their graceful, purposely exaggerated slimness. The results of Phloi's effort appeared oddly stunted beside them, but Khun Sai said never mind, not to worry, and that some day she would be able to do it with her eyes closed.

Some of the tasks were beyond her physical strength and Phloi only participated in their execution as a spectator. *Phalai*-polishing was one of them. Arms on the hefty side were required to raise and lower that bamboo pole with the huge chunk of quartz attached to its end, getting the stone to rub on the cloth and give its surface a glossy sheen. The women who took turns doing this chatted incessantly with Phloi and among themselves, and moved the pole effortlessly to a sort of rhythm, making the job look both easy and enjoyable.

Fanning also had its own rhythm. Fanning lessons usually took place in the evening. "Bear in mind you are fanning a person, and not a charcoal stove." This was one of Khun Sai's injunctions as she showed Phloi how to wave the long-handled feather fan at the silk length tied to the back of a chair, wave it in such a way as to keep the silk continually fluttering for as long as possible. "The longer you can keep it going the better." Then after the lesson one night she told Phloi, "I think very soon I'll be able to start you on fanning duty. Would you like that? You'd be positioned at this distance away from Sadet, who would be seated about where the silk is. And remember, you'll be fanning her, not a stove." This made Phloi giggle out loud. Imagine anyone mistaking Sadet for a stove!

But as Khun Sai had foretold, there had been more play than work. Play included accompanying Choi on her visits to residences of highnesses, Chao Choms and others, where her friends lived as members of the household. On the whole, though, Choi preferred taking her to Teng Row, where "you don't have to be so careful how you behave, where they don't tell you to keep quiet and not to do this and that all the time." Not all of the residences were big and beautiful, Phloi had noticed somewhat to her surprise. Some, in fact, were not only small but seemed on the point of tumbling down from old age and neglect. Other kinds of differences were no less eye- and ear-opening. At one residence, she listened with amaze-ment at the way its inhabitants spoke—it was Thai but with the tones all mixed up. "It's the Petchaburi accent," Choi later informed her. "The Chao Chom came from there, and all those Petchaburi maids came with her." At another Chao Chom's residence it was the southern speech, which sounded even more strange. Then at the third, which happened to be one of the most imposing build-ings, the dominant sound was that of the lilting northern dialect. Very pretty, Phloi thought. As pretty and as unique as the people who used it—the fair-complexioned women in the long *phasin* with their hair worn in a bun. The Chao Chom of this residence, a native of Chiang Mai, was called Chao Dara, Choi said, adding that "Dara" meant "star" in case Phloi didn't know. Then there were residences where one could buy things—scented water, sweets, savouries, silks, precious stones—almost anything. These places were always lively, not like some other residences where a more sedate atmosphere prevailed.

There was this one residence nearby. They passed it every day but never went in, because at this period a state of bad relations had been declared between its inhabitants and those of Sadet's house. While the adult members of both camps generally refrained from showing their ill feelings other than pointedly looking the other way or maintaining a disdainful silence at the sight of the enemy, the younger girls were apt to be more openly belligerent, and one day Phloi was present at a staring battle between Choi and a girl from "that place." Walking in opposite directions along one of the busy narrow streets, they had had to brush past each other. The other girl gave Choi a ferocious glare; Choi returned it, and the fight was on. There they stood, eyes riveted on eyes, each deter-mined to outscowl the other. A crowd soon collected around them, cheering them on: chairs were brought out for the opponents, who sat down without disengaging their locked gazes. Bowls of water and sweets were given them by their respective supporters. The crowd grew denser and noisier, the contest looked as if it might last all afternoon. After a while, however, an indignant Khun Sai appeared on the scene and succeeded, though not without some physical exertion and a string of verbal threats, in dragging Choi away. But by that time the other girl had shown signs of weakening, her glare having begun to waver slightly, and the neutral among the audience all agreed that Choi had won.

A naughty unruly child to most grownups, a terror to some of the children her own age, Choi was also one of the kindest human beings Phloi had known in her short life, and the most tender part of her big heart, Phloi had noticed during these first days they had toured the palace together, was always open to the poor, the weak, the unfortunate. The old humble women living out the last years of their humble lives in obscure corners of the Inner Court could depend on Choi to run errands for them, to treat them with sweet courtesy, to make them laugh and feel that they still belonged in this world. The younger children had Choi as their champion against the bullies, had her shoulder to cry on and her purse to dig into when they were hungry or desperately coveted a new toy. The stray dogs and cats—mangy ones included—roaming the Inner Court were all Choi's best friends. Even the grubs of coconut beetles—another palace speciality—were her best friends. These grubs were reared inside sugar cane sticks until they became fat and ready to fry. One day Choi brought home a stick and at bedtime smuggled it under the mosquito net, and Phloi fell asleep listening to the tiny greedy noise of the grub sucking at the juicy fibre of the cane. A few days later the stick had to be returned to the king's kitchen. Choi had wept watching her grubs being dropped into the boiling pan, and on the way back to the residence, tears rolling down her face, was stopped and questioned by several women if a close relative of hers had died.

Then the day came—the dread day, and not even Choi with all her resources and kindness could help. The morning was bright and sunny, not ominous in the least; then after breakfast Mother calmly announced that she was leaving today, now, saying she had already taken leave of Sadet the night before, while Phloi had been asleep.

Phloi did not let out a sob because she had no strength left. She was conscious of a terrible emptiness in the pit of her stomach, sweat on her body which had gone suddenly cold and the hot tears streaming from her eyes. Mother's face looked hazy, and her voice sounded muted, coming from far away.

"Please stop crying, my love, or I'll die. I have to leave you and walk the path of my karma, my bad karma. But I'm not leaving you for good. I'll come back soon and we'll be together again."

Mother was crying. Phloi could feel her tears on her cheeks as she kissed her. She cried with abandon, as always, and stopped crying with her usual decisiveness, quickly composed herself and went on to practical matters.

"I've left all my jewellery with Khun Sai. The list is with Sadet. They're yours now, to wear when you're a big girl. There's not a great deal of them, but enough to give you a good appearance among people. You will not lose face wearing them. The ruby pendant was a gift from Sadet, and the nine-gem ring from your grandfather. The rest—rings and bracelets and so forth—I bought myself. You may sell them or have them reset as you please, but do keep the nine-gem ring to leave to your children and grandchildren."

At the Sri Sudawong Gate she said, "Keep well, Phloi. Don't neglect your duties to Sadet. Do as Khun Sai tells you, and don't be a difficult child . . . Come, Phit, we must go."

"Phloi, let's have a race back," Choi suggested, and without waiting for an answer started off galloping away from the gate towards the interior. Phloi ran weeping after her, but on reaching the residence went straight to Khun Sai's room and would not listen any more to Choi, who was full of good plans for the coming afternoon.

Khun Sai asked her to help pluck the stems of the orange jasmine buds she was stringing into wreaths. Afterwards she told Phloi to take a nap and Choi not to bother anybody.

"Come and sit by me, Phloi," Sadet said later that afternoon, handing her a knife and a piece of ginger. "Here, will you peel it for me? The knife is not too sharp. Just right for you. I don't want you to cut yourself."

She showed Phloi the bowl containing pieces that had been peeled and carved, asking her opinion about them. "Aren't they pretty?"

"Yes, Your Highness," Phloi answered.

"Let's see, you pick out the prettiest ones." Phloi did so and put them on a plate.

"Look," Sadet said with a laugh, "they're all mine—the ones she's chosen."

Khun Sai shook her head. "I'm not surprised, Your Highness, what with mine looking so crude and rough beside yours. I used to do better, but my eyesight is so poor these days. Age," she sighed.

"Don't be silly," Sadet said affectionately. "You're several years younger than I am. It's not age but laziness. Sheer laziness." She paused, watching Phloi in silence for some time, then asked, "Do you miss your mother very much?"

"Very much, Your Highness."

"I know, and I feel for you. I would have kept her here for you if I could. However, Chachoengsao is not so far away, you know. Soon she'll be back with us again."

Lightly stroking Phloi's hair, Sadet instructed Khun Sai to look after her well.

To Phloi she said, "Come and see me often, and let me know when you need anything or feel troubled in any way. Don't shy away from grownups, Phloi. Children should realize that grownups have their welfare at heart. We want you to be good and to deserve all that is good."

And to the room in general, she said, "You people have no consideration for me. You take off whenever it's convenient and leave me with helpless children."

Khun Sai and the other attendants smiled among themselves, and carried on with their vegetable carving. Phloi vainly struggled to hold back her tears. They were not altogether sad tears, and were caused as much by Sadet's sympathy for her as by Mother's departure. Khun Sai, now looking distressed, would prefer to see more self-control in front of Sadet as a matter of principle, but Sadet herself was all in favour of letting the tears drown the sorrow "—as you would pour water on the fire to douse it."

When she thought Phloi had cried enough, Sadet sent for a box from her dressing table. There was a mirror fixed to the inside of its lid.

"You see?" Sadet said. "That's what we look like from crying too much. Not pretty, is it?"

Phloi glanced at the puffy face in the mirror and began to wipe her eyes. From among the articles in the box Sadet selected a gold bracelet with a charm attached to it—a lock with a ruby for the keyhole. Putting it on Phloi's wrist, she said, "There! I'm buying your tears with this. If you don't stop now these girls are going to join you. I know them—they dearly love a good cry—gives them a chance to show off their pretty tears."

Phloi bowed down with a heart filled with joy and gratitude, and did a rather awkward *krap*, nearly landing her head on Sadet's lap. There were still some tears left—the last lot—and her face was streaked with them.

Sadet laughed. "Didn't I pay enough? What a hard bargainer you are! Very well, you shall have this toy too." This was a musical box— the first one Phloi had laid her eyes on. Sadet wound it and put it on the floor. Its lid flew open; a bird of many-coloured enamel plumage flew up bursting into song, a performance it was to repeat for Phloi now and again throughout her life, sometimes in celebration of her happiness, sometimes to lessen the shock of a crushing event or make a heartache easier to endure.

ONE morning, a week or so after Mother had left for Cha-choengsao, Phloi found herself stepping over the threshold of the Sri Sudawong Gate into the Outer Court, where male visitors were allowed. It was a mid-month Buddhist holy day and on such a day—Choi had told her last night—her father and elder brother Nuang usually came to visit her, and wouldn't Phloi like to come along and meet them. "They don't always turn up," she had warned. "But even if they don't, it's fun to go and walk about and look at people and things."

The outer court was as bustling a place as it had been that other morning when Phloi, a typical wide-eyed clumsy stranger, made her unheralded first appearance inside its walls. Now she went zigzagging through the crowd almost as confidently as Choi the veteran, and when Choi, crying "There they are!" shot off like a magic arrow, Phloi followed her as she would on a playground; being no mean sprinter herself, she reached the goal at the same time as her friend.

Choi's father was a tall lean man with a gentle smiling face, a slender, less forceful version of his sister Khun Sai. Elder brother

Nuang, who must have had his topknot shaved off only recently—his hair had that comical sprouting look about it—grimaced in a cocky manner that reminded Phloi of her own brother Phoem.

Choi said, "This is my father," with great pride—the pride of a treasure-owner, which Phloi understood and appreciated, for in her undemonstrative way she too had her full share of the same pride.

Choi's father asked the familiar question, "What is your father's name, little one?" When she told him, his smile broadened in pleased recognition.

"I used to know His Excellency quite well," he said. "When both of us were young lads we often went about town together. I'll tell you this, little one, it would be hard to find a more generous man than your Chao Khun Father."

He had also known her mother. He described her as a palace beauty and inquired if she was still as beautiful, thereby making Phloi blush with pleasure and embarrassment.

"How is my Spotty?" Choi asked her brother.

"Ugly as ever," he replied with a smirk. "Maybe uglier. She had five puppies the other day—the noisiest puppies. Such a nuisance."

While Choi was excitedly jumping up and down, he turned to Phloi, aimed his smirk at her together with the remarks, "Are you a cry-baby? You look like one."

"Cry-baby yourself!" cried Choi, the defender of the weak. "Don't you talk to Phloi like that again, you hear? Cry-baby yourself!" she fairly snorted. To which her brother gave a superior shrug, mutter-ing unconcernedly, "Suit yourself."

"I brought you these persimmons," said Choi's father, pointing at the basket lying at his feet. "Share them with Phloi. And there's shrimp paste and a jar of roasted chili paste for your Aunt Sai. Your mother made it herself."

"Have you been a hard-working pupil, Choi?" he also asked. "Do you practice reading and writing every day?"

Smiling fondly at his son, he advised him to treat the girls with more politeness. "You're only a temple pupil, Nuang," he said, "and these girls are getting their training in the palace." The com-parison seemed to amuse rather than impress Nuang, who continued to wear the same self-satisfied expression in his treatment of the girls.

After the visitors had gone, the girls, in discussing their families, agreed with each other about elder brothers—how they stopped being reliable playmates soon after their tonsure, how they started putting on airs, swaggering about mistaking themselves for young men and therefore turned into ridiculous and tiresome creatures.

In actual fact, Elder Brother Nuang behaved reasonably well on subsequent visits—no more smirking or acting superior—and became the girls' ally to the extent of taking it upon himself to bring them their favourite titbits such as those very sour, very pungent pickles forbidden by their elders as being ruinous to the stomach.

All in all, what an excellent thing to have visitors from home. Apart from the pleasure of seeing them, and afterwards of distribut-ing the gifts they had brought among members of your crowd, their presence gave tangible proof that you were not so destitute, not entirely lacking in relatives and friends from beyond the walls—palace walls though they might be. No one from Khlong Bang Luang came to see Phloi. Nor did she expect them to. (Chao Khun Father in the Outer Court? Unthinkable!) Choi's father and brother were her only visitors during her first months in the palace, and they sufficed. They belonged to Choi and treated her, Choi's friend, as one of the family. It was natural for her to feel a sense of pro-prietorship about them. At any rate she could not have derived more enjoyment out of their more or less regular visits had they been her own blood relations.

How quickly the months had gone by. No news of Mother, but this did not upset Phloi. She missed her still but had stopped pining for her and, while looking forward to her promised visit with the eagerness of a loving daughter, took it as a matter of course that her mother, like the mothers of most girls in the palace, should be living somewhere else. She now shared the mosquito net with Khun Sai and Choi, and to go to sleep under it each night without Mother lying beside her no longer made her feel incomplete. She now bathed and dressed herself, and looked after herself at mealtimes, Mother would be pleased to know. She would also be amazed, Phloi thought, at how much she had learned about the palace and its people and, yes, its anecdotes, intrigues, feuds, scandals—she had no need to pester her with so many questions now. Palace idioms, slang and allusions had likewise lost much of their power to mystify. Now when hearing that hitherto cryptic phrase "like the Czarevitch reception," she understood that it meant something grand and lavish, requiring a great deal of preparation in advance (but without knowing that this dated from the visit of the future Czar Nicholas II to Bangkok some years back). When the word "fran," often ac-companied by a titter, was used to describe the close intimacy between two girls, Phloi knew, though she had but a vague com-prehension as to why it should cause comment, that they loved each other excessively (and with no inkling that the word represented a Thai pronunciation of the English word "friend").

Another month pass by. It must have been five months now since Mother took off for Chachoengsao. Then one evening, as Phloi was fanning Sadet and listening to her conversation with some of the women in attendance, Choi came up, and whispered in her ear, "I'll take the fan. Khun Aunt Sai wants to see you in her room." Phloi went, heard her mother's voice before reaching the door, dashed in and jumped on to her lap nearly knocking her over, and gave herself up to hugging and being hugged, kissing and being kissed, laughing and talking at the same time, and crying a little too. She asked Mother why she had stayed away so long. Mother said she'd had hundreds of things to attend to and that it was quite a job trying to arrange a journey from Chachoengsao to Bangkok—if this cousin of hers had not provided a boat she would have had to postpone the trip. She made Phloi stand up, remarking how she had grown, how pretty she was looking, that her manners had im-proved and that it wouldn't be long before she became a full-fledged Inner Court girl. The sympathetic Khun Sai laughed through her tears along with them, to be sure. The maid Phit wept through her laughter, so glad was she to see Phloi again, and to be back in the palace after months of being buried in the country, where "you couldn't see the moon and the sun," as she put it. The reunion would not have been complete without Phit's bawling and guffaw-ing, and without Mother having eventually to scold her. She told her to stop that nonsense and finish bringing in the baskets and parcels still cluttering the passage.

These contained gifts from the provinces—sugarcane, bananas, fresh eggs, salted eggs, dried fish, crispy fish, all kinds of paste and sweetmeat. She had selected the very best of everything to be presented to Sadet, Mother proudly declared. Khun Sai teased her about this, saying Sadet was to be envied for having such a wonder-ful maid, one who never stopped thinking of her welfare even while wandering in remote corners of the earth.

"Don't be so jealous," Mother retorted. "You're also getting the best Chachoengsao has to offer, my dear Khun!"

"And these are for you, Phloi . . . you like them?"

Like them? They were the sweetest, most delightful presents anyone could wish for—these miniature eggs, miniature fish, fruit and everything else, all real and edible, and resembling those for the grownups in every clever, meticulous detail. From the brown crispy fish the size of your little finger to the salted ricebird eggs no bigger than your thumb, not to mention the adorable baskets that came with them. Everything was a daintier, more perfect copy of its work-a-day original, everything looking so absurdly, so enchantingly real and toy-like all at once. And of course, what made them especially precious to Phloi was the thought that Mother must have had to spend days and days planning them, searching for them, making them (who ever heard of a shop selling salted ricebird eggs) and that she wouldn't have taken so much trouble if she didn't really love her! Mother had also brought plenty of each item to enable Phloi, in her turn, to give to her heart's content, and thus, while her elders had their chat, Phloi set about dividing up her riches, happily counting baskets and friends—the largest number of baskets having been set aside for Choi—and occasionally lending half-an-ear to the conversation.

". . . at least I've made a start," Mother was saying at one point. "Pho Chim was saying the other day we should buy a boat, go into wholesaling, bringing goods to and from Chachoengsao and Bangkok, you know. He says there's more money in that than just keeping a small shop over there. I think he's right."

"Who is this Pho Chim?" Khun Sai asked.

"A distant cousin. He's been helping me . . . Came with me on this trip . . . I did tell you about these cousins of mine in Chachoengsao, didn't I?"

"Yes, you did. But is this Pho Chim a good person, someone you can really trust? . . . Are you sure? . . . Perhaps I shouldn't be saying all this, but I love you like a sister, as you well know. I just don't want you to rush into anything without first weighing every possible outcome—good and bad . . . Then there's Phloi to consider."

"Precisely! I wouldn't be doing all this if it weren't for Phloi. Listen, Khun, it's for Phloi's sake that I'm struggling to make a success of this business. I want to be someone for her to lean on. I don't want her relatives across the river to say to her, 'Look at your mother. She's no good, she'll never amount to anything.' But since they won't lift a finger to help me amount to something, I've got to find help wherever I can . . ."

"All right, all right. You mustn't mind me, Mae Chaem. I'm like that proverbial toad who lives in a coconut shell and knows next to nothing about the ways of the world. Come, have a wash and freshen up, then we'll go and present your gifts to Sadet. She'll be so pleased. But then she'd be just as pleased if you had brought her only an egg."

When they were alone that night, Mother asked the question which had become a sort of tradition between them: "How big is your love for me, Phloi?" The answer, which never varied either, was: "As big as the sky, Mother."

This made her next question all the more startling: "How would you like to have a new father, Phloi?"

"I don't know," Phloi sincerely told her. "What about Chao Khun Father?" she asked.

No answer. Mother remained silent for a moment, then in a low voice, more to herself than to Phloi, she quoted the old saying about the fruit never falling far from its tree, and said that the tree in this case was unmistakably the one across the river, in Khlong Bang Luang.

FOUR

THAT time, Mother stayed in the palace for about ten days. Phloi saw her mostly in the morning and evening; during the day Mother had to go out on errands connected with her business. "There's so much to do and so many people to see," she kept saying. She brought back fruit and sweets from these trips into town, and never failed to gather Phloi into her arms, showering her with kisses as though they had not seen each other for months. She was looking young and beautiful, especially when her face was lit up with a certain dreamy smile quite new to Phloi. On the other hand, she often sighed, and apparently for no reason. But on the whole the smile predominated, which Phloi thought was a good thing.

There were no sad tears when they parted that second time, no feelings of fear, or anxiety, or loss. At the gate they said goodbye in cheerful spirits, content with each other and with their respective lot, and went their separate ways loving each other with that un-assuming love described by Phloi simply as being as big as the sky.

MOTHER had left; her next visit, and the ones after that, would come about in due course. Meanwhile the Inner Court was Phloi's foster parent, her home away from home, her school, her village; and the Grand Palace at large with its throne halls and offices, its pavilions and *chedi*s and giants, with the Emerald Buddha presiding in the royal chapel and the Guardian Spirit of Bangkok standing watch just outside its walls, was still her big city and, although she didn't know it at the time, the hub of her universe, a benign universe notwithstanding the *khlon*s, the ghosts and other intimidating types.

Benign, and to Phloi looking back on it years later, never tedious in its benignity but benignly generous in providing enough challenge, enough variety and beauty in its daily routine, and enough special fun-filled events of the kind that seem to be held with the extra purpose of highlighting one's memories of childhood.

One such event was the tonsure ceremony for Her Royal Highness the Princess Daughter. For weeks before this was due to take place the whole Inner Court lived in a heightened state of pleasurable anticipation. News and rumours and speculations about the ceremonials and festivities to come were eagerly sought, passed on and commented upon from morning till night: who had been selected to attend upon the princess in the procession, what costume Her Royal Highness would be wearing for each of the three days while listening to the chanting of holy stanzas, how many kinds of entertainment, what presentations, performances and spectacles could be expected, and so on and so forth. Preparing for the event was half the fun. Everyone, it seemed, was either engaged in getting the palace fair ready, or getting ready to go to the palace fair, or both. Old and young alike, the women of the Inner Court looked forward to putting on their best jewellery for the occasion; those who had pawned theirs were now trying to get them back at all costs, adding not a little to the general excitement by their frantic manoeuverings.

Choi and Phloi during these weeks could be seen with their loosened topknots bobbing up and down dashing from one spot to another to listen, inspect, interview, exchange and recount. Of all the roving pre-fair reporters (self-appointed, that is) they must be ranked among the most zealous, and the best informed, though they had their priorities and were not equally or indiscriminately interested in everything. The subject of diamonds and emeralds did not fire their imagination and they only touched on it perfunctorily. On the other hand, they were most knowledgeable, and rapturous, over the gradual and to them almost miraculous transformation taking place near the Amarindr Throne Hall, of bamboo frames, clay, tin sheets, paints and a few other mundane materials into Mount Kailas—Mount Kailas, the abode of the gods and centre of the coming ceremony, where the Princess would be having her ritual bath in a gilded pavilion, but also Mount Kailas, their own fairyland whose woods and glades and waterfalls were taking shape before their very eyes. The Amarindr Hall being on the other side of the inner wall necessitated some after-hour sneaking back and forth on their part—how else would they be able to keep up with the progress of the Mount?—but the gods must have been smiling on them for they were never caught.

The first day of the event saw the pair elbowing their way to the front line of the crowds waiting for the procession to pass on its way to the Outer Court of the Grand Palace. They waited for hours, drenched to the skin under the sweltering sun but with undam-pened high spirits. The conch shell trumpet finally sounded in the distance, telling them that His Majesty had seen the Princess Daughter into her gold palanquin and that they could now start craning their necks in earnest—and also standing firm on their appropriated bits of stone pavement against fellow parade-watchers, who were pressing and pushing on all sides. Choi was doing some pushing herself and yelling to Phloi that they mustn't lose each other. They were both laughing, and so were many people in the crowd.

The military band came first (no need to record that this was Phloi's first military band) playing a rousing march in the *farang* style; then columns of marching soldiers, eyes gazing straight ahead, guns aligned on shoulders, arms and legs moving in perfect unison. Choi and Phloi stared at them, then nodded at each other as if to say this was a good beginning, no doubt about it. The rat-a-tat-tat of the *farang* drums fading away was succeeded by the ting-tang-ting of the Java drums, which emerged at the head of another group of musicians, whose ancient dress furnished a colourful contrast to the soldiers' uniforms. The Java pipes filled the air with their heart-lifting notes as ranking officials and page-boys, their palms joined respectfully in a *wai*, walked slowly past the spectators. Next came the Victory Drum and Conch Trumpet Unit drumming and blowing in the midst of a waving white and gold forest of tiered umbrellas, sunshades and other lofty insignia of a Princess Royal. Mingled with the sound of the propitious instruments was the crowd's murmuring noise, rising at times into words and phrases.

"Where's the palanquin? I can't see it."

"You will in a moment—can't you wait?"

"Ah, here come the brahmins!"

The white-robed brahmins came strewing grains of blessed rice along the path. Some of them fell where Phloi was standing and she picked them up, though only to lose them soon afterwards.

"Oh look at the handsome cuckoos!"

They were a pair of charmingly costumed little boys carrying feathers in their hands to represent a pair of Indian cuckoos. A few paces behind them strutted the "peacocks," who were followed in their turn by two pretty little girls holding gold and silver branches. Then a sigh, a heart-felt chorus of "How beautiful!" went up as, preceding the long train of attendants—courtiers, bearers, pond maidens, fan maidens, and a retinue of maids-in-waiting—Her Royal Highness appeared, seated in the gold vehicle, herself golden and sparkling from topknot to the tip of her toes. Some among the spectators had tears in their eyes, and a few old women were paying respects and sniffling happily at the same time. When the vehicle had passed, those in the crowd who had friends and relatives in the procession started to point them out to one another, beaming and talking more loudly than before

Choi and Phloi did not stay for the end of the parade but scurried away as fast as they could and in a matter of minutes had joined the throngs of fair-goers jostling about the entertainment area behind the Emerald Buddha Temple.

Here was where the wire-walkers had Choi completely spellbound. She kept going back to them, gaping up at them and saying how she wished somebody would teach her to do it. All kinds of daring feats were being performed, and games, and dances—and a singing act or two that were rather boring. Phloi liked the comic shows best of all. She had to hold her sides from laughing so hard. A trio of clowns were her great favourites—a female character called Nang Kra-ua and her husband and their water buffalo. Nang Kra-ua, wore refined but ragged clothes, carrying a tattered parasol in one hand and a basket full of holes in the other. Her husband was armed with a stick with which to do battle with the animal, who looked and acted very much like the real thing—never mind his big feet protruding from underneath the cloak. The lumbering husband took to his heels, chased by the madly clumsy buffalo, while Nang Kra-ua panted after them, parasol and basket flying in all directions. They bumped into one another, rolled about, scrambled up. What a roaring fun fight it turned out to be! How the three enjoyed themselves and how the audience loved them!

"I'll become a wire-walker," Choi said, "and you a clown like Nang Kra-ua."

When it turned dark and the lights came on they headed for Mount Kailas, and did not leave it again until summoned home by Khun Aunt Sai. They went back the next night, and the next. Their fairyland at night was all aglow and throbbing with life. The lanterns and glass balls of fantastic colours swayed in the breeze, the leaves glistened, and the gods peered out from among the rocks and trees. There were many kinds of birds and animals in the forest as well as those marvellous creatures such as the half-man, half-bird *khinari*s. And, most wonderful of all, there were stories from the Ramakien, and the Inao, and the Prince of the Golden Conch being enacted by troupes of very beautiful and clever clockwork dolls on tiny stages round the foot of the Mount. Truly, one could spend hours and hours here without ever getting tired, or hungry, or sleepy. The morning after the event, Sadet was to remark to the gathering in the Veranda Room: "Why, Nang Phloi's got rings under her eyes from going to the fair!"

It was here at Mount Kailas that Phloi saw His Majesty for the first time. He came to the fair accompanied by the young princes and princesses and their royal relatives. Phloi had been so absorbed in what was happening on one of the tiny stages that she didn't notice people round her dropping to their knees. Choi had to pull her down, and none too soon. Raising her head after paying hom-age, Phloi found herself looking up at her king. He was standing so close she could have reached out a hand to touch his feet. This she did not do, nor did she dare let her eyes remain fixed on him for very long, but quickly lowered her head again. Her heart was pounding. She felt an

upsurge of joy, was gripped at the same instant by an overwhelmi
sense of awe, and through all this was mutely expressing her love,
loyalty and gratitude. These feelings were older than she was, had
been experienced by her forefathers and handed down through
the centuries, and would be bequeathed by her to the children and
grandchildren to come.

Some moments later, with her head still bowed low, she was given
a nudge by Choi. "Phra Chao Yu Hua has gone, Phloi, but our Sadet
is here."

"So this is where you've been hiding yourselves," Sadet said. "And
look at Nang Choi grinning at me as if we were playmates! Here," she
handed Phloi her betel box, "will you carry it?"

Somewhat swelling with self-importance, Choi and Phloi went
stepping after Sadet. Casting her eyes over the crowds, Choi was
prepared to throw gracious smiles at some people and subject others
to her best disdainful stare. After playing this game for a while, she
mumbled, "Why don't we take turns holding the box? I feel so silly
having nothing to do but make faces."

THEN there was the annual Loi Krathong on the full-moon night
of the twelfth lunar month. The biggest moon of the year, and that
year it shone in a clear, deep blue sky, on a night that was deliciously
cold. "Open the Side Gate!" The cries of the guards echoed like an
invitation in the lovely night. "Open the Side Gate!"

Following behind the royal party, the women and children of the
Inner Court—quite a large and exuberant entourage—trooped off
from the palace to the river bank, there to join the no less exuberant
crowds of people who had come from near and far, by land and by
water, to see their king and float their votive *krathong*s in his presence.

The *piphat* bands played on. And now the brilliant moon had
reached the point directly above one's head. Aboard the Throne Barge,
His Majesty put the flame of his taper to the fuse line connected with
another royal barge, the one with the seven-headed *naga* king for its
prow—the barge Ananda Nagaraj—and suddenly, in the twinkling of
an eye, a resplendent Buddha image appeared bathed in candlelight

upon a flower-bedecked altar set high in the centre of the *naga*'s body. The image grew in brightness as members of the royal family also lighted their candles. Then the *naga* glided away, its crew in their traditional red and green costumes lifting and dipping their oars in a slow stately rhythm, to the accompani-ment of a boat chant that seemed to drift over the river as though it were part of the breeze.

The *naga* was not the only royal barge taking part in the celebrations that year. In its wake there came the Sri Supanna Hong, or Glorious Gold Swan and several others, and these luminous barges, together with thousands of other boats moored or moving near them or farther out on the moonlit waters, together with thousands of *krathong*s floated from boats and from the banks, became as one vast shimmering tribute to the river Chao Phraya.

The *krathong*s, of course, were fabulous, ranging from the finely wrought replicas of royal barges, sea-going junks, river sampans and various other craft, to those that were content merely to represent their own simple beautiful selves: bowl-shaped vessels, made of banana leaves, bearing flowers, candles, joss sticks, along with the wishes and prayers of their owners.

"And the *sanuk thi sut* (most fun) part was when the fireworks went off." So Phloi was to tell her mother when the latter returned for another visit a few months after Loi Krathong. There were those that went off with a terrific bang, making everyone scream and laugh, and those that leapt up sky-high to blossom into endless showers of falling stars, and the ones you held in your hands—like holding sticks alive with fireflies, then the potted ones that sent up sprays of gems from the ground, and the kinds that went racing underwater, throwing off sparks and making gurgling noise all the way, and many, many more.

The greatest fun. The most beautiful. Phloi was full of superlatives in her account of the fireworks. "We the children," she said, "had the most fun," and Choi had some holes in her clothes where the sparks had fallen—she was tossing a few sticks about to frighten those squeamish women just a little and that's how she got the holes, but she didn't get burned or anything, a detail which was regarded by Phloi's mother as coming under the superlative "luckiest."

PHLOI always had a great deal to tell Mother when she came. She did not come very often, and never stayed very long. Then one day the maid Phit turned up by herself, muttering something to the effect that her mistress couldn't make the trip.

Phloi felt very disappointed at first, then more worried than disappointed.

"Is Mother sick, Phit? What is it?"

The maid hesitated before replying. "I'll tell you later."

Something in her tone and manner caused Phloi to imagine that the worst, whatever it was, had befallen her mother, and this made her cry; and Khun Sai, who was seated nearby having her morning rice, frowningly issued a stern command.

"Tell her what it is, Phit. What's wrong? What's the matter with Mae Chaem? Speak-up!"

"N-n-nothing, ma'am," Phit stammered, scratching the floor as if hoping to find the right word in the wood grain. "Nothing the matter, ma'am. You see, my Khun Chaem . . . well, she says for me to bring all these gifts for everybody. But she herself won't come, because she's ashamed . . ."

"Well?" insisted Khun Sai. "Ashamed of what?"

"You see, she's big with child—that's what it is."

"Ah." Khun Sai paused. "I suppose the child's father is that so-called cousin of hers, that—that Pho Chim?"

"You suppose right, ma'am."

Nothing more was said for a few long minutes, not even by Choi. During this time Khun Sai, having finished her meal, washed her hands and mouth, waxed her lips, and chewed betel, doing it all slowly, thoughtfully.

"Go and get something to eat, Phit," she finally said. "And you, Choi, go upstairs and wait on Sadet. Go now. Don't dawdle."

Alone with Phloi, Khun Sai started to talk about this and that, about setting up a family, taking a husband, taking a wife, having children together. A woman could have more than one man to father her children, she explained, and, knowing her dear Mae Chaem as well as she did, she was sure that everything would turn out all right. And

Phloi would remain permanently her mother's beloved one, Khun Sai had not the slightest doubt about it. That might be so, Phloi thought, but at the moment she could not rejoice in it, no matter how hard she tried.

The rest of the morning Khun Sai said not one word more to Phloi on the subject of Mother's new pregnancy. She found a series of small jobs for Phloi to do, keeping her constantly occupied, and incidentally preventing her from slipping away to get more information out of Phit.

She told Sadet what had happened. She didn't do it in Phloi's presence, but Phloi knew she must have done it from the way Sadet glanced at her when she went up to attend on her during luncheon. Despite her concern—Phloi could sense that too—Sadet chose not to discuss it; and Phloi, having been an Inner Court trainee long enough, understood and also chose to behave as she would on any normal, ordinary day.

In the late afternoon, when they all came together again, Sadet suddenly asked, "Isn't Choi old enough to have her topknot shaved?"

Khun Sai recovered from her astonishment to answer, "Yes, I think so, Your Highness."

"Good. I'll sponsor her tonsure. We must start planning, you and I."

Khun Sai made her respectful gesture of thanks, turned round to check if her niece had done the same and, seeing Choi was gazing out the window at some sparrows flitting about under the eaves, gave her a quick pinch on the arm.

"What about Phloi?" Sadet went on consulting with Khun Sai. "Would her Chao Khun Father mind my doing the same for her? I would like you to go to Khlong Bang Luang, Sai, and ask Chao Khun how he feels about it. Take Phloi with you when you go. She hasn't been back home for a long time."

And that was what Sadet elected to do with her concern for Phloi on that particular occasion.

To be going home, and then soon to be without a topknot—two joyful prospects indeed! But what about Mother? Was she faring so well?

The opportunity to question Phit came at night, before bedtime, while Khun Sai and Choi were still upstairs with Sadet. Phit said, "My little Khun, your mother is a long long way from being an old woman. She can go on bearing children for many years yet. It's nature. That's what it is. So don't you fret."

"This man Pho Chim—what is he like, Phit?"

"A sharp man, my darling. Too sharp and cunning for this maid of yours. But he must have his good points, or your mother would not have yielded to him, would she? She's got good eyes, good taste, your mother has. What she picks for herself can't be bad. Isn't that so? Hey, Nang Phit!"—when excited, Phit sometimes lapsed into her habit of addressing herself while actually talking to you—"Hey, Nang Phit, who do you think you are, babbling on like this? It's none of your business. Want some whip stripes on your back? Shut up, Nang Phit!"

"Where is Mother living now, Phit?"

"In the same house we've had from the beginning. At first there were just the two of us and a servant. Then Pho Chim and his sister Mae Plang moved in to keep us from feeling lonely—ha! Pho Chim said he brought his sister along so that people wouldn't tittle-tattle about him and your mother. Well, now there's nothing much left to tattle about, now that everyone can see they're living as man and wife."

"And Mae Plang—does she help you around the house, Phit?"

"What! Mae Plang help me?! She gives orders, that's what she does! Oh, she played the sweet and humble type all right when she first came. Couldn't do enough for your mother, you know, and oh so ready to agree with everything your mother said. All that has changed. Now we know the real Mae Plang. Now you'd think she was the mistress of the house the way she acts. If I were your mother I wouldn't stand for it. Poor thing, she loves her husband, so she has to please his sister too! But if that woman does not watch out, she'll get what's coming to her from me, from Nang Phit! And let me tell you, when I give that woman a lesson it will hurt, and even if they chain me and drag me off to prison it will be worth it . . . Ho, ho, ho, Nang Phit, how you talk! . . . Come on, Khun Phloi darling, stop worrying about your mother. In a few days Phit will go back to take care of her, have no fear. Come, my love, time for you to go to sleep. I'll tell you a nice story . . ."

The visit to Khlong Bang Luang took place a week after Phit had returned to Chachoengsao. Phloi got all dressed up for it under Khun Sai's supervision. The fineries were being worn not for the purpose of showing off, according to Khun Sai, but as befitted the occasion. She didn't want anyone to think that Phloi was not properly looked after in the palace. She also warned that Sadet and herself would lose face should Phloi's manners and behaviour be judged less than satisfactory by Chao Khun Father.

Accompanied by Mae Phaad, Khun Sai's number one servant, they left the Grand Palace, went along the wall and then across the road to Tha Phra landing, retracing in reverse the short route taken by Phloi and Mother some eight months ago.

The world at Tha Phra was a busy place full of strangers, some of whom with manners that could not possibly win Khun Sai's approval. It was very noisy, and not all of the noise was of the pleasant, cheerful variety. Some women vendors were hurling coarse words at one another evidently with great relish. Khun Sai quickened her steps, keeping her eyes averted and her face purposely blank.

Once in the boat, however, she forgot about such things as bad language and only concentrated on the safety of the journey. "Sit there in the middle," was her instruction to Mae Phaad. "Keep still or you'll rock the boat. Oh! help!" she cried out when the boat lurched forward, listing slightly to one side, then the other, as boats sometimes do.

Mae Phaad took up the cry. "Help! We're going down!"

From then on until they turned from the river into the more secure-looking *khlong* it was one exclamation after another, one of the most frequently heard being "*Ui*—spittoon's spilling!" a phrase very popular among excitable women in those betel-nut-chewing times. Phloi loved every minute of the riotous crossing. She took care not to laugh out loud too often, but was not above exchanging smiles of complicity with the old boatman, and now and again urging him with her eyes to make the boat swerve more than it needed to—for the sheer pleasure of having another spittoon go spilling wildly in the air.

Khlong Bang Luang this morning seemed smaller than the last time Phloi had been on it, and her house, which she had thought of as a remote, almost unreachable place, now stood only a short distance down from the mouth of the *khlong*.

Khun Choei and Pho Phoem happened to be hanging about the old landing pavilion. (Since Phloi had gone away, who else could Khun Choei have found to take her place except Pho Phoem, even if he was only a boy?)

"Mae Phloi, Mae Phloi! Mae Phloi's here!" they kept yelling and leaping about before and after dutifully paying respects to Khun Sai, whom they had never met but immediately recognized as someone important in Phloi's life.

On learning who these two youngsters were, Khun Sai looked mildly critical. No doubt she considered Pho Phoem rather boisterous and Khun Choei in danger of becoming like her half brother.

And how she beamed when Chao Khun Father remarked on Phloi's "much improved" manners.

"Really, Khun Sai," Chao Khun said. "You've been a good teacher to her. Anyone can see that. I'm grateful to you, and please be good enough as to go on looking after her. Be as strict with her as you like ..."

They had gone up to join him in the garden, where he was tending his collection of potted topiary trees, looking relaxed and as handsomely dignified as ever. He and Khun Sai had known each other for many years and they talked not only of Sadet's plans for Phloi's tonsure but of their young days and some people they both knew, understandably leaving out Mother altogether.

When Chao Khun Father had invited Khun Sai to go up and drink tea on the veranda, the three children followed after, but only as far as the steps, where they sat down to have their chat.

Despite Phloi's glowing description of the palace, Khun Choei was sure she wouldn't like to live there herself.

"All that crouching and crawling would make my body ache," was how she looked at it.

They talked of Mother. "Have you heard about ... ?" Pho Phoem asked.

"Yes," Phloi replied in a small voice, stole an embarrassed glance at Khun Choei, and was thankful to see her half sister looking unconcerned.

"Chao Khun Father knows all about it too," Pho Phoem continued. "Somebody told him. He's very angry. If she comes to the landing again I'm not to go down and meet her like I used to, he says, and if I do, I'm to leave this house and not come back."

Phloi was full of pity for her brother. To be forbidden to see Mother sounded like the worst punishment imaginable. But Phoem did not seem to be taking it tragically, perhaps because he was a boy, or perhaps because he felt that Chao Khun Father's anger would fade away in time.

"I sleep here in the big house now, you know," Phoem went on. "Behind Chao Khun Father's bedroom. When you and Mother left I wanted to move into Khun Chit's house, but Chao Khun Father wouldn't allow it. He said Khun Chit would make a bad boy out of me."

"And he's right," Khun Choei spoke up. "Khun Chit's always in trouble. He's naughty. He's awful."

Pho Phoem disagreed. "Khun Chit's a grown-up young man," he said in defence of his eldest half brother, a worthless rake in most people's opinion, but for whom he had a sneaking admiration. "He's different. You can't force him to be like us children."

"I hate him," Khun Choei declared in her vehement way. "I don't even want to look at him. Ugh! But Khun Big Sister worships him. She gives him everything he asks for—behind Chao Khun Father's back."

The reference to Khun Big Sister Un made Phloi realize with a sinking heart that sooner or later she would have to muster up her courage and face the lady of the house whether she wanted to or not.

She heard Chao Khun Father calling her name, and went up to the veranda.

"Let me look at you again," he said smilingly.

He had Phloi tell him about her Inner Court adventures, laughed at some of the things she said, and talked amusingly about himself when he had been Phloi's age. Phloi basked in his jovial mood and in his approval of her.

Turning to Khun Sai he asked her to convey to Sadet his respects and deep gratitude for all she had done for Phloi. He deemed it a great honour that this important event in his daughter's life—the tonsure—would come to pass under the patronage of Her Highness.

"I didn't think you would have any objection," Khun Sai said. "But of course Sadet would never dream of going ahead without first consulting you."

"Phloi's a very lucky girl," said Chao Khun Father. But then he went on, "Why don't you go in and see your big sister, Phloi? She'd like to see you."

The room looked exactly the same—murky—and gave off the same smell of scented flowers and perfumed candles. Khun Un this morning was not neatly applying wax to her lips but admiring some glittering diamonds on her fingers, her arm stretched out towards what little light filtered in through one of the slatted windows. Swift as lightning she brought the arm down at the sight of the intruder, and with her other hand slammed shut the jewellery box in front of her.

Her greetings were also characteristic. "Ah-ha, the court lady! You have nowhere else to crawl back to but here? Wherever you came from, I invite you to go back there!"

"I came with Khun Aunt Sai," Phloi said, rather pointlessly. What she meant was that she had come to visit and not to stay as Khun Un seemed to have deduced.

"Oh, you have so many relatives! You don't have to threaten me with them. I'm already frightened . . ." But curiosity got the better of her and she could not resist asking, "What are you here for?"

"Sadet sent us to see Chao Khun Father about my tonsure."

Khun Un burst out laughing, "Your *tonsure*?"

"Sadet wishes to do it," Phloi heard herself whisper.

"You don't have to tell me. I know. A high-ranking person like you must have a high-ranking princess to arrange these things—sure, sure, sure. It's just as well. My house is too small to hold all your mother's relatives who will want to attend the grand ceremony."

Phloi swallowed hard; then, not wanting to hear any more sarcasm about Mother, desperately changed the subject. "Chao Khun Father sent me in to see you."

"As if I didn't know that!" Khun Un raised her voice to a raging pitch. "If he hadn't would you have come on your own? Never! This is what I get from keeping tigers and crocodiles. They bite the hand that feeds them!"

Thus ended the dialogue—if that was the right term for such a lopsided exchange.

KHUN Choei took one look at Phloi's face and became vehement again. "I thought so! I knew she'd make you cry. She's horrible, isn't she? She likes hurting people and everyday she tries to make me unhappy. I tell you she has a demon's heart. I'll be glad when she dies!"

WHEN they said goodbye that day Khun Choei promised a visit to the palace "when I'm a little bit more grown up." Chao Khun Father patted her head and spoke in a trembling voice. "Take good care of yourself, Phloi. May you be happy and prosperous, my daughter."

As the boat came away from the landing with Pho Phoem and Khun Choei perched on it, Phloi thought to herself that in spite of Khun Un it was good to have been home. Leaning out of the boat she sent a last smile back at her brother and half sister, knowing they would be seeing one another again.

FIVE

ALTHOUGH the double tonsure of Choi and Phloi was to be held at the home of Choi's parents, preparations for it were mostly carried out at Sadet's residence, where it became for several months the focal point of interest, the pet project, the source of much bustling activity and enjoyment. The entire household led by Sadet herself pursued a common aim: that of setting up the most fitting and prettiest ceremony possible for their own Mae Choi and Mae Phloi, a pursuit at once worthwhile and abounding in *sanuk*.

At first Phloi did not feel quite as involved in the project as the grown-up members of the residence. Not that she did not look forward to the event. Having a topknot meant having to have it retwined again and again, when you'd rather be doing something else, and your head—except the knot, that is—needed to be shaved every so often, which could hurt, because the blade was not always as sharp as it should be. Then the hair around it must be plucked, and that always hurt! To have the thing shaved off once and for all meant freedom from all that bother, and, what's more important, to start growing a full head of hair amounted to proclaiming that you'd got through being a child and were well on your way to attaining adulthood, a stage of life reputedly less exposed to censure, scolding and punishment.

So Phloi had always been glad about the coming tonsure, even if in the beginning she was inclined to view the preliminary goings-on as her elders' affair, one that little concerned her personally. But she became more and more interested as work—and fun—progressed, and was full of excitement all through the final weeks of preparations. Many of the articles to be used and worn during the ceremony had been acquired—selected from among a number of possibilities after a series of consultation at all levels—and were now kept more or less on display in Khun Sai's apartment. It gave Phloi a thrill just to look at them, particularly the gold brocade *phasin*s, and the diamond-encrusted circlets for the topknots. Everything came in matching pairs, one set for her and one for Choi. Some of the articles were made at the residence, such as the collars, which, after having been cut to measure, sewn up and padded to a sufficient thickness, were ornamented with precious and semi-precious stones, and when finished were pronounced perfectly beautiful even by the most exacting connoisseurs.

More precious than the precious gems, more beautiful than the beautiful collars, were the enthusiasm, goodwill and loving kindness that came with them. Phloi appreciated this more keenly than Choi. (Choi could think and talk of nothing else these days except going home, and her home did sound like an enviably happy place, with no inhabitant like Khun Un to spoil it.) Without either parent to turn to at this time, Phloi nevertheless felt herself to be cared for, cherished, a person of some standing, thanks to Sadet and Khun Sai, thanks to the whole residence.

The tonsure party, after taking their leave of Sadet, set off for Choi's place one fine morning a week before the ceremony. Elder Brother Nuang came with two cabs to fetch them at the palace gate, and when every bundle and parcel had been stacked and every passenger seated to Khun Sai's satisfaction, away they went.

A better-travelled child might have described it as an uneventful journey along some quiet roads lined with trees, temples, houses and shops. To Phloi, who never went anywhere to speak of, everything it had to offer—the rattling of the carriage, the swirling cloud of dust stirred up by the horses and wheels, strollers crossing the road, pedlars with their portable basket-stores dangling from bamboo shoulder poles, glimpses of temple roofs and shop fronts—everything was the stuff of high adventure. And to cap it all the three of them—Nuang, Choi and herself—had a good laugh all the way. Or, to be more exact, they had a hilarious time trying not to laugh openly at Khun Sai's efforts to reform the driver.

"Don't do that!" she cried out every time he applied his whip. "Have you no pity?" she asked. "Stop it now! Oh, how can you be so cruel?"

Once she leaned out to shout similar admonishments to the driver of the other cab, and was very vexed when he smiled in response but otherwise paid her no heed whatsoever.

To her immense relief, Khun Sai found on arrival that the horses appeared to have suffered no ill effects from the trip. She did not, however, let the drivers go off without giving them a few more words of advice on the subject of compassion towards our fellow beings on this earth.

The house stood in a lane. To reach it they went on foot from the road, walking single file on planks laid out over the muddy ground. Choi's father, as ever cheerful and kindly, welcomed them at the foot of the outside staircase, and Choi's mother fell into Choi's wildly joyous arms at the top of the stairs. Everybody was talking all at once. Phloi, who somehow had never learned the names of Choi's parents, now heard Khun Sai call her elder brother either "Phi Nop" ("Phi" meaning older brother or sister) or Khun Luang ("Luang" being his title), and her sister-in-law, who happened to be her junior in age, "Mae Chan."

"Don't be so rough with me." Mae Chan laughed as her daughter gave her another squeeze. "Mind the stairs. We'll both fall down and break our necks if you don't stop this."

A few minutes later, leaving her mother and other elders to themselves, Choi took Phloi to the area underneath the house to see her beloved old bitch, Spotty, who turned out to be a warmly affectionate creature.

"You said she had puppies—where are they?" demanded Choi of Nuang, who had come to join them.

"We gave them all away. Spotty wasn't really interested in them and they were making such a racket."

"Couldn't you have kept just one for me?" Choi complained, kissing the bitch and being kissed in return.

"Disgusting," Nuang remarked. "How can you let that mangy animal lick your face like that?"

"I love her," Choi said, exercising her right to lavish affections where she chose. "I love her and I missed her very much."

"All right," Nuang conceded. "But come this way. I have something to show you."

He led the way to another corner of the sprawling area, stopped before a bench on which stood an assortment of earthen pots and jars and, waving his hand over them, grandly announced: "Needle fish. I breed them myself."

Nuang's needle fish looked very different from the ones Phloi had seen in *khlong*s and pools. They were much bigger and had pearl-white bodies and red-dotted tails.

"Do you keep them because they're pretty to look at?" she asked.

Nuang laughed. "They're even prettier when they fight. These are my champion fighting needle fish, don't you know." He scooped one out of a jar and put it by itself in another jar whose water he then churned into a current. The little fish swam against the current wriggling its sleek body with such style and daring that it made Phloi laugh with delight.

"I used to raise them myself," Choi boasted. "Those common ones?" her brother scoffed. "They're good for nothing. We don't touch them," this "we" being the true fish-fighting fanciers, his tone implied.

The father of the house was one of these. Emerging from behind a row of potted plants near a back staircase, Khun Luang sauntered up to the three youngsters, peered down into the fish jars, and was soon giving Phloi some good tips on how to spot a potential winner, how to train it, what to do when you had a sick fish on your hands, and so forth.

After the session with the fish Choi took Phloi exploring up and down staircases, in and out of rooms, back and forth across the main terrace from one pavilion to another. This was a largish house or rather a largish compound made up of several houses on stilts, linked together by the upstairs terraces and the rambling area underneath. The grounds were shaded by mango and other fruit trees. There were

potted plants and shrubs everywhere, and cages of cooing doves ⌐
under the eaves.

Phloi's stay in this house lasted some ten of her happiest days. It
was a happy-making house. It had a fetching aura of contentment
and generosity. A house where children found in their parents not
only respected elders but loving friends and genial companions, and
where servants, treated with sympathetic fairness, had become part of
the family. Here youth and age and superiors and inferiors, living side
by side, complemented and supported one another. Mutual affection,
effortless tolerance of human failings, a shared dislike of prolonged
conflict and tension—these were among the ingredients that went
into the making of this kind of harmony.

Naturally, friends liked coming to this house. And when it was
Khun Luang's men friends from the department dropping in after
work for a few hours on the terrace, Mae Chan happily saw to it
that they were well supplied with cheroots, betel-nuts, food and
refreshments. She did not join them on the terrace, but the men would
go to the kitchen quarters to chat with her. Most of them were old
friends and did not stand on ceremony.

If you happened to come by this house, more often than not you
would have been greeted by the sound of Mae Chan's laughter. Phloi
never once saw her in a bad mood. In fact it would be difficult to find
a jollier person, one more merry-tempered, more given to enjoying the
bright side of the situation, than Choi's mother, Mae Chan.

Khun Sai had a great fondness for her sister-in-law but did not hold
her in high esteem, considering her too lenient with children and
servants, too undemanding of herself and others. Determined to have
the household run like clockwork for the tonsure rites, Khun Sai many
a time was tempted to get very cross with its relaxed mistress, but in
the end would be won over by Mae Chan's infectious good humour.

Actually Khun Sai had little to complain about, because despite
their casual attitude, Mae Chan and her domestic staff possessed a
certain competence peculiar to themselves. They got things done
somehow—there was method in their mellowness, you might say,
and what with Khun Sai's own efficient management and the helping

hands of many friends, the house shone in spick-and-span readiness on the eve of the festive occasion.

On the morning of the first day, Choi and Phloi were taken to the back terrace of the house, where they were seated on low stools amid dragon water jars, scrubbing cloths, bowls of turmeric powder and other articles of the bath.

"I'll take care of your daughter myself," Khun Sai said to Mae Chan. "You do Phloi. She's easier to handle."

The bath lasted forever. Four servant girls besides Khun Sai and Mae Chan went scrubbing on and on and on. The scrubbing was followed by the pouring of water followed by more scrubbing. It was as if the skin were stubbornly resisting and must be taught a long, hard lesson.

I should not need another bath for years and years, Phloi thought. The skin wouldn't dare be dirty again after this.

More scrubbing. More water. Another rubbing of turmeric powder. Another rinsing. The tips of Phloi's fingers went pale and creased from the cold water. More scrubbing . . .

Halfway through this Choi staged a rebellion against the scrubbers. Khun Sai gave her a few smacks in retaliation. Choi cried and fought on. Their wrestling match—quite a lively affair it was—ended with everyone laughing, including themselves. The scrubbing was resumed . . .

When it was dried, the new raw skin, the colour of turmeric gold, received a coating of white powder.

"It stings," Phloi told Khun Sai.

"Only for a second," Khun Sai told her. "When I'm finished, you'll be very pretty."

"Have patience," Mae Chan said.

"I'm hungry," Choi declared.

The powdering was continued after lunch. Then it was time to get the two girls draped and bedecked in ceremonial garments. The gold brocade *pasin*, the finely-wrought but weighty belt, the thickly-padded, gem-mounted collar, the diamond-encrusted circlet—each piece of the costume proved as heavy to wear as it was splendid to look at. The girls, scintillated in gold and in beads of perspiration, had to be fanned continuously, and given cooling drinks of water and cooling words of encouragement. In time they became adjusted to the beautiful burden and able to move under it with comparative ease.

Meanwhile the guests had started to arrive. Most of them were friends and relatives, and quite a few had travelled a long way from far provinces for the purpose of attending this tonsure. They sat in the room where the monks would be chanting, on the roofed verandas outside or on the shaded part of the terrace. A hum of greetings and conversation was filling up the whole house.

In the dressing room, Choi raised her eyebrows at the mirror and let out a whoop of laughter, saying she had never seen anything so comical. As for Phloi, if truth be told, she who tended to consider herself pretty enough on ordinary days was very impressed indeed by what she saw in her mirror.

As soon as the monks arrived, the *piphat* band started to play. Time for Choi and Phloi to go forth and take up their honoured positions in the assembly.

Nothing but praises were heard as they made their way among the guests. Choi took everything in her stride, was not at all shy or flustered. If she hadn't been so formally attired, you might have thought she was at somebody else's tonsure. Behind her came Phloi, self-consciously demure in manner, no longer feeling so vain about her appearance but feeling all of a sudden rather lost and lonely, almost self-pitying, telling herself there was no one among the guests she could call her own, that not one of them was related to her in any way. Elder Brother Nuang, stationed near the threshold, smiled at her. He approved and was proud of her, the smile said, and this helped somewhat to bolster Phloi's sense of belonging. She followed Choi into the room and sat down beside her on the carpeted floor. In front of them were seated the monks in a row; behind them were some of the guests.

Phloi made the triple *krap* of reverence to Buddha, Dhamma and Sangha and, once the chanting began, concentrated on being a composed and absorbed listener. For a while she succeeded, then became distracted by certain voices and movements outside. Some more guests had just come up the stairs. There was a flurry of ushering and greeting. Turning her head discreetly, Phloi looked out of the door and saw—to her utter amazement and indescribable joy—her very own Chao Khun Father and Elder Brother Phoem. Could this be possible? Why hadn't she even dreamt of it? How was it that the idea had never entered her head that they might come? But no matter. They were here, and that was the glorious thing. Out of the corner of her eyes Phloi watched the other guests pay respects to her father. They looked very pleased, she thought, as though they had been waiting for him to come and preside over the ceremony. And she was not a destitute child after all, but the daughter of this distinguished person whom everyone regarded so highly.

Choi was grinning at her, sharing her unexpected windfall. Phloi grinned back and then, wishing to behave correctly for her father's benefit, gave her full attention once again to the monks' chanting.

"YOU have a pretty daughter, Khun Luang."

"I think Phloi is the prettier of the two, sir. Which is natural since she has such a beautiful mother." Having said this Choi's father looked more than a trifle embarrassed. But Chao Khun merely smiled and did not seem in the least offended by the reference to his estranged wife. He went on to admire Khun Luang's spacious, comfortable home. His host replied modestly that it was a little too small for the ceremony, and apologized for any faults His Excellency might find with the arrangements. Both men spoke of Sadet's great kindness, without which this auspicious double event could not have come about and the two of them, who had not got together for several years, could not have been reunited in so happy a fashion.

The chanting had been over for some time. The monks had been presented with offerings, had blessed the congregation and been escorted back to their respective monasteries. Choi and Phloi had been sitting with their fathers, but would soon have to retire to their room for a bath (another one!) and change.

"It's a superb costume you're wearing, Phloi," Chao Khun Father said. "But it must be very hot." Of course Phloi did not tell him that she had only started to sweat in earnest at the mention of Mother, that Mother had sent word that she had been prevented from coming by her poor health. She would save this last piece of news for Phoem, who at the moment must be roaming about with Nuang, probably getting acquainted with the champion needle fish.

"THIS is my friend, Choi. This is Pho Phoem."

"Who's Pho Phoem?"

"Why, my elder brother Phoem. I've told you about him, don't you remember?"

Phoem and Choi eyed one another.

"So this is Pho Phoem." Choi sounded unimpressed. "He's not so big. I can fight him easily."

"You talk too much," Nuang cut her off.

"But it's true," Choi insisted.

"Is she Big Noise around here?" Phoem asked. He had been acting rather reserved, but Choi's aggressiveness was beginning to make him feel at home.

"The biggest," Nuang replied. "We're all scared of her."

"KHUN Choei wanted to come," Phoem reported to his sister, "but Khun Un wouldn't let her. Khun Choei's going to have her topknot shaved too. In about ten days."

"Really? You'll have a lot of fun, then."

"I think it's going to be so-so, Mae Phloi. Nothing can be a lot of fun at our house. It's not like other houses . . . The other day Khun Un called me a menial, but Khun Choei said no, that can't be, and if I were, that would make her and Khun Un menials too, because we have the same father. So Khun Un beat her . . ."

Luckily, if there were people like Khun Un to spread suffering and gloom, there was also someone like Mae Chan to do wonders for your flagging spirits. "You're a good boy, Phoem," said Mae Chan, who had met him for the first time not so long ago but seemed to have detected in him all kinds of desirable qualities a growing young man should have. "Good boy," she repeated beamingly, slapping him gently on the back. "Have some more rice, Phoem. Have you tried this curry? You're a little too thin, you know—you should eat more rice. There's a good boy!"

THE children had had their meal, and now the adult guests were being served. Mae Chan had been overjoyed on learning that Chao Khun had agreed to stay on after the religious rites and dine at her house. Together with Khun Sai she had been busy concocting extra delicacies and having a special place set up for him. As the most senior guest, Chao Khun was to dine in lonely splendour, but he objected strongly to this treatment.

"You are not going to make me eat by myself, Pho Nop?"

"Please go ahead, sir."

"No, no. Come on, Pho Nop, keep me company."

"All right, sir."

The four young people came to wait on their fathers; and Chao Khun asked them which delicious dish he should have, there being so many and all looking equally tempting. When the children had made their suggestions, he laughed and said, "Each palate to its taste, I see. We'll just have to try them all, Pho Nop."

In the beginning, he had addressed his host by his title "Khun Luang," but had before long reverted to the more familiar "Pho Nop." Talking about old times while doing justice to the feast, he and Pho Nop mentioned several places the children had never heard of (among these, the Japanese Tea House on Bamrung Muang Road was the one that sounded most intriguing to them). From time to time, when the going got strictly adult, the two would drop their voices, then have a good chuckle together.

After the rice and side dishes had been cleared and the sweets brought in, Mae Chan, until now ensconced in the kitchen quarters, came out to pay her respects—and to be paid a compliment by Chao Khun.

"It has been many years, but you're still as beautiful as ever."

Mae Chan laughed her merry laugh. "And Your Excellency still speaks in the sweetest tongue. If I hadn't met Khun Luang first I might have followed you anywhere you wished."

Chao Khun said yes, that might have happened, and wouldn't have been nice if it had.

"It's not too late if you're still interested, sir," said Khun Luang obligingly. "It would be a great honour, sir, and I am not at all a possessive man."

"Don't be too sure he's not interested," said his wife in a menacing tone. "I'm not that old, and Chao Khun may be looking for a cook for all we know!"

Their dialogue and laughter mingled well with the *piphat* music, sometimes rising above it, sometimes serving as background to the gaily rippling melody. At other times they stopped talking altogether to listen to a particularly well-executed passage, and it was during one of these pauses that Chao Khun suggested to his host that, rusty though they were—neither had touched any instrument for years, they had confessed to each other earlier on—they should attempt a comeback and have some fun together, like in the old days.

"I'll take the *ranat ek*, and you play the *khong wong*. How about it, Pho Nop?"

Pho Nop was doubtful and extremely diffident, but after more cajoling, consented to have a try.

Members of the band were delighted to have them in their midst, and the guests readily turned themselves into an audience.

Pho Nop quickly regained his former skill after a hesitant beginning. He had been needlessly modest. His technique on the *khong wong,* a pleasing mixture of conventional rendering and witty improvisation, drew admiring comments from the audience and appreciative nods from fellow musicians. But it was Chao Khun's playing that brought a lump to your throat and made your eyes hot with tears of joy and sorrow. It was sorrow he started with. He told you of his broken dreams, of the days that had gone forever, of doubts and regrets and painful longings. As he sent the two beaters quivering on the bars, he—and you—could have been alone under a dark uncaring sky instead of at a party with bright lights shining everywhere. Time stood still, yet it also passed. You were not aware of it when the sad notes began to die away, but suddenly there came the realization that all was not lost, that hope could be restored and happiness recaptured. Now the *ranat* beaters went darting back and forth among the *ranat* bars like two butterflies, or like a pair of tuneful birds, or a couple of joyous souls laughing together in a garden. In the end the rest of the band joined in the celebration, with the cymbals ringing out in triumph and the drums giving forth their rousing cheers. A perfect ending, because it made you wish it didn't have to end.

That night Phloi went to bed exhausted and happy—ecstatically happy. Chao Khun Father, before leaving, had said he would come again tomorrow. She had not told him how much she loved him— they had never been very demonstrative with one another—but had searched for a way to express her feelings and ended up by taking a fan and then fanning him as steadily and smoothly as she knew how while he chatted with old friends and acquaintances. When he turned to her, smiled and said, "How very nice, Phloi. What a gracious little court lady you are," she had felt rewarded. He had understood her intention.

"I'm glad your Chao Khun Father came," said Choi, lying beside her under the mosquito net. "He's wonderful."

"So is your father. I wouldn't mind having your father as my father."

"Same for me. We can trade them any time."

"And Khun Aunt Sai said she'd never heard anyone play the *ranat ek* so beautifully. Are you very proud of him, Phloi?"

"Very, very proud, Choi."

"And so you should be . . . (yawn) . . . and tomorrow we'll have our topknots shaved. Happy day! But I wish we didn't have to get so dolled up . . ."

They were solemnly robed in white for the actual tonsure performance the following morning, then later on underwent another bout of elaborate costuming, this time for the *tham khwan*—the rites whose observance was aimed at preserving their beautiful and prosperous selves, bodily and spiritually. They were less interested in their invisible *khwan*s than in their conspicuously shorn heads, and could not help tittering at them. Yes, the sight did make them feel a little more grown up, but also absurd, and strangely bereft as well. After all, they had been wearing those knotted crowns virtually all their lives and needed to get accustomed to the new reality.

Chao Khun Father, at his loveable best, was there from start to finish and, as on the previous day, the other guests, in so many words and by their gestures, designated him leader of the gathering. On this occasion he gave Choi an exquisite gold ring in the shape of a serpent, and presented Phloi with two gifts: a pair of diamond-and-sapphire bracelets and an antique pendant with an emerald in its centre. He asked Phloi which of the two articles she thought the prettier, and smiled with satisfaction at Phloi's preference for the pendant.

"The bracelets cost much more. They're new. But the pendant, which belonged to your grandmother, has a rare beauty, though people nowadays don't know its value. They call such things old-fashioned. You have taste, Phloi."

Phloi was immensely pleased with herself, and with everybody and everything for that matter. It was indeed a totally, flawlessly happy day!

They left for the Grand Palace three days afterwards. Mae Chan would have liked them to stay longer. Khun Sai, on hearing this, predicted with a wry chuckle that a week more in this indulgent household and the two girls would have turned into a couple of bandits. Elder Brother Nuang, acting not at all like a bandit but more like an affable young gentleman, promised the girls he would come and visit them as often as possible. He seemed to be treating them as his equals these days.

KHUN Sai had hardly stepped inside the residence when she learned that Sadet had been asking for her. The maid bearing this message, after having conveyed it to Khun Sai, glanced at Phloi with a funny expression on her face before hurrying away on some other errand.

The meaning of the glance was revealed to Phloi—by Khun Sai on her return from the audience with Sadet. Mother had died in childbirth after being delivered of her premature baby, born dead. The cremation had taken place, arranged by her Chachoengsao relatives. Khun Sai, swollen-eyed and choking with sobs, did not try to console Phloi. The task was beyond her power—anybody's power—and must be left to the healing patience of Time.

SIX

FIVE years went by.

Phloi had by this time acquired the art of wearing a bodice cloth—had become, in other words, no longer a child but a young woman. She was sixteen. Round and about the Inner Court they called her a beauty, and they also said her character was good and her manners courteous.

At Sadet's residence she was known as a favourite attendant, if not the most favourite. (Some colleagues resented this and, prompted by jealousy, took pleasure in maligning her and finding fault with her, thereby giving Choi, forever Phloi's champion, the pleasure of dealing with them. Choi's forthright and big-hearted nature had remained intact over the years, as had her militant side, and in taking up Phloi's defence, Choi often forced the would-be fault-finders and trouble-makers to beat a retreat even before they had started to attack.) Certainly she was entrusted with more tasks and assigned longer hours than most of the other girls. She did not mind this at all, being of the opinion that she could serve Sadet a whole lifetime yet still not repay her for all her loving kindness.

During these five years Phloi seldom stepped beyond the Outer Gate. On the other hand, the Inner Court with its highways and byways, its maze of differing provinces, was still a vast territory to her and never lacking in adventure. She made visits and discoveries. She went everywhere, or virtually everywhere, either as Sadet's escorting maid carrying her betel-nut box, or with friends, or on her own.

She had been to the Yellow Room. How the child Phloi had wondered and speculated about this room! Lying as it did directly in the path between His Majesty's private apartments and the front chambers where he conferred with his ministers, this was the place where the ladies of the Inner Court foregathered to pay their respects as he walked by. A livelier assembly than this would have been hard to find. Everybody came, not only those who had no access to other royal audiences, either more formal or more intimate, but quite a few who did. They came early, well before the time His Majesty was expected to appear. Some remained more or less stationary once having comfortably seated themselves. Some moved about from group to group exchanging news and views both of their own and the outside world; some had business affairs to discuss, appointments to make, advice to seek and give; some came with pretty things—a new brooch, say, or an imported scent-bottle to show around—and some with interesting anecdotes to pass on; so one and all—young, old and middle-aged—contributed to the general animation, each in her own way. And although everyone kept her voice low and refrained from bursting into too-loud laughter, the collective sound issuing from their midst was wafted far along passageways and stairwells. From her seat in the corridor Phloi was occasionally summoned inside to join in the conversation, and once in a while to be given a present for no particular reason other than that the donor was kind and well-disposed towards her. With all the doors open, however, she had no need to enter the room in order to participate in the life going on within its walls, or to feel just as much a part of the audience when His Majesty came in.

For a minute or two before he appeared in the doorway no one spoke, and when he did, all heads and hands went down to the floor in the traditional act of homage. Crossing the room to the other side, His Majesty sometimes paused to say a few words here and there, and when he had gone out the noise resumed. Then the ladies prepared to adjourn, some to come back later on, while others chose to remain where they were, waiting for another audience when His Majesty should return from the conference.

And she had been to the Green Room or, more precisely, she had often accompanied Sadet when she went to attend upon the king in the Green Room at mealtimes. Here Their Royal Highnesses and other titled ladies had their regular seats and did not circulate at random as the party in the Yellow Room, and they talked and laughed in a quieter manner. The dishes were sent up from the royal kitchen wrapped in white cloth and sealed. From her vantage point in the adjacent pantry Phloi enjoyed watching those on duty, among whom were some of the princesses, go through the process of breaking the seal, unwrapping the cloth, carrying in the dishes and passing them from hand to hand until they reached the king's table. The routine movement had an easy grace, a pleasing rightness about it. It fitted in with everything, Phloi thought—with the green and gold walls, the upper portion of which had a narrow balcony lined with bookcases; with the king's chaise longue on which he often reclined; with the stately yet relaxed atmosphere of the gathering.

Phloi had no business to go into the royal bed chamber. But Khun Lady Officials in charge were friendly and took a sympathetic view of her curiosity. They let her in. There were no rules saying she had to walk on tiptoe and talk in whispers, but that was how she comported herself in there. She paid respects to the great tiered umbrella standing above the king's bed, to the bed itself, which stood on a dais, and to the other bed—Somdet the Queen's, which stood on the floor. She tried to memorize details of the positions, colours, shapes, and textures of what she saw round her for the benefit of those friends who had not had the good fortune of having seen them with their own eyes.

Where she had never dared to approach was the queen's private suite—the Blue Room. When Sadet went up to see Her Majesty, Phloi would wait on the lower landing of the west staircase. To climb further up would have taken her into that region guarded, nay ruled, over by Khun Tao, the Honourable Supreme Attendant, highly esteemed and greatly feared by all. The mere idea that Khun Tao might espy her lurking about was enough to deter Phloi from giving way to any inquisitive impulse.

During these years since her mother's death Phloi had had little contact with the family in Khlong Bang Luang, but lately her elder brother Phoem, now a junior official at the Treasury Department situated nearby in the Grand Palace, had been coming to meet her in the plaza outside Sri Sudawong Gate and give her news of home. He did not come very often, which did not surprise Phloi. She had gathered from his talk as well as from his telltale breath that he had made many friends and that drinking was a favourite pastime in his circle.

It was Nuang who came most regularly to visit her and his sister Choi—never less than twice a month except when unavoidably detained. From being a "temple pupil" Nuang had gone on to Cadet School and in a few months was to be made an officer in the army. The first time he had turned up in his red uniform (red like the lime chewed with betel leaf), Choi had greeted him with, "Heavens! You look like a walking lime-stick, Phi Nuang."

And so he did, somewhat, with his straight lanky body made to appear straighter and lankier by the tight-fitting tunic of blazing colour. He looked comical, yes, but endearingly comical, and rather handsome too, to Phloi's loving eye.

Until about six months ago Phloi had loved him like a brother and would have said so plainly if anyone had asked her. But not now. Now, should you have pointed out that she loved him with a woman's love for a man, and deeply, with her whole being, she would have vigorously denied it, and probably believed she was speaking the truth. For she had not given her new feeling an exact name—the feeling she had when Nuang was beside her, talking, then suddenly breaking off in the middle of a sentence to look at her with an expression that bore no relation to what he had been saying; or the feeling she had when she found herself counting the days, planning what to wear for his coming visit, going over in her mind what she would tell him, anticipating his laughing response and picturing to herself his lips and eyes when he laughed. The truth was that these past six months she lived as if the earth had just been recreated for her. She wondered at its beauty and newness. She exulted in the way the sun was shining and the wind blowing, in the sound of laughter, in the colour of her bodice cloth and the smell of her scented water. The last-named was truly astonishing: she had made it with own hands but had not discovered its real fragrance until now.

Some weeks back Phloi had started making excuses not to go out and meet Nuang.

"Are you sick or something, Phloi?" Choi demanded. "You're so absent-minded these days. And why don't you want to come out and see Phi Nuang any more?"

Well, that other time she had had a slight fever, Phloi mumbled her explanations, then there was the time Sadet had wanted her to do something—she'd forgotten what it was, and this last time she had promised to pay that girl in Teng Row a visit—surely Choi must have remembered . . .

Her new-found shyness with Nuang had come about as a result of that last meeting a few weeks ago, when Choi had questioned her brother as to his plans for after Cadet School, apart from becoming a soldier. Choi had laughed at his vague-sounding answer—"Oh, I don't know . . . might take a wife"—then teasingly asked if he had anyone in mind. Nuang had reddened and said yes, addressing his sister but sending Phloi a brief, sweet and solemn glance.

And since that day Phloi had not seen him again. She had been torn between her longing to see him and her shyness. The latter had won, supported by her belief that a period of absence would somehow do them both good—render them worthier of each other, perhaps.

"Oh, Phloi, Phi Nuang asked me to give you this," Choi said when they were alone together one night.

The parcel contained a large piece of plain silk—large enough to use as cover-sheet on a cool night, two bottles of perfume—one a clear European liquid and the other a Thai scented water with powder mixed in it, and a note.

The note came in the form of *phleng yao*, that love epistle in rhyme used in the courtship of those days. It was the first *phleng yao* Phloi had ever received. Her very own Phi Nuang had sent it. To hold it in her fingers gave her a marvellous feeling—a marvellously happy feeling, though not untinged with embarrassment.

Why this separation?—the *phleng yao* asked. Was illness the cause? Or was it some obscure anger? Once there had been smiles and laughter and joy. Alas, no more. Was she so jealous of her beautiful self that now she must needs lock it away for fear of prying hands and eyes? He of this *phleng yao* was like that earth-bound hare pining for the lofty moon, eager for even the palest light, the faintest gleam of hope. The two bottles were like his heart, bright and clear when he could see her, darkened and murky when she was gone. And like the plain silk with not one sprig of flowers on it, so his life was now but an aching, lonely emptiness . . .

"Well, I never!" Choi cried out in hushed tones, and laughing noiselessly, for fear of waking Khun Sai in the next room. "Imagine— Phi Nuang, a *phleng yao* composer! How funny!"

Phloi had gone pink all over. She did not know what to do or say, and so gave Choi a pinch in the leg.

"It's all right, Phloi. You don't have to be so shy with me. I've known it all along, you know."

But it would never do to let others share in the knowledge. Inner Court gossipers were not always harmless. One must beware of them. Phloi was therefore grateful, in the weeks that followed, that at least she had Choi to talk to. No, she never said it out loud, never tried to describe her love—that would have been an impossible task in any case. But she needed to mention his name and to say the most inconsequential things about him now and again.

One day it was Choi who brought up the subject of her dear brother.

"Phi Nuang is a good enough person," Choi said.

"He is," Phloi readily agreed with her.

"Nothing wrong with him," Choi went on, "except that he is too easy-going. He'll never make anything of himself, loving comfort as he does. As long as there is some fun and comfort, he's satisfied. It's a family trait, come to think of it."

No comment from Phloi. What she would have liked to do if she could, though, was to proclaim not only to Choi but the whole world that she would not have him any different from what he was, and that she dreamed of one day being allowed to follow him wherever he wished to go and be given the duty of making his life as comfortable as it would lie in her power to make it.

"When and if I marry," Choi announced airily, "it will never be to anyone like my brother or my father."

"Oh why not?" Phloi cried. "Yours is such a happy home, Choi. Your father has the kindest heart. He's so full of fun, and so good-natured."

"That's it." Choi gave an exaggerated sigh. "Father's so good-natured, the whole house is so good-natured. Nothing but the sound of laughter all day long. I'm tired of it. When I have a house of my own I want something different for a change. Some strife in the home—that's what I want. A brute of a man to fight with. A wife-beater. Or maybe a drunkard!" These horrible ideas seemed to amuse her a great deal and she chuckled with glee. "Yes, a drunkard will do. And I'll also find him plenty of minor wives. I'll fill the house with them, and when I go out I'll have a string of them walking behind me. I shall look very grand indeed!"

Frivolous Choi! But then she had never been in love. A few months younger in age, Phloi suddenly felt years older than her friend.

"Phi Nuang's coming again next holy day." Choi said. "Three days from now. Why don't you go and meet him, Phloi?"

No, not yet.

"Oh, he'll be disappointed again. He'll be so sad. He looked so sad the last time I saw him. Pitiful, really . . . By the way, Phloi, do you know that that was the first *phleng yao* he had ever attempted? He has such a hard time with the rhyming. Poor Phi Nuang, he's no poet. At one point in that *phleng yao* which you now know by heart—oh, don't blush, and don't deny you've read it at least a thousand times—well, at one point he got stuck and had to ask a friend to help him out over the next line . . . All for you, Phloi . . . You still don't want to see him?"

No, not yet.

"Well, if he goes and hangs himself, don't blame me."

Oh, no! How could Choi say such a thing, even in jest?

"If you don't come you'd better send a message or something. He's in a bad way, believe me."

The day before Nuang's visit Phloi spent all her spare time peeling betel nuts and rolling *phlu* leaves. When she had finished with them the nuts were more daintily sculptured and the *phlu*s more elegantly tapered than any nuts-and-*phlu*s had ever been. She put them, together with scented tobacco and three orange *champa* blooms, in an envelope made of banana leaves. On the day of Nuang's visit she handed the envelope to Choi without a word.

"Oh-ho, ah-ha! I think I'll take a bottle of smelling salts with me," said Choi. "I'll need it to revive Phi Nuang when he swoons with joy."

While waiting for Choi to return from Sri Sudawong Gate Phloi occupied herself with another task: the hemming of that cherished piece of plain silk. She had started it several days ago and now it was nearly completed. She planned to have it dyed in ebony and per-fumed to the right degree of fragrance. Then she would use it to cover herself in bed.

Choi eventually came back. But no interview took place that afternoon as each girl preferred to have the other initiate it. Phloi kept silent because she could not bring herself to confess her eager-ness even to someone very close to her, and Choi very likely because she wanted to teach Phloi a lesson for being so tongue-tied.

However, before bedtime that night Choi finally relented and spoke at length:

"Phi Nuang asked me to thank you . . .

"Phi Nuang said he would chew only one mouthful of the betels. The rest he would keep to gaze at and admire . . .

"Phi Nuang said you're an angel—an *apsara*. I asked him what he would do with this *apsara*. He said when he's an officer and can support a household he will come and fetch this *apsara* to go and live with him."

At this point Phloi ventured to interrupt her.

"I see, the matter is out of my hands. You two have settled it between yourselves. How nice!"

"Oh, Phloi, are you angry? You can't be. You know very well what I mean and how I feel. If he had fallen for some other girl, would I be so happy about it as I am? Never! He's my brother, isn't he? I wouldn't want him to set up house with a girl I couldn't bear, would I? This way, you and I—we'd become closer still—oh, you know what I mean, Phloi."

And Phloi had to laugh and say of course she knew.

A few weeks passed, during which time Phi Nuang sent more *phleng yaos* and Phloi pondered on when she would be able to muster enough confidence to go out and meet him face to face.

That day the question was resolved for her. Choi came back from Sri Sudawong Gate full of excitement as well as anxiety.

"You must see Phi Nuang the next time he comes," she declared.

"Why?" Phloi asked.

"Because he's been made an officer and they're sending him up north to be stationed in Nakhon Sawan. He doesn't know for how long. It will be his last chance to see you for a long, long time, so you must come . . . Now, now, don't look so mournful, Phloi. I won't have you break down like my mother. Phi Nuang says she's been shedding enough tears to drown us all. Don't you start crying too, Phloi dear. It's not as if he's being sent to his death."

With a sinking heart Phloi asked herself in silence if that possibility could ever be ruled out, remembering that carefree day five years ago when she had parted from Mother without suspecting that they would never see each other again.

Many a time, over the next four or five days, Phloi had to tell herself to stop making gloomy speculations about the future. There was enough work to keep her busy, at any rate, apart from her regular duties. Every free minute she had was spent collaborating with Choi in getting provisions for Phi Nuang's sojourn in the north. They made two kinds of chili paste and several kinds of sweetmeats—at times Phloi could not help smiling at her own supposition that though Phi Nuang might be old enough to fall in love he had not abandoned his childish habit of nibbling between meals; and they contrived to give the appearance for the benefit of the other girls at the residence that it was Choi, Nuang's sister, who was the leading spirit of this "food-for-Phi Nuang" programme, and that Phloi was only her willing assistant, as she should be.

About the silk cover-sheet which she had been using these past nights, Phloi decided to give it to Nuang to take with him to Nakhon Sawan.

When the day came the maid Phit had to be prevailed upon to help carry the good-sized box in which the large assortment of food and the parcel containing the silk had been packed.

Phloi had half-dreaded this farewell meeting with Nuang. What would he say to her and how would she answer him? Would he be pouring forth those ardent words like the honey-tongued Khun Phaen in the story? She sincerely hoped not—they were embarrassing enough when encountered in print.

What actually came to pass did not at all conform to the rather awkward situation she had vaguely sketched in her mind.

There was no constraint, for one thing. When he saw her stepping over the threshold of Sri Sudawong Gate, Phi Nuang came striding up and beaming at her as he had always done in the past, and she herself was so glad to see him that for the moment she quite forgot about their new relationship.

"Oh, Mae Phloi! It's been such a long time. I almost didn't recognize you. Are you well?"

Before Phloi could answer there was an interruption from Choi. "Really, Phi Nuang! If she were not well would she be here? You must be mad to ask such a foolish question."

"It is not a foolish question and it's not me but you who are mad. Isn't that so, Phloi?"

Phloi gave both of them an impartial grin.

Turning to the maid Phit, Choi demanded, "What about you, dear one? Are you mad too?"

"There are five hundred kinds of madness, Khun Choi," Phit replied sententiously, "and I am afflicted with all of them."

"Excellent, my dear Phit! As a reward I'll take you to that fruit stall over there and let you help me choose oranges for Khun Aunt Sai. These two think they're sane, so we'll leave them to fend for themselves."

"You've brought so many things, Phloi," Nuang said after Phit and Choi had gone.

"They're for you to take to Nakhon Sawan," Phloi told him. "Choi and I made them for you."

"And the silk—have you used it to cover yourself?"

"What a question!"

"But I must know. If you have, the silk becomes more valuable, most valuable. Well, have you?"

Phloi nodded, looking away.

"Then I'll treasure it as long as I live. It will never leave my side . . . I won't be gone for very long, Phloi. When I'm in a better position I'll come for you. Will you wait for me, Phloi?"

"I'm not going anywhere. I'll wait for you."

"And I for you. My parents say we should wait because we're both very young. They're right, of course. We are very young. But sometimes I feel as if my heart would burst from all this waiting."

Phloi could hear the note of anguish in his voice. He had really suffered on her account. Poor Phi Nuang!

"I'll wait for you, Phi Nuang," she repeated by way of consoling him. "You needn't worry about me."

She was somewhat relieved—and rather surprised—that they had been conversing in a normal ordinary way—or nearly so at any rate. She had been apprehensive of not knowing how to respond if Phi Nuang should wax too lyrical or passionate, like that romantic Khun Phaen of the legend.

"Why have you stayed away so long?" Nuang asked.

"I didn't want people to talk about me—about us. There are some who would like to see me behave in a certain way so they could start gossiping and bandying my name about. You know how it is."

"I do. I quite understood why you didn't come, but all the same I wanted to see you so badly that I wished you hadn't been so cautious . . . Do you trust me, Phloi? Do you believe I'll remain true to you always. You must."

"I do. I'm the same. What else did your parents say about us besides our being very young?"

"They're happy it's you because they love you very much. They say when the right time comes they'll present themselves to Sadet and your Chao Khun Father and request permission concerning us. They're pretty certain both Sadet and Chao Khun will grant it with pleasure. Everything will be done properly, they say, but I should work and try to get ahead and establish myself first. No need to be impatient, they say. There's time enough."

"I agree with them, Phi Nuang. I'm a little afraid myself . . ."

"Afraid of what, Phloi?"

"Of starting a household when I'm still so ignorant. Of making all kinds of blunders. Of making you grow tired of me."

"Tired of you? Never! Don't doubt me, Phloi. Oh, I wish I could take a knife and split my heart open to show you how true it is."

"Don't. It wouldn't be a heart but a fruit if you could split it so easily. How well you speak, Phi Nuang. Those pretty girls in Nakhon Sawan had better watch out for you and your sweet words."

"Don't you talk like that, Phloi! I won't have it, do you hear?"

Phloi laughed. It was difficult to believe that Nuang was going away. They went on talking of nothing and everything—nothing very coherent or profound, and everything had a significance all its own. They were together here and now. The afternoon sun shone brilliantly, the crowds in the courtyard moved as in a pageant, and neither the immediate nor the far future could intrude upon the present moment, so absorbed as it was in its own enchantment.

But the passing moment reclaimed them soon enough. Choi and the maid Phit eventually reappeared with baskets of various fruits. It was time to say goodbye and after that was said, time for the soldier to leave. Time for lovers to part.

Nuang's last words were an attempt at levity. "Take care of yourself, Phloi, and don't be such a cry-baby."

Walking away from him, Phloi was not in a tearful state, but felt drained, utterly vacant, as if she had been robbed of the very core and essence of her being.

When she turned to look back after having crossed over to the other side of the gate, Phloi saw that he was watching her. She knew that he would stand there looking after her until she had disappeared from his sight.

SEVEN

ABOUT a month later Mae Chan came to spend some companionably leisurely hours with her daughter, sister-in-law and Phloi in the Inner Court. These hours consisted generally of chatting, chatting while eating, and chatting while lending a hand to whatever communal chores happened to be going on at the moment.

The conversation at one point hovered on the subject of Mae Chan's recent trip to Bang Pa-in with Mae Chan doing most of the talking. She had travelled there with her husband Khun Luang and her son Nuang, and there they had parted, she and Khun Luang returning to Bangkok on the same boat and Nuang boarding another boat to go on up to Nakhon Sawan.

"What a hectic time I had!" Mae Chan said, laughing her merry laugh. "I was in such a state, I can tell you, what with being very sad to lose Nuang to the army and very scared that the boat might capsize—I never trust boats as you know, and Khun Luang added to the confusion by taking everything so calmly and insisting that I should be like him. 'Now let's have no more crying,' he calmly said. 'Your son's going to look after himself and he's not being sent away to be executed.' 'Of course, of course, he's old enough,' I said, but can I help it if I still think of him as a child? And you know, he is still like a child in many ways. Why, if his father and I hadn't been there to see to the loading and unloading he would have gone off leaving all his things behind—clothes, food and everything else except that little parcel he had in his hand. He was madly possessive about that parcel, clung to it all the way. 'What's in it?' I asked. 'Oh, just a silk cover,' he said . . ."

Mae Chan went on with her narrative, but Phloi had stopped listening to her. She thought of Nuang holding on to that parcel, then of his arriving in Nakhon Sawan and settling down and doing his job. She tried to visualize what it was like to be a soldier, but got no further than the terrible fact that a soldier was supposed to do battle and in the course of his duty might need to kill, or get killed. She could not imagine her gentle fun-loving Phi Nuang performing the act of killing, but as far as getting himself killed . . .

"What's the matter with you, Phloi?" Choi suddenly spoke up in a startlingly loud voice.

"Nothing. Why do you ask?"

"I thought you were crying."

"No."

"Are you sure?"

"Oh, Choi!"

"All right, I must have been seeing things. Don't mind me."

Mae Chan and Khun Sai, having directed a meaningful frown at their daughter and niece respectively, looked at each other, then at Phloi. Their eyes shone with affection and goodwill and Phloi felt like giving them a big hug. She refrained from the impulse, because it was obvious that while they might approve of this matter between Nuang and herself, both Mae Chan and Khun Sai deemed it premature to refer to the said matter openly in her presence.

Sadet, too, must have known about it—Khun Sai had few secrets from her royal mistress—and preferred to remain tactfully silent on the subject. (Except that now and again she was not averse to making such remarks as: "What kind of heavenly food have you been eating, Phloi? I've never seen you look so radiant.")

Before she left the Inner Court that afternoon, Mae Chan handed her daughter an envelope, saying: "Oh, I almost forgot. Nuang sent this the other day. It's for you."

Later on, Choi burst out laughing over her brother's message, which went, "Choi, please give the enclosed envelope to Phloi. I arrived safely in Nakhon Sawan. Am quite well. Nuang."

Phloi quickly claimed the enclosed envelope, put it away in her case, went about dreamily doing this and that the rest of the day, then finally, when everyone else at Sadet's residence had gone to sleep, took it to a far corner of the room and opened it under the light of a small candle.

She read and reread the letter, then folded it carefully and put it back in its honoured place among her valuable things. She went back to it the next night, and the next.

She did not light the candle now, but sat by the window looking out towards the luminous night sky, holding the letter in her hand. She could almost hear Nuang's voice murmuring those lines. ". . . You have my heart, Phloi. I beg you to keep it and not fling it away . . . I see your face everywhere and I think of you as I breathe in and out . . . Your *champa* flowers and betels have dried up. To me they are the loveliest of things. I keep them with me always. I wait for the night and when it comes I go to sleep with your silk cover that still has your scent, and then I'm not a poor man to be pitied any longer but one rich with happiness . . . Life in Nakhon Sawan is hard and lonely. How wise of our elders to suggest we should wait. I would not have forgiven myself if I had brought you out here to live. This rickety house I'm in is certainly not meant for a girl like you. And the food! I must thank you and Choi again and again for having supplied me with all those delicious pastes and sweets, for the food here is so tasteless when it's not crudely flavoured . . . My superior officers say in a year or two I should be transferred to a more comfortable place. So I try to be patient, and not to worry too much about those many men in Bangkok, men far better endowed than I in every way . . . As for you, you have nothing to worry about, for I will never change . . ."

Some nights later Phloi lit the candle again and after several hours and innumerable torn-up sheets succeeded in producing this reply: "Phi Nuang, I have received the letter you sent from Nakhon Sawan. I'm glad you are not sick or anything but sorry you don't like the food. Choi and I will send you more things to eat. Take care of yourself. I'm well. Everyone here asks about you. Will you be making trips to Bangkok once in a while?"

That was all. She signed her name to it, hoping that Nuang would somehow be able to read between those few lines—she could have filled tens of pages had she had the necessary talent and audacity to put into words all the thoughts and feelings she wished to convey to him.

Sending out love letters from the Inner Court was an enterprise not to be lightly embarked upon. If found out it could do grievous harm to your reputation, besides causing people whom you esteemed and held dear to be displeased with you—people like Sadet and Khun Sai. Going over what she had written, Phloi reassured herself that no one would ever be able to label it a love letter.

Nonetheless, on the day that they were to send food parcels to Nuang, she approached Choi very cautiously.

"Aren't you going to write him a few words, Choi?"

"What for? No one can read my writing anyway."

Phloi fell silent, then summoned up enough courage to say, "If you write, I can put my letter in the same envelope. Here, read it."

Choi did so, and said it was an absolutely blameless letter. "But," she added in a kindly voice, "all the same you had better play it safe and not send it. We can never be sure no one will get to know about it. And then, scandalmongers being what they are . . ."

Phloi saw the point, thanked Choi for being concerned for her sake, and tried vainly not to show how disappointed she was.

"Poor Phloi," Choi sighed, then perked up. "Tell you what. I will write him after all."

Choi's letter to her brother was as brief as Phloi's had been, and its message very much the same, except for an additional line at the end: "and Phloi sends you her best regards."

As a matter of fact, Phloi was perfectly content with it. She felt that that one single line was capable of carrying her unexpressed thoughts as fully as her own letter, which she now proceeded to tear into neat little pieces.

EIGHT

PHI Nuang had gone off to Nakhon Sawan. And Nakhon Sawan was certainly far enough, in Phloi's reckoning. Now it was being whispered in the Inner Court that His Majesty Phra Chao Yu Hua would be leaving for Europe!

Many elderly women refused to believe it. It was unheard of, they said; no Thai king had travelled to that remote continent, it was not traditional, not according to royal custom, and they concluded that it must be a rumour fabricated by some giddy young maids trying to impress the gullible.

But in this instance the elders were proved wrong. The whispering came to a stop as rumours turned into confirmed news capable of being discussed aloud; and after the visit was announced in the court circular even the most doubting old-timers had to accept it as a fact. His Majesty was to leave for Europe a few days before the festival of Songkran of the year 116 of the Bangkok Era (1897). It was incredible, they said, but true.

While Phloi understood that His Majesty was going on an important mission, she also thought about it in personal terms: that he would be far away from his loved ones, and that even the royals were not exempted from the pains of parting. The thought made her own separation from Nuang easier to bear.

The announcement about the king's European tour was followed by another of an equally unprecedented nature, albeit producing a somewhat different effect on the women of the Inner Court—the younger women, that is. This was the announcement that during His Majesty's absence Queen Saowabha would be ruling the kingdom in his stead. She would have the title of Somdet Regent—Somdet Phra Borom Rajini Nat—and the same powers and privileges pertaining to kingship.

How did they feel about it—the younger women of the Inner Court (and a few older ones too, for that matter)? Well, what they felt had some excitement mixed in it, of course, and pride. But more pronounced than either emotion was a sense of discovery, of awakening. Phloi felt it keenly. If the queen could become ruler like the king, it followed then that women as human beings were on the same level as men and could step into positions usually held by men if given the opportunity. That men were lords of their households and women more or less their dependents might be the prevailing situation but by no means an unalterable one.

She discussed it with Choi, who thoroughly agreed with her and later made the following declaration to Khun Sai: "You know what, Khun Aunt? I'm not afraid of men anymore. I'm a woman and a woman reigns over all in this land of ours."

"And if you don't shut up you'll get a coconut in your mouth to shut it for you," retorted her aunt.

But during the next months even Khun Sai had to admit that the palace had undergone a change, both in obvious and in subtle ways. The queen now reigned over all, as Choi said. She was the highest in the land, and at the daily ministerial conference of the Front Court it was she who presided over the proceedings. Her supremacy gave a new significance to the Inner Court, a kind of aura that seemed to relegate the Front Court to a secondary role whenever the two came together at social and official functions.

One of the changes within the Inner Court itself had to do with royal audiences. They had become much more informal. On most days, after the meeting with her ministers, Her Majesty preferred to see the ladies of the Inner Court in the Turtle (officially "Sivalai") Garden rather than in the more ceremonial atmosphere of the Upper Residence. Here it was more like a get-together than an audience granted by the most august personage. The ladies came and the queen chatted with all of them, and played croquet and bathed with them in the pool. Sadet went regularly, and sometimes Phloi went along as her escort carrying her betel-nut box and the tray containing her clothes and toiletries for after the swim. To be on duty at the Turtle Garden on these afternoons was pure pleasure, especially when photographs were being taken of the group, which happened quite frequently. The whole operation of setting up the camera and getting it to do its work was a show in itself: the mysterious black box perched on the three stilts, the pulling in and out of the various parts, the changing of the glass plates, the photographer's head disappearing under the black cloth only to pop out again and again, the signaling for everyone to hold still . . . The woman behind the camera, Soi by name, was a maid from Princess Orathai's palace; she had learned her craft from her brother, Khun Chaya, a professional photographer. The photo-graphs taken by Mae Soi were dispatched to His Majesty in Europe, Phloi was told.

At these gatherings in the Turtle Garden, Phloi noticed how Her Majesty always tried to put everyone at their ease, and if she used her authority at all it was to persuade them to enjoy themselves. She was gracious and friendly not only to the important ladies but to those not so high-ranking, and she was not only friendly herself but had a way of inspiring friendliness in her people—of keeping them united and not divided into contending factions. Phloi thought her very marvellous, so regal, and awesome and lovable at the same time.

Many months went by, and at last there came the glad news that His Majesty would be returning in the cool season and that the celebrations to welcome him would be grander than anything the capital had ever known.

The news threw the Inner Court into a festive mood. Excitement was in the air and you breathed it in the drawing-rooms and in the kitchens, in the gardens and in the streets, in Teng Row, in the *khlons'* quarters, in the tunnel. There were ceaseless comings and goings everywhere. Pavilions were being set up and decorated, banquets and entertainments organized and rehearsed. And among the younger women clothes were the dominant theme of con-versation and the main preoccupation. Seamstresses became the most sought-after beings; you paid them respects and pleaded with them and you were willing to pay as high as fifty baht for a blouse laced in ribbon or entirely stitched with bows and with leg-of-mutton (or as the Thais called them, leg-of-ham) sleeves.

Except for their girlish concern with clothes, Choi and Phloi behaved very much as though they were still ten years old instead of eighteen. Phloi could not help laughing at herself a little for so avidly looking forward to celebrating Phra Chao Yu Hua's return that she almost forgot to miss Nuang.

The actual events surpassed her expectations. They were more fun—more *sanuk*—to be part of, more beautiful to look at, more uplifting to the heart and soul than anything she could ever have imagined. She did not go all over town, did not get to see everything there was to see. That would have been impossible. But on that first night she was among the massive crowd gathered in Sanam Luang—Phramen Grounds—to offer homage and best wishes to His Majesty and watch the welcoming dances performed in his honour. The dances came later. At the beginning was the procession of the king's civil servants. Carrying candles in their hands and moving slowly four abreast, the civil servants approached the royal pavilion from a far corner of the grounds in a quivering ribbon of light that stretched and fluttered on as far as the eye could see. There was a hush as the candles came to assemble before the pavilion, then rose high above the heads of their carriers. Three times the candles were lifted and three times thunderous cheers went echoing up into the sky—Ho-he-ho-h-e-w!—started by the civil servants and joined in by the crowds. The cheering had barely died down when troops of monkey soldiers and demon soldiers suddenly appeared and really turned Sanam Luang into the city of Ayuthaya at the time of Rama's triumphal return. The dancing, prancing, whirling, masked figures filled the arena. But they were not fighting as they usually do in the other episodes of the Ramayana. Monkeys and demons, no longer enemies, rejoiced together on this most beneficent occasion. Phloi was totally immersed in their movements, a combination of disciplined formality and irrepressible antics. Then Choi beside her broke into a jubilant cry, "*Phra Ram ma laeo!* Here comes Lord Rama!" Lord

Rama and the other heroes of the long war entered in their chariots, and the gold in these magnificent vehicles and in the lords' sumptuous costumes glittered like stars come down to earth. Phloi had read poems describing such a happening, and was enthralled to be actually living through it.

Another unforgettable scene took place inside the Grand Palace. There had never been so many children in the Grand Palace as on that day, although the celebrations lasted many days. The boys came from Rajavidhyalai School and the girls from Sunandalai School, all looking adorable in fancy dress—in *farang* trousers and jackets, in Chinese mandarin coats, in Indian saris, and so forth. His Majesty gave a party for them in Sivalai Garden and they danced for him. The boys and girls in *farang* clothes danced in *farang* style. Phloi was told that one of the numbers was called "Lancer Song" and another "Sir Roger."

"Do you know that in Europe grown men and women dance together like this?" Choi whispered into her ear.

"I don't believe you," Phloi whispered back. "These children are sweet. But for grownups to hold one another like this for all to see? No, it won't do."

But Choi was very sure of her facts. "It's true Phloi. The *farangs* think nothing of it. I'm told that at Burapha Palace they dance like this for hours, hugging one another in front of everybody. I'd like to see it with my own eyes."

"I don't. And if I had to do it myself I'd die of shame."

THE most eagerly awaited event—an episode from the dance drama Inao performed by the famous dancers of the palace—also took place in Sivalai Garden. It was a private royal affair and Phloi considered herself blessed by good fortune to be among Sadet's retinue, and therefore a member of the audience. The dancers were the Chao Choms and the Chao Chom Mothers under the previous reign—under King Mongkut; they had retired from the stage many years ago, had become living legends, and Phloi had been hearing about their incomparable artistry ever since she had been in the Inner Court. That night they held her spellbound. After the first few moments she no longer thought of them with awe as venerable ladies of exalted ranks portraying the romantic Prince Inao, the lovely Princess Busaba, the dignified King of Daha, the gracious queens Pramai-suri and Madewi, and so forth. Age and position had been cast aside, had been transcended by art, and art in turn had been strengthened by love and gratitude. The venerable ladies existed for Phloi during those hours purely as dancers if not the very spirit of the dance. In later life, whenever she attended an Inao presentation, Phloi was to find herself wistfully remembering and saying to herself she had seen the best Inao of all time that enchanted night they celebrated the king's return in Sivalai Garden.

Another happening on that same night was also to be remembered by Phloi all her life—and surely by many others who were there with her, a happening which perhaps would have been described as "revolutionary" had that adjective been coined and in use at the time. And it was His Majesty who desired it and brought it about. It was he who announced that no seating arrangement had been made for that night's dinner (which preceded the Inao dance in the programme) and that all the guests would have equal opportunity to draw lots and take their chances as to who their respective partner would be—each dinner tray having been set to serve two people. Well, Khun Mon, a woman attendant, drew hers, and sat down face to face with His Majesty, and partook of the same royal food from the same royal dishes and bowls!

"*Mai koei pop hen ma kon*—never has such a thing been seen before," was how the elders described it, and they were to go on talking about it for a long time. Of course there were some who asked, "What will happen next?" in a vaguely apprehensive tone of voice, but on the whole they were moved by it. They believed it was a good thing, a wise thing—what Phra Chao Yu Hua had done. They understood that it was an expression of the love he had for his people high and low alike, and as regards Khun Mon, they said what a propitious omen for her to have been singled out by fate for such a high honour. To Phloi it was a most stirring and memorable sight—Khun Mon and Phra Chao Yu Hua sitting there together and sharing a meal like any two good friends. It aroused her sense of wonder, gave her a feeling not unlike what she sometimes had when watching the dawn of a new day.

One aspect of the event was brought up by Choi. As far as Phloi knew, Choi must have been the only one who was interested in it. "Poor Khun Mon," Choi said. "I pitied her that night. She must have been shaking all over from start to finish. Probably couldn't swallow a thing—must have been very hungry afterwards."

DURING the course of the festive weeks Phloi was reunited with her half sister Khun Choei, who had come to stay a few days with one of their numerous relatives in the Inner Court.

"How pretty you are, Mae Phloi."

"So are you, Khun Choei."

"I'm not really, but that's all right," Khun Choei laughed. "Except that Chao Khun Father is somewhat worried that he might never be able to dispose of me. It's quite possible that he'll be stuck with two spinster daughters, because Khun Un is determined not to marry but to remain guardian of the family's treasure for life and thereafter." They laughed together, both of them being no longer terrified of Big Sister Un.

"But," Khun Choei went on, "if she goes on like this—giving in to Khun Chit all the time, she'll soon have nothing left to guard."

"And what has Khun Chit been doing?"

"The same—loafing and squandering, and being nasty to wife and child."

"What! Khun Chit a father already?"

"That's right. Do you remember that little Phuang—her mother was one of Khun Un's maids? . . . That's the one. She's now our brother's wife—and suffering for it. He beats her when he doesn't get his opium."

"Opium!" Phloi cried out. And how could Khun Choei be talking about it so calmly!

But Khun Choei must have long ago learned to accept the situation. "Oh, yes, opium," she assured Phloi in the manner of a factual reporter. "He started on it with the excuse that it relieved his aches and pains, and now he lives for it. He's much worse than your brother Phoem, who only enjoys drinking and gets drunk fairly often but never violently. I worry about them sometimes," she added. "What will become of them when Chao Khun Father's gone?" She gave a sigh, then a smile: "And what about your future, Mae Phloi? Are you staying on here in the palace to fulfill the glorious and exalted destiny?"

Phloi knew what Khun Choei meant and protested loudly and somemnly that she had never entertained such a vastly exaggerated opinion of herself, and that it would be almost sacrilegious if she did. Khun Choei believed her sister; it was heartening to know that her Mae Phloi had not become overweeningly ambitious like some other palace women of her acquaintance.

Then they talked about getting Phloi back to Khlong Bang Luang on occasional visits. Chao Khun Father had not been too well this past year, Khun Choei said. She knew he would love to see Phloi—he asked about her all the time. He wouldn't want to take her out of Sadet's service and have her live at home with him or anything like that—no, of course not, he wouldn't be so ungrateful to Sadet after all she had done for his daughter. But if Phloi could come home once in a while it would cheer him up and, besides, in any case, Phloi should not cut herself off from her family—that wouldn't do, Khun Choei said. She said it not as a criticism of Phloi but as a loving sister who wished her well. Phloi wholly agreed in all this, saying she herself from time to time had thought about going home but had not carried out her intention due to several reasons—Khun Un's attitude for one, and then there was the practical side of it, getting someone to accompany her and that sort of thing. To journey back and forth between Khlong Bang Luang and the Grand Palace by herself was out of the question. If she were much older she would do it by just taking Phit along with her, but at present that would not look right either.

So together they made plans: when the homecoming celebrations for Phra Chao Yu Hua were over, Khun Choei would return home, get things ready for Phloi's visit (in all likelihood against Khun Un's wishes), then come to fetch Phloi. Sadet's permission would have to be requested. Phloi had no doubt that it would be granted, Her Royal

Highness being so understanding and so generous—a perfect patron really, she told Khun Choei.

How wonderful to have Khun Choei in the Inner Court! Anyone would be proud to show off such a distinguished sister, but apart from that it was marvellous to be with each other again, laughing together and chatting about home, about Sadet and Khun Sai and Choi, about food and clothes and everything. One subject, however, failed to get mentioned. Phloi did not try to tell Khun Choei how she felt about Nuang, not only because she didn't think the time was right for it but because she simply did not know where or how to begin her story.

Khun Choei and Choi liked each other from the first moment they met—as Phloi had always known they would. The three of them spent some time together every day, calling on friends, attending shows, touring the outer area of the Grand Palace. The maid Phit often volunteered to come along with them on these jaunts—to protect them from harm, she said, on account of the crowds these days being so mixed and you couldn't be sure what might happen.

"So you've become quite a palace person, eh, Phit?" Khun Choei remarked.

"Me?" Phit let out an ear-shattering laugh. "Never! They can't make a palace kind out of me—I'm too old to learn. I'm in the palace because Khun Phloi is here. When she leaves, I leave. Where she goes, I go."

Khun Choei was impressed. "How I envy you, Mae Phloi! I wish I had somebody at home with this kind of loyalty . . . Here, Phit. Buy some sweets with it."

Phit was delighted with the money. "Prepare yourself to eat a lot of sweets, Khun Phloi. Your wealthy Phit will feed you like you've never been fed before."

"Wealthy?" Phloi laughed. "On two baht?"

"Ah, but these two are turning into a big pile. I'm putting them on the lottery, and I know for sure which will be the winning letter this time. I saw a whole flock of herons in my dream last night."

"So what's the winning letter going to be?" Choi demanded.

"Why, *P-kangsu*, what else?"

"*P-kangsu*—that's the fish!" Choi said knowledgeably. "But you dreamt about birds."

"Those herons are fish-eating birds," Phit elaborated with some impatience. "Don't you know how to read dreams?"

"You've convinced me, Phit," said Khun Choei.

"From now on when I want to gamble I'll come to you for advice."

ONE night they went out to see a dance-drama presented in the Sahathai Hall by a group of His Majesty's civil servants. The Inner Court's dance enthusiasts had been looking forward to this event with a great deal of curiosity and a certain amount of skepticism ("What do these people know about dancing anyway?"), and Phloi, sitting in one of the back rows, could hear all manner of comments being whispered round her. Some of the experts thought the dancers were trying to do their best and ought to be commended on that score, while others regarded the whole thing as more comical than artistic, and these latter were tittering and being hushed by their more sedate companions.

Phloi was thus enjoying herself watching the action on stage and listening to audience reaction when suddenly she became conscious of something breaking in upon her absorption. She turned her head, prompted by some instinctive sense of direction, and found herself looking into a pair of eyes. They must have been watching her for quite some time before intruding on her consciousness. After that brief glance, which told her that the eyes belonged to a fair-skinned young man with regular features and dressed in the costume of a royal page, Phloi shifted her attention back to the stage; but the young man continued to stare at her—she could feel it. After a while it began to be irritating, and she turned to look at him once again—to frown at him rather, letting her annoyance show quite plainly. This, however, did not seem to deter him. On the contrary, he was smiling. Phloi quickly looked away, making up her mind to ignore his presence from now on. But that didn't work either, for she knew he was still there, his eyes remaining fixed on her. Really, she had never come across such a persistent starer! He had definitely spoiled the evening for her; she could not concentrate on the dance. The idea of leaving the theatre occurred to her, but there were Choi and Khun Choei to consider and she did not want to disturb them.

On leaving the theatre Phloi was well aware that they were being followed. If the Inner Court were not out of bounds for men, she was almost sure he would have crossed the threshold of the Twilight Gate and accompany them right up to Sadet's residence.

That night, instead of falling asleep thinking about Nuang as she had been in the habit of doing these past months, Phloi was kept awake going over the annoying incident in her mind.

She told Choi about it.

"Why didn't you point him out to me at the theatre?" said Choi. "I know how to deal with these oglers."

The next day Choi had a chance to apply her knowledge. They ran into him outside Sri Sudawong Gate. Phloi saw him first and had a suspicion—from the way he had been peering this way and that and from his expression on seeing her—that he had been lurking about on purpose.

"So that's him?" Choi murmured. "Come along, Phit, we're going to have a little fun."

Leaving Phloi at a safe distance, the two went and stationed themselves a few paces from him, then Choi spoke loudly to Phit: "Look here, don't you know that it's very vulgar to stare at people?"

"I do, I do," replied Phit as though she had been rehearsed beforehand. "Very vulgar."

"Very vulgar," repeated Choi in her most censorious tones. "Unspeakably rude. Something you never do if you're well brought up."

"My father and my mother, they didn't teach me right." Phit went on playing her part with gusto. "That's why I annoy people, drive them mad, too. Maybe I ought to be chained, and whipped, so I'd know better."

Here their impromptu little act abruptly came to an end, as the man began walking away, looking acutely discomfited.

"I'll give you a special reward when we get back to the Residence, Phit."

"No need to, Khun Choi. It was too simple—nothing to it at all."

Phloi strongly disapproved of their rough tactics and said so. The man could have fought back and made it embarrassing for all of them. Besides, Khun Sai would have a fit if she knew what they had done.

"Don't fret, Phloi." Choi was laughing and savouring her easy victory. "We've taught him a lesson. He won't bother you again."

As it happened, Choi's lesson had been a waste of effort.

The celebrations for his Majesty's return from Europe were over; Khun Choei had gone back to Khlong Bang Luang; weeks had passed and the man was still there; almost every time Phloi found herself in the outer area of the Grand Palace there he would be, prowling about and sneaking glances at her from a safe distance—safe because Phloi had succeeded in restraining Choi from going up to him and delivering some more of her dangerously scathing remarks.

Choi had also discovered what his name was. "It's Prem. Everyone calls him Khun Prem and they all seem to think highly of him. But if you ask me, I think he needs another lesson from us, don't you?"

"No, I don't." Phloi was most firm. "We'll just go on ignoring him. He'll get tired of it soon enough."

So when all the arrangements for her trip home had been made, Phloi felt doubly relieved. It was unlikely that this Khun Prem would pursue her across the river Chao Phraya, and it was to be hoped that her disappearance from the palace would persuade him to shift his attention elsewhere.

During these weeks she had been missing Nuang more than ever. Why couldn't it be he who followed her everywhere so faithfully? And why, oh why, had there been no news from him for so long? Perhaps he had been sent to some other post even farther away and more isolated than Nakhon Sawan. Perhaps he had taken ill, or been wounded—but no, no! that didn't bear thinking about. Most probably his letters had gone astray and—most comforting thought, this—they might turn up while she was away to welcome her on her return to the palace.

As for Sadet's permission, it was as she had expected. Her Royal Highness had not the least objection to her going home.

After making sure that Phloi would be properly accompanied on her travels, Sadet said to her in the presence of Khun Sai, Choi and her other attendants—it was during her midday meal: "It's good that you should wish to go to your father, to wait on him and add to his happiness. Gratitude towards one's parents is a noble virtue. I've brought you up, so naturally it makes me proud to know that you're a young woman of good character, though of course it's not only up-bringing and training that will make a person good or bad. Sometimes even the very best upbringing doesn't seem to help at all. Strange, isn't it?

"If you should ask to leave me for good because your Chao Khun Father needed you, I would still have to say yes, although I would have been very sad to lose you.

"Well, this time you'll be coming back. I suppose I can manage without you for a while."

Having finished eating, Sadet washed her hands and reached for a cigarette. "What! Only a couple left? And it was full yesterday. Who has been smoking my cigarettes?" Her glance swept over the faces before her, but each one was wearing an innocent look. "Don't think you can fool me! I can picture you all right." She took a cigarette, held it high and waved it to and fro a few times before striking a match to it. "You light it like this, nonchalantly, then you take a puff, like this, for all the world to admire—'Look at me, am I not smart?'"

It was a superb parody of the mannerism affected by certain smokers in the palace. The girls grinned at her and at one another, all except Choi, who laughed aloud.

"Ah, my impudent Choi. I amuse you, do I? Could it be you, by any chance, who have been pilfering my cigarettes?"

"Oh, not me, Your Highness!"

"Maybe not for yourself. But did you take them to give to your aunt?"

"Oh-oh!" Khun Sai groaned. "What have I done to deserve this?"

"I don't know. I only know that I've been too soft with all of you. And what do I get in return? You all take advantage of me." She gave an audible sigh. The girls went on smiling, some at one another, some at the floor, taking care not to do it too indiscreetly.

Sadet finally came back to Phloi. "I said I could manage without you, but perhaps I can't. We'll see. Go with my blessing, Phloi. Be a good daughter to your father. Obey him, and bring joy and happiness into his life."

NINE

CHAO Khun Father's residence looked small when Phloi first set eyes on it that time she went back home and stayed with the family for some ten days—much smaller than she remembered—and what had been an immense area between it and the landing pavilion also seemed to have dwindled to a merely reasonable distance during her absence. But the neglected appearance of the place was something real and not due to any discrepancy between a child's viewpoint and a grownup's standards. The pavilion had indeed seen better days; it was obvious that the house needed a coat of paint; and the brick and iron fence had started to lean towards the tawny water of Khlong Bang Luang whose gentle waves had been lapping against its base these very many years.

Chao Khun Father himself had been in poor health, and this, rather than his grey hair and his thin body—he had always been slim in any case—was what made him look a great deal older than when Phloi had last seen him.

"I'd like to keep you with me as long as I can," Chao Khun Father said. "You're going to share Mae Choei's rooms—isn't that right?... That's good—we'll be near one another... Have you brought a servant from the palace?... I see, so the maid Phit is still with you. I thought you had come by yourself and was going to ask Mae Choei to find someone to serve you while you're here.

"But it's difficult to get servants nowadays," he went on, musing. "Not like when your Chao Khun Grandfather was alive. Those days there were hundreds and hundreds of people living in the house under his care. There were his clerks, his oarsmen, his labour corps, his musicians and women dancers—a whole troupe of them, and relatives and hangers-on drifting in and out all over the place. Quite a household we were in those days—you should have seen the huge cauldrons we used for cooking rice, rows of them, like in a regular barrack . . .

"Yes, I had to let most of those people go after your Chao Khun Grandfather passed away. Impossible to keep them together. Didn't have the means to shelter them all."

"These days we're sheltering over fifty of them, sir," Khun Choei reminded her father. "I've counted them. Over fifty people are living in this compound, though sometimes it's so quiet you'd have thought it was deserted." She turned to her sister. "I'm afraid after living in the palace you might find it too quiet and lonesome here, Mae Phloi."

"It can be quiet in the palace too," Phloi said, "at times."

It was certainly quiet in Khun Un's sitting room—tense and quiet, with Khun Un's animosity jealously guarding the silence. Unlike the rest of the house, Khun Un's room was in every detail exactly as Phloi had remembered it, and its owner, as erect and immaculate as ever, seemed not to have moved an inch from her spot on the floor surrounded by her treasures where Phloi had last seen her many years ago.

She frowned at Phloi as at an intruder, then favoured Khun Choei, the instigator of Phloi's homecoming, with a look of acute displeasure.

"Listen to me first, Khun Sister." Khun Choei spoke rapidly, with a hint of defiance in her voice. "I didn't want to bother you, but Mae Phloi here felt she couldn't come into this house without coming in to pay you her respects."

Phloi performed a deferential *wai* which was ignored. She then asked Khun Un how she was and, receiving no reply, made no further attempt at communication.

Reaching for her dainty ivory box containing the scented wax, Khun Un began to varnish her lips with extreme care. She had evidently decided not to see, hear or speak for the time being, so after a while Khun Choei and Phloi came away, leaving her to her absorbing occupation.

"At least it's over and done with," Khun Choei summed it up. "But for a moment I thought she was going to be really unpleasant—and then I should have had to do something about it."

"Please try not to get into a fight with her while I'm here, Khun Choei."

"I'll try. But I'd like to see you try asking her not to give you any trouble while you're here, Mae Phloi!"

Phloi's old wooden house, where she had once lived with Mother and Phoem, had also been ravaged by time and was now occupied by Khun Chit and his family. If she had been alone Phloi would have sat down on the steps and cried—for her dead mother, for her childhood days, for the house itself, for Khun Chit's physical decline brought on by disease and opium which had changed him from a good-looking adolescent into this prematurely old, emaciated man with dark-circled eyes and greyish lips, and for his wife Phuang, so young to be wife and mother, so very much in awe of her sickly husband, and who referred to herself when speaking to him and to Phloi as *bao*—a servant, which position she had held from birth.

And Phloi became more depressed at the thought that Khun Un had not objected to her adored brother taking Phuang as his wife because she was confident that this meek and loyal girl would never rise up to usurp her powers as First Lady of the house.

But the children—a handsome boy of two and a chubby infant girl only a few months old—put joy back in her heart. She fell in love with them at first sight and they seemed to reciprocate her feelings. The boy hugged her in return and the baby held tight to her fingers while gazing into her eyes as if it had something to tell her.

"Just look at the little Khun!" Phuang cried delightedly, giving Phloi a sweet smile which made her look younger still. "She likes you, Khun Phloi. She knows Khun Aunt Phloi has come to see her. Don't you, little Khun?"

Phloi had brought along some gold trinkets as customary gifts for her niece and nephew. When she put the bracelet on the baby's wrist its father leaned forward for a closer look.

"How much does the gold weigh?" he asked.

Phloi couldn't quite believe her ears. She shot a furtive glance at Khun Choei, but the latter was keeping her eyes averted and her face blank.

Khun Chit repeated his question. "How much does it weigh?"

Phloi stammered out a reply, admitting that she didn't know exactly.

"Women!" Khun Chit grumbled to himself. "They'll buy anything that takes their fancy—never mind if it's not worth the price." But on the whole Khun Chit was very genial with Phloi, who behaved humbly and respectfully towards him as a younger sister should, and when this particular meeting came to a close, he told her to come and play with the children more often. "So that they'll grow to love you," he added graciously.

"I forgot to warn you," Khun Choei said on the way back to the big house. "And now it's too late. Khun Chit should not have been allowed to see the gold you gave the children. Too much temptation for him. No, I'm not exaggerating, Mae Phloi. Don't be shocked if your gifts turn into opium smoke within the next few days. You've learned many things living in the palace, and now you're going to learn a few more here in your own house, like accepting the fact that your own brother can sink so low. I can speak frankly with you. With other people I'm ashamed even to mention his name. But I've stopped having anxieties about him. I've become immune. It's his own karma after all, isn't it?"

"MY karma," Chao Khun Father said, "it's my karma that has brought me these two hopeless sons. Son Chit will go through life an overgrown bad boy. I've tried reasoning with him, pleading with him, whipping him. But no remedy exists that can cure him of his nature. Son Phoem is a little better, but still a long way from what a father can depend on. He shies away from responsibility. Oh, they like him well enough at the department, but he's not at all interested in getting ahead, you know. He goes to work at his convenience. Yet, he's old enough to start thinking about such things as wife and family, and settling down and making something of himself."

"DON'T worry about me, Mae Phloi."

It was Phoem's favourite rejoinder to his sister's oft-repeated suggestion that perhaps there was room for improvement in his mode of conduct, and he invariably uttered it with a breezy grin or chuckle.

Nothing wrong, he pointed out, with leading a carefree sort of life, doing nobody any harm and having plenty of friends, true friends who would never forsake him when he's down and out. Nothing wrong with spending the night in town occasionally or leaving the office when there's really nothing to do anyway. As to the business of taking a wife—well, Chao Khun Father, being a father, was obliged to talk like one from time to time, and Phloi was not to take his standard paternal view on this subject too literally.

"What would I do with a wife?" Phoem asked. "I spend all my money every month as a single man. If I had a wife she'd starve to death. Of course a rich wife might be the answer, but I have no time to go searching for one."

He came home roaring drunk one day, hollering and singing at the top of his voice and lurching crazily like a boat in a rainstorm. Luckily the maid Phit came along in time to deal with the situation in her usual capable manner.

"He doesn't have a bad voice I must say," was Phit's comment as she hauled him away before his rendition of the Song of Phra Wai at Close of Battle could disrupt Chao Khun Father's afternoon nap. She returned later to give her verdict: something about an empty stomach rather than alcoholic excess being to blame for his condition. She had washed him; fed him rice and boiling soup full of hot chilis and lime juice; and put him to bed on the bench under the mango tree near the kitchen quarters; and in an hour or so he should be as good as new. She had also given him a good talking to and believed he would not do it again, at least not while Khun Phloi and herself were staying here.

"By the way, Mae Phloi, you know my friend Khun Prem, don't you?"

Phoem asked this question during one of their pleasant brother-sister chitchats. (Phit's forecast was correct. He never repeated the alarmingly noisy and so shameful performance of that afternoon. And throughout her visit he did not once hang about in town but came back home every day to keep her company.)

Phloi started at the sound of the name, then casually replied, "No,

I don't."

Phoem looked surprised. "No? That's funny. From the way he talks I get the impression that he sees you quite often. He's a royal page—tall, slender, fair complexion. You must have seen him."

"Possibly." Phloi kept her tone normally conversational. "But you can't expect me to have learned everybody's name; there are so many people in the palace. And how did you get to know him?"

"Some mutual friends introduced us not long ago. He's a few years older than I am. Very nice man, Khun Prem."

Phloi nodded, asking no more questions. But Phoem had not finished describing his new friend. He went on and on.

"Comes from a good family—rich, too, much richer than ours. His Chao Khun Father's a tax collector I think. But he's not at all conceited. Never puts on airs like some of the rich fellows I know. He drops in to see me at the office all the time, always wanting to take me places and give me things, says he feels close to me as if we were brothers. I don't know why, but for some reason he's taken a great liking to me. I like him too, but then everyone does—he's such a gentle, likable person."

So is my dearly loved Phi Nuang, Phloi thought. She admitted to herself that while it made her feel uneasy to know that another man besides Nuang should be so interested in her, she couldn't help finding it somewhat flattering at the same time. And after all, this man Khun Prem had not done anything one could call offensive. As a matter of fact, it was rather sweet and amusing—the way he had gone to the trouble of seeking out her brother Phoem and ingratiating himself with him.

CHAO Khun Father, discoursing on the theme of matrimony while having his dinner, said to attendant daughters Khun Choei and Phloi, "Most of the young men nowadays seem to me just too spoiled and unstable to make good sons or husbands. I should like you to guard yourselves carefully and not plunge into any rash schemes. The result could be disastrous. Don't let your emotion be your sole guide. Listen first to what your elders have to say. We are concerned that you should build up a decent life. We came into this world before you, have seen and heard a great deal more than you. We speak to you from experience and you can't go far wrong by listening to us."

After a pause he suddenly asked of Phloi, "Any young men showing interest in you?"

Flushing a deep pink, Phloi hastened to respond with a brief "No, sir." What else could she have said? He had caught her so completely unprepared.

Chao Khun Father did not question her feeble denial, fortunately, but he warned her not to be so sure: living in a walled palace did not necessarily mean leading a secluded life hidden away from roving eyes. Girls of the Inner Court would always be a centre of attraction, he said, and the grounds on the public side of the inner wall full of young men come to admire them. He himself when still a royal page had loitered about the Earthen Gate waiting to gaze at the beautiful girl who was to become Phloi's mother. She had thought him an impertinent so-and-so at first—had flung many a look of scorn and exasperation back at him when their eyes met. But he had persevered, and won.

Chao Khun Father talked about Mother in an amicable tone of voice, as though she had been just an old friend. He made no mention of the rift between them, no hint of the fact that she, finding life intolerable under his roof, had left him, and then had died giving birth to a stillborn child by another man. Listening to his remembrances Phloi recalled some other old stories related to her by Mother at odd moments when they had all been living together in this old house, stories of how Chao Khun Father had been obliged to marry another woman because, being a dutiful son, he could not bring himself to go against his parents' wish, and of how, broken-hearted, Mother had sworn to renounce men for ever, only to be won over again when, after the birth of Khun Un and Khun Chit, Chao Khun Father had come back to plead with her. He could not make her his first wife, he had put it to her plainly, but would give her a position of which she would never have to be ashamed. Mother joined his household fully aware of her minor role. She knew her place and conducted herself accordingly, but this did not mollify Chao Khun Father's first wife, Khunying Uam, a lady of intensely jealous nature. On his part, Chao Khun Father also made every effort to keep the peace, but to no avail. Khunying Uam, refusing to compromise, spurning all attempts at appease-ment, parted with her husband and children and went off to spend the rest of her life on her ancestral estate at Amphawa.

Her eldest daughter, Khun Un, had blamed it all on Mother, had never forgiven her, and had done everything in her power, out of hatred and a desire for revenge, to undermine Mother's place in the house of her father, and in the end Mother, in her turn, had been forced to leave her husband and children like the Khunying before her.

Thinking about these sad events, Phloi grew afraid of what the future might hold in store for Nuang and herself. Then the fear was dispelled by her almost absolute certainty that Nuang's parents had not arranged for him to marry anyone else. If that were the case Choi would have learned about it—she was so clever at getting people to tell her the truth—and would have relayed it to her without hesitation.

With her mind on Nuang and Choi, she almost didn't hear Chao Khun Father asking her about their aunt Khun Sai.

Yes, she told him, Khun Sai was still with Sadet, and still kept a strict eye on all the girls at Sadet's palace. "A most worthy person," Chao Khun Father declared. "I have a high regard for her. Pity her brother hasn't got her strength of character. A very nice man, but one of these easy-going comfort-lovers with no ambition. If he had applied himself a little more earnestly he would have risen to the rank of Phraya or Phra instead of remaining only a Luang. What about the daughter who had her topknot shaved the same time as you?"

With a great deal of pleasure and ably supported by Khun Choei, Phloi commended Khun Luang's daughter to her father, using a collection of superlatives in her eagerness to convince him of Choi's worthiness.

Chao Khun nodded and went on to ask, "She has an elder brother as I recall—what's he doing now?"

"I think he's a soldier serving in the provinces, sir." Once again Phloi felt she had been caught unprepared (although she should have anticipated the question since they were talking about his family). She wondered, with a quickening heartbeat, if Chao Khun Father had heard about her and Nuang, but it turned out he was merely inquiring about an old friend's son and not a young man courting his daughter. He said, "That's good—to serve in the provinces when you're still young and can endure hardship. It should be useful to his career later on. But if he's like his father he won't get very far either."

Phloi listened to him in filial silence. She would have liked to, but didn't dare, defend Khun Luang and his son, but it seemed to her that their lack of ambition might well be what had made them so happy, and not only happy in themselves but able to dispense so much happiness to others. She was perturbed by Chao Khun's attitude towards Khun Luang's mixture of some fondness and too little respect which could augur ill for her cause, and even more perturbed by his pronouncement about Nuang's future. Did this mean that he would withhold his consent when the time came for Khun Luang and Mae Chan to approach him and request his daughter's hand for their son? She wished there were some way of bringing her Phi Nuang to Khlong Bang Luang so as to have him endear himself to her father, who would then look upon him affectionately as a son. She wished she could speak up and assure her father that Nuang might have been unambitious, but because of his love for her he was now trying hard to make something of himself, to become a man of substance for her sake—not that she didn't love him just as he was at present.

Phloi said all this in her mind while continuing to wave the feather fan gently over her father as she had been doing since the beginning of his meal.

KHUN Choei had been urging Phloi to stretch out her visit for as long as possible. "Your being here has done a world of good for Chao Khun Father—he hasn't looked so well in ages. And not only Chao Khun Father. There's me and the servants. We need you. You've been showing us how to do things properly the way they should be done—maybe I did make a mistake after all in not going to live in the palace. Do stay a few more days. The cook especially could do with some more coaching from you. By the way, the Javanese rice was delicious, and it's so exciting to think that the recipe has been brought back by His Majesty! But more than anything else I want you to stay on because I have been enjoying it so much."

Phloi oscillated between wanting to remain and to leave. It had done her a world of good too—to be home, to wake up and fall asleep in the house where she had been born, to serve her father and to have him tell her repeatedly what joy it gave him to have her here, to walk among the old fruit trees and flowering bushes, to laugh with Phoem and Khun Choei, play with her niece and nephew, watch the passing boats on the *khlong*—to have, in short, what palace life for all its richness could not give her.

On the other hand, she felt she owed it to Sadet and Khun Sai not to linger here longer than necessary. She also missed them and Choi, especially Choi. But, above all, she was anxious to get back to the palace because there might be a letter from Phi Nuang waiting for her.

Another consideration in favour of not extending the visit was Khun Un's resentment over her presence in the house.

"She's at it again!" Khun Choei muttered angrily when Phloi told her how Khun Chit now treated his half sister whenever she called at his bungalow. He had been quite cordial in his own way during her first days here; now he just said "Oh, it's you Mae Phloi," and disappeared into his room, leaving Phloi standing there under the balcony. And little Phuang, the last time Phloi had gone to see her, had looked at her mutely with tears in her eyes. Phloi had inquired after the children, asking if she might see them, and Phuang had given her this look before climbing up the stairs without saying a word. Phloi had wanted to follow her but thought better of it.

"Our Khun Eldest Sister has done it again." Khun Choei sighed, then gave a rueful laugh. "The last time you came she beat me with a twig after you'd left, because I'd been talking to you. I should be thankful she can't do that to me now . . . . Well, what can I say except please put up with it a few more days for Chao Khun Father's sake, and mine."

But Khun Chit and his wife Phuang were not the only ones who must reject Phloi in compliance with Khun Un's orders. There were also Khun Un's servants, and it was Phit who had to contend with them; and Phit's many qualities did not include forbearance. She came to Khun Choei and Phloi one night and spoke her mind. "I've had enough, Khun Choei. Let's go, Khun Phloi. I've been buying my food from the boats, did you know that? Don't want to go near the kitchen ever again. My ears burn up when I hear them curse."

"Whom do they curse, Phit?"

"Oh, they don't name names—they wouldn't dare, but I know who they mean and they know I know. If we don't leave soon I think I'm going to lose my temper and give each and every one of them a slap in the face. Won't that be fun? Won't their mistress just love it?"

Phloi said, "Calm down, Phit. We'll be going two days from now. Do you allow me, Khun Choei?"

"I don't want to," Khun Choei said. "But I have to."

PHLOI made a *krap* at Chao Khun Father's feet. He blessed her, gave her his fatherly words of advice, and asked her to convey his deep respects and gratitude to Sadet. Then he brought out a charming bracelet and handed it to her, saying, "I'm told it's the latest style and very popular with court ladies, so I bought it for you." After glancing briefly in the direction of Khun Un's suite, he went on, "You don't have to put it on now. It's for you to wear in the palace."

The bracelet was given with love and Phloi received it with a happy heart; and though it made her rather sad that Chao Khun Father was obliged to be secretive about showing his affection for her so as to avoid offending Khun Un, the happy feelings, being stronger, prevailed.

AFTER an audience with Sadet, the next thing she did on arrival in the palace was to take Choi by the hand, lead her to a secluded spot, and then to whisper: "Any news?"

"What news?" Choi asked uncomprehendingly.

"Please, Choi! Don't pretend. Don't joke with me. Have a heart, Choi!"

Choi stopped pretending, but that was no good either, because there actually had been nothing from Nakhon Sawan—no letters, no messages of any kind from any quarter whatsoever. "Though there might be before long," Choi said consolingly. "My mother is coming to visit us the day after tomorrow."

And that was sufficient to keep Phloi's hope alive. She slept well that night, and spent most of the following day giving detailed accounts of her trip to Sadet, Khun Sai, Choi and the other girls, skipping over such unpleasant items as her encounter with Khun Chit's opium habit and Khun Un's hostile little ways. Being back in the palace was like being home again, no doubt about it, but this time she couldn't help sensing its somewhat hemmed-in atmos-phere; walls were walls for all their graceful lines, and it would take her a few more days to accept once again the forbidding clanging sound of the gates closing at twilight as something ordinary and inevitable like the close of day itself.

As usual, Mae Chan came accompanied by a couple of bearers carrying all manner of baskets laden with fruit and other gifts.

"There you are, Mae Chan!" Khun Sai called out. "Have you had anything to eat? Come join us. We've just started."

"No more food for me." Mae Chan shook her head. "Not for awhile. I passed a *khanom chin* (noodles with various sauces) vendor by the gate. It looked so inviting so I sat down and stuffed myself—don't often get a chance to take my meals from these travelling-stores. Ooh, but isn't it hot today? And that was quite a long walk from the gate. I'm exhausted!"

"Have a wash, then. Make yourself fresh and cool. Then we'll talk."

Mae Chan nodded, took a dipper from the shelf and headed for the water jars in the backyard.

Phloi, who would have preferred the two elders to start talking right away or, more precisely, to have Mae Chan launch immediately into the subject of her soldier son without so much preamble, had to content herself with eating and now and again glancing at the visitor's baskets, some of which (it gave her pleasure to imagine) must have come from Nuang.

TEN

PHLOI pricked up her ears when Mae Chan re-entered, only to experience a mild disappointment. Mae Chan was talking about the weather, repeating her earlier remarks concerning the heat, and when through with that she shifted to the subject of scented water; she had taken a bottle from the shelf, poured out the liquid and was dabbing her face and arms with it. "What lovely perfume," she said. "You can never buy anything like this in shops. Not this kind of delicate fragrance. Who made it, Mae Sai?"

And Khun Sai replied, "Mae Phloi did before she went on her trip home. Nice, isn't it?"

"Mae Phloi is so accomplished," said Mae Chan, speaking as though Phloi were not present in the same room. "One could die peacefully having such a daughter—a daughter who would be a credit to the family, who would prosper and go unharmed through flood and fire."

Which was all very well, but not what Phloi had been waiting to hear so impatiently for the past forty-eight hours.

When she had put the bottle back on the shelf, Mae Chan spoke again. "I want to consult you about something, Mae Sai."

"Yes?" Khun Sai looked up from the betel nut she was in the process of peeling. "What is it? Go ahead. I'm listening."

Instead of getting on with it as she should, Mae Chan fell silent, casting a glance in the direction of her daughter and Phloi; then she reached for a cushion and, placing it on the floor, lay down with her elbows propped on it. "Oh, it's nothing urgent," she said carelessly, but not very convincingly.

A few moments of silence ensued, after which Khun Sai addressed herself to the two girls. "I'm not sure who are with Sadet this afternoon. Probably too few. Will you go up and keep her company, you two? And Choi, if she asks, I'll be in attendance later on. You may mention that your mother came to see me. And don't dilly-dally."

Once they were out in the passage, and before reaching the stairs, Choi said to Phloi, "You go on alone. I'll post myself somewhere where I can ambush my mother and get her to tell me why she came. Sending us out of the room like this, really! They ought to know I'd be devoured with curiosity and won't rest until I find out what it is!"

Upstairs in the Veranda Room, Phloi went on her knees to where Sadet was seated amid stacks of photographs old and new. As Khun Sai had feared, there was only one other maid attending.

Her Royal Highness smiled at Phloi. "I'm deserted as you can see. Where is Sai? What is she doing, do you know? . . . Is that so!" she exclaimed on being informed. "Family problems, I suppose. Sai has more relatives than anybody I know, and how she likes to play the Great Counsellor to them all! Here, Phloi, help me with these pictures. Let's put these good ones aside and choose some more. I want to have them mounted in a screen."

Phloi spent a wholly interesting hour going over the collection and listening to Sadet recounting anecdotes about court life in the old days. Only once or twice did she stare at the photographs unseeingly or hear Sadet's voice without catching her exact words.

She wondered if Mae Chan would think her too forward should she ask her point blank how Nuang was doing. Surely not. Mae Chan had known for some time how things were between her son and Phloi. She had been treating Phloi like a daughter. They were close to each other, she and Mae Chan, and they should have a nice chat together about Nuang. Why not?

But when Phloi finally got back from attendance, there was no Mae Chan in the room.

"She's left—has some errand to do in town," Khun Sai said in answer to her question.

Phloi gave an involuntary sigh.

Now Choi came in the door, looking weary and peevish at the same time, as though she had been in a fight and lost it.

"Where have *you* been?" Khun Sai inquired. "Were you with Sadet?"

"No!" Choi snapped back. "I went to Teng Row."

Khun Sai flew into a temper. "Don't you raise your voice with me! You're getting worse and worse every day. Why didn't you go up and wait on Sadet, may I ask?"

"I thought since Phloi was going she wouldn't need me."

"Meaning you can do as you please and never mind what your elders say? I'm like a tree stump you can pass over and ignore, is that it?"

"Oh, Khun Aunt!" Choi cried, then surprisingly broke down and wept like a child.

Khun Sai looked hard at her niece and when she spoke again her tone held no anger. "Did you see your mother before she left?"

"Yes," Choi replied between sobs.

"Go and wash your face," Khun Sai said quietly. "You look terrible."

"Tell me what it's all about," Phloi begged again and again. "What's happened at home? Anything I can do? It must be serious trouble to make you so unhappy. You and I have no secrets from each other. Come, Choi, you can tell me everything, you know that."

It took a long time but at last Choi produced a folded sheet of paper and thrust it into Phloi's hands. It was a letter from Nuang, and went as follows:

My dear sister Choi,

I'm in Bangkok for a few days but can't bring myself to come and see you. Don't be upset by what I'm about to tell you. I'm getting married next month.

Mother will come with me to Nakhon Sawan and arrange things with the girl's elders. Her name is Sombun. Her father, a Chinese Thai, died when she was a child. Her mother Mae Klai keeps a rice-and-curry shop in the market. I had my meals sent up from her shop and that's how I got to know Sombun and all her relatives. The whole family have been very kind to me, and Sombun treats me as though I were a deva for whom nothing is good. enough. Don't despise me too much, Choi, though I will understand if you do. I have no excuses. I was so lonely. I had been so used to having Father and Mother look after me and protect me with their love and care that I felt utterly lost when I found myself alone. I turned to Sombun and her people for family warmth and comfort. We became friendly, Sombun and I. I drifted on thoughtlessly and when I realized what I had done it was too late. Not to marry her now would make me the lowest of the low. If you asked me whether I love her or not I should have to answer yes and no. Yes, because she's my wife, and no, because when I used to dream about taking a wife it was never her or anyone like her whom I had in mind. But you know, Choi, though I'm filled with remorse and regret for what I have done I can't help thinking that perhaps it might be for the best after all. Sombun had no great expectations of me, expectations which I can never fulfil, weak and selfish as I am. Yes, I realize I may love someone very much and yet be able to cause her misery through my selfishness.

You may want to know what Sombun is like. She's younger than I am by a few years, a very nice girl, pretty enough by country standards, has been well-brought up and is competent in everything she does. Her country-girl manners only need a little polishing up but that's all. You'll like her, Choi, and won't lose face on account of her. When I told Father I wanted to marry her, he went wild, but calmed down and gave his consent after I'd explained. Even so he won't come to Nakhon Sawan with us but is willing to leave everything to Mother. Sombun's mother has asked for only 10 baht in gold and 80 chang in money for wedding gifts—which isn't a great deal and suits a poor family like ours.

Please tell Phloi I think of her always, but ask her to forget me. I did not accumulate enough merit in my former life to deserve her in this one.

> Your loving brother,
> Nuang

Phloi felt no pain at first. But her eyes were blurred—there seemed to have been a blinding glare as from an exploding lamp. She couldn't make out what was in front of her. The light must have gone out but she wasn't sure. Suddenly it became very cold and she had this sensation of slowly falling—it could have been in a dream. And like in a dream she was struggling against it. She made a desperate effort to stay on solid ground, to take hold of herself, to focus her eyes, to make things clear in her mind. *Phi Nuang has a wife.* She tried to give meaning to the simple phrase, but this required such energy, much more than she could summon up. She had to let it go. *Phi Nuang has a wife.* Other thoughts came tumbling about in its wake, helter-skelter. *She'll take care of him from now on. How will she do it? Does she know what he likes and what he doesn't? You have a wife, Phi Nuang. How can that be? I was going to be the one to look after you, to be your loving wife as long as I live. You've taken away my duty. Chao Khun Father never got to know you. Too late now. I'm not angry, or jealous. Phi Nuang getting married. Doing what's right. You tell me to forget. Like telling the sun to stop shining or the moon not to glow. You love her and you don't love her, Phi Nuang. My love. You'll follow the course of your karma, and I mine. Phi Nuang has a wife. How can that be? What's going to happen?*

"Phloi! Phloi!" Choi was shaking her. Whiffs of choking, an overpowering scent in her nostrils! Choi was forcing her to inhale from a bottle of smelling salts.

Phloi pushed it away. "I'm all right, Choi. Really I am. I was just going over the letter again. What's going to happen, Choi?"

"I'll tell you. Phi Nuang is going to marry a Chinaman's daughter and her mother sells rice-and-curry in the market. And you still ask me what's going to happen!"

Phloi paid no attention to Choi's fury. The hope which she had been carrying about with her for many months was stubbornly refusing to be cast aside and she must give it voice, even if for the last time. "Why the rush?" she asked. "Couldn't he wait a little?"

"The girl is two months pregnant," Choi said coldly. "So he decided to marry her. He pitied her. So noble—ha! But if he didn't come forth with the offer her mother was sure to take the matter up with his superiors. And that would have made a pretty story indeed!"

"You—you're being unfair," Phloi just managed to get the words out. "And it is noble of him. Please don't be angry with him, Choi. I—I'm not."

Choi stared at her. "Do you mean it, or are you just saying it?"

"I'm telling you the truth, Choi. It's—it's all right. I understand."

"It's not all right!" Choi was enraged. "And I will not understand! I know he's silly and weak, but to let himself drift into this kind of trouble—no, this is too much for me! And another thing, I am not going to enjoy telling people that my brother's wife's mother is a rice-and-curry vendor. No, not a bit!"

"There's nothing shameful about selling rice-and-curry for a living. You talk as though it were robbing and stealing."

"Oh, Phloi, I can't bear it. I'm mad! Mad! Mad!"

"Don't, Choi. You mustn't feel that way."

Choi opened her mouth, then shut it. She gave Phloi a long searching look. "Do you love him, Phloi?" she asked in a wondering voice.

"Very much."

"And you feel no anger, no hurt at all?"

"She's a woman like me, Choi. If Phi Nuang left her, how would she feel? What would become of her? Her whole life might be ruined and Phi Nuang would have been the cause. You wouldn't want that to be his lot, Choi. So you must stop blaming him. There are only the two of you, one brother, one sister. Don't let anything come between you and turn you into strangers . . ."

She kept on talking in that vein. The stupefying effect of Nuang's letter had not quite worn off; and, in her determination to pacify Choi, she was also, unconsciously or not, postponing the moment when she would have to come to grips with the reality of her loss. ". . . It's not as if I've never known any unhappiness," she calmly told Choi. "All this time, when I thought about Phi Nuang and me, I don't think I ever forgot to warn myself that it could end up this way." She said she wasn't going to stop feeling very close to Choi and that she would go on loving and respecting Choi's parents as though they were her own, and Phi Nuang like her own brother. "Wish him well," she pleaded. "There's enough suffering in the world and we shouldn't add to it, Choi."

And Choi listened and was touched by those words. Her voice softened as she said she would harbour no more ill will, no more rancour. She wished she could express all the love and esteem she had for Phloi. She tried to. Then she did an unexpected thing. Joining her palms together she lowered her head and made a *krap* in Phloi's lap, and this gesture of respect and affection from the heart acted on Phloi like a releasing agent. It jerked her out of her numbness. A penetrating ache welled up in her throat and the next instant she was leaning on Choi's shoulder and crying uncontrol-lably. Choi held her close, comforting her and sharing her grief, and did not let her go until long after her violent sobbing and shaking had ceased.

They were still sitting there together, in silence, when Khun Sai came down from Sadet's apartment. One glance at their faces told her enough of what had taken place, and after a few moments she spoke, but only to ask, "Have you had your bath, Phloi?"

Phloi was thankful for the ordinariness of the question, and answered her in an even voice, "Not yet, Khun Aunt."

"Are you on duty tonight?" Khun Sai inquired. "But go up anyway, will you? Have your bath first, and your dinner, then go up. Sadet has been asking after you."

THERE was no one else in the bathing courtyard, which suited Phloi's need to be by herself for a while. After splashing some water on her body she sat down in her wet *panung* and let her gaze roam about in the semi-darkness. The water jars, the trees and flower pots, the spires and rooftops in the distance—they were all here as on other nights. Did she expect them to crumble away after what had happened? Amazing how nothing had changed and this was another lovely night. Look at the brilliant sky. Look at the lights winking in the windows of the Upper Residence. Look at her own arms and legs: they had not been broken at all. Yet everything had changed, and she no longer knew where she was or where to go next. She had lost the way. She must get out of this desolate wilderness—but how?

Time went by and at last she pulled herself together, chided herself even. She had no business lazing about like this. She must finish bathing, get dressed, go up to Sadet. The thought of Sadet was a potent restorative—her beloved Sadet, her refuge, to whom she owed a lifelong debt of gratitude. No, she had not been deprived of her duty, which was to go on serving Sadet for the rest of her days. No need to feel so utterly lost and confused when she could hold on to this one constant in her life.

"COME and help me, Phloi," Sadet called out from her seat in the middle of the room. "I need your good eyes again. These rubies—let's choose them together. I'm having a brooch made."

Phloi went up and settled into a comfortable position on the floor. She picked out the loose stones from the cases in front of her, looking at them one by one and making her selection.

"I'm not all that fond of jewellery," Sadet said with a plaintive sigh. "But you can imagine how tongues would wag if I went about unornamented. So I wear them, without much enjoyment, which doesn't prevent me from fussing and fuming when they get lost or broken. Aren't we funny creatures, Phloi? How we cling to our possessions! And be it a precious gem or a worthless pebble, if we let ourselves become too attached to it we suffer when it's gone. We suffer all the same, yes, but even so it's helpful to be able to dis-tinguish which is which and not weep over a pebble thinking it a diamond."

She paused, perhaps expecting Phloi to say something, but Phloi could not think of anything adequate to contribute and therefore kept silent.

Sadet smiled at her and went on. "You're probably saying to yourself, 'Sadet is an old woman and has old-fashioned ideas. What does she know about us modern girls?' But believe me, Phloi, the young can profit by heeding the old. From having lived so long we've learned a few lessons, and if we try to pass them on to you it's because we'd like to help you achieve a good life.

"And by a good life I don't mean an exalted position in life. Many people here have suggested to me that you, Phloi, are comely enough and well-born enough and thus stand a good chance of rising to such a position in court and why don't I do something about it—such as installing you where you'll attract more attention. When they talk like this I just smile without saying anything. I've seen too much of the dark side of glory—that kind of glory. I've seen girls like you elevated into high prominence and seen them fall from grace, seen them surrounded by admiring fawners and seen those same fawners abandon them without any qualms. I want you to be happy, Phloi, but if your goal happens to be way up there I'm afraid you must look somewhere else for encouragement."

"I don't wish for anything," Phloi said with feeling, "except to go on serving Your Highness."

Sadet shook her head smilingly. "Oh, no, Phloi, that's not enough. You have your own life to live. So do all of us, but mine will soon be over, whereas you still have many, many long years ahead of you. We don't know what the future will bring but we do know that our good action here and now can only give rise to what is good in days to come, although we may not be aware of when or how. People who conduct their lives well are like those skilled and graceful dancers who keep in perfect rhythm with the music provided them by the *piphat* players. That's what I hope you'll be, Phloi: a consummate dancer on the stage of life . . . All right, Phloi, I've prattled on long enough. Now it's your turn. What have you been doing all day?"

"Nothing, Your Highness."

"I don't believe it. You girls are all alike, never want to tell me anything. The only one willing to talk to me is Choi; the only trouble there is how to stop her."

No sooner had Sadet spoken the last sentence than Choi came in the doorway, advancing briskly and looking her customary vivacious self.

Sadet greeted her with a laugh. "Are you doing the cock in Phra Lo, Choi?—'*The old man thought of the cock / And lo and behold the cock came to him*' . . . Now what have you got to regale us with tonight? Any interesting news I ought to hear about?"

"My mother came to see us this afternoon, Your Highness."

"You call that interesting? You make it sound as though no other mothers ever came here. Well, why did she come? Did anyone die?"

"Oh, no, Your Highness. On the contrary! My brother Nuang is taking a wife and so my mother came to consult Khun Aunt Sai about the wedding."

"My goodness, I can't believe your brother is old enough to marry. It seems only yesterday your mother brought him here to see me. The days and the months and the years—how fast they travel! No wonder I feel so ancient. And who's the bride?"

"Daughter of a rice-and-curry seller in Nakhon Sawan, Your Highness."

"How splendid! He'll never have to worry where his next meal's coming from for the rest of his life. And what did your mother have to say about it?"

"She just said she'd go to Nakhon Sawan and see to it, Your Highness. There's nothing else she could do."

"I think it's all very suitable, Choi. A boy like your brother—if he came to ask me for any of my girls I should have had to refuse him. Right, Choi?"

"Yes, Your Highness!"

Although she realized that Sadet and Choi were offering their duologue as a balm for her wound, Phloi could feel her heart beating irregularly while it was going on and could not help taking a deep breath when at last another topic was introduced.

It was quite late that night when the two girls took leave of Sadet and returned to their room. Phloi fell asleep immediately from sheer exhaustion. "One would have thought you didn't have a care in the world," Choi said to her the next morning, with a hint of reproof in her voice. "And there I was, tossing and turning all night from worrying about you."

That day, surprisingly enough, passed very quickly. The girls at the residence were tactfully sympathetic. All tried each in their different ways to solace Phloi and she forced herself to play along because she did not want to disappoint them, with the result that she really began to feel better as the day wore on. Then in the afternoon Khun Sai announced that Sadet would be accompanying Their Majesties on their trip to Bang Pa-in in a few weeks' time, which meant that most of Sadet's household would also be going and that there would be plenty to do to get everything ready, starting from now. She also, when they were alone together, let Phloi know how proud she was of her.

Several days afterwards Mae Chan came to the palace again to say goodbye before leaving for Nakhon Sawan. She treated Phloi with affection as always and, understanding that Phloi had learned about the forthcoming marriage, felt free to discuss it openly with Khun Sai in Phloi's presence. Phloi sat there, listening to them with com-posure, and found it astonishing that she should be able to do so.

ELEVEN

BANG Pa-in!

At that period, to most palace people in Bangkok, Bang Pa-in was something of a magical word. Even if you had never been there yourself the mention of its name conjured up visions of the greenest of green countryside to gladden your city heart and soul. Here the heat occasionally could be oppressive, but over there you would have the pure, fresh, cooling breeze all day long. Already in your mind's eye you could see the rice fields gently waving, stretching away to the horizon. You could see those fairyland lotus ponds with their pink and white blooms and drink in the vista of the broad river in all its moods: as it glittered in the sun, or reflected the many-coloured twilight, or turned quiet and mysterious under the stars. But perhaps the best thing evoked by the name Bang Pa-in had to do with the expectant holiday spirit, the getting away from old routines, the relaxed protocol, the carefree atmosphere. Bang Pa-in, to put it briefly, meant *sanuk*, *tunten*—fun and excitement.

And the fun, to be sure, began with the preparations. So many things to get, to make or have made for the trip. Clothes for rural living and out-of-town functions. Delicacies such as shredded pork, crispy bread, savoury lotus seeds and many others without which no journey starting off from the Inner Court would be complete. And medicines. To some women, especially older ones, food and clothes occupied a minor place compared with medicines, and you might have thought they were going to Bang Pa-in to open an apothecary's shop from the variety and quantity of powder, pills, ointments and liquid mixtures they were planning to take along. To Khun Sai, however, everything was important—food, clothes, medicines, utensils—not only for herself and her girls, whom she wanted to eat well, dress well, behave well, and remain in good health throughout the visit, but above all for Sadet. She wasn't going to have Sadet ask her for something in Bang Pa-in and find herself having to say, "Sorry, Your Highness, I didn't bring it from Bangkok."

She was kept busy, extremely busy, from morning till night, during those weeks; once in a while she would scowl or grumble, but on the whole you could see how much she was enjoying herself. To Phloi and Choi she delegated many special tasks. One of these, that of digging up and packing lumps of earth from the palace ground, went to Choi. According to Khun Sai, water in unfamiliar parts was never fit to drink—in fact, it could make you seriously, if not fatally, ill, unless you naturalized it, so to speak, by placing a token lump of earth from your native habitat at the bottom of the boiling kettle. Choi was intrigued by this bit of folklore and derived much entertainment value from it. She went around asking people, "Have you heard the story of my Khun Aunt, the Alien Water and the Miraculous Palace Dirt?"

Khun Sai and Choi were to travel to Bang Pa-in by boat, one of the many official boats assigned to transport most of the party and the bulk of provisions and other supplies. A smaller entourage, Phloi included, was to go by train, leaving Bangkok from the "sa-tae-chan" (the Thai word for "station" had not yet been coined at the time) situated in Hua Lamphong. When Choi heard about the arrangements she said what a pity Phloi would not be on board with the rest of them. "We'll have such fun, Phloi. There'll be just us—and only Khun Aunt Sai."

"Only me?" Khun Sai demanded sharply. "Meaning I have no power to stop you from having fun?"

"No, Khun Aunt." Choi beamed sweetly at her. "Meaning you're too kind-hearted not to let us enjoy ourselves."

"Ha-ha!" Khun Sai gave a sarcastic laugh, the kind she reserved exclusively for Choi. "I like the way you change your tune all of a sudden." To Phloi she said, "Don't you listen to her, my dear. It's a great honour to go in the same train as Their Majesties and the royals. I wish

I were going with you. I wish I were going by land. I never trust water, never feel completely at ease on a boat. Anything might happen. Just talking about it makes me feel nervous already."

"Oh, Khun Aunt!" Choi admonished her. "We're going in a big boat. It won't capsize or anything like that."

"Accidents can happen," Khun Sai said reminiscently. "Even to a royal boat. That time . . . also on a trip to Bang Pa-in . . . Queen Sunanda lost her life. I was there, accompanying Sadet in another boat. We were far behind and didn't actually see it happen. Two or three boats were involved in the collision but the queen's boat was the only one that went down. She was a good swimmer, the queen, but she must have got trapped somehow—she had gone inside the enclosure, you see, to bring out the princess, and at that moment the boat overturned. It was said that the men didn't dare go near where she was for fear of having to touch her—she being the queen . . . Or else they were in such a panic that they didn't think of righting the boat until it was too late. What a sad day that was. Our Sadet was inconsolable and for years she wouldn't go to Bang Pa-in. She loved Queen Sunanda very much, you know. Beautiful Queen Sunanda. She was only twenty—too young to die."

There were tears in Khun Sai's eyes and she wiped them with the end of her bodice cloth before going on. "I still get goose-pimples when I think about that day. Let's pray nothing like that will ever happen again . . . Now, girls, enough chatter. Back to work . . ."

One afternoon, about a week before the date of departure, Choi returned from a shopping tour with a couple of hats. "I've been told we'll need them in Bang Pa-in so I bought one for you too, Phloi. I think we've got everything, except maybe a new silk cover for me. My old one is full of holes. No time to make it myself either, so I shall have to . . ."

Phloi's eyes had gone misty at the word silk cover and she turned her head sideways to hide them. Choi continued chatting innocently, having forgotten about that other silk cover, the one in Nakhon Sawan, the one that had once made Phi Nuang feel rich in happiness, or so he said. What had become of it? Phloi could not help asking herself while fighting back the tears . . . Had it been thrown away, now lying buried among other unwanted objects? Or was it being used—something practical and convenient for the cool nights? And would this pain in her heart never go away? She had mistakenly believed that it had, that she had cured herself of it. Now she knew it had only retreated to some unknown corner within herself, waiting for the opportunity to assault her again when she least expected it.

Two days before she was due to leave for Bang Pa-in, Phloi received a package from Choi's house. In it was the silk cover and, between its folds, a letter from Nuang. The letter, another *phleng yao*, sang of his anguish at having to part with the silk, his acceptance of what his karma had decreed for him in this life, and his hopes for a happier encounter with her in the next one. The silk had lost some of its perfume with the passage of time, the writer would have her know, but his loyal sentiments towards her remained unchanging and timeless.

Choi was indignant. "It's too bad of Phi Nuang. To bother you like this when the whole thing is over and done with. Sending you a *phleng yao*—I wonder who helped him with the rhyming. Ridiculous! Don't pay any attention to it, Phloi."

"I don't," Phloi lied. She cried herself to sleep that night and, as is sometimes the healing effect of tears, woke up feeling quite well and ready to face the new day.

The party departing by boat for Bang Pa-in started off that morning. The streets and squares of the Inner Court were more animated and colourful than ever as chattering groups of women and girls came out of their houses and headed for the Outer Gate, those who were actually going away as well as those who were merely going as far as the gate to wish their friends a safe journey. Bright, eager faces were everywhere, and a lot of laughing and giggling all the way. Khun Sai laughed, saying she was growing more nervous by the minute. Choi laughed, telling Phloi not to miss the train tomorrow. Phloi laughed with them, perhaps not as gaily, but she did laugh and felt all the better for it.

The next morning, as Sadet's maid-in-waiting, Phloi rode in an Inner Court horse-drawn carriage from the Grand Palace to Hua

Lamphong; there, at an entrance which looked to her so enchantingly welcoming and full of promise, she alighted and went into the station carrying Sadet's betel-nut box and walking a few paces behind her. The whole length of the platform was lined with military and civilian officers, who bowed to or saluted Sadet as she passed by. Phloi's Chao Khun Father was among those present. He bowed to Sadet, and for a few seconds his eyes met Phloi's and they exchanged smiles and Phloi saw him tell his colleagues who she was. Phloi continued onwards, stepping ever more lightly, followed Sadet up into the royal coach and, after placing the betel-nut box beside her, withdrew and headed back for the car reserved for the maids-in-attendance.

Here the noise was terrific. The girls were greeting one another, chaffing one another, bumping into one another, moving about from seat to seat, jostling, nudging, laughing over nothing. At one point Khun Inner Court Guard had to take the matter in hand. "Keep quiet, all of you!" Her resounding command came from somewhere up front. "I'm ashamed of you. With all those important people out there, and you making this racket like sparrows returning to their nest! Phra Chao Yu Hua will be here any minute now—or don't you realize this is a royal outing? Mind how you behave!"

Phloi had a seat by the window next to a girl called Chamoi, who came from a neighbouring residence at court. A tireless talker, Chamoi seemed not only to know of everyone down there on the platform but to be related to most of them one way or another. She referred to them either as uncles (older-than-either-parent uncles; paternally younger uncles; maternally younger uncles) or elder brothers. "Oh, look, there's Chao Khun Uncle So-and-So and Khun Phra Uncle Such-and-Such, and do you see Khun Luang Elder Brother This? He's talking to Khun Elder Brother That." Chamoi knew them all, and all about them: the number of wives and children each of them had (or their eligibility as the case might be), their wealth or lack of it, their excellent qualities, weak points, problems, and so on. Her continuous discourse was accompanied or punctuated by her snuff-taking, putting the powder into the little U-shaped silver pipe and blowing it up her nose. Phloi listened absent-mindedly, looking out of the window at nobody in particular, but giving a polite nod now and then at her interlocutor, which seemed to be all that was needed on her part to keep the conversation going.

Suddenly her aimless gazing came to a halt. Over there, near a post, stood Khun Prem in his royal page uniform. In a split second Phloi registered the fact that he was looking straight at her, had started to move, was making his way towards this car. She beat a hasty retreat, leaning back as far as the seat would allow and inclining her head away from the window.

Now Chamoi had also seen him; she was whispering excitedly, "Oh, look, Mae Phloi! There's Khun Prem! Do you know him?" It did strike Phloi, preoccupied as she was, that Chamoi was claiming no family connections with Khun Prem. "They say he's the richest of the richest. I know several relatives of his. He's a descendant of Chao Khun Choduk. They're all rich, these people. You know them, Mae Phloi?"

Phloi shook her head while silently praying that Khun Prem would not stop and stare. Her prayer was answered. Khun Prem strode on past her window in the direction of the rear end of the train as the voice beside her continued its chirping.

"He's not bad-looking either. Not the hero-handsome type, that's for sure, but not bad."

Phloi gave a polite nod. She was glad when, with characteristic rapidity, Chamoi changed the subject.

"Do you know where you'll be staying in Bang Pa-in, Mae Phloi? Would you like to share a room with me?"

"You're very kind, but I think I'll have to be with Choi and the other girls from Sadet's residence. I don't even know which building we'll be in."

"Let's be near each other in any case. I like talking to you, Mae Phloi. You're not a trouble-maker . . . Oh! Phra Chao Yu Hua's here!"

The brass band was announcing His Majesty's arrival. The Guard of Honour gave their salute. The officials and all the others assembled on the platform had taken their proper position and were now standing at attention. In the attendants' car a respectful silence reigned.

On his way to the royal coach, His Majesty made several stops to hold conversation with his officials. Phloi's heart leapt up, as it always did whenever she found herself within sight and earshot of him, as he reached the group on the platform not far from her window. Sitting erect and still, she stole glances at the noble profile, careful not to do it too often or for too long, and tried to follow what was being said as much as she could. She did not hear every-thing, but enough to gather that the topics ranged from road-building and government in the provinces to the illness of some-body's wife and the schooling of somebody's children. Nothing is too big or too small for his wisdom and compassion, Phloi thought to herself. How blessed we all are that it is he who is our Lord of Life, that it is in him that the supreme power to preserve or to destroy has been invested. Silently she invoked all that was sacred in the universe to protect him, and when he had gone, she turned to Chamoi and smiled at her for no special reason. Chamoi smiled back; her thoughts must have been running along the same happy line and, for once, said nothing.

A few minutes later the train started to move forward. The sound of excitement rose up anew among the Inner Courtiers, many of whom had never before travelled by rail. The jerking, swerving motion was greeted by startled cries and bursts of laughter threatening to drown out the clattering of wheels going over points. Even Khun Guard was seen to be allowing herself a chuckle or two. As the train gathered speed the passengers poured forth more and louder interjections. *How terrifying! What fun! I feel dizzy! I can't see anything, can you? I had no idea we'd be going so fast. A storm—that's what it is—a storm blowing us all the way to Bang Pa-in.*

After a while they calmed down a little and became interested in the swiftly-changing panorama along the track. Many people living here on the edge of the city had come out to see the king go by in his train. Some had set up tables on which were arranged flowers, candles and joss sticks, and prostrated themselves as the train rushed by. Some itinerant vendors, apparently having just heard about the happening, laid down their shoulder-baskets and paid homage to the sovereign with a surprised and pleased expression on their faces. The train sped on. Soon the clusters of houses began to thin out, giving way to the green peaceful openness of the rice land, dotted here and there in the distance with small woods, bamboo groves, houses with attap roofs and temple spires. Some of the farmers working near the railroad track grinned at the passing train; some raised their clasped hands reverently above their heads; young children with sun-browned bodies and twinkling eyes looked shyly, or laughed, or shouted at the girls, and the girls were behaving very much in the same manner, each side equally interested and amused by the other. Some of the children were lounging on the backs of water buffaloes, presenting the very picture of cool comfort. Now quite a few of the Inner Courtiers were seeing those sturdy farmers' assistants for the first time in their sheltered lives, and their display of amazement was such as to cause a satirist among them to send up a cry at once very prim and very shrill, "Oh, my dear, the buffaloes have horns!" And now even Khun Guard was laughing out loud.

Once the novelty of train travel had begun to wane, Chamoi, who had been talking incessantly all the while, started to complain that all this chug-chugging and hurtling about was making her feel unwell. She took a couple of pills for it, leaned back with her eyes tightly shut, breathing heavily, then lapsed into a strange silence which Phloi welcomed at first but found alarming after it had gone on for some time. The other girls sitting nearby shared her concern, and all were hoping they wouldn't have to get out at the end of the journey carrying Chamoi between them down the precariously high and narrow steps, making a spectacle of themselves. Much to everyone's relief, Chamoi came to life again with her volubility intact as the train began to slow down; and before it came to a stop she was already apprising those around her as to who was who down there at the station waiting for an audience with Phra Chao Yu Hua and Somdet the Queen.

The provincial dignitaries on the gaily decorated platform were led by Chao Khun Governor of the old capital of Ayuthaya, of which Bang Pa-in formed one of the districts. On both sides of the dignitaries and behind them, overflowing the doors in the rear, and the edges of the paved area of the station, hundreds of men, women and children stood or sat on the ground, some having come from town, others straight from the paddy-fields. After their meeting with the officials, Phra Chao Yu Hua and Somdet went among the people, stopping for a chat here, there, everywhere. An old woman laughingly told the queen what had happened to her since their last encounter and the queen laughed back, saying: "Well, well, taking a husband for the first time at the age of sixty! What made you do it, Grandma Jaem?"

"My bad karma," Grandma replied, laughing harder. "My very, very bad karma, isn't that so and may it please Your Majesty, yes?"

Later in the day, at Woranat House, one of the residences of the Summer Palace, Phloi and Choi came together again, and had such a great deal to tell each other that it was as if they had been apart for two weeks instead of two days. Khun Sai had decided that the girls should stay in the palace to be near Sadet while she herself would be making a temporary home on the boat to see to the cooking and keep an eye on supplies and what not.

"Which is the best arrangement possible as far as you and I are concerned," Choi said gleefully. "We'll have all the excuses to go back and forth and roam about this lovely place. Oh, it's great fun here! Any number of ponds to swim in, and the river just over there. And we're going to practice paddling, do you know that, Phloi? As much as we like. Sadet has just said to me she'll want to go boating from time to time and we should turn ourselves into expert boat-women." A child surrounded with heaps of new toys could not be more enthusiastic about its lot than Choi was with hers at the moment.

"When are you going to grow up?" Phloi asked her.

"Never. No one in our family does. We may grow old but not up. Take my parents, or Phi Nuang—" she stopped short, giving Phloi a guilty, apologetic look.

"Go on, Choi," Phloi heard herself speak, sounding slightly unreal. "You mustn't be afraid to mention Phi Nuang's name to me. I'm all right now."

She didn't altogether convince Choi, nor herself. But then there were times when your feelings seemed to be going their own erratic way and you could never be sure of them. She did feel all right, to a degree. She was not dwelling in the past but confronting the present, and doing it readily, here in Bang Pa-in. She had locked up the silk cover with its vanishing scent and was not by any means trying to revive it.

The next few days flew by. Choi and Phloi agreed with each other that it felt as if they had been here a long time. They went swimming; they practiced paddling the boat to their hearts' content and had become proficient at it; they explored the gardens of the Summer Palace; they ventured outside palace grounds and had been three times to the shrine dedicated to King Prasad Thong, three times because Choi was fascinated by the fortune-telling system they had there, whereby you rattled the stick-box until one stick fell out whose number matched that of one of the prophecies, written in verse, printed on flimsy paper, and couched in terms so verbose and ambiguous as to mean anything at all you wanted it to mean. They went often to Khun Sai's boat: it was amusing enough just to observe how much Khun Aunt Sai was enjoying herself experiment-ing with new recipes, producing quaint but exquisite little bowls out of bamboo and coconut shells ("Sadet is so used to porcelain and silver I thought she might like to go rustic for a change") and, with the maids Phit and Phaad to cheer her on, indulging in buying sprees from the well-stocked floating market going up and down this stretch of the river. Such were the simple delights of Bang Pa-in, and simple delights were what Phloi needed at the time. Had Sadet foreseen this? Had she been worrying about Phloi and wishing these diversions on her? It would be presumptuous to think so, but nevertheless Phloi silently thanked her royal mistress for having brought her along on this trip.

Now came the day of Their Majesties' visit to a *wat* for a *kathin* ceremony—the offering of robes and other essential articles to monks at the end of Buddhist Lent. This *wat* had a most lovely name: Wiwek Wayuphat, meaning "where the quiet wind blows," but of course for today the quiet would have to yield to the festive since large crowds were expected to converge there for the opportunity of combining merit-making with watching the king and his family. Khun Sai's party, consisting of the maid Phit at the helm, the maid Phaad in the bow,

Choi and Phloi paddling merrily and Khun Sai herself in the middle, set out early in the morning so as to avoid being in the hot sun longer than necessary. Khun Sai had been fussing over what to take to the *wat* for their midday meal, until word got to her that Chao Khun Governor and his Khunying, together with other ranking officials and their wives, had asked to play host to the courtiers and would be providing boatloads of *khanom chin* enough for one and all. So they had come with nothing on board except Khun Sai's indispensable water kettle and cup. But it did not take long for them to start filling the empty space with lotus flowers and lotus stems, picking the latter as they would a vegetable, to be eaten boiled with fish in coconut milk or dipped uncooked in chili sauce with the next evening's rice. It was the same with the other boats, for they—these Inner Courtiers from the Summer Palace—were travelling through lotus fields, and lotus-picking was a most popular Bang Pa-in activity, especially with those who were doing it for the first time. Thus surrounded by nature's beauty and abundance they proceeded at a leisurely pace, feasting their eyes, stopping to collect more blooms and stems, bursting into song and sending greetings from boat to boat. It would have been impossible to remain lonely or sorrowful for long on such a morning. The simple magic of Bang Pa-in wouldn't have permitted it.

The sun was already high when they reached Wiwek Wayuphat. Up there in the *wat* compound, lining the walks leading to the chapel and the auditorium *sala*, crowds of devotees were waiting to pay reverence to the king and attend the *kathin* rites. Others stayed on in their boats, which were either moored along the embankment or slowly plying up and down the frontage of the *wat*. Khun Sai's party managed to weave their way into a nice spot under a big shady tree not far from the main landing pavilion and they too chose to remain on the river, something they didn't get to do every day back in the Grand Palace. All round them, on land and water, the scene was one of lively continuous movement. Dressed in its colourful best and with its faces wreathed in good-humoured smiles, Bang Pa-in had turned out in full force for the *kathin*. A sense of communal joy had taken over Wiwek Wayuphat. This merit-making, this giving-

and-receiving occasion, was meant for everyone—for the king and the royals, the farmers and their families, the gentry, the officials. And it was a social gathering for all, from the very old who must have been coming to this annual event more times than they could remember, to their great-grandchildren who were romping all over the place, more interested in fun and games than anything else.

In Khun Sai's boat it seemed to the passengers that only a few minutes had passed when the subject of food suddenly cropped up in their conversation and soon dominated it. They were still feeling light-hearted and gay, still enjoying the *kathin* sights and sounds, but their stomachs were demanding to be satisfied as well. "Must be the fresh air," said the maid Phit. "And all this paddling. I'd like to get hold of not one but two *khanom chin* boats." Actually they had been here for some time, during which the king had arrived and gone inside, the *kathin* gifts had been presented, and the monks had chanted and had their last meal of the day. It was now lunchtime for the laity, or should have been.

Choi was growing more restless by the minute. "Have they forgotten us?" she wailed. "I see a *khanom chin* boat way over there but by the time it gets here there won't be anything left. What shall we do? I'm starving."

"We could go up and eat in the *wat*," Khun Sai suggested, then changed her mind. "But wouldn't you rather wait and have a picnic in our boat? Much more fun. What do you say, Phloi?"

"Yes, let's wait, Khun Aunt. We don't get a chance to eat in a boat very often. You're not really starving, Choi, I'm sure a food boat will be coming along soon."

"I haven't got your endurance, Phloi. Oh, all right, let's wait. Anyway, if my hunger gets any worse I can always fall back on these lotus stems. Might as well, since I worked hard enough pulling them up. You know, they looked so slender and yielding I thought they'd be easy to pick, but not at all—you can sprain your shoulder doing it if you're not careful."

"The one and only time I ever came across easy-to-pick lotus stems was at Grandma Krut's field," Khun Sai remarked with a chuckle and then, apparently forgetting about food for the moment, launched into the story of Grandma Krut for the benefit of those who had never heard of this Bang Pa-in character, who had been dead and gone these very many years. "She was a rich woman, this Grandma Krut," Khun Sai narrated. "A rich woman who loved to brag about her wealth and about everything belonging to her as being of the best quality. She was also socially ambitious. Her great desire was to move in court circles, to become an intimate of the Summer Palace. Knowing how much the royals like to go on picnics in lotus fields she kept inviting them and all of us in the entourage to visit her field, insisting that it was the largest, the prettiest, the most luxuriant in all of Bang Pa-in. So finally a date was set and we all went. Her place looked all right, nothing extraordinary. Then we started plucking those stems. As you've found out, Choi, it needs a bit of strength to pull them out. Well, I was pulling hard and lost my balance when one of them came loose as soon as I touched it. I nearly fell backwards. And I wasn't the only one. It was happening all over the field. Then we caught on and had a good laugh. Yes, Grandma Krut had been anxious to make good her boast, had brought in plenty of additional plants and had them stuck in her field among the natural growth which must have been too scanty for her purpose! We hadn't been there an hour when patches in the field started to wilt right before our very eyes. Grandma looked a little shame-faced, but not for long. She was determined to have a successful party and went round doing a lot of picking herself and saying to us, 'Isn't this lovely? Aren't these very very succulent stems? Do try this sauce with them.' I think, you know, that the next day she was telling all her friends and enemies what a wonderful time the courtiers had had in her lotus fields. Which was true. We did have fun that day . . ."

Khun Sai paused, but before she could resume there was an interruption. An unfamiliar voice broke into their midst, saying, "How are you, Khun Aunt?"

They all turned to look. They hadn't noticed it until now, but here was a *khanom chin* boat bobbing gently alongside their own. In the stern sat a girl wearing a farmer's hat, and in the bow was Khun Prem wearing a friendly grin on his face. He was speaking again. "How are you, Khun Aunt? Do you remember me?"

Khun Sai looked puzzled for a minute, then cried with delight, "Oh, Pho Prem! I didn't know you were here. How nice! It's been many years since I last saw you, but you haven't changed. I'd have recognized you anywhere."

Thus occupied with the young man, Khun Sai was not aware that Phloi had gone pink and that Choi and Phit were looking at each other in consternation, with the latter clearing her throat rather loudly and meaningfully.

Khun Prem went on to say, keeping his eyes fixed on Khun Sai as though she were the sole passenger on the boat, "I was up there in the *wat* and happened to look this way. I saw you, and then it dawned on me you might not have had anything to eat, so I went to Khunying Governor and asked if I could bring you one of these boats. So here we are. What sauce would you like with your *khanom chin*, Khun Aunt? The fish sauce, or the *nam phrik*, or the . . ." he laughed. "I sound like a regular vendor, don't I? What I mean is, we're here to serve you."

Khun Sai was all smiles and gratitude. "You are kind, Pho Prem. We were just about to faint from hunger. Weren't we, girls?"

"I've lost my appetite, Khun Aunt," Choi said succinctly.

"Are you being difficult again, Choi? Well, I haven't lost mine. And everything looks so delicious. Let's eat, Phloi. What about you, Phaad? Come on, Phit."

The *khanom chin* girl had been busy with the noodles and sauces. Now she handed the plates to Khun Prem, who passed them on to Khun Sai, who then relayed them to the others.

Phloi looked at the plate she was holding in her hand, considering it from every angle. A small voice in her brain advised her to have nothing to do with it. "The situation is fraught with danger and haven't you learned your lesson?" the voice warned her. But she was very hungry and the *khanom chin* looked and smelled definitely tempting; besides, Khun Sai would be demanding an explanation if she didn't eat. Taking a spoonful she gave an extremely sulky Choi a few nudges, urging her to follow suit.

During the meal—and it was a particularly delicious meal—Khun Sai and Khun Prem kept up their conversation. Nobody else joined them, except for an occasional harrumph and mumbled comment from the maid Phit.

"... I'm so glad to see you, Pho Prem. And you're looking so well. Those days when you used to be brought to see us in the Inner Court you were rather a frail little boy, you know."

"... Would you like some more sauce, Khun Aunt?"

"... I've never forgotten your dear mother. What a lovely, generous person she was. We all loved her in the Inner Court. We were shocked and sad when she died. And how are your aunts, your father's sisters?"

"Khun Aunt Nui is quite well, but Khun Aunt Nian has been ailing, I'm afraid."

"Oh, I'm sorry to hear that. Give them my love and best wishes, will you? We used to see a great deal of one another when they were in the Inner Court, but we've lost touch since they went to live at home."

"They often talk of you, Khun Aunt."

"And I think of them always. Please tell them to let me know if there is anything I can do for them in the palace. And you too, Pho Prem, you must treat me like a real aunt and never hesitate to speak up when I can be of assistance to you."

"I thank you, Khun Aunt. And won't you let me do the same— make myself useful to you? You only have to send a message to the department whenever you have something for me to do—like getting transport when you wish to go out or running errands on your behalf outside the palace. I know it's not always convenient for you to leave the residence."

"Bless you, dear boy! You've made an old woman happy. But I have very few errands outside the palace. We old people, we live quietly from day to day, you understand, with Death waiting for us round the corner."

"But you're not old, Khun Aunt! Not at all! When I first saw this boat I thought it was full of young girls ..."

And so it went. Khun Aunt Sai and Khun Nephew Prem were undoubtedly charmed by each other, and from the way they talked and laughed together, so easy and natural, one would never have guessed that they had not met for years.

And one would have expected Khun Prem to linger on after the meal was over. But no. When everybody had finished eating he promptly took his leave of Khun Sai and went away without so much as a casual glance at anybody else in the boat. Phloi knew this because she had taken a few quick looks out of the corner of her eye. It was vexing to be neglected like this. How dared he, especially when she had resigned herself in anticipation to the discomfort and embarrassment of being stared at.

On the way back to the Summer Palace Choi demanded to know why her aunt should have been so taken with this stranger.

"He's no stranger," retorted Khun Sai. "I've known his family from way back, and him since he was a little boy. And why shouldn't I be nice to him when he took the trouble to be so nice to me? I'm not like you people, with your noses up in the air and not a word of thanks to him! Since when have you become so uppish anyway? I was so ashamed of you. Really!"

Phloi kept a bland face, as if not understanding that the reprimand applied to her as well.

Disregarding it altogether, for she knew her aunt was not really in a scolding mood, Choi went on to ask, "And who are his people?"

"He's the only son of Chao Khun Chanya and grandson of Chao Khun Choduk. Of the Department of the Left Harbour, you know. Mae Nui took me to their estate on Khlong Yom once. My dears, I can't tell you how fabulous it was. The gold in Khunying's room—chests of it stacked up on the floor! And countless servants milling around—both Thai and Chinese of course. I never knew Pho Prem's father but his Khunying Mother was one of the kindest women I'd ever met, though I was told she ruled her husband with an iron hand and he was terrified of her. She would have been proud of her son, who I'm sure will go far, just mark my word. He has everything in his favour, good looks, money, character. And so courteous in speech and manner. Whoever gets him is a lucky person."

"Right!" Choi nodded vigorously. "And since he's such a paragon and you such a good friend of his family, what about getting him for me?"

"Ha!" This interjection came from the maid Phit.

"My goodness!" Khun Sai cried, genuinely scandalized. "What are you saying! Just as well we're among ourselves. Crazy girl," she grumbled.

"I'm only being considerate," Choi said reasonably. "If I were lucky and won him for myself, with your help, you wouldn't have to worry about me any more, isn't that so?"

Her aunt gave a sigh. "Will you stop it? Whoever gets you won't thank me for it, and you'd make me lose face a hundred times a day. Do stop clowning."

Choi laughed. "Poor me! Even my own beloved elder won't give me a boost. It looks like I shall die a spinster in the palace."

A few seconds later she asked abruptly, "What about you, Khun Aunt? Why have you stayed single? Didn't you ever want to start a household of your own? "

Khun Sai uttered some loud exclamations, then said, "It's none of your business. Why should you want to know?"

"Because you've never told us and I've often wondered. You must have had plenty of admirers and a few must have been serious enough to propose. So what happened? Didn't you like any of them? Oh, do tell, Khun Aunt, there's nobody in this boat but us. Come on, please. What's the story? Why have you remained single?"

"Hmm, I don't know," Khun Sai said vaguely. "This kind of thing depends on your karma, I suppose.

"Maybe it's happened for the best," she went on. "Life would have been more troublesome, I'm almost sure. When you're old, to be without ties is better in a way. So it's hard to decide which was responsible, my good or my bad karma."

The others went on paddling in silence, waiting patiently for her to continue.

"Must have been about thirty years ago," she said quietly, "though it seems like yesterday. No use mentioning his name—we probably wouldn't recognize each other if we were to meet again. At first I wasn't interested at all but he tried hard, through our elders on both sides and through several people in the palace. One of the girls at the residence—again you don't want to know her name—became his greatest ally. She and I were very close, like you two, Choi and Phloi, and she proved herself quite a go-between, running back and forth between the Outer and Inner Gate, bringing me his presents and letters and all the time singing his praises. I was foolish enough to be carried away. Would have married him then if it hadn't been for my bad, or good, karma—whichever way you want to look at it. My father—your grandfather, Choi—wouldn't give his consent, you see. He said I was far too young and we should wait a few more years. I didn't mind. Things went on as usual for some time after that, with gifts and letters and occasional meetings—in public places of course and always with our go-between as chaperone. Then one fine day he sent me a letter—he couldn't go on living without me, wanted me to elope with him—he'd take me away and bring me back afterwards to ask forgiveness of our elders, assured me it would work out, and all. I was to meet him at the gate at such and such an hour on such and such a day. Well, you know I didn't do it. To betray Sadet's trust after all she had done for me—it was unthinkable. So I sent off the go-between to tell him he would just have to wait some more. That was all."

She gave a smile, signifying the end of the episode. But Choi was not satisfied. She demanded, "And is he still waiting? When are you going to say yes to him, Khun Aunt?"

Chuckling, Khun Sai answered in a normal voice, "No, I don't think he's waiting. After receiving my reply he went his way."

"What way?"

"He eloped with the go-between."

"Oh no!" Choi burst out laughing, with everyone joining her including Khun Sai.

"Yes, looking back, it was very funny," Khun Sai remarked. "But I did go through some miserable moments. How I cried! It's peculiar, though, when I think about it now it's as if the whole thing had happened to somebody else, to a young and foolish girl I used to know . . ."

Khun Sai probably did not suspect, or perhaps she did, how much her story had benefited Phloi. It was good to have this comradely feeling that there had been other broken hearts besides your own.

Be patient, she said to herself, the hurt will fade away in time, as it had in Khun Aunt Sai's case.

TWELVE

NOT long after that sojourn in Bang Pa-in, the court, back in Bangkok, discovered the bicycle. It started as a royal pastime, became and remained for some months the latest palace fashion.

Choi was among the first palace bicyclists, as would be expected. Surviving some quite nasty-looking cuts and bruises and her aunt's dark prophecies (regarding early death from a broken neck or some other unlovely accident), she went on to achieve such feats as riding with no hands or with only one foot on the pedal. She was appointed Sadet's instructor, and as a reward was presented with a bicycle of her own, a dashingly handsome model that caused heads to turn round with envy and admiration.

It was after her royal mistress had taken it up that Phloi decided that her turn had come. It was her duty if called upon to be able to accompany Sadet on wheel; she mustn't shirk it but must put aside her fears both of the machine itself and of looking clumsy and ridiculous falling off it. She took lessons from Choi, an inspiring if impatient teacher. She winced with pain when the maid Phit rubbed the *phlai* liquid on her damaged knees and swollen ankles. "What foolish-ness!" Phit kept grumbling and shaking her head. Once or twice, once after colliding with a gate post she had been determined to avoid, she cried in frustration and nearly gave it up. But gradually it became quite easy and, much to her surprise, simply wonderful fun!

Then Phloi began to wish she had a bicycle of her own to ride about, side by side with Choi and the other girls. Once born, this desire grew apace, became almost like an obsession. Absurdly childish of course, but there it was, she couldn't help herself.

So when her brother Phoem casually said to her during one of his visits, "Chao Khun Father told me to tell you that if there's anything you want from home to let him know," she jumped at the chance and spoke of her dearest wish. That is, she hesitated at first (out of the life-long habit of not bothering her father) but blurted out after Phoem had insisted, only mildly insisted.

And imagine her excitement and joy when her eyes fell on this beauty a few days later. She had come out with Choi to meet Phoem in the outer plaza and while she remained speechless, Choi fairly screamed, "Pho Phoem! Whose bicycle is this? Yours?"

Phoem smiled the superior smile of a conjurer. "It's for Mae Phloi. Do you like it, Mae Phloi?"

"Oh, Phloi, how marvellous!" Choi cried, clapping her hands. "Will you let me ride it sometimes?"

"But of course, Choi!"

"I can't wait to get back inside to try it," said Choi. "This is one of the best makes. German, you know. Wait till the girls see it, Phloi!"

Phloi stroked it gently, still not quite believing in her own good luck. To Phoem she said, "Please tell Chao Khun Father I'm completely overwhelmed. I prostrate myself at his feet with love and gratitude, and—oh, I don't know what to say—"

Looking at his elated sister, Phoem chuckled and said, "Actually, Chao Khun Father had nothing to do with it. I haven't talked to him—haven't got a chance to, but the bicycle's yours, Phloi. I'm giving it to you."

"Did you buy it?" Phloi asked doubtfully. "But you're always short of funds, and this must have cost plenty."

"I'm giving it to you anyway," Phoem repeated.

"My! My!" Choi exclaimed. "I had no idea you were so rich. Why didn't you buy me one too?"

"Because I didn't know you wanted it," Phoem quipped. "If you'd only told me I would have been only too happy to oblige. Well, girls, goodbye, I'd better be moving along. Enjoy yourselves."

"Wait," Phloi said, no longer excited. "Tell me the truth. Where did this bicycle come from?"

"Oh, don't look so serious, Mae Phloi, I didn't steal it ... If you really want to know, a friend of mine gave it to me, but I'm not keen about bicycling and you are, so I want you to have it. Now are you satisfied?"

"And this friend's name—is it Prem by any chance?" Choi asked.

"Well?" Phloi demanded. "Is it?"

And on Phoem's admission that it was ("I'm not supposed to tell you, you know. He asked me not to. You shouldn't have insisted," he had the nerve to say), she took Choi's hand and marched off without another word to her brother.

Back at the residence, Choi said half jestingly, half wistfully, "Perhaps we should have pretended not to know. After all, if people want to go scattering their money about and give us costly presents it's their own business, isn't it? We may as well get some fun out of them ... Anyway," she added in a sympathetic voice, "don't be so angry, Phloi. I've never seen you look so grim."

"How can I not be angry, Choi? Pho Phoem ought to know better. How could he do this to me—my own brother? Did he really expect me to accept that—that thing—from—from a stranger? If he had any sense of what's proper he should have refused it in the first place. And this Khun Prem—who does he think he is? And what kind of person does he think I am?"

She was also angry with herself. If she hadn't been so acquisitive, she reckoned, this wouldn't have happened. Now she'd learned her lesson. No more hankering after a bicycle—or anything else for that matter—ever again.

But the fates had decreed that she should have a bicycle of her own, their agent in this case being the irrepressible Choi. It came about in this manner:

There were just the three of them in the Veranda Room—Sadet, Choi and herself. Suddenly Choi was saying to Sadet in a doom-laden voice, "Mae Phloi is wasting away, Your Highness."

"Oh? What's the matter with you, Phloi?"

"Nothing, Your Highness. Choi is joking again, Your Highness."

"I am not, Your Highness. She's dying of grief and longing, Your Highness, and only Your Highness can save her."

"How, Choi?"

"By giving her a bicycle, Your Highness."

"Is this true, Phloi?"

Blushing, and not knowing whether to laugh or be very exasperated with Choi, Phloi had no choice but to make a *krap* at Sadet's feet.

"Ah-ha, so that's it! Here we have Phloi the Great Tongue-tied Bicyclist aided and abetted by Choi the Number One Self-appointed Intermediary. And soon everybody in this house will be demanding a bicycle of their own and making a pauper out of me, and we shall be known as the Bicycle Corps of the Inner Court. Well, well!"

Then she said Phloi could have the bicycle belonging to her and welcome to it. She herself had done enough bicycling to last her a lifetime.

There came other gifts after that incident, not for Phloi but for Khun Sai, and delivered not by Phoem but some women messengers— charming, innocent-looking gifts such as exotic fruits and flower bulbs from China. Khun Sai was always delighted to receive them, and on these occasions never failed to reiterate her high opinion of the giver for all to hear. She gloated over the rare plants, excitedly waiting for them to bloom.

Choi had this to say behind her back: "My aunt is nothing if not gullible. Doesn't she ever wonder why he's suddenly turned up after all these years?"

Then one day Phloi entered Khun Sai's room to find her in animated conversation with a particularly well-dressed visitor. She was about to withdraw when Khun Sai beckoned to her with a wide smile.

"Come in, Phloi. I'd like to present you to Khun Nui."

Khun Prem's Aunt Nui was bright-eyed and slightly-built. She was like a little bright bird, colourful and fluttering, and she had a unique way of speaking: it consisted mainly of interrogative statements uttered in her small, bright, tweety voice.

"So this is Mae Phloi?—Pretty. She's pretty, isn't she, Mae Sai?— I've been told Sadet is very fond of her, yes?—Why? Because she's a flatterer?—No? I see, diligent, is she?—And not one of these modern girls who think their elders are fools?—Loyal to Sadet, eh?

And grateful?—Can't stand people with no sense of gratitude, can you?—When were you born, Phloi, what year?—Five years younger than Nephew Prem. Not too young, right, Mae Sai?"

Talking about being grateful, that was how Phloi felt when Choi appeared in the doorway.

Khun Nui carried on with her questioning. "Choi, you remember me? Let's look at you. No, not pretty—Not pretty like Phloi, right?"

"Right!" Choi's reply was as immediate as it was chirpy. "No one's pretty like Phloi."

"You don't mind? My saying you're not pretty? It's all right?"

"I don't mind at all, Khun Aunt. It's true, isn't it? And what is true is deathless, right?" It did not seem to take Choi long to adopt the other's speech.

Khun Nui laughed. "Good! You and I can speak frankly with each other, or can we?"

"We can, Khun Aunt, we can. We'll have fun with our questions and answers, won't we?"

"We will. If we don't ask questions how are we going to get answers, right?"

"Right, Khun Aunt. Now let's see, what shall I ask you? Oh yes—do you know this riddle, Khun Aunt? What—"

"That's enough from you, Choi," Khun Sai interrupted. "I must warn you, Mae Nui, you tangle with this niece of mine at your own peril."

"Oh, I don't mind, Mae Sai. I like young people, don't you? I have a lot of fun with them, and they keep you young, don't you think?"

"Some elders don't," Choi volunteered. "They are against fun to start with—don't want it for themselves and don't want others to have it. They age quickly, these elders, or up and die an untimely death. And when that happens they often wrongly accuse us of having put a curse on them."

"Weren't you going some place, Choi?" inquired her aunt.

"Yes, as a matter of fact I was. I have an appointment with a *phalai* dealer in Teng Row. About time I got myself some new *phalai*s."

"Then why don't you be on your way and take your glib tongue with you?" suggested Khun Sai.

"I *was* on my way. I came in to fetch Phloi. We made this appointment together. So may we leave now?"

Permission was given by Khun Nui on the other's behalf. "You may," she said with a twinkling smile. "Why should you be cooped up in here? Going to buy yourselves some *phalai*s, are you? Good! Young girls should dress up—not like us, eh, Mae Sai? Nobody cares if we do or not, right, Mae Sai? Here, here's a present." Taking some money from her purse she handed it to the girls, who glanced at Khun Sai and, on receiving her go-ahead signal (a barely perceptible nod), accepted it with a respectful and appreciative *wai*. Always smiling, Khun Nui went on, "Buy a lot of pretty *phalai*s with it, will you do that? Garlic-skin weave is the best, isn't it? And mind you choose those patterns that stand out bold and clear. You have enough money? Is it enough?"

The girls assured her that it was and took their leave.

Coming out of the residence, Phloi asked: "When did we make this appointment, Choi?"

"We didn't. But we had to say something, didn't we? Otherwise we'd be stuck in there forever, right? Now we each have five *tamlung*s to spend. Is it enough? Is it enough?"

"And now we have to go and buy a few *phalai*s, I suppose?"

"And why not? Lots of *phalai*s. You know, Phloi, I get bored easily, but never with shopping for clothes. It's my most enduring passion—I can do it every day." Humming softly she went skipping along with Phloi trotting after her.

Presently she stopped and said, "Tell me, Phloi, did you have a dream recently about being bitten or crushed by a snake?" (According to an old belief, this means you are about to be united with your true love.)

"You do talk a lot of nonsense, Choi. What about you? Have you had this sort of dream yourself?"

"Never. And I don't think I ever will."

WEEKS passed—perhaps months, during which there were no more visits from Khun Nui. Her nephew was still sending occasional gifts to Khun Sai, and why shouldn't he? Phloi no longer wondered about his motive in doing so (apart from his natural kindness, that is). In fact she hardly thought of him these days. She was busy leading her peaceful everyday life and she was enjoying herself. At this period the Inner Court had a new fashion, the excitement over the bicycle having subsided: collecting ivory boxes, and she was involved in it like everybody else. An ivory box, used as container for lip-wax, had been part of a well-appointed betel-nut set for as long as anyone could remember, but without having any special distinction attached to it. Then one day His Majesty, while in conversation with Her Royal Highness Somdet Director-General, remarked on the eye-catching reddish patina, result of long usage, of the ivory box in her betel tray. Admiring it, he went on to observe how such a fine thing might be sought and valued as a collector's item, somewhat in the same manner as a smoker's pipe—meerschaum, for instance.

Thus the new fashion got started. And before long the word new became doubly apposite. For not only were the old boxes being collected, but brand new ones, whole series of them, produced alike by professional and amateur turners. Each of these collectors' series consisted of a number of boxes of diminishing sizes, from the larger-than-ordinary to the minutest no bigger than the tip of a child's little finger. Various new shapes had also been invented, not spectacularly dissimilar from the traditional persimmon type but possessing enough subtle points of difference to delight any connoisseur's heart. Choi and Phloi owned only a couple of boxes themselves, but with great pride and joy they helped look after (or played with as some might say) Sadet's collection, some items of which had small rubies, some emeralds, mounted in the centre of their lids. Even Khun Sai, normally not an avid fashion-follower, had acquired a few very good-looking ones, though she was always complaining she had no time to take proper care of them.

An ivory box exhibition and contest was held during the celebrations in honour of the investiture of Her Royal Highness Krom Khun Suphan Pakhawadi, and winners of the contest were awarded gold, silver and copper medals. By this time royal collectors were presenting their best boxes to His Majesty as they would their children and grandchildren so that he would bless them and endow them with auspicious names. The sets of boxes belonging to the royal consorts all had names given by His Majesty. He had chosen them and composed them into flowing, loosely-rhymed prose-poems, which the girls of the Inner Court enjoyed reciting to one another. One of these sets was called after royal ornaments and royal utensils—from tiara to sandals and from waterbowl to teapot. Another was given names of various fish, thirty-three in all, beginning with the mythical earth-supporting Anonda and the massive whale, and ending with the tiny needlefish and its slightly bigger friend, the fighting fish of iridescent hues. There was also the set named after flowers, with allusions to their distinctive fragrance woven into the phrases; and the one named after birds, not very many on account of this being a small collection, which was rather a pity, Phloi always thought. She loved the melodious lines linking together the prancing peacock, the chatty myna, the talkative canary, the stately swan and so forth, and wished there were more of them.

In her old age, when recalling these days, Phloi would sometimes label them the period of the ivory box, or sometimes she would refer to them as the era of Dusit Palace, since it was about this time that Dusit, situated some three miles from the Grand Palace, became His Majesty's favourite residence.

For many years there had been nothing there but a lone pavilion standing in the middle of its spacious parkland. Now there was the Vimanmek (Abode-in-the-Clouds) Mansion, with separate gardens for the queen and other members of the royal family, gardens named after different patterns of the blue-and-white Chinese porcelain then enjoying great popularity among Bangkokians: the Four Seasons, the Lotus, the Swan, the Small Characters, the Large Characters, the *farang* Kang H'si and so on.

Across the Jade Pool from the Vimanmek stood a traditional wooden house on stilts, decorated in simple style and complete with its own rustic-looking kitchen. On his tours of remote places in the kingdom, His Majesty had often been received in houses not unlike this one, and he must have had this one built so that when his friends from the country—he called them his personal friends, his *phuan ton*, came to see him in Bangkok he could entertain them in it, in a comradely atmosphere conducive to free interchange of ideas and opinions. Phloi had seen them on the balcony of this house, Phra Chao Yu Hua and his guests from the villages. They certainly looked comfortable and companionable together. The villagers were happy and proud to be with their Lord of Life and comported them-selves with great dignity, but you could see they also treated him as a friend with whom they could open up and speak what was on their minds.

That was one of the nicest things about Dusit. You had the opportunity to see the king more often than in the Grand Palace. You saw him on the balcony of the traditional-style house talking with his villagers and/or ministers of state, or in the park supervising the putting in of more trees and flowerbeds—he was a keen and knowledgeable gardener—or walking among the ferns and fountains in the plant-house adjacent to Vimanmek, or along the veranda of Vimanmek itself, a beautiful three-storey building with an approachable air about it, not so awesomely regal as the Upper Residence of the Grand Palace. Besides gardening, His Majesty when staying at Dusit took pictures in his spare time and developed them himself, and did his own cooking of *farang* dishes in the kitchen in the Long Building. It did your heart good to know he could come here for these recreations and to watch him stroll among the blossoming trees and the fruit trees of Dusit, either by himself or with his family and friends.

Choi and Phloi spent some of the happiest days of their lives here at Dusit, though there were moments when Phloi went in fear of its ghosts and wished she was somewhere else. There were ghosts in the Inner Court too, but you knew where you stood with them, so to speak. They were all royal ghosts, to begin with, and on the whole not given to unseemly manifestations. (No commoners died in the Inner Court except in an emergency, and in that case the ghost in question was always allowed, through certain religious rites, to leave in peace for some other dwelling outside.) You knew the places where they were likely to appear and could avoid going near there by yourself in the dark. When a prate (one of the several kinds of ghosts) sent up its shrieks in the middle of the night, you at least knew it to be a royal prate, and you prayed and poured water (an act of paying respects to the dead) and went back to sleep. Phloi had not had this experience herself but had heard others including Khun Sai relate theirs. Khun Sai had heard the shrieking a couple of times, and each time had prayed and poured water with all her power of concentration. Another time, however, she had done this only to discover the next morning that it had not been a royal prate after all but a flesh-and-blood cook's assistant screaming in her sleep. Choi had laughed at her aunt's mistake, but Khun Sai had insisted that her efforts had not been wasted, that some tormented souls somewhere in the Inner Court had received solace from her prayers and water-pouring.

All in all, it would not be far wrong to say that you felt relatively at ease with the ghosts of the Inner Court. Not so with those at Dusit, which were liable to materialize anywhere and whose identities and origins were completely unknown. According to some people, there had been a deserted *wat* here and during construction of the palace workmen had dug up large quantities of human bones from its cemetery. But nobody could point out the exact location of the old *wat*, so it might be easily be the spot where you least suspected and this was what made it so eerie. Countless hair-raising stories were told about these unfamiliar ghosts roaming about Dusit. Phloi didn't like hearing about them because they made her more afraid. In this she was the opposite of Choi who, even as she shook and shivered, enjoyed them immensely, either as listener or narrator.

One dark night, in a voice hoarse with trepidation and excitement, Choi said, "Listen, Phloi, it's happened again! At the Lotus Garden, night before last—those girls nearly died of fright!"

"Oh, please, Choi! I don't want to hear it. I'm terrified as it is."

But Choi went relentlessly on. "A lot of them saw it with their own eyes, Phloi. This girl who had a room downstairs saw it first. She happened to look out the window and thought it was a burglar crouching between two lotus pots. '*Khamoi! Khamoi!*' she yelled again and again, but it didn't budge. Then the others came, with lights. And there it was. Only the upper half of the body showing above the ground. A fat body, very dark skin and bald-headed. Rolling its eyes—enormous, protuding eyes swelling out of the head. Horrible!"

"I don't believe it," Phloi tried to cut her short. "What ghost would roll its eyes in the light, in front of everybody. It's unheard of !"

"You're hearing about it now," Choi continued. "There were many witnesses. One of them told me that the Princess Kao came out to watch, and that she prayed and poured water and gave it her blessing so that it would go away. Then she got angry and cursed it because it was so stubborn and kept rolling its awful eyes at her."

"Then what?" Phloi asked, curiosity getting the better of her.

"At the first sign of dawn it suddenly disappeared, but left its shadow behind on the tiled floor among the lotus pots. As the sun rose the shadow started to grow smaller and fainter, little by little, until it was no more."

Phloi might have listened to the story with a degree of scepticism, but no matter. It frightened her all the same.

Another night brought another story.

"Did you hear about the swimming ghost, Phloi? A few nights ago it came to the pool at Swan Garden and performed for Her Royal Highness." Choi mentioned the name of a princess then staying at Dusit.

"That's ridiculous, Choi. A performing ghost? Really!"

"So you haven't heard. Then let me tell you. The whole of Dusit is talking about it, you know."

"I'd rather not, Choi. Why don't you sing a song instead?"

But Choi was unstoppable. "The princess was there—" she began her story while grabbing Phloi's arm to make sure she had her whole attention "with two women and a child. She sat facing the pool and they with their backs to it. The women were talking and the princess listening. And then she wasn't listening any more but was peering at something in the distance. The women and the child turned round— and followed her gaze. After a few seconds the child screamed and fainted. Later it came to, but has been delirious ever since. Some say it might not live."

"How terrible, Choi!"

"The thing they saw in the pool was a black shape. It didn't look like any known living creatures on earth. Just a shape, a form. A formless form, you might say. And forever changing its contour, now bulging out here, now there. It grew quite large at one stage—the size of a water buffalo, then went heaving up and down until it reached the far edge of the pool. There it lengthened itself into something like a snake but not quite, slithered onto the ground, and made its way slowly up the pipul tree by the pool. Way up to the top branch. You know what happened then? It coiled itself, turned into a kind of black barrel, rolled down the branch and dropped into the water making a loud and prolonged splash. Now if you don't call that a performance I don't know what you're going to call it."

Choi's arms were covered with goose-pimples when she had finished telling her story. So were Phloi's arms, although she didn't want to believe what she had heard.

But soon after that, Choi said, "Will you come with me, Phloi?"

"Where?"

"Let's go for a swim in the Jade Pool."

"Oh, Choi, not after that story!"

"Why not? We're just as good as any ghost. If it can swim, so can we."

"Why don't you bathe in the daytime, Choi?"

"I did, for cleanliness. But now I want to show you how the *farang*s swim. I think I know how to do it."

"When did you ever get to see a *farang* swim anyway?"

"From a book, my dear girl, from a book. I saw it lying on Sadet's table when I was polishing. It's in English but you get enough information from the pictures. I can see the movements distinctly in my mind but I haven't had a chance to try them out. So come on, Phloi. The ghosts are busy elsewhere tonight, let's hope and pray."

"I'd prefer it if there were lots of other girls with us."

But the hour being quite late they found themselves alone at Jade Pool. The water looked irresistibly inviting, however. They went in, and after a while forgot to be scared of ghosts and had much fun trying to swim in the *farang* manner—that is, in what Choi understood to be the *farang* manner.

The night was lovely and cool, with a luminous sky and the air smelling of delicate scents from the night-blooming flowers. Walking back from Jade Pool after the swim Phloi felt invigorated, renewed, and at the same time full of peace and contentment. Then she heard Choi give a funny little sigh, and turned to look at her questioningly.

"What a perfect night," Choi said gravely, "and we've had such fun." She paused, stopped walking, and looked round. "Happy place—Dusit. In a few days we go back to another happy place, Sadet's residence in the Inner Court. Our home, in fact. We've been happy, haven't we, Phloi? We've had some good and bad times together, but on the whole we've been happy." She paused again, as if searching for words, then came out with "Oh, Phloi, how I do want things to go on like this—forever and always."

Phloi understood what she meant and responded feelingly, "So do I, Choi."

"But things are changing, Phloi. All round us. I don't often think ahead, but sometimes when I'm very happy I do—I don't know why—and when I do I end up feeling sad and confused. I see many signs of change, but what change will bring I don't know. To me the future is something dark and formless—like that ghost. Poor ghost. Come to think of it, it's more sad than scary."

"What's got into you, Choi? Don't look so solemn, and stop talking like that. If thinking about the future makes you sad, then think about something else."

"You'll be all right, Phloi," Choi went on being solemn. "You'll be able to adjust to the new. But I'm kind of obstinate and don't adapt easily at all. I can't imagine myself changing with the times. They compare Inner Court women to toads living under coconut shells, confined and sheltered. That's me, and I like it. I can't imagine living outside my snug protective shell. If the shell were not there I'd be lost. If the high walls of the Grand Palace should cease to be—"

"You're raving, Choi—stop it! Things change and nothing is permanent, yes, I know, but to say that about our palace walls which the royal forefathers built and our great grandparents have known—"

"Don't be so alarmed, dear Phloi. I'm not saying they will. But—you mentioned this yourself—as you and I have been taught, nothing is permanent. So it could happen. And if it should, what would we do, Phloi?"

"The question is beyond my poor brain. I won't think about it until I absolutely have to. In the meantime I'll pray that it will never come to pass. Now, Choi, it's time to get back. Start walking. This is an order!"

Choi laughed. "You sound exactly like Khun Aunt Sai. I'll race you, Phloi. To that white bench over there. Get ready. One-two-three—Go!"

THIRTEEN

ONE morning Khun Choei came to Sadet's residence in the Inner Court. As soon as Phloi saw who it was she dropped everything and ran up to greet her.

"Oh Khun Choei, how I missed you! It's been so long. Are you well? How's everybody at home? Chao Khun Father all right?"

"Wait, wait," Khun Choei said laughing. "Give me a moment to get my breath back. That was quite a walk from the Outer Gate, you know." Having said that, however, she began with hardly any pause to answer Phloi's questions about life in Khlong Bang Luang, which seemed to be going on in very much the same manner as before—peaceful on the whole, and never lacking in amusing little incidents when recounted by Khun Choei.

She stayed to lunch, the morning having passed so quickly. Khun Sai ordered special dishes for the visitor; these together with the many delicacies brought from outside by Khun Choei herself turned the meal into a feast. Everything tasted wonderful, and there was so much to tell one another and to laugh about together—a *sanuk mak* occasion, in other words. "You should come and see us more often," Choei said. "We need a new face now and again to liven up our old routine."

It was not until some hours later, when she was getting ready to leave, that Khun Choei revealed the main purpose of her visit.

"Chao Khun Father would like to invite you to come and see him," she said to Khun Sai. "Any day that's convenient for you. We'll send the boat to fetch you at Tha Phra."

A date having been fixed, Khun Sai went on to inquire, "Do you happen to know why he wishes to see me, Khun Choei?"

"I think he'd like to consult you about something but I don't know what," Khun Choei replied casually.

FROWNING up at the ceiling of her mosquito net, Phloi sought help from her roommate. "What do you think, Choi? What can it be—this 'something' Chao Khun Father's going to discuss with Khun Aunt Sai?"

But Choi's answer was absolutely useless. "Whatever it is," she said with a lengthy yawn, "it has to do with Khun Aunt."

Phloi sat up abruptly and blurted out, "And with me! It has to do with me and I'm dying to know what it is!"

Choi said sleepily, "We'll know in two days' time."

Phloi replied irritably, "And what am I going to do till then? I can't wait! I wish I could stop worrying about it, but I can't!"

Choi produced another yawn, then laughed. "Why, Phloi, I've never seen you like this. You're usually so calm and sensible. What's got into you?"

"It's very well for you to laugh. This doesn't affect you. If it did you'd be making a great fuss. And you wouldn't have let Khun Choei get away so easily with that 'I don't know what' of hers."

"True enough. But since we have no way of finding out, and to go on guessing all night long would only give us a headache in the morning, let's go to sleep, Phloi."

"You go to sleep, Choi. I can't. I feel wide awake."

"You know what, Phloi? It could turn out to be something quite unimportant, and then you'd regret having wasted your time worrying about it. Why don't you lie down, Phloi?"

Phloi lay down but continued making conjectures to herself. It could be, she thought, that Chao Khun Father had finally decided to ask Sadet's permission for her to leave the Inner Court and come back home. This sounded like the most probable explanation, especially when she considered the combination of his advanced age and his failing health. In fact she recalled that he had hinted at the possibility once or twice.

What would it feel like to live at home again after all these years? But first of all what a wrench it would be to part from Sadet, from Choi and Khun Sai, and to say goodbye to this dear and familiar place. She realized now how much she loved it, with its clanging gates and lofty walls and all. But if Chao Khun Father felt he needed her and wished to have her near him, then her duty would be to go to him, no doubt about that. And of course there could be nothing strange about living in one's family home. On the contrary, what could be more natural? Living at home would also mean having Khun Choei's constant companionship—how delightful! But what about Khun Un? So potent was this name that as soon as it flashed through her mind Phloi broke into a hot and cold sweat, stopped thinking reasonably and began to have nightmarish visions of life under the same roof with the reigning lady of Chao Khun Father's household.

ON the appointed day Khun Sai took off for Khlong Bang Luang early in the morning accompanied by her maid Phaad. Her first choice for an escort had been Phit. The dialogue between the two women which had resulted in Khun Sai taking Phaad instead—and thus frustrating Phloi's hopes of getting a full account of the visit from Phit later on—went as follows:

"You'll come with me, Phit."

"Not me, ma'am. Better to take Phaad."

"What! You're telling me what to do?! Why don't you want to come?"

"I'll do anything for you, ma'am, but I will not go to the house in Khlong Bang Luang with you and get us into trouble."

"What do you mean? We're not going to be there very long. No time to get into trouble."

"It won't take long for trouble to flare up, ma'am. I told you how things stood between me and those female scum. No telling what they might do to me, or I to them. You don't want to lose face, right? So it's better I don't go."

"Ah—I see. Yes, I remember now. It's been ages since I had a fight like that with anyone that I forgot what it could be like."

Khun Sai returned in the afternoon, and on entering the apartment proclaimed what a hot day it was, how exhausted she felt, and how her whole body had gone stiff from all that sitting in the boat. So first of all she was fanned, and when the perspiration had dried she went out to take a bath. Returning from the bath she disappeared into the bedroom to get dressed at leisure. Then she came back into the living room, reclined on the floor and was given a massage.

Meanwhile Phloi waited, doing her best to keep her impatience under control.

At long last the massage was over. Sitting up, Khun Sai said, "Come over here, Phloi," and handed her a parcel. "Chao Khun, your father, asked me to give you this. Look at it, my dear. Now you'll have something to carry when you go out."

Phloi undid the silk wrapping and exclaimed over the betel-nut box, a finely woven *liphao,* perfectly proportioned and ornamented with just the right amount of pink gold. Then she said, "But I seldom go out, and when I do it's as Sadet's follower carrying her box. I can't be carrying two boxes at the same time."

"It's a beautiful gift," Khun Sai declared. "And so sweet of him to think of sending it to you. Sooner or later you'll have occasion to use it I'm sure. So take good care of it."

Phloi thought to herself, *Surely, Khun Aunt Sai hasn't been summoned to Khlong Bang Luang just to bring me back this box. Not that I'm not grateful—and it shows Chao Khun Father now considers me a grownup, someone old enough to carry a betel box of her own when she goes out.*

Hiding her jittery state of mind as best she could, Phloi continued to wait for Khun Sai to tell her about the real business of the trip. She would have liked to question her outright but hesitated, afraid of committing an impoliteness. But after some time, despite herself, the words seemed to be slipping from her tongue of their own accord and she heard herself saying, "Why did Chao Khun Father want to see you?"

"None of your business, child!" Khun Sai answered in a rather shrill voice—predictably so—but, on seeing the expression of dismay on Phloi's face, went on in a gentler tone, "Don't mind me, Phloi. With old age I seem to be getting noisier somehow. Actually, your Chao Khun Father asked me to convey a message to Sadet, but since I haven't had an audience with her it wouldn't be right for me to go and broadcast it even to you. But you'll know soon enough—and it's not bad news, I can assure you of that."

The matter was thus closed for the time being. Phloi had no choice but to put aside her curiosity and shift to other topics. She asked after Chao Khun Father's health.

"Nothing wrong with him as far as I could see," said Khun Sai, "though I thought he looked much older than the last time I'd seen him. Which is natural—the passing of time and the impermanence of the body, you know." She paused and added, giggling, "I'm sure he also said to himself, 'Poor Sai, It's shocking how she has aged.'"

Later in the afternoon Choi drew Phloi aside and whispered, "What did Khun Aunt say?"

"She said, 'None of your business, child!'"

"Then it's definitely your business, child!" Choi concluded with certainty. "That was Khun Aunt's typical elders' evasion. They always want to keep it a secret from you as long as possible. Don't ask me why."

Her eyes popped out when Phloi showed her the box. "My, my, MY! It's grand enough for a Her Excellency the Than Phuying. What are you going to do with it, Phloi?"

Phloi laughed. "I don't know."

Lifting the box up and putting it down in a most ladylike manner, Choi opened it and took some imaginary wax from inside. Glancing haughtily at Phloi, she said, "Watch me closely, Phloi, so you'll know how to do it correctly if and when you become a Than Phuying—you never can tell." Having thus prepared her audience she proceeded with the performance, commenting on it as she went along. "This is how you apply wax on your lips—slowly, daintily. Remember to sit up straight, with your behind sticking out a little—like this, see? Raise your eyebrows ever so slightly, and let your gaze sweep round the room to make sure everybody's admiring you. Now bite on the betel leaf—again daintily, as if afraid to hurt it. Now the nut goes in, but don't start chewing just yet. Rub your teeth first with this pretty ball of tobacco, understand? You may deign to say a few words at this stage, taking the tobacco out to gesture with from time to time. When the tobacco has lost its flavour you should get rid of it. Down it goes into the spittoon! Never, NEVER push it to the side of your cheek, or you'll be accused of vulgarity and have your status as Than Phuying severely questioned. Enough. End of first lesson."

Phloi could not stop laughing for some minutes. Then she said, "I can't bear it. I think I'd have to stay away from Than Phuying Choi or die laughing."

"What's so difficult about being a Than Phuying?" Choi sounded full of self-confidence. "Except one thing—how to hug your husband in such a way that he won't go and get besotted over any minor wives!"

NEXT afternoon in the Veranda Room, Sadet was making jasmine garlands, assisted by Phloi and another girl. It was peaceful and companionable, an afternoon very much like most afternoons in the palace. Then the other girl took her leave, having finished her assignment and having been on duty before Phloi came to relieve her.

After a few moments had passed in silence, Sadet laid down her flower-needle, and said to Phloi, "Your father is asking my permission for you to get married. What do you say, Phloi?"

Phloi started, grew pale, had violent palpitations. She had expected some information from Sadet, but nothing like this. By force of habit she pulled herself together; it would never do not to speak when spoken to, especially by Sadet.

"I'm not ready, Your Highness."

"Why not? What's the reason?"

"I wish to continue serving Your Highness. The thought of starting a household has never entered my mind, Your Highness."

"About time it did—you're old enough. It's good of you to want to stay with me and I thank you. But we have to think of your future, don't we? What will happen to you when I die—since I'm not immortal. Not only am I not immortal, but the chances are I will not live to a ripe old age. Don't you remember what the Inner Court looked like when you first came to live here? Many more princesses than there are now, every palace was occupied, each with its princess and scores of maids-in-waiting and full of life and laughter. Since then—one death after another, so many deaths in so very few years, so many empty decaying palaces. Sad, but there it is—can't be helped. The point is that we princesses don't seem to be long-lived, Phloi, and when we die the girls who used to be under our care have to fend for themselves. Some do all right, others not so well. Now here's your opportunity to go forth and do well, build your future on a solid foundation. And it's not as if we're going to part forever. You can come and visit me as often as you like, you know—"

She paused, for Phloi was crying.

"Now look at you! Can't we have a conversation without the shedding of tears? You're as bad as the rest of them—snivellers all of you! I never know whether you're happy or miserable when you turn on the weeping act. Now let's start again."

Phloi wiped her tears and said the first thing that came to her head. "I don't know who it is, this person Chao Khun Father wishes me to marry."

"I was about to tell you," Sadet resumed, "when you rudely interrupted me with your boohooing. He's a very nice person of the right age, neither too young nor too old. His name is Prem, belongs to the Phraya Choduk family, immensely rich. Now are you satisfied? Do you know him at all?"

"I know who he is but have never spoken to him, Your Highness." Phloi's hands had turned icy cold, though she was not really surprised by the revelation. But did it make her feel glad, or what? This she could not answer herself. Her feelings on the subject of Khun Prem's behaviour had always been difficult to define.

"And so?" Sadet was urging her to go on.

For the sake of something to say, Phloi said, "I don't love him, Your Highness."

"Of course you don't love him," came Sadet's immediate retort. "How can you love him when you hardly know him? That's not important—as you go on living together you can grow to love each other. The important thing is that your elders, who love you and wish to see you settled and secure, have considered the match and approved it as most suitable. Do you, Phloi, consider it your duty to do according to what they deem best for you? To marry for love is all very well. But what happens when after living together you find you don't love each other any more. Love was the mainstay of your marriage, which falls apart when love is no more. But a marriage carefully arranged with parental love and goodwill rests on the support of that love and goodwill. It's the kind of support you can depend on and will remain with you always."

She paused, waiting for some response from Phloi, and asked again, "What do you say, Phloi?"

What could Phloi say? To protest was unthinkable—she could not do that to Sadet. But on the other hand, how could she say yes when she was still so confused in her own mind? And even if she wanted to say yes, she would have been too shy to do it.

What she finally said, hesitantly, was, "I don't know what he's like at all, Your Highness. And I'm also afraid, and I—I would like more time to think it over."

"Afraid? Of what, Phloi? Afraid you would fail as mistress of the house? Then you can stop being afraid. With the kind of training and upbringing you've had, coupled with your good birth, good sense, and ability, you have nothing to fear, believe me. As to the young man's character, rest assured it has come under close scrutiny and found to be satisfactory. Or do you think we elders are old-fashioned and therefore know nothing? Or perhaps you think your father likes him simply because he's wealthy? If so, you're wrong. Your father is not a poor man, and he's seeking happiness for his daughter, not trying to marry her off for money. Your father is a responsible and honourable man, Phloi. Oh, I know he made your mother unhappy, but I also know my own Nang Chaem and what a difficult woman she was, so I could never entirely blame him."

She stopped rather abruptly, then exclaimed "Oh, dear!" and continued in a decided tone of voice. "What a lot of talking I've done, but that's all from me, Phloi. Essentially it's none of my business. If you're not ready to comply, or if you want to rebel, or whatever you want to do, you'll take it up with your father. From now on it's between you and him."

Sadet and Phloi went on working on the garlands together, chatting about other things. Phloi understood very well that Sadet had not washed her hands of the affair but was letting her know that, ultimately, the right to choose Phloi's future must be exercised by Phloi.

AT first Choi was reluctant. "I might give you the wrong advice," she said. "Then you'd blame me afterwards."

"Tell me anyway," Phloi insisted, looking nervous and distraught. "I want to hear your views, though in the end I'll have to make up my own mind—nobody can do that for me. At this moment I'm in a daze. I owe everything to Chao Khun Father and to Sadet and I don't want to go against their wishes. If I did that I'd hate myself and it would be on my conscience till the day I die—ungrateful wretch! But Choi, how can I marry him? I hardly know him. I'm so scared. Help me, Choi. I don't know what to think."

Choi finally said, "I know what I think you should do. But I don't know if it's right or wrong. I think, Phloi, that you should do it—agree to it."

She laughed on seeing the surprised look on Phloi's face. "Yes, I know, that's an unexpected statement coming from me with my reputation for disobedience. Frankly, I'm not looking at this thing from the point of view of obeying or disobeying the elders. I'll try to explain myself. If I were to get married I'd choose a man who really and truly loves me and will not forsake me as though I were a mere trifle. Now Khun Prem has been courting you a long time. You ignored him completely and I treated him abominably in the beginning, remember? But did he give up? Never. He kept on following you around. He didn't change his mind in a hurry like someone we know. The constant suitor, if there ever was one! And now he's taken the matter to his elders and to your father, which strikes me as the right and natural thing to do. You see, Phloi?" She paused, and added, "I would like to see you settled with a good man, Phloi, a good man to whom you are someone worthy and not something insignificant to be easily cast aside at his convenience."

The last sentence did it. "Someone worthy . . ." It was true, Phloi could see it now, that a large part of her unhappiness over the break with Phi Nuang had stemmed from this: one day she had been important to him—or so she had been led to believe. Then, overnight, she had become nothing. She had not been angry with Phi Nuang, had not felt vindictive or resentful against anyone, but it had destroyed not only her romantic hopes but her self-esteem, had made her feel so abjectly worthless that she despaired of being of use to anyone in this world. It was Khun Prem's interest in her—although she had not returned it—that had restored a measure of confidence in herself. His persistent yet discreet courtship had been her moral support all along but she had not allowed herself to recognize the fact until now.

Phloi had always thought she was capable of any sacrifice where Sadet and Chao Khun Father were concerned—could even lay down her life for them. But no sacrifice was being demanded of her. To consent to marry the man they had judged suitable for her could not be termed a sacrifice, although it would be a risky venture—marriage is always that, in any case. Phloi was no longer afraid. Let the future come. She would willingly face any un-certainties or disappointments it might bring. She would submit her compliance to Sadet and Chao Khun Father as an offering of thanks. She reckoned it was a small offering, but felt happy and gratified that it should be within her power to present it.

She was about to say out loud how right Choi was when Khun Sai entered the room.

Khun Sai refused to believe that Choi had been advocating "doing what the elders think best." Phloi had to reassure her again and again that this was indeed Choi's position regarding this issue. Khun Sai then said, "Well, well, will wonders never cease! But what about yourself, Phloi? What is your answer?"

Phloi was too bashful to give a straight one. She said, "I don't know what to say, Khun Aunt. I leave it up to you. You've brought me up and you know what's best for me."

Khun Sai's face glowed with pride and pleasure, but her spoken words were about other things. "I don't dare make any decision for you, Phloi," she said. "Sadet is well-disposed to it today, but later on, if she should change her mind, or when she misses having you around, she might blame it all on me: 'It's all your doing, Nang Sai! Nang Sai, the go-between! If it weren't for you I'd still have Phloi with me. Now nobody looks after me and it's all your fault, Nang Sai!' So I'd better keep my mouth shut. The best thing is for you to talk it over with your Chao Khun Father first, and Khun Choei is coming to fetch you to Khlong Bang Luang in a few days."

There it ended. Khun Sai had nothing more to say on the subject, at least for the time being, much to Phloi's relief.

IN the ferry going home, Khun Choei said to Phloi, "When we get home, we'll go straight in to see Chao Khun Father. Afterwards you'll come to my room and we'll have something to eat, then I'll take you back to the palace. All right? No need for you to call on Khun Un at all. In fact, do me a favour and don't see her this time."

"What's the matter, Khun Choei?"

"As you know, Khun Un always says she'll never marry, that no one is worthwhile marrying, and that she'll live at home and take care of Chao Khun Father until death. But, you see, if she doesn't have a husband she doesn't want any of us to have one either. This proposal from Khun Prem has put her in an ugly mood—especially because Chao Khun Father is so delighted with it. And because he is delighted she doesn't dare cross him too openly but takes it out on the world in general and me in particular. I can more or less defend myself mainly by evading her, of course. But at the sight of you she's going to get hysterical, I'm sure of it. Which will be unpleasant for you and will upset Chao Khun Father. So I really think you should keep out of her way this time, Phloi."

"Anything you say, Khun Choei. But I still don't understand why she should take it like this."

"Oh, Phloi, I think deep down she would like to have a husband too. In fact, the more I think about it, a husband would certainly be a good thing for Khun Un. Wish I could find her one. The trouble is, one look at her 'I'm better than you' face and the prospective suitor is liable to run away!"

"What about you, Khun Choei—haven't you ever thought of marrying?"

"Don't worry about me, Phloi. I'm quite happy to remain single, especially now that you're going to be well-established and I can have you to lean on in my old age, and when I die you'll be able to give me a proper cremation!"

Chao Khun Father had been waiting for them on the balcony upstairs. He inquired about Sadet's health and Phloi's health, and talked leisurely about various inconsequential topics as though he had nothing else on his mind.

After a while Khun Choei excused herself, saying she had to see to the midday meal.

Chao Khun Father looked at Phloi for a moment or two in silence, then said, "You are a full grown young woman now, Phloi. Once I thought you were going to resemble your mother, but now I see the difference between you two. Her prettiness was of the flashier kind. She was something of a flirt, you know, and at her most attractive when in animation. But you're as beautiful sitting still as when you move about."

Phloi smiled at him but could not think of anything to say in reply.

Chao Khun recrossed his legs, cleared his throat and lit a cigarette. When he finally spoke it was in a low voice, as if he was anxious not to be overheard. "What did Sadet say, Phloi?"

"That—that she has no objection," Phloi stammered. "And that I should—give you the answer myself."

Chao Khun nodded without saying anything. He, too, seemed to have some trouble over his choice of words.

"What do you think of it, Phloi?" he said at last, and went on quickly without waiting for Phloi's answer. "I want you to know that I'm not forcing you. This is an important step in your life, and the decision must rest with you. But if you want my opinion I can only say

I find him most suitable in every way. If you have such a husband to look after you I'll be able to sleep peacefully. But, I repeat, it's for you to decide. If you have any doubts about it, tell me. Don't be afraid."

Phloi would have liked to express herself at length about her desire to bring nothing but comfort and peace of mind to Sadet and Chao Khun Father, and be a credit to them always; that she placed herself with complete trust in their loving hands and would willingly consent to marry Khun Prem or any other man of their choice and, once a wife, intended to fulfil her wifely obligations to the best of her ability.

But all she could say aloud was, "It's up to you, sir. I have no objection." Having said it, she felt her cheeks were burning, and kept her head bent low towards the floor.

She heard him chuckle—and knew he was pleased—and then heard his voice saying: "Don't feel so shy, my daughter. To marry is a normal thing, you know. I'm glad that I have an obedient daughter. Both of us must have made enough merit, Phloi, for you to be able to give me happiness, and for me to have lived long enough to see you securely established. Very well then, I'll let them know that we accept their proposal."

He fell silent again, and broke it only to remark, "I wonder where Choei is. She's been gone a long time." He smiled at Phloi. "She must be waiting to have a long chat with you, Phloi. I'd better let you go to her now, otherwise she might accuse me of wanting to monopolize you."

And with these few words he adjourned their meeting, one of the most momentous events in Phloi's life, even if it had not lasted very long.

Later in the day, when Phloi went to pay him respects before taking her departure, he gave her a purse containing money "to buy what you may need in preparation."

It was quite a big sum, and Phloi came away bewildered. How was she supposed to spend it? What sort of things were needed in preparation? She had no idea, and planned to deposit the gift with Khun Sai as soon as she got back to the palace.

Phoem was waiting for his sisters at the landing pavilion, chatting away with Phit, who had unwillingly accompanied Phloi to Khlong Bang Luang and was rather impatient to leave.

"I didn't go up to the house," Phoem explained, "because I didn't want to intrude. Didn't want to be shooed away from your important discussions." He had evidently been drinking but, while not altogether sober, appeared to be in sufficient command of his senses.

"Don't give me your silly excuses!" Khun Choei said severely. "Your sister has been here since this morning, but instead of coming to see her you've been gallivanting around as usual!"

"You're always scolding me, Khun Choei," Phoem said, smiling good-humouredly. "Actually I'm coming with you so we can talk all the way back in the boat. Anyway, soon we will be able to get together as often as we wish. No more lurking around at the Outer Gate, isn't that so, Phit?"

Phit gave a hearty laugh. "Oh, yes! The palace is growing more and more stuffy for me these days. I'll be so glad to move into a house where I can entertain you any time I feel like it."

Along the *khlong* during the journey back to Bangkok, the faithful Phit alternated between laughter and tears—she was in high spirits and it took very little either to amuse her or wring her susceptible heart. She laughed listening to Phoem describe how a certain person had been pining away for Phloi, living in fear of being rejected by her, unable to eat or sleep, teetering on the brink of death unless he should receive the good news in time; and she laughed at Phoem's despondent face when Khun Choei took him to task for talking nonsense and not behaving with the dignity befitting an older brother.

Later on her eyes grew moist as the three young people, whom she had known all their lives, drifted into a nostalgic mood and talked about their childhood days, and then reminded themselves that they were no longer children. They had been united as children and they felt closely united now, the three of them, though one was only a half-sister. What would happen to them in the years to come? Nobody could foretell. All things are impermanent, as all knew from the Lord Buddha's teaching. But all three vowed that in the midst of change and uncertainties they would remain loving and loyal always and never abandon one another.

"And you can count on me, too," said the faithful Phit, blowing her nose loudly. "I'll stick with you in sickness and in health till I draw my last breath—see if I don't!"

FOURTEEN

PHLOI lived the first part of those few months between her betrothal and wedding in a rather benumbed frame of mind, unable to connect her new position with her everyday life, unable to say if she was happy about it or not. Not that she was ever asked. The people who came to call on her seemed to take it for granted that she was. She had so many visitors these days. They had heard the good news—Khun Prem being so rich and eligible, and suddenly found her a much more interesting person than before. Friends and genuine well-wishers came and so did acquaintances desiring to become something more intimate. Then there were people who had clothes and jewellery to sell, and people who loved to be wherever other people congregated. They all appeared to be well-informed and usually had more news to impart than Phloi herself. And it was from them that she learned about Khun Prem's elders having been to see her Chao Khun Father to present him with engagement gifts, that these gifts were of fabulously high value, and that the wedding, scheduled to take place in the Sixth Month, would be one of the grandest of the year. It all sounded unreal to Phloi, and not particularly exciting.

She happened to be on attendant duty the day Khun Prem's Aunt Nui came to present engagement gifts to Sadet. Khun Nui did not eschew her interrogative style of speech even when addressing herself to Her Royal Highness.

"I am here to present the gifts to Your Highness. Are you pleased, Your Highness?"

Sadet said yes with a laugh. Khun Nui was no stranger to her.

The gifts were carried in by three little girls in their early teens, most likely relatives of Khun Prem, to judge from their looks and manners.

"Crystal, Your Highness," Khun Nui twittered happily. "Newly arrived from abroad. Quite rare, Your Highness?"

The three girls had to make several trips to the corridor in order to bring in everything. The room was now gleamingly cluttered with groups of bottles, jars, vases, trays, bowls, jugs, with and without stems, in graduated sizes, in contour round, oval, square, or oblong. The toiletry set had gold designs on all the pieces, whereas the altar set came with the "jackfruit spike" motif.

"Did you bring the whole godown, Nui?" Sadet asked. "You want me to set up shop selling crystalware, is that it?

Khun Nui giggled like the veteran court lady she was, bending her head low as if she was trying to conceal the giggle in her bosom. "Are you displeased, Your Highness? Pho Prem has asked me to present you with many, many gifts. He says they must be worthy of your great kindness. He's right, Your Highness?"

"And what's that?" Sadet pointed to a large magnificent bowl resting on an intricately wrought silver stand. "It doesn't seem to belong to any set. What do you use it for?"

Khun Nui went into another fit of decorous giggling. "I have no idea, Your Highness. But it looked so pretty I couldn't resist it. Right, Your Highness?"

When Khun Nui was gone, Sadet said to Khun Sai, "Look at all this. I've never seen so many gifts."

"It is as it should be." Khun Sai ventured. "To be worthy of your great kindness."

"Ah, Sai," Sadet said vaguely, half to herself. "You talk as if it's a question of bartering Phloi for things. If it were, I would never have to let her go."

She paused, and after a while spoke to Khun Sai in a business-like tone. "You'll look after Phloi's trousseau, won't you? Please make sure that it befits her position. Bear in mind she's marrying into a rich family, and let's not give them the slightest cause to feel that we haven't tried to do our best by her or by them. As to her jewellery, when the time is near you and I will choose it together from my collection."

"Yes, Your Highness," said Khun Sai, looking very pleased and serious and responsible.

"As to her toiletry set," Sadet went on, "I don't think I'll give her anything of mine, because what I have are either in pink gold or silver and they would clash with the gold niello her people across the river have always used. We'll talk some more about it, Sai. I'll need all the help you can give me. Remember, I'm marrying off a daughter."

"Yes, Your Highness," said Khun Sai, with a smiling glance in Phloi's direction.

TO all intents and purposes, Sadet's acceptance of the gifts served to formalize the situation. The news had been confirmed beyond all doubt that Phloi was now officially engaged.

The next few weeks saw Khun Sai busy putting together a suitable trousseau and Phloi now and again attempting to stop Khun Sai from "doing it too extravagantly." Phloi would express her opinion, and Khun Sai would counter with words to this effect: "Be quiet. We are not being extravagant. We are only doing what is proper for you and everybody concerned. Otherwise Sadet would lose face." So in the end Phloi kept quiet.

Days passed, bringing nearer and nearer the date of the wedding. Her new life would soon begin. It was not something remote and unreal anymore but a looming presence, of unknown shape and all the more terrifyingly real for being unknown. Phloi sometimes woke up suddenly in the middle of the night covered with sweat and with her heart pounding.

She confessed to her dear confidante, "I'm dreading it, Choi."

"So am I," Choi said. "It was a lot of fun at first—all these preparations for the wedding. You know how much I love buying things, especially with other people's money. But I feel very sad about losing you."

"You are not losing me, Choi. I'll be coming here to see you all the time. So that part of it doesn't worry me so much. It's this going off to live with a stranger that's giving me nightmares, Choi. I feel so helpless! What am I going to do? I don't know what he's like at all. And what shall I say to him when we meet?—Oh, it's awful."

"It is rather," Choi agreed. "Of course you're bound to get to know what he's like after living under the same roof with him for some time. But there's no way for you to become acquainted with him before that. No meeting after betrothal until the day the bride is delivered to the groom."

"Exactly." Phloi sighed, massaging her hands which had turned icy cold. "Two people who have never spoken a word to each other, all of a sudden thrown together, face to face, by themselves. Oh, Choi, I wish you could stand in for me. You're a better person to cope with this kind of situation. You could think of the right thing to say. You wouldn't be intimidated. Whereas I—I may just die of fright, who knows—" She sounded somewhat hopeful uttering the last sentence.

"Tell you what, Phloi," Choi said, trying to be helpful. "It's too late to worry. Just speak when you're spoken to and you'll be all right. If nobody speaks to you first, you keep quiet, see?"

DURING this time Khun Choei made frequent visits to the Inner Court, and from her Phloi learned the reason why the wedding would be held at Khun Prem's family place in Khlong Yom and not at her father's house in Khlong Bang Luang.

"I felt sorry for Chao Khun Father," Khun Choei said. "He wanted so much to have it at home—the first wedding in the family and he so very pleased and happy about the match. He would have loved to make it a really splendid affair in his own house, but every time he broached the subject to Khun Un she said it wouldn't be convenient because of this and that and the other."

"He didn't know why she was against it?"

"Of course he did, but he chose not to argue with her. In the end he just let the matter drop, and when Khun Prem's people suggested having the wedding in Khlong Yom he agreed that it would be more convenient."

"It's quite understandable," Khun Choei went on, "why he let Khun Un have her way. He's got to see her every day and it would have been unpleasant to have to come to blows. Even so, come to blows they nearly did when he asked her to bring out the utensils he wanted you to have for your new home."

"What happened?" Phloi asked with justifiable curiosity.

"He told her to choose from his gold niello collection a betel-nut tray, a toiletry set and so forth. She did, selecting the poorest pieces possible. When he saw them he was furious—but again he said nothing. He just demanded the keys from her, marched off to the cabinets and took out the very best ones. They're lovely, Phloi, you'll be pleased to know. Then he returned the keys, called for an empty chest, packed the stuff in it, locked it and had it installed in my room, to be sent to you on the day of the wedding."

"And then what did Khun Un say?"

"Nothing. She knew he meant business so she just shut up, and as far as he's concerned she's behaving as if nothing has happened. But she takes it out on me as usual."

"Oh, Khun Choei! You're in trouble on account of me again. I'm so sorry."

"Don't worry your head about it, Mae Phloi. I'll make a peace offering to her when I'm good and ready, and things will return to normal between us. I've been through it before. It's nothing."

Khun Choei also issued a warning about Elder Brother Chit.

"Ever since he knew who you're going to marry he's been pestering me to put in a good word for him. To start with, he wants me to tell you how he has always loved you, his darling little sister Phloi. He's going to be a persistent caller at your new home, I'm afraid. So do be careful. Don't believe everything he says and don't be soft-hearted with him. You're going to be generous with him, I know you, but remember, he's a shameless cadger and his appetite for spending money is insatiable. We don't want Khun Prem's family to look down on us, do we?"

Phloi said, "No, we don't."

"And we've got to keep an eye on Pho Phoem too," Khun Choei went on. "He and Khun Prem are good friends now—matter of fact it was thanks to Pho Phoem that Chao Khun Father came to know and like Khun Prem, but they'll soon become brothers-in-law as well as friends. And I just hope Pho Phoem will not abuse his position—we both know how irresponsible he can be at times . . ." She paused, not quite sure of the expression on Phloi's face. "You're not angry with me for saying all these things?"

"Of course not, Khun Choei. You're concerned for my sake and I'm very grateful to you. You're right, there's no telling what these two will do next. It does worry me, Khun Choei."

"No, no, there's nothing to worry about really. Just be careful, that's all, and firm. Scold them a little from time to time—it's good for them. For my part, I'll do my best to help keep them under control—" Khun Choei suddenly stopped here, and burst out laughing. "My oh my! Listen to me spouting advice as though I'd been married five times already!"

Another regular visitor to Sadet's residence these days was Khun Nui, who came principally to confer with Sadet and Khun Sai over the business of the wedding, but always stayed on for the pleasure of chatting. Choi called her Khun Aunt, and Phloi had now adopted this term of address, which pleased the good lady very much. Without having to be asked, she gave Phloi a few more facts about her nephew: that he had only one brother, Pruang, and only one sister, Prung; the brother looked after the family business and the sister was married; both of them had their own houses somewhere in Bangkok, leaving Khun Prem, after the death of both parents, sole master of the Khlong Yom estate, with Aunt Nui and Aunt Nian living in the same compound.

"Mae Nian is an invalid," Khun Nui remarked. "You'll like her, Phloi. She's quiet, not a chatter-box like me. You think I talk too much, yes? A bit annoying, yes?"

Phloi laughed. "Not at all, Khun Aunt. I love listening to you. You're so amusing."

"You flattering me?" Khun Nui demanded, beaming with pleasure nonetheless. "You don't talk much yourself, do you? Not like me and Mae Choi?" Turning to Mae Choi she gaily added, "You and I have a lot to say to each other, right?"

"A tremendous lot, Khun Aunt," Choi answered in the same spirit. "We get along famously and I know that if you had another nephew to spare you'd be glad to hand him over to me. Right, Khun Aunt?"

"Wrong, Choi. You're a delightful companion but would be difficult to handle as a niece by marriage, you agree?"

Choi said how could she not agree to such a straight-from-the-shoulder statement.

THE programme of the wedding day was discussed often enough by Khun Aunt Nui and Khun Aunt Sai in Phloi's presence and she knew that on that day she would 1) have an early morning audience with Sadet and take her leave; 2) then proceed, accompanied by Khun Sai, Choi and three other bridesmaids, to join Chao Khun Father at the Outer Gate; 3) journey to Khlong Yom to take up a brief temporary abode in Khun Nui's bungalow which, though situated in the same compound, stood far enough from Khun Prem's (or the main) house to be seemly for the purpose; 4) from Khun Nui's bungalow go to the main house to attend the chanting of the monks and make offerings to them; 5) come back to the bungalow to rest and get dressed for the ceremonial pouring of the lustral water, also taking place at the main house; 6) once again, come back to the bungalow to wait until the propitious hour when the bride would be presented to the groom.

Khun Sai said to Phloi apropos the use of Khun Nui's bungalow, "If your house in Khlong Bang Luang were nearer, I would have preferred that you go there after the offering to the monks and then after the water-pouring, but as it is, Mae Nui's bungalow will have to do, and I'm thankful it's at a decent distance from the main house. We should be all right there."

Sometimes Khun Sai's instructions regarding the wedding day made Phloi feel like a small child. "We should be all right at Mae Nui's," Khun Sai repeated. "I myself will be there all the time to keep an eye on things. So don't you worry, Phloi. You'll only have to do what I tell you and be prompt about it. No mooning about, you understand?"

Sometimes Khun Sai would go into great detail concerning what to do and not to do in the ceremony. Phloi could not remember it all. And it was not this or that particular detail she was worrying about anyway, but the whole event from start to finish and beyond. She grew more agitated as the important day drew nearer and lost her appetite and her sleep over it. She looked pale with dark rings under her eyes.

"Pull yourself together," Choi admonished her. "You don't want to die before the wedding."

"Perhaps that would be best," Phloi said.

"Don't talk like that!" Choi remonstrated, sounding not unlike Khun Aunt Sai. "You're old enough to know better. If you go on at this rate, not eating, not sleeping, you'll collapse—that's for sure. And what good will that do?"

"Oh, Choi, can I help it if I'm scared? Are they all like me I wonder?"

"I have not known many brides-to-be, but my mother was scared, she told me. Scared to death, she said."

"But, Choi, wasn't she acquainted with your father before their marriage?"

"Oh, no! They knew what each other looked like, but apart from that they were complete strangers. And then they wedded and have been living happily together ever since. So you see, Phloi, you can rest easy."

"But your parents are an ideal couple. What about the others? What about me? What if it turns out wrong for me—then what do I do?"

"Oh do stop wailing, Mae Phloi! If you don't know how it will turn out, why waste time agonizing? When you bet in a lottery, you don't give up the chance of winning right away, do you?"

But no amount of scolding or philosophizing could rid Phloi of her anxieties, just as no amount of wishful thinking on her part could slow down the passage of time to suit her convenience. The important day inevitably arrived on schedule and she had to confront it as best she could.

So here she was, up before dawn after a sleepless night, getting ready to leave her snug universe for the outside world and feeling not only very nervous but very sad, in fact even more sad than nervous. Khun Sai and Choi shared her mood. The former murmured something encouraging while her own eyes were full of tears; the latter was strangely subdued, saying very little. The three of them sat down to breakfast together, but none could swallow more than a few mouthfuls. Then they got dressed for the journey. Their clothes were elegant and festive, but their hearts remained heavy.

Now it was time to take leave of Sadet.

Climbing the stairs to Sadet's apartment, Phloi reminded herself again to behave calmly and sensibly. After all, she would be coming back here as a regular visitor. This was by no means the final parting, and she did so much want to show Sadet how well she could conduct herself, so that Sadet should have no worries as to how she would carry on the rest of the day.

Sadet was seated in front of the mirror combing her hair. She turned and smiled.

"Well, Phloi, all set to leave? I got up early to say goodbye to you, as you can see."

Phloi's good resolution chose to desert her at this very instant. She lowered her head to the floor and burst into tears. This was not the sensible performance she had planned and she did try to correct it, but the long-suppressed tears, once given an outlet, kept on coming despite herself.

Sadet said to Khun Sai, "One would think she's being taken away to be executed."

"Poor Phloi," Khun Sai, sniffling, muttered in a tremulous voice, and earned a reprimand from her royal mistress.

"It's for you to cheer the girl up, Sai, not make her feel worse. And why should you be crying? It's not your wedding."

She let a few moments pass before saying to Phloi, "This is an auspicious day and you mustn't spoil it with so much weeping."

Stifling a sob, Phloi stammered out, "I—I don't want to leave Your Highness."

"Phloi, oh, Phloi, you can cry until your tears turn to blood and still I won't be able to keep you with me. Come, stop crying, I have something to say to you."

At last Phloi recovered enough composure to sit up and pay attention.

Smiling, Sadet said, "My dependable Phloi, I can always count on you to listen to me."

After the briefest pause she went on. "I want you to know that I have enjoyed having you under my care. Looking after you has been an easy and gratifying task because you're so easy to teach, because you're amenable to reason and apply yourself diligently.

"Time and time again you have proved yourself a person of steadfast nature with a strong sense of gratitude worthy of your birth and upbringing. Your gentleness and tolerance should stand you in good stead in your new life. You are marrying a royal servant. Consider yourself as one also and live up to the honourable calling.

"Conduct yourself so that you'll be a great help to your husband and not a hindrance. Give him your support, Phloi. Praise him when he's praiseworthy, but don't be afraid to scold him when he deserves it.

"Your husband's happiness, your children's happiness, the good name of the family—all this should come before your personal comfort.

"I thank you for all you've done for me, and for giving me your love and loyalty. I wish you all the best. May you prosper in every way, live in good health to a ripe old age, and attain all that your heart should desire."

She picked up a small box from the dressing table and handed it to Phloi. It contained a brooch in the form of roses made with diamonds and rubies, and a pair of bracelets also encrusted with the two gems.

"A souvenir from the palace. Or call it some compensation for all the boring lectures I've made you listen to. They go with your wedding clothes, so you can wear them today if you wish. And if you should fall on hard times you could always sell them. Nobody would have the right to criticize you, for they are your own property and you can do whatever you want with them."

With her eyes full of tears Phloi made a *krap* at Sadet's feet.

"It's getting late," Sadet said. "You'd better go now, Phloi. Come back and see me any time you want to."

Going down the stairs, Phloi and Khun Sai overheard through the open door Sadet's voice calling the name of one of the maids-in-waiting, and then her complaint, "As usual, I call and nobody comes. Now that Nang Phloi's gone I'm never going to get any service in this place!"

"You see?" Khun Sai whispered, "she misses you already. She's going to be in a bad humour today and I'm glad I don't have to face her."

Choi and the other bridesmaids were already ready and waiting in Khun Sai's room. At Khun Sai's bidding, Phloi freshened up and tried to look more cheerful. Then off they went, out the gate of Sadet's residence, threading their way through the familiar narrow streets, turning this and that corner, passing familiar houses and gardens shimmering in the morning sun. They were the star attraction of the Inner Court this morning, and people came out to watch them go by, to greet them and shower the bride with best wishes. The bride was not responding very gaily to the cheering remarks. She was in a daze and could hardly see or hear them. Yet at the same time she was intensely aware that she was being taken away from them, these people, these voices, these houses and trees and stones, and she was filled with sorrow that it should be so. If she heard anything it was the voice of the whole place saying, "Don't go, Phloi. We'll never meet again as we do today. When you come back it will not be the same. It will never be the same again." How she longed to do the impossible—call off the trip, turn back and retrieve all that had ever been, but of course she kept going forward, plodding on, walking the path her karma had built for her.

"HOW pretty you look, daughter. How pretty you all look. Ah, I smell the lovely perfume! When there are Inner Court ladies present, the air becomes so fragrant." Thus Chao Khun Father complimented the girls. They had come out from under the arch of the Outer Gate. They paid their respects to him and exchanged greetings with Khun Choei, who was just as delectably turned out and delicately perfumed as any Inner Courtier. Chao Khun Father did not neglect to include Khun Sai in his eulogies. With his eyes twinkling he said, "You look like one of the girls this morning, my dear Khun."

And Khun Sai reciprocated with, "What about you, sir? Those guests at the wedding are going to mistake you for the bride's brother, you know."

Chao Khun had brought two carriages. Phloi rode beside her father, facing Khun Sai and Khun Choei on the opposite seat. She spoke very little during the rather long drive from the palace to Khlong Yom. She smiled at her three companions from time to time and replied to remarks addressed to her, but otherwise contributed nothing to their continuous and pleasant chatter. Most of the time she listened to them with only half an ear while gazing out the window at the passing scenes. She became somewhat more animated when at last the carriage turned into the drive of her new home and did observe to herself, in an objective way, that this was a large property, and the main house quite imposing with its wide marble staircase in front and a smaller one in the rear, with its colourful porcelain jars and blue-and-white pots standing round the front lawn and on the stairs. She saw many people walking about carrying things and looking busy, and noted, gladly, that there were plenty of tall shady trees in the compound. The carriage went past another building or two before coming to a stop in front of Khun Nui's two-storey wooden house where Phit, who had left the palace earlier, was standing at the foot of the stairs with a broad grin on her face, looking very much at home, very sure of herself.

Choi, descending from the second carriage, went up to Phit and said, "Excuse me, am I speaking to the lady of the house?"

Phit let out her famous guffaw. "Oh, oh, Khun Choi! Don't get me into trouble today, of all days!"

Upstairs Khun Nui gave them a warm welcome, calling out for tea and betel to be served and talking non-stop to Chao Khun and the others. She presented Phloi to her sister Khun Nian, who was frail and pale, and full of gentleness and charm. Phloi felt drawn to her, as Khun Nui had predicted she would.

Khun Sai would allow only a short rest from the journey. It seemed they had barely sat down when she started making everybody get ready to go to the big house, "Hurry, hurry! We must get there before the monks start chanting!" The girls tittered—they had never seen her so excitable.

They went up to the first floor of the big house, using not the front but the back stairs to make a suitably discreet entrance. The monks and some of the relatives and guests were in the central room with all its doors opening onto the front and the back verandas. Chao Khun Father was ushered in there, while Khun Sai and the girls, in accordance with the programme, settled in a smaller room adjoining it, also with the doors open.

When the chanting began, Phloi's thoughts flew back across the years to her tonsure ceremony. Phi Nuang's boyish face took shape in her mind, blotting out everything else. It was smiling at her, an encouraging smile, giving her the needed sense of belonging in a room full of strangers. With an effort she chased away Phi Nuang and that event of long ago from her remembrance and concentrated on the present moment. The rhythm of the chant had a calming effect and she felt thankful for the comforting nearness—of however brief duration it might be—of Choi, Khun Sai, Khun Choei and her other bridesmaids from the palace. Now the monks, having finished the Mangala Sutta, were going on to the Ratana Sutta and the Bojjhanga Paritta; Phloi listened to every word of them though she did not understand all the meaning, and became so absorbed that she lost all sense of time. When the chanting came to an end she was a little taken by surprise and only made her triple *krap* on the floor when she saw her companions were doing it.

A hum of conversation rose in the rooms and on the verandas in place of the chanting. Some of the guests were moving about and the servants were carrying more food trays from the kitchen below.

Khun Sai went to a door, spoke in a low voice to some people outside, then returned to instruct Phloi, "You may go out now, my dear. To present food to the monks."

Phloi's composure suddenly melted away leaving her hands and feet frozen. Everyone else was getting ready to leave but she herself seemed to have become paralysed. Khun Choei was whispering gently to her, "Don't be shy, Mae Phloi. We're all coming with you."

While Phloi was still summoning up her courage, Choi said, "Let's go, Phloi. It's the monks' last meal, you know, and they are not allowed much time over it. Or do you want to commit a sin by making them starve?"

With Khun Sai at the head of the group and Phloi surrounded by her bridesmaids, they proceeded to the front veranda on their hands and knees, weaving their way past the guests in the central room in a prim mannerly way demanded by the occasion, looking neither to the right nor left but keeping their eyes on the space directly before them, and seeming to be oblivious of the complimentary remarks about themselves made by admiring guests in voices varying from the clearly audible to the discreetly murmuring.

Khun Prem was waiting for the bride on the front veranda. Close to where he sat was a large silver bowl of steaming rice with a matching serving spoon resting in it, and there were ten monks' bowls standing in a row in front of him, one a votive offering to the Lord Buddha and the rest for the chanting monks.

A whispered last-minute advice from Choi: "Keep calm, Phloi, and make sure you get to hold the upper part of the spoon so that he'll never be able to bully you."

Prompted by Khun Sai, Phloi went to sit beside the groom, but took care not to get too close to him. Without glancing at her, Khun Prem moved a little nearer her, and automatically Phloi inched away from him, whereupon the groom made another slight movement which brought him closer to her still. Now he reached for the spoon. Phloi could hear the sound of his breathing and saw that his hand now holding the spoon was shaking, not conspicuously but definitely shaking. Mentally gritting her teeth she put out her hand, and as she did so Khun Prem slid down his own to the lower part of the handle. Whether he had overheard Choi and therefore was ashamed to show himself as a would-be bully it was difficult to say. Perhaps—and this was how Choi interpreted it afterwards—he wished to let Phloi know that she could bully him any time and he wouldn't mind it one little bit.

Phloi did not actually hold the handle but only touched it lightly, not to say gingerly, letting her fingers travel with it as it was maneuvered by Khun Prem from the silver rice bowl to the monk's bowl, scooping rice from the one and transferring it to the other, back and forth, again and again, until all the ten black metal bowls had been served. Such a long drawn-out operation, or so it seemed, but at last it was over and

Phloi was free to retire to the room where she had been sitting before. Once they had all got back safely inside this temporary refuge, Choi heaved a long heart-felt sigh.

"Oh it feels good to be back in here! I was shaking like a leaf out there. And it's not even my own wedding."

"Same here!" Khun Choei joined in fervently. "When I saw all those people I nearly turned back. Did anyone bring smelling salts? I need something to revive me."

Everyone—even Khun Sai—admitted how nervous they had been. But now they reverted to enjoying themselves, chatting and giggling (except Phloi, who was dreading other ordeals to come), not too loud of course, mindful of the monks at their meal and of the other guests scattered about in the central room.

Suddenly Choi cried out, "Look, Phloi! Look who's here!"

Phloi's heart leapt up at the sight of the newcomer, who greeted her with great effusion.

"My darling Mae Phloi! I'm so happy today! I can't tell you how happy I am!" The newcomer was none other than Choi's mother Mae Chan. She came in full regalia befitting the occasion. She looked happy and excited. The silk sash over her frilly blouse kept slipping from her shoulder and she had to swish it back every other minute, which did not seem to bother her at all.

Nor did she bother to defend herself when Khun Sai demanded, rather sternly, "Where have you been all this time?" but with a broad guiltless smile explained away her lateness: "It took me such a long time to get ready. It's not every day that I put on these fine clothes, stockings and all. Believe me, I was very careful to get everything right."

Choi laughed. "Is that why your sash keeps falling down, Mother? I must fix it when we get back to Khun Aunt Nui's. But don't get tangled in it now."

"It is rather a mess," Mae Chan conceded. "I don't understand it. I looked all right when I left the house." Returning to Phloi she said, "I'm very happy, Mae Phloi. It is as though my own daughter were getting married. But then if this were Choi's wedding, she would be jumping about like a monkey and making me feel embarrassed."

"That's not fair, Mother." Choi protested. "Give me a chance and I'll surprise you yet. Matter of fact, I've been watching Mae Phloi closely so that when the time comes I, too, can be a perfect bride. By the way, has anyone turned up to ask for my hand?"

Mae Chan gave a hearty laugh, but Khun Sai found it quite unfunny.

"That's enough, Choi! Save your antics for some other time and place."

"I'm so happy," Mae Chan said again for the third time. "And to think that Chao Khun himself came to invite us to be the bed-makers at this wedding. Such an honour! At first Khun Luang was very reluctant, you know, because he felt we were not grand enough. And we aren't! But Chao Khun insisted. He says rank has nothing to do with happiness. He wants us to do it because we are a happy couple, he says, and this would make it propitious for the bride and groom."

"And be sure you do it well," Khun Sai warned.

"Trust me, Mae Sai," said her sister-in-law emphatically.

Phloi kept silent while feeling immensely cheered by all this: by Mae Chan being so pleased about the marriage, by Chao Khun Father personally asking Mae Chan and Khun Luang to play an important role in the wedding and by their acceptance to do it. For she loved these two very good and kind elders and wished to remain close to them always.

The sound of chanting rose up again in the central room. The monks had finished their meal and were now blessing the congregation. When this was over the morning ceremony came to an end, and Phloi was escorted down the back stairs to return to Khun Nui's house, to have lunch and to rest before the water-pouring in the afternoon.

At the start of lunch, Chao Khun Father made some explanatory remarks in self-defence about the wedding arrangements. ". . . We could have done it at our house—perhaps it would have been more convenient. But not for the guests, though. They would have had to come by boat . . ."

Khun Choei and Phloi exchanged a glance that lasted but an instant, while Khun Nui said brightly and sincerely, "Oh but it is so convenient to marry them here, sir. I've told everybody at the big house not to come near here today because this is the bride's house. Please do treat it as your own, sir."

Nothing more was said on the subject, and very little about the water-pouring which was to begin in a few hours from now, except that it was bound to be a lengthy affair with so many relatives coming to give their blessings; and that the bride and groom would certainly get all stiff from having to sit in the same crouching position through the whole ceremony. That was all they said about the water-pouring. The rest of the time they just chatted pleasantly about this and that, nothing consequential, enjoying the food and the companionship, all except Phloi, who had grown nervous again and had no appetite for either food or conversation.

Later on, in the commodious room set aside by Khun Nui for the use of the bride and her retinue, while the girls were trying unsuccessfully to make Phloi feel easy and relaxed, Mae Chan came in to say that she and Khun Luang would be going home now, but would return before long for the water ceremony and stay on until the auspicious hour to make the bridal bed. Before leaving she said to Phloi, "Remember this. When the last guest has poured water and the ceremony's over, take care you're the first one to remove the Mongkol crown from your head and the first to step down from the bench. Be sure you do it before he does. That way he'll be afraid of you forever. So don't forget. Remind her, Choi," she added, and went.

"I don't believe it," Choi said. "And even if it were true, the question remains whether you ought to want your husband to be afraid of you or not. Do you, Phloi?"

"I don't know," Phloi replied. "I haven't thought about it."

"Then start thinking," Khun Choei suggested. "Time is running out. You're already half married."

"I don't feel up to thinking about anything," Phloi confessed.

Choi nodded understandingly. "I don't blame you. To find oneself a bride is enough to upset anybody. But to get back to this question of who is going to be afraid of whom. I don't see why it is necessary that the husband has to be afraid of the wife or the other way round. Can't they just live together without the one fearing the other?"

"I agree with you, Choi," said Khun Choei. "Some wives are so cowed by their husbands that they become like slaves. I don't like that at all. On the other hand, hen-pecked husbands are worse. They've turned themselves into most peculiar creatures!"

"If I had a husband," Choi went on, "I think I'd like to fear him a little. But the chances are he'd be frightened of me before I could do anything about it."

"Too true," Khun Sai joined in, chuckling. "It would be frightening having you as a wife."

"I'm going to shut up," Choi announced to the room at large. "I hate it when people take my flippant remarks seriously. Don't they know I'm going to be a spinster anyway?"

Khun Choei laughed. "You and me both. Never mind, Choi. We'll make ourselves useful by helping Mae Phloi take care of her children."

Phloi blushed, to be sure, but after a while found herself thinking about it with joy: to have one's own children to love and care for, to play with them, and watch them grow up day by day . . . She thought of Mother. She remembered her sense of wonder when as a little girl she learned from Mother how she had begun life inside her stomach, sired by Chao Khun Father. Mother had always been more straightforward than most grownups on the facts of life. And then about her birth. "It hurt more than I can tell you," Mother had said. "Then you came, and it was as if the pain had never been. Nothing remained but joy, the greatest I had ever known, when I looked at you."

If marriage consisted only of having children there would be no problem at all, Phloi thought. It was this role of a wife that filled her with anxiety. To go through life with this man who was a virtual stranger to her—how long would it take her to get to know him? To love and cherish and revere him? But what if he should turn out unworthy of love and reverence . . .

That question belonged to tomorrow, to the months and years to come. The thing to consider now was the immediate present. It was time to start getting ready again. Time to dress for the water-pouring. Put on the pendant her father had given her when she had had her topknot cut. The bridesmaids said it was too old-fashioned, but she loved it and Khun Sai was all for it.

Then it was time to leave for the big house again. Another walk among the trees, up the marble stairs, the sound of rustling silk accompanying them everywhere, past the central room full of murmuring guests through one of the open doors into another room.

The ceremonial bench stood gleaming in the middle of the room.

Phloi took up her place on one side of it, got into position, legs tucked under, arms forward, head bowed, hands joined in a respectful gesture, and smiled a wan smile at Choi, who had put herself close to the bench and was offering up some whispered words of encouragement.

She did not turn when Khun Prem came up to occupy the space by her side.

Chao Khun Father entered escorting His Highness the Prince, who proceeded to place the twin Mongkol crowns round the heads of the bride and groom, uniting them, and then to anoint their brows, after which he poured drops of water from the conch shell on their heads while giving his blessing and wishing them happiness and prosperity in their conjugal life.

He left, and the other guests started to file in one by one. Phloi was too bashful to look at them. She saw their hands and the conch shell, heard their voices, and felt the water on her hands and on her head—mostly on her head since the majority of the guests were rich in years and held in high regard by both families.

Choi's continuous whispering, delivered rapidly during the short intervals between comings and goings, kept her informed on what the guests looked like and what they wore—"Pity I don't know their names!"

She did not feel any ache or stiffness from all this sitting. The strain concentrated in her mind, leaving her arms and legs unaffected.

Time passed. The last guest had come and gone. Phloi hesitated, not quite sure of what to do next. Khun Prem remained quietly by her side. At last, Phloi took off the crown. Khun Prem followed suit. He waited, and did not get down from the bench until she had done so. His best men were tittering, very much amused by it all.

Phloi had another change of costumes after the water ceremony.

The spirits of Khun Prem's ancestors were enshrined in another one of the numerous rooms in the upper floor of the big house. Phloi was taken there to make offerings and to pay her respects to it.

The afternoon wore on, it was getting late and the sun would soon be setting—time for Choi and the other Inner Court girls to take leave of the bride and return to the palace before the closing of the Inner Gate. They were all on the brink of tears, Phloi in particular.

"We'll see you in a few days, Phloi," Choi spoke quickly and, not trusting herself to say any more without getting emotional, fled.

Khun Choei and Mae Chan kept Phloi company until evening came. At about nine o'clock Mae Chan went, saying it was getting near the auspicious time for the bed-making ceremony. Then about ten minutes to eleven Chao Khun Father and Khun Sai took Phloi to the big house to present her to Khun Prem.

Phloi would not be able to tell you afterwards how she ever got there, or what that night walk was like from Khun Nui's bungalow to the big house. All she would be able to recollect afterwards was the sound of *piphat* music coming faintly from somewhere, and the impression she had that most of the guests had gone home.

KHUN Prem was seated on the floor in front of the Chinese-style bed. He lowered his head, making a *krap* salutation to Chao Khun Father and Khun Sai on seeing them enter the room. The two elders and Phloi sat down and Chao Khun told Phloi to pay her respects to Khun Prem. When she had done this, he began to give the pair his blessing and counsel. He spoke in a low voice, but even if he had spoken louder Phloi would not have been able to distinguish the words, since at that point she could hear nothing clearly for the whirring in her own ears. After Chao Khun had concluded his talk it was Khun Sai's turn to give hers. She, too, spoke softly, but more briefly than Chao Khun. Then they both got up and left the room, shutting the door behind them.

Khun Prem and Phloi were thus left alone for the first time. Khun Prem had not glanced at Phloi once while the two elders had been blessing them, but had sat with his hands deferentially clasped apparently paying full attention to their words. Now he turned to her and saw that she was looking down at the carpet. Moments passed in total silence. Then he moved closer to her, and addressed her directly for the first time. What he said was most astounding. It was the last thing Phloi expected. He said, "Mae Phloi my dear, have you ever been to the Shrine of the Buddha Footprint?"

FIFTEEN

DURING the first week of her married life Phloi went out only once, and that was to accompany Khun Prem across the river to the house in Khlong Bang Luang, where together as man and wife they lit candles and incense sticks to the remains of Phloi's ancestors and paid respects to Chao Khun Father, whose gifts for the occasion included a pocket watch for Khun Prem and a ring for Phloi. (As Khun Eldest Sister, Khun Un was also present to receive the newlyweds' respects and make the customary presentation of a gift in return. Commanded to do this by her father against her will, she wore her surly look for the occasion and handed Phloi an ordinary little ring, a thin gold band decorated with some chip diamonds.)

Except for that trip Phloi stayed quietly at home with Khun Prem, and at some point during the week came to be aware of the way she felt about him. She would not call it love; it struck her as being not at all similar to that love which she had once experienced. She pondered on it, made some attempts at definition, and finally described it to herself somewhat as follows: *I feel myself as belonging to him. This is something absolute and unarguable. I belong to him completely and absolutely. I take him as my owner, as centre and mainstay of my life, forever, unless and until he himself should wish to cease being so.* Some women may prefer to stay free of such a tie, but Phloi happened to be that feminine type who finds assurance in it, and happiness in that assurance.

The second week saw our newlyweds go out almost every day on their respect-paying mission, there being so many esteemed elders on both sides. But Phloi went alone, of course, to Sadet's residence, Khun Prem being an adult male and therefore not allowed in the

Inner Court. Sadet's present for Khun Prem was a set of buttons engraved with her monogram. To Phloi she gave another sum of money—twenty *chang*.

She said, "I know you've got yourself a rich husband, but there's no harm in having your own money to start some business if you want to. This is honest money, honestly acquired, not embezzled or taken by force. You should prosper on it."

She asked Phloi what the new household was like and Phloi tried to tell her as much as she could, which turned out to be not a great deal since after all she herself was still a virtual stranger to Khlong Yom.

After taking leave of Sadet, Phloi went downstairs to pay homage to Khun Sai, who in turn gave her a bracelet, the value of which was assessed by Choi (behind her aunt's back) to be far below that of a memento presented to Khun Sai by the groom's family, in appreciation of her assistance in the wedding ceremonies.

Phloi's old friends came crowding into Khun Sai's apartment clamouring to hear her views on the matrimonial state. Choi put forward some blunt questions; Phloi got redder in the face, the girls sent up peals of laughter, and a merry time was had by one and all. But Phloi did not stay very long with them that time. She cut short her visit and hurried home, afraid that otherwise Khun Prem might get the wrong idea that she was still yearning for the palace and preferring to be there rather than home.

Home. Before now the word had meant Khlong Bang Luang. Now home was here, but it still seemed new and strange and incredible. She had never set foot in this place until not so many days ago, and now it had become her home!

One day when they had not been married for very long, Khun Prem handed her a rather enormous bunch of keys. Phloi's immediate reaction was entirely negative. She withdrew herself, shaking her head and said, "Don't give them to me! You keep them. I don't know . . ."

But Khun Prem interrupted her with a good-natured laugh. "I've been stuck with these keys since mother died and now I can turn them over to you—what a relief!"

"Everything in this house belongs to you," he went on quickly, before Phloi could put up any more arguments, "so who else should hold the keys if not you? When we have time we'll go over them together and I'll tell you where things are. All right?"

Keys were a minor problem compared with people. People lowering themselves to the ground at her approach had Phloi turning round looking for the person for whom the gesture was meant before realizing that it was herself. She would have to get accustomed to this deferential demeanour they assumed in her presence, learn to take it in her stride. And there were so many of them, such a bewildering confusion of new names and faces she'd have to sort out. Khun Nui had introduced a few of them to her—servants who worked in the big house and in the bungalow, but Phloi chose not to tell them directly what to do and to issue her few instructions through her maid Phit. Until one day that worthy person chose to do something about it. She put her foot down in her own well-meaning affectionate and peremptory way.

"You're a big girl now, Khun Phloi, and the lady of the house to boot. Why don't you give orders to these people yourself? If I keep on doing it they're going to get mad at me, you know. Might gang up on me and slap me to death or something. What do you have to say to that, my darling Khun?"

Phloi saw her point, and she began to behave more con-scientiously, more in keeping with her duties and responsibilities as mistress of a large household. For a start she set out to get better acquainted with its members. This would take some time since there were more than fifty of them, and since some of them were somewhat of a mystery even to Khun Prem. He could not tell her their names off-hand or how they came to live here. Some he knew vaguely as being related in some ways to the servants of his late grandfather, whose portrait in pigtail and Chinese costume was prominently hung in the central room. Once she had got over her shyness she found it on the whole enjoyable enough, or at least not as difficult as she had imagined.

She had no trouble at all getting acquainted with Thiap, the chief cook, whom everyone—including now herself—called Grandma Thiap. They were fast becoming good friends and each had a professional admiration for the other's culinary skills. When at work in her kitchen, Grandma Thiap wore an old faded *phalai* with nothing on top; when going off to consult Phloi in the big house she took along a bodice cloth, which she would fling around her torso any which way when reaching the foot of the stairs. She talked to Phloi in her faultlessly polite language, quite distinct from her colourful kitchen vernacular. When Phloi came to see her in her domain she showed her how to choose vegetables and fruit, told her what markets to go to for the best bargain in various items and advised her as to the prices of things from rice to shrimp paste and fish sauce.

Once she said to Phloi, "Beware of cooks, my respected Khun. They'll cheat you right and left if you don't watch out."

When Phloi laughed at this injunction coming from the horse's mouth, Grandma Thiap said without undue modesty, "I'm different of course. I don't indulge in that sort of thing—and I've been serving here since I was a chit of a girl. When I die you'll have trouble finding somebody like me, Khun Phloi."

Grandma Thiap and Phit took to each other like ducks take to water. "She's a trustworthy soul," Phit said of the other to Phloi. Like most good cooks—and Grandma Thiap recognized Phit as a member of this distinguished company—they loved to eat, and like many serious eaters they enjoyed drinking. Much to Grandma Thiap's delight, Phit also loved to sing, especially after a certain amount of imbibing. Theirs was a happy-making alliance, no doubt about it, even if it was a little on the noisy side.

Phloi went to see Grandma Thiap in the kitchen nearly every day, and sometimes made a dish or two in collaboration with her. Also nearly every day she paid a visit to Khun Nui and Khun Nian, to help look after the latter, to seek advice, or just for a little chat to pass the time of day.

There was another bungalow not far from that of the two aunts, a small one set not in the direct path but some way back from it, tucked away and partly hidden among the trees. Phloi had asked Phit, who seemed to know everything, whether she knew anything about this house, but this time Phit had no answer for her. She had meant to mention it to Khun Nui but kept forgetting, there being so many other things to talk about and because the house did not always attract her attention. It was usually very quiet, unlike most dwellings in the compound. Once Phloi glimpsed an old woman sweeping the steps but she had an errand that day and did not go up to speak to her. Another time she thought she heard a child's voice but was not sure.

One afternoon, while chatting with Khun Nui and Khun Nian, she did remember and inquired about it.

"By the way, Khun Aunt, who lives in that house?"

"Which house?" said Khun Nui.

Phloi told her, pointing in its direction. As a matter of fact they could pick out part of its roof from where they were sitting.

"Oh," Khun Nui said, and after a pause began, in her fashion, to pose some questions of her own.

"Such a big place this is, isn't it, Mae Phloi? So many people scattered about—confusing, yes? Takes a long time to know them all, don't you think?"

After a glance at her sister, the ailing Khun Nian remarked to Phloi with a charming smile, "I haven't wandered from my bedroom for ages. I'm not sure any more who lives in which house. But Pho Prem can tell you. He has to keep track of them."

During the following days Phloi could have gone up to the little bungalow and investigated for herself, but something—its nice quiet air perhaps—made her feel reluctant. It seemed to want to be left alone undisturbed, and so she let it be.

She could have asked Khun Prem, but the opportunity did not present itself. For he was sometimes away in the palace on duty, and when he came home they tended to lapse into the sweet-talk of young newlyweds, fooling and flirting with each other, the kind of exchange in which practical domestic queries would have been out of place.

Then there was her disinclination to pry or impose herself on others, and her fear of having her motive misunderstood by Khun Prem. She did not want him to think that she was over-anxious to unearth everything concerning this household in the shortest possible time when in fact she quite realized that, after all was said and done, she was but a newcomer who must tread always with tact and caution.

THAT afternoon Khun Prem was off duty. After a leisurely meal he asked Phloi for some betel nuts and she put the tray in front of him.

"I'm becoming a betel-chewing addict thanks to you," he said.

"Why is that?" Phloi asked.

"You make everything look so inviting, that's why. These betel leaves—most exquisite the way you roll them, and the carved nuts are a work of art. I can go on and on and if I were a poet I'd compose a *sakkrawa* in their praise. And it's not the appearance alone, but the flavour—the perfectly blended, subtle, gentle-on-the-tongue flavour! They're not like anything I've ever tasted before."

"And you must have tasted plenty before."

"Oh, enough to deter me from wanting to make a habit of it. I've had betels that are tasteless and dull, and those so tart they nearly burn your mouth. Now I have yours and they are heavenly. Don't be surprised if I become an addict for life."

Phloi smiled and looked away.

"How lovely you are, Mae Phloi—and growing more lovely every day. Your relatives are all attractive girls but none can begin to compete with you. They say your mother was a beauty, but Aunt Nui tells me she's plain compared with you."

"Oh, no!" Phloi cried. "She was the most beautiful woman I've ever known, and not only beautiful but full of life and charm and character."

"You loved her very much, didn't you?"

"More than anything in the world. I feel as close to her now as though she were still alive. I dream of her often, and sometimes I have this feeling that she hasn't really gone away—that she's somewhere near, watching over me . . ." She paused, wiping a tear but also laughing a little. "She would have been so pleased with you—a typical royal page with a sugary tongue to say all the flattering things to her and make her happy. She would have adored you and spoiled you, Khun Prem."

"She must have been a darling. If she were alive she would know that I, too, love her."

Phloi thanked him with a smile.

Khun Prem went on. "What about me, Mae Phloi? I've never asked you this before—how much do you love me?"

Phloi fell into silence. A simple answer of "very much" might have satisfied Khun Prem, but not herself. Finally she said, "You are so good to me. I have never in my whole life received so much kindness and consideration as I do from you. We live together and it's natural that we love each other. But over and above this I feel infinitely grateful to you. I'm in your debt. I owe you everything."

"No, No!" Khun Prem warmly protested, looking upset. "It's not true. You owe me nothing. It's the other way round. You could have found a husband a thousand times better than this one. If there should be any debt at all, then it is I who owe it. I'll make it up to you, Mae Phloi. I'll try in every way to make myself worthy of you."

Phloi felt a twist in her heart at these words. They reminded her too much of Phi Nuang, of so many things he had said and how she had believed in them and woven a whole dream future out of them. They would have started from nothing—she and Phi Nuang—and gone on, hand-in-hand, struggling, growing, building together. She had looked forward to enduring hardship and overcoming obstacles. She had never doubted that they would succeed, have all their wishes fulfilled, with everlasting love to give them courage and strengthen them at every turn. A romantic dream which had gone the way of most romantic dreams, vanished into thin air leaving not a trace. In the real here and now there was no hardship to speak of. She gazed at the pink-gold betel tray, thinking how in that vanished dream she and Phi Nuang would have had to save and scrimp and make sacrifices in order to acquire such a tray. It would have become a special tray, a cherished and meaningful object. She wished she could find some meaning to put on the tray she was looking at now. A pretty thing. It had been brought out from a cabinet where it had been residing with several others. More modest looking than its companions, it had for that reason been singled out as suitable for the wear-and-tear of everyday use . . .

"May I ask you something, Mae Phloi?" Khun Prem's gentle voice interrupted her musings. "Don't answer if you think I'm being too nosey. Did you love anyone before?" It was as though he had been following the trend of her thought.

Phloi hesitated. She didn't want to lie to him, but on the other hand she could not see what good it would do to bring up the subject.

She was still debating with herself when Khun Prem said quietly, "Forget I ever asked, Mae Phloi, because it makes no difference at all. Whether you did or not can never make me feel any different about you. I'll just go on loving you, that's all."

Phloi was deeply moved, and hastened to tell him what she really felt. "You are the only one for me, Khun Prem. No one can ever take your place in my heart."

He thanked her solemnly, paused, then went on, "And would you think less of me on account of things I might have done in the past? Bad things perhaps. Would you be very angry with me—would you even hate me, I wonder—if you should find out?"

They could have been hypothetical questions, though he sounded rather serious, Phloi thought. At any rate she felt she could reassure him, and did so without hesitation.

"How could I be angry with you over what you did or might have done before we met?—and we never really met until the day we got married. You can tell me about it if you wish, but if you don't, that's all right too. If it's over and done with, we won't worry any more about it, but if it's carried over into the present and has to be faced, then we'll face it together."

"You are so good, Mae Phloi."

Phloi laughed.

"Why are you laughing at me?" Khun Prem demanded. "Am I not allowed to admire my own wife?"

"I'm not laughing at you," Phloi said with another chuckle. "You reminded me of Choi when you said that, and sometimes when I think of Choi I can't help laughing out loud. Life is amusing to Choi, and when you're with her, it often is."

Khun Prem was not interested in Choi at the moment. He moved closer to Phloi, took her hand into his and said, "Are you sure you wouldn't be angry?"

Phloi reassured him once again. He gave her hand a gentle squeeze. When he spoke again it was on some other subject and in a playful tone of voice.

"Tell me, Mae Phloi, have you cast a spell on the people in this house? They all adore you and I'm very jealous."

Phloi laughed again. "I wish I had a spell to cast, especially on Grandma Thiap."

Khun Prem chuckled. "She's quite a character, isn't she?"

"Oh, she's wonderful! She's straight and honest and full of fun. And she's teaching me everything, you know. Without her you wouldn't be eating so well. I do like her very much."

"So do I . . . . You know what?" Khun Prem was grinning broadly. "Rumours had it that she was my father's minor wife."

"No!" Phloi exclaimed.

"It's not impossible or improbable." Khun Prem laughed. "In a household like this it often happens. Grandma Thiap was young once—though it is difficult to imagine."

"Did you ever ask her about it?"

"Yes, and, my-oh-my, how she scolded me for asking. She said I was bringing the lice of ill luck onto her head for suspecting that she wanted to rise above her station—she who was His Excellency's servant, who wanted nothing but to serve him loyally. She got quite worked up about it so I didn't pursue the matter."

"But all the same, she didn't really answer your question, did she?"

"No, she left me guessing. But one thing I must say for her. If she had ever been his mistress she never tried to exploit the situation. She has always been content to remain a cook—to rule over her kitchen and give us delicious things to eat. And they are delicious!"

He rose to his feet, pulling Phloi up with him, and suggested that they should go for a stroll round the garden and perhaps call in on the two Khun Aunts at their bungalow.

The sunlight was mild and pleasant at this hour in the afternoon and the soft breeze carried with it the fragrance from the *lamduan* trees. Around the trees several little girls were playing together and some were collecting the flowers which had fallen to the ground.

Khun Prem went up to ask them what they were going to do with the flowers and was told that these would be taken to "Khun in the Big House" for her to make into garlands. Some of the girls turned to glance at Phloi, their tanned faces creased in smiles. Phloi smiled back while reminding herself that she must tell Choi on her next visit to the palace that she had become the "Khun in the Big House"—quite a grand person, rather like the "Khun in the Gold Room" and the other Khuns of This or That Establishment in the palace! Choi would be sure to burst out laughing and come out with some wry funny remarks putting the epithet in its rightful place.

Leaving the little girls and the *lamduan* trees, they went on to look at the potted topiary plants. Like Phloi's Chao Khun Father, Khun Prem was very fond of his plants and enjoyed trimming and shaping them himself.

After this they walked along the path leading to Khun Nui's bungalow.

Then Phloi remembered, and she said, "Who's living in that house?"

"Which house?" Khun Prem asked, and when Phloi told him, he said casually, "Oh, there's a little boy living there who's quite sweet. Let's go and see him, shall we?"

They went strolling on. Upon reaching the spot they turned off the path and made their way among the trees to the house, which stood in a clearing surrounded by a low fence.

They climbed the steps to the balcony and, call it instinct or the result of past karma or what you will, when she saw the boy Phloi's heart went out to him immediately. He was grinning and waving his arms about, and jumping up and down in the arms of an old woman, who was trying to make him keep still.

"Let him come, Grandma Jaem," said Khun Prem to the old woman.

The boy came toddling up—he could not be many months past his first year. Having achieved a few paces he stopped and swayed on his chubby legs. Khun Prem called out to encourage him.

"You can do better than that, On! Come here, On, come!"

The boy came, but not to Khun Prem. He made straight at Phloi, and fell gurgling into her quick receiving arms. They laughed together,

On and Phloi, so delighted they were in each other's company.

Grandma Jaem, all smiles and shaking her head incredulously, exclaimed, "Why, he's treating her like an old friend!"

Khun Prem nodded in agreement, then told Jaem she could go off on errands of her own and leave him and Khun Phloi to look after her charge for a while. When the old woman had gone, and with On comfortably enthroned in her lap, Phloi looked Khun Prem in the eye as she asked him the inevitable question, "Whose son is he, Khun Prem?"

Khun Prem's answer came in a low quavering voice. "He's my son, Mae Phloi."

Obviously he was apprehensive of her reaction. But he need not have been, because Phloi had already anticipated the answer before posing the question. She had had her vague suspicions before, brought about by the evasive replies of Khun Aunts Nui and Nian when she had referred to this house, and later by Phit's unbelievable protestations of ignorance about its inhabitants. Then Khun Prem's awkward harking back to his "past" a short while ago had made her wonder again. The truth had struck her in all its plainness as she was walking up the stairs just now, causing her heart to sink not a little, and during the space of a few seconds many anxious thoughts had flashed through her mind, mainly on how best to adjust to the situation so that no friction would arise between Khun Prem and herself. The sight of On had rendered those thoughts quite unnecessary, wiped them out completely as a matter of fact. A most appealing, heart-warming creature if there ever was one, and when he suddenly dropped into her arms and gave her a laugh for a laugh she knew there would be no problems as far as she was concerned. She felt immensely relieved, then joyful. Why, they were fated for each other—she couldn't put it any other way to herself. She would love him like a son. Not out of a sense of duty, or a desire to do the right thing or to perform a meritorious act—no, nothing of the sort. She would love him—she was loving him—like a son, because—well, because that was the way she felt, because that was the way it was meant to be—

On was making some noises, carrying on a conversation in his fashion. It made her laugh again, and then she said to Khun Prem, "Why didn't you tell me before?"

"Oh Mae Phloi, I—I was so afraid you might be angry . . . Are you?" For although there was nothing remotely resembling anger in Phloi's demeanour, he just could not be sure.

"Angry? Why should I be? Because you have a son? He's your son, and that makes him my son too. Did you think I was going to hate him or what?" She turned On round, planted a kiss on his cheek, and whispered to him, "Dear little one, nobody in the world can ever hate you."

A few more questions and answers and at last Khun Prem was convinced that his erstwhile little secret not only failed to give rise to any bad feelings but was on the contrary enjoying a most enthusiastic reception. Breathing a sigh of contentment, he said he could sleep peacefully from now on.

Phloi had another question. She wished she hadn't, but there was no avoiding it.

"Don't think I'm just being inquisitive," she began. "But On's mother—who is she and where . . ."

"Don't bother about her," Khun Prem quickly interrupted. "She's gone. No, no, I didn't throw her out. She left of her own free will a few months before you and I were married. She wanted to go and live with her new husband, so I gave her some money and my blessing. She said I could have On and that she had no intention of ever coming back to claim him or interfere with his upbringing in any way."

"What are you going to do with him now?" Phloi asked, sounding already like a worried mother.

"With On? Well, now that you know, and don't mind, we'll go on as before. He's no trouble, as you can see. He's comfortable here, and old Jaem is a good enough nurse, don't you think?"

He was smiling. Everything appeared rosy to him, and he was unaware that his casual words rather took the joy out of his wife's mood.

To go on as before, Phloi reflected, *to grow up in this half-hidden bungalow while your father lives in the big house, to be treated as the son of minor wife . . .*

Oh no! Phloi moaned inwardly, conjuring up painful images from her own past. *A thousand times no!* Whatever rights she was entitled to in this house she would use them to protect On's childhood from that treatment—anybody's childhood for that matter.

"Please, Khun Prem," she said, "may I ask you a favour?"

"Ask me anything, Mae Phloi. You can have anything your heart desires. I only wish I could also give you the moon and the stars." He continued to speak airily, in the manner of one without a care in the world.

"Will you give On to me?" Phloi said simply. "Let him be my own son, let him live with me, his mother. Grandma Jaem will go on as his nurse, and they can move from here into our house . . ."

"Wait." Khun Prem held up a hand to slow her down, his eyes twinkling. "You would like to have On for your own son? But I hope not the *only* son."

Phloi's cheeks reddened, but she pressed on determinedly. "Do I have your consent?"

"My dear Mae Phloi," Khun Prem said in a changed voice. "I'm not sure if it's wise. On is my son and I love him, but I don't want to have him become a burden to you. You see, you know nothing of his mother's character. If he should turn out to be anything like her, you would have a lot of headaches, believe me."

"There is also the possibility that he may turn out to be like you," Phloi retorted smilingly. "You know I'm not a gambler at cards or lotteries, but I'm going to bet on On's upright and spotless character." She picked up the child, dandling him and saying, "Show your father what a good boy you are, On."

On laughed again in response, and Khun Prem said, "You're an angel, Mae Phloi."

Phloi shook her head. "No, I'm not. Apart from On being so irresistible I may be doing this more for my own peace of mind than anything else. Oh, Khun Prem, if you knew what it was like at our house in Khlong Bang Luang. I'll tell you about it some other time; it's a long story."

On's removal from the small bungalow to the big house was accomplished that day, and from then on Phloi took care of him personally, with Grandma Jaem's willing and able assistance, and On came to be looked upon as the first son of the house by one and all. "What a lucky boy!" they all said. "How lucky I am!" said Phloi to herself. She said it fervently. She regarded it as her great good fortune that On should have come into her life at this juncture. She felt she could not thank him enough. To start with, in pre-On days, although she had wanted to get to know Khun Prem in the shortest period possible and become not only wife but friend and companion to him, there had been times when she could not help feeling shy or reticent or over-anxious, as though he were still a stranger (which indeed he was, considering how recently their "acquaintanceship" had begun); but with On providing a common absorbing interest, a kind of camaraderie had sprung up between them so that Phloi now felt completely at ease with her own husband, and she considered this no small improvement in their relationship. At the same time the new responsibility of looking after On gave her a new sense of confidence and made her feel for the first time like a real *phuyai*—a mature person. Phit noticed this too, and she declared that Khun Phloi's *phuyai*-ness was so impressive that it made old Phit suspect herself of growing increasingly *dek*—childish, or even infantile, by contrast.

Two other On-induced happy consequences must be recorded. The first was that in adopting On, Phloi herself came to be adopted by Khun Prem's family. Not that they had not consistently shown her much kindness and goodwill from the very beginning. But she had nevertheless remained a relation by marriage, someone from "outside," whose true mettle they had not had enough time to observe and appraise. Not any more. They approved what she had done for On, liked her all the more for it and now considered her as one of their own without any reservation. Now Khun Aunt Nui never refrained from scolding her when Phloi deserved it—she would never do this to a mere niece by marriage for fear of having her good intentions taken the wrong way; and Khun Aunt Nian had abandoned the ceremony of getting out of her invalid's bed to receive Phloi but would hand her a pillow in case she, too, would like to lie down while chatting. The other happy consequence was Phloi being kept so busy she had no time to feel lost. For she had felt lost on countless occasions before On's advent, lost like a released cagebird who does not know what to do with its new-found freedom. She had longed for some boundaries, some restrictions, some Khun Sai to lay down a few rules, something to tie her down. Khun Prem had been no help at all in this respect: he always wanted to lavish on her more freedom, more leisure, more servants, more luxuries. But now she was tied down—looking after On was a full-time occupation, and she loved it!

"You're a strange woman, Mae Phloi!" Khun Prem said to her one day. "You can take it easy but you won't. Must you do all these things yourself for On? I envy him sometimes, you know."

"You shouldn't. He makes me love you more."

"That's all right, then."

"Besides, if it hadn't been for On I would get so impatient wait-ing, and you wouldn't like that."

"Waiting for what?"

"For the one who will be born!"

"Oh, Mae Phloi! When?"

"Oh—eight, nine months."

"Oh, Mae Phloi, my darling!"

He was overjoyed, and he wanted to know what sort of delicacies Phloi was hankering after in her new condition. Phloi asked for nothing but a few sour things such as a couple of unripe mangoes, and having said this proceeded to have her first bout of morning sickness straightaway.

SIXTEEN

"WELL!" Choi exclaimed. "Married yesterday and today you have a son who can walk!"

She gave On a hug (for On was extremely huggable) before asking, "Whose son is he anyway?"

And when Phloi told her, she cried out, "I knew it! I knew it! I always thought that husband of yours was too good to be true. And how like you to take it without any fuss whatsoever. So you just adopted him? Amazing!"

"More like he adopted me, Choi."

"Are you sure On is the only one?"

"I'm sure, Choi."

"How can you be sure? For all we know there may be half a dozen more hidden away somewhere—waiting to surface. You may find yourself having to build a large nursery, my dear."

"I may have to do that anyway, Choi. I'm going to have one myself. It's about a month now."

At this point Khun Sai appeared in the doorway, only to have Choi loudly yell at her. "Come in quickly, Khun Aunt! Something's happened!"

Khun Sai gasped." What—what's the matter?"

"Mae Phloi is pregnant, Khun Aunt!"

Khun Sai gave a weary sigh. "Is that all? You frightened me. I thought Phloi's house had burned down or some such calamity . . . Who's the darling boy?"

Phloi repeated the explanation she had already given Choi. Khun Sai blessed her lengthily and then the three of them chatted on until it was time for the morning audience with Sadet.

Phloi had more to tell her royal benefactress about Khlong Yom this time. It made her feel happy and proud to notice how interested Sadet was in her welfare and to hear her say how pleased she was that Phloi had come to see her. She was really in the best of humour this morning—until the subject of On was introduced. Then she flew into a temper and said that if she had known she would never have allowed the wedding to take place. She assumed that Khun Prem had forced On's mother to leave the house because he had wanted to marry Phloi.

Phloi tried to defend her husband. "Khun Prem tells me she left of her own accord, Your Highness. She wanted to go and live with her new husband, Your Highness."

"I don't believe it," said Sadet tersely. "He must have chucked her out," she went fuming on, "the poor girl. I am appalled! He could have kept her, that would have been the normal and kind-hearted thing to do. A man in his position can keep some minor wives. Nothing wrong with that. It's not as if Nang Phloi here would be jealous. I know you, Phloi. And be warned, Phloi! One of these days when he's had enough of you you'll find yourself in the same boat as that poor girl. Then I suppose you'll come running to dump your child here—like your mother. Heaven help me!"

Choi's eyes sought Phloi's, sending her a conspiratorial twinkle. But Phloi had a bland look on her face; she was cautioning herself not to say anything more that would further aggravate Sadet's temporary animosity (she knew it would not last) toward Khun Prem.

THAT was in the morning. In the afternoon—for she and On were spending the day in the Inner Court while Khun Prem was on duty in another part of the Grand Palace—Phloi found herself surrounded by the girls of her old crowd, all of whom were urging her to come with them to Bang Pa-in. The whole Inner Court had been talking about the trip to Bang Pa-in for weeks. They were all going, and Phloi must join them, they insisted.

Bang Pa-in had been chosen by His Majesty as the place to hold the cremation services for his beloved daughter Krom Khun Suphan.

"His greatly beloved daughter," one of the girls said reverently. "When she died he said death had robbed him of his 'daughter—companion in adversity.' And now that the time has come to cremate her he wishes to make it a truly special occasion."

"An event of such grandeur as has never been seen before," another girl chimed in. "If you don't come you'll regret it the rest of your life, Phloi."

"It will be such fun—*sanuk mak!*" they chorused. A most tempting invitation. Phloi's conscience, however, obliged her to point out that she was now a housewife. She had her husband and child to consider.

"Oh, your doting husband!" somebody snorted. "He'll let you do as you please."

Another voice took up the theme: "Anyway, he's sure to be accompanying His Majesty, so it isn't as if he'll be pining away for you in Bangkok."

"And you can bring On," Choi said by way of winding up the argument, "and any number of servants to help look after him. Plenty of room in the kitchen boat. Khun Aunt Sai will be delighted to have the pleasure of your company. Khun Prem will pay visits to the boat and you can pamper him with his favourite dishes. You see, Phloi, you really have no excuses not to come."

Phloi of course was dying to go with them. Her present enviable position of ease and comfort had not altered the fact that part of her soul still remained here at Sadet's residence, the Inner Court, the Grand Palace. After all these years how could it be otherwise? How could she cease to be an Inner Courtier from one day to the next? There had been moments during the past weeks (by no means a dull period) when she had been filled with nostalgia for the old life behind the high walls, and realized that if she were to be cut off from it altogether there would be a diminishing in her own life no matter how well-endowed it might be in other respects.

Which amounted to saying that she would feel left out indeed if she had to stay behind while her companions were attending the big event in Bang Pa-in To hear about it afterwards would be a poor substitute for being there herself as an eyewitness, a participating insider.

On the way home from the palace that afternoon she thought of how best to present her case to Khun Prem. But as it turned out she did not have to try very hard. It was Khun Prem who brought up the subject, giving her the news that same evening that he would be going to Bang Pa-in for the cremation.

"I don't like to leave you here by yourself, but—"

"But that's all right," Phloi finished the sentence for him, though not in the sense he had intended. "I can come along too as a member of my Sadet's entourage. Khun Aunt Sai is in charge of Sadet's kitchen boat and there's room in it for On and me and Phit and Grandma Jaem."

"But Mae Phloi, in your condition—"

"Oh, I'm fine!" Phloi laughed. "The river air will make me feel better still. And you can come and see us when you're off duty. It will be our second meeting in Bang Pa-in, you know. This time I promise not to ignore you. I'll even feed you, in return for the delicious *khanom chin* you brought me that first time—"

She looked at him smilingly and Khun Prem smiled back at her. He, too, would always treasure the memory of that picnic on the river.

SO one fine morning a week later Phloi, On, Phit and Grandma Jaem were among those present on the kitchen boat sailing merrily up the Chao Phraya on its way to Bang Pa-in. On was very much the star passenger. Choi and the other girls kept him supplied with delicious tidbits and romped about with him while Khun Sai, in between giving various directions to various people, called out warnings lest Pho On should fall overboard. As the boat went past Khwan Market, On fell asleep in the cabin, happily tired out, a smile lingering on his smooth cheeks, and after a while Choi followed his example—she had been packing till very late and had been up since before dawn. Leaving them to dream on, Phloi climbed out to the front deck, found a nice spot and sat down to enjoy the ever-changing panorama—the houses among the trees, *chedi*s and temple roofs, monks going by in their canoes and accepting food from devotees at piers and landings, people in ferries gaily gesticulating at the long line of the king's boats moving up river, children swimming, children paddling, the shimmering

Chao Phraya stretching out before her, serenely beautiful in the morning sun . . . She felt wide awake, excited, yet at the same time overflowing with peace and contentment. She thought of nothing in particular, but after a while her mind wandered back to that first trip to Bang Pa-in—her first train ride in the bargain! She recollect-ed all sorts of details: how thrilling it had been, for instance, to listen to His Majesty's conversation with the officials standing near her carriage window, and the cut and colour of the blouse she had worn to Hua Lamphong that day—not very many days after she had been heart broken over Phi Nuang's marrying another girl. Oh, but how strange: the blouse had remained so vivid, as though she had put it on only yeaterday, whereas the broken heart—what had become of it? The way she remembered it now, it could well have belonged to somebody else who had existed in some distant past. How could this be? She had loved Phi Nuang and had suffered because of him, yet here she was, thinking about it quite painlessly, without the tiniest quickening of a heartbeat. She could not understand it at all.

"And here's another mystery," said Phloi to herself. "Only a few months since the wedding but I feel I've been living with Khun Prem for a long, long time."

Shaking her head wonderingly, she gave a sigh and a smile, then went to help Khun Sai and the girls prepare the assortment of dishes required for the day's journey.

Their kitchen boat reached Bang Pa-in in mid-afternoon and was towed to its assigned mooring space in the *khlong* which ran along the back areas of the palace.

Khun Sai and Phloi spent the rest of the afternoon at Woranat House getting Sadet's apartment ready for her. The housekeepers and maids from the other residences of the Inner Court were also here, bustling about all over, for most of the royal family were com-ing to the cremation, so that Woranat House throbbed and hummed with the sound of laughter mingling with the noise of furniture being moved and footsteps along the corridors and up and down the stairs. Phloi was certainly in her element, so much so that Khun Sai had to remind her from time to time of her "condition" and not to overdo it.

The next day they all trooped off to the station to greet the arrival of the royal family and to accompany their respective patronesses to the palace.

At Woranat House, Sadet smiled with appreciation after glancing round her apartment.

"I can see you had a hand in all this. Thank you, Phloi... So you've brought On along, and the one in your stomach. Well, well, the more the merrier. It's good to know you're not far away, Phloi. But I also want you to be at the boat when your husband comes to visit you. Mustn't neglect him and give him the excuse to get rid of you. One never knows about these men...

"I'm glad you could come, Phloi. For my own sake and yours. This is an event to remember. You'll have a lot to tell your grand-children about it in the years to come..."

Two days later Phloi was back at the station. She stood on tiptoe, craning her neck, watching the funeral train as it approached the station and slowed down to a halt. His Majesty was there on the platform to meet it. The tall golden urn bearing the remains of his beloved daughter was in the first coach, flanked by the white-and-gold tiered umbrellas and other insignia of a princess of the realm. It was later carried aboard a royal barge to the landing pavilion of the palace, and thence to the Phra Thi Nang Aisawan Thiphya Asna, which His Majesty had had built in the middle of the lake. It was His Majesty's wish that it should stand here three days and three nights and there should be music and performances honouring the memory of the princess throughout the whole period, which would culminate in the cremation, with the collection of the ashes taking place the following day.

Pavilions had been erected for the occasion, and also walks and bridges to connect them and to link the Aisawan Hall with the embankment. There were separate pavilions for the Front Court and the Inner Court, and Phloi was among the Inner Courtiers, all dressed in white, attending the religious rites on the first day of the ceremony. A day to remember. Not so much on account of the rites as what happened afterwards. For after the rites were over and the monks had left, His Majesty came over to the pavilion where Phloi was sitting. Nobody had expected this and all eyes were fixed upon him. He went up to his daughter Sadet Phra Ong Klang, who was full sister to the princess in the urn, and embraced her. Then they wept together, father and daughter mourning their common loss and consoling each other. Phloi did not dare look but lowered her head to the floor making obeisance, with a lump in her throat and the tears wetting her clasped hands. "I have known sorrow before," she said to herself, "and it is certain to cross my path again. I will face it more bravely next time. For if Phra Chao Yu Hua, who is the Lord of Life of all of us, Most Revered and Powerful Lord, if even he cannot escape its shocks and pains, why should I, insignificant Phloi, be spared them?" She remained thus with head bowed to the floor until His Majesty had left the pavilion. She would never forget having witnessed those tears as long as she lived.

She told Khun Prem about it when he came to the boat. It was not every day that one saw Phra Chao Yu Hua in tears and Khun Prem fully understood why his wife should have been so profoundly moved by the incident.

Khun Aunt Sai gave her dear Pho Prem a warm welcome, treated him to a sumptuous feast, and remarked more than once that Pho Prem could always put her in a good mood.

Choi appeared after they had finished the meal. She came from the palace and was looking unusually worried.

"Have you heard about Somdet Phra Ong Ying Yai?" she asked. "They tell me she's quite ill."

Phloi could not believe it. "But Her Highness was at the station this morning!"

"That's right." Khun Sai nodded. "Be careful, Choi. If she's well and you go round spreading bad tidings you'll get a coconut in your mouth."

Ignoring her aunt's exaggerated reprimand, Choi continued with her news. "She was not feeling well but insisted on going to the station. She's got worse since then. They say she has a very high fever."

"Some people will exaggerate," Khun Sai said disapprovingly. "I'm sure it's just the change of air. The doctors will soon put her right again."

"Let's hope so," said Choi.

They went on to talk of other things, but Choi remained anxious and pensive, which was so unlike her. In fact, she only became her irrepressible self again when they all went paddling their canoes in the lake that night. This was the first night of the floats. The lake was shimmering in candlelight and the heart could not help but rejoice at such a beautiful scene. The floats—or *krathong*s—were presented in honour of the occasion by people from all walks of life including members of the royal family, civil servants and merchants, among others. The best ones would be given prizes by His Majesty and the judges would have a difficult time choosing them. One of the most elaborate *krathong*s was a perfectly detailed replica of a warship; another of a traditional Thai house; a third one, gaily bobbing after those two, was a model pavilion on which a full military brass band was staged. There were also *krathong*s depicting scenes from famous tales: a romantic episode from the story of Khun Chang–Khun Phaen; a frightening one featuring zombies from the saga of Phra Abhai Mani, and so on. One of the most impressive *krathong*s—Phloi and Choi agreed on this—had as its centrepiece the naga king in meditation. The exquisitely carved naga looked as though he was quite capable of suddenly uncoiling to reveal his magical powers for the lucky spectators. Then there were those clever floats—not only pretty but ingenious. The one with Nang Darani, the Earth, for instance, with actual water flowing from her long hair. Choi and Phloi, behaving like a couple of entranced children, tirelessly manoeuvred their canoe in and out among these fragrant candlelit *krathong*s and did not get back to the kitchen boat until very late.

The following day, feeling somewhat exhausted, Phloi did not go into the palace but stayed on board thinking she might take a nap in the afternoon. It proved too warm, however, so she took another bath, then relieved a kitchenmaid of a big bunch of onions and took them to a shady corner on the front deck where she set out to peel them in preparation for the day's cooking. She was absorbed in her little task, but after a while became aware that there was someone standing on the bank nearby. She glanced up. It was a soldier, who started visibly on seeing who she was and made as if to go away.

But he regained his equanimity a moment later and also his tongue. "Mae Phloi! I didn't know you were here."

Phloi was taking this unexpected meeting quite calmly. She smiled with pleasure, made a *wai* of greeting, and said; "You came looking for Khun Aunt Sai, right? Come on down, Phi Nuang."

Phi Nuang continued to gaze at Phloi for some seconds as though he could not make up his mind what to do. Then he carefully stepped down into the boat and settled himself on the floor in front of her.

"How are you, Mae Phloi? I've been assigned guard duty here. I was transferred from Nakhon Sawan to Ayuthaya some time ago, you know."

"I'm well enough, Phi Nuang, not ill or anything. You've grown fatter, haven't you? I almost didn't recognize you at first. How are you?"

"So-so. When you were getting married my mother wrote me about it. I wanted to come to your wedding but we were so busy getting ready to move."

Phloi turned to call out to Phit, who eventually appeared in response to the summons carrying On along on her hip. She opened her eyes wide and uttered a loud exclamation. "My dear Khun Nuang! So where have you been burying yourself all this time?"

Nuang chuckled. "Not far from here, Phit."

Phit had more to say to him, naturally, but she was cut short by Phloi's instructions to put On down and go and tell Khun Sai that she had a visitor.

Phi Nuang stared at On.

"He can't be your son, Mae Phloi."

"Definitely not, Phi Nuang," Phloi said giggling. "I have adopted him, though."

"I see. He's a nice-looking child. Mine is a little older but not as robust. Oh, but how he talks—a real chatter-box just like his Aunt Choi."

Khun Sai came out to join them, full of concern at first over the situation, full of relief afterwards. And when an hour or so later Nuang got up to leave, both Khun Sai and Phloi made him promise to come and see them again.

Phloi was also relieved. She was happy to have met him again, and happier still to know beyond any doubt that her feelings towards him were entirely friendly and no more. He would always remain a good childhood friend, Choi's brother, Khun Sai's nephew, son of Khun Luang and Mae Chan whom she loved and respected as her own kin.

ON the day of the cremation a procession af barges carried the golden urn with the royal insignias and the honour guard from the Aisawan Hall to Wat Prawet on the other side of Bang Pa-in Island. The funeral pyre had been erected on the site where as many bodhi trees had been planted as the number of years the late princess had lived. The *wat* was crowded and white was the dominant colour under a bright blue sky. Choi and Phloi observed the proceedings from their vantage point at the back of the Inner Court pavilion. From time to time during the rites they and the other maids-in-waiting would whisper to one another, mostly about Somdet Phra Ong Ying Yai and her illness, which had prevented her from attending the rites. Choi had heard from somebody that the fever had not subsided and that Her Royal Highness's condition had worsened to the point that she even had delirious moments when she uttered disjointed phrases in the *farang* language. While listening to the monks' chanting and to Choi's distressing news, Phloi offered up some silent prayers of her own, invoking all the sacred powers in the universe to restore good health to Phra Chao Yu Hua's daughter.

Then she felt a nudge on her arm. It was Choi again.

"Look over there, Phloi! Do you see what I see?"

Phloi's gaze followed the direction, and fell upon Phi Nuang standing in a group of fellow officers. She whispered back, "I forgot to tell you he came to the boat to see Khun Aunt. I happened to be there so we had a chat. He says he'll come again to see you."

"I can hardly wait!" Choi said meaningly. "Did it bother you—meeting him?"

"Not at all, Choi ... Oh, look, Choi!" Her eyes had been wandering and now her face broke into a radiant smile. "Look, look, there's someone else both of us know!"

Choi looked and made a disgusted noise. "Oh, it's only Khun Prem. And you're smirking, Phloi. Why, one would think you're the only woman here with a husband to show off!"

After the cremation came the collection of the ashes which took place the next morning; then came an interval of three days followed by the final merit-making rites. The mourning period had come to an end and colour was worn for the occasion. But alas, almost as soon as this was over Somdet Phra Ong Ying Yai died. Although her illness had been grave, it had lasted but a few short days, so her death seemed very sudden and came as a great shock to everyone.

Another golden urn had to be rushed by a fast train from Bangkok. The bathing rites were held. After that the urn was taken back to the capital by boat while His Majesty and the royal family made their return journey by train.

One funeral had just ended only to signal the start of another. One royal daughter had been cremated, and now another had taken her place in the golden urn.

On the kitchen boat going back to Bangkok a sadder and more mature Phloi sat contemplating the current, and the inescapable facts of getting born, falling ill, growing old and dying. It made her feel more insignificant than ever. Yet at the same time she dared sympathize with Phra Chao Yu Hua, who had to bear the sufferings which stemmed from those facts like any of his humble subjects, as powerless against the turning wheel of existence as the rest of us.

If only we could remember to live in awareness of those simple facts, she thought, and told herself that she might try harder from now on.

SEVENTEEN

"I'm so glad, Phloi," Chao Khun Father said during his visit a few days after Phloi's return from Bang Pa-in, a visit more or less in celebration of Phloi's pregnancy. "At last I'm going to have a grandchild to play with. My first grandchild—I'm very happy indeed!"

And Khun Choei was no less happy than her father. "It's so exciting, Mae Phloi! You can't imagine how much I'm looking forward to being a *pa* to your child."

She told Phloi about Chao Khun's dream. "Before we had known that you were expecting, Chao Khun Father dreamt he saw a big shooting star flash past our house across the river towards Bangkok. He said to me it must mean he would have a grandson. I thought nothing of it at the time, and then we had this wonderful news from you . . . Oh, I do hope it will be a boy."

"May it be as you say, Khun Choei. I, too, would like my first-born to be a son." Deep down she had no preference and would be just as satisfied with a girl, but all her nearest and dearest, especially Khun Prem, seemed to set their hearts on having her produce a boy, so Phloi felt she ought to oblige if she could.

Once in the course of the conversation Chao Khun Father talked about his health. "I don't know what's wrong with me these days. I don't sleep well and I've lost my appetite. Everything seems to give me indigestion. I've taken so many kinds of medicine prescribed by so many doctors. Absolutely no use. And now Mae Choei has put me on another herbal concoction. I doubt if it will do any good."

Phloi had already noted the tell-tale dark rings under his eyes and had wanted to ask if he had been unwell lately. Now she threw Khun

Choei an anxious questioning glance. The latter returned it with a tiny signal, a quick blinking which said "not now"; Then she spoke aloud.

"Please be patient, sir. The medicine is highly recommended by everyone. You must go on with it. Any ailment in elderly people, however mild, takes some time to cure."

"But she doesn't treat me like an elderly person," Chao Khun complained to Phloi. "You should see her order me about—as though I were a child. She forces me to see another doctor, take another pill, swallow another spoonful of this and that. I'm no longer a free man. She's my oppressor, Mae Choei is."

Khun Choei laughed. "You can see what I'm up against, Phloi. His Excellency fights hard to prevent me looking after him when he's not well. Perhaps you'd like to come and be my assistant oppressor?"

"No, no," Chao Khun said. "No need for Phloi to leave home and husband to assist you in anything, Mae Choei. If I were really sick, perhaps, but not now."

He sounded cheerful enough, but Phloi worried about him all the same. The next day her brother Phoem came to see her, carrying a note from Khun Choei, and its few brief lines confirmed that her worries were not groundless.

"I didn't want to discuss it in front of him," the note said, "so am asking Pho Phoem to bring you this. Not that I have a great deal to tell you. We still don't know exactly what it is. Sometimes he's very weak, and then he surprises us by appearing normal again—up and about as usual, like yesterday. To me the worst symptom is when he sinks into a kind of apathy and doesn't seem interested in anything, least of all getting well. Now don't you jump to conclusions that it must be something very serious. I don't want you to worry but take care of yourself and rest easy in your mind that we're giving him the best care possible. Do give Pho Phoem a good talking-to on my behalf. He's getting sillier every day."

Hoping her brother might be able to add a little more to Khun Choei's message, Phloi questioned him, got nothing in return, and nearly ended up giving him a "good talking-to" as requested by Khun Choei.

"What *is* the matter with Chao Khun Father, Pho Phoem?"

"Eh? I don't know. Is something the matter with him?"

"Oh, Pho Phoem! How can you *not* know? He hasn't been well at all."

"Oh, really? Last time I saw him—only two days ago—he was perfectly all right."

"I don't think you go home as regularly as you should, Pho Phoem."

"Now don't you start using that tone with me, Mae Phloi. I get enough of it at home. Why shouldn't I come and go as I please when nobody cares what I do anyway?"

"That's nonsense and you know it. Do act like a grown man, Pho Phoem."

"You all say that but you never never give me a chance to do it. Take Chao Khun Father. Has he ever entrusted me with an errand worthy of a grown man? Never! Take Khun Un. She scolds me as though I were a ten-year-old. And the same applies to our reprobate Elder Brother Chit. As for Khun Choei, who's several months my junior, she never leaves me alone for a minute. From her it's nothing but nag, nag, nag, all the time. Who does she think she is—my mother? And now you, my own younger sister, eager to take me to task as if I were a schoolboy caught at playing truant!"

"Calm down, Pho Phoem. It's because we care, you know. Khun Choei and I, we're your loving sisters and we want to be able to look up to you as our responsible, respectable, dignified, eminent, dependable elder brother. It's not nagging, it's caring."

In the end they were both laughing. Phloi could never keep up her role as Pho Phoem's reformer for very long, and Phoem's easy good nature was always easy to restore.

He was her most frequent visitor from Khlong Bang Luang, and when he did not turn up for a few days in succession Khun Prem would start to miss him. Phloi had cautioned her husband not to spoil him too much, and above all to refrain from giving him any more costly presents. She was afraid Khun Prem's family might think he was taking advantage of the rich friend who also happened to be his brother-in-law.

Khun Prem had laughed at her concern—her fussing over nothing as he put it—and given her a lecture on the subject. "We all know Phoem has his faults but we also know that he doesn't take advantage of anyone. It's not in his nature. In fact he's very proud. He's never asked me for anything, directly or indirectly. I gave him those things because I thought he might enjoy having them. What are a few gifts between friends who are also close relatives? In any case I feel I can never do enough for Phoem, and everybody understands this. If it hadn't been for his support for my case, you might still be eluding me. Right, my dear one?"

Khun Chit, though not a frequent visitor—and Phloi was thankful for this, had also paid his calls. The first time he came Khun Prem had not returned from the palace and he insisted on waiting for him. He made himself at home, sending his avid glance round and round the room, frankly appraising the price of every object in sight. Khun Prem came home to behave very politely, almost formally, with this brother-in-law, showing him every respect due to his position. Khun Chit in his turn was more than polite. He positively cringed in his desire to please. It was glaringly obvious that he believed in winning approval and favour with an obsequious attitude. Phloi felt not only embarrassed but frustrated: she wished she could find an opportunity later on to give him some words of advice, then realized she could never bring herself to do it, the notion having been too deeply instilled in her that she must not impose herself on the eldest brother, the first son of the Khunying wife of Chao Khun Father. She would just have to go on treating him with deference, for better or for worse.

He came again not so long after (thank heaven, Khun Prem was on duty that day) to "borrow" some money, which Phloi knew would not be spent on his wife and child as he would have her believe. He named a large sum, but Phloi managed to appease him with a much smaller amount. He snatched at it, his thin-veined hand with its grimy fingernails trembling with impatience.

And soon after he had left, an astonished-looking Khun Nui made her appearance. "Who was that I passed going down the stairs? Who is he?"

"That's—Khun Chit. He's—er—the son of Chao Khun Father and the Khunying. He's—my eldest brother. "

"Unbelievable!" Khun Nui exclaimed. "I thought he was a tramp and couldn't imagine what he was doing here. Is he an opium addict? Looks like one, doesn't he? Dear, oh dear, I've done it again, haven't I? I talk too much, yes? You'll forgive an old woman, won't you?"

Phloi had felt so ashamed on seeing Khun Nui, knowing she must have met Khun Chit on the way. Now Khun Nui's refreshing straightforwardness made her feel better, and Khun Nui's elocution style made her laugh, as it often did. They discussed Khun Chit's case but not for long, Khun Nui being so anxious to launch into her current favourite topic, which was Phloi's health.

These days she came to see Phloi all the time to inquire how she was. Phloi's mother, had she been alive, could not have been more solicitous. She wanted to make sure Phloi was eating well and sleeping soundly; she had a nourishing dish for Phloi; she had got the recipe from somebody who said it was just the right thing for young expecting mothers; and she had some advice to offer on what should be done in preparation for the "coming event."

For a spinster who had never taken much interest in childbirth, she gave out more advice and suggestions than any mother or midwife, and if in general they tended to be either of a vague or fantastic nature, nobody seemed to mind.

She announced on one occasion: "I've just thought of something. The white cloth, you know? We'll need lots and lots of it, won't we? Shall I get ten bales? Will that be enough?"

Another time she came out with: "It is extremely important that we stock up on the shells of horseshoe crabs. An absolute must, yes?"

"Yes? But what are they for, Khun Aunt?"

"How should I know? But I've been told you need them for when you give birth to a baby. Most indispensable, you understand?"

No, nobody understood. The doctors and midwives and the other experts were just as mystified as the uninitiated.

The "other experts" in this case included, among others, Grandma Thiap, the cook, and Phit, the handy-woman of all trades. The latter claimed she had assisted at the delivery of both Khun Phoem and Khun Phloi, not to mention those others in her native country village, and therefore knew everything there was to know; and Thiap, in her superior way, said she was not one for bragging, but that her invaluable experience and skills would speak for themselves when the time came.

One day, going past the kitchen, Phloi stopped to listen to these two converse on the subject.

"My dear woman," Phit was saying, "I'll admit you can cook, but having a baby is not as simple as scraping a coconut or pounding a chili paste."

"Are you by any chance," Thiap's voice was dangerously gentle, "calling me a damn liar?"

"Of course not, darling. It just occurs to me that as a virgin—and you are a virgin, are you not? So pure and innocent and all that?—you shouldn't be expected to know about these things."

"Sweetheart! For your gifted tongue I should give you a resounding slap right and left. I will restrain myself, however, for our Khun's sake."

Phit burst out laughing in great merriment. "All right, now tell me what you know."

"Well, Mae Phit, as I was saying when you so rudely interrupted me, the birth itself should be easy enough—it usually is for a young girl. The pain shouldn't last long, and she'll get over that in no time at all. Now you and me, at our age, we wouldn't survive—"

"Leave us out of it. Go on."

"So the important thing, the most important thing, is the heating after birth. The fire for the boards will need a deft hand to tend it to a nice even heat. We don't want to scorch her, mind you, but we do want to give her a good sweat. And the compress for her stomach must have the best stuff in it, needless to say. If all this is not properly handled the blood may turn bad. Even the brain. It could ruin your health for life. Or you could go mad. Now the medicine for after birth—"

"Yes, what kind of medicine?"

"The *ya dong* of course." This is any one of the various kinds of medicinal-alcoholic liquid made by leaving a cloth bag containing medicinal roots, leaves and other ingredients submerged in rice wine or arrack. "I've already made some for her, using my own famous prescription—"

"You don't say! Want me to try it first?"

"Why not? We'll try it together. She won't be needing more than half a bottle, and I've made three—"

Phloi came away, smiling to herself. She also felt a twinge of nervousness, and who could blame her, with all that blithe talk about pain and fire and madness and what have you.

During the first month, she had thought about the pain occasionally and had dreaded it, but even then love had carried the day, love for this child to be born that was of her flesh and blood, and as time went on any fear she might have experienced now and again had dwindled to nothing, leaving joy and hope to reign supreme. In truth, except for those few queasy days in the begin-ning, she had never enjoyed such a sense of well-being. It buoyed her up and made her feel simply invincible.

The night she was roused from a deep sleep by the first stirrings of the baby, she woke up Khun Prem, and then whispered to him in her excitement, "Hush, don't make any noise. It's kicking for the first time."

Khun Prem laughed, put a hand on her stomach, and laughed again. "What a powerful kicker! I predict a boy."

Several months went by.

Phloi was now feeling more clumsy than invincible, and rather ashamed of her enormous shapeless body. She didn't like to go out anywhere, would rather stay in her rooms, but Phit wouldn't let her have her way.

"Wellborn ladies have a difficult time of it because they do nothing but sit down or lie down. Girls in my village carry water and pound rice until the very last day and they have no trouble at all. You don't have to work, Khun Phloi, so you must walk. Go down to the garden and have a nice stroll. Pay a visit to the palace, why don't you? Move about, my darling Khun."

This counsel was strongly endorsed by Thiap. "That's right," she said, nodding her head vigorously. "Plenty of moving about. It won't do to get too fat."

These two certainly were a great help with their simple and sensible advice, and also in practical matters such as fixing up the delivery room, putting up the boards, ordering firewood and the like. Khun Sai, on the other hand, did not seem in the least in-terested in these details. The other day in the palace, she looked reflectively at Phloi's swollen stomach and started to plan the hair-cutting ceremony for when the infant would be a month old. She evidently preferred to skip its birth altogether.

At last the day came. It started at about two o'clock in the morning. Khun Prem was away on overnight duty in the palace and Phit, who slept in the same room with her mistress to watch over her in the absence of the master, jumped up and ran hither and thither doing several things at once, both the necessary and the totally irrelevant. At any rate the household was alerted and the midwife sent for. Of all the people in the house Thiap was the first one to come rushing in and the first thing she very wisely did was get the flurried Phit to calm down; then together they moved Phloi to the delivery room.

The midwife arrived, spruce, competent, inspiring confidence. She said with a pleasant smile, "Everything is going well, Khun Phloi. It won't take long. Trust me."

The first pains were not too unbearable, and there were intervals when Phloi could even manage an occasional smile. Then the reprieve was over and she started to writhe and moan despite herself; and Thiap, who was massaging her legs, moaned along with her out of pity combined with a sense of her own helplessness. Phit stood by ready with a cup of water, sweating profusely herself and muttering unintelligible phrases from time to time. Only the midwife remained unruffled. "Everything is going well." The serene expression on her face seemed to reiterate what she had said earlier.

Then once again the pain receded—another respite after all! Before dozing off with exhaustion Phloi heard Thiap's voice whispering to Phit. "Keep an eye on her while I go get a drink of something. The way I've been pushing, if there had been anything in my tummy, it would have come out by now!"

It was in the early dawn when Phloi emerged from the drowsy state to confront the last phase of her great labour. A head-on confrontation. She thought she would die, but even while thinking this she was conscious of Khun Nui's presence in the room and heard her voice in an undertone saying a prayer. When Khun Nui handed her a drink of blessed water Phloi accepted it obediently and drank it gratefully. Not long after this came the final outburst, the total explosion that robbed her of every consciousness except that of pain and her body felt as though it were being torn apart muscle by muscle. How long did this last? An eternity and a few moments. Then suddenly she took a deep breath involuntarily. The smell of birth with its peculiar pungency entered her nostrils. The absence of pain almost took her by surprise, as did the first wail of the newborn infant which rose to fill the space surrounding her. My child, she thought, smiling contentedly, and drifted into another sleep . . .

When she opened her eyes again she found Khun Prem by her side beaming down at her. "Mae Phloi! I came as soon as I heard. You have a son, Mae Phloi. A strong and lovely son. I'm so thankful!"

Phloi smiled back at him and glanced round at the other happy faces popping up here and there in the room that shone bright in the morning sun and smelled fresh and clean from the woodfire and medicinal herbs. One of these faces belonged to Khun Nui, who was holding the *kradong* with the baby in it. Conversing one-sidedly with the baby, Khun Nui brought the *kradong* over for Phloi to have a look.

The baby was red and wrinkled and adorable. Phloi believed she would have been able to endure ten times the pain she had gone through to bring him into the world. She had never known such great happiness existed. The planks on which she was lying were supposed to have become too warm, but she had no complaint. None at all. The fire was just right, everything was just right, she assured all those present, and she was feeling very comfortable never felt better in her life, really and truly . . .

Three days went by.

At the happy house in Khlong Yom this afternoon a little ceremony was taking place under the direction of Phit and Thiap. Its purpose was to drive away certain ghosts which, according to these two experts, had been lurking about waiting to harass the baby or even carry him off from those who cherished him. Malicious ghosts, but luckily not too clever, for you could fool them into believing that it was, in actual fact, a poor unloved baby, not at all sought after, and therefore not worth bothering about.

Khun Nui's assistance was required in this ceremony of deceiving the ghosts. She had been rehearsing her part and was eager to perform it.

Now Phit, who had been kneeling on the floor beside the *kradong* containing the baby, solemnly picked it up, rose to her feet with it and rocked it to and fro while stamping her feet in a menacing manner calculated to intimidate her unseen adversaries. "Three-day-old ghost child," she started to intone the formula. "Three-day-old ghost child, four day-old human child. Whose child is this? Come and take it!"

She repeated this three times.

The suspense had become unbearable for Khun Nui and she called out excitedly, "Is it my turn now, Phit?"

"Three-day-old ghost child, four-day-old human child," Phit brought the chanting to an end, and at the same time signaled to Khun Nui to go ahead.

"It's my child, Phit!" Khun Nui cried shrilly. "It's my child! Is it? Is it?"

Phit sank to the floor and laid down the *kradong*. Wiping the perspiration from her brow she said in a long-suffering voice, "You didn't quite conform to the text, madam. You're supposed to take the *kradong* from me after admitting that it's your child. If you keep on asking 'Is it? Is it?' the ghosts will suspect us of trying to hoodwink them."

"Is that so?" Khun Nui was both impressed and contrite. "What shall we do?"

"We'll start again," said Phit and, taking up the *kradong* for the second time, she went over the same routine as before.

"Isn't that my child, Phit?" demanded Khun Nui in another violation of the script. "Will you give it to me, Phit? Shall I take it, Phit?"

It was difficult for Khun Nui to give up her interrogative habit but Phit with infinite patience made her do it again and again and finally succeeded in extracting the accurate positive reply out of her.

A few days later Khun Choei came with baskets of various kinds of fruit for the new mother. She looked thin and worn out but otherwise was in high spirits. She told Phloi that Chao Khun's condition had improved a thousandfold since receiving the news about his grandson. "It's amazing, Phloi. He suddenly bloomed as if by magic. Khun Prem's message came at midday and in the afternoon he could sit up and eat with appetite—two bowls of rice gruel! I think he'll get well now."

"Have you found out the name of the illness?" Phloi asked.

"The doctor says it's ulcers in the stomach. I haven't told you about this new doctor we have, Phloi. A young man—quite a change from the doddering ancients we had to deal with before. His name is Luang Osot and he is both extremely good and extremely considerate. Chao Khun Father seems to be responding well to his treatment."

"I'm so glad you came today, Khun Choei," Phloi said. "I've been worrying about Chao Khun Father. It's a relief to know he's getting better."

"I really think he is, Phloi. And your son's good medicine for him. He longs to see him and would have come today if I'd let him. Now I must take a close look at this baby because he'll want to question me about it when I get home."

When she had scrutinized the baby, Khun Choei went on to say, "Well, I'm not very good at distinguishing newborn infants. They all look the same to me. What do you say, Phloi—who does he look like?"

Phloi laughed. "I can't tell either. But the people here have decided that he takes after me."

"And that's what I shall convey to Chao Khun Grandpa, who will be pleased to have his grandson resemble his daughter. Oh, I know! Wouldn't it be even better if I said the baby looked like him?"

"Why not? If you think it will help speed up his recovery."

"It will! Then you must somehow arrange for the resemblance to come true because I don't want to be branded a liar! By the way, if Chao Khun Father isn't strong enought to visit you, how soon do you think you can bring the baby to Khlong Bang Luang?"

Tapping the "fire planks" on which she was lying, Phloi said, "I don't know how much longer this heating business will go on. I'll ask the experts. But anyway, shouldn't we wait until the baby is at least a month old before taking him on an outing?"

"As you say, Mae Phloi. There's no hurry, and who knows, by then Chao Khun Father might be fit enough to make the journey here. I have great confidence in Luang Osot. He's really a wonderful doctor, Phloi. Not only able but compassionate, you know. He's made me promise that when I notice a change for the worse in Chao Khun Father—however slight—I will send for him immediately. He's willing to stay all night with the patient if need be."

Phloi was delighted at the note of admiration in Khun Choei's voice and the pink tint in her cheeks as she spoke of Luang Osot, and could not help asking, though careful to make it sound casual, "Tell me more about him. Where has he sprung from?"

"Oh, he's with the Department of Royal Physicians and quite highly regarded." This information was given with a great deal of enthusiasm. "Chao Khun Father has known him for years. I called him in after we had tried so many other doctors without getting anywhere."

"You said he's a young man. How old is he?"

"He's eight years older than me. A childless widower. His wife died about a year ago. He's really a very nice person, Mae Phloi," she added, and failing to discern Phloi's smile at this unsought testimony, went on expanding a little more. "He's solid and dependable. No nonsense about him, yet at the same time he's consistently gentle and courteous."

This is very good news, Phloi thought happily to herself. *She likes him. My dear sister Khun Choei has found someone at last.*

But as the conversation turned to other topics Phloi did not try to guide it back to the estimable doctor. Further questioning would have been inopportune at this stage, and Khun Choei might consider it too inquisitive on her part.

The fire planks grew rather hot after Khun Choei had left, but in her light-hearted mood Phloi scarcely felt the discomfort.

The next few days brought more visitors. From the palace came Khun Sai and Choi, bringing many gifts including a multitude of Inner Court delicacies.

"Did it hurt terribly?" was Choi's first query.

"Yes, but I don't remember it now. I only know it did."

Shuddering, Choi said, "The mere idea scares me to death. I would have screamed the house down! And look at you now. Are you being roasted alive?"

"It's a little hot, Choi. But what can I do?"

Choi emitted a groan from the heart. "This is definitely not for me," she declared. "My mind's made up. I shall have to take a vow and resign myself to perpetual spinsterhood. No husband, no childbearing. It's just too frightening for me. I'll become a *mae chi* (lay nun)—that should solve the problem."

"Don't waste your time listening to nonsense, Phloi," said Khun Sai. "Sadet is very happy for you and sends her best wishes. 'Tell Phloi to take care of herself and the baby,' she says. And the girls want you to bring the baby to the residence as soon as you can. You have a fine son, Phloi."

Choi moved closer to the baby and started to poke him gently here and there. Then she exclaimed with delight, "Oh, look, isn't he sweet! Look, Phloi, he's smiling at me!"

"Rubbish," said her aunt. "He's too young to smile."

"Well, he did!" maintained Choi. "Too young or not. Quite a roguish smile too. What are you calling him, Phloi?"

"He hasn't got a name yet. Khun Prem wants Chao Khun Father to think up one for him."

"What about 'An' as nickname in the meantime?" Choi proposed. "'An,' younger brother of 'On.'"

Phloi liked it, and from that day onwards the baby was called An (pronounced as in "fun") as Auntie Choi had suggested.

On came in to see his younger brother An every day. He could sit patiently for a long time by the *kradong*, fixing his eyes on the baby and doing nothing to disturb him in any way. Watching the two of them together, Phloi felt relieved and full of contentment. Having her own son had not affected her relationship with On, had not lessened her love for him. If anything, it had deepened her understanding of On's plight and increased the tenderness in her feelings towards him.

A whole month elapsed during which it appeared to Phloi that An was getting bigger at a marvellously fast rate—*to wan, to khun* (growing by day, growing by night), as the saying goes. Nor had it taken him very long to acquire certain individual mannerisms all his own, she found to her fascination. He had his favourite posture while suckling at her breast, when lying awake or sleeping. Awake, he would sometimes solemnly contemplate his own hands and feet in the manner of some diminutive sage which never failed to amuse Phloi. He certainly was a constant source of entertainment and Phloi wished his proud grandfather could come and see what an interesting and funny little creature he was.

But another week passed, and another, bringing not very encouraging news from Khlong Bang Luang. The amazing improvement in Chao Khun's health at the time of An's birth came to an abrupt end and since then he had had several setbacks. Then one day Khun Choei sent a note asking Phloi, now that the period of her post-natal recuperation was over, to bring An to visit Chao Khun, and to stay as many days as possible. Phloi consulted Khun Prem, who not only approved but promptly started making the arrangements for the trip and on the appointed day personally escorted his wife and son across the river.

They got there at midday. Chao Khun Father was still asleep and Khun Choei settled them in her rooms for the time being. Later, after Khun Prem had returned to Bangkok, Phloi and Khun Choei debated the same old question of whether Phloi ought to see Khun Un and pay her humble respects to the eldest sister. As usual, Khun Choei was strongly against it, but Phloi went anyway, her desire to do the right thing being fortified by the belief that Khun Un surely would not be so overbearing with a mature married woman and mother as she had been with Phloi the youngster.

But Khun Un's first words on seeing Phloi were: "Ah, the millionaire woman come to see me in my room! Not afraid of getting tainted by my poverty?"

"I've just arrived," said Phloi evenly, resolved not to be offended by Khun Un's malevolence. "After unpacking I came to prostrate myself at your feet."

"So you heard about Chao Khun Father's illness," Khun Un said in that heavily sarcastic tone of voice she enjoyed adopting for such an occasion. "But if you aim to sit around waiting for your share of the estate, let me tell you that he's not *that* sick!"

She paused, spat betel juice into the spittoon, and addressed herself to one of the cupboards standing sentinel along the walls. "The vultures couldn't wait—they're here already."

At this point Phloi had no other alternative but to beat a retreat.

Khun Choei laughed when Phloi recounted the foregoing scene to her. "Didn't I warn you, Mae Phloi? Vultures indeed! She's impossible, this eldest sister of ours. And she's worse these days on account of Chao Khun Father—you know, because he's so excited about your son. Oh, she's on the warpath all right and we're in for some fun!"

When Chao Khun Father was awake Khun Choei and Phloi went into his room, Phloi carrying An on a cushion, which she placed beside him on his bed. She was shocked by his appearance—shocked and saddened. He had grown so frail, his eyes were hollow, his cheeks sunken, his body nothing but skin and bones. *No, no,* she told herself, *I mustn't cry. It would make him lose heart.* So she forced herself to put on a cheerful countenance and chat pleasantly about this and that for his benefit.

Chao Khun himself made no attempt at hiding his emotion, at holding back his tears as he murmured, "Dear little one, too little to be brought so far. But now that you're here, let's keep you here for a while."

He kept stroking the baby and could not keep his eyes from him. "You said he looked like me, Mae Choei. Not true at all. I'll tell you who he looks like. Your beautiful mother, Phloi. Oh, why did she have to die so young . . ."

His face was tear-stained and his eyes were shining brightly through the tears, shining whether with joy, sorrow, or fever, or a mixture of everything it was impossible to tell. Phloi in any case looked away, her throat constricted, and for the sake of something to do picked up a feather fan and waved it slowly back and forth over the bed.

Thanks to An's presence Chao Khun got better again, starting from that very day, and on the third day he was well enough to sit up and hold the baby on his lap. At the end of the week his doctor Luang Osot examined him and was astounded. If he continued to mend at this rate he should be as good as cured in another ten days or so, Luang Osot said, adding that this wonder drug called "An" was more effective than anything he had prescribed or would be able to prescribe for Chao Khun.

Phloi relayed the glad news to Khun Prem, telling him he could expect them home in about ten days, that Chao Khun Father could now walk about over short distances, that he was out of danger and on the road to recovery. Perhaps he would even be able to come and see them in Khlong Yom sometime soon.

Then one morning, when Phit had carried An to Chao Khun as usual, Phloi, who was still in her own room combing her hair, heard Phit's voice shouting for help. When they got there, Phloi and Khun Choei saw their father lying on his back on the bed, his face ashen. Phit told them briefly how Chao Khun had been so happy to see An, and then all of a sudden he had cried out "I'm fainting," and fell backwards. Khun Choei rushed out to dispatch a steward to fetch Luang Osot. Phloi held Chao Khun Father in her arms giving him smelling salts and Phit started to massage his legs. He died a few moments later, still in her arms, before the doctor could get to him and while Khun Choei was still out of the room.

EIGHTEEN

THE period between Chao Khun's death and his cremation, which took place about a year later, could be given the name Disaster as far as the house in Khlong Bang Luang was concerned. The family quarrel over the disposal, or rather the non-disposal, of the estate erupted not long after Chao Khun's body had gone into the urn. Khun Un claimed that nothing had changed: Chao Khun being survived by her mother the Khunying (although this lady refused to come to the funeral rites from beginning to cremation) gave her the right to continue as absolute mistress of the house. In short, she saw no need to divide up the inheritance. And this ruling had the full support of Khun Chit and was fiercely opposed by Khun Choei, who wanted her share decided upon once and for all so as to be liberated from Khun Un's autocratic ways.

Much as they sympathized with Khun Choei, Phoem and Phloi had no wish to get embroiled in the dispute, which was creating enough unrest and unpleasantness among the inmates of the house without their intervention. Nor would they have considered themselves entitled to intervene had they wanted to.

But to go back to the day Chao Khun died. Khun Un strode into the room full of people, paid no attention to Khun Choei, who was sobbing her heart out, paid respects, dry-eyed, to her father's body, then turned to glare at Phloi and in a voice full of hate spoke loudly for all to hear: "Now are you satisfied? Chao Khun Father was all right but you had to come and kill him! Don't bother to squeeze out those tears. You can't fool me!"

So Phloi reckoned it would be best not to spend more time in this house than necessary. The bathing rites were due to take place in the

on, then the placing of the body in the urn and the evening
 ǝg to follow. And then she would be able to leave. She felt
..... ely safer when Khun Prem arrived. He would protect her from
harm, shield her from danger, and escort her home in one piece. But
to make doubly sure she also took the precaution of steering clear of
Khun Un's wrathful path, removing herself as far away as possible from
where Khun Un could see or hear her.

With so much happening the hours passed quickly, and now in the
centre room where the urn stood the evening rites were drawing to a
close. The monks had finished their chanting of the Phra Abhidhamma
and were being served tea. Some of the guests were preparing to leave
while others were still exchanging news and pleasantries. Phoem and
his friends had set up their chess boards—they would be playing far
into the night and the dead would not be so lonely. Khun Un, with
Khun Chit trailing behind her, had repaired to some other room
somewhere, which was lucky for Phloi, as she wanted to go to the urn
and pay her homage before leaving.

She went up on her hands and knees to sit before the urn. She had
not been grieving over her father's death, perhaps because of lack
of opportunity, for it had been such a hectic day. She had cried this
morning, but more from a sense of shock than anything else and
because the others were crying and their tears were infectious. His
death had come as a shock, though while holding his lifeless body in
her arms it had flashed through her mind that death itself was not as
terrifying as she had imagined. He had gasped for air, breathing hard
for a few seconds, then he had stopped breathing and passed into a
state of apparently complete relaxation, with traces of a smile on his
face—left over, it would seem, from his last happy encounter with An.
Phit had helped her ease his body onto the bed before dashing off to
fetch Khun Choei, carrying An with her on his cushion. After that
had come the turmoil of the funeral preparations. Chao Khun Father
was dead. People had come to pour water into his hand, prostrate
themselves at his feet and take their leave of him. The undertakers
had arrived from the palace bringing the urn, the tiered umbrellas
and other appurtenances; the body had been bound and placed in the

urn. The funeral music. The monks chanting. Everything had revolved round the fact that he was dead. Yet it was only now, as she sat before the urn to say goodbye to him for the night, that the meaning of the fact became clear to her. The realization that she had lost him smote her with an overwhelming force as she sat facing the graceful urn rising toward the ceiling before her. How it shone and glittered in the candlelight! She stared at it as though she had never seen it until now. The musicians were playing again, for the last time tonight, and now she could hear every haunting note of the *pi*, every lamenting beat of the drum. Joining her palms together she lowered her head to the floor. A chill went down her spine and she shook uncontrollably. She wept for a long time, isolated in her sorrow, in a kind of oblivion, unaware that the other people in the room had stopped chatting and that some were crying quietly in sympathy with her. When she returned to consciousness of the surroundings she heard Khun Prem's voice murmuring some soothing words. He helped her up and led her from the house to the landing pavilion where the boat was waiting with Phit and An already on board.

"He'll always be with you, Khun An my sweet," Phit said between her sobs. "He'll be watching over you. I can still see him smiling. His thoughts were with you until the last moment, my dearest."

Phloi returned to Khlong Bang Luang, invariably in Khun Prem's company, to attend the seventh-, the fiftieth- and the hundredth-day rites. She went to the *wat* for the cremation, and she took part in the collection of the ashes and in the merit-making subsequent to that event. At all these functions she purposely behaved like a guest—an obscure one at that, never putting herself forward as a presiding daughter of the deceased. To do otherwise would only make Khun Un flare up again and Phloi did not want any unpropitious incident to occur if she could help it.

It was not too difficult for Phloi to avoid coming into contact with Khun Un, unlike Khun Choei, who had the misfortune of living under the same roof with her.

During those months, whenever they found themselves alone together, Khun Choei would lapse into tears while Phloi would do her best to console her. Khun Choei said on one occasion, "I would have packed up and left if Chao Khun Father's body were not in this house. I don't care about the money. She can have my share. I can live on what Chao Khun Father gave me while he was alive. It's not very much but I don't mind being poor. What I do mind, and what hurts so much, is the way she lashes out at me, her own sister. You can't imagine the nasty, wounding things she says to me, Phloi. And now she's even commanded the servants not to serve me—I have to get my own food and everything—but they have to spy on me, and report to her every word I utter, every movement I make. Khun Chit fawns on her and makes up stories about me to make her hate me more.

"He's so creepy and horrible! Phoem is the only friend I have left in the whole house but what can he do? Oh, Phloi. I can't tell you how awful it is. Sometimes I wish I were dead!"

"Don't, Khun Choei, don't take it to heart, I beg you. When the funeral is over, you come and live with us."

"Thank you, dear Phloi. But no. You have your family. I would only be a burden."

"Never, Khun Choei, and if you're thinking about Khun Prem, let me tell you that it was he who first suggested this idea. He doesn't want you to go on suffering in this house any more than I do."

Khun Choei remained silent for some time, then she said, "Let's discuss it after the cremation." But instead of discussing it, she sent Phloi a note through Phoem. He arrived with it one morning a few days after the merit-making service following the cremation.

"Mae Phloi," the note said, "I'd rather you hear about it from me than from other lips. When you read this I will have gone. Luang Osot is coming to fetch me. I'm sorry to be causing you loss of face from having a sister who eloped. But I think you'll understand. I don't know where his house is or what it's like, but I'd be willing to live in a shack with nothing to eat but lumps of salt—anything is better than to go on living in this house. When I'm a bit calmer I might come to see you, if you'd let me."

"Poor Khun Choei," Phloi murmured, then looked at her brother. "Did you have any inkling beforehand?"

"No, none at all." Phoem shook his head. "I only found out this morning bright and early. She left in the middle of the night, so they tell me."

"Has Khun Un been told?" Phloi asked.

Phoem gave a small chuckle. "You wouldn't have asked if you'd heard her remarks on the subject. Rather loud and shrill, I must say. All the way to the mouth of the *khlong* you could hear her. When I left the house she was still going on and on and on. She enjoys being abusive, as we all know."

"Poor Khun Choei," Phloi said again. "What are we going to do about it, Pho Phoem?"

"I don't know. But if you want my opinion, I think it's a good thing. Nothing to worry about. Khun Choei has gone to lead her own life. She'll have her own house to run, children to bring up and so forth. I may be wrong . . ." he paused, and went on hesitantly, "but it seems to me the main cause of it was not her squabble with Khun Un. It was Chao Khun Father's death that did it. She looked after him for a long time, you know. It was her occupation and his death took it away from her and she became a lost soul without it. A boat without a rudder, that's what she was like, drifting about aimlessly. Luang Osot had been helping her take care of Chao Khun Father. They like each other, but apart from that she feels especially close to him on account of his involvement with Chao Khun Father. He's been her partner, if you like. I'm not surprised she eloped with him. Oh, my!" He stopped abruptly. "I talk too much!"

"No, no, Pho Phoem. It makes sense. Do go on."

"Really?" Phoem laughed. "First time I've been paid such a compliment. But I have nothing more to say."

"Tell me about Luang Osot. What's he like? Does he love Khun Choei very much?"

"To tell you the truth, Mae Phloi, we've exchanged only a few words, he and I. He's so quiet and reserved, at least with me. No, I can't tell you what he's like."

"That's it. We know so little about him. Khun Choei tells me he's very nice, but she hasn't known him for very long either."

"I wouldn't worry if I were you, Mae Phloi. Khun Choei's not a fool, and she has enough income of her own to live comfortably—for a while anyway." He fell silent, and resumed half jokingly. "Actually, I should be doing some worrying about myself. Now that Khun Un hasn't got Khun Choei to persecute, It's most probable that she will appoint me her next victim."

Phloi nearly spoke up to invite him to come and live in her house just as she had done with Khun Choei. She discarded the plan immediately, however, because it wouldn't be the manly thing for Phoem. It would have been all right for Khun Choei, a defenceless woman, but Phoem ought to be more resourceful and able to sband on his own feet.

As if he could read her mind, Phoem laughed and said: "No, I wasn't intending to ask if I could move in with you. You won't have to bother about me, Mae Phloi. A single man like me has simple needs—accommodation presents no problem to him."

"What are your plans then?"

"Nothing at the moment. I'm not exactly living in the lap of luxury in Khlong Bang Luang but I'm used to it. Anyway, I can always decamp if things get unbearable. You know me, Mae Phloi. I'm easy."

When he had left, Phloi went on reviewing the situation to herself. She quite agreed with Phoem's assessment that it was a good thing. She would even go further than that and say it was a matter for rejoicing: Khun Choei, free and independent, settling down with a man of her own choice. Whether her life with him would be a happy one remained to be seen, but this could be said of most couples including Khun Prem and Phloi. And this "elopement"—was it really so scandalous? Phloi did not think so. Even if it were, people would forget about it soon enough. Khun Choei was after all not an adolescent but a grown woman. She had been an exemplary daughter to her late father and now she had taken steps to build a new life of her own. Only a few die-hard scandalmongers would find anything to snigger about in Khun Choei's action. One result of that action—a very happy result, Phloi thought selfishly—was that she had no reason now to visit the house in Khlong Bang Luang. She had intended to do so from time to time for Khun Choei's sake, had made up her mind to risk being shown the door by Khun Un. That resolution could now be scrapped—what a relief!

Months passed without any more news from Khun Choei. Sometimes Phloi would feel like going to see her—she had heard that Luang Osot's house was situated somewhere on Tanao Road, but would desist from carrying it out fearing that Khun Choei might not feel ready just yet to renew her old ties even with somebody very close to her. Or she might even be annoyed. In the end Phloi decided to wait and let Khun Choei make the first move herself. Khun Prem concurred with her on this, saying he was certain Khun Choei would never cut herself off from Phloi.

"Give her a little more time, Mae Phloi, and she'll be here of her own accord. Not only Khun Choei, but even Khun Un will come to you one of these days. Mark my words."

The latter part of Khun Prem's prediction was made half in jest, and Phloi could not help laughing at the extremely unlikely vision of Khun Un suddenly materializing in her sitting room.

There was much laughter in Phloi's house at that period, and peace, and contentment, and An continued to get bigger and bigger at an amazing rate. They were blessed with good health and no one doubted that they were also endowed with good character and intelligence. They got along very well together although from time to time Phloi had to stop On from giving way so readily to his little brother.

Chao Khun Father having died without giving his grandson An an official name, Phloi took him to her royal benefactress and asked her to do the honour.

"The father's name is Prem and the mother's name is Phloi," Sadet said, thinking out loud. "Prem and Phloi . . . The fashion nowadays seems to be polysyllabic names, so I suppose we have to follow it . . . Prem and Phloi . . . I've got it. Let the boy's name be 'Praphan.'" Along with the name she also gave An a gold pendant. It had her monogram engraved on it, which signified her gracious acceptance of him as a page in her retinue.

Khun Prem was delighted with the new name, but when Phloi

suggested that he should also give one to On, he said "Why can't we go on calling him On?"

"We can and we will," Phloi replied, somewhat impatiently. She didn't like it when Khun Prem appeared uncaring about his eldest son. "But, at the same time he should have an official one as well. Sadet has thought up such a lovely name for An. Praphan. You must try to match it for On."

Khun Prem laughed. "Why don't you do it yourself? You're his mother, and you're the literary one in this family. I'm no good at this sort of thing."

"That's not true at all," Phloi retorted. "You're just being modest, and you're teasing me. Go on, I insist!"

But he kept on refusing, smiling obstinately. Finally Phloi came out with "Praphon" and he said cheerfully, "Fine! Fine! That goes superbly with 'Praphan.' I like it very much."

And Phloi said to herself, "He loves On, as any father loves his son, but with me he pretends he's indifferent to the boy in order to increase my sympathy—to make me pity On even more, love him even more. He means well, but it's a trick all the same. And so unnecessary, considering how I already feel about On. We must have a heart-to-heart talk soon. I'll tell him to stop being cagey and show On how much his father cares for him."

That summer—An was now over a year old—Phloi started her second pregnancy. Khun Prem had been just as excited as she had been over her first one. He had wanted a son and his wish had been fulfilled. This time he asked Phloi to give him a daughter, a simple request, his tone seemed to imply, and one which Phloi should have no trouble in granting.

The summer months passed uneventfully. The rains came. And it was toward the end of the rainy season of that year, when the weather was already starting to turn cool, that it happened. The time was late at night. Phloi had been fast asleep and woke up with a start. Khun Prem was standing by the bed, his hand on her arm, gently shaking it, and he was speaking in a voice that sounded far away. "Wake up, Mae Phloi. Come to the window."

Phloi sleepily obeyed. Khun Prem put an arm round her shoulder and with the other pointed outward at the sky. Phloi looked and at that instant all her drowsiness fell away. She blinked at the sight. She gaped at it in consternation. It had a big round head—this apparition in the sky—round and palely reddish behind a veil of mist, and a tail, a long luminous tail as wide as a door panel, and the glow emanating from the whole thing made the stars nearby appear dim and insignificant.

"What is it?" Phloi whispered, shivering.

"A comet," Khun Prem whispered back, drawing her closer to him. "How enormous it looks."

"Oh Khun Prem, according to the old people this is a bad omen. I had no idea it would be so huge. Look at the tail stretching way over there, nearly touching the horizon. Is it really a bad omen? Is that why I feel so depressed? What's going to happen, Khun Prem?"

"Probably nothing," Khun Prem answered, not too confidently. "I'm told by people who study *farang* textbooks and know about these things that it is a natural phenomenon though a rare one. Even so, I can't help feeling uneasy either. I suppose they'd call me old-fashioned and superstitious."

They continued to watch in silence. After some minutes Khun Prem with a deep sigh suggested they ought to get back to bed. He soon fell asleep, but Phloi lay awake for a long time, nervously opening her eyes now and again to glance out of the window. It was still there, an eerie menacing glow in an otherwise peaceful sky, an ominous sign if ever there was one.

The next day the whole town talked about it. It could bode nothing but ill. It might be a portent either of death—death of some exalted personage—or of some terrible disaster such as a famine or a plague. No precise forecasts, no definite predictions, but a general sense of anxiety, not to say of fear, prevailed.

Also a great deal of sheer excitement over the novelty of it all, though this soon waned, for as it reappeared night after night—it lasted nearly two weeks—the comet became less of a sensation and people began to get used to having it up there with the other stars.

During this time Khun Prem would come home from the palace bearing more information of the scientific kind to relay to Phloi; what the astronomers had learned about comets; the name of this particular one; similar occurrences to date; the reason why the present phenomenon appeared so immense to our eyes; and so on. All this knowledge was very interesting, Phloi found, but it did not serve to dispel her premonition.

One day, on arriving home, Khun Prem said, "Your comet has nothing to do with us after all."

"Why do you say that?" Phloi asked.

"The news came to the palace this afternoon. The King of England is dead."

Phloi put a hand on her heart. "Oh! You see? It was a sign. That a death would occur—death of a mighty, exalted person, a king, a Lord of Life. But the King of England must have accumulated much, much merit, Khun Prem, so that even we in *Muang Thai* could see the sign. What was his name?"

"King Edward VII," Khun Prem told her, then gave a chuckle and went on. "You know, Mae Phloi, the comet can be seen not only in *Muang Thai* but all over the world. And all over the world there are subjects of the King of England. *Muang* England has many colonies: *Muang* India, *Muang* Burma, *Muang* Malaya and many others. The king was going to *sawankhot* (go to heaven), so it's quite right that his subjects everywhere should know about it."

"I've seen his pictures," Phloi remarked. "A fat *farang* with a beard. Not to be compared with our Phra Chao Yu Hua in nobleness and dignity. He's not my king but I'm sorry he's dead. May his soul find peace and happiness. I'm sorry, but I'm also relieved to know that the sign didn't point to our land."

"Me, too," Khun Prem admitted. "I caught the comet fever from you, Mae Phloi. Now I feel much better."

A few days later the comet, which had started to orbit away from Earth—and had been growing smaller and smaller—finally disappeared from view.

Not long afterwards Khun Prem remarked to Phloi one evening, "No audience today, Mae Phloi. Phra Chao Yu Hua was not feeling we...

Phloi immediately asked, "What was it—anything serious?"

"No, no, only a slight indisposition. He went on working but kept to his private study. He'll be all right in a day or two."

Five or six days elapsed without Phloi hearing any more concerning His Majesty's health. The royal residence at the time was Amphon Sathan Hall in Dusit Palace. Khun Prem stayed there when he was on overnight duty.

That afternoon he was supposed to go off duty and return home, and Phloi had a meal prepared for him as usual. But the afternoon, then the evening came and went without any sign of Khun Prem. Phloi waited for him half the night, finally went to bed and willed herself to sleep but with very little success.

The next morning saw her still waiting, still fidgeting, pacing to and fro, peering in the direction of the gate, watching the driveway. It was not Khun Prem, however, but Grandma Thiap who returned. She had been to the market and she was wailing as if her heart would break.

"The king is dead," she told Phloi. "The whole market is stricken. Nobody's selling or buying."

Phloi sat down trembling on the platform at the foot of the stairs. But within seconds she found herself refusing to believe it. Of course Khun Prem's absence from home indicated that some event of great import had transpired in the palace. But not necessarily the king's death. His condition might have worsened—that must be it! The market rumour must have been grossly exaggerated. The king dead? The Sun of our Universe had ceased to shine? The Most Venerable Bodhi Tree under whose protective shade we all lived had fallen down? No, she could not bring herself to accept it.

"Don't, Thiap," she said uncertainly, "Don't say it. It brings bad luck."

With her head touching the marble step and crying harder than ever, Thiap swore that that was what they were saying in the market. Then she left Phloi and went to tell the others, and it was not long before the sound of weeping could be heard from every corner of the compound.

Back in her room Phloi hesitated before the clothes cupboard,

ɔt so long ago she had worn mourning clothes for
ther, and now . . . She stopped and told herself off
would Khun Prem say when he came home to find her
at like a rabbit, panicking over nothing? He would soon
ring good news, Phloi reassured herself. She resolved to go
on wai.. for him before doing anything, believing anything—to go
on hoping despite everything, including her own heavy heart.

She went to station herself at a window and looked out over the
fence at the road beyond. Still no sign of Khun Prem. The road looked
desolate. The sky was overcast, the air felt chilly though the October
north wind was not blowing today and not a leaf stirred. From the
road Phloi turned her glance to the sprawling group of wooden houses
across the *khlong*. Outside one of them an old woman with a bent back
was crying to herself as she climbed up the rickety steps. Phloi averted
her gaze while protesting silently, "No, no, it's not true! You must have
heard it in the market like Thiap, but I tell you it's not true!" Her eyes
went in search of a more cheerful sight from another house nearby—a
jolly young couple lived there, Phloi had often seen them laughing and
teasing each other. They were there now, sitting in the doorway with
their feet resting on the lower floor of the small balcony. The girl's head
was buried in her arms. Her husband was comforting her and at the
same time wiping his own tearful face with a *phakhaoma*.

Phloi quickly withdrew from the window and went seeking refuge
in the centre room. Here on one of the walls was hung a portrait
of Phra Chao Yu Hua, an enlarged photograph taken on one of his
European tours, showing him seated at a window, dressed in *farang*
clothes, wearing a *farang* hat. He was leaning at the window and
smiling straight at you, smiling his characteristic smile, brimming with
loving kindness, radiant in benign powers and kingly virtues. Phloi
sat down before the portrait, drawing solace from it, and she was still
there when Khun Prem came back. He walked in and sat down beside
her. There was no need to ask him any question. He was crying. Phloi
had never seen him cry before. She paid reverence to the portrait, then
laid her head on his knees and burst into tears. Her sorrow was not
less than what she had felt at her own father's death. She also realized

that this was a far, far greater loss. As to what consequences the loss would bring she would not presume to guess, but she had no doubt that they would be far-reaching and of high significance.

When she had calmed down a little, Khun Prem said to her, "I must get back to the palace, Mae Phloi. I'll just have a quick wash and change. The Bathing Rite will be held this afternoon, then the procession of the urn from Amporn to the Maha Prasat in the Grand Palace. A new reign is starting. One must be careful of what one does, how one behaves, these first days of transition. Somdet Phra Borom... uh, I mean the new Phra Chao Yu Hua spent the night at Amphon— he didn't go back to Saranrom Palace at all. We were all kept quite busy. A great deal of commotion everywhere as you can imagine, and I haven't had a thing to eat since I don't know when. I'd better have a bite or I'll faint from hunger this afternoon."

At the mention of hunger Phloi was suddenly reminded of her duties. Drying her eyes she went off hurriedly to get things ready for Khun Prem's bath and send down instructions to the kitchen for a quick meal to be prepared and served. Opening the cupboard to get some clothes out she started to cry again. This time she did not bother to wipe away the tears. The king was dead. She was mourning for him, so was her husband, so were other people throughout this land who loved and worshipped him.

She sat with Khun Prem while he ate. He could hardly swallow his food and pushed away the plate of rice after taking only a few spoonfuls. They talked about what had happened, and this was what Khun Prem said to Phloi, "On Monday His Majesty sent a letter to the ministers regretting his inability to be with them—he always did this when unavoidably prevented from granting a ministerial audience. But he was well enough to go on working and walking about in his private apartment. On Thursday he didn't leave the bed chamber, but even then nobody in the royal household was unduly alarmed. He'd been working hard and needed a rest—that was the general impression.

"On Saturday morning the ministers were stunned when the doctors informed them of his critical condition. The message was conveyed in great haste to the crown prince, who came immediately from Saranrom Palace. We were filled with anxiety and fear, yet we clung to our hopes . . . But in the afternoon he lost consciousness. The end came at midnight. His family were there in the bed chamber—they had been keeping vigil all those hours.

"The whole palace was in tears. Some of the Chao Choms fainted. Dr. Poix spent the next hours running round ministering to these ladies—he nearly collapsed himself from sheer exhaustion.

"I cried as I have never cried before—not even when my own father died. Our greatly beloved Nai Luang—there was never anyone like him. You and I are privileged to have been born under his reign, Mae Phloi."

When Khun Prem had gone back to Dusit Palace and left her by herself again, what Phloi would have liked to do was to go to Sadet and be near her. She didn't do it, however, knowing that to present herself to Sadet at such a time would hardly be appropriate. The day dragged on, growing more dismal and oppressive. Then at some point in the afternoon the thought crossed her mind that the procession of the urn must be starting presently and she could go and watch and pay her homage and that would be the best thing she could do at such a time.

Together with Phit she set out in a cab towards Ratchadamnoen and along the way saw many fellow citizens, on wheel and on foot, heading for the same destination, dressed in mourning black carrying flowers, candles and incense sticks in their hands and with deep sorrow etched on their faces.

Leaving the cab at Chang Rong Si Bridge, Phit and Phloi walked on to the Inner Ratchadamnoen Avenue and sat down on the kerb as soon as they came upon available space. There were masses of people on both sides of the road, yet it was very quiet. All were waiting in silence, patiently. Near where Phloi was sitting stood a young soldier, one of the guards stationed along the route from Dusit to the Grand Palace. He held himself very straight, hands resting on the rifle butt, his face immobile, but his eyes were full of sadness like those of the people waiting behind him.

The sky darkened as they waited. Flashes of lightning streaked across black rainclouds in the distant and the rumbling of thunder broke the prevailing silence. Nobody stirred, however, except to make room for new arrivals. At last came the moment they had been waiting for. Phloi's flesh tingled at the sound of the funeral music mixed with the sobbing of the people. Now the procession had crossed Makhawan Bridge, and the long lines of candle-holders made the road gleam under the dark sky. The people lighted their own candles and prostrated themselves as the ceremonial palanquin bearing the Golden Urn came past. The weeping grew louder as though vying with the lamenting flutes and drums in the cortege. Phloi held her candles and incense sticks in trembling hands, waiting for the palanquin to reach the stretch of road in front of her, and when it did she bowed her head to the ground at the same time as those near her. Raising her head again she happened to glance at the soldier and saw the tears streaming down his face, such a young face, strong and sunburnt, a country lad no doubt. She had not wanted to break down in front of so many people, but seeing the soldier cry she could no longer contain herself. She cried with him, with abandon, and with the other strangers surrounding her, bound together with them in one common bereavement.

The Golden Urn had disappeared behind the walls of the Grand Palace. The crowds were making their way home. Phloi remained seated for a long time, then rose to her feet and walked slowly, gazing across the distance at the familiar towers and spires of the palace, remembering her first day there and thinking how very long ago it seemed. She felt that today marked the passing of an era in her life. She had come to the end of one journey and must begin another, but darkness had fallen and she could not make out what might lie beyond it.

There was another flash in the sky followed by claps of thunder, and then the rain came pouring down in a blinding torrent. Phloi went on walking slowly. Phit understood and did not try to hurry her. They got into the cab soaked to the skin and rode home in silence, and Phloi, weary and dejected in spirit, did not care if her clothes were wet or dry, or whether the air had turned cold in the rainstorm.

RAMA VI

NINETEEN

IT was in the afternoon and Phloi was watching her sons romp about on the front lawn of her house in Khlong Yom—her three sons, one of them her stepson whom she loved as she loved the two of her own: On now over seven, An about five, and the three-year-old Ot, conceived under the reign of King Chulalongkorn, Rama V, (also known as Phra Buddha Chao Luang) and born at the beginning of the reign of King Vajiravudh, Rama VI—during the week of the cremation rites for His Late Majesty, as a matter of fact.

Now she was expecting again. While carrying Ot she had incorrectly guessed his sex but had not been disappointed to have another son. This time she positively yearned for a daughter and had been praying and making pledges of offerings to deities and spirits, soliciting their goodwill and assistance in making her wish come true.

It was natural that Ot should have been thus nicknamed, following On and An as he did, and his official name "Praphot," given him by Khun Prem, likewise was meant to furnish a pleasing alliterative sequence to "Praphon" and "Praphan."

Phloi had already picked a name for her to-be-born daughter: Praphai, and Khun Prem had laughed with amusement at this manifestation of confidence on her part, and said, "Better have another name handy in case it turns out the same as last time."

Phloi laughed with him but remained confident.

Khun Prem had done well in his civil service career and had been twice promoted. At the beginning of the new reign he had been raised from an ordinary page to a ranking one, with the title of "Nai Sanong Ratchakhit," and then just as Phloi had begun to get accustomed to hearing people address him as "Khun Sanong" he had got himself another promotion. This had come about shortly after the coronation, an affair of unprecedented splendour bringing together the greatest number of royals from foreign lands ever before seen at any single event in this part of the world. Having distinguished himself in the performance of his duties during the coronation, Khun Prem had been awarded a chestful of medals and soon afterwards had been invested with the rank of "Phra" with the accompanying title of "Boriban Phuminat." The day he received his Certificate of Rank, Khun Prem said to his wife, "Being called 'Khun Sanong' wasn't so bad, but being called 'Khun Phra Boriban' makes me feel terribly old. Come to think of it, I am getting on. Look at this." He touched his temples, which showed a perceptible sprinkling of grey. "But I don't mind being looked upon as an old fogey as long as you, Mae Phloi, will disregard all evidence to the contrary and go on treating me as a young man always. So for a start, I forbid you to call me 'Khun Phra,' and if you disobey I'll leave you and find myself a new wife."

Phloi laughed delightedly. "Listen to you!" she exclaimed. "Calling yourself old and threatening to get a new wife all in the same breath. Get as many new ones as you want, as if I ever tried to stand in your way!"

She stopped laughing, and went on. "You're not the only one growing old around here, you know. In fact, I feel much older than you. In spite of the grey hairs you seem to be getting younger and younger every day."

She was not entirely chaffing him. Not long after the demise of His Late Majesty another tragedy had struck. Sadet had died. She had been taken ill one day and died only a few months thereafter. Nursing her newborn infant son, Phloi had taken him with her to the palace to stay with Khun Sai and Choi at the residence during the funeral rites held at the Dharma Sangwet Pavilion in the Grand Palace, and after the cremation she had visited them again, to comfort them and be comforted, to mourn with them and remember with them. Many of Sadet's erstwhile attendants had left the residence after the cremation and moved away from the Inner Court, from behind the high walls of

the Grand Palace to begin a new life outside. But Khun Sai and
had elected to stay on. Without Sadet at its centre the residence
wore an air of desolation and neglect, but it remained their true home
and they could not imagine themselves living anywhere else.

With Sadet's death Phloi's world had come apart once more and
once more the pieces had been put back together again somehow.
Slowly she had recovered from the blow, adjusted to the changed
shape of her world and gone on pursuing the course of her karma.
Emerging from her sorrows that time Phloi had felt like a full-fledged
elder. She had lost her mother, her father, and now Sadet, her revered
and beloved Sadet, her protector and refuge, and must now assume
the role of an elder herself, must rely on herself, must be someone the
young people, particularly her own children, could rely on—not only
for material help but for counsel and moral support, for sympathy, for
compassion . . .

And Khun Prem? It was true about his giving the impression of
getting younger. The new court was a youthful court with its own style
of work and play and everyday living, and Khun Prem had adopted
the style, adopted it with ease in his own natural, unself-conscious
way. Even his gestures and movements had become different, Phloi
noticed. They had acquired a kind of *farang*-like jauntiness, she would
say. He had also given up betel-nut chewing and Thai cheroots and
taken to smoking *farang* cigarettes; and he had formed the costly
habit of drinking *farang* whiskies and wines, which Phloi found
disturbing—not the expense but the habit itself. She wished he
wouldn't do it but never felt bold enough to come right out and say
so. As though to forestall her criticism, Khun Prem had more than
once extolled the superior quality of these *farang* drinks (no harmful
stuff in them, he assured her) and talked about social drinking and
civilized living and so on and so forth. He spoke eloquently, but to
Phloi liquor still meant liquor.

Another big change was in his attitude toward clothes. He who had
paid little attention to what he wore now fussed over every item—hat,
shoes, jacket, *phanung*. He'd bought stacks of new *phanung*, silk ones
and cotton ones and sought out the best materials for his jackets to

wear with them. In the old days a page when going inside—among the ladies of the court, that is—had been allowed to wear only cotton *phanung* and had been obliged to run his fingers through his hair so as to muss it up a little and not look too neat and handsome. All that had changed. Because His Majesty was a bachelor, the "outside" had become the centre of activities, and it was here that the best-dressed people congregated, sometimes looking as though they were competing for prizes. On the whole Phloi was amused by Khun Prem's sartorial enthusiasm, though when he pondered aloud the idea of sending his jackets by steamer to be laundered in Singapore ("they do it so much better down there, my dear") she did think he was going too far, and dealt with the situation by keeping silent while at the same time continuing to have the jackets washed and pressed at home as though he had never hinted otherwise.

Following another fashion Khun Prem had bought a motorcar and hired a Malay to drive it—with Phloi's unmixed approval. She felt not a little proud when out riding in this vehicle with its shiny brass fittings. It looked very smart and clean and went much faster than the horse carriage. Though forsaking the latter in favour of the motorcar Khun Prem had not abandoned the horses, but had, in fact, bought a few more for his stable. He had joined the Wild Tiger Cavalry Corps, a creation of His Majesty, and riding was now one of his great pleasures and passions. Phloi went in constant fear for his safety because he would be venturesome and ambitious and insist on trying new stunts.

But the change in her own home paled into insignificance when she reflected on the difference between the Inner Court then and now. Many another residence besides Sadet's had become empty. His Late Majesty's queens and some of the Chao Chom Mothers (royal consorts not of royal blood) had moved outside to live in their private palaces and mansions all over the city. A number of lady officials and *khlon*s remained inside and the old customs continued to be maintained, but the streets were deserted, the windows shut, and signs of withering and decaying confronted you at every corner. Where had the chatter and laughter gone? Phloi asked herself as she passed by the dear old landmarks on her way to see Choi and Khun Sai. Where was the throbbing vibrant Inner Court that had once been the hub of her universe?

As to her old family home in Khlong Bang Luang, Phloi had had no news since Phoem had moved out soon after Khun Choei's sudden departure with Luang Osot. Phoem had taken a wife, a girl named Yuan whose father was a small trader with a house in Ban Khaek Road. Phoem had crossed the river with his few earthly possessions and moved in with her. He still worked in the same department and had also received a rank and title: from plain Nai Phoem he had been promoted to Luang Phanwichan. Almost everybody including Phloi now called him Khun Luang Phan or simply Khun Luang, omitting the titular name when it was not necessary to use it.

As Phloi was sitting there watching the boys play and letting her thoughts wander back and forth between yesterday and today a rickshaw came to a halt outside the gate. A middle-aged woman dressed in subdued colour in keeping with her years climbed down, paid the Chinese puller and walked in. The afternoon sun being at such an angle, her face was obscured at first. Phloi watched her approach incuriously—in this house someone or other was always dropping by to call on a friend or a relative living somewhere in the compound.

When she recognized who it was she jumped up and dashed forward shouting "Khun Choei! Khun Choei!"

She was beside herself with joy and so was Khun Choei. They were both laughing and crying at the same time.

"Why didn't you come see me before, Khun Choei? I missed you so. How are you? How's everything?"

Khun Choei sat down, pulling Phloi down to sit beside her. "I've been longing to see you too, Mae Phloi. But give me a glass of water first. I'm so hot and thirsty. Let me rest a while and I'll answer all your questions."

Phloi ordered refreshments and called to the boys to come and meet their aunt. Khun Choei hugged each of them in turn, but her specially big hug she bestowed on Ot. "I think I love him best," she said when they had bounded off to resume their play. Then she laughed and chided herself. "I hardly know them. How can I be so partial? I've turned into such an old woman, Phloi. You mustn't mind me."

"And your children?" Phloi asked.

"None. Would have brought them if I had. And none by his first wife, so I take it he can't have any children. Considering our straitened circumstances, perhaps it's just as well."

Khun Choei had grown thinner, her once-fair complexion had been darkened by the sun, and her hands had become coarse and broad-knuckled. It was obvious that her personal appearance was not one of her preoccupations. Yet she looked very well, Phloi thought. She talked and laughed gaily and her eyes sparkled—they were the eyes of a healthy and happy woman.

"Why did you stay away so long, Khun Choei?"

"I meant to come. I planned to come. But in the beginning there was so much to do and I kept putting it off. Then time simply flew by— weeks into months into years. We also had to make trips upcountry . . . Anyway, things are better now and I'll be coming to see you often, if you have no objection, that is."

"How can you say that! You must never neglect me again, Khun Choei. You must come very, very often and bring Khun Luang Osot. Tell me about him, about yourself, your house, I want to hear everything."

"Not everything, my dear. It's such a long story. But I'll tell you about that first day, Phloi, the night and day of my elopement. What a day! He took me straight to his house in back of Tanao Road. I nearly wept when I saw it. It looked so small and shabby and not at all inviting, to put it mildly. I stood in a narrow lane, a long narrow twisting muddy lane with uneven wobbly planks to walk on, and in this lane the houses were built close together with very little space between them—so close that a chicken cannot land on the ground, as they say. So close you could hear what your neighbours were saying and when they hurled curses at one another it came over loud and clear. And there were pools of stagnant water everywhere. I almost broke down at the foot of the stairs but I didn't because I loved him and felt sorry for him and didn't want him to feel bad.

"We went up and I had another shock. He had been living alone since his wife's death, you know, and the house was a veritable rats' nest. The amount of sweeping and scrubbing I put in—you'd have been impressed, Mae Phloi!

"The first time I went to the market, by myself, carrying the basket myself, I felt very embarrassed, but I got used to it quickly, and if you'd seen me, Phloi, you would have thought I'd been doing it all my life!"

Khun Choei paused and laughed at the way things had turned out for her.

"We've known some hard times," she went on, not complainingly but by way of keeping the record straight. "We can't afford luxuries. We have to skimp. But all in all you can also say we've been happy. No fights, no tension, no friction, no heartaches. Khun Luang Osot is a good man, and he's so sweet and considerate. To this day he's never uttered an unkind word to me, although I must have deserved a few now and again!

"He wouldn't touch my money. Didn't want people to say he was after my fortune. It wasn't much of a fortune! But when his department was dissolved after the last reign ended and we were really hard up, I had to put my foot down and make him use it to set up a medicine shop. Now we've rented a place right on the road and we're living there too. It's more convenient."

Khun Choei living in a shophouse, Phloi said to herself. *Incredible! It would have been more believable if all this were happening to me.* She wanted to hear more details, but to ask for them outright would have been an imposition, so in a roundabout way she inquired, "Is the shop doing well?"

"We make enough to live on," Khun Choei said. "It won't make us tremendously rich, that's for sure. We have two girls to help us but Khun Luang and I do most of the work ourselves. Sometimes I'm at it all day long and half the night—crushing the ingredients, mixing them, making the pills, labelling, and so on. Once in a while we go to the provinces to sell and buy—sell our medicines and buy those herbs you can't get in town. And that reminds me—" From a parcel she had brought with her Khun Choei took out several envelopes containing various kinds of pills and powder. "I thought you might be pregnant again, Phloi, so I brought this especially for you. Take it when you feel faint, or tired or dizzy. The rest are for children's ailments. This one is a laxative, and this you give them when they have a fever . . ." Khun Choei went over the medicines one by one, then gave a chuckle. "I'm not trying to pass myself off as a doctor, my dear. I'm just a doctor's wife who loves to give away pills and advice.

"Not that we have very many patients, Phloi. Most of them are poor too, some poorer than we are. The rich ones are flocking to doctors practicing *farang* methods. So we don't always get paid. Never mind. One does what one can to give help when help is needed."

Khun Choei talked of being poor as something ordinary, as nothing shameful or repellent. Certainly nothing terrible like, say, an incurable disease. She talked with characteristic frankness and naturalness. Her manner towards Phloi was the same as it had always been—that of a genuinely affectionate and generous elder sister. And if you expected her to resent having to live in a shop-house and ride in a rickshaw— resent having become the poorer sister, in other words—you would have been wrong. Khun Choei resented nothing. She didn't put on any act either. No defensive haughty act, nor, conversely, a sweetly humble one to rouse pity and curry favour. Not that Phloi ever suspected for a minute that Khun Choei would be capable of such pettiness, but it is eminently satisfying to have your faith in people you love and admire affirmed again and again. No, poverty had not reduced Khun Choei's inner dignity. She accepted being poor but was not crushed by it. Adversity had failed to give her bitterness, envy, or self-pity. If anything, it had brought into play a quality of hers which had been under-employed in the old prosperous days: courage. Courage worthy of those ancestors who had proved themselves so valiant in the battlefields of long ago. They would have applauded the way Khun Choei was conducting her own battles, Phloi thought. They would have been very proud of her.

Now the three boys had had enough of tumbling about and came to join their mother and their aunt. Phloi gave them a little lecture on how they must always obey their Khun Aunt Choei and treat her with great love and respect, and the boys were pleased to show their interest in Khun Aunt by pulling and tugging at her legs and arms and fighting for a seat in her lap.

Khun Choei played with her nephews for a while, then she said, "I almost forgot, Phloi, when I heard you had a new son I wanted to send him a welcoming gift . . . Here, I've brought it with me."

Phloi had a lump in her throat. She recognized the gold necklace-and-pendant Khun Choei took out from her betel-nut bag to put round Ot's neck. Khun Choei had worn it as a child. She had taken it along with other belongings in her flight from Khlong Bang Luang to Tanao Road. She could have used it for a more practical purpose. But of course she wouldn't. She would rather make a gift of it to her nephew, to her Mae Phloi's youngest son. Giving was an expression of her love, and Khun Choei would go on giving. The recipient of her gift in this case was equal to the occasion. Ot, as he had been taught, joined his palms together and lowered his head and hands onto her lap, expressing his thanks and respect at the same time.

After a while, though, polite manners gave way to love of fun, and Ot began to treat his new-found aunt like an old friend. He jumped up and down, skipped round her, urged her to join him in a race and ended up singing a song for her.

The afternoon wore on. Khun Prem came home from work and was greatly delighted that Khun Choei had at long last returned from her self-exile. The two caught up with each other's news and had a long and pleasant chat together. Then Khun Prem excused himself to go up to the house, and as soon as he was out of sight, Phloi said to her sister, "How does he strike you, Khun Choei?"

"What?" Khun Choei was puzzled. "How does he strike me? He looks all right to me. Nothing wrong with his health, is there? He looks quite healthy."

"That's not what I mean. Do you think he's changed a great deal?"

"Well, he's a little older. So are we all. But . . . yes, perhaps he has changed. More bubbling, more volatile than he used to be."

"That's it. You've noticed it too, you see. Sometimes I wonder if he's not becoming a little too volatile. I think I rather prefer the Khun Prem who was steadier, more solid. But it could be that I'm just too old to keep pace with all this change."

Khun Choei laughed. "Change in manner and style, Mae Phloi. It's the new style of talking and walking and gesturing—different from what we were used to when we were children. Nothing to worry about. You're not old and Khun Prem is all right, even if he's changed his style somewhat. You should in any case be thankful you have a healthy and not a sickly husband. As for change, you and I know that time passes and we can't force things to stay the same. Now when we were children . . ."

They went on chatting and had not run out of topics when Khun Choei got up saying it was late and she had to get home. She promised to come again soon and bring her Khun Luang with her. As Phloi said to Khun Prem afterwards, it had been the most heartening reunion. She rejoiced in Khun Choei's happiness, and talking with Khun Choei had made her feel easier in her mind about many things.

Another afternoon found Phloi paying Choi and Khun Aunt Sai a visit at the residence. She brought them fruit and sweets and they had some palace titbits for her to take home. The three of them chatted together and had refreshments and then Khun Sai retired to her bedroom for a nap. She had lost much of her old verve and had become rather frail and Choi's main occupation these days was looking after her.

"Do you remember, Phloi? One time at Dusit Palace we talked about change and how life as we knew it and what we saw round us might one day disappear?"

"Of course I remember, Choi."

"I think it has disappeared, Phloi. I'm a survivor here from another age. It looks like I'll die here—like one of those old women we used to know when we were children."

"You're not so old, Choi . . ."

"Say no more, my dear Phloi. If you think I'm contemplating going outside to get myself a husband like the others, forget it. For one thing I can't leave Khun Aunt. And for another I can never leave my cage, for I'm a caged bird who will perish if you release me. I've always been good to the old people—made a lot of merit that way, so I hope that in my extreme old age some kind-hearted youngster will be ministering to me."

Choi laughed; her sense of fun—her love of *sanuk*—was very much in evidence as always, though Phloi thought she could detect a glimmer of doubt and anxiety in her eyes. But Choi would never complain, she would never let her friends see how troubled she felt. There was a core of toughness in her character that prevented such a revelation. Phloi did not worry too much about her, however, for she never doubted Choi's strength and resourcefulness. No matter what happened, Choi would rally, would walk her chosen path with head held high, enjoying herself and giving joy to others. These days they did not get to meet very often, what with Phloi being immersed in housewifely duties and Choi busy making herself useful to her seniors staying on in the Inner Court, but they remained the closest of friends, and this friendship was one of the few things both felt they could be certain of in this changing world.

During those first years of the new reign Phloi spent most of her waking hours looking after her children, her husband, her people in the house. She rarely attended official functions. Generally speaking, the women seemed to have receded into the background compared with in previous years when they had been very active in court circles, especially following the time when Her Majesty the Queen (now the Queen Mother) had ruled as regent during His Late Majesty's European tour. Now most of the important occasions seemed to be predominantly masculine affairs and Khun Prem usually went to them without asking his wife to accompany him. Phloi did not mind in the least. She much preferred staying home with the children.

When the time of confinement drew near she made her preparations, but except for fervently hoping and praying for a daughter she took everything very calmly—after all, she had done it twice already. Khun Prem had wanted her to see a *farang* doctor, and she had absolutely declined. She did not even ask what nation-ality *farang*—he could have been English, French, American, or whatever else for all she cared. Why use *farang* methods when herbal medicine and the heating boards for afterbirth had carried her through so successfully? She had been so forceful in her argument that Khun Prem had been obliged to let her have her way.

As it turned out, she nearly died. Her labour pains, unlike on the two previous occasions, dragged on abnormally, subsiding only to begin again and again, increasing in severity but leading to nothing. Finally her suffering reached such an unbearable point that she collapsed and lost consciousness. When she came to she felt weak and thirsty, but the pain had gone. She asked for water. Khun Prem put the glass drinking pot to her lips, and she sucked at it, relishing every drop. Then she saw a beard. It belonged to a tall *farang* standing over her, smiling down at her.

"I sent for him," Khun Prem said in a low voice. "He got here in the nick of time. How lucky we were, how very lucky. He had to use instruments to deliver your baby, Mae Phloi. There was no other way."

The *farang* doctor put his fingers on Phloi's wrist, then he spoke to Khun Prem.

"He says you're doing fine," Khun Prem relayed the message to his wife. "He wants you to try and go back to sleep."

"And the baby?" Phloi asked.

"It's a girl, my dear. That's what you wanted, isn't it?"

"Praphai, my daughter," said Phloi to herself as she drifted into sleep.

A few days afterwards Phloi learned from Khun Prem what the *farang* doctor had told him. Khun Prem said that she had been in grave danger, it had been an extremely complicated and difficult birth and that she would not be able to bear any more children.

TWENTY

PHLOI was an invalid for several months. "And no wonder," commented the faithful Phit, now called Granny Phit by most people in the house. "All this comes from your giving birth to Khun Praphai the *farang* way. Without proper heating after delivery the blood turns bad and causes plenty of trouble." But Phloi quite realized that she would not have been alive today if Khun Prem had not sent for the *farang* doctor that night. Throughout her illness Khun Prem proved himself the most solicitous of husbands. If she had asked for the moon he would have tried to get it for her. He not only hurried home to be by her side but he stayed home night after night, something that had not taken place too frequently over the past few years. Cheered by his attentiveness, Phloi couldn't help thinking that deep down he had remained the same man and was not turning into a stranger as she had now and again feared.

Beside Phit and Khun Prem there were also Khun Choei and Choi and Phoem to nurse and coddle her and make her feel that to be ailing certainly had its compensations. Khun Choei and Luang Osot came to see her all the time, bringing Thai prescriptions to supplement *farang* remedies and render them more efficacious; Phoem looked in nearly every day and Choi was shuttling to and fro between Phloi and her old people in the palace, occasionally spending the night or a few days at Khlong Yom to keep the patient company.

Time passed and Phloi recovered. She had not gained back all her strength but she was well enough to lead a normal life, and to resume having anxious thoughts about her husband who, she felt, was drawing further from her again.

"*Samakhom*," Thai for "society," was a new word to Phloi. *Khao samakhom*, "joining society," was, according to Khun Prem, a must if one wished to prosper in life. Prosper or not it was Phloi's observation that Khun Prem's *khao samakhom* activities consisted mainly of cultivating a taste for the sumptuous and the showy, of coming home late, if at all, reeking of alcohol and cigarette smoke, of going out with lots of money to gamble with and to lose it all, and, last but not least, of lapsing into some daydream of society while at home with his wife and not hearing a word of what she was saying to him. Society was what he liked and Phloi did not want to deprive him of it, but it hurt to be treated like a table or chair, like something which might be necessary or even indispensable but needed no loving care in handling because it was such a durable fixture.

Perhaps Phloi would have been fairly content with being a table had Khun Prem been lavishing his loving care on the children. Khun Prem, of course, was doing no such thing. He might love them in his own fashion but he spent hardly any time with them and showed very little interest in them. The children were probably too young to feel sensitive about this, but they had Phloi to feel it on their behalf.

Lovely children they were at this stage, all four of them, especially Praphai. Praphai at two was a real enchantress, a cuddly talkative enchantress prettily chirping out phrases in her sweet voice and displaying a remarkable vocabulary for her age. Phloi had been a quiet child, close-mouthed almost, and Praphai must have inherited this gift of the gab from her grandmother. She was also on the way to becoming quite a scholar. Now that the two older boys were going to school Phloi had started giving reading lessons to Ot at home, and Praphai had been joining these sessions of her own accord. Reciting the names of the letters of the alphabet had been a delightful game to her and now she was actually learning to read.

Phloi could be described as loving all her children equally in that she observed a strict impartiality in dealing with them. On the other hand she felt differently about each one of them. On—for the very reason that he was not of her own flesh and blood—engaged her sense of pity more readily than the others, and when it came to impartial treatment she always put more thought into it where he was concerned, taking special care that he should not feel in any way inferior to the other three. Concerning On's position in the house, nobody questioned it any longer. They had stopped asking "Whose son is he?" He was simply one of the sons, without qualifications, and to the younget children he was simply their eldest brother. On was a gentle obedient child and he was very good to Phloi; he was such a good son, such a devoted son, that sometimes Phloi found herself tempted to take his side even when she shouldn't. Unlike On, An, could be stubborn and unruly, and given to tanrums and outbursts of violent temper when thwarted. This ungracious streak in her first-born's character bothered Phloi not a little and she tried her best to rectify it, using persuasion as well as sterner methods. As for Ot—something about Ot made Phloi love him in a special way (though she kept this to herself). Ot had a sense of humour all his own, and his own way of reacting and responding to experience. He was prone to laughter, so many things seemed to him funny, or ridiculous, or absurd, among the most absurd being himself. Three boys, three different temperaments. On handing over his toy to An because the latter coveted it, On loving that toy dearly still but loving even more to give it to his brother; An easily bored with his own toys, eagerly pouncing on the new acquisition; and Ot, uniquely detached, unconcernedly letting his toy be taken away by whoever wanted it—he could always find another one to play with straightaway.

Loving them all, Phloi nevertheless would admit, if pressed upon, to feeling more deeply concerned with Praphai than with the boys. Because Praphai was the youngest, the last child she could have and, most importantly, because she was the only daughter. In her daughter Phloi could see herself starting out in life all over again, growing up in body and soul, going through joys and sorrows, dreaming dreams. To her daughter Phloi had transferred all the dreams she had dreamed for herself, and more, for she would like her daughter to have all the things she had lacked and be blessed with more happiness than she had known.

All of them—Praphai and the three boys—were very attached to their mother. They told her their cherished secrets and shared their triumphant moments with her and when miserable they came to her for comfort and consolation. They brought her the gift of love every day and made her a proud and happy mother.

But she longed to have them just as close to their father—or at least closer than they were. They scarcely knew him, and he them. If Khun Prem at this period seemed distant to Phloi he was virtually inaccessible as far as the children were concerned. Once in a while he would be in an affectionate mood and start fraternizing with the children, but as they were not accustomed to his company, the children tended to be bashful with him. Then Khun Prem would lose interest-—he didn't have the kind of patience needed to reach a child's heart. Other times, urged by Phloi and eager to do her bidding, the children would go to their father and then they too, on their part, would lose interest on finding him, though kindly enough, not at all inclined to frolic with them—he happened to have other things on his mind, as he usually did. Phloi often despaired of bringing them together, but the instincts of the natural mother would not let her stop trying.

On one occasion, after considerable hesitation, she said to Khun Prem, "Please don't misunderstand me. I don't presume to teach you how to be a father, but I think you ought to let the children see more of you, get closer to you, so they won't feel lonely and neglected."

"You think too much," said Khun Prem in his good-natured way. "They're too young for any such feelings. When they're older they'll get together more with their father. Plenty of time for us to get acquainted."

"But Khun Prem," Phloi grew more persistent. "The children want their parents near them. I know. I was their age once."

Her husband laughed. "They have you with them all the time—"

"That's not enough," Phloi interrupted. "I'm only their mother. They need their father too. A father's care has great importance, perhaps a greater importance. Children are attached to their mothers when they're very young, but as soon as they're old enough to know—"

"Let me ask you something, Mae Phloi." It was Khun Prem's turn to interrupt, and his voice had taken on a note of vexation. "Have the children been complaining or do you just think they should be?"

Phloi's sensitive ear caught the undertone and she knew that to pursue the matter further would only lead to a futile argument, so she brought the subject to a close by saying mildly, "Of course they haven't been complaining. It may be that I think too much, as you say. Don't mind me, Khun Prem." And with an inward sigh of disappointment she steered the conversation on to other topics with no apparent difficulty.

She could always bring a gleam into his eyes by asking after his horses. For it was his horses which seemed to interest Khun Prem much more than his children or anything else. When the Wild Tiger Corps and the Tiger Cavalry had been created under the new Sovereign's direction, Khun Prem had been among the first courtiers to join up, becoming a dashing Mounted Tiger officer in addition to being a high palace official with the rank and title of Phra Boriban Phuminat. Phloi had been pleased; the Wild Tiger movement was greatly favoured by His Majesty and in her opinion it was very commendable indeed that Khun Prem should be following his Lord and Master so enthusiastically. And how superb he looked in his full-dress uniform. The Mounted Tiger uniform, incidentally, did rather outshine those of the other Wild Tigers. She had been pleased, and then, as mentioned earlier in these pages, she had started to feel afraid for his safety as a dedicated horseman with unlimited aspirations. Khun Prem's passion for horseback-riding must have been lurking secretly all these years, unknown even to himself, biding its time, waiting to burst into the open. Once it had done so it claimed and absorbed all his attention. When he came back early from the office he would make straight for the stable to admire his splendid imported animals and discuss their welfare endlessly with the groom. He rose before dawn for his morning ride, came home radiant, elated, especially when he had attempted yet another new feat more challenging than the last one and succeeded at it. Or even when he had not. For Phloi's fears had now been substantiated. He returned home one morning covered with bruises and cuts. Phloi cried out in horror on seeing him, and suffered for him when he said one of his arms might have been fractured. Her shock and sympathy gave way to amazement however when she realized he was laughing gaily while recounting this "little" accident. "*Mai pen rai*," he said with an exuberant grin. "It doesn't matter. It's nothing at all, my dear Mae Phloi." Khun Prem—a would-be crack-rider! Who would have guessed it in his early youth.

Looking at her thriving children, Phloi often indulged in making conjectures about them, picturing them variously engaged at some point or other in the years to come. You never can tell how people will turn out, including your husband and children.

"Tell me, On, what would you like to be when you grow up?"

"Oh, I'm going to be a soldier," said On with absolute certainty.

"And be taken far away from me to some remote camp," Phloi noted to herself somewhat plaintively. Aloud she asked, "Why do you want to be a soldier?"

"I want to march and drill and learn to shoot. Maybe I will ride a horse too like Khun Father."

"And what about you, An? What are you going to be?"

"I don't want to be a soldier," An replied after pondering the question. "My teacher says I speak well and argue well, and ought to be a lawyer. So that's what I want to be—a lawyer."

Phloi was not sure if she wholeheartedly approved of teachers making such suggestions to their very young pupils. All the same, making your living round and about the law courts was probably a little better than soldiering in back-of-the-beyond places.

"Now it's your turn, Ot. What do you have to say? What will you be when you grow up?"

"Nothing," Ot said laughing and vigorously shaking his head. "I won't grow up. I'm going to stay like this with you."

Phloi laughed with him but felt obliged to put in a few practical words. "We all grow up," she said. "We pass from childhood to adulthood, from being a *dek* to being a *phuyai* who must work, earn a living . . ."

"I know," Ot cut in. "I don't like work. I won't be grown-up. I'll be a child. On and on and on."

"I want to grow and grow," Praphai announced in her sweet voice. "I want to be tall and pretty like Mother." The announcement was acknowledged with a hug and a kiss from Mother.

The happiness that Phloi derived from her children was abundant beyond measure. Funny to think how in those pre-wedding days she had been full of misgivings, had so dreaded having to leave Sadet and the girls in the palace to go and live with a man, a stranger, and look how that stranger had now become part of her—indivisibly part of her. While daunted by the prospect of becoming a wife, however, she had never had any real qualms about becoming a mother, had in fact looked forward to motherhood and endowed it with much glamour. But the real thing, she found to her delight, far surpassed her expectations, fanciful as they had been. To be sure she had gone through some bad days and nights on account of the children. That time, for instance, when On had stepped on a nail and the wound had festered and his temperature had shot up most alarmingly. Each occurrence of children's disease, be it mumps or chicken pox or measles, had nearly put Phloi herself on the sick list. Her nerves were too well attuned to the children's aches and pains and they could not run up a fever without her intently willing the excess heat to pass from their bodies into her own. Never mind. These anguished moments were but a small price to pay. The children had recovered and she had survived to reclaim her happiness in their recovery.

Phloi counted among her blessings that she had Luang Osot to depend on when there was an illness in the family. Childless himself, Khun Luang loved children and was devoted to his nephews and niece and took pride in the fact that he was one of their favourite grownups. They might have been afraid of other doctors, but not of this one. When they shrank from his medicine he could always charm away their fears by some clever bargaining or gentle coaxing. He never scolded. He told them stories and made them laugh. When one of the children fell ill the rest would wait for Khun Uncle Doctor's visits full of pleasure and excitement. Even the patient, unless too sick, looked forward to being entertained by him.

Luang Osot had been treating her children for some time when Phloi at a long-sought opportune moment brought up the subject of fees and so forth with Khun Choei.

"Your Khun Luang doesn't seem to want to talk about it," she told Khun Choei, appealing to her. "What should I do? What do you say?"

"What do you want me to say, Mae Phloi?"

"I think he ought to charge something. I can't let him go on doing it for free, you know. It's his profession and he would be getting something if they were somebody else's children. Perhaps if you would have a word with him . . . Will you?"

"I can't," Khun Choei said serenely. "If I talked to him about it he would be very angry. But if I were you I wouldn't speak to him either, because he would be very hurt if you did, and hurting somebody's feelings is worse than making them angry."

Phloi gave a helpless sigh and began again. "What about me? I'm taking advantage of everybody and it's not good at all. If I were very poor and could not afford to pay it would be another matter, but seeing that I can it's only fair and right that I should."

Khun Choei looked at Phloi thoughtfully before answering. "Don't forget we are sisters, Mae Phloi. Think about it. I'm your elder sister and your children are my nephews and my niece, mine and Khun Luang's. Isn't it natural that we should all help our nieces and nephews and attend to them when they're sick? Money has nothing to do with it. If you were poor I would be doing it for free, as I'm doing now. The question of money doesn't enter into it when we are sisters, loving each other as we do, but for me to accept money from you would amount to our having stopped being sisters and becoming estranged. I can't have that. If I should stop regarding someone as my blood relation because of his or her poverty you would criticize me severely, wouldn't you? Well then, I would be equally blameworthy to do it on account of her wealth. I dare speak like this because I love you very much, Phloi."

In the last two phrases Khun Choei called herself "*phi*," meaning "elder sister" (or "elder brother" as the case may be). She hadn't done this in a long while; she generally used "*chan*" (one of the many words equivalent to "I") in talking to Phloi. Her choice of this particular first person pronoun, unconscious or not, deepened the meaning of what she said. There was nothing more to discuss. It only remained for Phloi to accept the elder sister's true sentiments with understanding and gratitude.

Phloi's life in the early years of the new reign thus revolved round her family and a few close friends, having its ups and downs inside the domestic border, with little or no involvement in what went on beyond it. Only once in a while she was made to realize what a homebody she had become. Like that time Khun Prem floated this question at her out of the blue: "Mae Phloi, if I danced in a masked play, what role would suit me?"

Phloi reacted with a giggle. Khun Prem dancing in a *khon*—dear me! "Where and when, pray tell?"

"Don't laugh, Mae Phloi," Khun Prem said unsmilingly. "I'm thinking of taking lessons."

Khun Prem learning the khon *dance!* No, Phloi could not believe her ears.

"What's all this, Khun Prem? Why should you want to dance the *khon*?"

"Nai Luang likes it," Khun Prem answered briefly.

This provided sufficient reason for Phloi. If His Majesty liked it, it was all right, it was a good thing. With her upbringing Phloi had a firm belief in the righteousness of royal policy and in court officials doing their duty and acting in loyal accordance with it. She couldn't help feeling embarrassed, though, visualizing Khun Prem strutting (or stumbling?) all over the stage.

Her embarrassment turned to utter astonishment at the next piece of information imparted by Khun Prem.

"Our present Nai Luang is very fond of the theatre, Mae Phloi," Khun Prem said, "all kinds of theatre—*khon*, *lakhon*, everything. He performs in it too, you know."

Phloi gaped at her husband. She remembered during the last reign, during the festival celebrating His Late Majesty's return from Europe, there had been a beautiful and unprecedented performance—unprecedented because some of the Chao Chom Mandas (royal consort mothers) had taken part in it. Phloi recalled the great excitement this had aroused and how exclusive the presentation had been, with nobody from outside in the audience. "Now Khun Prem tells me His Majesty himself is performing!" Was this the beginning of a new tradition? Phloi would have to bestir herself and try to catch up with the advancing world. At the moment she could not yet take it all in, but she desisted from questioning Khun Prem any further as she did not consider it proper for her to discuss casually so lofty a subject.

A month or so went by. Phloi assumed that Khun Prem's *khon* lessons had started in the meanwhile, but one day he said to her, "Mae Phloi, I've been thinking it over and I've decided that I'm too old for this dance. There are enough agile young fellows to do it and I'll just let them carry on without me. But it's all right, Mae Phloi. I could perhaps join the talk-plays, the *lakhon phut*. His Majesty is also very interested in them."

Phloi was relieved to hear about his decision. "But what are these talk-plays?" she asked. She was familiar with the sing-plays (*lakhon rong*), such as those staged by the Pridalai Troupe, but she had never seen a talk-play and had no idea what it was like.

"I'll take you to one, one of these days," Khun Prem promised. "The actors and actresses are dressed like ordinary people and they speak like us—they don't sing or dance."

"Is it fun?" Phloi inquired. "It sounds to me like a game we used to play when we were children, pretending to be grownups and speaking like them—"

Khun Prem laughed. "Oh, Mae Phloi. I must get you out of this house more often, before you become hopelessly old-fashioned. A talk-play can be quite amusing if you know how to watch it. I must take you."

Phloi didn't mind at all being called old-fashioned. She said laughingly, "Of course I haven't moved with the times like you. I'll never be able to keep up with you, Khun Prem. You're such a modern young man. And looking younger and younger everyday."

Khun Prem beamed at her. The expression in his eyes brought back memories of the days when they were first married.

"Do you really think so, Mae Phloi? Do I really look young to you?"

"Why should you care what I think?" She was sounding rather girlish herself.

"I do care," he said earnestly, placing a hand on her arm and holding it. "It's very important because you are important to me—the most important person in my life."

"You see, Khun Prem?" She smiled at him, mocking him a little. "You even sweet-talk like a young man."

Ignoring her banter, Khun Prem went on in a bemused tone of voice. "I must confess I have this fear of old age, Mae Phloi, and the knowledge that it's creeping up on me makes me feel so discouraged sometimes. But if I still have you, my own Phloi, to go on regarding me as a young man, things aren't so bad. I only have to think of you to feel uplifted, unafraid. So do tell me again—make me feel good. Do I really look young to you?"

"Why of course!" This was uttered in that coquettish accent of a young bride pretending to be peeved; but the next phrases were spoken in more sober tones. "Why should I flatter you, my dear? It's a fact, and it's also a fact that I'm the one who has aged."

The hand on Phloi's arm tightened its grip. "That's not a fact. It's a figment of your imagination. For me you're not a day older than when I frst saw you. You're more beautiful, that's all."

All those doubts she had been harbouring about her place in Khun Prem's life were washed away by those few words. They were like precious water, those words; they cleansed and refreshed and nourished her heart. In that instant her homely existence was wondrously lit up, all aglow in many coloured illumination, and she felt confident and ready to confront tomorrow and whatever it might bring in its destined course.

TWENTY-ONE

PHLOI had never revisited the old house in Khlong Bang Luang in all these years since the funeral rites for Chao Khun Father, but she often thought about it and its mistress. As time went by the bad features in her remembrance of Khun Un faded away, and when she thought of her now she saw her not as the tormenter who had never passed up an opportunity to hurt and humuliate her but as Elder Sister Un, born of the same father as herself, whom she had not met for a long time. She wondered how Khun Un was keeping and was interested to have more news of her. Khun Choei herself had encountered Khun Un only once and that was at the funeral of their Khunying Mother in Amphawa, some three years after Chao Khun Father had passed away. No reconciliation had taken place there between the two sisters: Khun Un had refused to talk to Khun Choei who, in her turn and in her unsubmissive fashion, had kept as far away as possible from Khun Elder Sister. And after that, with both parents dead, Khun Un had become sole ruler with absolute power over her Khlong Bang Luang domain. Her favourite brother Khun Chit and his family lived there with her. And Khun Un must be giving Khun Chit a big enough allowance, Phloi reckoned, because Khun Chit never came to see her any more—he usually came when he wanted some money, and the last time was ages ago. *It's best for me not to get involved in the affairs of Khun Chit and Khun Un,* Phloi sometimes told herself. But her sense of family prevailed. They were her half brother and sister after all, and they would continue to be her concern no matter what.

Then one afternoon she and Phoem had a long talk about them. Phoem was in his habitual mood, relaxed, jocular, at peace with himself and the world. Phloi gave him an assortment of savouries, sweets and fruit to eat as she always did when he dropped by after work. Reclining on the veranda after having done justice to everything on the tray, Phoem said he was a lucky man to have a sister who was a good cook and house manager and even luckier to have a wife ditto. (Phoem was always singing his wife's praises: she not only kept a comfortable home for him but ran her own business most efficiently, and best of all she was a generous woman, never nagged, never carried on like some of your jealous and domineering wives.) He chatted about many things with Phloi, then at one point he was rambling on about the swift passage of time—how it seemed like yesterday he and Phloi and Khun Choei were scampering round the old orchard by the *khlong*, and look at us now! Phloi, a matron with four children, he and Khun Choei quite settled down and middle-aged. Heavens!

Phloi then asked if he had had any news about Khun Chit and Khun Un.

"From time to time I hear something," Phoem said. "And what I hear is never good news."

"What have you heard, Khun Luang?" (While Khun Prem had emphatically requested not to be addressed as "Khun Phra" by his wife, Phoem very much appreciated having his sister call him by his rank of Khun Luang.) "And why haven't you told me before?"

"Because I didn't want you to worry about it—you're such a worrier, Mae Phloi. Khun Choei and I talk about it sometimes when I drop in to see her and we agree not to burden you with it."

"What is it, Khun Luang? Is anything the matter with Khun Un?"

"Khun Un is the same old Khun Un. That's what's the matter."

"Don't be so mysterious. Tell me."

"Ah! " Phoem gave a sigh. It seemed to weary him having to elaborate on this topic. "Some of the servants from Khlong Bang Luang come to see Khun Choei and me now and again. They say Khun Chit is like a god in that house—more like a devil I should say. Khun Un is completely under his thumb. She adores him and is afraid of him at the same time. Once he asked for and got a sizeable sum out of her to start a business, he said, and Khun Un willingly gave it to him."

There was a silence.

"And then?" Phloi asked.

"And then the money was gone in one day." Phoem went on. "He can never have enough, our Khun Chit, with his enormous capacity for drinking, smoking, gambling and I don't know what else. That day, he crossed the river with the money he got out of Khun Un, went to his favourite betting place and didn't leave it until he'd used up the whole pile. He has a genius for spending, I must hand it to him. Khun Un was furious when she found out, but not for very long. He's done it again and again since then."

"Khun Un is a very rich lady," Phloi said. "And he's the only brother living under her care. Of course she has to go on looking after him, but it can't make a serious dent in her great fortune."

"Don't you be too sure, Mae Phloi. Having a brother like Khun Chit is like having a hundred brothers throwing your money away with both hands. I've been told Khun Un has sold nearly all of Chao Khun Father's rice land and has started to sell some of the diamonds and gold to keep him in funds. The servants say he no longer asks her for money but demands it, and if she doesn't give in fast enough he threatens her. He gets nice and drunk first, you see, then goes on a rampage to the big house and threatens her till she gives in. It looks to me that if she doesn't stop giving in she'll soon have nothing left to give."

Phoem had been right. The news did upset Phloi. It did not make her feel vindicated to learn that Khun Un might be heading towards certain disaster. On the contrary, she recoiled from the possibility as being against the natural order of things. Khun Un's maltreatment of herself in the old days seemed to Phloi more in keeping with that order, easier to account for, than Khun Un having to cede authority to Khun Chit and being terrorized by him. That was shocking. And she had misjudged Khun Un, Phloi reflected, had wrongly thought her completely heartless, stooping to help only those who fawned on her, while all this time she had been helping Khun Chit, giving him another chance over and over again, although Khun Chit long ago must have stopped making any pretense at fawning. She certainly had a weak spot for him, and this Phloi found endearing. It showed Khu Un was capable of *metta*—loving compassion. But what bad karma, what misfortune, that she had chosen to bestow her *metta* on the one person who was beyond its redeeming power. What would happen next? How to stop Khun Chit from plunging her into ruin?

But Phoem had not quite finished.

"Another thing," he said. "Khun Chit has taken several other wives. The old place is swarming with his women *and* his numerous children. It's quite a mess."

"What about his first wife Phuang?" Phloi asked.

"Oh, I imagine she's still there. From servant she was promoted to wife and now I suppose he's made her servant again."

"Dear, oh dear! " Phloi let out a helpless cry.

"Wives and children aren't so bad, Mae Phloi," Phoem con-tinued. "But lately Khun Chit has brought some peculiar types into the house. Drinking companions, fellow opium-smokers, hangers-on from the gambling dens, hoodlums of all description. He collects them, enjoys their company, shelters them in his old family home. Chao Khun Father's home is like a bandits' hideout these days, the servants tell me. It's quite jolly at night, with all the noise and goings-on."

"And Khun Un can't do anything about it?"

"She tried to at first, but Khun Chit never listened to her, and now I think she's too terrified of those men. What can she do, one woman against that lot? So she hides herself in the big house. Khun Chit and his thugs revel in her defeat and grow more demanding than ever. They have fun menacing her."

"And what does Khun Choei say about all this?

"What can she say, Mae Phloi?"

"Isn't she going to do anything? She can't cut them out of her life— they are her full sister and brother."

Phoem chuckled. "Khun Choei said to me that if she showed her face at Khlong Bang Luang now either Khun Un would accuse her of crawling back to her for money and throw her out, or Khun Chit would be afraid she and Khun Un might become reconciled and therefore would squeeze Khun Un all the harder lest she should have anything left to give Khun Choei."

"So Khun Choei can't do anything—is that your opinion, Khun Luang?"

"I have no other, Mae Phloi. Some well-meaning relatives have also asked Khun Choei to go to Khun Un and have a good talk with her, warn her, plead with her, get her to take a firm stand and so forth. Khun Choei didn't tell those relatives how useless that would be. But she told me. Would Khun Un listen to the younger sister whom she loathed? Never. She's a stubborn creature anyway—you can't teach her anything. Khun Choei did worry about it, Mae Phloi, but she has come to the conclusion that there is nothing she can do except adopt the principle of *ubekkha*, and view the matter with equanimity. Let Khun Un follow the course of her karma. She will awaken one day. That's the only thing we can do, Khun Choei says."

"So we wait for that day. But it may come too late. 'While you wait for the beans to get brown, the sesame seeds get burnt.'" She quoted an old saying.

Phoem laughed. "I think so too, unless you do something about it. Why don't you go and have a talk with Khun Un, Mae Phloi?"

"ME!" Phloi screamed. "How can I do that?"

"I thought so," Phoem laughed again, his good humour fully restored. "We are like those poor mice in the story. Which one of us is going to tie the bell round the cat's neck?"

How true. Laughing with him, Phloi felt as though the redoubtable Khun Un of their childhood was scowling at them, accusing them of trying to interfere with her life.

"So now you know," Phoem said, "why Khun Choei and I wanted to spare you. But take my advice, Mae Phloi, and don't lose your sleep over those two. You can't do anything to change their ways, so why worry? When there's nothing you can do, do nothing, that's my motto. Just go on behaving your own self as well as you can, which, if you ask me, is difficult enough. In my case, even if I should want to help anyone, I wouldn't have the means to do it. I'm thankful, though, that I don't need to ask anybody for help except my dear wife. And speaking of her I think I'll hurry home after I leave here. I miss her—I haven't been home for three days."

"Oh Khun Luang!" Phloi exclaimed. "Where have you been?"

"Oh, here and there. Staying at a friend's house, then at another friend's. Don't frown, Mae Phloi. You know my wife doesn't mind. She calls me her little oriole." (The ability of this bird, this *nok khamin luang on*, to sleep anywhere is celebrated in a famous Thai song.) "When I come home she greets me and never fails to set a beautiful tray of food before me. My friends are green with envy, as they should be!"

Phloi gazed at her brother, shaking her head at him, but smiling at the same time. This funny brother of hers! Amazing the effortless way he could get happiness out of life—he made it seem so simple, really.

"You and your friends," she remarked. "You have more friends than anybody I know." Which was not surprising, as his gregarious-ness went hand in hand with a tolerant and unexacting attitude towards his fellow beings. And when some old friends, having risen to higher and more responsible positions in the world, moved away from his happy-go-lucky circle, Phoem never bemoaned the change. He took it as a matter of course, wished them well, accorded them due respect, and went his own way as before. His relationship with Khun Prem rather fell into this category. He now addressed his brother-in-law as "Khun Phra," and referred to him as "Than"—"Excellency." They remained friendly as always but did not spend as much time in each other's company as in the old days.

"Sometimes I think you care for your friends more than for your wife, Khun Luang."

"My wife doesn't think so, Mae Phloi. From the very beginning she has understood about me and my friends. She knows I'll always come home. Actually, my going out with friends is less trouble for her than my bringing friends home. Every time I do that she drops everything else in order to give us a sumptuous feast. I'd better not do it too often or she won't have any time left to look after her business."

"You're lucky to have an accommodating wife, Khun Luang. Some wives might frown on this habit in their husbands." Phloi was thinking of herself—feeling rather hurt sometimes when Khun Prem didn't come home.

It's not a question of accommodating, Mae Phloi," Phoem agreed, "but of understanding. You know, many people didn't think much of her at first. They said I shouldn't marry beneath me. But I've never doubted I've made the right choice. A wife of my own station might well have been one of those demanding females, and if she happened to be rich people would say I'm a parasite living on her. Bad for my reputation. No! With this ideal helpmeet of mine I can breathe free and easy."

"And I'm glad to see you well and happy, Khun Luang. But tell me about you and your friends. What do you do with them?"

"What do you do with your friends? You get together. You talk. You help one another when you're in trouble. You eat together, and when you discover it's too late to go home you spend the night at your host's place."

"You only eat together, Khun Luang?"

"Very well, Mae Phloi," Phoem gurgled. "We eat and drink together if you prefer. What else do you want to know?"

"And you meet regularly?"

"Why not? We make plans to meet here or there, or sometimes we just drop in—it doesn't matter."

"But what have you got to talk about day after day, night after night? Tell me about some of your conversations. What sort of subjects?"

Phoem laughed. "You're so inquisitive, Mae Phloi. We talk about anything and everything. I'll give you one fascinating example. Potted topiary trees. What do you think of that? Some of us are serious fanciers and collectors of potted topiary trees. I don't belong in that class but I do have some lovely ones and am getting more all the time. Funny about these plants—when I was a child I could not understand what the grownups ever saw in them, but now I go for them myself in a big way. Our latest craze, though, is doves. I started keeping them not so long ago but I've been having wonderful luck. My birds have been beating their opponents at every contest."

"Oh, Khun Luang! " Phloi cried. "The poor birds. And you're committing a bad deed, making them fight."

"Wait, Mae Phloi. They don't claw each other to death or anything like that. It's a cooing match, my dear girl. The birds remain in their respective cages. We take them to the arena near Wat Saket, hang the opposing cages side by side and start the birds cooing against each other. That's not a bad deed, is it?"

"Well, maybe not. But how do you judge it—how do you pick the winner?"

"Easy. The contestants aim to outcoo each other, right? It's not only the volume of course, but the rhythm, the melody, the artistry of it that makes the whole thing so fascinating. And they not only coo, you know. They curse, harangue, tease and taunt and thrust and so forth—the dove language is quite rich and subtle, you understand. Pretty soon, the better bird is gaining advantage: it is cooing wittily, cheerily, sonorously, while its opponent starts to make some ugly noises, as people do sometimes when they feel they're losing the argument. The fight goes on and this second bird gets madder and madder. Now it is raving and ranting and beating its wings against the cage, wanting to lunge at its adversary probably with murder in its heart. It has made a fool of itself and lost the game. The first bird is clearly the victor. Just like us humans, don't you think? Lose your temper and you shall lose the battle. He who keeps calm shall conquer."

Phloi laughed. "How nice to be able to find a moral in the cooing of birds."

"You can find it in everything I think," said Phoem complacently, "if you look closely enough. A dove in a cage is easy to observe—it can't fly away, and then of course it doesn't lie or use so many tricks to conceal its true self. We may be more devious than the birds, but a moral for them is in essence a moral for us."

"You'd make a good preaching monk, Khun Luang. I could imagine you delivering a sermon full of proverbs and parables. Do you go often to the *wat*?"

"Now and then, but not to listen to sermons. I go to chat about topiary plants with my learned monk friends. They've taught me a lot. They're not averse to passing on their knowledge to others."

Phoem's contentment came easy to him; the things he wanted were those he could get without too much effort, and he never seemed to yearn for the unreachable. He contended against no one, had no interest in amassing wealth and did not even try to hold on to his possessions. Power, fame and such-like had no attraction for him. He would be perfectly satisfied to remain a Luang the rest of his life—good enough for me, he always said. Phloi had a feeling her son Ot might grow up to be like his uncle, and while this speculation worried her somewhat (for naturally she would like her son to have some ambition) it also gave her a measure of assurance about Ot's chances of personal happiness in his adult life. She was in fact more concerned about An, whose overbearing ways reminded her too much of Khun Un. An knew his mother loved him. He liked that but he hated having to share her with his brothers and sister. Phloi was obliged to scold him quite sharply sometimes. As for On, Phloi often found herself looking for points of resemblance between On's character and Khun Prem's, but then there was still much in Khun Prem's character that kept eluding her. Phloi during this period spent not a small portion of her time musing upon her children's future, her own having ceased to intrigue her very much, not like in those bygone adolescent days in the Inner Court. She studied their individual character and behaviour in the hope that she might be able to weed out those questionable traits which could mar their prospects for a good life in the years to come. In general and to put it briefly, she wished to do her best to help build a bright future for them all. But could she? What should her best consist of? The more she pondered the question the less confident she became. How could one be certain of the future in any case? Her so-called best plans might well be dotted with flaws and errors for all she knew, and what she deemed the right course of action could still fail to bring the desired result. What to do? In the end she did what dear Khun Aunt Nui had been advocating for some time—consult a fortune-teller, or rather this particular fortune-teller who had been a regular caller at Khun Nui's bungalow for years and years. He was a blind man, a Chinese who spoke Thai with an endearingly comic accent. Khun Nui called him her *"sinsae,"* a Chinese word—which had been assimilated into the vernacular—meaning doctor, teacher, professor as well as fortune-teller.

That afternoon they all gathered round the blind *sinsae* on the balcony of Khun Nui's bungalow. He commenced with On. After securing the date, the day of the week, the month and the year (of the twelve-year cycle) of On's birth, he touched the boy's face, stroking it, going over its contour and features including the ears-—he seemed to dwell longer on the ears. Then he said, shaking his head and sighing:

"He glow up hab toubung."

Phloi went pale at this pronouncement. She came near to telling him to stop then and there—she didn't want to hear any more. But curiosity won out over apprehension and she asked, "What sort of trouble, *Sinsae?*"

"Ah, he will go to pisung. But not to wolly. He go to pisung but come out again."

On to be put in prison? But that's preposterous! Her gentle blameless On—who could ever connect him with a future of crime and imprisonment? Something must have gone wrong somewhere in the *sinsae's* calculation. Fortune-tellers, Phloi reminded herself, like the rest of us, are not infallible. All the same, it's disquieting, to say the least, to be told you have a son destined to go to jail.

The *sinsae* also spoke of On being too uncompromising and that this would be the cause of his "trouble." Since Phloi had never detected anything of the kind in her son's behaviour she again dismissed the prognostication as being wide of the mark.

When An's turn came, the *sinsae* foresaw a prosperous future awaiting him. An would "glow up" to become someone of consequence with lots of subordinates deferring to him and he would win recognition and honour. This is more like it, said Phloi to herself. The *sinsae* knows what he's talking about after all.

He also predicted that An would quarrel with his brothers, that there would be a rift between him and them, though followed in time by a reconciliation. As for Ot, the *sinsae* did not have very much to say about him apart from describing him as a good boy (as if Phloi didn't know!) and speculating that he would not be as long-lived as the others. The *sinsae* was not asked to read Praphai's future that day, Khun Aunt Nui having ruled that the little one was still far too young to have her fortune told.

"Phi On's going to jail! Phi On's going to jail! " An yelled, bounding down the steps of Khun Nui's bungalow. He was jubilant about it and teased On without mercy. Phloi had to reprove him quite severely before he would stop harassing his poor brother, who was looking on the verge of tears.

With a reassuring smile Phloi told On not to take seriously what the blind *sinsae* had said but to put trust in one's own good karma always. Inwardly she resolved to do everything she could to prevent the prediction coming true. (Absurd prediction, but what mother would not be made uneasy by it?)

Meanwhile, she wished On would change his mind about wanting to be a soldier. But as time went by, it became increasingly doubtful that she would be able to do anything to divert this particular course of destiny. On stuck to his declared preference, and when Khun Prem heard about it he agreed that it was a good idea. In due course he arranged to have On enrolled in the primary school for future cadets, a boarding school where the pupils were allowed to go home on weekends. On looked sweet in his uniform, and Phloi forgot her misgiving when she saw how immensely proud and happy he was to be wearing it.

After On had settled down in his school Khun Prem turned his attention to the younger boys. Phloi told him about An wanting to be lawyer, adding that she was not too enthusiastic regarding the choice but if that was what he wanted she would go along with it. She said at the moment Ot talked only nonsense but that he was perhaps too young to know his own mind.

"Law is not a bad profession," Khun Prem remarked. "Having a lawyer in the family can be quite useful—help keep swindlers away for one thing."

Then he said something which made her heart sink. "The difficulty is lack of schooling in our country. Not very much choice. Nowadays people send their children abroad to be educated. I think we ought to do the same for An and Ot. When they come back to serve they'll stand a better chance of getting ahead."

"Is it necessary, Khun Prem?" Phloi ventured to ask. She knew about their Royal Highnesses and other royal sons journeying to Europe for their studies. They were destined to help govern the country and one of them now sat on the throne. For them it was perhaps necessary. But she could not see why An and Ot should be taken away from their mother and sent across the oceans to acquire knowledge in a *farang* land. She suspected Khun Prem (though she didn't say it) of entertaining an exaggerated idea of their sons' importance.

"It is rather necessary," Khun Prem replied. "I know it will be hard for you to part with them, but as we love our children so we must consider their interests first and be prepared to make some sacrifices for their sake. If we keep them here it will amount to holding them back, impeding their progress. Our country is developing fast. Those who are not well-educated will soon lag behind." He paused and gave a chuckle. "Do you know what, Mae Phloi? My English is so inadequate that sometimes when His Majesty speaks it I can't follow him at all. When he says something and people laugh I just look blank. What else can I do? I don't dare laugh along with the others, because if he should ask what I was laughing about I would lose face, wouldn't I?—having to admit I didn't know."

"I think the children are too young," Phloi said resolutely. "You can't send them away now. They don't know how to look after themselves."

"Don't get excited, Mae Phloi. Who says anything about sending them away *now*?"

Phloi felt a little better. "When do you plan to send them?"

"Oh, we can wait a few more years. During this time they'll be learning more English. I'm thinking of transferring them to another school—a missionary school."

"Oh Khun Prem! And have my sons converted to the *farang* church?"

Khun Prem laughed. "Going to a *farang* school doesn't mean you're obliged to forsake your own tradition, Mae Phloi. With your guidance, and mine, our sons will understand they're there to gain knowledge, not to give up their spiritual belief handed down to them by their ancestors."

Not long after this, An and Ot started attending a *farang* school, where they were taught English in preparation for going abroad for further study. Phloi was thankful she still had them with her before and after school hours and tried not to look ahead to when these hours would have to be sacrificed on the altar of higher education.

Now the passage of time brought her another sad loss. Choi came to see her one day dressed in mourning and looking distraught. On seeing Phloi, her face contorted and dissolved into tears. She had come to tell Phloi that Khun Luang her father was dead. The two women, friends from childhood, cried quietly together. Khun Luang had been one of Phloi's beloved elders. She had not seen very much of him in recent years, but this did not make her feel any less lonely at the thought that he was no more.

"Had he been ill, Choi? I've heard nothing about it."

"It happened suddenly, Phloi. He fainted. His heart gave out. That was all. Mother sent word to me at the residence. I didn't tell Khun Aunt Sai—didn't want her to collapse from shock. I lied to her that Father wasn't well and I'd have to go home and see him."

"Can I do anything, Choi?"

"Nothing, my dear. I came to let you know we'll have the seventh day rites for him next Thursday."

"I'll come, Choi. How's your mother?"

"Inconsolable. She says she'll come and live with me after the cremation."

"Oh, and what will happen to the house?"

"She says she'll rent it and use the money to live on."

"Phi Nuang will be looking after her too, won't he?"

Choi made a grimace. Her voice, when she spoke again, sounded strained. "Phi Nuang's staying at the house for the funeral, but don't ask me what he's going to do. We seem to have grown apart, my brother and I. And Mother says her son listens more to his wife than to his mother. I don't know what to say, Phloi."

"But Phi Nuang is Mae Chan's only son. He'll want to do everything he can for his mother. It is his concern, whether he has a wife or not."

"My mother doesn't like her son's wife. Never has. The feeling is quite mutual I must say. But anyway they have several children and wouldn't have time to look after an old woman. I have all the time in the world! And actually, it would be more convenient to have Mother with us at the residence. I wouldn't need to scurry back and forth between her and Khun Aunt, who's growing more crotchety with age and behaving more and more like a child. Mother's easy, though, and that's a great help. It will be all right, Phloi. I still have enough strength to look after both of them—and a few other venerable ladies living out their days behind the venerable walls." She paused. "But today I need your company, Phloi. Do you mind if I prolong my visit and just babble on about nothing?"

"I want you here with me as long as you can spare the time, Choi, the longer the better for me."

Choi had dried her tears but lines of sorrow remained on her face. Taking some betel nuts from the tray, she said, "I'm around my old ladies so much that I've become old like them. They are my karma, my destiny. There is nothing else for me in this life. Tell me, Phloi, who will take care of me when my turn comes?"

"I'll take care of you, Choi."

"Silly girl!" Choi retorted in that half-serious half-mocking voice Phloi knew so well. "You're going to be just as old and feeble as I am. You'll be tottering and I'll be doddering and won't we have plenty of *sanuk* propping each other up!"

"Really, Phloi," she went on, "there are times when I want to run away, far, far away. But where would I go? I wouldn't last a day outside. Do you know what I find dreary beyond words? The very atmosphere of the Inner Court. When you and I were young it was heavenly to breathe in that atmosphere. How beautiful everything looked to us then, didn't it, Phloi? And merely to be there was exciting, was it not? Now the place is crumbling away. It reminds me of those lines: *'Thung dieo ni mi tae phra prang plao; phra phan klao niphan nan nakna.'* (Now the towers are desolate, for our Lord has long departed.) Very few of our royals are left. Most of those who could do it have gone to set up new residences and palaces outside. Among us serving maids, some are clever enough to have found new mistresses in new palaces.

But I'm a poor hand at manoeuvring so have no choice but to remain. Sadet's residence is like a melancholy ghost. The impermanence of things is getting me down, Phloi. I wish Somdet Phra Phan Pi ("Somdet of a Thousand Years," Her Majesty the Queen Mother) had chosen to stay. If she had, the Inner Court wouldn't be deteriorating so fast. But I don't think she'll ever move back inside from her Phya Thai Palace."

"By the way, Choi, I've heard Somdet Phra Phan Pi is in poor health. Is that true?"

"She's been ailing ever since His Late Majesty passed away. I haven't seen her myself, Phloi, but they tell me she's lost interest in everything. She can't even walk by herself now, so I'm told, and has to be supported or go in a wheelchair. But most of the time, they say, she keeps to her bedchamber, taking her meals and granting audience inside the screen."

"And Phra Chao Yu Hua of this Reign, will he not take up residence in the Grand Palace again?"

"I doubt it, Phloi. He seems to prefer the other palaces and only comes to the Grand Palace for state ceremonies. At the beginning of the reign he did stay for a while in the White Room in the Upper Apartment. There were some lively goings-on then."

"What goings-on, Choi?"

"Oh, those pages attending His Majesty, you know. Every morning they crowded round behind every window to peep down at the girls, and let me tell you, there was as much ogling from the ground as from the windows—and any amount of giggling. I went near the spot everyday to watch the show. Great fun."

"Same old naughty Choi," said Phloi, laughing. And Choi went on chatting away as she had said she would, and was looking much more like her old cheerful self when she finally took off late in the afternoon.

TWENTY-TWO

IMPORTANT news concerning the outside world reached Phloi now and then, at random, mostly through Khun Prem. She usually listened to his accounts of them in a neutral frame of mind. They did not seem to have very much to do with her. But once in a while Khun Prem's reaction to an event would strike her as so unexpected that Phloi, because she was interested in her husband, became interested in the event itself.

She heard about World War I from Khun Prem and paid little attention to it at first. The *farang*s were fighting among themselves in far-away Europe. Nothing to be afraid of or get excited about. None of our business which battles were won or lost by which side. As the war progressed, however, her own business—that of running the house—began to show disturbing signs here and there. To put it baldly, it was costing her more money than before to feed and clothe the people under her care. The price of imported stuff rose first, and it was not long before the price of local goods started to go up and up, too—even rice! She wondered if the country was entering a period which the old folks referred to as the time of *khao yak mak phaeng*—"when rice is scarce and betel is dear." She recollected Khun Sai's complaint many years ago about the price of mackerel having climbed from one *lot* (not even one *satang*) for one bamboo basket containing three tiers of the plumpest fish, to one *pai*, or three *satang*s per basket with less fish in it. And now Phloi was having to pay out two whole *pai*—six *satang*s!—for a basket of only a few mackerels.

"Why is everything so dear, Khun Prem?"

"Because of the *farang* war, Mae Phloi."

Phloi frowned. "This word again! I keep hearing it wherever I go. The war's way over there. What has it got to do with our rice and fish?"

Khun Prem laughed. "So you don't believe me. But it's true my dear. As a result of the war we have to pay more for imported goods and since we Thais are quite partial to them and buy quantities of them, Thai goods consequently go up in price as well. But be of good cheer, Mae Phloi. I haven't told you this before but our own family business is also making more profit, so you have more money to spend. It comes out even, you see."

Phloi shook her head. "No, I don't. It's good of course to be earning more. But I tell you it's no laughing matter the way money flows out of the house nowadays. And we have so many people to take care of. Really, Khun Prem, I can't help worrying."

Now Khun Prem displayed a confident smile and said in a soothing voice, "You won't have to worry much longer, Mae Phloi. Soon things will get back to normal. It shouldn't be long before the Germans win the war. The end is in sight."

"You know already who's going to win?" Phloi asked doubtfully.

"Why not?" Khun Prem demanded right back, with the superior air of someone in the know. "I follow the news every day. It's obvious the Germans have the upper hand. The English and the French are going to find themselves in bad trouble this time. You mark my words." He paused and added, "I'm betting on the Germans."

"You seem to be siding with them," his wife remarked.

"It does look like it," Khun Prem admitted, then gave a chuckle before continuing. "The English and the French have been big powers for so long—and how they did try to lord it over us! The Germans on the other hand have never done us any harm. We'll see, Mae Phloi, we'll see."

The war did not end as quickly as Khun Prem had expected. This did not seem to disturb him and he went on rooting for Germany, extolling the superiority of German weapons and fighting prowess whenever the subject came up; and when another town was captured by German troops he never failed to relay the news to Phloi, who invariably forgot its strange name almost as soon as she had heard it.

Well, Khun Prem kept this up for many months. Phloi could not say exactly when his enthusiasm began to wane. It must have happened when she wasn't looking, or listening. At any rate she became aware at some point that her dear husband had been oddly reticent on his favourite topic for some time now and was no longer voicing his opinions with so much vigour.

Then one afternoon he came home early, jumped out of the car asking where Phloi could be found and on finding her proclaimed, "Our *Muang Thai* has made a declaration of war!"

It sounded very important, very grand, and the expression on Khun Prem's face matched it perfectly, as though he was personally responsible. Phloi couldn't quite grasp the full meaning of the phrase however, and she said, "Really? And then what, Khun Prem?"

For a moment Khun Prem was looking vague himself, but then he hit upon an answer: "Well, we're going to fight too, I think."

"On whose side?"

"The Allies. Police were rounding up German nationals last night. They've confiscated German properties including B. Grimm Company and all the German ships."

Phloi was extremely puzzled. "But Khun Prem, do we want to be on the losing side? I always hear people say the Germans will win."

"Hush, Mae Phloi." Khun Prem looked round as if afraid they might have been overheard. "That was just idle talk, Mae Phloi. Everybody knows the Allies will win. They have right on their side. The Germans are in the wrong and are bound to be defeated."

They both remained silent for a while. Then Khun Prem said, "Mae Phloi my dear, from now on please don't go round saying what you've just said ever again. Remember we have joined the Allies and the Germans are our enemy."

Khun Prem himself became from that day onwards a staunch supporter of the Allies' cause, our cause. Our victory is assured, is round the corner, he would declare with certainty and passion, citing this German retreat and that German loss in support of his pronouncements. Sometimes he coupled the demeaning prefix "*ai*" with the word "enemy" or "foe," alluding to the Germans as *ai satru* or *ai khasuk*. Occasionally he called them *ai Han*. The Huns, he explained, were an ancient savage tribe, cruel, brutal, inhuman, not unlike the present-day Germans, our enemy.

Then came the official proclamation calling for volunteers to join an expeditionary force being organized. Thai soldiers were to go and fight in Europe for the first time in history! Khun Prem lived in a state of high excitement throughout this period.

"What a pity, Mae Phloi" he said, his eyes all aglow. "If I were still young I could be marching off with them. Oh I wish I weren't so old."

Phloi couldn't help chiding him a little. "I'm never sure how young or old you see yourself, Khun Prem. You seem to shift back and forth as the mood takes you."

Khun Prem tittered shame-facedly and said no more about his old age—or youth, whichever it was. But his boyishly spirited response to our country's participation in the Great War continued unabated.

The day our soldiers left for Europe he didn't get home till the small hours of the morning. He had been seeing them off on their historic journey and afterwards had been celebrating. Despite the lateness of the hour nothing would do but he must relive the events for Phloi's benefit. He also told Phloi about the Ceremony of Cutting of the Wood in Intimidation of the Name (*Tat Mai Khom Nam*) which had been preformed as in bygone days. He had seen His Majesty in the traditional red costume of an old warrior king holding the ancient ceremonial sword in his hands. The sight had sent Khun Prem's heart pounding. Even now, he said he could feel the old fighting blood racing through his veins. He kept on talking, rhapsodizing, his eyes sparkling and his speech very heroic sounding. Phloi was amused to observe this side of him—she had never suspected its existence. At the same time she was just a tiny bit put off by so much bravado in a grown man and caught herself impulsively wishing the Allies would lose because she would like to see Khun Prem's face in defeat. It was only a momentary wish, inspired by nothing more serious than a wife's whim to have her husband taken down a peg or two for his own good.

One day—this was not too many months since the soldiers' departure—Khun Prem returned from work unusually early. Phloi heard his voice coming up from downstairs shouting her name. It startled her at first, then she detected its merry notes and waited calmly for him to appear.

He burst into the room beaming from ear to ear.

"Didn't I tell you, Mae Phloi?"

"What is it, Khun Prem?"

"The war's over! Germany is totally crushed."

Phloi greeted the news with much relief. Now surely the prices would go down, as would Khun Prem's war fever. One thing she must say for the war, however: it had given her new insight into Khun Prem's character. That he had strong likes and dislikes despite his gentle manner she had always known, and now she knew how easily he could change his mind about them, and in all sincerity too. He had been strongly in favour of Germany, then had changed his mind upon His Majesty having made it clear that the country was going to war on the side of the Allies. Phloi was reminded of these lines often quoted in the Inner Court of her youth:

Our Lord says it is beautiful and we say it is beautiful.

Or are there any among us to say that it is not?

"Chao wa ngam ko wa ngarm pai tam chao,

Ru khrai lao cha mai ngam tam sadet?"

But—and this must be repeated—Khun Prem's sincerity was never in doubt. His lips never uttered what his heart did not believe. When he said something was beautiful he truthfully thought it. He believed it through and through, with his whole being.

The war was over. In Europe there were victory parades and processions, and the Thai contingent took part in some of these. Khun Prem was thrilled and enjoyed talking about them at great length. When the soldiers arrived back in town he was there in the front line of the cheering crowd, and the ensuing weeks saw him actively involved in the various homecoming celebrations—so much so that he had no time left for anything else. And when that phase had passed he promptly took up another engrossing avocation. A fund was set up for the Royal Navy to acquire a new battleship; the public was asked to subscribe to it and Khun Prem became one of the most enthusiastic and energetic fundraisers.

"Don't forget to wear your badge, Mae Phloi."

The badge had a silver filigree elephant, in a kneeling position and holding up its trunk, pinned on a red and white ribbon. You received it when you made a donation to the fund. Khun Prem had given generously, in his own name as well as in the names of his wife and children.

"Why do we have to wear it, Khun Prem?"

"To persuade more people to join the campaign and to express our patriotic feelings. This ship is going to be the biggest we've ever had. We'll show the other countries we're not so far behind them."

"Aren't people buying this badge, Khun Prem?"

"Yes, but we must try to get more and more people to donate. We'll tell them that even Ya-le has donated," he added with a smile.

"Ya-le? Who's Ya-le, Khun Prem?"

"Haven't I told you about Ya-le—His Majesty's pet dog, Ya-le? He started life as a jail dog, you know. He was born in the prison at Nakhon Pathom. His owner presented him to His Majesty when he saw how the dog and the king took to each other at first sight. So now Ya-le lives in the palace, and I think Nai Luang much prefers him to some of his human subjects. I think Ya-le knows this too. He's terribly clever. He's bitten off chunks of my clothes in front of Nai Luang, just to put me in my place, I suppose, but when we're alone and I want to smack him he turns on his charm, wagging his tail and looking at me so tenderly I don't have the heart to do it. Well, Ya-le has also given to the Fund. Tell the others about it, Mae Phloi. Makes a good story. We must try to do all we can to get more people to give more—until the goal is achieved."

Phloi appreciated the importance of the campaign, and even more she appreciated the nature of Khun Prem's involvement in it. He was behaving laudably of course, while at the same time, Phloi thought, also like a child with a new toy. "But for that matter," Phloi said to herself, "my brother Phoem's the same with his toys—with the plants and the doves and what not. And not only my husband and my brother but their men friends—there's something of the little boy in all of them, in the most mature of them."

On the whole those were the carefree days, and not only for the perpetually young-at-heart men of Phloi's personal world but for the country at large. The endeavours of the older generations in previous reigns, the manifold tasks of nation-building carried out by them, the wisdom and perseverance and foresight which had gone into their efforts, had borne fruit, and the Thai people living under the reign of Rama VI in those years before, during and after the Great War were going through very good times indeed. There was peace and prosperity. There was material comfort, attended by the comfortable, not to say complacent, feeling that all was well and would continue to be well. In the cosy security of the present very few bothered to have doubts about the future. And as for people in smart society, it looked as though the only problem they had to worry about was how to outshine their fellow denizens. Phloi did not compete in this race; and although her own life was comfortable enough, she had Khun Choei and Choi with their daily struggles to remind her—if she had needed reminding—that hardship existed and not all were blessed with good fortune in this golden land of hers.

One incident served as another reminder. That afternoon she was alone in the bedroom mending the boys' clothes. A servant girl entered to say "somebody is here to see you, ma'am."

"A man or a woman?" Phloi asked uninterestedly.

"A woman, ma'am. She says she is your sister."

"Can't be," said Phloi. "Where is she?"

"I've asked her to wait in the front veranda, ma'am."

Wearing a dark green *panung*, with a grey silk shawl draped over her blouse, with a pink gold betel-nut purse lying by her side, the woman was waxing her lips when Phloi came up to the veranda. The sight of the woman, of that gesture—the finger moving slowly over the lips, sent Phloi's mind rushing back into the past and suddenly she felt very small, very diffident.

"Khun Phi," she said in a tiny voice.

Khun Un smiled at Phloi, the first smile Phloi had ever received from her.

"Khun Phloi. I haven't seen you for so long. Are you well?"

Phloi answered that she was, using the very polite ending *chao kha* and stammering rather badly—it had startled her to be called "Khun" by Khun Un.

"Let me look at you," Khun Un said. "You're even prettier now than ever. Motherhood becomes you, gives your skin a lovely glow."

Phloi then asked her what errand had brought her to this part of Bangkok.

"No particular errand," replied Khun Un. "I've been thinking of you, and so I came to visit you. There are only a few of us brothers and sisters, and as I get older I feel I want to see more of you. Khun Phra still at the office?" So she had heard about Khun Prem's pro-motion, Phloi noted to herself. "Where are all the children?"

Phloi told her the boys were at school and sent for Praphai to come and pay respects to Khun Aunt. A few minutes later the child came skipping to the door, and on being introduced lowered herself to approach her mother's eldest sister on her hands and knees. Khun Un embraced her and sat her on her lap; and Praphai seemed to enjoy being fussed over and proceeded to chat with Khun Aunt as though she had been a regular visitor. Astonishing, Phloi said to herself.

"Pretty child," declared Khun Un. "Like her mother. You're going to be a celebrated beauty, my little niece."

The compliments did not greatly excite Praphai, who was anxious to get back to her playmates and took her leave on being permitted to do so; the compliments did not interest Praphai's mother, who said nothing aloud but kept on asking herself what could be the real reason bringing Khun Un across the river all the way from Khlong Bang Luang to Khlong Yom after all these years. Khun Un asked after Phoem, and whether Phloi saw much of him.

Then she inquired about Khun Choei.

Phloi made suitable answers to her various questions.

"I don't get to see them as you do," Khun Un remarked, implying by her tone that they were to blame for this lack of contact, not she.

Phloi politely waited for her to continue.

"And it's no use my having a younger brother living with me," Khun

Un went on. "He gives me nothing but trouble."

Again Phloi waited, and at last Khun Un said, "What I came to see you about—but this will give you worries, I'm afraid—"

"Oh, not at all," Phloi hastened to say. She felt more at ease now that she knew that Khun Un did have a motive in coming to see her. "Please tell me and let me do whatever I can for you," she quickly added.

"It's so difficult to tell—" Khun Un began, and paused. "I do so dislike having to trouble you—"

"No, no, you mustn't feel like that," Phloi assured her again. "Please go on."

After contemplating the floor for several seconds Khun Un permitted herself a sigh, then spoke in a low voice, "It's on account of Pho Chit, as always. If you can't help us, we're sunk." She lapsed into silence again.

"Tell me what it's all about," Phloi urged.

It took Khun Un a little while to come to the point. "It's about our Khlong Bang Luang house," she finally said. "You see, Pho Chit wanted money to start a timber business but I didn't have enough so he asked me to mortgage the house. I couldn't refuse him—how could I not help my brother, whom I love? The business did badly and had to close down, and now the creditors are pressing us. If we can't find the money we will lose the house, lose our family home. Oh, Mae Phloi, can you imagine how Chao Khun Father would have felt, and Chao Khun Grandfather? And what loss of face for us all!"

"How much money do you need?" Phloi asked. She had no trouble understanding Khun Un's problem, and with another part of her mind she noted that Khun Un was speaking more straight-forwardly and no longer calling her *Khun* Phloi. She was glad about this.

"I think eight thousand baht should put us in the clear," Khun Un answered. "Then I will make you the holder of the mortgage so as to prevent Pho Chit from getting us involved in any more mad schemes of his. He wouldn't dare to come and pester and prey on you the way he did with me."

Phloi told Khun Un she would give her what was needed to pay the debt, then went on to ask, "But apart from that, is everything all right with you? Do they look after you well in Khlong Bang Luang? It's not too lonely for you living by yourself in the big house?"

Phloi's promise of financial assistance lifted Khun Un's spirits, but it was Phloi's questions about her personal welfare which wrung her heart and brought tears to her eyes. What could she say to this person who had every reason to hold a grudge against her, every reason to gloat over her downfall, but instead was giving her the sisterly and human sympathy she had done nothing to earn? She started to speak through her tears, but could not do it at first and went on crying quietly. Phloi murmured some consoling words, taken by surprise at the tears no less than she had been at the unexpected visit.

Wiping her eyes, Khun Un spoke at length, pouring her heart out to Phloi and this was the most surprising thing of all.

"Forgive me, Mae Phloi," she said. "Forgive me for what I did to you, for all the wrong I ever committed against you. I know now how wrong, how despicable I was. And so stupid. With my stupid pride and arrogance I only listened to those who kowtowed to me, and now they laugh at me for being a fool. I've lost everything, all for Pho Chit's sake, and he has only contempt for me. Not one grain of gratitude, or decency, or pity. Let me tell you what happened the other day. He wanted me to sell that lovely set of the gold-lined teacups, the last family treasure I'd managed to save from him. I refused. Do you know what he did then? He broke the glass case and smashed the whole set to bits . . ."

She started to cry again, and Phloi said to herself, "She has been wounded and is suffering, and I must do all I can to help her."

"Where is Khun Chit living now?" she asked when Khun Un had calmed down.

"Here and there, with one wife here, one wife there. He only comes to see me when he wants money. I don't expect to see much of him from now on—now that I have nothing left to give him."

The farther Khun Chit stays away the better it will be for all of us, Phloi thought. Aloud she said, repeating her earlier questions, "And are you all right living alone as you are? Do you have enough good people looking after you?"

"I look after myself, Mae Phloi. Oh, there are still some people hanging about in the compound, Pho Chit's people. I don't know what they do but they're certainly not serving me. No one is except my maid Prik. She's the only one I have and she's getting ga-ga. Some days I have to boil my own rice and wash my own clothes. It's not a comfortable life I'm living in my old age, but I have no one to blame but myself. I wish for death sometimes to rid me of my miserable existence." And with the last sentence she lapsed again into tears.

"Don't talk like that, Khun Phi," Phloi said, and paused to steady herself for what she had to say next. She had made up her mind as to what she must do. No one was in a better position than herself to extend a helping hand to Khun Un and rescue her from a deprived and lonely old age. Khun Choei was not equipped to do it. Nor Phoem. Only she could do it. How Mother would have laughed at the irony of it all, Phloi thought, but with her kind heart, Mother, too, would have approved. Chao Khun Father would have been enormously pleased—in fact, he would have expected nothing less from her. But perhaps the most important reason for the action Phloi was about to take was that she herself would not be able to live peacefully with herself if she were to shirk it.

She said to Khun Un, "I'm worried about you living all alone like that with nobody to take care of you. We have room enough here. Why don't you come to live with us?"

Khun Un stared at her one-time victim. Incredulity was written all over her tear-stained face.

And then, calling Phloi "Mae Khun Mae Thun Hua," a term used to express the speaker's great affection and admiration for the addressee, she said, "Do you mean it? Are you really saying you want me to come and live here?"

Phloi repeated her invitation, saying she would fix up one of the bungalows, that it would be no trouble at all and she only hoped Khun Un would find it convenient and comfortable enough. She couldn't help giggling a little when Khun Un said how "good" she was, because it reminded her of Choi; and she had to suppress a smile, again thinking of Choi, when Khun Un voiced her fear that it might prove too burdensome for Phloi having to put up with an old woman like her. Choi had been looking after *her* old people, Phloi said to herself, and now *my* turn has come. How tickled Choi would be when she heard about this!

As for Khun Un's fear, Phloi would have liked to point out (but of course did not) that after having put up with Khun Un's youthful wrath and survived, she should be able to handle Khun Un's tamer old age with no great difficulty.

The news spread fast. Soon after Khun Un had left, the faithful Phit came limping up looking alert and suspicious.

"They are talking in the kitchen about your sister being here. Has she gone? Now which sister could it be if it wasn't Khun Choei?"

"It was Khun Un who came, Phit."

Phit joined her palms together and raised them high towards the heavens. "The impossible has happened! I never thought I'd live to see this day. And what did she come for?"

"She came to visit me. And—and she is to be pitied. She's old and alone and unhappy. She has no one to look after her. No one at all, Phit. So—so I've asked her to come and live here, Phit."

"Oh-ho, Khun Phloi, are you joking?!"

"No, Phit."

"Oh, oh, oh, I'm going to faint . . . And what did she say?"

"She has agreed to come. She'll move here in four or five days' time. We had better get started cleaning up On's old bungalow. You will help me look after her, won't you, Phit?"

"Hmm, I guess so. She's your sister, after all. But what about that woman Prik—that poisonous trouble-maker, is she coming too?"

"Yes, Phit. She's the only one who hasn't abandoned Khun Un."

"I guess I shall have to forgive that creature too, but not after I've taught her a lesson. Oh, yes, I must. She has it coming to her, Khun Phloi!"

Two days later Khun Choei came. She had heard this astonishing rumour and came rushing to get the truth from Phloi's own lips. Phloi confirmed it for her.

"You're playing with fire," Khun Choei warned.

"The fire has gone out," said Phloi with a smile. "You can touch Khun Un now without getting your hand burnt."

Khun Choei laughed. "I suppose you're right. Actually, Mae Phloi, you have my full sympathy and support. She threw away her pride and came to you for help. I'd have done the same if I were you. What I'm afraid of is that Khun Chit will try to follow her here."

"Me, too, Khun Choei. I'll have to be very careful with him. We may have to resort to using Khun Prem as our protection."

'That's it, Mae Phloi, put Khun Prem in the front line of defence."

"Well, Mae Phloi," Khun Choei said before departing that day, "I do think you are making merit and I rejoice with you. When she's settled down I'll come and see her to make amends. You can count on me to help you, Phloi."

The news was greeted with a burst of laughter from Phoem. "And I'll bet our mother is laughing, too," he said. "There in the land of the ghosts she must be having a hilarious time over all this. But I'm not surprised at all. To dispense kindness is your obsession, your vice."

"Oh, Khun Luang! What are you accusing me of?"

"Or let's put it this way. Compassion is your passion. While other women indulge in gambling or buying jewellery you get your pleasure from helping people. And why not?"

Khun Prem approved of what his wife had done. He was also pleased with himself.

"What did I tell you, Mae Phloi?" he said. "Didn't I predict that Khun Un would come to you of her own accord? And now my prediction has come true!"

TWENTY-THREE

ALTHOUGH she had been forewarned, Phloi's heart sickened on being told by Khun Prem the time had come for her to start making preparations for the boys' departure.

"My friend Phra San has been assigned to our legation in London. He'll leave in about four months and An and Ot can travel with him. We're fortunate to have someone like him to keep an eye on our sons."

Phloi knew it would be useless, but she could not prevent herself from pleading with her husband. "Can't we wait another year or two, Khun Prem? They're still frightfully young."

Khun Prem's answer came as no surprise to her. "Now, now, Mae Phloi, be reasonable. We've gone over all this before. It's for their own good and we mustn't try to hold them back. They're at the right age. It will be easy for them to get into an English school and derive full benefit from their experience. The longer we wait the more difficult it will be."

Phloi then made another request: that her sons should not have to attend so many classes but spend as much time as possible at home with her during the next four months. This request was granted.

An was in raptures about the coming trip and could talk of nothing else. Ot on the contrary took it very calmly, almost indifferently. Phloi asked him if he was not excited to be going abroad, and he said, "Not really. Anyway, Phi An is excited enough for both of us." Then he demanded, "Why isn't Phi On coming with us, Mother?"

Phloi hesitated, and ended up not answering. She had of course wished to give On the same opportunity as the younger boys, even if it would have meant parting with three instead of two sons all at once.

She had talked to Khun Prem about it, and he had replied, "I'd like to have On go on at the Military Academy. He wants to be a soldier. It doesn't make much difference at this stage whether he's here or abroad. After his graduation we'll see."

She had also asked On what his feelings were on this subject.

"I wouldn't want to go now," he had said. "I much prefer to finish my study and get my commission as quickly as possible. And with An and Ot leaving I'd rather be here with you anyway. You'd be lonely with all three of us absent at the same time."

One week gave way to another, and another. Another month went by, another day wore on. Phloi's heart grew heavy every time she glanced at the two steamer trunks standing so prominently in the corridor. One day the boys went to have their passport pictures taken. Another day came and the whole family sat for group photographs to mark the ocasion. Then Khun Prem took his sons to Badman Store and John Samson Store to buy *farang* clothes for them. How grown up they looked in these clothes! They were no longer Phloi's babies. The babies were gone forever, never to return, and now these two young lads would soon be leaving home. Phloi tried to cure herself of her melancholy mood by keeping busy. She arranged and rearranged the two trunks, which made her feel worse rather than better. She ordered a large wooden box from a Chinese carpenter and filled it with tins and jars of shredded pork, candied tamarind, savoury lotus seeds, and countless kinds of preserved fruit for the boys to eat on the high sea and in the strange land.

Khun Prem said something about An later going on to France for his law studies while Ot was to remain in England the whole time. This sort of elaboration did not interest Phloi very much, preoccupied as she was with the question of sheer distance, the great unknowable distance which was to separate her from her sons. England or France— what did it matter? To her it was all the same, a far, far away place, and very cold, a hundred times as cold as our winter here, or so she had heard. She would not be there to protect them from the cold, or the hunger, or any other hardship they might have to face. She told herself not to paint gloomy pictures and kept reminding the boys to write often, regularly, so that the people at home would not feel so cut off from them.

The date of the departure was finally fixed. The eve of the departure finally arrived. They all went to bed early that night for the boat bound for Singapore was scheduled to sail well before dawn the next morning. After spending some hopelessly wakeful hours in bed, Phloi tiptoed out and into the boys' room. Enough light pouring in through the open windows enabled her to see their faces and observe their even breathing under the mosquito net. It would seem she was trying to commit this sight to memory. After a while she sat down in a chair near their beds and closed her tired eyes. Ot must have woken up at some stage, for the next thing she knew he was seated in her lap with his head on her shoulder, a favourite position of his from way back. Phloi held him close to her, drawing solace from his warm body, swallowing her tears and thinking that the warmth would have to last her for a long time to come.

She dozed off. Her legs had gone numb when she was woken at the touch of Khun Prem's hand on her shoulder. "It's time, Mae Phloi."

Phloi slid Ot from her lap, waking him up. On and An were walking about looking sleepy still. Phloi sent her glance round at all of them one last time before going off to get dressed.

The rain was falling in a fine steady drizzle as the car turned into the gate of the wharf at Thanon Tok. They got out and walked on the moist ground, making their way to the steamer looming ahead against the purple pre-dawn sky. Its lights were on, illuminating puffs of smoke spurting from its funnels. There were people milling about on the upper deck and a giant crane was hoisting crates from boats moored along its side. Breathing in the smell of oil and coal, Phloi held on tight to her sons' hands, and only let go when Khun Prem, having seen to the luggage, herded them across the narrow footbridge linking the bank and the steamer. On board, Khun Phra San, who was of the same age as Khun Prem but of a plumper and shorter stature, came up smilingly to greet them. Phloi paid him her respects and entreated him in a trembling voice to look after her sons, to scold them when they were naughty, to treat them as though they were his own children.

"You have nothing to worry about," said Phra San. He see
an altogether kind and good-natured man, Phloi was glad to n
Turning this way and that between the parents and the sons, he went
on talking cheerfully. "Khun Prem's sons are like my own. We're going
to stick together, aren't we, boys? When you want anything you'll tell
me, won't you? Khun Prem and Khun Phloi please set your minds
at rest. They're by no means too young to travel, and I tell you these
fellows grow up fast. Before you know it you'll find yourself with two
full-grown sons. Nice-looking boys, both of them."

Khun Choei, Luang Osot and Phoem came up to join them. Luang
Osot's going-away presents to his nephews were miniature Buddha
images encased in gold-framed lockets. "Keep them with you always," he
enjoined the recipients. "Remember the Lord Buddha's teaching, and
pray that its benign power may protect you against harm." Khun Choei,
her face about to crumple into tears, handed the boys a few packages
containing their favourite sweets, and Phoem gave each of them a *takrut
salika thong*, a type of amulet designed to bring forth loving kindness
towards the wearer. "A few years from now you'll have the *farang*
girls running after you, thanks to these *takrut*s," he told his nephews.

Then they all went to look at the boys' cabin, which adjoined that of
Phra San. Khun Choei poked her head in, then withdrew immediately
exclaiming, "Oh dear! It's only big enough for a cat to wriggle and die.
I feel suffocated on their behalf."

Phloi silently agreed with her as she took in the beds looking like
two narrow shelves one on top of the other, the minuscule basin for
washing up, and the one small round hole in the wall serving as a
window. Noticing her fallen face, Khun Prem hastened to cheer her up.

"It's only for a few days' journey, Mae Phloi. Once they get to
Singapore they'll change to a much bigger boat. They'll have a
wonderful time on it."

"Yes, yes!" Phra San eagerly supported his friend. "There'll be plenty
of room, please rest assured, Khun Phloi. It will be fun for them. You're
not to worry about a thing, Khun Phloi."

"I'm so grateful to you, Khun Phra," Phloi said, and went on
worrying.

Having inspected the cabins, the party returned to the deck and stood about chatting, listening, looking, waiting while the minutes inexorably ticked away.

Now the loading was done. The racket connected with that activity had died down. There was a lull, a silence, a feeling of sadness in the chilly air. Phloi had nothing to say really—she would rather cry, but tears would have been inauspicious, even a bad omen perhaps—so, controlling herself she managed to whisper to Ot, "Behave yourself. Don't climb over the railing or you may fall into the sea," and to An, "look after yourself and your little brother."

Ot nodded, while An bit his lip trying to act brave. An who had been so excited about this trip was looking quite pale, very much like a typical child about to be separated from his parents and already having pangs of homesickness.

Suddenly the air was filled with a most startling sound. It was the whistle blowing. Two shattering blasts of it in quick succession. A flurry of movement and then some official appeared asking those who were not passengers to please disembark. Phloi felt her legs giving way, regained her balance, and was the last one to kiss the boys farewell. Holding them in her arms, feeling them snug and warm against her, she could not bear the thought of letting them go. Khun Prem gave her shoulder a few pats, and after a while helped her up and led her away.

From the ground Phloi looked up at the travellers. She heard commands in some *farang* language coming from the bridge up above followed by answering shouts from somewhere in the lower decks. Holding On's hand, pressing it, her face upturned, Phloi peered across the distance at the spot on the upper deck occupied by the two boys and Khun Phra San. Khun Phra was waving and smiling—but oh, how small the boys looked! Decidedly too small to be taken away from their father and mother. And now, alas, it was too late to reclaim them. The whistle was blowing again. Then the vessel started to move, to the accompaniment of the ringing of bells and the churning of the water; and after a short while it was no longer alongside the banks but in the middle of the river, on its way to sea. The figures behind the railings grew smaller and smaller. Another moment passed and nothing could be seen of the boat save some green and red lights burning dimly out of the dark expanse and these too were finally swallowed up.

For many days afterwards, the house looked to Phloi a dreary place, arid, lifeless, as if a drought had spread over it and nothing would ever bloom again. One unintentional glance at the boys' beds, or their old clothes, or their favourite dishes, would start her longing for them, or send her off to cry quietly by herself. No one could comfort her. Least of all Khun Prem. Now that he had effected the boys' departure, Khun Prem quite happily went back to the care of his horses, and when it occurred to him to say some soothing words to his wife he tended to repeat himself over and over again, which was rather tiresome. Apart from missing them she worried about their safety, and when a rainstorm brought thunder and lightning she would imagine the ship sailing through the same kind of weather, only much worse, much more dangerous and she would suffer agonies until the sun shone again.

The day the first news arrived was a red-letter day for Phloi. The earth became liveable once more. She felt indescribably uplifted, and extremely grateful to the postman for having delivered this picture postcard to the house.

An's salutation was in a most correct form: "I make obeisance at your feet, dear and esteemed Khun Father and Khun Mother." Then came the message in his neat handwriting: "I have arrived safely in Singapore. This is the picture of the hotel where I'm staying. We sail in the big boat tomorrow. Today Khun Phra took us riding in a motorcar and we saw many tall buildings. I hope you are all well. I miss you very very much."

The bottom half of the card was adorned with Ot's straggly lines: "*Mae cha* (mother dear), I've seen two sharks already. I called Phi An but he came too late and didn't see them. It's very hot here and full of Chinese, more Chinese than at home, but not one can speak Thai. Strange, isn't it?"

The postman became a very important person in Phloi's life. How eagerly she awaited his next visit! She expected him to turn up in

morning, then the morning having passed she looked forward to
ééing him in the afternoon. Days passed and he still had nothing for
her; but at the point where she began to feel really desperate he came
with another letter—bless him!

The letter was from Ot, telling her that An was still feeling weak,
having been seasick and unable to swallow anything solid for days.
"The name of this town is Colombo," he went on to inform her.
"*Khaek*s (Indians) are all over the place. A lot of them come up to
the boat. They smell mouldy and make a lot of noise. The captain
says to close all our doors and windows because they are very clever
at stealing. I don't understand what they are yelling about. Khun
Phra says they have things to sell and they want to take us to see the
sights. Khun Phra is very kind. He teaches me to eat the *farang* way.
Mae cha, do you know *farang*s spoon their soup out and away and if
you scoop it toward yourself you're doing it wrong? And we eat lamb.
Ugh! Smelly! I want to put lots and lots of mustard on it to kill the
smell but Khun Phra says that's rude. Funny."

The postman called fairly regularly bringing news from other ports;
and then he began to gladden Phloi's heart with letters from England.
An was now living with an English family, preparing himself for
enrolment in a boys' school. His letters were invariably neatly written
and their contents revealed his commendably serious intention to
succeed at what he was doing. Khun Prem took the letters to his office
and proudly showed them to his friends. Phloi appreciated them no
less than her husband, but she had to admit to herself that she rather
got more pleasure from what Ot had to say because he told her what
she wanted to know. From Ot she got some idea of the grey days in
England and the difference between what she considered "winter"
here and the real thing over there, and how they lived and what they
ate and that sort of thing.

"They buy a leg of meat every week," Ot told her in one of his letters.
"We have some on Sunday and then the rest of it for six more days,
sometimes hot, sometimes cold, and on Saturday we have the meat
from near the bone, all chopped up. Then we begin another leg on
Sunday, you see. I think there is something good about being far from

home because living here I know how comfortable it is at home. But don't you worry, Mother. I am very well and they look after me well, but I miss you so much, that's all. I can't help it. I miss you, I do!"

Khun Prem was critical of his younger son's epistolary efforts. "Look at all the mistakes," he said. "The boy's so untidy. And how he rambles on and on about nothing." But Phloi always put forward a good argument absolving Ot of his short-comings, at least to herself. What if he crossed out words and left smudges all over the page? He would outgrow these childish failings in time. In the meanwhile he wrote often, and that was the main thing.

As time went by Phloi grew more or less accustomed to not having An and Ot at home. She also became much less of a homebody not only because she had two children less to look after and the other two required less supervision but because Khun Prem had been taking her out more often these days. Perhaps he wished to distract her from pining for the boys, or perhaps it had become fashionable to go about with your wife to the various official and social functions. At any rate he seemed to like having her attend them together with him and Phloi quite enjoyed herself at these occasions although she didn't think she would, greatly miss them if Khun Prem had decreed otherwise.

One leisurely afternoon, in the course of a domestic conversation, Khun Prem paused to contemplate his wife for a while, then said, "May I ask you to do something for me, Mae Phloi?"

"Of course. Have I ever said no? What is it?"

"It's this. Our Nai Luang doesn't favour the short haircut for you ladies. He's all for the new style. Wouldn't you like to let your hair grow and—"

Phloi didn't let him finish. "Oh, Khun Prem!" she cried out. "I'm too old to change. I'd only look ridiculous!"

"I don't think so," said Khun Prem in the tone of one who knows best. "I don't think you're too old, and I think you'd look even younger and prettier with your hair long and done up nicely in the new fashion. I mean it, Mae Phloi. I can imagine you at a royal audience . . . His Majesty noticing you and approving, and the other people gazing at you with admiration."

He was being quite persuasive, Phloi had to admit. Nevertheless his request called for a gibe and she gave it to him, with a smile: "If you want a younger and prettier wife, why don't you get yourself a new one? I shall not stand in your way."

"You're only saying that. If I really took a new wife you'd make my life miserable with your jealousy. Anyway, even if you meant what you said, I still wouldn't be interested. Taking another wife is such a bother. I want *you* as my new wife, Mae Phloi, a more youthful and more beautiful Mae Phloi. That's for me."

Sweet of him to say all that, but even so she would like to think it over a little bit more. She would ask Khun Choei's opinion. She could always depend on Khun Choei for sane, sensible advice.

And Khun Choei, when she came to see Phloi a few days later, agreed with Khun Prem though she expressed herself in less ecstatic terms. "Yes," she said, having surveyed her sister in the manner of a strictly impartial judge. "Yes, I think you should do it, you know. It will be all right—you're still young enough."

"What about yourself?" Phloi countered. "You're only a little older than me. Why don't you do it too?"

"Leave me out for the time being, Mae Phloi. Let's have *you* try it first, shall we?"

Thus it came to pass that Mae Phloi acquired a new hairdo for herself after having worn it short all her adult life—ever since the tonsure of her topknot, that is. She was self-conscious about it at first, inevitably and unavoidably so, but had to confess that it did make her feel somewhat younger—prettier too, perhaps.

One day, in the course of another sisterly get-together, Khun Choei took another good look at Phloi, who was fixing her long hair in front of the mirror, and said, "I know what, Mae Phloi. There's something else you must do now that you're so fashionably coifed."

"What are you suggesting *now*, Khun Choei?"

"That you scale your teeth, make them white again, you know. Your present hairstyle and the betel-stained teeth don't go together somehow. In fact, they clash horribly. So let's polish them, shall we? Come and sit over here, Mae Phloi. I'll help you." It was typical of

Khun Choei to start implementing her plans the very minute she formulated them.

"You think so, Khun Choei?" Phloi spoke uncertainly from the mirror. "Won't I look pale and bland with white teeth?"

"No, no!" Khun Choei clucked impatiently. "You look almost like a *maem* (European woman) with this new coiffure. And a *maem* with betel teeth is unheard of. There's something incongruous about the combination. Come on, Mae Phloi, let's not waste any more time."

They spent the whole day at it, taking time off for lunch (with no post-prandial betel-chewing as on other days), and succeeded in their task. Phloi's front teeth had been sufficiently polished so that their natural whiteness was now revealed, much to Khun Choei's satisfaction. The rest could be similarly achieved without any great difficulty, she said, adding, "Oh you look so charming, Mae Phloi!"

"But they'll turn black again," Phloi remarked, sounding wistful, smiling at the mirror then at Khun Choei.

"Not if you take care of them every day" said Khun Choei encouragingly. "Besides, I'm told that once you're used to having white teeth you will not feel like chewing betel as much as before."

When Khun Choei had left, Phloi bathed and changed and waited for her husband to come home.

Khun Prem got back, exchanged a few casual words with his wife, bathed and changed quickly and, after a few more casual words, dashed off for the stable where he remained until dinner time summoned him back to the house.

The meal over, Khun Prem was relaxing talking to his wife about horses and other pleasant matters. Suddenly he stopped in mid-sentence.

"What have you done to yourself?" At last came the question Phloi had been waiting for. "You look different."

"How?" Phloi asked.

"I don't know. Prettier, yes. But that's not exactly what I'm trying to say. I don't know what—"

Phloi laughed.

"Oh-ho!" Khun Prem exclaimed. "I see, I see. No wonder you look so different. And beautiful, Mae Phloi!"

"You like it?" said Phloi shyly.

"Of course I do. Who wouldn't, Mae Phloi? Who wouldn't like to see his wife looking so attractive . . . Khun Choei suggested it, eh? Very good, very good. Splendid idea. You really look marvellous, Mae Phloi."

As always, Phloi was pleased to have done something that pleased him. These days she did take more interest in her personal appearance, and when they went out together she and Khun Prem made a handsome couple. Handsome, and definitely *samai mai* (modern).

At heart, though, Phloi did not feel as *samai mai* as her clothes and hair style would have you believe, and when Khun Prem came out with remarks about her old-fashioned ideas, whether jokingly or reprovingly, she usually laughed, tacitly admitting to them without fuss or bother.

When they went to the fair at Wat Benchama Bophit—the Marble Temple—Phloi felt like a member of the older generation all right, and while enjoying herself very much she kept casting her mind back to the past. She had attended this fair under the late reign. His Late Majesty had initiated this annual programme with the purpose of raising money for the maintenance of the edifice he had had built. The young Phloi had thought it the grandest fair ever. Now she could see that that had been but a small beginning. There were under this reign many many more booths and pavilions, all sumptuously decorated, and the old fairground had never been so brightly-illuminated as this. In fact, the Wat Benchama fair was now the social event of the season—the gayest, most glittering, most glamourous. An absolute must, to be among those present, to see and to be seen. The men and women in the crowd looked as though they didn't have a care in the world and never would, Phloi thought, and they were talking and laughing together with a kind of frankness new to her. They were not exhibiting the rather coy mannerisms which they had once tended to affect when thrown together in public.

That year, Phloi went to the fair only two nights, but Khun Prem regarded it as his duty to be there every night. No one could accuse him of not performing this duty wholeheartedly and well. He went early and came home at dawn. He also contributed to the success of the fair by spending a great deal of money. Too much, Phloi thought in her old-fashioned way, but did nothing to restrain him from using his own money as he saw fit. That sort of interference would have required a certain kind of boldness she did not possess.

A tolerant, uncomplaining, not to say indulgent, wife was Phloi, and always anxious to do what was expected of her by her lord and master. Within reason, that is. Once in a while she begged to differ, like that time Khun Prem wanted her to go and present herself to Her Highness Phra Worakanya.

This was after the cremation of Somdet the Dowager Queen Mother, which was followed after a not so very long interval by the cremation of the royal brother Somdet Phra Anuja Heir Apparent to the Throne, whose death occurred during his visit to Singapore. The Great War had been over, the soldiers had returned and their homecoming celebrated many times over. It came after all those events, the news that His Majesty had got engaged to Her Highness Phra Worakanya. Phloi first heard it from Khun Prem, who brought it home straight from the palace. Then she heard it again and again from everybody else she happened to meet. The thrilling news spread fast, and pretty soon there wasn't a photographic studio in town which didn't display a portrait or two of the princess in their windows. The young and not so young society ladies wasted no time in adopting her favourite mode of attire: waisted overblouse worn very long, almost covering the entire length of the *pha chongkraben* (thus making this traditional piece of garment, when viewed from a distance at least, look very much like a European skirt); stockings and heeled shoes; and for the hair, chignon and velvet or silk headband. In such style did the young and not so young women deck themselves who did not wish to fall behind the latest fashion.

Now among the wives of the king's officials quite a few had already gone to present themselves and attend on Phra Worakanya. Phloi however had not done so, and one day Khun Prem brought up this matter with her.

"When are you going to do it, Mae Phloi?"

"Join the frantic rush to attach oneself to a rising star? I've seen this sort of thing before, Khun Prem. I think I'll wait a while."

"Why must you be so contrary, Mae Phloi?"

"Not at all, Khun Prem. It's only because I don't like flatterers and fawners that I don't want to become one myself. You and I, Khun Prem, will always be loyal to the throne, as were our grandfathers and grandmothers before us. We are Nai Luang's loyal subjects and it follows that we're going to be loyal subjects to his wives and children. We don't have to prove it by joining the rush for favours, do we? In any case, we owe loyalty to all his wives and should not declare exclusive allegiance to only this or that particular personage."

"I think this reign will have only one queen, Mae Phloi. He has been educated in England and the English *phudi* (well-born; of noble birth) do not have several wives."

"I'm not arguing with you, Khun Prem. He may be going to have just the one as you say. If so, all the more unnecessary for me to go and present myself to her. For if there were to be several, perhaps as wives of the king's servants we might be called upon to choose among different entourages ... So you think we'll have only one queen, Khun Prem? Hmm, I don't know. I'm not altogether convinced, Khun Prem. Frankly, I feel the palace ought to be filled up. It would look rather bare and empty with only one royal consort, don't you think?"

A few days later Khun Prem told his wife how glad he was about her decision not to "join the rush." Phloi asked him what had made him change his mind, and he said, "Well, I thought I'd go and see what it was like and now that I've seen it I can understand why you want to stay away. Masses of simpering people—I don't know where half of them sprang from. While we were waiting I listened to the conversation round me. I had no choice. They were clamouring to be heard and they had so much to say-—all about themselves and Her Highness. How they had known her since she was a child, or a baby, how they had carried her in their arms and blah blah blah. Then she came into the room and they gathered round her and paid her such overdone compliments that I didn't know where to look. Some of them had tears in their eyes—they were so overcome with joy that they couldn't restrain themselves. They made my flesh crawl."

"And what did Her Highness say?"

"She smiled. What could she say? Anyway, I wouldn't have been able to catch anything she might have said. The sound of those joyful tears falling all round her was so deafening."

Phloi laughed with amusement. Then she asked, "Do you think she believed it?"

"I shouldn't think so, Mae Phloi. If common people like us could see through it, why wouldn't she? She has a more refined eye. But what could she do? They were so assiduous in seeking her audience it would have been churlish not to grant it. If she thought their compliments insincere she couldn't very well come right out and spurn them, could she? A gracious princess doesn't behave like that. When we don't like somebody we can show it if we want to, Mae Phloi. But someone in her position cannot. It's not done.

"I'm glad you weren't there, Mae Phloi," he added. "She might have thought you were no different from those people. I wouldn't have liked that at all. What loss of face that would have been!"

"I have something to confess, Khun Prem," said his wife in a confessional tone of voice. "Please don't say I'm mad, will you?"

"I won't," Khun Prem chuckled. "Even if I should think so I'll keep quiet about it."

"Actually," Phloi began. "Actually, I've been dying to get a good look at Phra Worakanya. I'm so happy about the royal engagement.Who wouldn't be? It's marvellous that we're going to have a queen at last! I've stayed away from her audiences not because I'm uninterested. Not at all! Does she look like her photographs, Khun Prem?"

"You'll see for yourself, Mae Phloi. I'm getting tickets for this play Nai Luang is staging. He's acting in it and so is Phra Worakanya."

"Tickets, Khun Prem?"

"Oh, yes, tickets are being sold to the public and the proceeds will go to help maintain the Wild Tigers."

An astonished Phloi put a hand on her heart. Phra Chao Yu Hua performing in a stage play in public? She trembled in anticipation, because for her the sovereign was a lofty being, an object of high reverence, and when one wished to gaze at him one did so with the utmost discretion: one kept lowering one's glance and never fixed it on him for too long or in too bold a manner; and she simply could not imagine how she would go about watching him do his part as though he were a mere actor. Oh dear! She went on to ponder other points, such as why with his untold wealth Phra Chao Yu Hua should need to raise money for the Wild Tiger Corps. Or if it was his pleasure to have us contribute and share with him he could have commanded some royal troupe of dancers to put on a show for us. That would have been more than sufficient, Phloi thought. But the most astonishing thing of course was the fact that Her Highness Phra Worakanya would also act in the play. Now Phloi had seen the Pridalai Troupe productions, which had an all-women cast—except for a male clown or two, who counted as clowns rather than as males. But Her Highness would be doing a role together with real men playing male parts, and she a future queen, and even though Nai Luang himself would be in it . . . Dear me! I must adjust my thinking, Phloi told herself, and bring my mind up-to-date and not hark back to the old ways I happen to be accustomed to. Must try to be like Khun Prem, who was talking about this coming event quite placidly, as though there was nothing perplexing about it at all.

So she summoned up some aplomb and asked him, "What sort of play is Nai Luang staging, Khun Prem?"

"Its title is '*Phong-phang*,'" Khun Prem answered. "He wrote it himself. A speaking play not a singing one. I'm told it's very good." (A *phong-phang* is a kind of fishtrap with a net attached to stakes, which, depending on the tide, are raised or lowered from their positions on the river or canal banks.)

On the appointed evening, Phloi put on such finery as she considered appropriate to the event. She had a ticket to a play entitled "*Phong-phang*" (she found the idea of a fishtrap in this connection mystifying), but in her heart she was going to attend a royal audience. And you couldn't really quarrel with her attitude. The theatre was situated in Phya Thai Palace and His Majesty would be there. Although he would be assuming the guise of a thespian and she that of a spectator, Phloi knew for certain that she would not be carried away by his artistry, no matter how accomplished it might turn out to be, to the extent that she would forget about the man behind the actor.

Khun Prem and Phloi arrived at the theatre well in advance of curtain time, as did most of their fellow play-goers, among whom were Their Royal Highnesses, other members of the royal family, ministers and other high-ranking officials with their ladies and a host of other prominent men and women. There were also quite a few *farangs*—"diplomats," whispered Khun Prem—and Indian and Chinese merchants. "Everybody's here," said Phloi to herself. She was gratified to note that the atmostphere did not differ so very much from that of a grand state function. The people round her were conversing, when they conversed at all, in undertones, and their main activity, Phloi could tell, was waiting. Looking poised, expectant, ready, they were all waiting like herself for the moment Phra Chao Yu Hua would appear.

Yet those few moments immediately after the curtain rose saw Phloi breathing normally again having darted a quick nervous glance round the stage and registered the fact that His Majesty was nowhere in sight. Her sense of relief lasted but a short while, however, for he soon came in. Enter Nai Luang, and right away Phloi instinctively bent forward, lowering her head, composing her arms and hands into the gesture of rendering homage. But she caught herself in time, suddenly conscious that no one nearby—certainly not her own husband— was moving in unison with her. They were watching the play. She marvelled at the apparent ease with which they had entered into the spirit of the occasion. She straightened up and tried to follow the dialogue but soon became engrossed in watching Nai Luang instead. "How noble, how handsome," she thought. "A kind of inner light radiating forth, a presence not of the common run of men." She went on watching, entranced. "He reminds me of the late Queen Mother. Oh, he's so very like her!" Here Phloi felt a tingling in her skin, for her feeling of love and awe had remained undiminished throughout these years as regards that august lady, Somdet of the Upper Palace,

Somdet Regent, Somdet Phra Borom Rachini Nat, then in her last years Somdet of the Thousand Years, the Queen Mother. "Remarkable resemblance," Phloi repeated to herself. She made a renewed effort to concentrate on the play, but when His Majesty in an aside threw a glance at the audience she dropped her gaze, and when the other actors stepped close to him and talked to him just as you and I would talk among ourselves, she couldn't help trembling a little and feeling afraid for them. Of course they were only play-acting and not *really* behaving as his equals and thereby exposing themselves to all manner of misfortunes, but even so . . .

When Her Highness Princess Worakanya made her first appearance, Khun Prem gave his wife a gentle nudge, quite unnecessary, for who wouldn't recognize her immediately? "Quite attractive," remarked Phloi to herself, thinking that she had seen more beautiful princesses in her young days in the Inner Court, then reproaching herself for entertaining such a thought and making such a comparison, for letting her mind stray into irrelevancies instead of keeping it on the "Fishtrap." With close attention therefore Phloi watched Phra Worakanya portray her role and before long was filled with admiration for Her Highness, was amazed at how easy she made it all seem, moving and smiling and talking so naturally and confidently without the slightest trace of self-consciousness. Phloi could just see herself trying to do the same, or rather she could see herself shaking and stammering, or fainting altogether with fright should she have been called upon to attempt it. But however superbly Phra Worakanya was acting her part Phloi still could not regard her as anything but a princess and future queen, and when a man approached too near her and spoke to her with familiarity, Phloi had to stifle an impulse to mutter, "Oh, no! Don't!"

The scene she would never be able to forget came just before the end: His Majesty embracing Phra Worakanya and the latter saying, "When did you fall in love with me?" and his reply, "That day I saw you at the painting exhibition in Bang Pa-in."

Phloi was so stunned she didn't make a move when the band struck up the royal anthem. Khun Prem had to prompt her. A dazed Phloi then rose to her feet, and afterwards followed her husband in the jostling crowd through one of the exits to stand waiting for the car in front of the theatre, shivering a little in the night air which had turned chilly.

On the way home, in answer to Khun Prem's question, she said, rather evasively, "It was good. But I'd never seen anything like it before, you know, so I had some difficulty keeping up with the plot."

She wasn't going to tell him about her various reactions which had been quite extraneous to the play itself, and which no doubt would only make him shake his head and say, "Oh, Mae Phloi, you and your old-fashioned ideas!" But she would tell Choi about tonight (and how she was looking forward to their next meeting!) and they could discuss it together. Choi would understand.

As the car turned into the gateway of their home, Khun Prem said, "I had a marvellous time. And I thought Nai Luang was the best actor of them all. He left all the others way behind him."

TWENTY-FOUR

SOME extracts from Ot's letters to *Mae cha* (mother dear):

"It's snowing, *Mae cha*. The first time for me! Before that it was so awfully cold my bones nearly broke, but now it's a bit warmer. Snow doesn't shower like rain, *Mae cha*. It drifts down in tiny flakes, slowly. You remember that day you and I were sitting together near that big kapok tree and its fruits were ripe and bursting into white balls, all fluffy? Then the storm came and the wind blew the white fluff off the tree and it floated everywhere in the air and we could see it so clearly because of the dark sky? Snow falling is something like that, *Mae cha* ..."

"... Phi An has gone off to France and here I am at my school and its VERY cold. And no fire. But plenty of rules and you can't do this and that, and the boys teased me and made fun of me, but they don't do it any more. They stopped doing it when they saw I didn't mind at all. Phi An would have hated it. You know how he hates being teased ..."

"... I didn't tell you but at first I couldn't eat school food it was so bad. But I got hungry and now I eat everything and ask for a second or third helping sometimes. They give you plenty to eat here. You don't have to worry about me starving, Mother dear."

"Before I came to school I used to sit around thinking about you and getting so homesick, but now there is no time to sit doing nothing by myself. Every day they keep me doing this and that all the time. No spare time at all. I go to chapel, I go to class, I play games. You must all play games here, everybody, unless you're sick. After games I bathe, then the bell rings and I do my homework. I go to bed early and get up early to take a cold shower. This was painful at first but now I'm used to it."

"We live in different houses and each house has a teacher looking after us, and a boy who's head of house. He is very powerful, this boy. He can command us to do things and we must obey him and he can punish us when we do wrong. I'm all right in class. I have no difficulty at all in arithmetic because I've done it all in Bangkok and my English is much better now, but I have to work hard at Latin to catch up with the other boys. What a crazy language this is, Mother dear! Take the word 'table'—it keeps changing all the time. It's just a plain table when you don't want to do anything with it, but bang on it and it's no longer the same. And the table you go to and the one you come from are not the same either, do you know that? Then there's the table you talk to. "O Table!" Isn't it fun? When I come home and you see me talk to a table you'll know that I'm not mad but only using the good knowledge taught me in England . . ."

". . . It doesn't seem like I've been here very long, but actually I have. I'm glad because it means the day will soon come when I'll be going home to be with you again. I hope you miss me, but not so much as to make yourself unwell."

". . . You're not to worry about my going to *farang* church and singing *farang* hymns—some of the hymns are quite lovely. This is part of school, and it doesn't stop me being a Buddhist. I say the prayers you taught me before going to bed every night and pay reverence to the Buddha image given me by Uncle Khun Luang. You should be happy that if anything happens to me I'll have not one but two heavens to go to, one Thai, one *farang* . . ."

". . . Phi An's come over from France and we're on holiday here with some Thai friends. You'll be interested to know that we've been cooking Thai food and stuffing ourselves. They've made me chief cook because I know a little more than they, having learned a few things from sticking close to you around the kitchen at home, you see. The *farang*s here use rice to make a sort of pudding (definitely not my favourite sweet) and buy only a handful of it at a time. Not like us. When we buy rice, the shop assistant cries, 'How are you going to eat all that?' Not all our Thai dishes come out exactly Thai but they're gobbled up all the same. We have no problems with the simpler dishes.

Sweet pork, for instance, we can produce with the greatest of ease. Now success has gone to our heads and the other day we even made a beef curry! You would have laughed, Mother dear."

"We had to use anchovy for shrimp paste, and I nearly scalded my hands squeezing dried coconut—had to use very hot water to get any juice out of it. Chili and shallot and garlic we had, and some spice. For *makrut* (kaffir lime) peel we substituted lemon peel. No *kha* (*alpinia galanga*) was to be found, but the most sorely missed ingredient of all was lemon grass. We'd have given anything for a few stalks of it! I went to the chemist's shop and bought a bottle of lemon grass oil and sprinkled a few drops into the pot. Then as the pot started to boil Phi An shook his head at it saying it didn't look like the real thing without some *makua phuang* (a pea-sized variety of eggplant) so I added tinned peas and this did indeed improve its appearance. You probably wouldn't have recognized it as *kaeng phet nua*, Mother dear, but it was *phet* (hot) enough with all that chili and we ate it all up with great relish. Some *farang*s in the house came to the kitchen to see what the commotion was about and we invited them to join us. They gulped and choked and sweated but bravely and politely said it was delicious. Last winter I bought red and green pepper used for Christmas decorations, sauteed it and feasted on it. My *farang* friends suspected my stomach was lined with copper. . ."

". . . More about food. We do go to Chinese restaurants in London but of course we don't get to London very often. Chinese food is 'safer' than Thai in that it doesn't smell so strongly. At home we're not conscious of it but over here people sniff the air around them looking mystified, not to say indignant, and move away from you, and you that the garlic you have eaten is filling the atmosphere with its distinctive odour which most English *farang*s find offensive. Fresh garlic (when only a few cloves are used) isn't so bad. It's smell doesn't last so very long. The longest-lasting effect is from those highly valued delicacies from home such as roasted chili paste and savoury rice. You can clean your mouth a hundred times and gargle and suck sweets and do all sort of things and yet cannot get rid of the smell. It doesn't seem to come from your breath alone but from every pore in your body.

One day in London, Phi An and I had some bread on which we spread your roasted chili paste (delicious!), then we had to go somewhere in the Underground. Our fellow passengers sent inquiring glances demanding to know where the alien smell was coming from. They finally edged away from us. I didn't mind. We had lots of space to ourselves. I tell my *farang* friends that just as I now enjoy lamb and love cheese I'm sure that if they happened to come and live in our *Muang Thai* they would in time grow to like our garlic omelette, roasted chili paste, fish sauce and other tasty Thai delights. And, speaking of fish sauce—you asked what foodstuffs we'd like to have from home. Well, fish sauce would be fine. Without it our Thai cooking can fall flat as you know. We tried making it once, didn't get very far, no-thing came of it except a very peculiar smell. The neighbours started to complain in earnest and we had to bury the whole experiment at the bottom of the garden. Kaffir lime, lemon grass, various curry pastes—all this would also be most welcome . . ."

This last letter earned the following comments from Ot's father: "He goes on and on about food and not a word about his study. I don't understand this son of yours, Mae Phloi."

Smiling at her husband, Phloi offered no argument, and began planning in her mind how best to pack the herbs and spices and bottles and jars for the next shipment to Europe. Getting homegrown and homemade food supplies to her sons in that distant land was one of her most enjoyable and satisfying occupations during those years. Unlike Khun Prem, she was not bothered by the fact that their younger son Ot was not as serious-minded as his brother An. An's letters continued to show his sense of purpose and determination to get on in the world. Good for An. But Ot had qualities of his own, and if he chose to write home about everyday topics such as food, well, why not? Phloi reflected smiling to herself. Food is im-portant, and cooking a kindly, friendly enterprise. During this period, calling at her house you sometimes came upon Phloi surrounded by lovely-smelling ingredients and numerous servants from the very old to the very young helping her chop and peel and pound. The scene was quite lively and conveyed the impression that a festive meal for hundreds of friends was being prepared.

One of the members of Phloi's household who greatly enjoyed participating in the food programme for Europe was Khun Un, Khun Eldest Sister Un now contentedly settled in the bungalow which had housed On before his discovery by Phloi. Yes, contentedly, peaceably settled, much to the astonishment of those who had rightly looked upon her as one of the most combative ladies they had ever encountered. Phloi had been surprised on the very first day Khun Un moved from Khlong Bang Luang to this house, surprised to start with, and then filled with pity. She had not realized till that moment to what deplorable extent Khun Un had been ruined by the brother she had loved too well. There she was Khun Un, sad-faced but dignified, arriving at her new home with a few small chests. Phloi took one look at these, could not quite fit them in with her still vivid childhood memory of Khun Un seated upright in her room where the silver and gold treasures were kept, and immediately offered to send servants across the river to fetch the rest of her things, only to learn the heart-rending truth from Khun Un that there was nothing else left to be fetched.

Phloi vowed to herself then to do everything she could for Khun Un, to provide for her and make her as comfortable and happy as could possibly be done.

And before long it became obvious that Khun Un had lost all interest in accumulating worldly possessions. Peace and quiet was all she sought, and when Phloi inquired how she was she would say she had never felt so well in years. She lived quietly in her bungalow, attended by her loyal retainer Granny Prik (who, as her one-time enemy Granny Phit said, "has also mellowed") and a servant girl provided her by Phloi. Her face always lit up with pleasure when Phloi came to see her at the bungalow, and she behaved with Phloi in a sisterly way, intimately and unceremoniously, that is. But when Khun Prem came to call she would assume a formal deferential manner towards him, as though he were a high-ranking guest entitled to receive her homage. Her head would be respectfully lowered when she put her palms together in a *wai* before him, and she used a most polite form of address in conversing with him, and all this made Khun Prem feel extremely uncomfortable.

"Mae Phloi," he said, "will you please ask your eldest sister not to place me so high. It's not right. I'm her younger brother, a junior person to her. She shouldn't treat me this way."

"Don't you like it?" Phloi said. "To have your wife's older sister honour you with a reverent *wai* and call you 'Excellency'?"

"Don't joke, Mae Phloi. She shouldn't do it. It might bring me bad luck—might even shorten my life! Do something about it, Mae Phloi."

Phloi never did. She could not picture herself going up to Khun Un and advising her how to behave. She wouldn't know how to begin. At any rate, Khun Un had chosen to "cast off her fangs and claws" as we say in Thai and behave genially (in her own fashion), and we should rejoice, Phloi thought. Of course she didn't have to be that formal with Khun Prem and accord him all that reverence, but given time Phloi was sure she would come round to treating Khun Prem the way he would like to be treated—as a younger brother.

Then one fine afternoon Khun Choei came to visit. She and Phloi went up together to Khun Un's bungalow. They climbed the stairs to the balcony and sat down, and Khun Choei paid her respects to the eldest sister in a manner most properly humble.

Khuh Un had been talking to Praphai—she doted on the child— and showing her the art of peeling *maprang*, a kind of fruit, egg-shaped and rather resembling an apricot in size and colour. She smiled at Phloi. She did not look at Khun Choei.

"I'm sending a plate of stripe-peeled *maprang* to you this evening," she said to Phloi. "Praphai is too young to handle the sharp knife, but she'll soon be old enough to start learning to do it. Next season, perhaps."

Her voice betrayed no emotion—which made it all the more chilling. Phloi stole a look at her, swallowed, hesitated, and finally mustered up her courage to say, "Khun Choei wanted to come and see you, Khun Phi . . . and—and I came along."

"I only have one sister left, Mae Phloi," Khun Eldest Sister replied without lifting her eyes from a *maprang* she had just selected from the basket. "And you wouldn't have come to sneer at me and gloat over my misfortune."

"Oh Khun Phi!" Khun Choei cried, turning her anguished face to Phloi, who could see that she was very near tears. "Please, Khun Phi! I have come to see you and pay my respects."

Khun Un was speaking to Praphai. "You see, darling, this is how one holds the knife. Watch me closely. I don't press it too hard and I keep it steady as I guide it over the fruit. Look at these lines, the pattern is lovely, isn't it?"

Praphai laughed with delight.

"Mae Phloi," Khun Un continued. "You were good and kind to give me this house to live in. It suits me very well. But when some exalted personages appear under its roof I can't help feeling that they must find it too small and shabby to deserve their presence."

Phloi the intermediary didn't know what to say. She looked at the floor and reflected with wonder that both Khun Choei and herself were still very much in awe of their big sister. Khun Un might have lost a fortune but she had retained her ability to make them feel like a pair of naughty children caught in the act once again of some wrong-doing.

And then, after sneaking a glance at Phloi, Khun Choei made up her mind. Leaving her corner of the floor, she approached Khun Un on her hands and knees and lowered her head together with her joined palms at the other's feet, following which gesture, she said, "I beg your forgiveness, Khun Phi. I have caused you much displeasure and made you angry and unhappy. Censure me as severely as you like. But do please forgive me and let the bad karma between us be resolved."

No reply from Khun Un. You could have heard a pin drop as she went on peeling the *maprang* for Praphai's benefit.

Khun Choei turned to Phloi again, mutely appealing for help, and the latter lost no time in coming to her rescue.

"Please, Khun Phi," Phloi said to Khun Un. "Don't be angry with Khun Choei any more. Let bygones be bygones. I beg you to grant me this request. I have very few relatives and it is my dearest wish that they love one another and live together in harmony."

Looking up from the fruit and the knife in her hands, Khun Un fixed her eyes on Phloi in silence.

"Mae Phloi," she finally said, "since you have taken it upon yourself to ask me, I'll not refuse you. Let me say this, however: after Chao Khun Father died, I considered it my duty to take charge, to be head of the family for my younger brothers and sisters. I've come to realize how badly I treated you, Mae Phloi, and you must have hated me at times. With good reason. In spite of that you never breathed a word against me, never hit back, never did anything to hurt me. Your behaviour was irreproachable. Deep in my heart I knew how good you were and that's why it was not difficult to swallow my pride and come to you seeking your help when I was down and out. You have been a true sister, Mae Phloi. The bonds between us have never been broken.

"It was an altogether different matter with my very own, my *full* sister, my willful, thoughtless, heartless sister. *She* had no regard for my position, not the slightest consideration for my feelings. She didn't care how much I suffered when she defied me and hurled insults in my face. I put up with it, though—her defiance, her insolence, her ill will towards me. Then she ran away with a man and that was the last straw! She, a daughter of our family, capable of such an act! Oh, I was sick with shame for all of us. I vowed to myself then that I would cut her off from my life—till death and beyond. And that was that . . .

"Now I must part with that vow. You have done so much for me and I'm forever in your debt, Mae Phloi. You ask me to let bygones be bygones. Very well, Mae Phloi." Here she let herself come to a pause and, turning to Khun Choei, who had been sitting with her head inclined towards the floor, said, "Sit up and make yourself comfortable, Mae Choei. All is forgiven. What's past is past. Now you may come and see me whenever you want."

On their way back to the big house, the two women had a good laugh together.

"I behaved very well, didn't I, Mae Phloi?"

"Quite well, Khun Choei. I was so afraid you might flare up the way you used to and spoil everything."

"Oh, no, I wouldn't have dared. What a woman! The proverbial

335

tiger who never loses its stripes, eh?"

"And who can always frighten us. Right, Khun Choei?"

"Oh, definitely, Mae Phloi. When the tiger flashed those eyes I was right back to being ten years old again. I was doing something awfully bad and I got caught and there was no wriggling out of it."

But if Phloi found it amusing that Khun Un could still with her old magic reduce Khun Choei and herself to a couple of cowering youngsters, she couldn't help feeling disturbed by another familiar manifestation of Khun Un's character. This had to do with the way Khun Un, in order to acquire happiness, had a need to single out a favourite to expend her love on, to coddle, to spoil outrageously. At Khlong Bang Luang, Khun Chit had had this dubious honour. At present it was Praphai. To love is to give; with Khun Un this meant smothering her darling niece with gifts—gifts of all categories from food and jewellery to praise and support. Take the simpler matter of food. Praphai had had a bad stomach on several occasions as the result of Khun Un overfeeding her both in quantity and variety. Sometimes she would turn down the proffered titbits and when pressed to change her mind fly into a rage more violent than the situation warranted; or she would capitulate so as to avoid hurting Khun Un's feelings. Either outcome was harmful to her digestion as well as her character.

Praphai might be pretty as a picture, smart, and charming when she liked, but she was also a temperamental child who could be difficult to an unbecoming degree. Pampering was the last thing she needed.

Phloi, to be sure, exercised great tact in her effort to curb Khun Un's influence on her daughter. With Khun Choei and Phoem she voiced her concern openly. Khun Choei gave some practical advice but Phoem, by treating the matter lightly, was not unhelpful either.

"Please don't bring her anything next time, Khun Luang," Phloi told him when Phoem came bearing another present for Praphai. "She's already overindulged by our big sister. And I'll tell you something else. She's in danger of becoming like her aunt. I can see the resemblance more and more every day."

And Phoem laughed at her, saying, "You're imagining things, Mae Phloi. Praphai's a lovely child. She'll never be like Khun Un. But what's wrong with having Praphai turn out to be another Khun Un anyway? We get along fine, Khun Un and I. So Praphai and I will be great pals too. I have no objection to that."

"Don't joke, Khun Luang. It's not that I despise Khun Un. I don't. Not at all. It's just that she's had a lot of unhappiness in her life, and I—I don't want to see Praphai suffer . . ."

"Don't be such a worrier," Phoem interrupted her. "I'll tell you who I think Praphai takes after. Our dear mother, that's who. Sudden explosions of both tears and laughter. Quick-tempered, you know. Difficult at times but a good sort on the whole. So what is there to get agitated about?"

Phloi did allow herself to feel more reassured, but not to give up her concern altogether, her children being after all a major occupation with her.

That afternoon, though, the main topic of the conversation between Phloi and Choi (who had taken a day's leave from her elderly charges in the Inner Court and come to relax at Khlong Yom) was not about Phloi's children but about what Bangkok at that period was most interested in, namely, the king's future bride.

The interchange on this popular topic that afternoon at Khlong Yom went as follows:

"Have you heard the latest, Phloi?"

"Probably not, whatever it is."

"Nai Luang has broken off his engagement to Phra Worakanya."

"Oh, Choi, are you sure? Khun Prem was talking about the wedding plans only the other day. He even mentioned the guest list. The *farang* royals are to be invited too, he said."

"I heard it from the inner circle, the most reliable sources, my dear."

"But perhaps it's only a temporary break and soon we'll be hearing that they've got re-engaged. Not impossible, you know. Remember the old days, Choi? Remember the Chao Choms who we thought had fallen from favour but who became favourites again?"

"Yes, and I also remember the Chao Choms who fell and never rose again. Anyway, they didn't have to get engaged first in order to get to be Chao Choms. Some of them surprised us by suddenly becoming one, remember? But once they had attained to this position they continued in it, favourite and non-favourite alike. Now, when the betrothal is broken off . . ."

"I still can't believe it's broken off. I hope not. She's a lady of great dignity, every inch a person to whom you and I would gladly and willingly pay our reverence."

"According to my sources, there will be another princess to take her place."

"Oh? Which one?"

"Someone very close. Her younger sister."

"Yes? What is she like? Have you seen her?"

"Yes, and so have you. At Phra Nang's residence, don't you remember? She's much prettier and livelier than her elder sister, who's rather reserved—of great dignity, as you say, but quiet and somewhat distant, don't you think? The younger princess is a darling, a charmer in the nicest sense of the word—really and truly has a winning way about her. Everyone who knows her adores her. I'm very happy for her I must say."

"Why don't you join her retinue, Choi, and get yourself promoted to Khun Lady Elder?"

"Why stop there? Why not Khun Lady Chief Attendant? Can't you just see me swaggering about showing the whole palace what it means to have power?"

Phloi related Choi's news to her husband that same evening. He raised his eyebrows in surprise, then said, "It can't be true. Tell Choi not to listen too much to those old women or she'll get to be like them. They have nothing to do so they tittle-tattle all day long. The Rise and Fall of Royal Favourites—that has always been one of their pet themes. But this reign is not going to have several queens and hundreds of Chao Choms. He's lived abroad among *farang* royals. It's going to be just one wife for him. Like me, come to think of it."

Be that as it may, Choi's sources proved to have been reliable nonetheless, and it was Khun Prem himself who confirmed the news for his wife only a few days afterwards. He also said on that occasion, "It's just as well you didn't go to be presented to her."

To which Phloi replied, "If had known I would have gone."

"Why, Mae Phloi?"

"So I could go and see her now, I suppose. Now that she's no longer the bright star of the moment, most of those people who have been crowding into her reception room will probably stop going. There should be a few of us left to keep her company at such a time."

Khun Prem brought more news to Phloi during the following weeks, about Nai Luang's engagement to Phra Worakanya's younger sister, and about the raising of the latter's rank from Mom Chao to Phra Ong Chao. He did not overtly urge his wife to go and attend on our new future queen but he never stopped singing her praises: What a marvellous beautiful person she was, good-hearted, talented, gracious, a noble lady through and through. She must be, Phloi reflected, for not only my husband but other people, men and women of all ages, are saying the same thing about her and it's plain to see that they love and admire her and, like me, rejoice in all sincerity in her rise to the top.

Still, Phloi had not forgotten the dedicatory poem at the beginning of the book *Sakuntala*, a verse-drama written by His Majesty, a copy of which Khun Prem had brought home from the palace not very many days before the fall of Phra Worakanya:

". . . as Dusayan, vowing
his constancy to Sakuntala,
asks her to take his ring,
so I ask you, my beloved,
to accept this gift of verse
as testimony of mine to you.
But we differ, Dusayan and I—
for he has his forgetful moments
whereas I shall know of none.
Till the rivers cease to flow,
till the sun and the moon are no more,
till death comes . . ."

TWENTY-FIVE

AND then there were those months which saw Phloi immersed, often with an accompanying headache or an aching heart or both, in the task of restoring the old property in Khlong Bang Luang. For some time she had not thought a great deal about it—except in nostalgic terms as her "home" in that tender sense of the word. She had let Khun Un have the money to get it back from the creditors and had continued to regard it as Khun Un's inheritance, to do with as she pleased.

Then one day Khun Un said to Phloi—she had walked all the way from her bungalow and up the stairs to Phloi's sitting room in the big house to say it—"I came to talk to you about our place in Khlong Bang Luang. I'm going to transfer the deed to you. I want you to be its owner, Mae Phloi."

Assuming that Khun Un had the loan on her mind, Phloi hastened to assure her that there was no urgency about the payment whatsoever, that Khun Un should let the matter rest and hold on to the property which, when and if she felt like selling it, would fetch a sum far exceeding the small loan of 8,000 baht.

"And if you transferred it to me, Khun Phi," Phloi added, "you know what people would say. They'd say I only asked you to come and live here because I had designs on it."

"Ah, what people would say." Khun Un laughed. "But they would say anything true or untrue who dearly love to gossip. So let's forget about them and concentrate on our own business. I can sell this house, but I don't want to. From our forebears it has come down to us and I want it to be passed on to our grandchildren. But now, in our lifetime you're the most appropriate person to have it, Mae Phloi. That's my decision and I'll go ahead and make the arrangements. There is to be one condition, though: Praphai is to inherit it from you and not your other children . . ."

Thus it transpired that Phloi became the rightful owner of the family estate in Khlong Bang Luang, and was obliged to do something about it. The first thing she did was to ask Phoem to accompany her across the river and have a look at the old place together. They set out one day from Bangkok and as the boatman steered the ferry from the river into the *khlong*, Phloi's heart began to beat faster with expectation, excitement, and a measure of pride.

"Who would have foreseen this?" Phoem was saying. "You as the mistress of our Khlong Bang Luang house. Did you ever dream it could happen?"

"How can you ask such a question?" Phloi rebuked him. "We were children of a lesser wife, don't forget."

"All is impermanence," Phoem quoted.

No doubt. But it gave Phloi a jolt all the same on being confronted with another illustration of this noble truth a few minutes later. The boat had reached its destination and here was the landing pavilion with every sign of impermanence and decay written large all over it, especially in the way it was leaning precariously to one side. For a brief moment Phloi wondered whether it would collapse under her weight. Evidently not yet. There were even two Chinese hunkering on its steps, one cleaning vegetables out of a basket and the other washing a piece of ebony-dyed cloth. They did not pay any attention to the newcomers but went on doing their chores as though this were a public landing place and Phoem and Phloi merely two more citizens using it for their own purpose like everybody else.

The courtyard, too, had been put to use—perhaps by those same Chinese on the steps, for there were lengths of newly dyed and newly washed cloth spread out everywhere under the sun. Phloi stopped before this blue-black vista and turned in dismay and uncertainty to her brother, who said, "Never mind, Mae Phloi. This is usually the fate of abandoned property. Come, let's go on with our inspection tour."

They did not go inside the main house where Chao Khun Father had lived and died and where Khun Un for so many years had reigned over all from her sitting room "where the silver and gold are kept." They remained standing near one of its twin staircases which had sunk a few inches into the ground, gazing at it in silence.

"I left here not so long ago," Phoem remarked after a while. "How could it have fallen into this appalling state in such a short time?"

The house is dead, Phloi said to herself. *It has been left to die and here's the corpse, a friendless corpse which no one has even bothered to throw a rag over.*

Actually there was plenty of life peeping out from among the broken tiles, chipped balusters and the gaps left by the missing panels in the windows. Life from some bo trees and banyan trees sprouted from under the eaves. Fat spiders ambled across the stained walls. Pots and pans, and stoves, and clothes, were scattered about on the veranda . . .

"Come on, Mae Phloi," Phoem said. "We can't stand here forever."

More signs of human habitation appeared along the way. The path through the garden was strewn with garbage, fresh and not so fresh. The potted topiary plants, once the pride and joy of Chao Khun Father, had outgrown their pots and had clotheslines strung between some of their branches. Now here's a group of children—whose children could they be?—sitting and playing under the old cork tree, as Phloi and Khun Choei had sat and played ages ago. The dear tree looked fine, flourishing, serenely impervious to the change in its surroundings.

Phoem and Phloi trudged on until at last they came to stand before the wooden house—Mother's house, dilapidated but still in one piece, in a manner of speaking. One of the stilts had rotted away to the point of being nearly separated from the ground. The rest were in various stages of disrepair and looking as though they wouldn't be capable of holding up the sagging upper floor much longer. As her glance went roaming over the desolate scene Phloi involuntarily peopled it with remembered shapes and forms and sounds and scents out of her vanished childhood; and a picture came to her mind of the young Phoem and Khun Choei and herself chasing one another with shouts and laughter from stilt to stilt, and Mother sitting there in her favourite corner, working on Chao Khun Father's cheroots, smiling, beautiful, alive—

"Khun Phloi," a voice was calling her and she turned, wiping her eyes, to find a woman standing a few paces away, a thin woman, middle-aged—no, in actual fact youngish, but with a haggard face which made her look at first glance older than her years.

"Khun Phloi," the woman repeated, stepping closer to pay her respects to the visitors. "Don't you remember me, ma'am? I'm your servant Phuang," she announced, smiling and crying at the same time.

"Oh, Phuang!" Phloi exclaimed in an anguished voice "You're so thin I didn't recognize you at first. Have you been ill, my dear?"

Khun Chit's wife, calling herself a servant as always, shook her head and said no, she had not been ill.

"And where's Khun Chit?" Phoem asked.

"I don't know, sir. He went away—been away a long time—and never came back once. I don't know where he is."

"In a way, a very good riddance," was Phoem's comment.

"And my niece and nephew?" Phloi inquired. "Are they well? Where are they?"

Phuang started to cry harder, and between sobs she told of her two children: the baby girl had died and Khun Chit had taken the boy with him. Phloi consoled and comforted her as best she could while her heart cried out in pity for this fellow creature, a wife and mother like herself. Would Phuang have been better off if she had married a man from her own circles? Phloi believed so. To her mind it had been a cruel fate indeed which had condemned poor innocent Phuang to be chosen and raised to the status of wife to a master like Khun Chit. A worse husband than Khun Chit would be hard to imagine. At least she had had the two children to love and care for, but now she had nothing, an abandoned childless woman existing from day to day, in poverty, in a deserted house.

"Anyone else from the old crowd still living here?" Phloi inquired further.

"No, ma'am. They died or moved away. There's a family living in the kitchen quarters. I know them. They had no home and asked if they could move in and I let them. I was so lonely, ma'am."

She was afraid Phloi might be displeased, and looked more cheerful on receiving the assurance that she had done nothing wrong. "I'm glad you have some company," Phloi told her. "And Phuang, I want to thank you for staying on and keeping an eye on things."

"But I'm not much use, ma'am," said Phuang. "A woman, living by myself. Sometimes I tell strangers not to use the landing but they never listen to me. I don't know what to do."

"It's a big compound and you need some help to look after it properly. I'll see to it right away, Phuang. Don't you worry."

Before departing, Phloi gave her sister-in-law all the money she had in her purse—50 baht, saying she would be sending more in a day or two.

She went on thinking about Phuang long after the boat had left the landing, and it was Phoem who brought up the question of what was to be done with the estate. In his opinion she ought to sell it and be rid once and for all of the multifarious problems she would have to deal with as its owner. Phloi didn't think she could do that, take the easy way out. Khun Un would be furious, for one thing. Here even Phoem had to admit, laughing as he did so, that he, too, would rather not have to face Khun Un's wrath in whatever form it might erupt. Both finally came to the conclusion that there was no alternative but to have the place cleaned up, repaired, and main-tained; and, on being asked to do it, Phoem said yes, he would help her and take on the job of supervising the whole operation.

He then said, "Khun Chit may come back once the house is habitable again. Have you thought of that?"

Phloi sighed. "If it were he and he alone, it would not be so bad. After all, he's Chao Khun Father's eldest son and has every right to live there. But his followers! What can we do, Khun Luang, to keep them away from the house?"

Phoem mulled it over for a while, then broke into a grin. "If those hooligans came along with Khun Chit," said he, "They would be met by a few of my own, and these are much more efficient at their business than Khun Chit's gang. We will outbully the bullies, Mae Phloi, that's what we'll do. What fun!"

The predicted (and predictable) return of Khun Chit to Khlong Bang Luang came about in due course, some time after work had started to get the house back into shape.

"Don't worry, Mae Phloi," Phoem said to his sister after telling her the bad news. "I'll move in with him. And you'd better stay away from Khlong Bang Luang until things are settled between the two of us. You're too soft-hearted with him."

Phoem disappeared from Phloi's view for a month, during which he sent word now and again to allay her anxiety. The gist of his message seemed to be that matters were progressing satisfactorily, though he didn't give her any details.

Then one day he came himself and with a smile of self-congratulation announced that he and Khun Chit had come to a perfect agreement.

"First of all, " he recounted, "I told him he could stay, on the condition that he wasn't going to bring in any of his loutish hangers-on. And then I made up a set of petty rules and regulations that he must abide by—"

"And he agreed?" Phloi broke in, sounding very skeptical.

"Well, he had no choice," Phoem explained with a chuckle. "I had my people with me when I made my propositions to him, you see."

"What people, Khun Luang?"

"You don't know them, Mae Phloi, but maybe you've heard about them. They're from Bang Lamphu, part of the famous—or perhaps notorious—Bang Lamphu gang,

"Khun Luang! Since when have you become a gang leader?!"

"Not me, Mae Phloi. I'm not their leader but they consider me their friend. I happened to came across them in the past when they were hard up, and I helped them. Since then whenever our paths cross they say to me, 'Any time you need our help, just tell us. You tell us to strike, we strike; you tell us to stab, we stab.'" He paused and gave a hearty laugh. "Don't be alarmed, Mae Phloi. It won't come to that, ever. Their presence alone was enough to scare Khun Chit into complying with all my wishes."

"I see you've been having fun, Khun Luang. Go on, tell me more."

"Poor Khun Chit," Phoem continued. "The peaceful life was probably too much for him. He got very drunk one night, kicked up a great row, and threatened to burn the house down unless I gave him money—lots of money. He screamed at me to come over here and get it from you and bring it back to him immediately. Or else!"

"I had no idea you were having such an exciting time, Khun Luang. And then?"

"I let him rave on a bit while I brought out my own bottle and started tippling in earnest, pouring the stuff out and downing it at great speed. I could not hope to fight him sober, you see, so I had to hurry to catch up with him."

"And you caught up with him, no doubt."

"Not only that. I outdistanced him in next to no time. Then when I was good and ready I challenged him to a race: who would be the first one to set the house on fire. I had all the sticks and kerosene and matches in front of me and I said, 'Watch me! See how fast I can do it!' Now you can guess what happened next."

"No, I can't. Evidently there was no conflagration or we would have heard of it."

"You don't understand us serious topers, Mae Phloi. It's like this: when the other fellow gets more drunk than you, you sober up somehow. And that's what happened to Khun Chit. He became quite rational when he saw the state I was in. He began to soothe me and reason with me and implore me not to do anything rash. He withdrew his threats and said let's talk as friends and brothers. I was quite touched. Then we had a few more glasses together and went to bed."

Phloi couldn't help wondering what would have happened if somehow Khun Chit had not sobered up. To her question on this point Phoem answered, "Who knows? I might have done it—started a bonfire, drunk as I was."

"Heavens!" was all Phloi could say.

"Anyhow," Phoem went on, "Khun Chit became really tame after that. He was even nice to his wife."

"And then?"

"And then he got bored. He couldn't bring in his rowdy friends. He

346

had to behave. He's not used to the quiet life, I tell you. So the other day he came up to me and said he was leaving, for good, going to live upcountry, and would I ask you to look after Phuang because he had no means of keeping her. Then he left, and that was that. I think he meant it, Mae Phloi, about not coming back."

"You see, Mae Phloi," Phoem concluded. "Your method of doing good deeds for bad folks may be noble and all that, but in many cases you can waste a lot of time and money without getting results. In many cases the quickest remedy for badness is a dose of those bad lads from Bang Lampoo."

After Khun Chit's departure Phoem moved back to his house but made frequent trips to Khlong Bang Luang, sometimes in Phloi's company but more often on his own, for he turned out, surprisingly enough, to be most conscientious concerning his role as supervisor-manager of the restoration project. He was also most scrupulous with Phloi's money and would not spend one *satang* more than he absolutely had to. Phloi could not get over this and one day remarked to him, "Are you like this with your own money, Khun Luang? You must be richer than I thought." To which he replied, "My money never stayed with me long enough for me to do anything with it, Mae Phloi. So now I turn over my salary to my wife and she gives me a daily allowance."

"How much, Khun Luang?"

"One *salung* a day." (1 *salung* = 25 satangs.) "Don't laugh, Mae Phloi. It used to be one *fuang*," (half a *salung*), "before she took pity on me and raised it. She says if I had more I wouldn't come home. It's her little joke—she knows I don't need one *satang* in my pocket in order not to come home."

In time, the house in Khlong Bang Luang fully recovered from its sickness—for that was how Phloi regarded the decay that had threatened to engulf and destroy it. To see it now, looking like its former winsome self again, gave her that happy sense of gratification she would have felt were she to visit an old beloved friend whom she had helped nurse back from the brink of death to health and vitality. She loved taking her family and friends there to spend the whole day, pottering about, picnicking, relaxing. She loved the place for the memories of childhood it evoked for her, and also for what it would be some day, a home belonging to the children of her children, a home built by their ancestors and passed on to them through her.

She wrote to An in France and Ot in England about it. Ot's letters, in their turn, were full of references to it, although, as he said, he had never been there even as an infant. "One of the first things you must do when I get back is to take me to Khlong Bang Luang," he had written in a recent letter. "I'm so happy for you, *Mae cha*. I always knew from the way you used to talk to me about it how deeply attached you were to the old place."

In the same letter Ot also touched on a subject which had been puzzling his mother lately: "I plan to cross over to France and see Phi An next holiday," Ot's letter went. "He doesn't write to me very often, but enough to make me feel I ought to go and see him, and try to bring him down to earth. I get the impression from the things he says that he's up in the clouds thinking too many cloudy thoughts . . ."

Ot did not elaborate what these were, but Phloi suspected they must be similar to those expressed by An in his letters home, and it was these thoughts which had been puzzling her. Such as:

". . . To compare the difference between this country and ours would be like comparing sky and earth. I think the reason they are so far ahead of us is because the people are allowed to take part in the government of their country . . . They have no kings, and are not divided into royals and commoners . . . They are equal before the law . . . They elect their representatives who meet and thrash things out in order to find the best solutions . . . The government that doesn't do well gets criticized and if it doesn't improve must quit and let others do it . . . Everybody here is interested in how his country is managed . . . Everyone has a chance to say what he thinks and to do what he's capable of doing . . . The students in my class would like me to tell them how we do things in our country, but I avoid talking to them on this subject . . . We're so backward—it would have been embarrassing . . . When I look round me and observe how advanced they are I think of our country and this sometimes makes me feel depressed, sometimes inspired . . ."

Phloi might have been puzzled, but Khun Prem was very proud. He said, "You see, Mae Phloi? What did I tell you about the advantages of sending our sons abroad? Would An be talking so intelligently if he were at school in Bangkok? Remind me to take it to the office tomorrow. I'd like to show it to some friends."

"Are you sure that's wise? said Phloi, a little uncertainly. "Young men will have their strange ideas. I don't understand them, but I have a feeling some seniors in your department might disapprove."

"What ideas, Mae Phloi? You mean about government and all that? But that's perfectly all right. His Majesty himself is always discoursing on these themes. I've heard him on many occasions. I think he wishes to educate us. He's introducing new ideas to us, but he also says it will take time, that it has to be done gradually, cautiously, otherwise they will do more harm than good. He has set up the Dusit Thani City Scheme in the palace expressly for this purpose—to demonstrate how the business of government is conducted abroad. Some ignorant people are saying the Dusit Thani is nothing but a doll's town and our Nai Luang is playing with it as a child might. But the truth is, he's using it as a model, a demonstration. He wants our people to open their eyes to new ideas, to be more advanced. Your son An wants the same thing, Mae Phloi."

To be more advanced? Phloi had but the vaguest notion what this signified. An said our *Muang Thai* was backward, but to her mind it had been advancing so fast she could never hope to keep up with it. She was thinking of the change in the social climate, or, to be more specific, the change in the behavior of young girls in our society. Nowadays young girls and young men went about together unchaperoned by their elders. When she saw them at the winter fair, held in the parks of Chitrlada Palace, she asked herself, "Is this advisable?" and was inclined to answer in the negative. She saw them and heard them and, really, the way those pretty young things gave shouts of laughter and made bantering remarks to the men! Well-brought-up Thai girls should not appear so bold, so forward, and they should not try to ape the manners of *maems* (*farang* girls)—it did not become them.

Choi did not agree with her. After hearing Phloi's views on the subject Choi burst out laughing, and said, "If I hadn't been born so long ago I'd be just like them, probably much more so. Luckily for my friends I feel too old to change my ways. We belong to different eras, that's all—we and the lasses of today. At least you are wearing your hair long, Phloi, while mine remains old-fashionedly short. At least you look modern, but if your fashion-minded husband knew what goes on under the smart hairdo he'd say you're hopelessly behind the times, my dear!"

TWENTY-SIX

THE day came when her fashion-minded husband urged Phloi to discard what she had been wearing all her life—the *phanung* or, to give it its full name, the *phanung chongkraben*. The phrase he used was "*loek nung pha*," which could also be construed as "stop wearing clothes," so naturally Phloi cried out, "What! *Stop wearing clothes*?" And Khun Prem, laughing, explained that he merely wanted her to give up wearing the *phanung* and start wearing the *phasin* instead.

"What!" Phloi exclaimed again. She didn't say it was a most preposterous suggestion but that was what she thought. Had Khun Prem forgotten that the *phasin* was the costume of the women of the north, as distinguished from the women of the central region?

"What's got into you, Khun Prem?" she demanded. "I'm not a Lao, you know." For, like most Bangkokians in those days, Phloi tended to refer to the people in the north as "Lao."

This time she was corrected by her husband. "Don't call them 'Lao,' Mae Phloi. We are all Thai. The people of the north are citizens of Siam just as much as we are. And what have you got against the *phasin* anyway, may I ask?"

"Nothing at all," Phloi answered truthfully. "I think it's very pretty. When I was in the Inner Court there were lots of northern girls at the palace of Phra Raj Chaya, and I always thought they looked so nice and pretty in their *phasin*s. Phra Raj Chaya herself looked gorgeous in it, especially at full-dress functions. You should have seen her gold brocade *phasin*s, Khun Prem. They're truly magnificent!" She paused and went on to further clarify her position on the matter. "Yes, I've always thought it a pretty costume—but I've never wanted to wear it myself. I was perfectly happy with the *phanung*, and still am. Why should I give it up?"

"His Majesty favours the *phasin*," was Khun Prem's reply, which explained everything. "Her Royal Highness has started wearing it and the maids in her entourage have followed suit. It's time you did too, Mae Phloi."

"I'm too old to change," said Phloi with an air of finality.

"Same excuse again!" Khun Prem sounded aggrieved; then he went on pleading with her. "Listen to me, Mae Phloi. Please do it for me, Mae Phloi. I'm asking you. It wouldn't be so important if I were in another ministry. But I work in the palace and I do know what he likes. Picture to yourself this scene, Mae Phloi: you turn up at court wearing a *phanung* while all the other ladies are dressed in their *phasin*s. How will it look? Think of it."

"I have no *phasin*s," said Phloi lamely, already sympathizing with Khun Prem despite herself.

"I'll get you some," Khun Prem responded breezily, smiling, relieved.

The very next day he brought home dozens of them. He seemed so pleased with himself that Phloi did not have the heart to tell him she thought all of them too girlishly colourful for her and that she would look ridiculous in them—a matron trying to pass for a sixteen-year-old and failing conspicuously. When he had left the room, Khun Choei, who was visiting her sister that day, said, "We can exchange them easily enough, Mae Phloi. I know the owner of a *phasin* shop very well and she'll let you choose what you like. But now let's see how you look in it. Put one on, will you—any one will do. Just for fun."

Phloi being curious herself did not need much prompting. She put one on and regarded herself in the full length mirror and then both she and Khun Choei burst out laughing.

"I don't think I'd dare to go out in this." Phloi said, "I wouldn't even know how to walk in it."

But *mai pen rai*—never mind. The new fashion would pass, the faithful *phanung* might be temporarily eclipsed but would reassert itself in the long run. This was what Phloi and Khun Choei believed. Little did they know that the *phasin* had come to stay, or, for that matter, that it would eventually be joined by the skirt, the slacks, the shorts, and all.

In the meantime, it was not long after Phloi had got somewhat accustomed to seeing herself in a *phasin* that Khun Prem ceased to take much interest in what she wore. The reason for this was obvious: he was too busy himself keeping up with the latest mode in men's fashion. Phloi would never forget the day he came home to get dressed for a party given by a colleague to celebrate his new home, a gift graciously bestowed on him by His Majesty. There was Khun Prem darting out of the car, bounding up the stairs with an armful of parcels, saying, "New clothes for the party," in passing, and then, after some time, reappearing to pose before her with a cheerfully confident expression on his face and asking her, "Don't I look handsome, Mae Phloi?"

After staring at him unbelievingly for a few seconds Phloi recovered sufficiently to drawl, "Ye-es." She was a tactful wife, but even so she could not prevent herself from adding, "You put on all this to greet *Phra Angkhan* perhaps?"

Angkhan is the name of the planet Mars, and *Phra* an honorific to signify a deity, and *wan angkhan* means "Tuesday." Now that day happened to be a Tuesday and the traditional colour for the day is pink. For a man to drape himself in a pink *phanung* had always struck Phloi as foppish enough, but here was her husband covered in pink from head to toe. His pink silk *phanung* was topped with a pink silk jacket while his legs were encased in pink silk stockings and his feet in pink satin shoes, and—would you believe it?—the felt hat on his head was dyed pink! To be fair to him, it must be recorded that the walking stick in his hand, though polished to a high gloss, had not been painted pink.

"It's the latest style." Khun Prem informed his incredulous wife. "Everybody will be wearing it at the party."

"Ah." His wife nodded her head at the explanation. "And if it were to be held tomorrow, a Wednesday, all you men would be all in green? Jacket, *phanung*, hat, shoes—everything green?"

"Why, yes."

"And resplendent in red on a Sunday. I see. The women will look so dull and drab next to you, won't they? They can never hope to compete with you from now on." Khun Prem gave a chuckle as Phloi continued, "Fortunately you have a light complexion, Khun Prem. It can accommodate either the Tuesday pink or the Sunday red, otherwise you might look like that Khanang in the last reign." Phloi was alluding to a Negrito who had been brought from the south by His Late Majesty; he had been a well-known personality in the palace, somebody quite unique, and the startling contrast produced by his dusky skin against the flaming red of his garb had served to accentuate the uniqueness.

Khun Prem was not chuckling now. "I went to a lot of trouble to have these clothes made," he said in a plaintive voice. "I dress with care but my wife looks at me and she's reminded of Khanang! So you don't like it?"

"Oh but I do, I do," Phloi lied shamelessly, though she couldn't help laughing. "I just can't find words to express my appreciation. Give me time. But I can tell you I'll be looking forward to seeing you in the other six colours of the week. I can't wait!"

Khun Prem shuffled about without saying anything for a minute or two; then he left, rather abruptly, for the party, and a few more minutes after that Granny Phit came waddling up to Phloi and inquired, "What was the pink creature that flashed by just now?" When Phloi told her, she said, "My goodness! It was my own master and not some weird character escaped from a Chinese opera."

This particular vogue in men's wear did not last long; in Khun Prem's case it was a sartorial experiment spanning a few short weeks before he reverted to the customary blue or grey silk or cotton *phanung*, with the white or cream jacket on top. He had a new hobby, though: collecting walking sticks. Half the male population of Bangkok, or so it seemed to Phloi, were doing it, pursuing it with a fixation past their wives' understanding. All species of walking sticks were being collected, but the most highly prized, the most zealously sought after, were those made of *mai kaeo*, or China box-tree wood. Khun Prem had in his possession several of these but was always on the look out for more. When he heard of the existence of another fine specimen of *mai kaeo* walking stick he would not be able to eat or sleep until he had tracked it down. If it were not for sale he would go to look at it anyway, to contemplate its beauty. If the owner consented to part with it he would pay any exorbitant price for it.

"Better than spending my money on another woman, eh, Mae Phloi?" He would forestall her criticism with some such facetious remark.

As though I would know what to say to him if he chose to throw his money away on another woman instead of another cane, said Phloi to herself.

The most incomprehensible aspect of Khun Prem's obsession with these sticks, to Phloi's mind, was the way he kept them imprisoned most of the time in their tin sheaths filled with oil, bringing them out only to polish, to admire or exhibit to fellow collectors before putting them back in oil again. Even that most sane and sensible of men, Khun Luang Osot, even he had fallen prey to the walking stick fever. His wife Khun Choei was just as nonplussed by his advanced condition as Phloi was by her husband's.

"He's crazy about them all right," she told Phloi. "Lucky they're all gifts from friends—if he had to buy them, we'd soon starve. Come to think of it, we may yet starve, because he's not at all interested in human patients these days, but if you have an ailing stick, bring it to him and he'll cure it free of charge. He'll spend the whole day dipping it in oil and rubbing it and rerubbing it and I don't know what. He's turned into a stick specialist. Many people bring their sticks to him for his special treatment. Amazing, isn't it?"

Among the men who had not developed a passion for the walking stick was Phloi's brother Phoem. He preferred, he said, to stick to what he termed his living hobbies such as plants and birds, especially the latter, whose individual habits and behaviour he enjoyed observing. He also believed that the main driving force behind some wealthy collectors of the walking stick was not love for the thing itself but the desire to show off their wealth through its acquisition. It was a kind of contest, Phoem said, and these men might as well stack up their money to see who had got the biggest pile and be done with it. As for him, he added, he had other uses for money when and if he had any to spare—getting drunk on it, for instance.

It was true that a number of rich Bangkokians of that period behaved as though their main objective in life was to flaunt their wealth. They had many ways of doing it of course but the most obvious favourite was to cultivate lavishly extravagant habits in their mode of living. They built palatial homes and filled them with costly objects, some of which were beautiful and others merely opulent. They dressed, ate, drank, and smoked expensively, and sometimes they achieved tasteful elegance with their money—not that it would have bothered them if they did not, for taste was not all that important to them. They did bow to the truly elegant and glamourous people who were to be found at court and the circles nearest to it. The gentlemen and ladies of the court set the style in everything; in their privileged position they were admired by everyone, rich and poor alike. They were admired and praised and looked up to; they were imitated, emulated and envied; but resented, they were not, generally speaking. In those days of peace and plenty, the sense of well-being was pervasive enough to give the whole society a genial atmosphere free from tension and jealousy. You could emulate the rich if you had the temperament for it, or you could live the good life your own independent way. If your ambition was to serve the king, you would find that opportunity at court was open to people from all walks of life regardless of financial or social status. Peasant or aristocrat, with or without the advantages of wealth or birth, you could climb up the ladder of fame and fortune on your personal merits and talents; this had been demonstrated frequently enough to justify your hopes and expectations.

The reason the court was so accessible was because His Majesty himself was the soul of broadmindedness. And also of sympathy and generosity. His subjects everywhere talked about this and marvelled at it. They said he had a heart most compassionate and all-embracing, and no matter who you were if he knew you needed help he would give it to you in every way he could. If you went to him and said you had no land he would give you a plot of land; no house, and he would give you a house. "Our Nai Luang gives and gives and gives," Phloi once said to her husband, and she compared him to Phra Vessantara in the Ten Lives of the Lord Buddha—the noble Vessantara who embodies the virtue of giving. Regarding this her husband begged to differ slightly. "Phra Vessantara gives away what he has," Khun Prem said. "Our Nai Luang is capable of doing more than that. Let us say you appeal to him for a large sum of money, and he hasn't got it. He will give it to you anyway, paying you in instalments as though you were his creditor. I've seen it happen, Mae Phloi."

And then, after a pause, Khun Prem went on, "He has such a kind and generous heart that I haven't the heart to ask him for anything. At first I toyed with the idea of requesting that An be made one of his sponsored students. He would have agreed, you know, but I've changed my mind. He's already paying for so many students going to school and university abroad and I don't want to add An to his burden. Yes, he gives and gives and gives again, and he spends very little really on himself. People round him eat very well but I've seen cold and tasteless food on his tray. I've seen holes in his trousers too. Sometimes when he does his writing he wears only a piece of red cloth. There's a glass of barley water and a glass of fragrant water on his desk. When he's finished them he doesn't ask for anything more. I often think that even someone like me could well afford, in all humbleness, to volunteer paying for his personal living expenses, which wouldn't cost more than that of an average monk."

Born under the reign of His Late Majesty Phra Buddha Chao Luang (King Chulalongkorn), Khun Prem, in his own words, had never ceased to feel like a child throughout that reign in his relationship to his king, a happy child, perfectly cared for, lovingly protected, but all the same a child, timidly, tremblingly in awe of the Most Important, the Supreme Elder of his world. The mixture of awe, adoration and reverence in which he had held His Late Majesty had been an inborn, inextricable part of his emotion; and to the question "How do you love your king?" his instantaneous answer would have been "Like a father." At the king's death his grief had been greater than at the death of his own father, for not only had he lost a father but the world round him had suddenly gone dark. That's what it had felt like, Khun Prem said. With the present king, whom he had known as a young prince, as crown prince and then as king, he didn't feel so timid but, as he told Phloi, he found it much more difficult to explain his love for him. Sometimes he'd try to do it, and in the course of this very con-versation, he tried again.

"I love him as my Lord of Life. I'm loyal and grateful to him as to his ancestors who made it possible for our fathers to prosper and attain happiness in their days. I also love and admire him immensely as the most brilliant man I've ever met, and the most erudite. He's so well-informed on a vast number of subjects and his knowledge seems to me so inexhaustible that I feel there can be no end to what you can learn from him, this extraordinary teacher of teachers. Then sometimes I have this feeling, Mae Phloi, that all the love I have for my wife, my children, my clan, my country—all this is there in my love for him—and I could do anything for him, including giving up my life. It's this love that spurs me on. My personal ambition is mixed up in it and so is my wish to improve myself so that I can be of greater service to the nation, be a worthy servant of he who leads all of us in serving the nation. But there are also times when I see some people take advantage of him, abuse his kind heart, and in his goodness he is blind to the wrongs committed against him by these people, and I'm filled with sorrow and pity and want to shield him from harm as though he were a defenceless child. Other times, though, when he's in a gay mood, playful, mischievous, laughing and teasing and joking with friends, smiling his beautiful smile, then I'm completely enthralled, utterly under his spell. You might say I fall madly in love with him as though he were a girl. When he's in this mood to be with him is pure enchantment."

"And when he is displeased?" Phloi asked. "Displeased because you've done something wrong, how do you feel?"

"Awful, of course. Mortified. He doesn't scold you in front of other people, you know. Doesn't want you to lose face. He lets you have it afterwards, in private, and then he can be very angry indeed, and because he doesn't scold without reason, you know you deserve every bit of it."

Phloi loved to listen to her husband talk about His Majesty. Of late, however, Prem didn't have much to say on the topic which most women in Bangkok considered to be the most exciting one concerning their Nai Luang, and it was Choi of the Inner Court who kept Phloi the housewife up to date on it. On her recent visit Choi startled Phloi with her news that the rank of "Phra" had just been bestowed on two ladies. Phloi had never heard of a woman being given this masculine rank and asked, "Do they work in a ministry like other male civil servants?"

Choi giggled. "No, my dear hopeless Phloi. Their post is somewhat like that of a Chao Chom under the late reign, if I may put it like that."

"Then why not call them 'Chao Chom?' Phloi said. "To address them as 'Khun Phra' sounds very strange."

"Not at all," Choi disagreed. "It's smart and modern. It's His Majesty's way of honouring his ladies. There are so many Chao Choms anyway, and they belong to a past era. Besides, a Chao Chom stays put, right?—unless they become a Chao Chom Mother—whereas a Phra may be promoted to a Phraya and a Chao Phraya. It's a great boost for womankind, dear Phloi."

"All right, all right, Choi . . . And what's happened to Her Royal Highness?"

"Nothing. She remains where she is. Her situation has not changed."

"I was given to understand that she would be the only one royal consort."

"It doesn't look like that now, does it?" Choi said contentedly. "I'm in favour of plurality in these royal matters, aren't you, Phloi? I only wish some of them would move into the Inner Court so the place would come alive again. These days it is sometimes as quiet and eerie as a cemetery."

Months passed, during which Phloi heard about new developments on this subject—from Choi mostly, but from other sources as well, including her shopkeepers. The words "rise" and "fall" figured prominently in these reports—not so very different from the old days after all. Then there was news about a pregnancy, about a royal title being invested, and about the title of "Phra Borom Rachani," or "Queen," being conferred. Time marched on, relentless as ever, bringing change in palaces, in the streets, in the home. At Phloi's house, tidings were received from Europe: An in France had passed his first-year law examinations, while in England Ot had finished school and would be entering university. At home, On had a few more months to go before graduating from the Military Academy and donning the uniform of an officer, and Prapai was growing up so fast that Phloi warned herself, with motherly forethought, to start getting ready to cope with the difficult business of looking after an adolescent daughter. As for the change in her own person, Phloi noticed one bright morning the first two grey strands in her hair. This gave her a mild shock, from which it didn't take her too long to recover. She accepted the sign, reflected once again on the immortal truth about ageing and mortality, and exercised a greater care than usual in choosing her garments for the day, not in defiance of that truth but in compliance with it.

TWENTY-SEVEN

"WE have a soldier in On and will have a jurist in An, so what profession should Ot be training for? Have you thought about it, Mae Phloi?"

"Ye-es. Khun Prem . . . Why don't we ask him what he would like to do, Khun Prem?"

"All right. But I don't trust him, you know. He might have in mind something fanciful and utterly useless. He hasn't told us what he's going to study at university, and we'd better make sure it's something he can build a reasonable career on. You write him, Mae Phloi."

Phloi promptly did so, and in time received Ot's answer which read, in part:

"When we were children, Phi On knew he wanted to become a soldier, Phi An was already a budding lawyer at school, and I was the one without future plans. None whatever. Didn't even want to grow up particularly. Just wanted to go on being your son and having you near me. To tell you the truth, I'm not much more ambitious now than I was then. But I don't suppose Khun Father would approve of my coming back just to loaf round the house, would he? Anyway, I thought and thought (never thought so hard in my life, believe me) about the subject I should pursue at university, and then—at last!— the phrase *rian nangsu* came home to me. 'Ah-ha!' I said to myself, "that's what I will do. I will 'study books.'

"The formal name for this is 'literature' and I shall be doing a lot of reading and writing. This is a respectable and honourable course of study, it being considered difficult and exacting enough by all those who ought to know, please assure Khun Father."

When he had read this, Khun Prem made a wry face, and said, "Didn't I tell you? Reading and writing indeed! What does he want to be—a clerk? Though I suspect what he really wants to do is nothing at all. An idler's life of ease and comfort, that's what he's aiming for."

"Khun Prem," Phloi said, "you're always saying how fond Nai Luang is of reading and writing. Then why can't Ot serve him along these lines when he comes back from England? I do think he should join your ministry, Khun Prem. It will be nice to have someone in our family carry on in the palace after you're retired. And it will be an honourable move on your part to place a son in Nai Luang's service, a son who's been educated at an English university, like him."

Khun Prem laughed. "Have you thought it all out carefully, or are you temporizing?"

Phloi laughed with him. "I'll say yes to both questions."

"I think you're indulging your son as always. All the same I have to admit I do see your point . . . Very well, let him go on with his reading and writing then. I have no objection."

"What a contrast to when I was a schoolboy!" Ot wrote from his university. "The back and the palm of a hand—that's the difference all right between my past and present existence. After being treated for so long as a child liable to go astray unless kept under strict surveillance and told what to do and what not to do and when to play and when to work, I suddenly found myself a free man, and it was utterly delightful and quite a shock at the same time, so that the first few days I rather went round and round in a daze. The impressive looking porter of my college kindly corrected me in the middle of our conversation: 'You don't "sir" me, sir,' said he. 'I am the one to do that to you, sir.' My daily gaucheries made me flinch but they were brushed aside with a 'not to worry, sir' by my man-servant who looks upon them as being well within the pattern of clumsiness exhibited by new undergraduates year after year. He—this excellent man—comes with the rooms assigned me by the college. Imagine, a bedroom and sitting room to call my own! No bell-ringing to summon me to the 'classroom' as such, only suggestions and advice by *achan*s, or professors, as to what books to read and what lectures to attend, and then I have this excellent man to look after me. What does he do? He keeps my place tidy and my clothes clean, he brings breakfast and tea and when I have guests to dinner he serves it in the best English style. He gives edifying answers to my questions concerning the customs and conventions observed by the university in general, and this college in particular. As a rule he gives his advice only when I seek it, but sometimes when he believes I need it he will give it to me unasked but in the most subtle and unobtrusive fashion. He also sees to it that I don't neglect my study. He lays out my books on the desk and hovers about until I finally settle down to work before leaving me for the night. He lays out my clothes as well, when I'm invited to a function, and if I change one little item—the handkerchief, say—he apologizes then for not having chosen it in the first place—and I know his feelings have been somewhat hurt. Actually he does know best, and to be correctly dressed for any occasion I only have to leave everything to him . . . Are you getting tired of hearing about him, darling Mother?"

On the contrary, Ploy was enjoying herself. She felt very grateful to this *farang* who had been serving and taking such good care of her son. She was interested to know (for Ot went on speaking about him) that he excelled in rowing (Ot had decided to take up the sport), and that although he spoke the best English he could also, under appropriate circumstances, perfectly speak what was called "cockney" English, a very interesting linguistic phenomenon, Ot said. It's good to know these things about a person who's close to one's son, Phloi thought—to know that he has many accomplish-ments but above all to know that he is considerate, dependable and kind. On the whole, Phloi noted with a mother's satisfaction, Ot was leading a good life. That he was doing well enough scholastically she had already gathered from other sources. Ot himself said he felt he had learned not only from books but from the brilliant minds with whom he came into contact every day. "If I hadn't come here I wouldn't have had the opportunity to meet them—I'm very lucky indeed . . ."

In less than three years Ot would come back home, and An in less than two. Phloi's heart leapt up at the prospect. Quite a number of days to go yet but for Phloi it was not too early to start thinking about turning some of the rooms in the upper floor into living quarters for the young men, until they should marry, that is. When that time came, they would each have their own separate houses in the compound. That would come later. Meanwhile Phloi went on planning for the not too far future and looking forward to when she would be standing on the pier waiting for the boat bringing An home and then, another twelve months thereafter, Ot would be with her. Ot would not have changed very much, Phloi imagined, but she was not so sure about An.

Ot had recently crossed the channel to see his brother in France and had written the following:

"... Frankly speaking I find some of Phi An's friends rather a strange lot. Thai friends with strange fanciful notions, Annamese friends with radical ideas, or *farang* friends with hollow cheeks, uncombed hair and wild eyes expounding theories too deep-sounding for me to understand. Phi An says these are far-sighted men, men who will play important roles in the future, but for my part I'll be glad when the time comes for Phi An to part with them and go home to be with you..."

While Phloi pondered the above passage her husband said, "Don't you worry about An, Mae Phloi. Ot never has a serious thought in his head, that's why he can't understand why anyone should be serious about anything, you see. It's Ot we've got to keep an eye on. An's never given us a moment's anxiety. I'm very satisfied with him."

Phloi had her own opinions concerning these two sons of hers but chose not to voice them on this occasion. Being satisfied with the children is one thing, she reflected, and keeping an eye on them is another—it is something we go on doing, it's part of our loving them. As regards sons, she and Khun Prem had another recurring subject of conversation these days: On's graduation from the Military Academy. They were now proud parents of a young army officer. On said his dream had been fulfilled and his aim hence-forward was to try to acquit himself honourably in his chosen career. Phloi rejoiced with him and gloried in his success, but she didn't like it at all when she learned that his first post would not be in Bangkok but in Ayuthaya.

"Oh, On! You're leaving me. What am I going to do?"

On laughed. "Ayuthaya is next door, Khun Mother!"

"Even so . . ." Phloi began, and tailed off. Gazing at On's radiant face, she felt a pang in her heart. *How young he looked. No longer a child, but still so young, so full of confidence and his hopes—and so vulnerable. Please let no misfortune befall him.* She said an inward prayer, remembering a young officer who had gone to serve in Nakhon Sawan and what had happened to him. Ayuthaya might be closer, but would it not be just as ridden with pitfalls for inexperienced young men thrown on their own resources for the first time?

"I can't help it," she confessed aloud. "I would much prefer to have you with us a little longer." She sighed. "You will be careful, won't you? When you have problems and are not sure what to do, promise you will consult your parents first. Don't make hasty decisions; you might regret them afterwards."

On listened attentively to her as he had always done. He left for Ayuthaya a few days later with her blessing, and although he would be back in a week or so on his first visit, the big house with its numerous inhabitants seemed sadly empty to Phloi after his departure.

On had been stationed in Ayuthaya for some time when one day the following scene took place in his parents' house in Bangkok. Khun Prem, back from the ministry, came into the sitting room where his wife was in the process of hemming a vest, and inquired in a voice full of cheer, "Whose vest is that you're making, Khunying?"

"Are you talking to me, Khun Prem? What is this—another joke?"

Khun Prem gave a joyful laugh. "No joke, Mae Phloi. You're going to be a Khunying very soon—this Coronation Day, as a matter of fact. I'm practising saying it, Khunying!"

"Oh!" Phloi cried. "Are you being promoted to a Phraya? Oh, I'm so happy for you! Phraya what?"

"Phraya Botamal Bamrung," he announced. "Sounds rather nice, don't you think? Doesn't look bad as a signature either. I've tried a couple of experiments with it."

Bending her head down Phloi confided a fond smile to the vest in her hands. Khun Prem at that moment was like a child with a brand new toy and she loved him dearly. Now he sat down close to her, saying, "Are you very happy about this, Mae Phloi?"

Phloi answered him from the heart. "More than I can say, Khun Prem. I never dreamed that I would one day be a Phraya's wife. Such a great honour."

"And my dream, Mae Phloi, has always been to make you feel proud that you have not chosen wrong in marrying me. For myself, being your husband is more than good enough. If I try to achieve anything beyond that it is for your sake, and I'll go on trying, Mae Phloi, for you deserve the best."

"Oh, Khun Prem, you don't have to woo me after all these years!"

"I have no one else to woo, don't you know?" He gave her back a gentle stroke, planted a light kiss on her cheek and, humming a tune, went off to have his bath, leaving the new Khunying to blush by herself.

During the next few weeks Khun Prem was a much-admired, much-congratulated man in his circles of friends and relatives. At a festive family gathering Khun Un presented her brother-in-law with a heavy gold ring set with a large ruby, saying Chao Khun Father had intended it for a son upon his being conferred the rank of Phraya but since it was extremely unlikely that either Khun Chit or Phoem would reach that goal she deemed it most fitting that Khun Prem should have it.

Choi, of course, dropped everything and rushed over from the palace. "Is Khunying home?" she called in a booming voice climbing up the stairs, then at the doorway sank down to her knees and declaimed, "Khunying, *chao kha-a*!" dramatically stressing the polite ending. "Humbly I pay you my respects, *chao kha*. I place myself under your protection. May your merited fortune spread its beneficent power over me!" Phloi pronounced her mad as ever; they laughed and chatted away as usual, and at one point Choi said, "I must admit I underrated Khun Prem. He truly impressed me as an unimpressive young man when we first met—the type that wouldn't get very far, you know. I'm happy to have been proved wrong. Tremendously happy, Phloi!" To which the other responded with a quiet but heartfelt, "So am I, Choi!"

Phloi the happy wife co-existed at this time with Phloi the devoted mother anxiously waiting for further news from France and there came at long last An's letter informing his highly revered parents (An always wrote the most properly decorous Thai) that he had booked his passage and expected to reach Bangkok towards the end of next month. *An definitely coming home!* His mother recited the joyful phrase to herself. *He's coming back! We'll be together again!*

"... My professors and several friends urged me to stay on and do a higher degree," the letter went on, "but I've decided against it. I want to start putting myself at the service of our country as soon as possible. There is so much to do. So much needs to be done in order to push our country forward. Many problems exist which must be solved, and solved quickly, before it's too late.

"I'm looking forward so much to coming back and being with you again. I've been away quite a long time and I hope you will not find me changed for the worse, and if I should cause you displeasure in any way I hope you will forgive me. The French have a saying: to understand all is to forgive all, and I know I can always count on your understanding."

Happy and excited as she was Phloi couldn't resist making a few remarks on the way her son talked about "our country." As though he were coming back to run it single-handedly, she said. And what's all this about causing displeasure anyway? Such an unexpected subject to get mentioned on such a happy occasion. Khun Prem just chuckled, saying the letter typically reflected An's thoughtfulness and foresight.

"I'm glad he's decided to come home and start working right away," Khun Prem said. "I think this son of ours will go far, Mae Phloi. Who knows, he might one day become one of the big men of this country."

"He sounds big enough now," Phloi said lightly. "Almost too big for me."

"Spoken like a mother!" Khun Prem commented. "You would stop your children from growing up if you could, wouldn't you?" He paused for a moment, then went on to talk of his plans in connection with An's homecoming. Apart from the physical installations and improvements such as getting new furniture and putting in more bathrooms and ceiling fans, he also wished to introduce a few changes in their daily routine. For instance, instead of taking his meals seated on the floor on the veranda or in the sitting room, often by himself with Phloi in wifely attendance, he would now eat in the dining room downstairs, at the dining table, together with wife, sons, and daughter like a *farang* family. "We should adapt and adjust our ways a little, don't you agree, Mae Phloi?" His wife was agreeable, seeing no harm in using chairs occasionally, or even partaking of *farang* dishes with *farang* knife and fork once in a while. She was also delighted to have Khun Prem turn his enormous energies and enthusiasm to domestic matters for a change. And indeed Khun Prem worked hard during the ensuing weeks, enjoying himself immensely too, and when the job was completed, proudly accepted Phloi's compliments that without him An's bachelor suite would not have looked as attractive and comfortable as it now did.

An landed in Singapore in due course. After spending a few days there he boarded a ship bound for Bangkok.

Phloi had been too excited to get much sleep the night before, but *mai pen rai*—no matter; she awoke that glorious morning feeling all was right with the world and herself the happiest of beings. Khun Prem, too, was in unshakably high spirits, chuckling at anything and everything. "Let us go, let us go," he sang out the words, hurrying Phloi and Praphai into the car although these two were just as eager as he to get to the port. On arriving there they were greeted by Phoem, Khun Choei and Luang Osot, and everyone agreed it was preferable to come and wait here rather than at home. They had more than an hour to wait, standing in the shade provided by the godowns, cheerfully conversing among themselves, exchanging smiles with relatives and friends of the other passengers and peering into the distance for the first glimpse of the boat.

When it did emerge into view, Phloi's eyes were filled with tears and she watched it approach through them, tightly gripping her handbag and umbrella, breathing intensely and unable to utter a sound.

Khun Prem was talking, and so were the others. Some were already shouting greetings into the air. Then it was Khun Prem's voice again, rising jubilantly above the rest. "Look, there he is! My word, how he's grown!"

Slowly the boat was coming nearer. Now Phloi could pick out her son from among the lines of people crowding at the rail. An was gazing in their direction, searching for his family—now he'd seen them—he was waving to them—he was turning to tell some fellow passengers about them—An in his *farang* clothes, smiling gaily, waving and gesturing—An come home at last.

Phloi had dried her eyes, got herself under control, but later on they all went up to the deck and when An came to her she threw her arms round him and cried openly. "Mother, Mother," An said to her in a whisper. "I missed you so much. Now I'm home. To stay, Mother." This made Phloi very happy, and she cried harder, before finally calming down and reluctantly letting go of him. They all crowded round him and the reunion became quite a merry affair with the light-hearted questions and answers and the jesting remarks interspersed with bursts of laughter. To come and meet the boat, and welcome your son home after years of separation, this must be the most wonderful outing of all, Phloi thought.

Then An said, "Excuse me a moment," strode off to a group of *farang*s standing nearby, and returned bringing with him a *maem*, a *farang* woman, and introduced her to Khun Prem. "This is Lucille, sir." Khun Prem looked a trifle startled as he shook hands with the girl and plainly bewildered when she spoke to him in a foreign tongue which was not even English. When Phloi's turn came she followed Khun Prem's example and held out her hand but at the same instant the girl swooped down on her, crushing her in a hug and kissing her noisily on both cheeks. Phloi was blushing scarlet at this *farang* treatment when she heard An's voice saying, "This is my wife, Lucille. We got married after I'd passed my exam. I didn't tell you before because . . ." He went on saying something about not wishing to worry them and knowing they would love her like a daughter and so on—irrelevancies adding nothing to, nor detracting from, the significance of the main issue. That succinct phrase, "This is my wife," was enough to make Phloi feel faint with disappointment. No, not because Lucille was a *maem*. The operative word here was *wife* rather than *maem*. If she had known beforehand, Phloi would have taken the marriage as a normal stage in An's progress through life, and would have set about building him a suitable nuptial home in the family compound. But this was a blow—to be surprised like this, to be suddenly handed a daughter-in-law when all the time she had been looking forward to welcoming a son home, to fussing over him, to mothering him after having been deprived of his nearness for many long years. She would have reacted in the same way had An brought home a Burmese wife, or a Mon, or even a Thai. Well, perhaps not quite, for the presence of a European daughter-in-law in a Thai household was bound to bring forth a special domestic situation.

Now An was talking to his wife, and then she began to pay respects to the family in the Thai manner. Joining her palms together she performed a learner's awkward *wai* to all of them, one after the other including Praphai—An must have neglected to instruct her about letting his little sister *wai* her first.

And now Phloi asked herself what to do next. She stole a glance at Khun Prem, looking to him for guidance, but he was gazing at the sky, his face an impassive mask. The others were just as unhelpful. Khun Choei and Luang Osot were busy talking to each other while Phoem was grinning at a Chinese cabin-boy who happened to be walking by. And Praphai? As one might have expected, Praphai was staring at her newly acquired sister-in-law from abroad, her eyes twinkling with curiosity and enjoyment. For her it was great fun—*sanuk mak!* Phloi watched her in trepidation, hoping she wouldn't do anything more untoward, but sure enough, the staring was soon accompanied by the giggling. This, however, gave Phloi the opportunity to do something, which was to scowl at the child; and it also served to rouse Khun Prem from his reverie, for which Phloi felt thankful. "Are we ready to leave? "Khun Prem muttered. "I'll go and see if they've finished the unloading."

He was about to go but Phoem was quicker. "Let me do that for you," Phoem volunteered and took off hastily. A moment later Khun Choei and Luang Osot also left, mentioning an appointment in town and promising a visit to Phloi's house in a day or two.

During the ride home neither Khun Prem nor Phloi had very much to say. Praphai was well-behaved—subdued, that is—which made her look rather sulky. Fortunately An was voluble enough, switching easily back and forth between French and Thai, explaining Bangkok to his wife, explaining (if you could call it that) his wife to his parents. "In a few months Lucille will be speaking Thai fluently," he informed his parents. "She's a bright girl, and quite a good linguist." He also said she was very happy to be here. Phloi smiled. To make up for Khun Prem's aloofness—he had relapsed into his pensive pose—and her own inability to converse for the sake of conversing, she smiled. She smiled, now at her son, now at her daughter-in-law, now at her husband. It was the longest, the most exhausting automobile trip she had ever taken.

TWENTY-EIGHT

"YOU'RE up very early this morning, Mae Phloi," Khun Un said to her sister who had come to see her at the bungalow.

Phloi admitted she had not slept very well. (Neither had Khun Prem, though Phloi didn't mention this to Khun Un. "Need you ask?" Khun Prem had snapped at her late last night. "You don't *really* know why I can't sleep? You don't have to be so sarcastic, Mae Phloi. You think it's my fault because I sent him abroad to be educated. You expected me to foresee this—that he would bring back a *maem* wife, is that it?" But Phloi had not been blaming him at all. She had said nothing, in fact; she had merely asked what was bothering him.)

"Are you upset because of the *maem* daughter-in-law?" Khun Un asked, and went on without waiting for a reply. "Don't be. What's done is done. There's nothing you can do about it. I think she's sweet-looking and, knowing you as I do, I think you're going to be quite fond of her, Mae Phloi."

Phloi was less concerned this morning with her personal sentiments, present or future, towards her *maem* daughter-in-law, and more with the urgently practical question of what to feed her.

"She seemed rather repelled by our food last night," Phloi reported to Khun Un. "She ate hardly anything. So what sort of *farang* morning food should I get, Khun Phi? I don't want her to starve. An didn't eat very much either, out of consideration for her, I suppose. In fact it was a dismal meal altogether, with the table groaning—I shouldn't have made so many dishes, and nobody eating and Khun Prem grouching . . . So what shall I serve her this morning, Khun Phi?"

"Bread and butter," said Khun Un. "Bread will keep her from going hungry."

Good, said Phloi. Bread was easy. Khun Prem, too, took a piece of toast now and then, with butter and jam, although his staple morning fare was rice gruel with a few side dishes.

"You might also send for some *farang*-style dishes from that Chinese cook-shop across the road," Khun Un went on. "Just don't forget plenty of bread. *Farang*s eat bread as we eat rice, you know."

When Phloi got back to the big house the first person she met was An. This was the first occasion since his return that Phloi found herself alone with him.

He said, "It's wonderful to be back! I was so excited and happy I couldn't sleep a wink last night."

Phloi said, "Is Maem—" then broke off and started again. "Is you wife awake, son?"

"She's getting dressed. Let's go and see her."

"Oh, let her finish dressing, son. I'll wait for you in the dining room."

"No, no. She'll want to see you. She's fallen in love with you, Mother!"

The two women smiled at each other, Lucille sweetly, Phloi rather timidly. Lucille in her dressing gown making up her face, Phloi sitting carefully on the edge of a chair, appreciating her daughter-in-law's prettiness. Pretty as a doll, was her silent verdict. White and pink skin, hair the colour of copper, eyes pale blue almost like glass—pretty in a very striking way, but maybe not the kind of prettiness that grows and grows on you, that increases as you observe it. Then she spoke to An.

"Please ask your wife what she would like to eat this morning."

An laughed, and proceeded to act as interpreter.

"She says some bread and coffee would be fine, Khun Mother."

"Is that all? Are you sure, son?"

"Yes, and for me, too. It's the French 'morning rice,' Khun Mother."

Now Lucille, her face still unfinished, went to the clothes cupboard and opened it to show the contents to her mother-in-law.

"Lucille would like you to choose a dress for her," said the interpreter.

Phloi obediently did so, or to be more exact, she pointed at the first one her eyes fell upon, something pink. A very pleased Lucille took it out and laid it on the back of a chair, and returned to the application of creams and paints on her eyes, cheeks and lips. *All this for going downstairs?* Phloi marvelled to herself. *What will she put on her face for an outing?*

Aloud she said, "Please tell your wife I think she's very pretty," and a moment later almost wished she hadn't. For as soon as An had rendered the compliment into French Lucille came rushing up to her, and embraced and kissed her again and again.

"She says it's you who are so very pretty, Mother."

Phloi had the presence of mind not to stiffen or flinch, not to recoil from this French demonstration of affection. She made a mental note, however, to suggest to An at the first opportune moment that perhaps he ought to warn his wife not to do this sort of thing in public. Well-bred Thai people, especially those with a strict sense of decorum, would consider it unseemly behaviour. She did not have time to pursue these thoughts much further because Lucille, instead of going back to the mirror, remained standing in front of her, talking rapidly while fingering the tail end of her bodice cloth—*I hope she's not going to pull it,* Phloi said to herself, placing her hand on the knot just in case—and examining her *phanung* with great interest. Professional interest, An explained. "She would have become a coutouriere if I hadn't persuaded her to marry me instead. She thinks your costume is unique and most charming, Khun Mother. Two pieces of cloth, no seams, no buttons, no pins. So simple yet so elegant. She says if she puts them on they're sure to fall down. But she'd like you to teach her how to do it."

"I will—later on," Phloi replied quickly. "Tell her they do indeed come loose when you're not accustomed to wearing them. She'll need some practice." Here Phloi was blushing at the possibility of Maem Lucille and the Thai garment parting company in front of servants and visitors. "Nowadays," she continued, "the *phasin* is the fashion anyway—and the *phasin* is more like the skirt. I only wear this around the house." She paused, and rose. "I must go and see about food," she said, and hurried away, feeling she was becoming too much of an object of curiosity to the two young people.

From his seat in the dining room Khun Prem looked at her and demanded peevishly, "Where have you been, Mae Phloi?" And when Phloi told him he snorted. Phloi would have preferred him more amenable this morning but she also sympathized with him for not feeling on top of the world.

"Excited, aren't you?" he said cuttingly. "Just couldn't wait to start coddling the new daughter-in-law!"

"An asked me to go in and talk to her," Phloi said in a conver-sational tone, "so I did."

Khun Prem helped himself to some rice.

"What are they doing now? " he finally asked.

"Getting dressed," Phloi answered, adding casually, "She's a pretty girl."

Khun Prem didn't take kindly to this innocuous remark. "Pretty! Pretty!" he spluttered. "For you it's always the question of pretty or not pretty. How about asking if it's proper or or not proper, good or bad, right or wrong? But oh, no, you're not interest-ed. It's always pretty or not pretty—that's all you women care about. Bah!"

Phloi told him she did not mind his shouting at her, taking it out on her. He had her sympathy, she said. At the same time she could not see how losing his temper was going to solve anything. It would not change what had already happened. "If you go on this way you'll only hurt An's feelings," she ventured to say, and felt he was perfectly justified in his retort, which went, "And what about *my* feelings? Did he care about *my* feelings when he took a wife without a word to me?" But when Khun Prem hit out at Ot ("And why didn't Ot tell us? He must have known about it.") she felt he was being unfair. "It wouldn't have been right for Ot to tell on his brother, would it?" she said, and then, looking through the open door she dropped her voice to a whisper. "Here they come. Please, Khun Prem . . ."

Khun Prem glanced briefly at the newcomers before returning to his rice bowl. He was not to be left in peace, however, for Lucille headed straight at him, smilingly speaking French and extending her hand. Khun Prem took it but not without shooting a sour look at his wife, a look which said, *What a bore, all this hand-shaking!*

Phloi flashed a bright smile at him, only to get a frown in return—he would not be humoured.

An had noticed that look and he said, "The French shake hands when they meet, sir." Khun Prem, upon receiving this information, uttered a petulant "Tcha!" and this prompted his wife, in an effort to prevent his expressing himself further, to ask of her son, "Even when they live in the same house and see one another every day?"

"Hand-shaking is a polite custom with them, Khun Mother."

Khun Prem's huffy comment, "So much politeness that the hand may get broken!" came out before Phloi could produce another phrase to forestall it. So she gave another smile, this time aiming it at her son, and launched into some small talk for his sake. An stammered a reply while his father went on sulking at his rice. An fidgeted and flushed as Phloi chatted with him, doing her best to help him regain his poise. Meanwhile Lucille, blessed by ignorance of the native tongue, poured coffee and buttered a slice of toast, smiled, and began to sip and munch with obvious enjoyment. *She dunks her bread in coffee,* Phloi noted to herself, *and now my son does the same, dear oh dear! Another polite custom among the French?*

Afterwards Khun Prem said to his wife, "I'm going to write Ot today, *now*, and tell him that one *maem* daughter-in-law is enough for me and if he brought another it would shorten my life. I'm going to forbid it, do you hear? If he insists on bringing one back he's no longer my son—that's all there is to it!"

"But Khun Prem," Phloi said. "Ot has shown no signs whatever of wishing to take a *maem* wife."

"So you're clever at reading signs, are you?" Khun Prem's voice rang with irritation and heavy sarcasm. "So An gave you plenty of signs and you knew what he was going to do! Why didn't you tell me?"

He made Phloi laugh to herself.

"Oh-ho!" Ot wrote to his mother some time later. "Did I ever get a sermon from Khun Father! I hope he's pleased with my answer which I have just posted. I've given him my solemn promise never to wed a *farang* woman. I've even told him that if and when the idea of taking a wife should occur to me I would ask him to get me one.

"Phi An and Lucille were neighbours who fell in love and lived together before they could get married—that's the story in brief. Her parents are not rich people. They like Phi An and have never objected to the romance. I think somebody in that family also started a rumour to the effect that Phi An was a prince come abroad incognito for his studies. When I visited him I was made to feel somewhat noble myself thanks to the rumour.

"Lucille is a nice girl, but of course she will have to adjust to our Thai ways, and you're the one to help her do this, Mother dear. Khun Father will be too busy, and Phi An in some ways is more French than the French.

"You may rest assured there'll be no foreign wife for me. Too many problems for all concerned and I'm a coward and don't like problems. I'm not saying that I believe mixed marriage is doomed from the start. On the contrary I don't see why a Thai and a *farang* who love each other should not be able to lead a happily married life together. So what am I afraid of? Let me try to draw you a picture of what I think could happen. Let us suppose a *maem* falls in love with me. Ah, but is it really 'me' we're talking about? No, it is this fascinating stranger hailing from the exotic East she has read and heard so much about, who wears bejewelled costume in his home country, is waited on hand and foot by numberless servants, whose family owns tall buildings in town and elephants in the forest. For my part, I find her beautiful and desirable and tell myself I cannot live without her. I treat her more gently and speak to her more sweetly (we Thai men are adept wooers) than my *farang* rivals. I pay her more compliments and bring her more gifts and, to cut a long story short, we become lovers, we get married and then we come back to live in *Muang Thai*. Before long she finds life in our country not as colourful and exciting as in that fabulous land of her imagination. In fact she finds it not only unglamourous but un-comfortable, if not downright unsanitary. She suffers from the heat and the mosquito bites. She's disgusted with our insects and lizards and the mere thought of snakes gives her nightmares. And she misses her *farang* friends. As for me, I begin to compare her with the Thai girls and discover flaws in her manners, her complexion, her figure, her temperament, etc., and while she tries vainly to tolerate the smell of shrimp paste I start to get fed up, as it were, with the flavour of milk and butter. . . It all adds up to a climate not exactly favourable to marital bliss, to my way of thinking.

"Anyway, I'm in no special hurry to present you with a daughter-in-law of any skin colour. I suppose I'll get to be a bridegroom one of these days but in the meanwhile am perfectly content to go on being your bachelor son."

Ot's letter amused his mother and filled her with joy, but it also made her feel a little apprehensive of what might possibly lie in store for An and Lucille.

Arriving under separate cover, Ot's letter to his father proved an unqualified success. When he had read it Khun Prem burst out laughing delightedly. "Ah, this is a son after my own heart," said he in a gloating, vindicated tone of voice, as though he had never thought otherwise. Phloi was glad to hear this, but it struck her as funny nonetheless, and she turned her face away to hide her smile.

Soon after his return An was taken by his father to pay respects to the family's esteemed elders as well as colleagues and friends in both official and non-official circles; His Majesty being on a visit to Singapore during these weeks, Khun Prem had more time to devote himself to this and other parental duties. An's wish to start serving his motherland without delay was fulfilled when the Ministry of Justice readily accepted him and assigned him to a post suitable to the education he had received from abroad. Khun Prem thought his son had done very well and was proud of him, and, as time passed, he grew accustomed to Lucille and treated her with his customary kindliness and goodwill. Phloi breathed a sigh of relief over this development. A genuine peace-lover, she liked having people round her get along together.

Lucille and Praphai got along very well. There was a great deal of affection between the two of them. The problem here was how to stop Praphai from copying Phi Lucille's demeanour and deportment—how, in other words, to dissuade the girl from aspiring to be like a *maem*. Praphai crossing her legs *maem*-style looked definitely uncouth to

Phloi and she sternly ordered her to uncross them. Praphai's protest of "But Phi Lucille does it, so why can't I?" elicited the following answer from Khun Mother: "She's a *maem*. That's the way *maem*s and *farangs* sit. But you're a Thai, and it doesn't become you." Praphai's experiment with French cosmetics made Phloi raise her voice, something she rarely did: "Go and wash your face at once! Wash it off, do you hear me? At once!" And Praphai, with tears falling down her painted cheeks, insisted she had done nothing wrong. "Phi Lucille says they all do it in Paris."

"And pretty soon they'll all be doing it in Bangkok," An said to his mother later on in answer to her complaint. "Bangkok's very fashion-conscious, I've noticed. I wouldn't worry about Praphai, Khun Mother." Smiling fondly at her, he added, "And you, Khun Mother, you would look even more beautiful with some rouge on your cheeks!"

"Just because you have a *maem* wife," Phloi said, "don't think you can turn me into a *maem* mother. And I won't have Praphai paint her face. She looks preposterous!"

An laughed good-humouredly. "Praphai's growing up. You can't stop that, Mother. And the girls of today are different from when you were young. There have been a lot of changes since the war, and more changes are in the offing."

I accept change as a condition of life, Phloi reflected, *but I don't have to like all changes. In fact I find some changes wasteful and ridiculous!*

In the midst of change, Phloi, like many others, went on trying to preserve and make secure, accepting change while desiring constancy and continuity . . .

"I have great news for you, Mae Phloi!" announced Khun Prem in an exultant voice when he came home from the office one afternoon not long after His Majesty had returned from the trip to Singapore. "Great news, Mae Phloi. Her Highness is expecting!"

Her Highness referred to in this instance was the Chao Chom who had accompanied His Majesty on his visit to Singapore and who was to be elevated to a royal consort rank of Phra Nang.

"Isn't it the most glorious news?"

Yes, indeed! The most glorious, joyful, happy news for the whole nation. The coming of the first offspring of this reign. The people of *Muang Thai* had been waiting to hear this news for over a decade.

"Oh, I'm so happy for Nai Luang!' Khun Prem went on, talking to himself as much as to his wife. "Childless all these years…What joy it must give him…There have been too many deaths in the royal family. It's tragic for them and for all of us that Nai Luang has lost all but one of his brothers of the same Queen Mother, and as you know, Mae Phloi, his royal brother Thun Kramom Iad Noi does not enjoy the best of health…Now this great auspicious news, this good fortune for Nai Luang and all of us. An heir at last! Our Nai Luang is still in his prime, so he will have many years to train his successor to the throne . . ."

Khun Prem was ecstatic. What he envisioned was as beautiful as any mirage could be, and he did not suspect it could dissolve into nothing.

That year, 1925, or Buddhist Era 2468, Phloi did not attend the Coronation Day ceremony. She waited for Khun Prem to come home from the Grand Palace to tell her all about it. It was very late when he did get back, and the first thing he said was that something extremely unusual had happened. He was puzzled, and so was Phloi when she heard it. This was what he told her: "From now on Nai Luang will be residing in the Grand Palace. He has chosen to stay in the Chakraphat Throne Hall from now on."

"What!" Phloi exclaimed. "In the Chakraphat?"

"Yes, in the Chakraphat. That's where he's going to live, not at Phya Thai Palace any more. You can imagine how astounded we were, Mae Phloi. There we were after the ceremony was over and then suddenly he came out with this decision!"

To a stranger who might ask, "What's so surprising about that? He's the king—why shouldn't he live in the Grand Palace?" the answer was, firstly, His Majesty had never taken up residence inside the Grand Palace. There were several royal residences in the city beside his principal home, the Phya Thai Palace, and he had stayed at all of them, but never had he brought his personal household to any residential hall within the old walls of the Grand Palace. Secondly, the Chakraphat was *not* a residential hall, not anymore, had ceased to be many long years ago, but was now more of a shrine, used only for ceremonies of high sacredness. The last king to have lived in this throne hall, which had been built at the same time as the capital itself, was the third monarch of the Chakri Dynasty, King Phra Nang Klao Chao Yu Hua, Rama III, who ruled the kingdom from 1824 to 1851.

"Why Chakraphat?" Phloi wondered aloud. "What could be the reason? I think I can understand why he should want to stay in the Grand Palace—so that the royal baby would be born there, thus increasing the propitiousness of the occasion . . . But why Chakraphat?"

"Exactly," Khun Prem said, "when he could have chosen any other residence more comfortable and more appropriate. But no, he has set his heart on the Chakraphat. You know what, Mae Phloi? I think he wishes to be near the spirits of his forefathers, to recreate the past, to relive history. He's had the ancient utensils and articles brought out and arranged as of old all round him." Khun Prem paused, frowning slightly, searching for words, then he went on, "Tonight he seemed to me like a traveller longing to go home after years of wandering, and somehow it made me feel uneasy, Mae Phloi."

After a few moments' silence, Phloi, in a wifely attempt to dispel his anxiety, however vague, said to her husband with a smile, "Let's look at it this way. The Grand Palace will be lively again like in the old days. Choi must be elated about this. The whole Inner Court must be wide awake, I'll bet. . ."

They went on chatting. Mention of the Inner Court put Khun Prem in a reminiscent mood and he chuckled over some remembered scenes from their young days. Made him feel young again. Not for long, however. In the middle of a conversation that stirred up memories— and illusions—of youth, he suddenly winced and complained of an aching shoulder—sign of creeping age—and ended up asking his amused wife to massage it. By the time he went to bed, Phloi noted, Khun Prem had begun to get used to the idea of his beloved sovereign settling down in the Chakraphat Throne Hall. She herself had come to accept it as nothing so out of the ordinary after all.

It was some three or four days afterwards that His Majesty was taken ill.

Khun Prem took it lightly. Upset stomach after a Chinese meal, he told his wife, before giving her the really exciting news from the palace: according to the doctors, the long-awaited birth of the royal infant should occur in about ten days' time. "Get ready to celebrate, Mae Phloi. Let us rejoice, Mae Phloi." And Phloi was just as thrilled as her husband.

Another day passed, followed by another... His Majesty did not get well.

"Abscess in the stomach, Mae Phloi. Diabetes. Complications. The doctors are worried."

"No improvement today, Mae Phloi . . ."

Phloi shared his anguish and she prayed with him. "I've been praying as I've never prayed before, Mae Phloi. I've placed my supplications at all the shrines. Oh, please protect him. Please let him come through this danger and make him safe again . . ."

Khun Prem was tearful. Then he joked, so as not to weep. "I've even sent a warning to Thao Hiran Hu, Mae Phloi. Doesn't he always claim that no harm will come to Nai Luang as long as he's there to guard him? Well, I've told this Thao Hiran Hu if anything happens to Nai Luang I'm never going to speak to him again!" (This Thao Hiran Hu had appeared to Nai Luang in a dream many years back, at the time when he was still crown prince on a visit to the ancient capital of Sukhothai. In the dream, Thao Hiran Hu had volunteered to be Nai Luang's guardian spirit, and the request had been granted. Since then Nai Luang had never journeyed or stayed anywhere without having this self-appointed guardian spirit close by. Phloi had seen a statue of Thao Hiran Hu at Phya Thai Palace. There was also a small one kept in the royal car, according to Khun Prem.)

More days elapsed, dark days whose oppressive gloom failed to lift even when Ot's letter arrived from England with its cheering message: ". . . and so it won't be too long now before I can get on the boat and sail home!"

Then one afternoon Khun Prem came back from the palace and said to his wife, "Have you heard? The royal infant was born this morning."

"A prince, Khun Prem?"

"No, a princess," he answered wearily.

"Has His Majesty been informed?"

"Yes, though he already knew. The conch-shell sound was absent from the music celebrating the birth. He could hear it in Chakraphat and knew without having to be told that a daughter was born, not a son."

"Has he seen her, Khun Prem?"

"She was brought to his bedside. He touched her, with tears rolling down his cheeks."

Khun Prem looked worn out. He had been going with very little sleep and his eyes were bloodshot. Phloi would have liked for him to take some food and a short nap before returning to the palace, but he said he couldn't swallow a thing and that sleep was impossible.

He didn't come home that night, nor the following morning. It was Choi who brought the news the following morning: *"Sawankhot laeo"*—His Majesty has gone to heaven.

Phloi was shaken. She was not overwhelmed by grief as she had been at the death of his royal father, but she was shaken and her heart filled with pity and sorrow. And mixed with these emotions there was also something like fear, fear of the unknown, of the changes that were bound to come in the wake of this portentous event to affect her life and all our lives in this land.

"A star fell as he departed," Choi was saying. "I happened to be in the courtyard and I saw it. A star as big as a coconut shining down on the Chakraphat Hall. So bright that the roof tiles looked as if they would burst into flame. People were rushing to the Twilight Gate thinking the palace had caught fire. Then all of a sudden the sky went dark . . ."

The two friends spent the morning together, talking quietly, keeping each other company in the lonely hours after Nai Luang's death, and waiting for Khun Prem to come back with more information.

But they were not to hear anything more from Khun Prem's lips on that particular day. He came home, entered the room where they were, but after glancing at them walked on without speaking and disappeared through another door. After a while they went looking for him, and they found him in the altar room, lying unconscious before the portrait of Nai Luang. He had fainted while paying homage to his king.

RAMA VII

TWENTY-NINE

TIME passes more quickly as you get older, and this applies in my case, Phloi told herself. But perhaps it was not merely age but the way events came crowding in on her at this period of her life, allowing her little time to pause and gaze about and take note of time's passage. Whatever the cause or causes, she often lost count of the days, was astonished to be confronted with the end of yet another week, or month, or year, and felt disoriented as though waking from a vivid yet confusing dream. Though it was more like a nightmare sometimes. It still frightened her when she thought about that day when she had come upon Khun Prem lying crumpled on the floor in the altar room. Khun Prem had collapsed from physical exhaustion; equally he had been devastated by grief. Phloi spent the first days—or weeks?— under the new reign nursing him. He recovered in due course; that is, the doctor pronounced him well enough again and he went back to work. But he looked old and sad, was so dull and lifeless, so apathetic about everything that Phloi went on keeping an anxiously watchful eye on him.

She recalled his attempts over the past years to convey to her the quality of his love for our late Nai Luang. He had once said, "I have this feeling, Mae Phloi, that all the love I have for my wife, my children, my clan, my country . . . all this is there in my love for him . . . I feel I can do anything in the world for him including giving up my life. It is this love that spurs me on . . ." She also recalled believing him with half a mind while with the other half wondering if perhaps he was not being a trifle too emotional and rhetorical. Now, watching him in his bereavement, giving him support and solace as he bore the burden of his loss, she understood the truth of the feelings he had not always been able to put into words.

There was another truth, although this did not occur to Phloi—the truth that fifteen years back Khun Prem had been at the right age to prove himself and find self-fulfilment, given his background and character, in serving his Lord of Life with dedication, with selfless, unquestioning devotion. He had come into his own during that new era, had eagerly adapted himself to it, sailed along in it with great zest and enjoyment, and in the process had garnered both worldly success and personal happiness. Now another era had begun, but he no longer possessed the energy to thrust forward and meet its challenges. He was and would always remain an unswervingly loyal servant to the throne, but time had taken its toll; he was not the vital young man he had once been and while he went on performing his duties conscientiously it was never with the same enthusiasm.

Phloi did all she could to help him regain his interest and joy in life. She took heart every time he gave a small chuckle, regarded it as a victory when she could induce him to talk with some animation on any topic at all, and although she still had her fears for his safety when he went horseback-riding, she felt thankful that he had not abandoned this favourite recreation. He went galloping off every morning, usually heading for Lumpini Park, where public celebrations marking the fifteenth anniversary of His Late Majesty's accession to the throne were to have taken place, and when he came back drenched in sweat but unharmed and looking more alert and like his former self, she would feel relieved and more hopeful about his condition.

Then there was Ot's homecoming. He had written to give the date of his sailing and Phloi busied herself getting his rooms ready for him. But there had been other things to absorb her attention: important functions to attend in connection with the start of the new reign and also the obsequies for His Late Majesty, not to mention again her anxieties about Khun Prem's health, so that when the actual day came it almost took her unawares. Driving to the station—Ot was arriving by train from Singapore—she could not get over the fact that it was really happening. Ot will be with us and things will get better from now on, she told herself, glancing at her husband beside her. Khun Prem was already looking much better.

"Dry your eyes, Mother darling," Ot whispered in her ear. "They'll say you're a cry-baby, you know." And Phloi laughed as he released her from his encircling arms and turned to exchange greetings with the others. She fixed him with her eyes as he talked to his father, grinned at his brothers and sister, laughed with his aunts and uncles. He had grown quite tall, taller than Khun Prem by several inches, and there were shadowy lines of shaved hair round his lips and jaws. Of course he was different from her little boy who had left home many years ago; and yet he had not changed at all, Phloi felt, not in the essentials, not where it mattered.

Ah, and he had not brought "anybody" back with him—she had been casting surreptitious glances up and down the platform, and he had smiled knowingly and murmured, "As you can see, I'm still single. But please stop looking overjoyed—Phi An might get jealous."

Back home at the family feast, Ot, smacking his lips and uttering cries of a connoisseur's delight, did more than justice to every dish brought before him. The meal over, the conversation going convivial as ever, Ot leant back in his chair smiling a satisfied smile, and they all laughed to see him looking the very picture of relaxed contentment.

"I'm never going to leave home again," Ot declared at one point. "Home is *Muang Thai*, and it is just right for me."

"And what's all this I hear about *muang nok* being very *sanuk-sabai* ?" asked his Uncle Phoem. (*Sanuk* is fun; *sabai* is relaxing, and comfortable; *muang nok* is the "land out there," usually Europe and other *farang* continents.)

"*Sanuk-sabai* to visit," Ot said. "On a temporary, not a permanent, basis. We enjoy ourselves there, Khun Uncle. We have lots of fun and we appreciate the wonderful things they have to offer. We stand awed before their marvels and all that, but ultimately, as outsiders, Khun Uncle. Here the earth and the sky belong to us, and the rains and the heat. The smells are not all fragrant, but no matter—they are the smells of home. The rice paddies, the trees, the roadways—all are part of us and we of them. The pretty sights as well as the not so pretty—

some are pretty messy but we can tidy them up if we wish to. All the way on the train I looked out the window watching my country go by and I didn't get tired of it. It comes down to the question of where you belong, I think."

"My dear boy," said Uncle Phoem, "That's exactly how I feel. Most probably I shall die without having set foot in those distant lands, but I don't mind. As you say, home is *Muang Thai,* and I don't get tired of it either. The only thing is, never having been to *muang nok* myself, I can't very well argue with people who give nothing but glowing accounts of it, and am obliged to hold my peace, which is no fun for a chatty fellow like me . . . Now let's hear what you have to say, Ot. Tell us about the differences between *muang nok* and *Muang Thai.*"

"Quite a tall order," Ot said. "It would take me more than a year. Well, let's see. Where should we begin? How about the difference between the rich people of *muang nok* and the rich people of *Muang Thai.* The answer is, the *muang nok* rich are many times richer; that's the difference. The very rich over there are so monumentally, colossally rich that they would consider what we call a very large fortune here somewhat laughable. On the other hand, our poor people are much more fortunate than theirs. Life in a cold climate can be brutal when you don't have money. Here food is easy to come by—fish in the water everywhere, fruit and vegetables growing wild, a bowl of rice-and-curry costing practically nothing. Here with the sun shining a poor man in a loin cloth sitting under a shady tree is cool and comfortable. His wealthier neighbour may even be dressed the same way, for rich or poor, we all like our cool comfort, don't we? In a severe English winter you'd freeze to death if you didn't have enough clothes. Here a homeless man finds free accommodation in a *wat*—plenty of space underneath the monks' quarters, on the pavilions, or along the verandas and corridors. Yes, nature is much kinder here, and also the way of life . . . I've seen the poor districts of *muang nok* on dark wintry days, outside and inside. There may be ten people sharing one tiny flat, cooking, eating, washing, sleeping and everything else in these dingy cubicles with all the doors and windows shut to keep out the icy wind. When you step in, the stench from so much concentrated living hits you like a blow between the eyes. They rarely bathe—a bath costs money which they can ill afford, and they can't take a dip in the *khlong* or river like we do here to freshen up. It's too cold anyway . . ."

"And what were you doing in the poor districts?" Khun Prem asked.

"Paying visits, sir," Ot replied. "I went as a visitor, and also as a student. You sent me abroad to get an education, so I thought I should try to learn as much as I could."

Then Khun Prem asked his son if he had also seen something of life among the English *phudi* (well-bred people; members of the upper classes). Ot had, and he talked about being invited by some university friends to stay at their ancestral homes in the country during vacations. Vast properties, he said, stretching "beyond the limits of the ear and eye," and the houses themselves as grand and gorgeous as palaces. He described the English *phudi's* substantial breakfast, their decorous tea, and their formal and meticulously-served dinner, and he dwelled at some length on the subject of their gentlemanly sports, the seasonal fishing, shooting and hunting.

"They pursue the fox on horseback?" Khun Prem asked.

"The hounds pursue the fox," Ot said, "and the hunters follow the hounds that pursue the fox. The hounds catch the fox, and kill it."

"What for?" Khun Prem inquired.

Ot was not quite sure either. "Because the fox is destructive and therefore must be destroyed," he said hesitantly.

"But can't they just shoot it?"

"Oh, Khun Father, that would be unsporting, ungentlemanly, sacrilegious. You could be ostracized for such an act."

"What? For shooting a mere dog?"

"Not a mere dog, sir. A fox. That would be a most serious breach of fox-hunting etiquette. Pheasant-shooting and quail-shooting also have their own conventions, their rites and rituals. No shooting out of season, no shooting at birds which are sitting or walking on the ground. Some of these birds are quite tame, having been raised on the premises, and they have to be stirred up to take flight in order to get shot at."

"There must be lots of woods and forests," Phoem remarked.

"They are private properties, those woods," Ot said. "Only the owners and the guests and those with licences can shoot in them. These sports cost money, Uncle."

"What if I, a poor man, should want to shoot a few birds and catch a few fish for either fun or food?"

"You sneak in, sir, and try your luck. If caught you'd be fined or sent to jail. Not very many years ago you might even be sentenced to death."

Raising his hands palm-to-palm above his head, Phoem intoned, "O may I reborn in *Muang Thai* in my next life and not a poor *farang* in *muang nok!*"

Khun Choei was less interested in sports and more curious about the English *phudi's* good manners. "Are they very different from ours?" she asked. Ot said certain details differed, of course, and generally speaking the English *phudi* were inclined to be more reserved, but on the whole he thought the essence of polite behaviour must be the same everywhere. "When I first landed and didn't know very much about the English I just behaved the way my mother taught me, and it worked perfectly well, I think." He beamed at her and Phloi smiled back, thinking this was one of the happiest days of her life.

He himself might not be aware of it but that was Ot's speciality: making his mother happy. He did it in many ways, and the least casual of which were by no means the least appreciated, such as his asking her to change the buttons of his jacket or to help him with his *phanung*—a costume which could look inelegant when done up by an unpractised hand—or to cook him a favourite dish he had been missing and fancying during his absence from home. After the long absence he was content to stay home, pottering about, lazing, reading. He enjoyed, above all, being near and keeping his mother company. Many another young man in his position was itching to go forth into the world and get started on a promising career, while with Ot, living from day to day seemed quite blissful enough. Phloi gave him some spending money—though he never asked for it—a hundred baht or two hundred at a time. He seldom spent it on himself but would, and frequently did, empty his pocket of it to help you out when you were in trouble. Phloi had no objection to his unworldliness and deep down she loved having a son near her as opposed to his spending so much time in an office or barracks. That nagging sense of duty, however, told her it was only right for Ot to have a profession. and since Khun Prem didn't seem to take any interest in the matter, she felt obliged to remind him.

"We did talk about Ot joining your ministry, Khun Prem. Have you thought any more about it?"

"My ministry?" Khun Prem gave a weary sigh. "I don't know what's going to happen at my ministry. Let's wait until things are more settled, Mae Phloi." After a pause he asked, "What would Ot like to do? Have you any idea?"

"No, Khun Prem. We haven't talked about it."

"Why don't you have a word with him then?" Khun Prem seemed relieved to be able to entrust to his wife this parental task. And then he surprised her by saying, "Frankly, I don't see any real need for Ot to go seeking employment. I should think we have sufficient means to keep a son at home. Phloi disagreed. "It's not a question of means. That's not the point at all. You and I have known several young men whose parents have means to keep them at home who became victims of the aimless life and turned into wasters. We don't want that to happen to Ot."

And what did Ot himself think about it? Khun Prem had asked her to discuss it with him. Phloi did so, but it wasn't a very fruitful discussion as far as practical purposes were concerned.

"What would I like to do?" Ot laughed. "Nothing, of course."

"Oh, Ot! Please be serious. You can't idle away your time like this indefinitely. You must do something."

"Well then, whatever you say, Khun Mother. My training has been such that I'm prepared to do anything as well as nothing."

"Oh, you're no help at all," Phloi wailed. "You're just as bad as your father."

"All right, Mother," Ot said soothingly. "I'll find something. But please, may I go on being your happily jobless son a while longer?"

Phloi didn't press him because she didn't want to do it unconvincingly, though she suspected that Ot already had a pretty shrewd insight into her heart of hearts as regards his staying at home versus his sallying forth in pursuit of a career. The matter could be postponed in any case. It was the time of the cremation rites for His Late Majesty. The funeral pyre (Phra Meru) was set up in the heart of the city. The preparations for the events and the ceremonies themselves kept Khun Prem occupied, busy to the exclusion of other activities. He was on duty every day and every night, working at a gruelling pace, which must have been good for him, for after it was over he looked much healthier and was in better spirits than Phloi had seen him in many months. The real recovery had begun, she thought to herself. But then—and this happened not too long after the royal cremation— came the winds of change blowing through the royal offices, especially Khun Prem's ministry, the Ministry of the Palace. "Most of the pages will have to go," he told his wife. "I think all those of the Bed Chamber. And some departments and divisions are to be dissolved."

"It's natural, Mae Phloi," he opined. "Change of reigns brings changes everywhere, particularly in the Royal Page Corps. His Majesty naturally prefers to have his own pages, those who have been with him in his entourage from the beginning. It's quite understandable. But I can't help feeling sad about those depart-ments that will be scrapped. The place won't be the same again. So many old friends will be gone. Those who have private means and those who have found new masters are all right. Those pages are all right, too, who've been endowed with grants and gifts by His Late Majesty. Some of the pages are also named beneficiaries in his royal will and should be getting a few extra hundreds of baht in addition to their regular pensions. But there are so many others not so fortunate. Many. You see a lot of woebegone faces at the ministry these days, Mae Phloi."

As time went on, news of this nature increased and multiplied. Phloi heard about it every day, from her husband and from various friends and relatives, about this or that department being discontinued and about some people they knew being retired from office. She was told it was necessary to reduce the number of officials so as to cut down expenditure in order to "balance" the budget, because, "you see, we are in a state called 'economic depression.' Money has become harder to get hold of, and therefore we must spend less, you understand." Phloi would listen uncompre-hendingly. Things for her household could be bought more cheaply nowadays. Surely this could not cause hardship to anyone? As to the country not having enough money, she found this the most difficult of all to grasp. All the money, all the silver and gold, all the wealth in all the twelve royal treasuries—*sip-song thong phra khlang* was the ancient term used by Phloi—where had it all gone? Besides, now that we had paper money, why not print more of these notes to pay people instead of doing away with their jobs? A much simpler and kinder step to take, one would have thought . . .

The word "balance" was being used and abused by experts and laymen alike. *Dulyaphap* in Thai was a long name for the condition we were trying to achieve. A popular verb came into being: *thuk dun.* When a person *thuk dun,* it meant he was retired or made redundant in the interests of the "balanced budget."

One afternoon Khun Prem came home to announce to his wife, "*Chan thuk dun sia laeo,*" or, "I've been balanced out." Before Phloi could say anything, he went on, "I was instructed to lop off some seven hundred and fifty baht from our salary allocation. I could have let a few clerks go, but that would have been too awful. It so happens that my salary is exactly that amount, so I've decided to tender my resignation. Now the budget is quite nicely balanced," he added with a dry chuckle.

THIRTY

KHUN Prem was enjoying his food again, and he was sleeping like a log and talking and laughing cheerfully. He was like a man who, after no little hesitation, plunges into the cold waters in the cold season and emerges physically and mentally braced.

The above description held true for only about a month, however. If he could have gone back to work then, maybe that state of well-being would have lasted for some time. But he was in retirement and, unless he found some other occupation, was doomed to face the years ahead with nothing to do except enjoy unrelieved leisure. He didn't have the talent and stamina for it, and tedium began to set in after the first month. Now there was Khun Prem staring blankly into space, or aimlessly pacing to and fro in the compound, or lying down after lunch but unable to fall asleep, or riding off more recklessly than ever to vent his boredom, or erupting into a rage over some trivial incident . . .

"But why?" Phloi put the question to her brother Phoem, who had been "balanced out" soon after Khun Prem had resigned. "Why hasn't it made you miserable and bad-tempered too? You're even happier now, if anything."

"Well, Mae Phloi," Phoem said. "The relationship between my job and me was never serious to start with, so its disappearance from my life has not left any gap to speak of. Then I have my friends and my hobbies, and not having to go to work every day gives me more time for them, which is fine with me. Khun Prem is in another category. You can't compare us."

"I think you can help him though," Phloi said. "Come and see him more often. Cheer him up. Maybe you can get him to take up some of your hobbies."

Phoem looked doubtful. "We're old friends and brothers-in-law and all that, Mae Phloi. But our paths have diverged—he in his highly responsible position and me on my humble rung of the ladder, you understand. And then of course there's the difference of taste and temperament."

"Try anyway," Phloi insisted. "It does worry me—seeing him like this. I'm afraid he's going to make himself ill again with all this moping about. Do try, Khun Luang."

A few weeks went by, and one day Khun Prem could stand it no longer. Phoem had been paying him another protracted visit. "What's got into that brother of yours, Mae Phloi?" He sounded quite exasperated. "Doesn't he have anything else to do except come here to pester me? He wants to take me here and there. He says I should start raising birds, can you imagine? He seems to think we should be boys together again. Really, if we hadn't been friends for so long I should be very annoyed with him."

And Phoem dropped by a few days later for a chat with his sister.

"His Excellency is bored all right," he said. "But I can't do any-thing about it. If I tried harder he'd kick me out of here for sure. I can't solve the problem for you, Mae Phloi. You'll have to do it yourself, and I think you can."

"But how?" Phloi was ready to do anything.

Glancing cautiously to the right and left, Phoem said in a whisper, "Why don't you get him some young girls?"

Laughing, Phloi said, "Is that all, Khun Luang? Very well. But it's not for me to supply them, Khun Luang. If Khun Prem wants minor wives, let him find them himself."

Phoem eyed his sister. "Are you jealous, Mae Phloi? Shouldn't be. We're all old enough."

"I'm not jealous, Khun Luang. But I wouldn't know how to go about it."

"I'll tell you, Mae Phloi. You surround him with these young maids, you see. Have them move about prettily where he can't help but notice them, all right? Have them get him a drink, fetch the papers, bring food and so forth. Then at night, when he says he's tired, one or two of them can massage him while you make some excuses—it's too hot, you say, or anything you can think of, and leave them alone together. Keep this up and pretty soon you'll have a new Khun Prem, younger and sprightlier than ever before."

"No," Phloi said firmly. "Khun Prem will have to make his own arrangements. I will not start plotting things for him—it would be immoral somehow."

With a smile Phoem delivered his verdict: "It all boils down to jealousy. You just won't admit it."

Phloi was unable to get across to her brother that while his proposed remedy might be the very thing for Khun Prem, as Khun Prem's wife she should not be expected to have to concoct and administer it herself. That would be too much. Really, Phoem could be so insensitive sometimes!

She was genuinely concerned nonetheless, and willing to see the remedy given a try. So she finally had a talk with Khun Prem himself.

"What is the matter, Khum Prem? Please tell me."

"I don't know myself, Mae Phloi."

"If you haven't been feeling well, perhaps you ought to see a doctor."

"What for? I have no sickness—not the kind that doctors can cure, anyway."

"If there is anything you would like to have, Khun Prem, or anything you would like to do, anything at all, that would please you, make you happy, you'll go ahead and—and please yourself, won't you? I have no objection at all. I mean it. Whatever you want to do—"

"To do what, Mae Phloi?"

"Well—if you would like to have someone to—to serve you . . ."

"Hmm, I thought so! It's a minor wife you have in mind for me. You needn't have bothered, Mae Phloi. My condition is not that bad. I'll tell you if it reaches that stage . . . Ah, yes, I've been feeling empty and depressed and I don't know what to do with myself. But it will pass and in time I'll get used to not having the old office to go to . . . A minor wife!" Khun Prem grimaced. "If you wanted to cut short my life, that would do it."

And that was the end of that talk.

Another cure for his boredom was suggested to Khun Prem by Ot. It, too, was rejected.

"I said to him," Ot reported to his mother afterwards, "'why don't we go into business, sir, you and I? Let us become merchants. Why not?'"

"Why not indeed?" Phloi said. "And what did he say?"

"That he's been a civil servant all his life and knows nothing about buying and selling, and that especially with me as his partner, we'd go bankrupt in no time."

"And what did you say to that?"

"I said, 'I think you're right, sir.'"

Like father like son, Phloi commented to herself, with some vexation mixed with much tenderness.

She worried about them, yes. But would she change them if she could? She had always been proud of Khun Prem—Khun Prem, His Excellency Phraya Botamal Bamrung, respectfully addressed as Chao Khun by one and all; she had been proud of him, had admired him and looked up to him and rejoiced in his successes; now she had her worries about his health, his moods, his behaving like a child in various ways, but at the same time she felt he really, wholly, belonged to her, her very own Khun Prem, and this rich, warm feeling was something she had but rarely experienced during his more active days. As for Ot, the little boy in Ot had been refusing to grow up and grow out of his carefree boyhood, and this was plain enough to his mother. He should get a job, this was her sensible wish, yet lurking close to this wish was her foreknowledge that she would miss him very much when his work should claim him as theirs had claimed On and An.

She had no worries about On and An not behaving like mature persons—*phuyai*—that's true. Especially An, who, when Phloi gave him some typical motherly advice, was liable to remind her along these lines, "Oh, Khun Mother! I'm not a child any more. I'm a *phuyai*. I know what I'm doing."

That was what he said in answer to Phloi's remarks on the subject of friends: "Be careful about choosing your friends, son," and "Don't let your friends lead you down the wrong path, son," and some other mild maternal phrases like that.

The subject had come up during their little discussion, initiated by Phloi, having to do with An's habit of going out by himself and leaving Lucille at home, which the latter considered a grievous fault in a husband. She had felt neglected and hurt and had been telling Phloi about it. Although Phloi herself had not condemned this sort of behaviour in her own husband ("Oh, but you and I are different, Khun Mother!" Lucille had pointed out), she fully sympathized with her daughter-in-law. She wanted Lucille to be happy in her adopted country and to live harmoniously with her husband and the rest of the family. Between Phloi and Lucille there were no problems at all; they liked and understood each other though on certain matters they might hold different views, one being a Thai woman and the other a French woman—a Thai-speaking French woman, for Lucille was a good linguist. Lucille had a frank, outgoing nature. To be in this country had filled her with excite-ment, and in the beginning everything had lived up to her expectations. She had had the time of her life and An had been the most adoring of husbands. Now the novelty had worn off. She accepted this and was settling down to a more routine role of house-wife. But her unthoughtful, inconsiderate husband—must she tolerate this situation? Oh, it wasn't fair. She felt so lonely. She was homesick. She also complained about the mosquitoes and the heat and other inconveniences—complained, in fact, very much like that imaginary *farang* woman living in *Muang Thai* as depicted by Ot in one of his letters to Phloi. Phloi blamed her not at all. She could imagine herself feeling wretched living in *muang farang!*

"Lucille and I understand each other, Khun Mother," An said casually, with easy confidence. Then he went on to explain his social life: "One must have many friends if one wants to get anywhere in this country . . . I was away for so long—hardly knew anyone when I came back—and had to start finding my way again . . . I need the support of my friends, Khun Mother . . . We get together and we enjoy ourselves, but our meetings are not always for amusement alone. Their wives are content not to follow them everywhere. If mine tags along it will look absurd."

That was when Phloi made the already mentioned remarks about choosing one's friends with care. She let An's reply (". . . I know what I'm doing, Khun Mother") go unchallenged. That is how it should be, she reflected, and let's hope he does know what he's doing.

An was regarded by everyone as a young man with a bright future. He had everything going for him, they said: he was well-bred, well-educated, purposeful, as clever as he was hard-working, and so on. At times, though, Phloi couldn't help wishing him to be a little less sure of himself. Above all, she wished he'd get rid of those wild ideas he'd written home about while a student abroad. She had hoped he would leave them behind where they belonged, but no, he'd brought them back home with him along with his academic degree, ideas which seemed to Phloi most unsuitable in a man of his position. She could only hope that the fact of his having them would never reach the ears and eyes of the country's elders and royals. If it should, she thought, the consequences could be decidedly bad not only for himself and his immediate family, but other relatives and friends associated with him.

An said on one occasion, "There are enough men with ability and expert knowledge in this country, but they don't rise to where they can exercise effective leadership because they haven't got the push and pull needed in our society. So what have we got? We've got men with little competence but lots of family influence together with old men with obsolete ideas running the country for us. No wonder all they could think of doing when confronted with a problem was to throw people out of work. As if that would solve anything!"

On that occasion, Khun Prem was somewhere else in the compound and therefore not part of An's audience, which consisted of only Ot and herself. Phloi felt thankful about this.

"Who would you bring in to provide the solution?" Ot asked, a faint smile playing on his face.

"As I said, we have people to do it, but they're kept outside the exalted circle. They're powerless."

"What about yourself, Phi An? Would you be a problem-solver for our country?

Ot's careless tone and the smile that went with it did not please his elder brother, who nevertheless went on expounding.

"All our problems can be traced back to the system under which we operate, under which this country is governed. You yourself, Ot, must realize how hopelessly antiquated that system is. This is the root problem. It must be solved first before you can begin to tackle anything else. How can a backward system cope with the problems we have today? Look at the mess we're in already. The system must be corrected for the good of the whole country."

"Take it easy, Phi An," Ot murmured, then without a pause began in a normal voice to talk of other things.

Phloi's uneasiness concerning An and his ideas did not assail her too often, occupied as she was with the day-to-day business of overseeing a sprawling household. Her anxiety over her one and only daughter Praphai was a different matter. She felt it frequently indeed. An, after all, did not try to tell her how our country should be run every time they met, whereas Praphai could upset her merely by being her ultra-smart and modern self.

Modern children, conservative parents, youth, age, time past and time present, a conversation on these recurring themes between the two old friends, Choi and Phloi, went as follows:

"My dear Mae Phloi, do stop fretting. Be your age, sit back and enjoy contemplating the young . . . Such a pretty girl, Praphai, even if she does wear those bizarre clothes." Choi was referring here to the *farang* mode of short skirt and loose shapeless blouse, the current rage among the style-conscious of Bangkok.

"It's not only her clothes, Choi, but everything about her—her manner, her attitude, the way she walks, talks, laughs, everything. Half the time I have no idea what she's talking about—it could well be in a foreign language. It's not so bad when she's alone with me, but when her school friends are here, I listen to them and feel like a creature from another earth."

"Not another earth, just another age . . . You remember how Khun Aunt Sai used to scold us, Phloi? We could never be graceful enough, well-behaved enough, lady-like enough, we were always falling short of the high standard she set for us. When she didn't scream at us she'd mumble and grumble away like what you're doing with Praphai. But we never did pay much heed, did we? I didn't, anyway, and look at me now—haven't I turned out quite respectable? Not very graceful or lady-like, perhaps, but indubitably well-behaved."

"Perhaps not as well-behaved as all that, but the same old Choi, as full of fun as when she was ten years old with an untidy topknot on her head. In a way you haven't aged at all, Choi."

"On the contrary, Phloi, I've aged in *all* ways, and that's the only way to do it, I've found. Much more fun than striving to remain eighteen forever."

"You *would* turn it into fun, Choi."

"Well, it is, you know. When I chat about my infirmities to my palace friends, they laugh, and we compare notes on getting a little harder of hearing and the old eyesight playing tricks with us and so forth. Sometimes we sound like we're competing in an ageing contest. You know, when we were children I couldn't wait to get rid of my topknot and become a young woman. Now I can't wait to be sixty and have the youngsters come to pour water on my hands, paying respect and asking for my blessing. It's very exciting, the thought of reaching so venerable a stage!"

Phloi did not always find it easy to maintain equanimity of mind where her children were concerned, but a talk with Choi never failed to take her nearer it. It had been a few years since Khun Aunt Sai's death, followed shortly by her own mother's, and now Choi was all alone, but by no means a poor lonely woman—not with that open mind and generous heart and that stubborn courage she was endowed with. Phloi often gave thanks that their respective courses of karma had brought them together and kept them together, as permanently as could be in the impermanent scheme of our existence.

Time passed, fleeting days and weeks following one another in a more or less routine manner, giving no sign, presaging nothing. That day saw Khun Prem, astride his horse, go off early in the morning as on previous days. Phloi watched him go, then resumed her morning chores including seeing to his breakfast and his clothes. When nine o'clock came and he had not returned she thought he was unusually late. It was only a few minutes after this that she heard noises coming from the floor below, people running and talking. Before she had time to rise and go down to investigate, Ot entered, sat down on the floor beside her and spoke rapidly. "Khun Father has had an accident beyond Lumpini Park somewhere in Khlong Toey. I'm taking the car to bring him back."

He dashed off without waiting for her questions. She had none to put to him in any case. She could not utter a sound then or after he had left, and she went on sitting there, feeling now hot, now cold, trying to think, trying not to think, trying to keep calm while her heart was racing. She was still there, seated at the same spot not far from the tray containing Khun Prem's clothes, when at last the car came back. She could hear it braking to a stop down below, she heard the doors bang and human voices, then heavy footsteps coming up slowly. It was Ot again, Ot and some men carrying Khun Prem into the room and lowering him onto the settee while she sat there, staring. She saw that Ot's face was streaked with tears and heard him say, "It was too late when we got there—he'd fallen—it must have been instantaneous . . . You don't mind my bringing him back here, do you?"

Ot said that because he knew about the belief held by some people that when death occurred elsewhere the body should not be brought back to the house but taken straight to a *wat*.

"This is Khun Prem's house," Phloi said vaguely. "This is where he should be."

Ot wept, holding her close to him. Phloi was dry-eyed. This could not be real. How could it be? How could she accept it as real? No, no, it could not be. She could not force herself to believe it.

The whole day was unreal. The house was suddenly crowded. So many people came to pour water on Khun Prem's hands, paying their last respects. Members of the family, cousins close and distant from all over, some of whom Phloi hadn't seen for years, some she barely knew. The people from the palace came, and the centre room was transformed into the funeral hall. The monks arrived; the evening chanting of the Phra Abhidhamma took place. Phloi greeted the guests, accepted their condolences, lit the candles, asked the servants to bring tea to those arriving late, and so on. Some of the friends and acquaintances remarked how good and brave she was, but Khun Choei and Choi rightly suspected she was in a state of shock, and they consulted and decided to spend the night here to watch over her.

THIRTY-ONE

PHLOI did not feel too lonely while Khun Prem's body remained in the house. The funeral services continued, with the chanting of the Phra Abhidhamma being held every night starting from the first day and ending in the seventh-day rites, after which there was a week's rest before the chanting was resumed every seventh day until the fiftieth-day rites; then another period of the weekly chanting which culminated in the hundredth-day rites. There was a great deal to do on all these occasions: flowers to arrange, offerings to prepare for the monks, food to plan and cook and serve to the monks and the guests and all the people who came to help in any way they could—relatives and friends, Khun Prem's old sub-ordinates from the ministry, former retainers and members of their families, and so on. Phloi was kept busy throughout these months. The aching sadness in her heart was always there, surging up at odd moments, although she had come round to accepting the reality of Khun Prem's death, and of her own life, which from now on until it should cease must be lived without him.

From the very first day, from near and far, and from many unexpected quarters, Phloi had been receiving all sorts of help, material, spiritual, moral, which comforted her and sometimes moved her to tears. She was more grateful than she could say, was unable to convey her feelings in words that would do justice to the kindness being lavished on her. With Choi and Khun Choei, though, she didn't have to try to be articulate. They understood her, as she them. They came often during this period to spend a few days at the house, especially when there were many things to be done for the rites. They slept in her room, they chatted before going to bed, always had a lot to say to each other, and they cheered her up without attempting to do it directly. Phoem also came to stay, sharing Ot's bachelor apartment, picking up some more English phrases from Ot and sprinkling his conversation with them much to the amusement of Choi and Khun Choei. The latter's husband, Luang Osot, busy as he was with his patients and his pharmacy, never missed an evening chanting and was more often than not the last one to leave, sometimes quite late at night after having a game or two of Thai chess (*mak ruk*) with Phoem.

Khun Un had not got over the tragedy. She had been beside herself with grief that first day, and till now could not speak of him without tears running down her cheeks. Calling him her benefactor, a bo tree spreading happiness over her head and protecting her from harm, she said she would never again find such a thoroughly good man in this life, and her sorrows were all the harder to bear because his sudden departure had robbed her of the last opportunity to express her gratitude—not that she could ever repay him for all he had done for her. If he had been ill for a few days, she could have nursed him day and night, she said. She was greatly indebted to Phloi, but infinitely more to Khun Prem, she would like you to know. For he was no blood relation, yet had treated her as though they had been born brother and sister. . .

"There goes the Lady Mourner," Khun Choei whispered to Choi as Khun Un went passing by the back veranda where they were sitting amid the flowers and the trays of candles and incense sticks. This must have been about the tenth week after Khun Prem had passed away.

"She does put in a great amount of weeping," Choi agreed. "Poor thing. Many a time I've felt like joining her and had to restrain myself."

"But why?" Khun Choei asked. "Why not cry when you feel like it? I do, but I can't carry on like Khun Big Sister Un, that's all."

"Listen, my dear," Choi said. "You and Khun Un can cry as hard as you like. Khun Un's old enough and you are happily married to your dear Khun Luang, and both of you are Phloi's sisters. And if Phloi hadn't cried we'd have had to beat her until she did, wouldn't we? People expect you to be stricken when your husband dies. But me, if I shed one tear too many, people would start asking: What was Khun Prem to *that* woman anyway? And *that* would cast doubt on my hard-won reputation as a spinster, and I will not have it!" She stopped abruptly, then went on, "Oh, oh, if Khun Aunt Sai were here with us she'd say, 'Enough of your silly nonsense, Choi! Stop it now, do you hear me?'"

She paused, kept silent, no doubt in deference to Khun Aunt Sai's memory, but not for very long. "Ah," she sighed, placing a set of candles in the tray in front of her, then mused aloud on life and death in her irrepressible fashion. "Quite a business—this living, isn't it? We jump about, loving one minute and getting angry the next, laughing, crying, bickering, reaching after this or that prize, each in our own way. Then we die, and it's the same for everybody. No more jumping about . . . When I'm dead, though, there won't be any tears for me. I can see you all laughing when you think of me after I'm dead, as you're laughing now . . . But you know, those I have loved have not really died, not while I'm still alive. I have them with me in my thoughts, in my heart, and since I'm not dead yet they live on. They're part of me as long as I breathe and remember . . . Take Sadet—how many years has she been dead? Never mind—I still do things the way she liked it, and I take care not to cause her displeasure. It's the same with my father and mother. And when we come to Khun Aunt Sai—my dears! She pursues me now even more implacably than she ever did in the flesh. I used to be able to escape her vigilance from time to time, but now I have this feeling she's watching my every move. Like at this very moment . . . Yes, yes, Khun Aunt, I heard you. No more drivelling. I'll stop now before Khun Choei and Phloi and all these good people suspect me of being madder than I actually am . . ."

After the hundredth-day rites there was an interval before the cremation took place, and during the two days preceding the cremation day there was the Kong Tek ceremony. This is a Chinese merit-making rite for the dead, a main feature of which is the burning of paper replicas of everyday earthly possessions such as money, clothes, tables and chairs, houses and cars. Observance of this funerary custom is not uncommon among Thai families with Chinese connections. Amid the usual collection awaiting the ritual burning stood a group of profferings which some people said would surely come as a complete surprise to Khun Prem. Phloi had had an inkling of it beforehand from overhearing, a week or two prior to the ceremony, the following conversation between her brother Phoem and her son Ot:

"I tell you, Ot, it's going to be a lovely Kong Tek. That Chinese is an artist and he's done us proud. Everything is so well-made, especially the two cars. Superb! Khun Prem will look smart and dignified riding in them in the Beyond. But—but something is still lacking—"

"What else should we get, Khun Uncle?"

"Horses. We must send your father some horses. I'll get our Chinese to make a string of them, nicely saddled and everything, and a stable too. What do you say?"

"But Uncle, what if he should have given up horseback-riding after what happened? He might think we're mocking him."

"You have a point there, my boy . . . Ah, I know—what about some comely lasses to serve him and keep him from feeling lonely Over There? He never had any in this life. About time, don't you think?"

"I don't know, dear Uncle. What would Khun Mother say?"

"Oh, she wouldn't mind. Your father might, though. He never had any use for them, always said they'd shorten his life, but now that he's dead it shouldn't make any difference. Anyway, if he doesn't want them, when I join him yonder I'll just claim them for my own."

So there they were, at the Kong Tek ceremony for Khun Prem, the charming paper maidens, standing in a many-coloured row, each with an identity tag attached to her gown, for Phoem had thoughtfully invented names for them as well; and Choi, on seeing them, remarked in a rather loud whisper, "If I had known I would have contributed a few cradles and some baby things." And Phloi was smiling through her tears.

It was not until after the cremation that Phloi had a long uninterrupted session with her sorrow. Early in the morning she had made another journey to the *wat* with her children and close relatives, collected the ashes and returned to the house. The small urn had been placed on one of the altar tables, and after paying their respects the others had left. Now she was alone in the room where Khun Prem had once been, with the urn containing his ashes standing on the table before her, thinking she'd stay here a while before getting on with the various jobs of the day. But she didn't leave. She remained a long time in the silent room, with its empty seats where the monks had sat, with the wreaths drooping on the walls, and Khun Prem's walking sticks gathering dust in their old corner.

Our allotted years in this life must come to an end—she didn't need to be reminded again, but knowing it did not prevent her from crying for her dead husband or from asking of the surrounding emptiness what she was to do with the days and nights stretching ahead of her. The allotted years could seem endless. She looked long at the urn as though seeking its guidance, but only the past would speak to her. Away from the urn, beyond the walls of the sad room, she could see the sunlit river at Bang Pa-in—two girls in a boat, with the maid Phit and Khun Aunt Sai—a young man in another boat . . . How delightful to see it again, like coming across an old picture unexpectedly. But the picture soon wavered, grew indistinct and then was no more. There was nothing left but bones and ashes.

Now On came back into the room, to take leave of her and return to Ayuthaya. They cried together. On had shared her grief in silence before. They had no need for words during these moments.

Then On said, "I'll be back next week, Khun Mother." Next week, when the merit-making for the ashes would be held.

"I wish you didn't have to go, my son," Phloi said. "When are they going to transfer you to Bangkok?"

"Maybe next year, Khun Mother. Not before then, I'm afraid. I'll come home as often as I can. I want to be near you and have more time to take care of you."

Thoughtful, gentle, modest On had become perceptibly more so since Khun Prem's death, whereas An had been conducting himself with more authority especially when dealing with his brothers and sister. He had been less confident during the first days following the tragedy, and on the day it happened had been just as dazed and confused as everybody else. It was Ot, surprisingly enough, who had taken charge generally and organized everything and everybody, including Phi An. When the others had recovered and things started to move along smoothly, and An had assumed the important elder brother's role, Ot had reverted to his habitual easy-going ways.

The merit-making for the ashes took place on the appointed day; and some time after this post-cremation rite Phloi found an opportunity, when her sons and daughter were present together, to hold a sort of family council about family properties. Khun Prem had handled these things. She knew nothing about them and wanted one of her sons to carry on. She asked On first, he being the eldest.

"I think An is the person to do it," On was quick to suggest. "He has the ability, and the added advantage of knowing the law." To An he said, "You're the most suitable person from every point of view."

"Shouldn't we first consider the question of inheritance?" An asked, sounding indeed like the legal man he was.

"Khun Father made a will," Ot spoke up, addressing the ceiling rather than anyone in particular. "He left everything to Khun Mother."

The information was new to An, and he said, "Really? I didn't know. Why haven't I been told, Khun Mother?" You would have thought he was interrogating a witness.

"I—I don't know," Phloi stammered. "The will was in your father's desk. Ot and I found it going through his papers. It makes no difference, because—because all I have I consider as also belonging to my children. After reading the will I didn't think any more about it. Haven't thought about it again until now."

"I see." An now spoke in softer tones. "Well then, it's up to you, Khun Mother. Whatever you want to do—"

"On's right and I agree with him entirely," said his mother quickly. "You're most suitable in every way. I'd like you to look after our family business, son."

After a few moments' silence, An said, "If you really want me to do it, Khun Mother. I don't know how well I'll be able to manage it, but I'll try my best. That's all I can say."

"I'm sure you'll manage it very well, my son." Phloi was greatly relieved. Then she went on to broach a related subject. "Perhaps you'd like your brother Ot to help you? In fact, I think that may be a good idea—your having Ot as assistant."

An gave his younger brother a look before coming back to Phloi. "If you don't mind, Khun Mother, I'd prefer to do it alone at least for the time being. It's less complicated that way. A better idea would be for Ot to get himself a proper job, establish himself in some career, do something useful for a change." To the half-smiling Ot he said, "Don't take it amiss, will you? I'm saying this for your own good. In my opinion you've had enough time to decide what to do with your life, and really, if I were you I'd be bored to death loafing about at home. You're highly qualified, dear fellow. It's time you put your knowledge to some good use, for your own sake, for the family, for the country. I didn't want to say anything before, didn't dare in fact, because Khun Father himself never brought it up. But now that he's gone and since I'm your elder brother—"

"You feel duty-bound to be like a father to me." Ot finished the sentence with a good-humoured twinkle, then turned to his other brother. "And what have you got to say, Phi On?"

"Not a thing," On answered with a laugh.

"What? You don't want to be a father to me, too?"

"Can't do it, Ot. Sorry. You're too old for me, and too well-educated. Besides, you're so contrary that if I preach something the chances are you'll go and practice the opposite."

An frowned at both of them. "You're too lenient with him, Phi On. You should be helping me put some sense into him…Listen to me, Ot— conceit will get you nowhere. Seriously, there are plenty of openings for someone like you, if you'd only make up your mind and stop playing the gentleman of leisure. It's so out-of-date anyway. We're in for some real changes in this country, let me tell you. The day will come—"

"Tell me, Phi An," Ot interrupted him, "Who are these people engineering the changes to come?"

Glaring at his brother, An said sharply, "Don't change the subject. Or do you want to stop talking about it and go on loafing? Very well. But let me say this. When there's a chance to go forward, it's idiotic not to take it."

Phloi always found it unsettling when An used that tone of voice, but she knew he meant well, and she could see how Ot's insouciance might further ruffle his brother. "Ot, dear," she said tactfully, "do try to be a little more serious and not take everything as a joke. An's your elder brother. He cares about you. It's natural he should give advice when he believes it would be to your advantage."

An seemed mollified, but only momentarily, for instead of holding his peace Ot chose to declaim a Bali phrase: *Brama chaloka,* the opening words of the invitation to a preaching monk to start delivering his sermon.

"May I leave now, Khun Mother," said An with dignity, in a well-controlled voice. "About what you want me to do, I'll get started as soon as I can. We'll be talking more about it, of course. Just the two of us, so that nobody's time will be wasted."

"You shouldn't tease him, Ot," Phloi remarked after An had left the room. "You know what he's like. And lately he's become more irritable. I don't know why."

"I don't blame him for getting mad at you," said Praphai, who idolized her Phi An. "You can be so maddening sometimes, Phi Ot!"

"I know," Ot concurred readily. "I don't blame him either, little Praphai. But I don't do him any harm by making him mad. They say it's good for the kidneys if you lose your temper once in a while, so in actual fact I help keep Phi An healthy."

"You see!" Praphai cried. "Joking again!"

"I'm also useful in another way," Ot went on.

"What?"

"People compare me with Phi An and his virtues shine more brightly. I set him off, black setting off grey, making it look nearly white. Now that's useful, I'd say."

"Oh, Phi Ot! . . . May I go now, Khun Mother? I'm going shopping with some friends." She strode off, so pretty in her modish clothes.

"You think I'm good for nothing, Khun Mother?" Ot asked.

"Not at all, son. But I don't understand why you don't want to show what you can do. An's right, you know. There are plenty of openings for someone like you. Why aren't you interested?"

"I don't really know," Ot confessed. Then he gave a funny smile. "But I know this. Life gives us so little time. It's terrifyingly short. Each day that we're still together is very precious to me."

THIRTY-TWO

IN her young days in the Inner Court Phloi had heard the old women talk about it (keeping their voices secretively low), some believing it to have reached us from the Lord Buddha, while according to others it was King Phra Buddha Yodfa, founder of the present Chakri Dynasty and of Bangkok as capital of our land, who himself had made this prophecy that his Chakri House ("Chakri" had been one of his titles) would endure one hundred and fifty years before losing its royal power. Phloi had listened politely to the old women, thinking, "Here they go again—how they just love these prophecies and predictions and whatnot." The 150th anniversary of Krung Ratanakosin (city of Bangkok) had seemed to her such a long way away, and there had been a host of other more thrilling things to engage her attention at the time.

Now the date was approaching, and there was a revival of interest in the old prophecy—widespread interest, not just among the old folks. Phloi had not believed in it before, and she did not believe in it now, but whereas she had not bothered about it in the past, its present status as the most popular gossip was making her feel uneasy despite herself.

"It's not pleasant at all," she said to her brother Phoem one day. "It's not auspicious. Why do people like to talk about it so much? Do they really believe such a thing could happen? It seems wildly improbable to me, yet it preys on my mind because I keep hearing about it all the time."

"I don't believe in it either," Phoem said. "And I find it strange that our royals should take it seriously."

"How do you know? Who told you that?"

"Nobody. But if they didn't, would they have decided to have the 150th year of the era commemorated on such a grand scale? We had the 100th year celebration, yes, and I'm told that was quite a splendid affair, but nothing like what we're going to have. My question is: why not wait till the year 200 to have another one? Somehow it seems to me that this betwixt-and-between figure of 150 doesn't by itself deserve the significance being given it."

"Speak for yourself, Khun Luang. Why, the whole of Bangkok is excited about it. The people who are gossiping about the prophecy are also getting ready to go to the fair and watch the parade and what have you. My daughter Praphai is already fussing about what she's going to wear . . . No, Khun Luang, I don't see anything unusual in our royals wishing to hold great celebrations this year. And there'll be rites and ceremonies to prevent any possible ill luck—"

That's what I mean, Mae Phloi. They are concerned about the possiblity."

"I see—yes. I see your point, Khun Luang. But there's nothing wrong in taking precautions."

Weeks went by during which Phloi had not discussed the prophecy rumour with anyone else, not given it much thought for that matter. She was more concerned with matters nearer home—a potential domestic crisis. Things were going badly between An and Lucille. They fought in front of Phloi sometimes, flinging French words against each other—one didn't have to understand the words to know that they were hurting each other. According to Praphai (once Lucille's aper and admirer, now her chief critic), Lucille had been consorting exclusively with her *farang* friends and looking down her nose at the Thai people. Knowing how the girl worshipped her brother, Phloi didn't believe everything she said about her sister-in-law, and, noting An's habit of going out by himself night after night, returning very late if at all, Phloi also felt his wife was entitled to send up a few complaints and protests. She hoped the situation would improve in time. What else could she do? No one had asked her for advice or assistance. It was after all their private affair and she could not butt in and start ordering them to behave themselves.

Then one day Phoem came to see her again, and what he had to tell her made An's marital tiffs seem a most trivial issue by comparison. Phoem started out with what they had discussed on his previous visit. The old prophecy continued to be talked about, he said. But this other rumour was much more worrying. It had come to his ear from several sources, for he had friends and acquaintances in many different circles.

"What other rumour?" Phloi asked.

"I'm told there's a group of people plotting to overthrow the royal power."

Phloi cried aloud on hearing this. "Impossible! It can't be true!"

"It's what I've heard, Mae Phloi. It's hard to believe, but—"

"Impossible!" Phloi repeated. "No! And even if this rebel group existed—which I refuse to believe—they would never succeed. Our royals are protected by their merit, and their loyal subjects and all those close to them who have sworn allegiance and have taken the Water of Loyalty would never allow it. The plotters would be condemned."

She was ready to dismiss the awful rumour, but Phoem had not finished. He beat about the bush at first, but finally had to let her have the most important part of it.

"I've also heard, Mae Phloi, that An might be involved with this group."

Phloi was aghast. She cried out again, shrilly this time. "What are you saying, Khun Luang? My own son! The son of my flesh and blood whom I have reared from the moment he came into this world! How could you, Khun Luang!"

"Take it easy, Mae Phloi. We're still discussing rumours. I knew you wouldn't like it but I had to tell you. If they had mentioned On's name or Ot's I would have laughed at them. But An is full of strange ideas, you must admit."

"No, no, Khun Luang!"

"Tell me, Mae Phloi, do you know all his friends, and do you know about his activities after office hours?"

"Why should I? He's a grown man and a respectable official. He doesn't need his mother to spy on everything he does!"

"So you don't know. But calm down, Mae Phloi. You're trembling."

Phloi was shaken to the core of her loyal soul. A phrase she had heard in her childhood flashed through her mind: *Tat hua chet chua khot* (Behead seven generations!) That had been the fate meted out to the conspirators against the Lord of Life in ancient times. Like her ancestors of those times and her parents and grandparents she believed in the sacredness of the Water of Loyalty and the oath-taking at the Drinking Ceremonial. The inviolability of the royal power was her creed, and had the rumour been about An plotting against his own mother she would not have been half as shocked.

"What am I going to do, Khun Luang? I don't believe it. It can't be true—but—oh, I don't know—I don't know anything any more—"

"Let's hope it's not true. But if I were you I'd talk to him anyway, Mae Phloi . . . If it is true, all the more reason for you to stop him before it's too late. But, I repeat, it may just be rumours."

An was leading such a busy life that Phloi didn't have the opportunity until several days later. He came into her sitting room one afternoon to keep her informed on what he had done regarding some family property. Phloi listened with half an ear, put in one or two perfunctory questions, and when he was through, asked him to stay for a chat since she had not seen him for quite a while. Having had to wait so long for this moment, she launched into her subject without too much preamble.

"You spend so much time with your friends, my son. Who are they, these friends of yours?"

"Oh, some are from the department, some are old school chums, some I met in Paris—" He stopped short, eyebrows raised. "But why do you ask, Khun Mother?"

"I've heard some disturbing rumours, my son." She paused, and began anew. "Sometimes we are influenced by our friends without realizing it—and there are good friends and bad friends. I'd like to remind you again please to be on your guard and not let yourself be led to the path of wrong-doing."

"Khun Mother!" An exclaimed in a voice of injured dignity. "What's all this? Are you implying that my friends and I are frequenting bars and brothels? Is that what you've been hearing about me?"

"I know you have no such vices, my son. The rumours I've heard are not about drunkards but about some people who may be drunk with too many heady schemes for this land of ours. I'm anxious you shouldn't be mixed up with them, that's all. Gratitude and loyalty to our benefactors have been one of the principles we live by—both your father's family and mine. Our royals have bestowed on us untold blessings and we have served them well and faithfully, on my side for hundreds of years and on your father's side since his father came here from China—"

Phloi had been rehearsing a much longer speech, but An cut her short. Laughing, he said, "Are you afraid I may be planning a revolt or something? "

"No—no, it's not—" Phloi faltered, taken aback by the question.

An came to kneel in front of her. Looking into her eyes, he demanded, "What gave you this idea, Khun Mother?"

"Those—those rumours, you know—"

With this eyes remaining fixed on her, An said, "I know you love me and are concerned about me. I'm sorry you've been upset. Please stop worrying about my being led astray by friends, Khun Mother. Your son's not so easily led. And please trust me. I feel about our ancestors as you do. I'll never betray them. With all my heart I wish to be worthy of them, and of you and Khun Father. Do you believe that?"

"I do," Phloi said. "The rumour upset me, I must confess. I've heard you air your views about our country, you know."

"I feel strongly about our country," An spoke in his earnest voice, "loving it as I do. But at the same time I am His Majesty's loyal subject and I feel deeply and forever beholden to him. What can I say to convince you beyond any doubt? Let's do it like this—" He lowered his joined palms and head on Phloi's lap, and after making this gesture of obeisance he said slowly, "I swear to my mother whom I love and revere above all else that I will never be party to any plot or plan to harm our sovereign and his family in any way. If I break this oath, may—"

"Don't!" Phloi placed a hand on his lips. "You don't have to swear. I believe you."

An thanked her with another *krap* on her lap. Then he went on, "I wish to be useful to our country, Khun Mother, to do all I can as an honest and loyal subject for its progress and prosperity. Won't you give me your blessing and wish me success?"

"I do, my son."

He took hold of her hands and pressed them to his cheek. Then he took his departure.

Phloi felt better after that talk, but she couldn't help wondering why An had taken it so calmly. After all, the rumour had maligned him and he should have been angry—that would have been more in keeping with his character and temperament. However, when she saw Phoem again some days afterwards she merely told him what An had said, leaving out her impression of his manner during the interview.

"I'm relieved to hear it," Phoem said. "But the rumour about the plot itself hasn't died down, Mae Phloi. What's more, I've been told by a person who never lies to me that it's true."

"I still don't believe it!" Phloi frowned. "If it's true, why isn't anything being done about it?"

Phoem's answer was vague and confused enough. "Maybe because too few people are in the know, though I have a feeling—just a tiny feeling, Mae Phloi, that our elders in high places are not entirely in the dark about it."

"Then why don't they do something? I don't understand it, Khun Luang!"

"I don't either, Mae Phloi. Strange goings-on these days. On the one hand you hear these disquieting rumours, and on the other, wherever you go you keep bumping into so many gold clips inscribed with various royal monograms. Every jacket has at least one or two clips, but on some jackets you see a whole glittering row of them—makes you think the wearers must have been rushing round from one palace to another." He paused, shaking his head in wonder. "Perhaps our royals have faith in these clips they have given to their followers."

"What do you mean, Khun Luang?"

"That those who wear them can be trusted."

"I've come across quite a few of those clip-wearers, Khun Luang.

I've seen how with the greatest of ease they put on or take off their attachments, depending on circumstances."

"We humble people can see that, Mae Phloi, but viewed from up high things are bound to look different, I dare say."

Phloi nodded, knowing what he meant. Then she said, "But to get back to your rumour, Khun Luang. You want to know what I really think? I don't care what you're going to say, but I think it's a lot of nonsense. You can go on telling me what you've heard, but I'm not going to believe it."

Phoem laughed. "Actually, Mae Phloi, I can't believe it myself. Oh, it will fade away, I'm sure, like so many other rumours we've had before."

The above conversation took place not very long before the 150th Ratanakosin Year Celebration, which lasted several festive days and nights. The sky was bright and clear and the streets at night were beautifully lit up. Bangkok was looking joyous and magnificent and was having a grand time. Phloi celebrated the occasion more quietly than most. She went out once, got dizzy in the dense crowd and was glad to get home.

"Don't you want to go to the opening of the bridge?" Praphai asked her mother one morning. This was the Memorial Bridge, our first bridge across the Chao Phraya River. Phloi said this was an auspicious day for all of us but she would stay home and look after the house, and let the children and servants go out and enjoy themselves. Later on, though, talking to Choi and Phoem about it, she did envy them a little—they had had so much fun going everywhere and seeing everything there was to see. When Choi told her about the processions at the inauguration of the bridge, Phloi said, "I wish I'd been with you. I wish I had your energy, Choi."

"Great fun," Choi said. "And you know, Phloi, nowadays I feel much safer in a crowd than when I was a young girl. No horrible young men to bother me. When they see me coming they disperse and give me room to pass by. Very nice."

The celebrations were over. The 150th year of the Ratanakosin Era had arrived. No misfortune had befallen, and the old prophecy was soon forgotten by everyone including Phloi.

THIRTY-THREE

THE celebrations were over. The hot dry month of April wore on, then a few drizzles came in the first weeks of May, heralding the year's rainy season with assurances that nature was going about its predictable cycle. But towards the end of May a domestic change occurred in Phloi's household. Nothing very grave, and yet she wished it had been in her power to circumvent it.

"Lucille would like to go and visit her people in France," An told his mother one day. "I've made the arrangements for her."

"Oh—" Phloi was surprised. "Have you thought carefully about it, my son? Husband and wife shouldn't part from each other too long, you know." Except for that time she had gone to Khlong Bang Luang to nurse her ailing Chao Khun Father, and the few times when Khun Prem had made trips to the provinces on civilian duty, or on some occasions with the Royal Tiger Corps under Nai Luang's leadership, Phloi had never lived apart from him. Of course, Lucille's case was different. Such was also An's opinion.

"She's homesick, Khun Mother. It's understandable."

"How long will she be gone?"

"Six months, Khun Mother."

"Six months!" Phloi's voice was full of concern. "That's very long."

"I'd like to ask a favour of you," An went on. "During Lucille's absence, should anything happen to me, will you please have Ot get in touch with her and forward her whatever funds I may have that belong to me."

"Oh my dear!" Phloi cried. "What on earth has made you bring this up? You're too young to have such thoughts."

An laughed. "Anything can happen, Khun Mother. Don't look so startled. We should be prepared for any eventuality."

"At any rate there's no need for you to tell me what to do 'in case anything should happen.' I would take care of Lucille. Really, An, you ought to know that!"

From An's account it would seem to be Lucille's own wish to take this trip, but Phloi got a different story from Lucille herself.

"Of course I miss my people," Lucille said. "And I get homesick for Paris from time to time. But not to the extent that I want to leave my home here. The idea never crossed my mind to go away. I'm married to An and my place is here with him. But he kept saying to me—'Why don't you go, Lucille? Do go, Lucille.' Go, go, go. He's made it quite plain he wants me to go, so I go."

Phloi sighed. "An said it was your idea. Now you tell me it's his."

"Darling Khun Mother!" Lucille's smile was tender and full of understanding. "I know how you feel. You love your son. And me, I also have your affection; I know that. You want us to be happy together . . . Oh, Khun Mother, I'm going to miss you so much!"

"An said you'll be away six months. Then you'll come back and we'll be together again."

Lucille gave another smile, a wistful smile. "Perhaps I'll hurry back before then—if An still wants me."

Phloi didn't go to see her off the day she left—in early June it was. They said goodbye at home. Both were in tears. Lucille gave Phloi a long loving embrace, and for once Phloi was equally demonstrative. She pressed the girl close to her, blessing her and comforting her and kept repeating she mustn't stay away too long. Then An came and said it was time to leave. As she watched the car go out of the gate, Phloi asked herself whether she had done enough for Lucille, and if she had given the girl her love from the very beginning, would it have helped to keep her from having to leave today?

An was a changed man after Lucille's departure, much more relaxed and cheerful. Some nights he did not come home at all, and some days Phloi only had a few brief glimpses of him as he flitted in and out, but every time they got together she would be struck by the transformation that had come over him. He told her he had a great deal of work to do and many people to see, and she mustn't worry when he was absent from home. He seemed to enjoy being a single man, Phloi remarked wryly to herself.

Then came that morning—the days had gone by swiftly but it was still in the month of June. Phloi was lying awake in bed. She would get up in a minute but meanwhile was planning her day and listening to the birds and the familiar sound of doors and windows being opened on the floor below, when suddenly the morning calm was disrupted by heavy footsteps tramping up the stairs and Phoem's voice yelling, "Mae Phloi! Mae Phloi! Get up. It's happened!"

She came rushing out, and Phoem told her, "A revolt! It's happened, Mae Phloi!"

Phloi sat down on the floor and gaped speechless at her brother.

"We were wrong, Mae Phloi. We didn't believe such a thing could happen. A revolt. A rebellion. They've done it."

"Are you sure it's true, Khun Luang?" She could think of nothing to say that would make sense.

"Unfortunately it is. Here, read this." He took from his pocket a piece of paper and handed it to her. "The rebels' proclamation. Read it yourself."

Phloi did. She nearly gave up when she was halfway through and had to force herself to go on. She was horrified by what she read. "It's not true at all!" her soul cried out in protest. These violent words— incredibly violent. What were they trying to do? Destroy everything she believed in? No, no, they would never succeed with her! She would dismiss it.

"Who are these people?" She spoke in a cracked voice as though she had been shouting. "Who are they—this 'Khana Rasadon?'"

"I know only a few—not all of them." Phoem went on to name a few important names in the Khana Rasadon, the People's Party, none of whom was familiar to Phloi.

"What are they going to do with Nai Luang? Are they going to kill all the royals? What's going to happen?"

"I don't know, Mae Phloi. I don't think anybody does. I only know

423

these people want a constitution." He said the word in English, pronouncing it the Thai way: *khon-sati-tu-chan*, which could mean a *sati-tu-chan* person. Very confusing. He made a few attempts at explaining this *farang* word, but Phloi didn't find it very helpful.

"The People's Party would like to place Nai Luang under the law, Mae Phloi."

"What for, Khun Luang? Nai Luang has never broken any law. He's the one who makes the law. I don't understand."

"They want some other people to make the law, Mae Phloi."

"And if Nai Luang refuses?"

"That's it, Mae Phloi. That's the big question. Nai Luang is on holiday in Hua Hin. I think they've sent a delegation there."

"Any news about Their Royal Highnesses?"

"I hear some are under arrest."

When Phoem told her the names, Phloi recalled that of late there had been some talk about their owners being unpopular with certain groups of people. These might welcome the news, but to her it was at once sad and terrifying.

"May the Lord Buddha protect them! Oh, Khun Luang, it's awful! Why oh why, Khun Luang?"

"In an upheaval like this what can you expect, Mae Phloi? Even people like us may get caught up in it—there's no telling what will happen."

Now Ot came into the room and sat down with them. In answer to Phoem's question he said with a smile, "Yes, Khun Uncle, I've heard. I've been hearing about it for some time."

"Tell your mother about this *khon-sati-tu-chan*, will you? I tried to, but I think you can do it much better. Give us a lecture on it, Ot."

"You don't really want to hear it, do you, Khun Mother? I think we'd better wait anyway, Khun Uncle. No telling what sort of *khon-sati-tu-chan* they might be cooking up."

Looking at Ot, Phloi suddenly went cold. *Where is he—where's An?* At a time like this he ought to have come home. He had left the house last evening or the evening before—she wasn't quite sure, to stay overnight with some friends, but she didn't know where. She hoped he was not roaming the streets at this moment. Not safe at all—anything could happen. Phoem must have been thinking the same thing, for he was saying to Ot, "Where's your brother, An?"

Ot glanced smilingly at his mother, and Phloi answered for him. "He often spends a night or two at his friends'. I don't think he's home, Khun Luang."

Then Phoem and Ot exchanged the following few words.

Phoem: "I see."

Ot: "Phi An and his friends must be celebrating."

Phoem: "You mean . . . ?"

Ot: "Yes, that's what I mean."

Phoem, sighing: "I thought so."

And Phloi cut in, speaking sharply, "What are you two talking about?"

The two men looked at each other. Phoem took it upon himself to give the answer. "What we talked about the other day, Mae Phloi. An is involved with these plotters."

"I don't believe it!" Phloi shrieked at them, tears rising in her eyes. "He swore he wasn't . . . Ot, tell your mother it's not true! I *know* it's not true. Say it, Ot!"

"I don't know what to say," Ot said in a low voice, "unless you want me to lie to you."

With tears streaming down her face, Phloi poured out her words in a voice shaking with rage. "Ot! How could you! You can say anything against your brother in fun—I don't mind. But this is too much. I won't have it, do you hear? I won't have it! Don't you love your brother at all? Have you no heart? How could you! He's your own brother, he's my own flesh and blood, and you're accusing him of the most dreadful crime. If he's capable of it, so are you!"

Ot kept silent, looking down at the floor.

"Stop crying, Mae Phloi," Phoem said. "Forgive me, I've made you unhappy. This is no time for us to quarrel, Mae Phloi."

He left after a while, saying he'd go and find out what else had been happening. The rest of the day passed quietly at Phloi's house. Nobody else came to see her. The whole capital city seemed shut down—

Bangkok holding its breath, waiting. And Phloi waited and waited for An, nervous about his safety and at the same time wanting him to come home to give her all the facts and dispel her doubts. But she was to be disappointed. He didn't come home that night, or the following day. And on this second day rumours were rife, and they were all bad: rumours about Nai Luang bringing in the provincial forces to quell the revolt—fierce battles expected, bloodshed in the streets of Bangkok; the rebels going to put all our royals in a boat and sink it in the ocean; and that all properties belonging to our royals and the rich people would be confiscated, all sorts of rumours seemingly designed for the sole purpose of creating terror in the hearts of the listeners.

An didn't come home until the third evening.

Phloi and Ot had been talking about him at the dinner table.

"Haven't you any idea where your brother might be?"

"Whatever I say you'll scold me again."

"Oh, Ot, I was so frightened that day . . . Well, do you know?"

"Phi An is not one to go after amusement at a time like this. If he's not home, it must mean he's engaged in some important work somewhere. I wouldn't worry, Mother. He'll be home soon."

"I just want to know where he is. And if you do, perhaps you can go and see him."

"I don't know *exactly* where he is, darling, but I can guess, and if he is where I think he is, I don't think I'll be allowed in to see him."

Phloi was about to chide him for making a mystery of it when An walked in.

"Oh, there you are!" she cried with joy. "We were just talking about you."

An had rings under his eyes, but he was looking wide awake and full of cheer. Smiling, he surveyed the food on the table. "How very nice! I'm famished. Looks like I'm going to have a proper meal for a change!"

While Phloi was happily filling An's plate, Ot smiled at his brother. "Congratulations, Phi An," he said.

"Thank you, Ot, thank you." He sat down at the table. "I knew you'd understand and be pleased about it. From now on *Muang Thai* will never look back. From now on all who have ability, be they well-born or not, will have equal opportunity to serve their nation . . . What about you, Ot? Why don't you come and help us? We can use someone like you."

Ot smiled down at his rice plate before asking, "Everything going well, Phi An? Any more news?"

"The best of news," An answered proudly. "Nai Luang has agreed. *Muang Thai* will have a constitutional monarch. We've done the right thing all along, and I'm immensely relieved."

"Why, Phi An, did you think he would refuse?"

"Well, one couldn't be sure."

"I'm surprised. I shouldn't have thought there was any doubt about His Majesty's consent. I took it for granted that he would give it."

"What made you so sure?"

"You've just said it yourself, Phi An. All educated people would understand and be pleased. Now you know very well that our Nai Luang is a highly educated man, more so than most of us I should think."

An concentrated on his food in silence for a while. Then he said, "May I say something, Ot? As an elder to a younger brother, may I give you a word of advice?"

"You certainly may, Phi An."

"I'd like you to be careful of what you say from now on. Don't blurt things out as you please and when you please the way you've been doing. I don't want to see you get into trouble."

"What?! All right, Phi An, I'll try not to. Now may I also offer you a piece of advice?"

"Of course, Ot. Let's hear it."

"Don't go around saying what you just said to me. People would lose faith in you if you did."

"What do you mean, Ot?"

"Your objective is to change the ancient regime to a democracy. I don't know how you're going to translate 'democracy' into Thai, but under it, freedom of speech is recognized, is it not? Under the old system one could get a coconut rammed in one's mouth for speaking against the established order. You don't want that, right? So if you went round forbidding people to speak their minds, wouldn't that be contrary to what you stand for and ultimately defeating your purpose?"

An laughed—he was definitely in a genial mood. "Have patience, Ot. Changes for the better will come, and we'll make them come as fast as possible. But we're still at the critical stage, you understand—after all, this is only the third day. A measure of control is necessary. At this turning point we must make sure that our people take the right road."

From her seat at the head of the table Phloi smiled at her two sons, thinking it hardly mattered if she understood next to nothing of what they were talking about. The only thing that mattered at the present moment was that An was home safe and sound—an occasion for celebrating, not for quibbling. Anxious that their conversation should not take an undesirable turn, she put in a playful word. "Are you two arguing again? If you are, I want you to stop it immediately, this very minute."

They both laughed, and Ot said, "Sorry, Phi An. I rather overdid the freedom bit."

"Not at all, Ot," said An, "I'm glad you're interested. And seriously, why don't you come and work with us? Think about it and let me know, will you, and I'll talk to my friends and our elders."

Phloi shot a warning glance at Ot who, understanding her message, gave no direct reply. Nor did An seem to be expecting anything of that nature. He went on with his meal, greatly enjoying it. The evening passed without any discordant note.

Phloi let a few days elapse before demanding a clarification from her extremely busy son—thankful as she was that he had returned unharmed and uncharged with any crime, she nevertheless felt he owed it to her. So when the right opportunity arose she asked him a straightforward question: "Did you know about it from the beginning?"

Avoiding her eyes, An stammered out his answer, "I suppose you could put it like that . . . But—but I wasn't one of the original planners

. . . That day I was summoned by one of the leaders, a man I greatly respected. He had errands for me to carry out . . . Otherwise I wouldn't have been involved—-"

"All right," Phloi interrupted him. She could see he was ashamed of having been disingenuous with her, and that was enough—she didn't want to embarrass him any further. "I'm glad it's over and everything settled peacefully. But you shouldn't have gone to such length as to swear, you know. Lucky I stopped you just in time. A false oath brings ill consequences."

An's self-confidence had returned; he said reproachfully, "Meaning you still consider it a rebellion—an act of treason, *kabot?*"

"I don't know what else to call it," said Phloi.

"Khun Mother," An spoke in an earnest voice. "I swore to you in good faith. What we were planning to bring about had nothing to do with treason and everything to do with the good of the nation. Never for a moment did we wish to harm His Majesty and the members of the royal family. Most of the leaders come from families which have enjoyed royal patronage for generations, like ours. Some were not entirely happy about what had to be done but felt it was necessary for the sake of the country as a whole. Our loyalty to Phra Chao Yu Hua has remained intact throughout, and if anything, it has increased since he has granted his approval on the change to bring this country into line with the civilized world."

"What about the proclamation?" Phloi asked. She still felt repelled by *that* piece of writing. "The proclamation you people put out on the first day. It says things that are untrue, using hateful and violent language."

"I agree," An admitted. "I didn't like it at all. The argument of those who were for it was that the people had to be won over and strong words had to be used to persuade them to believe in our cause. But even so, I must say it was a mistake that could have been avoided. I hear we're going to ask His Majesty's pardon. We're going to admit our fault and I hope we'll be forgiven."

"That's better," Phloi said approvingly. "I didn't know you people had sought a royal pardon. I'm so glad!"

"Now, Khun Mother," An went on. "I'm going to ask you a favour.

"Yes, An?"

"When you refer to what happened that day, please don't call it *kabot* (revolt, rebellion, treason). "

"What do you want me to call it, my son?"

"*Kan plian plaeng kan pokkhrong* (change of system of government)."

"I may not be able to remember it, son—it's so long."

"Call it *patiwat* (revolution, coup d'etat.) then. It's shorter."

Phloi had had no news from the Inner Court since the *kan plian plaeng kan pokkhrong*, and she welcomed Choi with great delight when that veteran Inner Courtier came to visit her one quiet afternoon after the situation had returned to normal. The first thing Choi said was, "I nearly died of fright, you know."

And Phloi countered with, "You're exaggerating. I looked at it this way: if we stayed quietly in our own home, nobody was going to come and bother us."

"Ah, my dear Mae Phloi but you are a mere householder whereas I am a Khun Inner Courtier, you understand? To be living in the Inner Court in the Grand Palace on that particular day was no laughing matter, let me assure you. The minute the news broke they locked all the gates. For two days we were shut in behind the walls not knowing what was going to be done to us. I was surrounded by hysterical women behaving as if the end of the world had come. I tried to calm them but ended up more terrified than any of them."

"Isn't it wonderful that everything is over?" Phloi said with feeling. "The bad luck has passed."

"Do you believe so, Phloi? Do you think it's really over? That's not what I've heard."

"Oh, Choi, don't say that!"

"But you, Phloi, have nothing to worry about. Fortune's darling, that's what you are. You must have accumulated a lot of merit in your former lives to be so well favoured in the present one. Born into a good family, grown up into a beautiful girl to marry a worthy man who rose to be a Phraya thus making you a Khunying, and now mother of a successful son."

"What are you raving about, Choi?"

"Well, isn't An one of the originators of the plan? It's not a secret any more, Phloi. I'm told by several people that An is one of the important new men."

"He never told me. And I haven't noticed anything exceptionally successful about him. He has the same old position at the ministry."

"He's destined to become a big man, don't you worry, Phloi."

On her subsequent visits during this period, Choi tended to assume a kind of composed, somewhat formal manner when conversing with An—didn't tease him or joke with him any more.

Choi's not the only one to have changed towards An, Phloi remarked to herself. *Luang Osot and Khun Choei are also treating him rather distantly. They used to take a proprietory interest in his doings and to be affectionately concerned about him, and now they barely ask after him when they come to see me. Then there's Khun Un. She's decided to place An where she once placed Khun Prem, or even higher. She's holding him in such high regard that it's embarrassing, even annoying at times. I mustn't rebuke her, though, or she'll be hurt. And what about Phoem and Ot? Must these two invariably change their conversation, conducted these days mostly in a whisper, when An goes over to join them? Praphai's the only one who hasn't changed. An's already a demigod to her so she merely goes on worshipping him as before.*

Then On came home from Ayuthaya. He had had no leave for two months, and he hadn't been home two minutes when his views on the change of government became all too obvious to Phloi. The conversation on the subject took place almost immediately upon On's return between him and Ot, with Phloi listening to them in silence and thinking how fortunate the other brother wasn't home.

"I regret not being in Bangkok that day," said On, looking more angry than regretful.

"What would you have done, Phi On?"

"Anything to uphold the sacredness of the Oath of Loyalty."

"What could you have done singlehandedly when so many approved of what was being done?"

On's clenched jaws became more pronounced. "Ha! If only we had some real man to lead us that day . . . I would have followed him to the bitter end, Ot. Whatever the outcome it would have been a more honourable thing to give a good fight than to let them have it all their own way without putting up the least resistance."

"Phi On," Ot said gently. "Don't think too much. Nai Luang has granted his royal consent. It's over, Phi On."

There was a hard stubborn glint in On's eyes Phloi had never seen before. "Did he grant it willingly, Ot?" he growled. "Or did he do it because he took pity on his people and didn't want to see them take up arms to kill one another? He is our Nai Luang, endowed with kingly compassion—he couldn't have commanded us to go ahead and fight them. But we could have done it for him unasked."

"He has declared his approval of the new system of government, Phi On."

"I'm not so sure," On said brusquely. "I don't think the time has come."

"Umm," Ot murmured, eyeing On reflectively and quoting that French phrase: *"Plus royaliste que le roi."*

Some hours later Phloi and her three sons—An had returned from the office—sat down to their evening rice together. Stealing glances at On and An, Phloi warned herself that this might turn out to be a difficult and uncomfortable meal. She did not anticipate anything more, was not prepared at all for what happened only a few minutes after they had taken their seats.

At the beginning, An, still basking in his triumph and prone to look at the world with a friendly eye, had been perfectly oblivious to On's glowering at him with bitter resentment. Phloi had been making a valiant effort to guard the table against mention of the dangerous subject; she chatted about everyday matters, keeping it light and neutral. But she was fighting a losing campaign, for On was determined to give battle and he got his chance when An said to him, "Well, Phi On, you haven't told me yet what your fellow officers in Ayuthaya think about it?"

"Think about what?" On asked darkly.

"The change, of course—the change to the new regime. I'd be

interested to know if the majority feel we've done the right thing."

"I have no idea what the others think," On replied in a chilling voice. "But I do know this. One officer is very much against it. I am that officer."

"Oh, Phi On!" An exclaimed, genuinely distressed. "But why, Phi On? Will you please tell me why?"

"Very simple. Because it is treason, and I am against treason, against anything and anyone connected with treason."

"Do you call it treason, Phi On?"

"Yes. They who have acted in violation of the Oath of Loyalty are guilty of treason, and even our own brothers, if they are guilty of this crime, must cease to be our brothers!"

An rose from the table. "As you like. If you don't want to consider me your brother, that's up to you . . . For that matter, you're not my mother's son—"

On stood up and with a flick of the hand sent a glass crashing on the floor. Ot got up too, and placed restraining hands on On's arms as their mother cried, "An!" at the top of her voice. "An! Take back what you said. You must apologize to your brother and I want you to do it now."

An looked at his mother, at On, then at Ot, who gave a slight nod urging him to do as he was told. An complied. He said, "For you, Khun Mother . . . I'm sorry, Phi On," and walked out of the room.

On stood still for a minute, gritting his teeth, then he gave way utterly. He came up to Phloi, put his head in her lap and broke into tears. Phloi's thoughts and feelings were in a turmoil and all she could do was stroke On's hair. On's sobbing was the only sound in the room, but inside her muddled head Phloi could hear Khun Prem's voice saying, " He's my son, Mae Phloi . . . My son On . . . Since you want him, he's yours now . . ."

THIRTY-FOUR

THE scene had left Phloi shattered.

Family unity she counted as one of the treasures of life. She had built her home for it on the foundation of love and kindness and tolerance. What was she to do when her sons turned bitter enemies before her eyes? They had hated each other then and Phloi, who loved them both, had been made to suffer more than either. She suffered for both of them. She took pity on both of them. Far be it from her to take sides.

On had deliberately provoked his brother. An had hit back in the cruellest way possible. In making An apologize to his brother, Phloi told herself she was not taking On's side but reassuring him where he stood in her affection.

"... *My son On ... He's yours now, Mae Phloi.*"

It had always been so since the first day Khun Prem had brought them together. He had been her son, never a stepson. That was the truth of their relationship which An's remark was meant to belittle. She could not have allowed that, for An's sake as well as her own.

Far be it from her to take sides. But was she also not aware that she strongly approved of On's adherence to his loyalty? The kind of loyalty she understood and believed in, the kind that had been upheld by generations of her forbears and ingrained in her heart and soul. An was made differently, he saw things from a different angle and in a different light, but he, her own flesh and blood—he too had claim on her compassion, love and support.

She felt torn and tugged this way and that as she sat there stroking On's head. At last he was calm again, calm enough to speak. "I have no other mother but you," he said. "You're the only one I have."

"Yes, my son." Phloi smiled at him. "You're my first son, my first beloved son. Nothing can change that. But you must forgive your brother. He was not himself and didn't know what he was saying. He is your younger brother after all. Forgive him, On, Do it for me."

On made a *krap* in her lap, then left the room. After a while Ot left his chair and came to sit at his mother's feet. Hugging her knees, he said, "My darling, from now on you must try to harden that soft heart of yours a little."

"Yes, Ot?"

"Because with this new thing affecting our lives there will be more problems for you to face, more estrangements, more unexpected scenes and unheard-of events."

"What new thing, son?"

"It's called *kanmuang*—politics, darling. Politics has come to our land. It was here in this room just now."

"Was it responsible for what happened between your brothers? Dear me . . ." Phloi sighed. "What made them act like that I'll never know . . . Oh, Ot, your mother doesn't understand anything." She put a hand on her brow, wiping it as if to clear her mind, but when she spoke again she sounded more wearied than ever. "I feel so old and ignorant. I don't know what's what anymore. You must be my guide, my teacher. Teach me. Explain to me what politics is about."

"I don't think I'm going to prove a competent teacher," Ot said. "I've been trying to explain it to myself. Very difficult going, and with unsatisfactory results. It's such a vast and complex subject."

Nevertheless he did attempt a few simplifications and generalizations, such as:

"Before politics, Phi On was doing his soldiering and Phi An his law, each in his own special field, not interfering with the other's line of business, not called upon to do so. Enter *politics*, and they find themselves thrown together, for politics is one huge all-embracing field; politics widens horizons, pulls down walls and invites everybody in. A soldier and a lawyer can meet here to work for the common good of our country—our *muang*—or to disagree as to what that common good might be and fight to the death for what they think is right. Politics gives everyone the right to differ, the right to his own conviction, be he soldier or lawyer, prince or commoner.

"Politics is progress, is civilization, is justice and therefore marvellous, some say; politics is a dirty business, others will tell you. You can put up arguments for or against either side. Politics ennobles, politics corrupts. Politics inspires you with high ideals, gives you the freedom and the opportunity to fulfill yourself, to enjoy the satisfaction of being master of your own destiny rather than having masters to arrange your life for you. Politics also sets brothers against brothers, even sons against fathers. Murders have been committed in its name and in its name great and glorious deeds for mankind have been achieved. Enduring friendships have been forged through politics and through it you can lose all your friends, your money, your liberty, your life."

After weighing the pros and cons, Phloi asked, "Why should we have it then?"

"Because it's here, Mother. Doesn't look like we have any choice but to live with it. It came to us when it did, apparently because the time was ripe for it to do so. If it didn't come then it would have come some other time. A nation changes as it grows, like us humans. I only hope the change goes smoothly and not too many people get hurt."

"Why do you say that, Ot?"

"Well, I'm reminded of that old pond near our house. You remember, I called to you to come and look at it one day—the tide was rising, the pond was fresh and full that day, and the whole fish population turned up to celebrate the new waters. Such a pretty sight. Presently, along came people with their nets, and plenty of fish got caught. I hope not too many people let themselves get so carried away by our new political pond that they forget how dangerous it can be."

Phloi nodded. "An did say something about this being the critical period. We are at a turning point, he said."

"Yes, Mother. Let's pray the critical period doesn't last too long, and that we'll make the right turning."

"I pray that none of my children will get caught. I'm concerned about my children."

Ot smiled. "And I'm concerned about *you*, Khun Mother. You must be brave and strong, my darling. If you are, I'm sure you'll see us safely through."

On left the next day to return to his regiment. Looking at his haggard face when he came in to say goodbye, Phloi suspected he had not slept at all the night before. They chatted in the usual way, as though nothing disastrous had come to pass. As he went out of the room a thought flashed in Phloi's head: perhaps she might not see him for a long time. She instantly chased it out as something undesirable that must be got rid of at once.

Phloi's life with politics during the ensuing months did not radically differ from her former life without it. She was, however, very much aware of its presence in her house when the men in her family gathered about her. Phoem came to call on her and Ot more often than ever before. Or rather, he came to see Ot to have long talks with him, but he did not entirely neglect Phloi. When An was present, he would be polite with him, as though An were a guest and not a nephew. His uncle's changed manner toward him had not escaped An's notice—he didn't have to be particularly observant as Phoem made it obvious. He seemed a little annoyed but did nothing about it; it was the conspicuous way Phoem and Ot would change their discussion when he came into the room that really disturbed him.

One day he questioned Ot in Phloi's presence.

"What do you and Uncle talk about anyway?"

Ot laughed. "What else, dear brother, if not what everybody else all over *Muang Thai* is talking about these days?"

"Well, what is it?"

"Don't you know? Politics, Phi An, politics. What else have we got to talk about? The air is thick with political news. So-and-so is going to be arrested, so-and-so may have to be got out of the way, there'll be an armed clash between such-and-such factions, and so on. Uncle is full of this news. I'm just his appreciative audience. He's very entertaining."

"*Akuson* news," An said.

"What? What news?" The word *akuson* (bad, sinful, malicious) was not unknown to Ot, but this was the first time he had ever heard it employed in this context.

"*Akuson* news," An repeated scornfully. "All lies."

Ot burst into a laugh. "How appropriate! How resonantly appropriate! I must remember to say to Khun Luang Uncle: 'Sir, you've been spreading *akuson* news.' He'd love it."

"Must you be flippant about everything? Get it into your head, Ot, that the problems we're facing now are nothing to joke about. Tell Uncle to watch his tongue. He must not talk too much. It's dangerous."

"I know, Phi An. I tell him that all the time and I will tell him again. I don't think he'll take my advice, though. Ever since the coming of freedom and democracy Uncle has given up all his other hobbies—his doves, his topiaried trees, his caladiums, his crotons, all, in favour of politics. It's his only hobby nowadays."

"I see," An said in a low voice.

"He never talks politics with me," Phloi said, sounding as if she was trying to defend her brother.

Smiling, Ot explained, "On this important subject he says it's not much fun talking to you. He prefers me."

"Ot!" An snapped. "Do you understand what I just said?"

"Yes, Phi An, it's quite clear to me. And I'll warn Uncle, though I don't guarantee he'll listen to me."

Phoem did listen to his nephew. He was a little more cautious after Ot had warned him—not very much, but a little more.

Time passed, during which Phloi often felt something must break soon because there was so much tension one kept hearing about. There was also too much freedom for her peace of mind—freedom of this and that and the other swirling about the atmosphere, freedom, especially, to stage a revolution against everything and everybody. She was both befuddled and intimidated by these words: *seriphap* (freedom), *patiwat* (revolution), and others like them, words making up the new speech everyone was learning, sometimes without much comprehension. She was appalled to hear about pupils staging a *patiwat* against their teachers, and temple boys against the monks who had been looking after them. "What's our *Muang Thai* coming to?" she murmured to herself. When Choi came to see her and made jokes about these new-fangled notions saying, for instance, that if Khun Aunt Sai had been alive today, she, Choi would have served her a memorable revolution, Phloi did not laugh. Her sense of *sanuk* was not at all receptive to revolution.

Meanwhile she had heard nothing from On except that he was well. He had not come home to patch it up with his brother, but Phloi kept on hoping. While the estrangement weighed heavily on her heart she kept assuring herself that with time the two would one day come to understand and truly forgive each other and be reconciled. She only had to be patient.

THAT morning in October, 1933, it was not yet noon when An reached the house. He had rushed back as soon as he had heard. He went straight to Phloi and tried to keep his voice steady as he talked to her.

"I have something to tell you but please don't be alarmed."

Phloi replied calmly, "Tell me anything, An. I feel nothing can alarm me any more."

"We were afraid this might happen, and now it has. I came home to tell you because I don't want you to be frightened by rumours."

"What is it, An?"

"Soldiers from Khorat and some other units up north have moved down to Don Muang. They've now occupied Don Muang. They've sent an ultimatum to the government demanding certain changes."

"What changes?" Phloi asked uninterestedly, thinking, *Politics again! How tiresome.*

"Changes to satisfy themselves. The government is not going to yield. They can't use this sort of coercion on a legitimate govern-ment."

Thinking of what had happened last year, Phloi was not entirely convinced. However, she merely said, "And if the two sides can't agree?"

"Then the two sides will have to fight. Most of the Armed Forces are loyal to the government, I should think."

"You mean . . . a civil war?" Phloi began to feel alarmed in spite of herself.

"It could come to that." An sighed. "Let's hope not." He paused, gave another sigh, and went on reluctantly. "I have something else to tell you. The soldiers in Ayutthaya have joined the other side."

Phloi's heart skipped a beat. "On . . . ?"

"Yes, Mother, Phi On's in this with them."

"Oh my son, my son, what are we going to do?"

"I know you love Phi On very much, but there's nothing you can do. You must resign yourself to the fact that you can do nothing. He's old enough, and he's responsible for his own misguided actions—for his own karma, if you like."

But you're wrong, An, Phloi thought when he had left her. *There's so much I can do for your brother. When he was a little boy he would come to me when he got hurt, for me to dry his tears. He may be a grown man now but I can still give him solace when he needs it. If there was fighting and he got wounded I could nurse him. Where are you now, On? Where is he? Oh please don't let him die. I can help him, do you hear, An? Why do you call it his misguided action? I'm in no position to judge who's right or who's wrong. Are you sure you're absolutely in the right, An? . . .*

The following day—it was in the afternoon, as Phloi was wondering about On's whereabouts and feeling downhearted and miserable—Ot came in to sit down beside her. "Darling, I have another piece of bad news for you." He was smiling, though, as he said that.

"What now?" Phloi asked in a tired voice.

"It's about Khun Luang Uncle this time."

"Which Luang—Luang Osot? What's the matter—is he sick or something?"

"No, Mother, the other Luang. My Uncle Phoem. He was arrested this morning. As soon as I heard I went to the police station. He was in a cell but they wouldn't let me go near him. No visitors allowed."

Phloi was so stunned she could hardly talk. Finally she asked, "What has he done?"

"I'm not sure. It seems an aeroplane of the provincial forces was flying past his house and Uncle Phoem was in the street looking at the sky, jumping up and down gleefully, yelling, 'It's the end now, folks!' And later in the morning the police came and took him away." When he finished speaking Ot broke into a giggle, and was scolded by his irate mother.

"Don't you dare laugh! Your uncle is a prisoner behind bars and you laugh! Nothing like this has ever happened to our family. If your grandmother were still alive this would have killed her. Oh Khun Luang, oh Pho Phoem, what terrible karma has brought this about!"

"I'm sorry, Mother," Ot said contritely, but added, "I couldn't help laughing—the whole thing struck me as very funny . . . And Mother, you mustn't think of it as a shameful thing. If he was arrested for theft, or embezzlement, yes, that would have been a disgrace to the family name. But his shouting was a kind of political act—or must have been taken as such by the police, so it makes him a kind of political prisoner, and this is not looked down upon, Mother. Why, some even regard it as an honour. Uncle might even brag about this experience when he comes out."

This was entirely new to Phloi, that you could be honoured for having been put in jail.

"Politics gives me headaches, " she said. "Your uncle was acting in his usual high-spirited way without meaning any harm. It was heartless of those who arrested him . . . What about his wife, did you see her?"

"She was sobbing and sobbing. She's sent him some food but we don't know if it will get to him."

"What are we going to do, Ot?"

"Why don't you have a word with Phi An, darling? He knows a lot of powerful people. He could go and explain to them about Uncle's natural high spirits and essential innocence and ask them to intervene on his behalf."

Phloi talked to An that evening.

"I did tell him to be careful, "An said. "In a way it's a good thing he's arrested. It will teach him a lesson."

Of course, Phloi was furious. "How can you say that, An? He's my brother, my only brother, and you expect me to abandon him—leave him in that cell? If you can't or won't help him, will you be good enough to send me to see someone who can? I will prostrate myself at the feet of this person and beg him to help my brother."

"Please, Khun Mother," An said in his sensible tone of voice. "Of course I will help. But we can't rush things, especially not now. I'll find out what should be done, what must be done, what's the right way to go about it. It doesn't sound to me like a very serious case. It will be all right, Khun Mother. Stop worrying about it."

The next few days saw Phloi spending most of her time sitting in front of Ot's radio listening to the news of the fighting. For it had come to that. Thais were fighting Thais, each side branding the other as enemy of the nation, each side professing its loyalty to His Majesty and proclaiming this loyalty to be the reason and inspiration of its action. From inside the Inner Court Choi sent news that His Majesty and his party had left Hua Hin by special train for Songkhla farther south, which information only served to increase Phloi's confusion and anxiety. She had had no news at all from or about On.

Phoem's incarceration at the police station lasted five days. Upon his release he came straight to see Phloi and Ot. "I'm all right, Mae Phloi, I'm all right." Indeed he appeared to be his buoyant self. I got five days for my five words—what do you think of that, eh? They put me in there without ceremony and they let me out equally without ceremony."

"Don't talk about it, Khun Luang. You can forget it now. Your bad luck is over. But do be careful from now on, won't you?"

"Did you think I was afraid, Mae Phloi?" Phoem went on expansively. "Never. I've lived a long time and I've been through a lot, so I don't scare easily. So let them put me inside again if they want to. They can't change the way I feel about things in five days or five years. They can kill me—then maybe they can stop me from speaking my mind."

"You've come out stronger than when you went in, Uncle," Ot told him.

"No, Ot. I'm the same as before. I just won't have people try to bully me, that's all."

He stayed until An came home that day but would only exchange a few conventional words with him. On later occasions An seemed to take the hint and would discreetly withdraw when his uncle came to the house.

Soon it became apparent that the government side was winning. The forces from the provinces, now generally referred to as "rebels," began to retreat to the north, pursued by government soldiers. Still no news about On. Phloi dared not speculate what his future might be; she only allowed herself to hope that he was still alive and that she would see him again.

THIRTY-FIVE

TO the majority of the people it was a political incident which had little to do with them. It did not affect them personally as it did Phloi and women like her who had sons or husbands taking part in the fighting. For Phloi the affair turned into a tragedy when, with the defeat of the faction now called the rebels, her son On emerged as one of the officers now being imprisoned somewhere who would in due course have to stand trial for treason.

Phloi beseeched An to help his brother with tears running down her face, and when An, while trying to comfort her as best he could, was obliged to tell her he could do nothing at this stage, she cried harder, and charged him with still harbouring rancour against his brother over an old quarrel. "Please help him for my sake," she implored. "Or if not for mine then for your father's sake." She was like a drowning victim clutching at any twig floating by.

"The quarrel has nothing to do with it," An assured her. "In fact I felt very sorry about it the next day and have been wanting to make it up with Phi On. But he never did come back . . . No, it has nothing to do with my not being able to help get him out of this, Mother. This is a big issue, Mother. It is of the utmost gravity and lies beyond my power to intervene. He's going to be tried for treason. You know as well as I do how extremely serious that is. I'd like to mention a few other points. One is that I'm being watched, which is understandable under the present circumstances. If I went round actively trying to secure help for Phi On I would definitely come under suspicion. Now, I would do it if I thought there was any chance at all to get him out. But even if there was a chance I would still ask myself another question: would Phi On himself want me to do it? The answer to this is no, he wouldn't. You and I know his character very well. He did what he did believing in the rightness of it—that he was misguided is another matter. And he's true to his friends. If by a miracle we could get him out, would he be willing to leave his less fortunate friends in there? I believe not."

Phloi had to admit he was right. After a few moments of silence she asked, "Where is On. Do you know?"

"No, Khun Mother. They've been separated and put in various places . . . Why?"

"I'd like to go and visit him."

"Oh, please, not yet. It's—it's too soon . . . you might be—misunderstood."

"Can't a mother visit her son? What's become of our *Muang Thai*, will you tell me?"

"Please, Khun Mother. Phi On is not the only son you have. Spare a thought for your other children."

"My duty is to help *all* my children when they're in trouble."

"They may forbid visitors at present."

"Let's find out. If they do, they do. But I must try to get to see him."

At this point Ot came into the room, walking softly, almost on tiptoe. Nodding at him to come and keep their mother company, An took his leave quietly.

"Ot, my son," Phloi said to him. "I feel as if the sky had fallen on my head. I'm having a nightmare, Ot."

"Pinch yourself, Mother, maybe you'll wake up."

"If I could only wake up."

Then Ot spoke to her softly, as to an unhappy child. "Darling, I have something to give you, but you must promise not to cry any more. I feel so sad when I see you cry. Give me your word you won't cry and you can have it."

Touching his head affectionately, Phloi smiled. "All right, treat me like a cry-baby. I deserve it. What have you got for me? A sweet? A toy? I promise not to cry, so please give it to me now."

It was a crumpled piece of paper. It was a note from On, written to his mother from a field in Bang Khen, near Don Muang, "a field," the note said, "belonging to all of us on both sides and now we must try to destroy one another on it."

He begged her forgiveness for doing this without having consulted her. He tried to explain what made him do it. "Please believe my sincerity, that I'm doing this not in order to gain power or glory for myself. All my life I've been taught to be grateful and loyal to Phra Chao Yu Hua, by you, by my father, by all my teachers. I cannot imagine my life without having these feelings to guide me. They are the creed I live by. My duty as a soldier is to defend the land, defend the royal power, to give up my life if need be for my king."

He did not want her to think for a moment that he liked what he had to do against his fellow Thais. "Every time I shoot or order the shooting it's my own heart that's the target. I'm sinning against my own brothers—that's what it feels like. I want to run away sometimes but I can't, can't leave the men under me, can't leave my officer friends. We've sworn to die together. When I glimpse running figures in the distance I realize they, too, were my friends until not many days ago. We too swore to die together, were all the king's men together, some of them could well have been under my command, some my superior officers, some my former teachers. It's agony having to fight them.

"I long to be with you, my most revered and beloved mother. We will be together again, this is my dearest wish, but if it doesn't come true, please know that my last thoughts will be with you. I'm filled with sorrow I cannot describe. Forgive me, dearest Mother, for having caused you so much trouble."

Putting the note down wearily, Phloi asked, "Where did you get it, Ot?"

"A farmer brought it this morning. He said a young officer gave it to him some days ago, gave him some money too, but he was so busy fleeing the scene of battle he couldn't get to us sooner . . . And now, Mother, don't forget your promise not to cry, because here is *another* letter from Phi On to you."

"Oh, Ot, give it to me quickly . . . Who brought this one?"

Ot handed her the second letter. "Uncle Phoem did, though he refused to tell how he got it—he just smiled, looking quite proud and calling himself a clever man."

This second letter was written after On had surrendered. He was now in a prison somewhere in Bangkok—he wouldn't say where. "Please don't try to find out. Don't try to come and see me. The authorities are watching everybody's movements and you would be creating problems for yourself and for An and Ot as well. I'm ready to accept the consequences of my failure and hope to do it without having to make things worse for my younger brothers. Perhaps I shouldn't even be writing you, but I felt I had to, otherwise you would worry too much. So this is to let you know that I'm in good health, I have everything I need and I'm not at all unhappy. I miss you very, very much, but there will be time, I tell myself, for us to meet again, there will be time for me to express my love and respect at my mother's feet in person."

There was a postscript: "May I repeat—please don't come to visit me. I feel quite calm, but I don't trust myself not to break down in front of you, and I don't want to do that."

"Mother," Ot said, "I think I'll let you cry after all. It will make you feel better."

There were no messages from On during the trial; all the information Phloi had was what she read in the papers and what was relayed to her from various sources by her two younger sons, her relations and friends, who shared her anxiety, gave her every support and encouraged her to go on hoping, even though, as the trial proceeded, all signs were pointing in only one direction: guilty as charged. The question—the most vital question—was how severe the sentence would be.

Meanwhile Phloi learned that Their Majesties would pay a visit to Europe. The news did not unduly arouse her curiosity. They had been to America some time ago and the purpose of that journey was for His Majesty to receive treatment for his eyes. She understood that this trip, too, would be taken for medical reasons. Now it was Phloi's hope for her son as well as for the other defendants in the trial that Nai Luang's clemency would prevail in the end, considering how they had proved their loyalty to him to the fullest degree. Ot had told her this was wishful thinking, that the government would have the last say, not Nai Luang, but Phloi would not let him convince her. The news of Their Majesties' coming trip did not dim that hope. They would be gone for only a few months, as she was given to understand.

Phoem, however, was of a different opinion. On the day of Their Majesties' departure Phoem had been to the farewell audience at the royal landing. He dropped by to see Phloi afterwards, dressed in his civilian full dress uniform and dying of thirst from the heat of the sun and the warmth of the costume.

Phloi expressed her surprise at his having been there, for as a rule he was never too keen about attending these formal occasions. "I'm not surprised you're surprised," Phoem said. "I never did like attending these functions. Haven't got the right temperament for it, and then my back would ache from having to bow to so many people—they being Their Excellencies and me a mere little Luang. And then, Mae Phloi, one day after the change of government, I decided to attend the royal audience at Chitrlada station—it was the day Phra Chao Yu Hua returned from Hua Hin. If you'd been there you'd have cried, Mae Phloi. I'd never seen such a meagre turnout for our king in all my life. 'Where's the usual crowd gone to?' I asked myself. The station looked so sad and deserted. Well, since that day I've not missed one of these occasions."

"And what about today?" Phloi asked. "Did many people come?"

"We had a fair-sized gathering, Mae Phloi, I'm happy to say. But it was not a happy occasion, not at all." And then he said it. "I felt it was the last time—I felt I'd never have another chance to see them again."

"Are you sick or something, Khun Luang? What made you think you won't live to bid them welcome when they return?"

"What I mean to say is that I don't think they'll return, Mae Phloi."

"What! What are you saying, Khun Luang?!"

"Listen, Mae Phloi. I watched Phra Chao Yu Hua as he glanced round at all of us. There was such a sad expression in his eyes, Mae Phloi. Then when he was on board, standing on the deck and waving to us, I could see his gaze sweeping the skyline. He was taking leave of his palaces, Mae Phloi, and something told me he was committing the sight to memory because he would not see it again. I don't think it was my imagination, Mae Phloi."

"Stop it, Khun Luang. I can't bear it. There's no earthly reason why he shouldn't come back."

'There is, Mae Phloi. There has been disagreement between Nai Luang and the government on a number of things, don't you know?"

"No, I don't. As far as I know Nai Luang has been most graciously agreeable to their plans and proposals and appointments and what have you. And in fairness to the government, I must say they're treating him with respect and reverence."

"You wait and see, Mae Phloi. Nai Luang and the government may be aiming for the same goal, but this doesn't mean they see eye to eye on how to fulfil it. Nai Luang is as democratic as any of them, if not more, and—I don't know—perhaps the government would prefer to have him not so democratic and leave them to be democratic in their own way."

"You make my head ache, Khun Luang."

"And my own too, Mae Phloi." Phoem smiled and, leaving democracy alone, went on to chat about more mundane matters.

The trial went on. The sentences were passed. Not all at once, but case by case, a few at a time. Life imprisonment . . . Twenty years . . .

When the inevitable day came, it was Ot who broke the news to his mother. Everything went black at that instant and when she came to she found herself in Ot's arms. He led her to the bed, made her lie down, and from the betel box he took the bottle of smelling-salts and held it near her nose. Phloi kept her eyes shut for a while, opened them to see the ceiling sway above her and shut them again.

"Don't go away, Ot," she murmured. "I'm not feeling well."

Gently waving a fan over her, Ot said, "I'm not going anywhere, darling. Lie still and don't talk."

Some minutes went by. Then Phloi asked, "Does An know?"

"Yes, Mother. In fact, he asked me to tell you. He said he couldn't do it himself. Couldn't bear to look at you." Ot handed her a handkerchief. He sat by quietly while she wept in sorrow and pity.

She couldn't understand it, she moaned, why they should want to have her son executed when they had given many others the gift of life—life in prison, yes, for a great number of years or even till death. She had feared that that might be the punishment meted out to On—that was the worst she had feared, and now she would have welcomed that fate as good fortune.

"Phi On was not merely obeying orders," Ot said. "According to all evidence he was much more seriously involved than many others. Phi On himself confessed to his active role, Mother."

"I must go to him," Phloi said.

"Of course. But you must first of all make yourself well and strong."

Phloi sat up. "There's nothing wrong with me. I feel all right now, Ot. We must arrange to go and see him as soon as possible."

Throughout that day and the following day Phloi's close friends and relatives came to visit her. They left it to her to start discussing On's case. Phloi talked openly about it and they consoled and comforted her, although she could see that they were not feeling any more hopeful than she was. In the end, however, she did find a flimsy something to cling to, thanks to Phoem and his stubborn optimism.

At first she had protested to his "Keep calm, Mae Phloi."

"How can I, Khun Luang?" she sobbed. It was so callous, so unfeeling of him to suggest it. "If he were dying of an illness perhaps I'd be able to accept it, but I can't resign myself to—to this."

"I'm not asking you to resign yourself," Phoem went on serenely. "I say keep calm. The judges have delivered the sentence, but it's not going to be carried out today or tomorrow, you understand. On lives, Mae Phloi. There is time to get the sentence commuted."

"How, Khun Luang?"

"By submitting a petition for mercy to Phra Chao Yu Hua."

"You really think there's hope, Khun Luang?"

"Mae Phloi," Phoem said, doing his best to sound like a wise old man, "as long as we can breathe we can hope, my child."

THIRTY-SIX

THE next day saw Phoem back at his sister's house. He had spent most of the night thinking about her and On, and he came expressly to make sure she was not making herself ill with worries, to prevent her from despairing, to go on with his good work and convince her that all was not lost. He made no more mention of the petition for mercy, but he would remind her (here he dropped his voice to a whisper although there was no one else about) that the execution of the condemned men could not take place without a royal command and in his opinion Phra Chao Yu Hua would thoroughly go over every detail before consenting to affix his signature to it, and in his considered opinion it was most unlikely that Phra Chao Yu Hua would consent easily.

"After all, Mae Phloi, this is no ordinary crime. The so-called rebels are not armed bandits who have robbed and murdered. Some of them were in high positions, even exalted positions, others have friends and former colleagues in all sorts of key places. The affair is not a simple one, as we now know, and though the court has decided, the carrying out of the sentences requires delicate handling on the part of the authorities. I think if Phra Chao Yu Hua chooses to have the death sentence commuted no one will dare go against his wish."

Phloi was grateful to her brother for his encouraging words while recognizing that the rosy views they expressed were based on no other source but inside his own head. "I haven't lost all hope," she said. "But I don't want to let myself be lulled by false hopes, to be over-optimistic and then to be deceived." She sighed. "Oh, Khun Luang, I feel I've aged a great many years and I've cried so much I have no tears left. We mustn't forget, Khun Luang, that in everybody's eyes On has committed treason, and the penalty for that act . . ."

"No, Mae Phloi," Phoem interrupted her. He was brimful with confidence. "I want you to think back to the year 130 of this our Ratanakosin Era—only twenty odd years ago, you know—and remember what happened that year. It caused the greatest stir, it was something much more sensational than the recent trouble insofar as the person of the king was concerned. A conspiracy to assassinate our lord and sovereign! Think of that, Mae Phloi! And were any of the conspirators put to death for their crime? Not one. Nai Luang in his infinite mercy let everyone live. A few of them were imprisoned, yes, but these were freed under a royal amnesty towards the end of his reign. Have you forgotten all that, Mae Phloi?"

No, but somehow she had not thought of it until now. The 130th Ratanakosin year, yes, she remembered it very well. Early in the sixth reign it was, His Late Majesty King Vajiravudh having ascended the throne only the year before. She remembered Khun Prem telling her about it, his voice trembling with emotion. A band of army officers and civilian officials plotting against Nai Luang, but the plot had been discovered in time.

"Let us give thanks to the Lord Buddha and all that is sacred in the universe, Mae Phloi." The plan had been to shoot him at the Bangkok Noi station as the train brought him back from Nakhon Pathom, but he had been protected by the gods and his own glorious merit. Later on it appeared that the list of the conspirators had been tampered with, resulting in the absence of many names that should have been there. The ones whose names had remained were arrested and tried, but as Phoem said, our late Nai Luang, the embodiment of compassion, had decreed that there be no death penalty . . .

Phloi remembered, and took heart. The light of hope, flickering on and off, refusing to be extinguished, shone a little brighter once again.

She could make out a ray of light in the dark gloom of the future. She could feel a warm radiance emanating from the kingly virtue of benevolent and loving compassion.

On would live.

She thought of what the blind fortune-teller had told her many years ago: On would go to prison but he would come out again.

Fortune-tellers aren't always right . . . Sometimes they are, though. Quite often they are . . . amazingly often.

On would live.

A royal pardon. Nai Luang's clemency . . .

"KHUN Mother," An took her hands and held them in his. "I know you're planning to go and see Phi On. You're having Ot arrange the trip without saying anything to me because you thought I might not like it. Mother, you don't realize how much I feel for you and for Phi On. You think I don't care? I do. Please believe I do! The only thing that worries me is that the visit may make you feel worse instead of better. I'd like you to bear in mind always that Phi On is a prisoner, and be prepared to see him living in certain conditions altogether unfamiliar to you which you may find unpleasant, even shocking. I'd like you to prepare yourself so you won't be distressed by what you're going to see at Bang Khwang."

Phloi asked herself how it could be possible for her not to feel distressed at the sight of On languishing away in prison, but to An she said, "I'll be all right, my dear. I've adjusted myself to the fact that your brother is not living at home."

"Let me know a few days in advance, "An said, "and I'll get a motor launch to take you there and back. Ot will go with you, of course."

Phloi looked after him as he walked out of the room, wondering if he, too, would not like to come with her. She believed he wanted to, she believed he cared for his brother, but she also believed he would nonetheless feel obliged to stay away, because he couldn't be sure what On's reaction to his visit might be, or perhaps because he had to be careful lest his colleagues in the new regime, especially the more important ones, put a wrong interpretation on such a visit; and she came to the conclusion (not for the first time) that uninterested as she was in this new thing called politics, it persistently refused to leave her alone. It had started to interfere with her life long before she had been forced to take note of its existence. That it had been responsible for putting On where he was today she had no doubt at all. It had also taken An away, though he lived here in the same house with her. Oh, he had his filial piety still: he loved and respected her, he was grateful to her and was concerned about her, but . . . but all the same there was virtually no contact between them. He loved her as a mother while keeping her at a distance as a person. Under the spell of politics—oh, yes, she blamed it!—he had come to regard her as a survivor from a past, and far from perfect, era, someone with fixed antiquated ideas who could never understand what he was doing. He had little to say to her these days, nor to Ot for that matter, (perhaps because Ot understood too much?), and there was a distinct coolness between him and his Uncle Phoem. The inconstancy of human relationship was something she had become acquainted with quite early in life, but it had never manifested itself to her in so blatant a manner and with such disturbing frequency as over this past year. Here Phloi was also thinking of some of her friends, or rather of a number of people she had counted as friends. One group of friends had arbitrarily dropped her after the change of government; another had come flocking to her house, bringing excessive goodwill and an ill-concealed expectation that friendship with An's mother would provide access to An himself, hence to his eminently promising niche in the new scheme of things, hence to a few more doors of opportunity for themselves. How these people must have been confounded by On's role in the recent event! At any rate, now that On had been tried and convicted, the opportunity-seekers had stopped coming to see her . . .

She thought of what Khun Choei had said to her during their conversation one day recently. ". . . The impermanence of things has been getting me down, Mae Phloi. If I didn't have a husband to look after I think I should renounce the world and go take up the meditative life somewhere. I feel eighty years old, hopelessly out-of-date and fed up with the present."

Choi, however, subscribed to the view that since impermanence was permanent, so to speak, why worry? And anyway there was a fundamental sameness about all change—the details might differ and the cast of characters acting out the truth of impermanence kept changing, but this made it all the more interesting. Once she had been rather terrified by the Great Impermanence but now she derived much comfort from it. On hearing this, Phloi, who was not deriving comfort from anything whatever at that moment, said, "I wonder if you're capable of feeling unhappy at all, Choi!" And Choi replied, "Oh, sure, but every time I open my mouth to tell you about it I'm reminded that your unhappiness is greater than mine, so I keep quiet."

Two days before she was to go to Bang Khwang Phloi received another note from On (brought by Phoem, who, as on the previous occasion, enjoyed keeping everybody guessing as to how he had got hold of it), telling her he had no other regrets save for having caused her trouble and unhappiness, and that he was not afraid to die— "though I would have preferred death on a battlefield." He assured her he remained in good health, had enough to eat and was being treated as well as could be expected. He wrote of what he had learned from prison life: "We political prisoners are kept together and apart from the other categories. We're thrown together from morning till night and not surprisingly we have made some new discoveries about one another. A prison is a great place for unmask-ing you, for stripping you of veneer and guise and pretence, a place where you come to appreciate people you never thought much of before, which is all right, but also the place where you lose respect for people you used to regard very highly, which can be a sad and upsetting experience." The letter ended with a prayer that if there were rebirths, he should be born her son again in all of them.

They set off early in the morning for Bang Khwang—Phloi, Ot, and an errand boy to help carry the baskets of food for On and his friends. Boarding the waiting motor launch at the Tha Chang Wang Na landing, they travelled north over the peaceful Chao Phraya. From the landing to the mouth of Khlong Bang Lamphu, then from Bang Khun Phrom to Samsen, Phloi's gaze fell on the several palaces along the way—they belonged to our high-ranking princes of the realm, these graceful mansions standing among trees and lawns in their spacious compounds. Phloi had been to some of these palaces in their heyday and had felt herself in a storied land where all was light, colour and gaiety. Most of them were now closed up, uninhabited except for a few caretakers, and they were looking so forsaken and rundown this beautiful morning that Phloi's heart ached for them. On such a morning on the Chao Phraya, you might be on your way to a prison to visit a son under sentence of death, but your thoughts could keep going back to the days long past, the days of giggling boatfuls of Inner Court girls on their way to Bang Pa-in, of candlelit flower floats under a bright moon, of processions of the royal barges with their fabulous prows moving to the accompaniment of the boat chants. You could still hear the singing, the rousing rhythm, and see in your mind's eye the boatmen in their red costume raising and lowering their gilded oars . . . The Chao Phraya of lovely moments, of haunting memories, Phloi thought with a sigh as the ordinary everyday craft took her nearer and nearer to On. They had passed under the Rama VI railway bridge, a comparatively new sight on the river, having been opened only a few years back at the beginning of the present reign; now came the mouth of Khlong Bang Khen, succeeded by Wat Khema and after that, Bang Tanao Si.

Then Bang Khwang at last. Ot, who had been keeping silent out of respect for his mother's mood, touched her arm gently as if not wishing to awaken her too abruptly. "Here we are, Mother."

Phloi cringed from the sight of the prison. She had not expected it to look comfortable, but neither had she come prepared for the grimness of it. There was an air of finality about that grimness which she found depressing beyond words. She glanced at the other visitors, at the men, women and children who had arrived in other boats, drawing solace from their presence and mutely extending to them her heartfelt sympathy. They all made their way together to the massive gate of the prison, entered, and after the necessary formalities went to wait in the visiting area parallel to the long barred enclosure looking safe enough to house some fierce beasts of prey. They waited, and after some time heard the noise of opening doors in the back, of the guards shouting something or other, and of iron chains dragging on the floor.

Prisoner On lowered his head on the rough bench behind the bars to pay respects to his mother. Phloi quickly looked away from the chain he carried with him, felt a sob rising in her throat but managed to produce a smile of sorts, and to utter a few words.

"I missed you so much. Are you well, my son?"

On's voice was cheerful enough. "I'm quite all right, Mother. It's so good to see you. I'm so happy you're here, Khun Mother." Then he turned his attention to Ot. "How are you, Ot? Many thanks for having the food boxes sent. We've been getting them, and let me tell you they're greatly appreciated. Prison fare needs to be somewhat supplemented, as you may have guessed."

"What food-boxes?" Phloi asked.

"Ot has hired a woman living near here to do some catering for us occasionally, Khun Mother."

"You didn't tell me, Ot . . . That's very nice . . . So you have enough to eat then? Do you need anything else?"

"You're not to worry, Mother. I live quite well here, really."

"We've brought you lots of food, son. You can share it with your friends."

"Wonderful! I'll tell them it's from you."

That was the tenor of their conversation for the whole of that all too short visit: resolutely unemotional, yet there was no strain, and the pleasant, seemingly inconsequential remarks served perfectly well to convey their love and concern for one another. A few yards away from the spot assigned to them, an attractive girl was crying openly, and the young man behind the bars was saying to her across the space that separated them, "Please don't cry, Anong. I'm going to be all right, you know . . . I want you to take good care of yourself . . . Look after our children, Anong."

Sharing the girl's sorrow made Phloi feel more able to cope with her own. It was not until afterwards, during the journey back to Bangkok, that she broke into uncontrollable sobs, and this, incidentally, happened just after Ot had commended her on her "excellent behaviour in front of Phi On."

As the days went by Phloi became increasingly hopeful that the death sentence would be commuted. All the news she received, even from those who had been sceptical, pointed in that direction. She would now accept the lesser misfortune of On being in prison and do her utmost to make things as easy as possible for him under the circumstances.

Alas, there was bad news at the same time, bad for everyone, whether or not they had a son in prison. A sense of impending doom came over Phloi when she first heard of it from her brother Phoem.

"Didn't I tell you, Mae Phloi, that day Nai Luang left for Europe? I said it looked as if he would not return, didn't I? I told you that if Nai Luang and the government could come to no agreement on—on a number of things, he would choose not to come back. Well, it looks like they can't and Nai Luang is not coming back. He's going to abdicate."

"It's not possible, " Phloi said hoarsely.

"It is nowadays, Mae Phloi."

"And our *Muang Thai*, Khun Luang, what will become of it? Who is going to be our Nai Luang then?"

Phoem made a few conjectures. There being no more royal sons left of Queen Saowabha, the Queen Mother of the late Rama VI and the present monarch, Rama VII, the succession, he thought, would go to the line of Queen Sawang Watana, but of course he couldn't be sure.

According to An, everything was being done by the government to avert a crisis.

"Everything, Phi An?" Ot smiled oddly when he asked this question.

"Yes. We've explored every avenue and made every conceivable effort. We don't want him to abdicate, you understand."

"There's one thing you haven't tried, Phi An, and that's to let him have his way for a change. Why don't you try it?"

"I see you're being flippant again, Ot."

His Majesty's abdication became an established fact in the hot month of March, 1935. It was Ot who broke the news to his mother.

"I don't want to believe it," Phloi said feebly. "I don't want to see our country in this situation. Oh, Ot, it is a great, great pity."

"It is indeed, Mother. Democracy hasn't been with us for very long, and now we've lost one of its staunchest champions."

RAMA VIII

THIRTY-SEVEN

PHLOI, aged over fifty, had started to call herself a *khon si phaendin*, a person of four reigns, having been born in the reign of King Chulalongkorn, Rama V, and at present a loyal subject of King Ananda Mahidol, Rama VIII.

As a *khon si phaendin* she considered herself very much an elderly type, especially this morning as she chatted with Ot while studying a photograph of the king—the new Nai Luang—which Ot had obtained for her at her request. She talked to Ot about the old days, recalling the occasions on which she had seen the late Prince Father of Nai Luang, had paid homage to him, had had the opportunity, to observe him at close quarters. She referred to Nai Luang's Prince Father as Thun Kramom Daeng, "Daeng" being his nickname and "Thun Kramom" an epithet signifying the highest princely rank, and she told Ot they had all loved him—everyone who had known him, including herself.

"Nai Luang looks so much like the prince," she said, giving the photograph another scrutiny. "You'd say they came out of the same mould." Then she sighed, and spoke of what had been on her mind since the day His Royal Highness Prince Ananda Mahidol, not quite ten years old, had been proclaimed king, the eighth monarch of the Chakri Dynasty.

"Oh, Ot," she said, "I feel sorry for him somehow. Look at him, our lord and master. How dear he is! But oh so young, so little, so defenceless. I feel as though a son or a grandson were being bullied."

Shaking his head affectionately at her, Ot said, "Come, come, darling. To bully Nai Luang would definitely be unconstitutional. I know how you feel about him. You not only love him as Nai Luang but you feel very very protective towards him. But don't worry too much, darling. He's being very well protected, very well looked after, you know."

"Oh, I'm aware of that, my son. But think of it . . . . Think of little boys his age running about, living in a carefree sort of way, eating, playing, having fun, being themselves—oh, you know what I mean. Then think of Nai Luang on the throne—a magnificent life, I grant you, but full of restrictions and difficulties such as we ordinary mortals can never know and can only guess at. Even in the best of times and having the right age for it Nai Luang's lot is an arduous one, Ot. But when you're an innocent boy and our country is not what it used to be . . . That's why I can't help feeling the way I do . . . ." Feeling very much the way many old people feel towards the young ones who are most precious to them, she might have added.

Thus Phloi began her life under the new reign—a loyal and loving subject, not in awe of her new Nai Luang (at least not in the way she had been of his grandfather and uncles before him) but personally and deeply interested in his welfare, following closely the news about his progress at school abroad and waiting for the day when he would return to his kingdom.

The new reign had brought good news, good enough for Phloi. The death sentence issue would not be re-activated. On would live, and Phloi had made up her mind not to yearn for his early release but to accept the inescapable fact that he would be deprived of a normal existence for some years to come. Like any mother Phloi would like to see him enter monkhood, for a time, then marry a suitable wife and have children like other men, but for the moment to have him alive and well was blessing enough—that, and being able to go and see him and send him gifts as often as she wished.

Meanwhile other people in her household needed her care and attention, the old ones particularly. Phloi had nursed Khun Prem's two aunts through their last days. Khun Nian had died about a year after the change of government, and Khun Nui not long after her sister had gone. Now there was Khun Eldest Sister Un, still living withdrawn from the world in her small bungalow in the compound exactly as she had been doing since her removal here from the ancestral home in Khlong Bang Luang, dressed in exactly the same mode as she had always dressed since the days of her youth, seated erect—though not so erect as last year—and immaculate, on the floor amid her tea things and betel trays which now seemed an extension of herself. Khun Un had aged, but because she had never changed her ways she continued to give an impression of per-manence and durability. She was also as devoted to Praphai as ever, though the girl had somewhat outgrown their close relationship and was always criticizing her aunt for treating her like a child.

The other important senior member of Phloi's household was the maid Phit—Granny Phit to everyone from the Khunying to the gardener's youngest child. Granny, retired after untold years of service, had been given her own living quarters not far from the main house and was now served in her turn by a personal maid assigned exclusively to her. She could hardly move about but this didn't seem to bother her at all. Her mind was alert and she had yet to grow bored with living each day as it came. Phloi dropped by to chat with her all the time, doing it to give as well as to receive pleasure. Phit was her special link with the past. Who else could reminisce so amusingly, so heart-warmingly, about Mother and Chao Khun Father, or about the way things had been, going back to a bygone era even before Phloi had been born? Granny Phit made the long-vanished days as fresh as yesterday; she also made the present more flavourful by sprinkling a lot of the past on it.

And she loved to discuss Phloi's children, one of her favourite themes being how they resembled or differed from this or that parent or grandparent. She'd said this about An: "He may look more like you, Khun Phloi, but there's plenty of Khun Prem's character in him. Excitable, earnest, full of determination ... and always this great liking for the latest and the newest. I don't mean women. Khun Prem was blameless on that score."

And about Ot: "He has inherited some of his father's features but in heart and mind he takes after your brother Khun Phoem in many ways, except he has more wisdom. . ."

"What about Praphai?" Phloi once asked her.

"Ah . . . she's a flirt, like your mother."

"Like my mother!" Phloi cried. "Granny, what are you saying?"

Granny Phit chuckled benignly as she went on pounding the betel nuts in her small brass mortar. "Yes, my darling Khun Phloi, you have a beautiful daughter who is a flirt like your mother, good woman that she was. So you've got to keep a strict eye on that young lady, haven't you? Pity I can't help you now that I'm so old and feeble."

Phloi's method of "keeping a strict eye" on her one and only daughter in this first year of the new reign consisted mainly of not allowing her to go out at night without a brother to escort her. Ot obliged from time to time, but since he'd rather stay home if given a choice the honour usually fell upon the more sociable An. In the daytime Praphai went gallivanting with her girl friends quite freely—with only one condition: she had to tell her mother where she was going. This was the new custom, the new freedom adopted by the younger generation, and the confidence of it, the audacity of it, had not ceased to amaze Phloi (with her memories of life behind the Inner Gates) although she had more or less adjusted herself to living with it.

One of the most exciting words in Praphai's young world must be the word "party" (pronounced *pati* with the accent on the last syllable), it seemed to Phloi, listening to her daughter talk both prior to and after attending one. In the old days, Phloi reflected, we only had the tonsure, the wedding, the ordination, the funeral rites, calling them all *ngan*—"*ngan* wedding," "*ngan* funeral," and so on (*ngan* means "work," and a great deal of work is indeed required at these gatherings). But now there was this *ngan pati*, sometimes to celebrate a birthday or a wedding anniversary (she and Khun Prem had never had this kind of *ngan*), but very often, to her knowledge, it was for no other purpose but itself—*ngan* for *ngan*'s sake.

She sought further elucidation from Ot.

He laughed. "What do they do at a party? Why, you want to go to one, Mother? To dress smartly and go to eat and drink and gossip away with a lot of people? To dance, too, perhaps?"

"*Farang*-style dancing?" Phloi asked.

Then she learned something new about her daughter. "Of course," Ot said. "Our Praphai is getting to be quite good at it now, coached by Brother An, no mean dancer himself."

Phloi's first reaction was to feel peeved. Why hadn't the girl ever told her? Why had An kept it from her? And why should Ot talk about it in so casual a manner? For her daughter to go dancing like the *farang*s was not to be taken lightly in her view.

However, old-fashioned as she was, or maybe because she *was* old-fashioned, Phloi knew better than to demand the impossible—and to want to understand all about the young people of today would be demanding the impossible. So after letting Ot have his say: "They all do it nowadays . . . There's nothing improper about it, . . . Anyhow, Praphai's always chaperoned by a brother," she dropped the subject.

NOW, under the new reign, a new experience for Phloi: Praphai would be giving a party—here in this house!

"Next month is my birthday, Khun Mother. Will you give me something, please?" "But you always get a present for your birthday, daughter. What would you like this year?" "A party, please, Khun Mother. I've been to so many parties and I should give one in return. Right, Phi Ot?"

"Right, little sister."

"So may I do it, Khun Mother? Throw a party, invite my friends here? . . . Oh thank you, thank you, oh Mother, you've made me so happy . . . And you won't have to do a thing, you won't have to lift a finger. I'll do everything myself, I'll arrange it. Phi Ot will help, won't you, Phi Ot?" "Gladly, little sister." "The front lawn of this house is a perfect place for holding a party. I should have thought of it before. Oh, it will be *sanuk mak*—great fun, Khun Mother. You'll enjoy it . . .'

Praphai's pre-party exuberance infected the entire household. Khun Un beamed her approval, the servants readily entered into the spirit of the thing, Ot the jolly and able assistant grew jollier still, and Phloi, repeatedly told to do nothing except hold herself in readiness to grace the affair as guest of honour, compliantly relaxed and, somewhat to her own surprise, looked forward with amuse-ment mixed with curiosity to her first *ngan pati*.

It came. Here it was. As the late afternoon sun was setting, the birthday girl stood in the middle of the lawn surveying it with satisfaction before the arrival of the first guests. The long, gleaming buffet table looking tasty as well as tasteful, the strings of lights ready to be switched on at the coming of dusk, the gramophone and records in their corner, the tables set not too far apart to accom-modate thirty to forty people, everything as neat and trim as could be, yet gaily welcoming, imparting an air of friendship and fun. The birthday girl, radiantly young, happy and beautiful in the softest shade of pink, wearing round her neck Khun Mother's present (the antique ruby pendant which Chao Khun Father had given Phloi on her tonsure day long ago), was being watched in her turn by Khun Mother, who was seated at a table placed a little farther away from the others as befitted her respected position. She was watching with satisfaction also. And with maternal pride.

Really, Phloi thought to herself, *I may be annoyed with her from time to time, but on the whole I must say I'm pleased. Look how poised and graceful she is, greeting her friends, talking and laughing charmingly and so naturally with the men as with the girls—and how astonishing the way she has of making each one of their gifts seem like a rare treasure. At this age, and in this sort of gathering, I would have felt so helplessly self-conscious, awkward . . . And they're all right, these young men and women . . . Nice manners, well-spoken, you can tell they've had a good upbringing—although they and I, let's face it, don't have very much to say to one another, and with my failing memory I'll never be able to remember all their names . . .*

Phloi was having an interesting time at the party even if these nice young people in themselves did not greatly interest her. With one exception, as it turned out. From the first moment he stood out from the rest of the nice young men, doubtless because he was the only one wearing the traditional *phanung* and five-buttoned jacket—the others were attired in the latest *farang* trousers and coat-and-tie. He had just arrived and had not yet been brought to Phloi's table to be introduced to her. She watched him as he chatted with Praphai, and discovered it was not so much the costume (plus the handsome face) that was holding her attention, but a distinctive something about him, a certain air, a combination of easy dignity and good-humoured gentleness in his demeanour. She didn't expect to find it in one so young. She thought it very attractive and appealing.

Praphai brought him over and smilingly said, "Here's Than Chai Noi, Khun Mother, or perhaps I should say Than Chai Sitthidet," and left them together.

"Please call me Noi, Khunying. Everyone does."

His Serene Highness Mom Chao Sitthidet or Than Chai Noi sat down beside Phloi. They talked. They chatted on and on. Guessing rightly that Phloi would like to know it, Than Chai mentioned without being asked the name of His Highness, his father who had died a few years ago. Then Phloi asked the other question usually asked by an elder of a younger person who was his mother, which Mom (non-royal consort of a prince), and was delighted to learn that Than Chai's mother and herself had known each other in the Inner Court, the lady having been a maid-in-waiting in the Upper Palace while Phloi had been at Sadet's residence. They talked of the Inner Court, of Than Chai's mother, his younger brothers and sisters, and of Phloi's children. Than Chai said he had met An and Ot in Europe and they had been friends ever since, then one day he had been presented to Praphai . . . and now he and Phloi were chattering away like two old friends . . . And what sort of work was Than Chai doing? Oh, working for the government like most. Head of a departmental division. Nothing glamourous, but quite enjoyable.

"May I interrupt?" Ot's voice broke into the conversation. Beaming at them, he said, "Shall I take him off your hands for a while, Mother? If you want some food, Than Chai, you'd better come with me before those boys and girls clean up everything."

Phloi urged him to go and help himself. He did, returning with two platefuls for both of them, and sat down to eat with her.

Later she said to him, "Please come and see us again, Your Highness. An usually works quite late. Praphai is just as often out as in. But Ot and I are always home." She smiled. "If you don't find it too boring in an old woman's company—"

Than Chai laughed. "You're not old. But even if you were I wouldn't be bored. I like old people's company. I grew up in it, you know."

IT was now midnight. The last guests had gone home and the air had turned cool over the quiet lawn. The party was over but its laughter lingered on, accompanying Praphai when she came into her mother's room to thank her again, to make a *krap* of gratitude and give a crushing, loving hug. It had been marvellous fun, thanks to Khun Mother.

"I didn't do anything," Phloi said. "You did it all yourself, daughter. And anyway, you don't need to thank me. When my children are happy, I give thanks."

Then she said, "Your friend Than Chai Noi is such a dear."

"I knew it!" Praphai giggled. "I knew you'd love him. He's the elders' sweetheart. It's that absolutely melting old-world courtesy of his that none of you can resist!"

"Whatever it is, he's very nice ... Ask him to come again. Anytime."

More laughter from Praphai. "Oh, Khun Mother! Don't you know he wants to see me every day? A standing invitation from me and he'll want to move in bag and baggage ..."

This sort of startling remark made one feel more than ever like an elderly *khon si phaendin*, Phloi said to herself, looking after her daughter as she went tripping out of the room, humming a tune.

THIRTY-EIGHT

PHLOI did not know whether her daughter had done what she had asked her to do—to reassure Than Chai Noi that he would always be welcome at their house. It didn't matter really, for Phloi herself had made that offer of hospitality the day of the party and since then, in any case, Than Chai had become their most regular visitor. If it was on a weekday he would drop by after work; on a Saturday or a Sunday he would appear earlier and stay on for hours, quite often sharing the evening rice with them. On presenting himself at Phloi's house he would invariably ask to see her before anybody else, and Phloi, if her daughter was home, would send for her immediately to come and "attend on Than Chai."

Apart from using a number of honorific words of the court language (such as *sawoei* instead of *rap prathan* or *kin* for "to eat;" *sadet* instead of *ma* or *pai* for "to come" and "to go;" *prot* instead of *chop* for "to like") when speaking to or of him, Phloi's children treated Than Chai with the same comradely familiarity as they did their other friends—yet another instance of the modern behaviour, Phloi supposed. She herself would never dream of regarding him as just another ordinary young man, and in his presence always comported herself with especial care, assuming the correct deferential manner. Not for nothing had she been reared in the Inner Court, a manner which was at once modest and dignified, gracefully decorous as well as respectful, a manner which had become instinctive with her, an expression of the love and reverence for her kings past and present and their royal descendants. Than Chai on his part showed the humility of a younger person and accorded her every gesture of esteem as he would his own elder relatives. When these two met they would both be very quick in paying respects to each other, both wanting to be the first one to execute the *wai* with the result that they very often did it simultaneously. Underneath all these courteous attitudes they had a great liking for each other. Than Chai came to Phloi's house not only as her children's friend but because he very much enjoyed being with her. As for Phloi, when he was absent for a few days she would miss him and ask after him as if he were one of the children, and if she knew beforehand he was coming she would carve some fruit and prepare a savoury especially for him—it gave her much joy to feed him and see him take pleasure in her work with the fruit and in her cooking.

On one occasion, with an indulgent smile, Praphai teased her after Than Chai had left. "You are besotted with him, Khun Mother."

"I'm not besotted with anyone," Phloi protested. "He has a lovable character and I love him for it. Nothing wrong in that, is there?"

On that same occasion, Praphai also said, "Actually Than Chai is very nice and I'm glad we're friends. I'm quite fond of him."

Phloi dwelled happily on those remarks for days. They might have been casually uttered, but never mind, they encouraged her to hope all the same. She would consider herself blessed with good fortune indeed were she to have a son-in-law like Than Chai, one she could talk to like a son, one who would look after her and be attentive to her in her old age. Than Chai made it plain enough (short of spelling it out in a formal declaration) that he aspired to that position. It only remained for Praphai to make her choice. Phloi tried to deny to herself that Than Chai's noble birth had anything to do with her hopes, which only showed that it did (otherwise, why try to deny it?) and that while she genuinely admired and felt a tender affection for him as a human being, she was also immensely pleased at the possibility of having her daughter marry a man of royal blood and of herself being grandmother to their children.

Praphai's other suitor—for Than Chai had a rival, and how Phloi wished it weren't so!—was An's friend and colleague from the same ministry whose name was Sewi. Khun Sewi was some years older than An and some ranks higher. His physical appearance was not unpleasing, and his manners proper enough—except, Phloi thought, for a little trick he had of avoiding your eyes when he should be looking straight at you. That, and the rather stilted way of speaking he affected when addressing her . . . *But I mustn't be overly critical.* This was what Phloi usually ended up telling herself. *Than Chai's my favourite candidate but I mustn't be pre-judiced against Khun Sewi. The ultimate decision lies with Praphai and I have no right to interfere.*

Khun Sewi was not a sedulous visitor, not like Than Chai, but every time he came he never failed to cause Phloi worries on Than Chai's behalf, not so much on account of what he did or said, but because Praphai was so obviously impressed with him.

"You like Khun Sewi?" Phloi asked her once somewhat unnecessarily.

"Yes, I do, Khun Mother. He's so intelligent and so know-ledgeable. I always feel I've learned something after chatting with him. He makes my other friends seem so frightfully young and frivolous."

"He's a much older man," Phloi remarked.

"Which makes him more interesting, and at the same time more dependable."

"So you like him," Phloi said, unable to keep the anxiety out of her voice. "To what extent, may I ask?"

The question drew a prolonged laugh from Praphai. "Meaning you want to know if I'm in love with Khun Sewi?" She laughed again, paused, and continued. "The answer is no, Khun Mother. I love nobody that way as a matter of fact. That sort of love that would have to last a long time—am I capable of it? I'm not sure at all. I don't believe I'm ready for it, you know? So I'll wait a while. When it happens you'll be the first to know, Mother dear!" she added airily.

She had clarified where she stood vis-à-vis love and marriage. There was nothing very much Phloi could say, then, by way of giving advice or suggestions as to what sort of partner she ought to consider for that relationship that would not sound as though she were prodding her daughter to find a husband. Phloi would never do that; the mere notion made her blush.

Meanwhile she had Ot to deal with.

Ot could not bear the sight of Khun Sewi. One day, after that visitor had departed and An and Praphai had also gone off on their respective errands, Ot stole back into the living room and, eyeing his mother reprovingly, demanded, "Have you been nice to that odious man again?"

"What do you want me to do—shoo him away when he comes to call? Don't be childish, Ot. Just because you don't like him you can't expect me not to welcome him when he pays us a visit. In all fairness to him, he has done nothing wrong."

"Not a thing," Ot conceded, then went on, "except that he's conceited and pompous as well as sly and sneaky, and the less we have to do with him the better."

"Your brother An has a high regard for him, Ot."

"Is that why you have to be so cordial with him? Are you afraid of Phi An or what? Phi An's entitled to his opinions and you to yours, and you're the mistress of this house."

"And therefore," Phloi retorted, "I have certain duties, one of which is to make my children's friends feel welcome here."

"I wish you'd make an exception of this man," said Ot, sighing and sulking at the same time. "I really do. I can't trust him. Have you noticed how he looks at the objects in this room sometimes—pricing every one of them? Ugh! And don't say I'm exaggerating became I'm not."

In her effort to maintain her "neutrality" Phloi refrained from admitting that she, too, had been bothered by those appraising glances, and merely said, "Some people are like that. Let's not be too censorious, my son."

For several months Praphai, unbeknown to herself, kept her mother on tenterhooks. She was always glad to see Than Chai, she helped Phloi prepare special dishes for him, told Phloi what he particularly fancied, had long talks with him, laughed with him, took him along sometimes when she went out with her girl friends. On the other hand, she was equally glad to see Khun Sewi, looked forward to his visit upon learning from An that he would be coming on such and such a day, dressed up with care for him, hung on to his every word when he talked to the others, and sang his praises when he had left.

Her conduct towards both men was forthright and irreproachable, and she could hardly be blamed if it should alternately fill her mother with hopes and fears.

Ot finally stepped in. If Phloi could not forbid this (to him) objectionable man her house, *he*, Ot, could take his sister *out* of the house. To the cinema, to shops and restaurants, to see friends, to go for a drive—with Than Chai of course. Always with Than Chai. Ot, the man who would rather stay home if given a choice, came to be seen everywhere about town, the indefatigable escort and chaperone of Than Chai and his sister, both of whom appeared to be enjoying every minute of being together.

During this period of his intensive campaign to promote Than Chai's cause which, to judge from Praphai's enthusiastic cooperation, was producing good results, Ot even took to behaving towards Khun Sewi with a little more kindliness, no doubt considering him the losing opponent in the race. Ot was always magnanimous in victory.

It was not surprising then that Praphai's friends and relatives had started to discuss Praphai's future in no uncertain terms. Khun Choei and Phoem came to lunch with their sister one day and talked of nothing else. Both had been Than Chai's ardent admirers and supporters and they were no less happy for themselves than for Phloi over the prospect of Than Chai becoming one of the family.

"You're jumping to conclusions," Phloi cautioned them, though she was smiling and heartily agreeing with them that her dear Than Chai was indeed a paragon. ("And he's not a poor man, either," Phoem had said, showing he was not neglectful of practical matters.) "Praphai has yet to make up her mind, you understand, and she says she's in no hurry. So I don't know what will happen. It's up to her."

"How independent the young people are nowadays, " Phoem said. "Not like the way *we* were, eh? Everything arranged for us."

"Think again, Pho Phoem," Khun Choei admonished. "Every-thing arranged for us—ha-ha! What a short memory you have. As I recall it, no elders told me to pack up and elope with my Khun Luang. I did it all on my own."

"Well—" Phoem began but was not allowed to finish.

"And so did you when you took a wife," Khun Choei went on. "Mae Phloi here had a conventional marriage, but I wouldn't call it 'arranged.' Tell me, Phloi—if you hadn't liked Khun Prem well enough would you have married him? I doubt it. And neither Sadet nor Chao Khun Father—convinced as they were that Khun Prem would make you a good husband—would have forced you to do it against your will. You're quite right about not putting pressure on your daughter." Khun Choei nodded approvingly. "Anyway it's only a matter of time, my dear. Those two are destined for each other."

Phloi certainly hoped so. And now that Khun Sewi did not seem to figure so importantly in the contest as he had a few months ago she felt more optimistic than ever.

Such being her state of mind she nearly fainted when a few days later An sprang the following request on her: "Khun Sewi has asked me to approach you on his behalf. With your permission—if you have no objection—he would like to have his elders come and pay respects and ask you for Praphai's hand."

Phloi had to take a deep breath to restore her calm, and it took her a few more moments to get her speech back. "Wait, An," she said. "Don't go so fast. This is so sudden. I didn't know . . ."

"Sewi has made his intention known to me for some time, Khun Mother. You must also have noticed that he's very fond of Praphai. And I'm sure you agree with me that he's a worthy man in every way."

"I know very little about him, An."

Khun Sewi had never talked about his father or mother, and Phloi for some reason had never asked him who they were. Rather strange, this, since it was habitual with her as with most elderly people to inquire as to who the parents of their children's friends might be.

"His father's dead," An now informed her. "He was a merchant with a big house on Si Phraya Road, where Sewi now lives with his mother and their relatives. They are a wealthy family, Khun Mother."

"And what was the father's name?" Phloi asked.

An hesitated. He swallowed before answering. "His name was Hong. Nai Hong Sae Tae. Mother's name is Sin. Sewi doesn't use 'Sae Tae' any more. His last name is now Techasin."

"*Luk chek* (a child of Chinese parents)." She realized it was the wrong thing to say the moment she said it.

"What of it?" An returned rather sharply, perhaps to make up for his hesitation at the beginning. "He's as Thai as you and me. Surely it can't be counted as a demerit to have a father named Hong Sae Tae. And don't I myself pay reverence to *my* Chinese ancestors on *my* father's side?" He paused, and continued in his serious and reasonable tone of voice. "If you ask me, I must say I'm all for him, Khun Mother. Praphai's future would be assured, secure, with a man like Sewi. He has the advantages of a good education, he's holding an important job— quite high up in the ministry and will go higher, I'm certain of it, and furthermore, he's rich enough so that we don't have to be afraid he might be after Praphai's fortune. Taking everything into account I shouldn't think you'd lose face having him as your son-in-law, Khun Mother."

Stifling a sigh, Phloi said, "Have you told your sister?"

"Not yet, Khun Mother. I thought I'd talk to you first. She's downstairs. I'll go and bring her."

Blushing prettily, Praphai's answer was to the effect that, should her mother approve, she, Praphai, was agreeable, as she considered Sewi one of the "best" men she had ever met. Upon hearing this, her mother cried out involuntarily, "What about Than Chai Noi?"

"Than Chai and I are very good friends," said Praphai in a gentle voice. "I know he's a good man in every way, but I do think he's far too young for me. In a marriage the man should have maturity. He should be guide and leader."

Phloi struggled on in spite of having lost the battle. She didn't think Than Chai was either too young or too old—he was at the right age, in fact. Remarkably mature, exceptionally intelligent, a refined man, a generous man, a noble man in every sense of the word. She said all this, then asked her daughter whether she was sure of having "thought everything over carefully."

Praphai looked down at the floor, remaining silent. Her brother took it upon himself to reply to Khun Mother.

"I like Than Chai very much," An declared. "He has one shortcoming, though."

"What is it?" Phloi bristled, ready to come to defence of Praphai's rejected suitor.

"His name," An said evenly. "Close association with royalty is suspect nowadays. Perhaps not so much for you, but it would make things a bit difficult for Praphai and me."

"I've thought about that," Praphai said, echoing Phi An as always.

Incredible! Phloi mused afterwards. *Not so many years ago Than Chai's lineage alone would have made him most eligible, and today they deem it the least desirable thing about him!* Royalty not in fashion at the present time—that was what it amounted to. Phloi nonetheless felt pangs of disappointment over her daughter's choice (even as she fervently wished it to be the right one), but then she was never what you'd call a very fashion-minded person.

Before setting the date for Khun Sewi's elders to come and carry out the ceremony of asking for her daughter's hand, Phloi had a meeting with Than Chai. She was moved by his behaviour, which bespoke sympathy and understanding for all concerned. Before they took their leave of each other, she said to him, "Please don't feel too badly, Your Highness. Let's accept it as the result of our karmic past. I'll find somebody else for you, somebody who will be more worthy of you than Nang Praphai," which had made Than Chai smile.

Phloi saw him rarely during the ensuing months—he was understandably obliged to stay away, and she would have missed him more keenly had she not been so occupied with the changes taking place in the house. Praphai had decided not to move to her fiancé's house after the wedding but to bring him to live here. The wedding date had been fixed and Praphai's new home was now under construction. Khun Sewi was financing the building, and Phloi was providing a piece of land in the compound. Quite a large piece, and this had meant, first of all, the demolition of the wooden house which had been inhabited by the late Khun Aunts Nui and Nian. Glad as she was not to be deprived of her only daughter's proximity after her marriage, Phloi had mourned the passing of the old house, had tried to save it, but in the end had had to let it go for various reasons. Then it was discovered that more land was required—for a lawn, a garden, a garage and so forth. Khun Un's house, standing in the path of expansion, had to come down. This, however, presented no problem at all, for its occupant was more than willing to come and live in the big house with her dear Mae Phloi. She chose a small room on the lower floor for her new abode, after having refused Phloi's offer of a spacious suite upstairs, saying her old bones would prefer not having to negotiate the long flight of stairs.

Khun Un was not sentimental about the bungalow which had been her home for so many years. She was, on the other hand, quite ecstatic about her future nephew by marriage. On being informed of the engagement, she had enthused, "Oh, how lucky you are, Mae Phloi. He has everything—wealth, honour—well, everything! I'm so very happy for you!"

"I didn't choose him, Khun Phi," Phloi couldn't resist saying. "He's Praphai's own choice."

"She's made the right choice," Khun Un said emphatically.

Khun Choei's reaction had been vastly different from that of Khun Big Sister Un. To begin with she thought it "unbecoming" of Praphai to let herself be seen all over town with Than Chai and then get engaged to Khun Sewi. Then she questioned Phloi's wisdom in consenting to have her daughter marry a man whose "origins we know nothing about." She was inclined to believe Phloi had been overindulgent and if her daughter ran into marital troubles in future she'd only have herself to blame. Having delivered all this, Khun Choei, with barely a pause or change of tone, went on to say, "But I'm babbling like an old fool. The man may have great qualities which have escaped my notice and I need to get better acquainted with him. In the meantime, since he's halfway to becoming my nephew I'll just accept him and be partial to him on principle."

And Phoem? Well, Phoem's disappointment over the engagement was perhaps not so profound as his sister's but he did have strong feelings about his future nephew-in-law. He didn't elaborate but chose to express them in one succinct word. "Pfui!" That was all he said.

As might have been expected, Ot greeted the news with disbelief, fury and horror. His mother did her best to pacify him and succeeded to a large extent. Ot recovered his sense of proportion regarding the betrothal, but saw no reason to change his mind about the character of Praphai's betrothed.

"I don't trust him."

"Please, Ot, we've gone over this before."

"He's enamoured of your money rather than of Praphai."

"He has money of his own, Ot."

"He wants more. The more he has the larger his appetite for it."

"Hush, don't get excited again, please. Do try to be civil to him when you meet him face to face, and help me keep this house nice and peaceful."

"It's possible that I may have to seek peace elsewhere when he moves in. The dislike is mutual, if you're interested to know, and he's not trying to conceal it either. He's also decided to look down on me as a parasite because I haven't got a job."

Phloi could have said, "Get one then," but she didn't.

Then there was On. He, too, had to be appeased, as Phloi discovered on her first visit to Bang Khwang after the engagement. He had heard about it from Ot; he knew about Praphai's fiancé; his feelings were hurt because he took it almost as a personal affront that his sister should have preferred Khun Sewi to Than Chai Noi, though for this he blamed An rather than the girl herself.

"An had nothing to do with it," Phloi reminded him.

"Praphai worships her Phi An," On countered. "He didn't have to try to persuade her with words. She knew who had his backing and she was influenced by it. So I can't help thinking that if our side had won perhaps An wouldn't have been so willing and eager to have this man as his brother-in-law."

But as they went on talking On grew more reconciled or maybe resigned; and then he let her in on a piece of news that instantly drove Praphai's engagement from her mind, made her feel suddenly young and strong, and covered her face with tears of joy. The news was by no means confirmed but On said his fellow prisoners were pretty sure it would be; the government was considering a policy under which they, the prisoners, would gradually be removed to a rehabilitation centre, where they would undergo a re-training programme for a period of time, then released. "But anything can happen," On warned her, "so please don't expect too much."

Phloi couldn't help it. She was beside herself, she was in raptures. "I'll tell An about this when I get home," she said. "He knows many influential people and they should be able to speed things up."

"Please," On begged her solemnly, "don't try to get help from them. Let us not owe those people a greater debt of gratitude than we need to. Let's wait rather than ask them for special favours, Khun Mother."

Respecting his wish Phloi made no mention of this matter to An. She went on waiting, but with greater expectations; she went on praying, with greater fervour.

In the meantime the building and decoration of the nuptial home went on apace, reaching completion well before the wedding day. Praphai sailed through the engagement months with the greatest of ease, with gaiety and confidence. Talk about leadership! It was she who led and Khun Sewi who followed. He indulged her every whim. She merely had to say she wanted something for him to make it materialize within the shortest time possible.

On the day of the wedding her self-confidence was supreme. That was how it looked to her timid mother, who had been a bundle of nerves on her wedding day. She got up early, Praphai did, and was busy all morning long getting the house ready for the *ngan*. Her mother, watching her being coolly energetic about it all, was at once impressed, intrigued and confounded, and when they sat down together at lunchtime, remarked, "You're bustling about as if this is not your wedding day, daughter."

Laughing merrily, Praphai said, "If I shyly kept to my room you'd have had to do it all yourself. It would have been so tiring for you."

In the afternoon a small contingent of young ladies (Praphai said she had "recruited them for bridesmaids") were with the bride in her room as she got dressed for the water-pouring rite. Phloi went in there with the intention of lending a hand, listened to the girls' light-hearted chattering for a while and left them on seeing that her assistance was not needed.

Nor did she have a great deal to do later on as mother of the bride, in spite of the fact that this was a big wedding, or perhaps because of it, together with the efficiency with which the three of them—An and the bridal couple—had organized everything. Although there were many relations and older family friends attending the ceremony these were far out-numbered by the high-ranking people, military and civilian, who had been invited by An and Khun Sewi and whom Phloi was meeting for the first time. After some minutes' interchange of greetings and civilities with these important guests she left it to An to carry on hosting the affair and went to join Choi and a few other older folks seated in what one might call a spectators' corner.

"What do you think of your guests, Phloi?" Choi whispered to her. "Those grand personages of the new regime?"

"I don't think they've had time to get used to being grand," Phloi whispered back. "That's why they look so awkward, poor things—not at all sure how grandly or not so grandly they ought to behave at a gathering like this."

"Yes," Choi agreed, "It is difficult when you rise too rapidly to a high position. It does take some getting used to before you can take it in your stride and be natural about it."

Choi and Phloi were the last ones to go in and pour the water. Thinking of Khun Prem, Phloi had tears in her eyes as she tilted the conch shell over her daughter's head while wishing her happiness and prosperity. But she felt shy somehow about pouring it on Khun Sewi's head and was about to aim the shell at his hands when he quickly thrust his head forward. Phloi then did her part properly, including giving him her blessing.

Choi said afterwards, "Your hands shook. What was the matter? Having qualms about giving your daughter to him?"

"Stage fright, Choi. My first time, you understand. An got married abroad, as you know."

"Everybody says you're getting an ideal son-in-law, Phloi. So wealthy, so highly placed and so forth. Now you'll have to make yourself a worthy mother-in-law to him, won't you?"

"How, Choi? Do tell me!"

"Oh, easy. Since he's a big man, you'll have to act big yourself, otherwise there'll be a clash of styles. Then you must give him the impression that you side with him, especially when he and his wife have their little disagreements in front of you, but behind his back you must instruct your daughter not to let him have everything his own way. And tell her not to trust him but to pretend she does—that's a good motto I think, men being what they are. Tell her she must exercise control over him but to do so in a subtle way so that he will not feel oppressed."

"My dear Choi, you want to get me into trouble with both Praphai and her husband, is that it?"

"You asked me to tell you how to be a worthy mother-in-law and I did my best to oblige. Too bad you don't think much of my well thought out advice. What a waste of effort!"

"Too bad you have to leave me, Choi. It's such a comfort to have you near me at this wedding."

Choi had to get back to the Inner Court before dark. Phoem also left almost immediately after the water-pouring ceremony, pleading a headache. The elders among the guests (including those grand personages although some of them were not so old in years) went home early leaving the young people to help the just-married couple celebrate. The wedding party was held on the front lawn. The trees around it, hung with coloured bulbs, glowed and glittered under the starry sky. The sound of laughter filled the air, mingling with the music as though written into its melody, and the girls in their silk dresses seemed to be gliding about in perfect consonance with the rhythm of the song.

Phloi sat watching the scene with Luang Osot and Khun Choei and the three of them agreed that it could well be a beautiful episode from some unnamed play. The time was close to ten o'clock. The astrologer had given eight as the auspicious hour for the bed-making ceremony and eight minutes past ten as that for the presentation of the bride to the bride groom. Luang Osot and Khun Choei, chosen by Phloi to be bed-makers, had performed their ritual task; Phloi had been waiting to do hers, and while enjoying the lovely sight of youth enjoying itself she was also keeping an anxious eye on the clock. When it struck ten she started to glance round the lawn in order to send signals to her daughter and Khun Sewi that it was time to set out for their new home where, in the bridal suite, she, Phloi, would "hand over" the bride to the groom as she herself had been handed over to Khun Prem by her Chao Khun Father many years ago.

Presently they came up to her, with An leading the way. An spoke with the air of a master of ceremonies: "Now is the auspicious time for you to present the bride to the groom, Khun Mother." And Phloi rose, making ready to go off with them to the nuptial home. But An went on, "We can do it here, Khun Mother. No need to go the house."

"What?" Phloi asked as Khun Choei and Luang Osot exchanged looks. "*Here* on the lawn?"

"It's all right, Khun Mother," replied An, while the bride and groom smiled at Khun Mother. "So you won't have to walk all the way to the house. And then after the presentation these two can get back to their guests."

Phloi sat down again, not quite knowing what to do, then got control of herself and proceeded to murmur phrases at the couple, who had seated themselves at her feet and were now looking up at her, each with hands joined in the attitude of receiving the blessing she was bestowing on them. It wasn't what you might call a full-dress presentation—Phloi would not have given a long speech even in a more conventional setting but she would have had a little bit more to say. When it was over they made a *krap* of grateful thanks and then Praphai, laughing, took hold of Khun Sewi's hand and led him back to the centre of the lawn.

"Praphai and Sewi plan to enter their house the way the *farang*s do it when they get married," An informed the three elders. "The groom will carry the bride into the house. It's a *farang* custom."

Upon being thus apprised Khun Choei started to cough and when An had walked away she said in an amused tone of voice, "You have a *maem* daughter-in-law, Mae Phloi, and now you have got yourself a son-in-law who's very *farang*."

Mae Phloi shook her head in astonishment. "A grown girl to be carried like a baby—I've never heard of a more embarrassing custom!"

"I must say, Mae Phloi," Khun Choei declared, "that this is the most remarkable wedding I've been to. First time I've seen the bride handed over amid guests and greenery . . . By the way, what did you say to the bride and groom? You were mumbling and I didn't catch a word."

"Nothing memorable, Khun Choei. I said whatever came to my head—may they live together happily and so on, you know. It wasn't much of a presentation."

"I'm on their side," Luang Osot put in. "The presentation ceremony was meaningful in the old days when the bride and groom hardly knew each other, but you can't expect them to take it seriously nowadays when they've been seeing each other all the time before the wedding. That's why just now I found it all the more heart-warming to see Praphai and her young man receive your blessing, Khun Phloi. They haven't abandoned the old custom but have adapted it to suit the prevailing conditions, you see."

"Why!" Khun Choei exclaimed. "I didn't know I had such a modernist for a husband . . . Why didn't you carry me up the stairs the day I moved in with you?"

Luang Osot chuckled. "Because nobody told me about the custom, that's why. However, I can make up for lost time and do it tonight if you want us to amuse our young friends in the neighbourhood."

A FEW months had gone by since Praphai and her husband had settled into their new home. In the beginning Phloi had dropped by fairly regularly for a chat with Khun Sewi, until his insistence on turning this into a strictly formal visit had finally discouraged her from continuing the practice. Maybe he only meant to show special respect for his mother-in-law, but must he be so excessively polite about it? It made him appear all stiff and strained and Phloi couldn't help feeling she was imposing on him. She had wanted their relationship to grow closer and more comfortable, but as he had never relaxed with her she in her turn had begun to feel ill-at-ease with him.

Praphai was happy, and this was much more important to Phloi than the fact that she couldn't warm to her son-in-law, nor he to her.

Praphai as a married woman was also much more comprehen-sible to her than Praphai as a smart young thing had ever been. But not wholly comprehensible. That would be asking too much.

"I've decided not to get a cook," Praphai announced one day soon after the wedding. This was followed by a request, "May I have food sent from your kitchen to our house, Khun Mother?"

"Yes, of course," answered Phloi. "That's convenient enough. But I do feel you should be looking after the meals yourself. That's the wife's duty, a most important one, you know."

With a charming laugh, Praphai said, "I won't have time, and Khun Sewi doesn't really want me to do it. He's so easy to feed too, and anyway he says he'll never get more delicious food than what you provide, Khun Mother!"

Is this the way a modern married daughter looks after her household? Phloi asked herself, and answered, *Yes, let Mother do it, that's the way!*

And then, three months after the wedding, here was Phloi broaching the subject that had been constantly on her mind for some weeks.

"When do you think I'm going to be blessed with a grandchild, Praphai?"

"Not yet," was Praphai's quick, laughing answer. "Khun Sewi feels the same way. We both want to go on enjoying ourselves without the burden of parenthood for a while."

"But there's little choice in the matter," Phloi said wisely. "When it comes, it comes. Some people long to have children but have to accept their fate and wait and wait, sometimes for years. With others the first child comes in the first year of marriage. It's according to your karma."

This elicited more amused laughter from Praphai. "No, Khun Mother," she said, "not karma. It's according to when you plan to have it. Birth can be controlled these days," she explained "Whatever your karma, you don't need to have a baby in the first year of marriage if you don't want to. You can postpone it until you're ready to have one."

Phloi felt a chill down her spine. It seemed to her a cruel and unnatural thing to do. She was moved by the thought of her grandchild wanting to enter this life but getting thwarted by control at every turn. Poor, hapless, pitiful thing!

THIRTY-NINE

ALL Bangkok was eagerly awaiting Nai Luang's return to the kingdom. All Bangkok was yearning for the sight of him and for the opportunity to pay homage to him in person. Some years had passed since his accession to the throne at the time of which he had been attending school in Switzerland, and this would be his first visit to his people. They missed having Nai Luang close to them. They kept abreast of his health and his progress at school; it made them proud and happy to hear what an intelligent boy he was and how lovable in every way, and their longing to have him in their midst was like a real *krahai*—a veritable thirst. The news of his coming, though not for a permanent stay since he still had to finish his studies, gladdened the people's collective hearts as no other event had done for such a long period; and in their common joy they put aside their disagreements and felt better disposed towards one another. In Phloi's family circle Uncle Phoem was chatting with Nephew An in a more friendly spirit than he had shown since the advent of the new regime; he even accepted An's invitation that they should go along together to greet Nai Luang on his arrival, and didn't turn a hair when An said Khun Sewi would also ride with them in the car; his thoughts so concentrated on Nai Luang that he clean forgot his aversion to his nephew-in-law.

Phloi was not going with them. She had made her own plans. On that day, she and Ot would go and fetch Choi at the Grand Palace, then the three of them would proceed to station themselves at some strategic spot along the Phramen Grounds (Sanam Luang) and wait to pay homage to Nai Luang as he went past in the royal car. Choi of course could easily remain behind the palace walls, in the vicinity of the Emerald Buddha Temple, for Nai Luang would be coming there from the royal landing. But she said it would be much more fun outside: she wouldn't have to behave so primly and while waiting to feast her eyes on Nai Luang she could go round buying things to nibble on and striking up conversation with strangers if she should feel like it. At first she rather doubted if Khunying Phloi ought to come with her. "Your son An might consider it undignified." Then she was afraid Phloi might not be hardy enough to rough it on the pavement. Phloi bade her to rest assured on both counts. "Very well then," Choi finally said. "On the day of Nai Luang's arrival you and I will pretend we're still a couple of youngsters at a parade instead of two elderly women who ought to know better and stay home."

So here they were on the important day, threading their way in and out of the shades of the tamarind trees along Ratchadamnoen Avenue, careful not to be stepped on or have their bags snatched.

"Isn't this fun, Phloi?" Choi asked.

"I've never seen so many people," said Phloi. "It's exciting all right, even a little intoxicating!"

"Don't you dare stage any fainting spell around here, Phloi! Keep an eye on your mother, Ot. Catch her if she falls . . . Will you let me pass, my dear sir?" The last sentence was addressed by Choi to a young man loitering ahead of her and obstructing her path. But he didn't seem to hear her and so she prodded him with the ferrule of her umbrella. How he jumped! He turned, and on seeing his assailant, gave a laugh.

"Why are you in such a hurry, Khun Aunt?" He was very good-tempered about it, and talked to Choi with an easy familiarity as though they had known each other all their lives. "You didn't have to attack me, you know, Khun Aunt."

Later on, another young man talked to Phloi as she stood in the shade by herself while Ot was engaged in a chat with some people a few yards away and Choi was buying an iced drink from a Chinese vendor. Their eyes happened to meet, Phloi's and the young man's, and he gave her a friendly smile and walked up to her saying very politely, "Don't you want to go and wait over there nearer the street, Khun Aunt? If you stay here I don't think you'll get to see Nai Luang when he passes." Phloi told him she definitely planned to be in the front line and thanked him warmly for being concerned about her. *There's a lot to be said for the young people of today,* she thought. *They might not be in awe of their elders as they ought to be but they were certainly self-assured, and in their own fashion quite well-mannered really, and not at all lacking in consideration.* She looked round; it made her feel refreshed, rejuvenated even, seeing so many youthful faces in the crowd, smiling, expectant faces—faces of hope and of the future, she said to herself, faces turned towards a new horizon, under a new reign . . .

How long did they wait? But they were not mindful of the time. Nor of the heat. "Listen," Ot cried. Now they could hear the cheering come over faintly from the distance. The king had landed! Nai Luang was here! . . . Now the procession must have left the landing. Nai Luang was on the way to the Grand Palace. The cheering continued, faded away . . . Nai Luang had gone inside. The royal anthem had never sent up more rousing echoes.

A big white cloud had appeared overhead, toning down the fierce glare of the sun. The air was suddenly cool; there was a lovely breeze blowing.

"Do you feel the beautiful cool air?" Choi was saying. "He's brought it, Nai Luang has brought it with his noble merit. He will spread the shade of happiness over us. Long may he reign!" Phloi, her throat constricted, could not say a word.

The crowd was getting bigger all the time, for those who had seen Nai Luang near the Grand Palace were thronging down Ratchadamnoen elbowing for room to stand and wait for another opportunity to watch him and greet him. They were by no means ready to call it a day. They had not quite quenched their thirst.

Chaiyo! Chaiyo! The cheering had started again. He must be leaving the Grand Palace. He's coming! *Nai Luang ma laeo!* It won't be long now . . . There! Can you see? . . . There, he's coming! *Chaiyo! Chaiyo! CHAIYO!* The triumphant cry grew louder with each passing second and some youngsters near Phloi were leaping into the air and laughing. These were shouting the loudest when at last the royal car came in sight, then passed slowly by. Phloi did not shout with them and she hardly noticed the soldiers on horseback riding in front. Her heart was pounding and her eyes, through the tears, were fixed on her little Nai Luang. How little. How young. "My dear lord! My dear lord!" she murmured. He remained in her eye-range for a few brief moments, long enough for her to be touched to the quick of her being, and for her memory to receive and retain an indelible image of innocence and purity. Were he not Nai Luang he would still be loved for himself, she thought. But he is Nai Luang through and through and can be nobody else. He looks at his loyal subjects and shines forth in noble merit, young and little as he is amid the uniformed grownups.

Joy filled her heart, and love, and mingled with it was that indescribable feeling of protective and tender pity . . . Our little Nai Luang . . . Our dear lord . . . May all the sacred powers of the universe watch over him . . .

"I *love* him!" Choi proclaimed in a booming voice, waking Phloi from her reverie.

"We all do, Choi. You're not the only one. Everybody loves him. He's our Nai Luang."

"I love him as Nai Luang and yet not as Nai Luang," Choi tried to explain. "I'm not afraid of him at all. I *simply* love him. And just now I wanted so much to rush out and hug and kiss him."

"Auntie Choi!" Ot exclaimed, laughing. "You'll watch that impulse, won't you? Not that you'd ever be allowed to get that close to him."

No matter. Choi and other citizens like her might not be able to get as close to Nai Luang as they would have wished that day but they could hold him close to their hearts, which was what they did. Like Choi, they were not in awe of him but simply loved him. They had brought their loyalty to welcome him home and now that they had seen him that loyalty had been strengthened with love—the kind they felt for their dear young ones very close to them, of the same bloodstream as we say in Thai. The love was nothing new but their feeling it for their sovereign was new and this gave another dimension to what is called *khwam chongrak phakdi* (love and loyalty) from a citizen towards a king. The good feeling permeated the air and endowed that day with a freshness that lightened the heart and the spirit. At Phloi's house hours afterwards Nai Luang continued to be the dominant subject of conversation—as he no doubt did at most houses in the city that night. They talked happily about him, agreeing and feeling united with one another, and Uncle Phoem continued to behave towards Nephew An with avuncular affection as he should, which for Phloi was a most heartening sight indeed; and she could imagine the same kind of scene unfolding in other homes: relatives and friends coming together again who had been growing apart these past few years—perhaps enemies might even be making up, who knows. She thought it wonderful and all due to Nai Luang being here, and that this day was of great auspiciousness, an omen presaging a beneficent time for all of us.

Hence a good omen for On's future. As days went by Phloi felt ever more hopeful about it. Some of On's fellow prisoners had already been released. She rejoiced with them and their families. At least for them the anguish of separation was over. And, noting On's optimistic frame of mind when she went to see him, she found it easy to wait patiently for his turn to come out, to be reunited with her, to be a free man again, to start life anew.

In the larger sphere beyond Phloi's domestic boundaries the political situation looked brighter, not so clouded with distrust and antagonism as before. The gentler spirit of compromise, and of forgiving and forgetting, seemed to be making a comeback. Apolitical as she was, Phloi could not help thinking that perhaps what An termed our "critical period" would be over at last.

Time passed, bringing other omens, other portents. It was after Nai Luang had left to continue his schooling in Switzerland, and while Phloi was still complacently waiting to hear the good news about On, that Khun Un was taken ill. She never had any use for doctors, but with a recurrent fever and the pain in her chest keeping her from getting any sleep she finally submitted to an examination.

Phloi froze with horror on learning that it was cancer of the breast and the malignancy had gone beyond any medical or surgical help. No hope of recovery. The end would come soon. The doctor shook his head sadly. Khun Un must have been aware of it for some time but she had left it too late. There was nothing to be done except make her as comfortable as they could, relieve her pain, minimize her suffering as much as possible.

"Has the doctor told you?" Khun Un asked with a smile when Phloi went in to see her.

Phloi could say nothing.

"He didn't want to tell me at first," Khun Un went on. "Didn't want to give me a shock. I had to prise the truth out of him . . . Birth, old age, sickness, death . . . We must die some day—"

"Oh my dear Khun Phi!" Phloi cried out. "Why didn't you let us know? Why, oh why? In the early stage it could have been cured. Oh, Khun Phi—"

"No use regretting, Mae Phloi. If it had been a growth on my finger I wouldn't have minded letting everybody know and look at it. But it's in my breast, Mae Phloi. How could I, an old maid, not feel shy about it?"

So it was her spinster's modesty that had made her keep it a secret and caused the fatal delay. *Oh, my poor dear sister,* Phloi moaned inwardly. It was heart-breaking to think that if Khun Un had not found the idea of marrying so repugnant, if she had been a wife and mother, had breast-fed a child, she would not have felt embarrassed about showing her illness.

But how calm she was. The knowledge that she was going to die had not only not terrified her but given her this new calmness in facing life. She had no regrets, no anxiety, no fear. She was only anxious not to impose too great a burden on others, especially on Mae Phloi, her principal nurse. When the pain came she would try to hide it. A low moaning sound now and again, a contraction of the brow, that was all she would permit herself.

Meanwhile, apart from the vicissitudes of individual destinies, the country's "critical period," instead of coming to an end, had been worsening since Nai Luang's departure. Politics rearing its ugly head again, as far as Phloi was concerned, and Phoem, she noticed, had resumed his political whispering sessions with Ot and, to her dismay, had again distanced himself from An and Khun Sewi.

He dropped by one day, Phoem did, saying he came to see how Khun Un was faring. But before going in to see the patient he had a long talk with Ot, conducted in low voices, both of them looking unusually perturbed. Afterwards Phloi insisted they tell her what was going on.

Phoem said, "I didn't want to worry you, Mae Phloi. You have enough worries what with Khun Un and all . . . I was just telling Ot what I heard today. Twenty or more people have been arrested, Mae Phloi. Military and police officers, and a few royals."

"Not again, Khun Luang! And the royals too? Oh, when will all these troubles end? What is it about this time, Khun Luang?"

"Another rebellion, Mae Phloi."

"Another? You talk as though it were a normal thing. When we were young a rebellion was something almost inconceivable. Oh, I'm so confused. I don't know who's on the right or the wrong side any more."

"Hush—hush, Mae Phloi! Do be careful of what you say. Two mighty people in this house have no doubt whatever which is the right side. So you can't have any doubt either. If you did—well, they won't arrest *you*, but they might have *me* arrested."

"Don't be sarcastic, Khun Luang. I don't like it. I don't want you to feel like that about your own nephew and nephew-in-law."

"Don't be angry, Mae Phloi. Bear with me. Anyhow, in this sort of situation you might find me in jail again."

"Most likely, Khun Luang! I shall have to move somewhere near Bang Khwang. My son is coming out, but my brother may be going there soon if he doesn't keep his mouth shut."

"Mother dear," Ot spoke up quietly, hesitated, and went on sounding not very happy having to say it. "Mother dear—about Phi On coming out—don't expect too much."

"What do you mean, Ot?" Phloi asked with a sinking heart.

"The situation being what it is, they've stopped the re-training programme—Oh, please don't be alarmed, Mother. I don't mean it's anything final. They've stopped it for the time being—so the process may take longer than we thought."

"Don't let it get you down, Mae Phloi," Phoem said. "Don't brood on it too much or you'll ruin your health—I already have one sick sister and that's enough!"

Phloi tried, but could not make herself feel any less depressed. *Oh, On, what have you and I done? Surely this time it's other people's deeds that we're paying for. How much longer must we go on paying? Must I resign myself, give up hope?* But the convergence of events being what it was, while worrying about On she went on giving Khun Un the best of care throughout the ensuing weeks. Khun Choei was a great help and comfort, coming to nurse her sister nearly every day and sometimes spending a night or two with her.

Khun Un never cried, and she would console Phloi and Khun Choei, who could not always suppress their tears when they had to watch her suffer without being able to do much about it.

"It's not so bad—it will soon be over. Don't grieve for me—I'm quite all right—and thank you, my dears, for taking such good care of me."

She was not sorry to be leaving this world, but was concerned about leaving Praphai, and she kept saying to Phloi, "You'll look after Praphai, won't you?"

Once she said, "Praphai looks like you, Mae Phloi. I did not love you when you were a little girl. My loving Praphai so much is a kind of compensation for that." Then her face twitched with pain, and when it had gone she said, "Don't cry, Mae Phloi. I'm merely suffering for the bad action I've committed."

She must have also accumulated enough merit, however, for she did not have to suffer too long. The end came a few months after that first examination. She had gone to bed one night and never woke again. There was no trace of pain on her face that morning and she looked as though she had been enjoying a well-earned rest.

She had repeatedly asked Phloi not to hold the funeral rites for her longer than two weeks and, respecting her wish, the family cremated her on the fifteenth day following her death.

A very tired Phloi also needed a rest, emotional as well as physical, and Ot, realizing this, had been withholding from her the latest news from Bang Khwang. But of course he had to tell her, and one day he made himself do it.

"It's my bad luck to have to be the bringer of unhappy news," he said.

"What is it this time, my son?"

"About Phi On, darling."

"He's not going to be released?"

"No, and what's more, he and the other prisoners have been sent to an island in the south. He asked me not to tell you because we were having the funeral rites for Khun Aunt and you already had enough to worry about."

"You see, Ot, even when he's in trouble he's concerned about his mother . . . What else did he say?"

"That you should be glad because he'd have a little more freedom on the island and the sea air is fresher."

"Glad, Ot? Then sad again? No, I don't dare to feel anything at the moment . . . Please keep in touch with him, Ot, and find out what he needs so we can send them to him."

"He'll get in touch with you, darling."

Phloi turned away without another word. She went into her bedroom and lay down, thinking to herself how exhausting it could be just to go on living.

FORTY

SO she resigned herself and gave up her high hopes. In fact at this point she was afraid of hope. Once bitten twice shy—and she had been bitten not once but more times than she cared to remember. Ot kept reassuring her that from all reports the prisoners were better off on Tarutao Island than at Bang Kwang. She was glad to hear it, but shied away from envisaging any brighter prospect for her son On.

In this state of mind, living in a big house inhabited by scores of people, she often felt far away from everything and everybody. Never from Ot, however. Ot was and would always be there, close to her . . . . So close that it was hard to tell when she began to notice that lately he had not been his usual self. Her son Ot who loved to chat on gaily about any inconsequential subject and laugh and joke at the slightest provocation—something had happened to him, made him listless and gloomy and strangely quiet.

Khun Aunt Choei had also sensed this transformation in her nephew. She came to visit one day, and this was the first thing she said to Phloi, "I passed Ot just now. He was either daydreaming or grouching, I don't know which. What's wrong with him, Phloi? What's eating him these days?" She paused, and went on to make a guess. "Maybe he's fallen for a girl. You think he's in love, Phloi?"

Phloi started. It had not occurred to her. Ot in love! But why not? Most natural thing for a man his age. She was amazed at herself for not having thought of it. Ot loving someone, Ot taking a wife. All of a sudden she turned into a possessive mother—she didn't want to share him with anybody! Then in the next instant she got control of herself, felt rather ashamed of herself, and rebuked herself for having

494

let herself become so clinging to Ot as to neglect his future, his personal happiness as head of his own family. In any case, she reflected, whether it was over a girl or something else, it was her business to find out and try to help him.

"You don't seem very cheerful these days. Aren't you feeling well, my son?" This was the opening question she put to him.

"I'm all right," was Ot's reply. "Quite well and healthy."

"But you have something on your mind. What is it, son? Could it be that you have fallen in love and can't decide whether to tell me about it? If so, please tell me. Whoever she may be, if she's your choice I'll go and ask for her hand."

Ot laughed with great hilarity, and said if he could find a girl like his mother he'd marry her but so far he hadn't. Then he stopped laughing, and with a sigh said that as a jobless man dependent on his mother he was in no position to contemplate marriage anyway; he'd been thinking about his unemployed state and "it's so depressing."

Phloi then said soothingly—and with a sense of relief, "Then why don't you find some work to do? Anybody will be glad to have you."

"I don't think so, Mother. I might not know how to flatter my boss and he might find me objectionable and throw me out and that would make it worse—"

"There you go again," Phloi cut him short, remonstrating with him, "'fighting the fever before you have it.' If you really want a job we have friends and relatives who could help you."

"Don't talk to me of relatives," Ot said, with distaste in his voice. "It's my relatives in this house who are poisoning my days. If it weren't for them, if there were only the two of us here I could go on living like this in perfect contentment till the day I die. But they won't let me be. Because I don't trot off to an office every day they despise me, *and* delight in letting me and the whole world know that they despise me, that they consider me a drifter, an absolute good-for-nothing."

To Phloi's knowledge neither An nor Praphai nor Khun Sewi had said or done anything to deserve this accusation. At any rate, nothing could be simpler than for Ot to get himself a job, Phloi said. He could become a civil servant like everybody else. Plenty of civil service jobs for a man of his background and education.

"Ah, Mother," said Ot, "don't forget I'm in close touch with my brother On. You don't think that's held against me? It is, you know." Well then—Phloi had another suggestion: he could start a business of his own, work for himself.

"Me??" Ot cried. "Run a business?" He, a business ignoramus and too old to start learning; he, who had been taught from the cradle onwards to grow up and enter government service and rise to be a big man with lots of reverent followers to pay him homage—how could he become a mere merchant?

"Oh, it's so wearying when you go round and round like this," Phloi finally said. "I can't argue with you, son."

"Then let's not, Mother." This was said with a good-humoured smile, "And let me solve the problem my own way."

Regarding the contemptuous attitude on the part of his "relatives in this house" towards him, Phloi at first tended to believe that Ot had been exaggerating, and she suspected that Ot's dislike of Khun Sewi had a great deal to do with it. She also wondered if perhaps he had not developed some sort of complex on account of his joblessness. However, she came to change her mind later, after having had time to observe the situation. Ot's grievance was real enough, she concluded, and this was confirmed for her by a conversation she happened to have with Praphai one day. They had been chatting about Khun Un—how she had been preoccupied until the last days of her life with the welfare of her great favourite. That Praphai had married and settled down made no difference—Khun Un had gone on full of protective concern, and she had asked Phloi to look after Praphai as though this would not have been the most natural thing for Phloi to do. "It's because she loved you very much, daughter," Phloi said. This made Praphai giggle with pleasure, and then she went on to remark casually, "Good thing she loved me and not Phi Ot. If she did, she would really have to feel concerned."

"Why?" Phloi asked innocently.

"Because Phi Ot is such a lay-about. He's done nothing. He won't amount to anything."

"Don't underestimate him," Phloi advised. "Anyway he's your elder brother, and I'm sure once he's decided on a career he'll make a success of it."

"Ah," Praphai smiled. "But when will he decide? That's the question, isn't it? Will the day ever come? It's strange how he's not at all like Phi An." And when Phloi, coming to Ot's defence, cited his good qualities, she laughed lightly. "Oh, Khun Mother, you always side with him. And he knows it. That's why he feels free to loaf, wasting his time and not doing any work. Khun Sewi says it would worry him to death if he had to idle his life away like Phi Ot—but then he's not frivolous like Phi Ot. He says a man leading this kind of meaningless existence is not worthy of respect and if Phi Ot weren't his brother-in-law he wouldn't like having to consort with him."

Phloi felt a sudden surge of anger and she spoke out sharply commanding her daughter to tell that husband of hers not to go round meddling and making mischief and bringing unpleasantness into this house with his uncalled-for, disparaging remarks about another person. And then Praphai, looking guilty, tried to make amends by mumbling something about her husband meaning no harm, that he merely wished to see Phi Ot improve himself, make something of himself, that, in short, her husband's heart was in the right place where Phi Ot was concerned . . .

A few more days went by and it was An who, while chatting with his mother one afternoon, once again brought up the subject of how Ot should conduct his life.

"What are you going to do about Ot, Khun Mother?"

"What do you mean, son? What has Ot done now?"

"It's a question of what he has not done, Khun Mother. You can't allow him to go on doing nothing forever. He must have an occupation."

"You're his elder brother, son. Why don't you talk to him?"

"I have, but you know how impossible he can be. He either clowns or turns sarcastic. Only you can do it, Khun Mother."

"Do what, son?"

"Tell him to get a job."

"I did, but maybe not convincingly enough. Actually, his not having a job causes no one any trouble as far as I can see, apart from the fact that he's a great help to me around the house. He is, you know. And then I also feel there's enough money in the family for one son not having to earn a living. Ot spends very little anyway," she added. Nothing in what she said could be called a valid reason for maintaining Ot in his present easeful status. Phloi realized this, but chose to speak her mind nonetheless.

As was to be expected, An reproved her for taking too much interest in Ot's day-to-day comfort and too little in his future career. "One's knowledge gets rusty like any other tool," An said in the course of his longish sermon. "If Ot doesn't start applying it soon it's going to be too late. I don't want to see my brother go through life a useless loafer. So much time and money has gone into educating him. It would be an awful waste."

He's sounding just like his father, Phloi thought. *It's uncanny—could have been his father going on and on like this.* She felt a pang in her heart and for a few moments the memory of her dead husband was more meaningful to her than any problems of the here and now.

But now An stopped talking, abruptly, because Ot had come into the room. And Phloi resumed paying attention to the present.

"Go ahead, Phi An," Ot said, smiling. "I think I can guess what you've been discussing. Let's hear it all. No good doing it behind my back when it concerns me."

So the discussion continued, with An being well-intentioned, sensible and elder-brotherly, with Ot being prone (as An had put it earlier) to clown or turn sarcastic, and with Phloi enjoining her younger son to behave responsibly and not evade the issue.

A stage was reached when Ot, in all seriousness, said, "You're right, it's time I became a wage-earner. Now how do I go about getting a job?"

"That's more like it, Ot!" An was very pleased. "I'll help you find something suitable. That's no problem at all."

Ot had a question, "Nowadays you have to belong to groups and cliques in order to get placed anywhere, isn't that true, Phi An?"

"My dear fellow, things are not so different today from what they have always been. But if having friends in the right places is important, we do have them. Sewi, for one. He'll be only too glad to help you."

"We'll leave Sewi out of this if you don't mind. If he were to have any part in my employment he'd never let anyone forget it, least of all me. He'd hold me in his debt forever and lord it over me in this house. Not that he is not doing it already but it would be much worse if he were justified."

An refrained from contesting this point and continued urging his brother to take the right action of abandoning his aimless routine in favour of an honest occupation.

Ot then surprised his two elders with the following disclosure, which was prefaced with a sigh of resignation: "As a matter of fact I have applied for work at the Ministry of Public Instruction. They've accepted me and I should start in a few days. As a second grade civil servant in the probationary category. Is that all right?"

"That's great!" An cried with delight. "That's how I started out, you know. But why didn't you tell us from the beginning and save all that palaver?" He took Ot's hand and shook it vigorously. "Congratulations, old man! I'm very happy for you, really and truly!"

When An had left them, Phloi queried her younger son. "Yes, Ot, why did you have to go into all that rigmarole instead of just telling us you've found work?"

"I wanted to make it clear that I did it without my relatives' help."

"If An had helped you, he would have done it because of his sincere concern for you—would have gone about it as a loving brother. Don't you trust his sincerity, Ot?"

"I do, Mother, absolutely—it's not Phi An I'm thinking about. Phi An's not only sincere, he's guileless, so guileless he's easily gulled by his so-called friends."

Letting the matter drop, Phloi went on to say, "I'm so glad you've been accepted at the ministry."

"Are you really? Do you mean it?"

"Certainly I mean it. Why shouldn't I be glad?"

"I don't know. But I can't help wondering who's going to keep you company and run little errands for you and take care of you and serve you, now that I'm going to be a working man like everybody else."

He knew well enough what her feelings were, as opposed to her reasons, but his tone was half joking, and Phloi, too, made herself speak lightly. "Your ministry is not far from home and you'll be here mornings and evenings and so, my dear son, I don't see myself being deprived of your service at all."

ON his first morning as a civil servant, before leaving the house for the office, Ot advised his mother to warn the whole house not to do their laundry today, for the clothes would not get dry. An un-expected action is said to bring on unexpected rain, and his setting out to work was sure to make this an exceptionally showery day.

Now it was already the second week after that unexpected event. It was late afternoon and Ot, back from the office, was helping himself to some choice savouries prepared by his mother and chatting with her between mouthfuls when his Uncle Phoem walked in and sat down with them, saying, "I see you're feeding your hard-working son, Mae Phloi. Well, Ot, how goes it at the ministry? And how soon will you get to be a big man like the rest of them?"

The nephew groaned. "Uncle, Uncle, give me time. I've only been there ten days."

"Oh, I'm not being impatient. What I really want to know is what kind of work they've given you to do, but I thought I'd put in the 'big' question for good measure, to make it an auspicious interview, don't you know."

Smiling at his mother, Ot said, "I don't think I can go up in the world fast enough to satisfy my exacting family." And to his uncle: "I can't tell you what kind of work because there has been no work. I'm still waiting for them to give me something to do, and in the meantime I read the newspapers all morning long, every column including the ads, then I go out to lunch, come back to my desk and give the papers another close study, then it's four o'clock and time to go home. Do you think I can rise to a high position on this routine?"

"It is a very good routine," his uncle replied, nodding sagely, "and many have risen to great heights on it. If you do too much you may make mistakes and that's bad. If you do nothing you have no occasion to do wrong and therefore you get your yearly raise, and before you know it you're up there, a big shot, all due to having followed the routine of tea-sipping and newspaper-reading at your desk."

"Khun Luang," Phloi said, "I'll thank you not to lead your nephew astray. And don't you laugh, Ot, it's not at all funny. It was not through laziness that your father rose to be a Phraya."

"Khun Prem was a worker all right," Phoem said. "And my, how he suffered when work was taken away from him! He was a work addict and that's bad, too. I tried to help him but he was too far gone. And now he's gone, and I'm still here—Mae Phloi's exasperating brother."

The subject of how to succeed as a civil servant thus faded away, yielding place to reminiscences about Khun Prem. At times, Phloi said, she felt that it had happened so very long ago and had vanished—her life with Khun Prem—leaving her nothing to hold on to, but more often she felt the nearness of his presence—of him talking to her, advising her, walking with her, and the sense of his still being here with her was of such utter reality that he might not have died at all. Phoem was not surprised by what she said and he cited the many times he had done this or restrained himself from doing that because Mother seemed to have been there nudging him along or holding him back. *So where are they now, our loved ones?* Phloi asked. *Khun Prem has gone, but where is he really?*

Turning to his nephew, Phoem said with a grin, "You remember, Ot, those comely maids we despatched to keep your father company in the Beyond? I think they must be languishing away because he won't spend any time with them but keeps coming back here to hover round his wife. I shall claim them when and if I ever die, but by then they'll be too old for me."

FORTY-ONE

OT had not waited in vain. They gave him, in due course, some-thing to do at the office. He loved his work, loved it for a couple of months, during which he'd come home and talk about it with his mother, discussing its various aspects and expounding his opinions and ideas with her as though she were an educationist and not a housewife who had never been to a formal school. His interest quickly went beyond the confines of his assigned task to embrace the way they should link up with other tasks in other divisions and departments; he became, in brief, interested in how the whole civil service system operated. He admired certain tried and true elements in it, saying they were so flexible and practical, and at the same time he would like to see a few others taken out or improved upon. Fired with enthusiasm, he laboured far into the night, consulting books and making notes, and planned to submit a list of suggestions to his immediate superior. Oh yes, for a few months he was an ardent second grade official (probationary category) of the Ministry of Public Instructions who yearned to, and believed he could, con-tribute his little bit for the common good. And then at some point, enthusiasm, waning rather rapidly, gave way to indifference, which in its turn brought on lassitude. Those few inspired months became a thing of the past. Now he came home looking tired and bored, and Phloi did not like it at all. She did not want to think that his initial excitement had been that of a child with the latest toy, didn't want him to take his job lightly and fail at it and become the butt of scorn and ridicule.

She would talk to him this afternoon, cheer him, tactfully tell him to mend his ways and apply himself consistently and diligently as his father, a model civil servant, had done.

Ot came home at the usual time and after he had had his
spoke to him along those lines. With a fond smile Ot told l   ..ε
could never hope to be the man his father had been and she should
not compare them—ever. Then he said, "I suppose you think I'm just
being lazy. Maybe you're right."

He went on to elaborate on the theme, admitting that he was
particularly lazy about fawning on the masters and making himself
charming to colleagues with influential relatives in the seats of power.
Nor could he summon the required amount of energy to look earnest
and busy when there was nothing to do. "And when there is something
that ought to be done and nobody's doing it I mustn't try to do it
either, because if I should by chance do it well, that might show up
somebody else's incompetence and I could create enemies that way,
you know."

As Phloi kept silent, he continued, "As I understand it, in my father's
time he and his friends helped their subordinates as a matter of course,
giving them generous support and encouragement in their jobs. Well,
I've had no such luck. And rather than beating my head against the
wall I have chosen to retreat from the wall and do nothing. Phi An
might say I'm making excuses for my laziness. The truth is, I'm also
lazy about making excuses."

He then went to plant himself in front of a window, gazing sombrely
out of it at the green trees and the blue sky.

"No, Mae Phloi," Phoem said to his sister a few days later, "I don't
think he's lazy. On the contrary, he takes his job seriously, or did.
He was eager to do some real work—not the right kind of eagerness
where he happens to be. Anyway, his attempts were foiled and he
got frustrated, disillusioned, and that's all there is to it. He is quite
plainly ill-suited to the job and I have a feeling he may quit any day
now. When he does, don't you be severe with him, Mae Phloi. Have
confidence in him. I do. I'm sure he'll find something else more in
tune with his temperament, and he'll be good at it."

Thus forewarned, Phloi showed no disappointment when Ot came
in one afternoon to tell her he had resigned. She had been decorating

the flower stands to be placed before the Buddha images, and she went on doing it while addressing the stands in front of her. "If you and your job do not get along well together, it's better to part."

"Aren't you surprised at all?" Ot demanded. "I thought you'd scold me."

"I'm only surprised you didn't say a word to me before."

Ot came to kneel beside her. "Forgive me. I should have talked to you first, but I didn't want you to advise me against it, then find I had to go against your advice. As a matter of fact, when I left you this morning I'd made no plans. It was after some hours of sitting dumbly at that desk that I suddenly felt I couldn't bear it one more day. I was thoroughly fed up, and thoroughly disgusted with myself, too, for having cheated the government by doing nothing and getting paid for it. I was ashamed to face the ghosts and the angels and myself. So here I am."

Now An happened to come in at this moment, and he said to Ot with a smile, "You look like a little boy in quest of a present. You must be sweet-talking Mother into giving you something, right?"

The smile vanished as soon as he learned what Ot had done. "What foolishness!" he spluttered. "What has got into you? What made you do it? And why didn't you consult me first? What was the difficulty anyway? Whatever it was it couldn't have been anything serious. You should have given yourself a little more time to get used to the idea of working—"

"Phi An," Ot said, "you can call me a lazy good-for-nothing if you want to. I don't mind."

While An was shaking his head in vexation Phloi hastily produced an untruth for the sake of peace. "Ot asked my advice, An, and I told him to go ahead if he was unhappy in this job and look for another one more suitable of him. I feel it's not too late for him to start all over again."

An frowned. "You do spoil him, Khun Mother. You should have made more effort, Ot, instead of giving up so easily. There's so much you can learn."

"I didn't know you wanted to send me back to school," Ot said, grinning. "There has been some misunderstanding obviously. I went there to work, and there was no work, so I left."

An heaved a profound sigh of annoyance. "I can't talk to you when you put on that flippant tone. I shouldn't have tried—it's utterly useless."

"He's right," said Ot, looking after his brother's back as he went grumbling out of the room. "You do spoil me. So now what are we going to do?"

"You're going to look for another job, son, and I'm going to keep nagging you to do it. I want to see you settled before I die."

"Ah—yes, and what am I going to do if you die? Can't imagine life without you, can't be philosophical about it, so I pray that I should die before you."

"Nonsense. Let's get back to the subject of work. You will start looking, won't you, without delay? You must have an occupation, my son."

"You're getting to be a real work-advocate like Phi An, darling. Anyway, I will find something, I give you my solemn promise. Meanwhile, I beg you to spare yourself the trouble of trying to save my reputation among my critics in this house. It won't hurt me to be branded a failure—it might even improve my character."

Some ten days went by.

Ot did make a move. He and Uncle Phoem, he told his mother, would take a trip to the South together, to explore job possibilities and get more news of Phi On at the same time. Would Khun Mother approve? Phloi was all for it; and the next few days saw her busily, and with loving care, packaging food, clothes and medicine for Ot to take to her prisoner-son on Tarutao Island, although of course she could not be sure if Ot would be able to find a way of getting them to their destination.

The day before the start of the journey Phoem dropped in to say goodbye to his sister.

"I want you to behave yourself on this trip," she playfully warned him. "No painting the town red, no drinking spree or anything like that, do you hear?"

"Oh-ho!" Phoem cried in mock horror. "Do you think I resemble Khun Chit that much?"

They laughed together and chatted awhile about their reprobate brother. Where had Khun Chit disappeared to anyway? According to his deserted wife, Phuang, now caretaker of the house in Khlong Bang Luang, he was reportedly living somewhere in Ban Pong with some other wife or wives but that had been some time ago. She hadn't heard from or about him for ages. Was he alive, or dead? A reformed character, or the same old Khun Chit? Or perhaps he was in jail? Anything was possible.

"We don't know where Khun Chit is," Phoem said. "We do know where On is but we can't get to him. By the way, Mae Phloi, you did know about some prisoners escaping from Tarutao, didn't you? . . . Oh, yes, they did, but On wasn't one of them. I was so disappointed."

Phloi, on the contrary, was relieved. "He could get into worse trouble trying to escape and getting caught."

"I don't know, Mae Phloi," Phoem mused. "If I'd been exiled on that island I would have tried anything to get away. The pursuing guards and I could have some fun together instead of moping about on the beach."

His sister looked at him doubtfully. "I think you have a secret longing to be taken prisoner, Khun Luang. Anything to make life more exciting. Maybe I should not let Ot go with you—you shouldn't be trusted to look after anybody."

"You have nothing to worry about," Phoem said brightly, "because it's Ot who's going to look after me on this great expedition."

OT was away for over a month; he came back looking thinner, tanned, and very cheerful.

"Any news of On?" was the first important query put to him by Phloi.

"He's still there and he's all right," Ot told her. "It took some doing to find the right contact who could get the packages through to him. Now he's got them, and some money too. And here's a letter for you, darling."

After she had finished reading it Phloi remained silent, her mind tuned to On's voice echoing in the distance and feeling sad because he was there and not here, but at the same time feeling thankful that he was still there, alive, and as well as could be expected under the circumstances. More freedom on the island, On said, and the air so wonderful it's like being on a holiday. Except for the hardship, of course, but that's nothing unusual for a prisoner. And, at times, acute loneliness, almost unbearable, loneliness of an incalculable magnitude such as he had never experienced while behind the walls of Bang Khwang jail. At other times there was a loss of all meaning and direction, and he became like a piece of flotsam buffeted about by the waves. Those parcels brought with them Khun Mother's loving kindness, reviving his capacity for hope, strengthening his will to go on, protecting him from despair and illness. All would be well and the time would come when he would be allowed to serve his beloved mother again and express his reverence and gratitude to her in person. That was his prayer, and now he must close and get the letter to the person who was to take it to Ot. How good Ot and Uncle Phoem had been to him. He would try to repay them in this life if he could, though he would remain in debt to them always.

When Ot had read the letter he murmured to himself, "Living on the island has made a writer of Phi On." Then aloud, "He's all right, you see. He'll come through, Mother. I hope to go down there again and get more supplies to him. At the moment he's well-stocked and the money should come in handy when he wants extra material comfort." He paused, and smiled. "Now what about me? Don't you want to know what happened to me? And didn't you miss me at all these past weeks?"

His mother laughed, having missed him not a little these past weeks. "And was it fun, Ot?"

"Great fun, Mother. Exciting, interesting, eye-opening. I should do it more often—get out of Bangkok, go to the provinces, learn more about our country, spend more time in the hills and the forests. Nature is so rich down there, and yet there's so much poverty, much more in evidence than in Bangkok. On the other hand, the millionaires of the South could burn bank notes for amusement and be no less wealthy the next day. I don't think I could ever become a millionaire, but what would you say if I should decide to go and work there?"

"I'd have no objection," said Phloi sincerely.

"I ran into an old school friend," Ot went on. "He owns a couple of mines and some other businesses. He's offered me a job."

"And you've accepted?"

"I told him I'd think about it and let him know. I would have preferred something nearer Bangkok. Don't want to be too far away from you."

His mother, determined to be cheerful and sensible about it, said, "You mustn't miss a good opportunity because of your concern for me, do you hear? That would turn me into an obstacle and I won't have it. And you wouldn't be too far away in any case. It's not all that inconvenient to travel back and forth between Bangkok and the South. I could come and visit you—that would be a nice change for me. I'd like that."

Nothing more was said on the subject by either son or mother on that occasion. Nor was it brought up again that day. Nor the next.

More than a month elapsed and still Ot had not made up his mind. He had reverted to the quiet life at home, but it did not satisfy him as before. Since his return from the South he seemed to have lost the knack of taking it easy with enjoyment; he was restless, yet reluctant to take any step that would mean leaving home. During this time, while not looking forward to it, Phloi prepared herself for the day when he might come to tell her he had decided to take up the good friend's offer.

IT came. Whether or not it would have come had the following incident not occured was a question to which there could be no definite answer.

They happened to find themselves all together that afternoon, mother, sons, daughter and son-in-law, at one of those ordinary, unplanned, placid domestic gatherings with refreshments and chitchat. It started to cease being placid when Phloi, remembering, asked An to get some money from the bank, mentioning the fact that she was going to buy a new car. A new car? An was surprised. What's wrong with her present one? Plenty, Phloi told him. It broke down so often, something always went wrong with it—old age, you know. She and Ot both thought it would be more practical to get a new one. He had not noticed anything wrong with it, An maintained. Ot, who had the use of Khun Mother's car, then urged him to go and make a closer inspection so as to assure himself of its dilapidated condition. Thereupon An turned on him.

"Listen, Ot, if you want to drive a beautiful new car and can afford it and pay for it out of your own pocket, it's your business. But I cannot approve of your wasting Khun Mother's money."

"It's my idea," Phloi quickly interposed. "Don't blame Ot."

"I'm blaming no one. I'm only saying that we're all old enough to provide for ourselves, and not to sit and eat, sleep and eat, doing nothing but living luxuriously off the common fund of the house."

"Meaning me," Ot said.

"Meaning you," said An. "You're taking unfair advantage of the others, you know."

"How?"

"As I said, you sit around doing nothing while the rest of us work to earn our living. What you spend comes out of the common fund, have you ever thought of it? Of course, everything in this house belongs to Khun Mother, but some day—" he hesitated a moment or two, "—some day it will have to be divided among her children, and you, Ot, will be getting an equal share even though you will have already profited from it. If that isn't taking advantage of the others, what is?"

"Phi An—I never—never thought—" Ot stammered, turned pale and did not finish the sentence.

"An!" Phloi intervened again. "We're discussing cars, not legacies. And with me sitting here you talk about dividing up the property. Have you no consideration for my feelings at all?"

"You can always use our car, Khun Mother." This interruption came from Sewi, the son-in-law.

"That's right, Khun Mother," Praphai promptly joined in. "There's our car, and there's Phi An's car. Two cars available for you in this house. No need whatsoever to get another. Waste of money, really."

"Khun Mother is not to be allowed a car of her own? Must she borrow one every time she wants to go out, Praphai?"

"Not borrow, Phi Ot. We offer it to her. We want her to make use of what we have. All we possess we put at her disposal—she doesn't have to borrow anything from us. We want to serve her, repay her for what she has done for us. She's looked after us all these years, and now as grownups we look after her, strive to do all we can for her."

"And I, doing nothing for her, still have to be looked after like a child, to be fed and clothed and taken care of by her—is that it, Praphai?"

"It's not my place as your younger sister to censure you, Phi Ot."

"Thank you, Praphai. Thank you, Phi An. It's no small thing, let me tell you, to be made wiser as regards one's sisters and brothers. Well, very soon things are going to be different, and no one should have cause to accuse me again of taking advantage of the others."

He paused and, seeing that no one had anything further to add or detract, walked out.

Ot left for the South a few days later.

Phloi would have liked him to join his friend as a business partner. She would put up the necessary capital, but Ot declined. He'd rather go empty-handed, as it were, and start from scratch.

When they took leave of each other Phloi gave him her blessing in broken phrases. Have a safe journey, Ot. Take care of yourself, my son. She patted his head and kept repeating herself without knowing it. Keep well. Come home as soon as you can. Keep well. As soon as you can get leave come back home for a visit. May you succeed and prosper. Come back soon, come back soon.

Ot said, "And you must come and see me. As soon as it can be arranged and you're ready, I'll come back and fetch you, Mother. It will be a nice change for you, as you said. You'll like it, Mother."

When he was gone Phloi felt forsaken by the whole world. Alone in her bedroom she sat down at the dressing table and from a drawer brought out the music box given her by Sadet many years ago—the day her mother had gone away. A gift of loving kindness, a balm for a child's lonely heart. She wound it and the bird began to sing. It was a sad song she heard coming from the little creature's gilded throat. She put her head down on the table and shared its grief.

FORTY-TWO

EXTRACTS from one of Ot's letters to his mother:

"Work going well . . .

"I've just sent off another package of provisions and some cash to Phi On. He, too, is getting along quite well on his island resort. . .

"Separated from you I feel close as ever to you, as much part of your flesh and blood and heart and mind . . . Knowledge of the important things in this life I've received from you, and for this I'm eternally grateful—honesty, loyalty, fairmindedness, compassion towards our fellow beings, all this and more . . . I feel you're here with me in spirit, guiding me, keeping me on the path of right thinking and right action . . . I've always known this but living far away from you has sharpened my awareness of it, of how blessed I am to have been born your son . . .

"The sun is going down over the hills and the birds fly past my veranda on their way home. The view is lovely at all times but particularly enchanting as dusk approaches. I never get tired of watching it. You'd love it too. . .

"The surest way to get rich quick down here is to marry one of the mining heiresses. Naturally most of them have already been snapped up but there are still two left for us late-comers. One is over fifty, blind in one eye and with teeth set far apart reminding you of bridge posts. Her rival, a young lady aged seven, has a perpetually running nose and a distinguished, ear-splitting voice. I've been eyeing them speculatively and would appreciate your motherly advice. . ."

If Granny Phit had been alive Phloi would have taken these letters to her room and read them to her. They would have laughed together, wiped away a few tears together, missed Ot together, and felt all the better for it. Granny Phit died of old age, like a ripe fruit dropping effortlessly from the tree, not long after Ot had left for the South— Granny Phit, who had moved into this house the same day as Phloi the bride, who had been present at Phloi's birth and at the death of Phloi's mother, who had loved this earthly existence and taken its wayward joys and miseries in her stride. Now she was gone. Yet another well-loved landmark had been blotted out. Another unfillable void in Phloi's world.

Choi, who seemed to know instinctively when she was most needed, paid frequent visits to her friend during this period, and proved, as always, an antidote to the despondent mood, a refreshing rain shower to the parched soul, a renewer of belief in the possibility of happiness. Sometimes Phloi only had to look at her to laugh with delight. There she'd be, seated smiling on the floor, amazingly, preposterously, endearingly the same Choi, resistant to change, her hairdo the same short style she had always worn since her tonsure, dressed in the *phanung* and bodice cloth (no *phasin*, no *farang* skirt, thank you very much) whose colour combination was prescribed for that day of the week in the best tradition of the Inner Court of a half-century ago. The garment had the Inner Court fragrance, and so did the powder and scent she put on her skin (to Phloi, one of the most evocative smells on earth) and when she left the room the floor and the air above it would continue to proclaim her recent presence. But while she might look a figure from a bygone era, Choi lived very much with the hard realities of today, coping gaily with them—none of this bemoaning the passing of the golden age; and when she aired her problems it was only to assure Phloi that everybody had them—a small consolation perhaps, but helpful nonetheless.

One night they had this conversation in Phloi's room when Choi came to stay with her:

"Ah—worries, worries. Be thankful you have no children, Choi."

"But Phloi, I often wish I had a few worries like yours to brighten up my life. Woe is me, who have no parents, no children, no Sadet, no Khun Aunt Sai—my brother is alive but we don't see each other. Ah, one can suffer because one has nobody to worry about."

"You don't, though, Choi. You don't suffer."

"Perhaps not so much on account of having nobody to worry about as on account of having no money to speak of. You haven't got that worry, Phloi, and can pursue your other worries in comfort. You don't have to struggle to make ends meet, to stretch the baht to it's farthest limits—"

"Choi, you know very well if you need money—"

"Wait. Luckily I still have a roof over my head and I don't have to pay rent, but one of these days I might be ordered to get out of Sadet's residence. You never can tell."

"Then you would move in with me. But what about your old house?"

"My father died a poor man, Phloi. In fact, Khun Aunt Sai had to help pay for his cremation. Phi Nuang sold the house, didn't I tell you? I went past it the other day and thought I'd look in. I shouldn't have. Some Chinese weavers have taken over the place and turned it into a cloth factory, and I'm sure their business is flourishing, but the place has gone to seed, Phloi, so shabby and filthy and stinky—what used to be a nice *khlong* running by the house is now a garbage dump. And the house itself—oh Phloi, you would have cried, the house is falling apart, rotting away. It was so sad-looking, Phloi. I wept."

"I know exactly how you must have felt. But look here, Choi, if you haven't got enough money to live on—"

"Oh, but I do! I still have a little something left me by Khun Aunt, please note. I know you have a heart vast as an ocean, but for the time being I think I can survive unaided. I take in some sewing from a shop, I do the monks' robes for them, and I also make scented water and bottle it and sell it. Then, once in a while I'm asked to arrange flowers for some important occasion or other. Oh, I get enough to eat."

"Choi, please let me help. What if you should be taken ill?"

"I could dispose of some of my old trinkets and live on the proceeds for a while. Those things will last me for some time, and I'll try not to outlast them. And so, my dear Khunying Phloi, stop looking tragic. I'm all right. Just wanted to remind you that we all have our troubles so that you won't feel so lonely in your suffering, that's all."

Regarding Ot and the scene between him and his brother and sister, which Phloi had recounted to her in full, Choi had this to say: "Those three children had been living together in peace until the fourth person came along. Beware of this person, Phloi."

She did not mention Khun Sewi by name. "I feel I'm sowing enough discord telling you to beware, but beware. I mustn't interfere in your family affairs."

But of course Choi was considered one of the family and therefore she had every right to speak her mind when believing something had gone amiss in the family.

SINCE Ot's departure Khun Sewi had been coming to the big house to keep Phloi company nearly every day, either with Praphai accompanying him or by himself. Rather sweet of him, Phloi generally thought. He doesn't want me to feel lonesome, he's become less stiff, he's putting himself out, it looks like he finally wishes us to move closer together, to be friends and not just in-laws—perhaps all this time he's been deterred by Ot's glaring antipathy. Ah, but what would Ot say if he knew what had been going on behind his back? I don't trust him, Mother—that's what Ot would say. You've been nice and kind to that odious man again, Mother—he doesn't deserve it. But Ot, he's the husband of my daughter and I should treat him like a son...

There were times, however, when Phloi had to admit to herself that she would prefer Khun Sewi to be less assiduous about dropping in on her, and when his visit threatened to drag on she would catch herself praying he would go away soon.

And now there were times, while in conversation with him, when she would be reminded of Choi's "Beware, beware..."

He said to her one day, "I can't help feeling concerned about Khun An. He's looking so tired."

Now this came as a surprise to Phloi, and she asked wonderingly, "You think so, Pho Sewi?"

"He's been working too hard, Khun Mother. He works hard at the office—he's one of the most dedicated and the best men in the department and I'm full of admiration for him. And when he comes home he carries on with his work for the family. Quite a gruelling schedule."

"What work?" Phloi asked again.

"Well, he manages the property for you. That's work. Not heavy work, admittedly, but complicated enough to make demands on his time and energy. If you permit me, I'd like to suggest you find somebody to help him, to lighten his burdens. He could do with a little more rest. Poor Khun An."

With a slight frown, Phloi remarked, "Funny, he never said anything to me about having too much to do."

"Of course not!" Khun Sewi gave an all-knowing smile. "My esteemed brother-in-law is not one to complain. Once he's agreed to do something he gives it everything he has, without a murmur, especially when it's for you, Khun Mother. And it will never occur to him to get anybody else to help him, unless you suggest it. I've been thinking, Praphai's not all that busy and I'm sure she'll be willing to lend a hand."

"Oh, no, Pho Sewi," Phloi said firmly. "That's out of the question. I'm not going to take Praphai away from her wifely duties. She has her own home—she has you to look after."

Silence for a moment or two, then Khun Sewi said in a soft, gentle voice, "You have been infinitely kind to me and I will never be able to discharge my debt of gratitude to you in full, but won't you please allow me to pay back a little by making myself useful to you and to Khun An. I can't go to Khun An and offer him my service—he might think I'm trying to poke my nose in his business, but if it's your suggestion I think he'll welcome it."

Phloi said she would talk it over with An.

ONE night after dinner, in answer to his mother's questions, An said, smiling a pleased smile at her concern for his well-being, "I'm not working too hard at all, Khun Mother, and I feel perfectly all right, not in the least tired. The work I do for you is anything but arduous— collecting rent, putting money in the bank, drawing it out for you, and yes," he laughed, "keeping the accounts in order. Every baht and *satang* received and spent is all there in the book, scrupulously recorded. Don't want anybody to accuse me of cheating you, you know. But what made you think the job might be too much for me?"

"No, it's not that. I just thought if you'd like to have more spare time I'd get somebody to help you."

"Who do you have in mind, Mother?"

"Well, what about Khun Sewi?"

"Sewi? Why Sewi?—Wait a minute. Is this your own idea?—Ah, I see. I should have known. Praphai sounded me out some time ago on this very same subject, but I deliberately ignored the hint. There's no reason why Sewi should have anything to do with the handling of your money."

They both remained silent for a few minutes, and then came this question from An, "What do you really think of Sewi, Mother?"

"I think he's a good man," Phloi answered spontaneously. "And as son-in-law he behaves properly, sometimes so very properly as to be touching. It's me, An, who's not a very good mother-in-law to him. I reproach myself for not being able to feel more at ease with him."

"I used to think I knew him quite well," An said. "Now I'm not so sure. In fact, sometimes I don't understand him at all, and, what's more disconcerting, I'm beginning to find my own sister hard to understand. For one thing, she's getting to sound more and more like Sewi."

Phloi saw nothing wrong in that. "A wife who loves and respects her husband tends to sound a little bit like him. We should be glad they get along well, my son."

"Do they, Mother? I should qualify my statement. She sounds like him, but not without an effort. She says certain things and you get the impression that she doesn't really want to say them but has been made to—that she's extremely reluctant about uttering those words which are not her own."

Phloi then cautioned her son not to say or do anything which might cause a rift in the family. "Remember, An, it's a delicate thing, this relationship between in-laws."

An assured her of his abiding peaceable intentions, made some remarks on the "difficulty of learning the true character of another human being," then left it rather abruptly and turned to more enjoyable themes.

Several days had gone by during which Phloi did not discuss the management of her property with anyone. She was perfectly content to leave well enough alone.

It was Praphai who brought it up again one peaceful afternoon. Her opening question went something like this: "Have you any idea at all where you stand financially, Khun Mother?" And Khun Mother gave a sigh, followed by an evasive answer. "Your Phi An takes care of everything for me. He's very efficient, as you know." Next came Praphai's remarks to the effect that Phi An by himself could not be expected to think of everything and oversee everything and that there might be leaks here and there he had not detected, and what a pity if that were indeed the case.

Oh, how Phloi was annoyed with her daughter! She proceeded to list An's undoubted virtues such as thoroughness, punctiliousness, scrupulousness, integrity, rectitude and what have you. And then she said rather cuttingly, "I thought you worshipped your brother. Am I to understand that you don't even trust him?"

Now it was Praphai's turn to sigh. "Oh, Mother, you know I didn't mean it like that. Frankly, I didn't want to talk to you about—about those things at all, but then—" She didn't quite know how to go on, and while she was forming her words, Phloi put in a few of her own.

"Loyalty to one's husband doesn't have to mean blind obedience. A wife who feels that her husband may be acting wrong or thinking wrong should warn him. That's true loyalty. Being a good wife does not preclude being a good sister. Sometimes it's very difficult to keep the peace among our nearest and dearest, but we mustn't give up too easily, Praphai."

Now Praphai was ready; she had decided to tell Khun Mother about it. She said, "Khun Sewi has been prodding me to propose this and that to you and Phi An concerning the family property. He's constantly after me to take more interest in what he says will be mine one day. He's afraid that my ignorance is going to rob me of my rightful share or something like that." She gave another sigh. "Money, money, money. I've never known anyone to be so obsessed with it like Khun Sewi. It's true, Mother. I'm not exaggerating. You don't know what it's like when he keeps harping on money matters. It makes life so dreary. It's quite awful."

It must be, Phloi thought, but aloud she spoke as a mother should. "Money's important," she said, "and since you never knew anything about it except how to spend it, Khun Sewi is doing what's right if he's teaching you to handle it with more care."

"Ah!" Praphai gave a dazzlingly sardonic smile. "But I'm not handling any money, Mother. He keeps it all and doles out small sums to me from time to time. How could I have thought him so generous! But he was generous in the beginning. Now when I want to buy something nice he usually objects and we argue about it. We've had so many fights over money. You didn't know that, did you?"

Phloi shook her head in dismay, but while sympathizing with her daughter she nevertheless proceeded to give such positive advice as, "You mustn't give way to your emotions, Praphai. Try not to provoke him, my daughter. Behave calmly, don't lose your temper." And Praphai's answer to all that was, "You can't imagine how aggravating he can be, Mother, especially when he argues like a tricky lawyer who's a pompous orator to boot. Well," she added, "now you know. It hasn't been easy for me, not at all easy."

Eyeing her handsome but not very cheerful daughter Phloi thought here was a good opportunity to have another talk on the subject dear to her heart. "Children," she began, "bring happiness to the home. When you have children—"

"No, Khun Mother." Praphai was quick to dispel any false hope Khun Mother might be entertaining in that direction. "I take comfort from the fact that at least Khun Sewi and I are childless and that if we should find it impossible to live together we could part without having to agonize over the question of children."

"Praphai!" Phloi was shocked. "How can you talk so glibly about it! You've had a few arguments with your husband and you talk about parting from him! Where did you get this attitude? Not from my upbringing!"

"Time was," Praphai said calmly, "when what the women felt was not considered very important, not even by the women them-selves. By and large they were regarded as belonging to their husbands and not as individuals having their own lives to live. It's not like that any more, Khun Mother. I have but one life, and I'm not going to waste it in an unhappy marriage. I'm in favour of happiness, Mother."

"We all are," Phloi said impatiently. "The important thing is how we should go about getting it. Happiness is not something you demand, my dear child. It's not grabbing but giving that brings true happiness. When you love someone, you give of yourself to him—that's happiness."

Then Praphai suddenly asked, "When you married Father you didn't love him, did you?"

And Phloi answered, "I must have loved him without knowing it, otherwise I don't think I would have consented to marry him. I know now I've never loved anyone but him."

"It's nice to be so sure," Praphai remarked, gave a rueful smile and brought this rather desultory conversation to an exceedingly unsatisfactory conclusion as far as Phloi was concerned, by adding, "You see, I'm not sure at all that I love Khun Sewi."

FORTY-THREE

PHLOI came down to her morning rice one fine morning to be informed by a solemn-faced An that another war had broken out in Europe. Germany on one side against France and England.

Same as last time—in the year 2457 of the Buddhist Era. And who did An believe would win this time? Phloi asked, and the answer—"Germany, of course," given in a positive tone of voice, made her laugh because it reminded her so much of Khun Prem at the beginning of that other war. An talked about Germany's overwhelmingly strong position in international politics and went on to forecast a short war, and the likelihood that our *Muang Thai* would not be adversely affected by it. Phloi was not too disturbed by his news except to feel human compassion for the *farang*s who had the bad luck of having another war thrust upon them. *Farang*s in general. And it was not until An, after finishing his breakfast, was about to leave for the office, that she suddenly remembered: Lucille! Lucille was still in France. "Oh An, how remiss of me not to have thought of her right away. What news of her, An? When is she coming home?"

"Lucille and I are divorced, Mother. We decided on it not long after she left."

"Why didn't you tell me, son? Oh, why didn't you tell me? Oh my poor Lucille. . ."

It was as much Lucille's decision as his, An assured his mother. They had agreed on it being the best solution; he had meant to let sufficient time elapse before telling Mother, wishing to break it to her gently.

Phloi asked, "Does Praphai know?"

An replied, "She's known all along, Mother."

"No wonder—" Phloi began, and stopped.

"No wonder what, Mother?"

Feeling disinclined to discuss Praphai's case (the less said the better, in her opinion), Phloi gave a vague answer and waved him off to work. She herself went on thinking about Praphai, about Praphai and Sewi, An and Lucille. The momentous happening in Europe had quite receded from her mind.

She remained indifferent to the war throughout its early phase, and so did most of the people round her; even Phoem seemed to be unmoved by the blitzkrieg and had, surprisingly and most uncharacteristically, very little to comment on the fall of France.

But before long she began to realize how much the world had shrunk over the past twenty-five years, so that events erupting in what had been a remote spot on the face of the globe could now swiftly affect the lives of people here in *Muang Thai*. A war was being fought among the *farang*s and now *Muang Thai* was demanding that the French return to Thai sovereignty some of the territories along the Mae Khong River which they had taken away. The claims had been formally submitted and now there were public demonstrations supporting those claims in the streets of Bangkok and in other cities and towns all over the country, masses of citizens proudly and cheerily marching along, carrying banners with stirring phrases painted on them such as "WE THAI WERE BORN WARRIORS" and "WE WILL FIGHT IF OUR TERRITORIES ARE NOT RETURNED." Phloi felt the excitement, but more as a spectator rather than a participant. She prayed hard, though, when fighting broke out in the border areas at the height of the dispute, praying for her nation's cause, for the safety of the soldiers and sailors, and above all for a speedy and peaceful settlement. Ot wrote from the South advising her to mind her age and not go marching about but be content to evince her patriotism in a more sedentary manner. Phloi gathered his heart was in the right place even though he had not been doing much shouting against the enemy.

Nor had Phoem, and this struck Phloi as definitely odd. She asked him what was the matter. "Have you gone pro-French or what, Khun Luang?"

"Never!" Phoem cried. "I still remember how I felt when they wrenched those provinces from us, young as I was, in the year 112 of our Ratanakosin Era." He paused. "But, it's funny, I can't explain it, Mae Phloi. I can't explain why I haven't been able to drum up much enthusiasm about all this."

"Don't you want to reclaim our lost territories, Khun Luang?"

"Yes, yes, Mae Phloi, but at the same time I can't help feeling sceptical about the outcome. If we should get back those provinces, how long would we be allowed to keep them? The French have fallen but they still have friends. I don't think they're going to be forsaken by their friends. I hope and pray, Mae Phloi, that the plots of land we might get back will not cause us to lose more plots later on."

"You're not sure who will win the war in Europe?"

"I'm not sure of anything. But war brings losses and all involved in it can be losers. I feel uneasy about our *Muang Thai*, Mae Phloi. War is getting nearer us, I fear. I'm afraid. But you know what, Mae Phloi? It's not the *farang*s I'm afraid of these days but the Japanese."

"But I don't understand, Khun Luang. Why should you be afraid of the Japanese? They've never troubled us in any way. I think they're nice people—polite, you know, not so very different from *Khon Thai*. Take Dr. Takeda—such a nice, kind gentleman, and a good doctor, too. I went to see him a couple of times and he was so good to me."

"Oh, Mae Phloi! Oh, Mae Phloi! You haven't the faintest idea what I'm talking about, do you? You know one kind Japanese so you think the whole Japanese nation is like him. Let's talk about something else."

Whatever apprehensions he might have about the Japanese at this time Phoem expressed nothing but thankful relief when at last the Thai-French conflict came to be resolved under Japanese mediation. Cessation of hostilities. The provinces of Phra Ta Bong, Siemrat, Champasak and Lan Chang were handed back to *Muang Thai*. The terms of the settlement had apparently been effected to everyone's satisfaction.

Calm was restored and the war clouds looked like they were moving away. How lucky they were! Then, after a few short months, the clouds returned, closer, darker, more menacing. No one wanted to believe what they heard, but everywhere in Bangkok people were asking one another, Is *Muang Thai* going to be invaded? What's going to happen to us? What are we going to do? Official announce-ments read over the radio day after day affirmed the country's desire, resolution, determination to maintain and safeguard its neutrality—*khwam pen klang*—(being in the middle). As the days went by, the tone of the announcements became more intense, almost desperate. Then came another series of announcements and these really put fear in Phloi's heart. They had to do with this new law made for the defence of the homeland in the event of enemy attack. Peace-loving as it was, their country must now hold itself ready for violent action, when and if necessary. The people should be ready to set fire to their own homes and paddyfields and plantations in carrying out their duties as citizens against the invaders, whoever they might be.

"We must be prepared for the worst," An said. "It may come or it may not, but if it does we'll face it. In the meantime, Mother dear, stop listening to the radio if it upsets you so much. No use making yourself ill with worry. Don't be afraid. You're not alone. There are many of us in this house and we will take good care of you."

Ot wrote again, telling Mother his work was keeping him unbelievably busy at the moment; he had planned a trip to Bangkok and had to cancel it at the last minute. Not a word about the terrible news and rumours, Phloi remarked to herself. Doesn't he know? Hasn't he heard? Our country is in danger and he says nothing about it!

As for her brother Phoem, how he could be so light-hearted at a time like this was beyond her. He even joked about this poison gas business. "Have you got any in your possession, Mae Phloi? If you do you could make plenty of merit by donating it to the authorities to use against the enemy. Make merit with your generous gift of the poison gas—sounds good, doesn't it?"

Phloi remonstrated with him, telling him to stop laughing and start worrying. "War is no laughing matter, Khun Luang!"

"You're right, Mae Phloi, and today's war is a lot deadlier than the old version. If by worrying we could get it to bypass us, we should worry with all our might. Ah, Mae Phloi, if only it were in our power to alter its course, though if you ask me what that course is, I can't tell you. What are you frightened of anyway? If the war should overtake us and you and I should get killed, what of it? We would have lived long enough on this planet Earth. If death comes not today it comes tomorrow, in peace as in war."

"I'd prefer it in peace... I don't know what I'm frightened of, but I am. I can't help it. Listen, Khun Luang, you won't leave me if anything happens, will you?"

"Perish the thought, Mae Phloi! What do you think I am, my one and only little sister?"

And on the night it happened he was there with her. He came straight to the house as soon as he heard. It was the seventh of December. An, Khun Sewi and Praphai had gone out to watch the rehearsal lighting for the coming Constitution Day celebrations and then to a party afterwards. Phloi was in bed when he arrived. He roused the servants to open a front door for him and sent a maid to wake her up. A few minutes later found them together in the sitting room where only one small light had been switched on; and in the semi-darkness Phoem said to her in a low voice, "They've turned into soldiers, Mae Phloi. The Japanese in our town. They're walking about in their army uniforms."

Phloi peered at him uncomprehendingly. "It can't be, Khun Luang."

"I've seen them, Mae Phloi. Soi Sap was full of them."

"What were you doing in Soi Sap?"

"That's my business. After seeing them I hurried away and went looking for some officer friends who might be able to tell me more about it. Couldn't find one, but I talked to some of their men. The Japanese are coming, they tell me. You understand now, Mae Phloi?"

She understood and her heart was pounding. "Oh Khun Luang! What are we going to do? Where can we go? And where are all my children? Oh, Khun Luang, help me."

Phoem was disgusted. "Don't act like a scared rabbit. Keep calm. Don't panic, please."

"I don't know how I can keep calm!" She took a deep breath. "How can you expect me to keep calm?" Another deep breath, then she asked, "What about your wife? Shouldn't you be with her?"

"We've got a houseful of relatives. She's all right, probably sound asleep at this moment. You're alone here. I'll stay with you at least until An comes back."

Phloi felt very grateful. She sat down with him and together they waited, mostly in silence, for An and Praphai to come home. In the stillness of the night they heard a car or two roaring past and the roosters chorusing their pre-dawn chants from time to time, but otherwise nothing. Nothing extraordinary seemed to be taking place in this part of the city. At last a car came in the driveway and Phloi went to the window to call down to it. Praphai, its sole passenger, got out and came up to join her mother and uncle.

"Khun Sewi and Phi An were called away from the party," she told them. "Khun Sewi says everything will be all right and you're not to worry, Khun Mother. The Japanese are here as our friends."

"How could he know?" Phloi said doubtfully.

"He has many Japanese friends," Praphai said, yawning. After a few minutes she rose. "I'm so sleepy. May I go to bed, Khun Mother? If there's anything, please send someone to wake me up."

When she was gone, Phoem said with a chuckle, "Why don't you follow your daughter's example, Mae Phloi? Everything will be all right, you see. Her husband says so."

"I don't think I can sleep, Khun Luang. I'm not made of iron and steel like these modern people."

They waited until morning and went down to breakfast. It was some hours later that An finally appeared. He looked awful, as if he had not slept for a week instead of only twenty-four hours. He sank down in a chair, looked at Phloi, and said, "We've lost our country to the Japanese—" Then he cried without restraint, sobbing like a small boy.

Phoem quickly went to him and put his arm round him. "Courage, dear boy. Let's talk about it first. What happened? What's going on?"

An dried his tears and told them, in broken sentences. "Japan has declared war on England and America . . . Japanese forces entered *Muang Thai* last night. They sent us an ultimatum . . . They would attack if we didn't let them pass. . . We had to yield—there was—there was no other choice. . . We were caught off guard—no warning—we've had no warning, not the slightest . . . very few people seem to have known what was coming—"

His uncle said, "We've become Japan's vassal, is that it?"

"That's not how the foreign diplomats put it," An replied. "They say we still have our independence—as Japan's 'ally.' But I feel as you do, Uncle."

Uncle and nephew looked at each other, thinking the same thoughts, and Phloi, watching them, was very glad to see them united again, even if in sorrow and despair; and for a minute or two she forgot about the Japanese soldiers. Then she started to tremble: Ot and On in the South! An said there was fighting in the South! She grew frantic and Phoem had to scold her. "Stop snivelling over your grown sons, Mae Phloi!" And An pointed out how far away both On and Ot were from the scene of the fighting, which by now should have ended in any case.

As Phloi quieted down, the two men, their voices heavy and low, their faces clouded with anxiety and hurt and shame, resumed talking about the situation. Phloi did not try to follow them. She felt the subject was too big for her, beyond her power to grasp. Not for her to make any judgment or decision. How she was to cope with it she would leave to the menfolk. They would guide her. She would do her best, keep to the path of doing right, and let the deeds good and bad that she had committed in this and other lives bring on whatever consequences for her to face in the uncertain days ahead.

She was the first to see Sewi enter the room in his customary stealthy way. Unlike An and Phoem, he was looking hale and hearty, not in the least tired or dejected. He smiled at them, and at An's question, "Any more news?" his smile broadened.

"Nothing more, An, except more assurance from the Japanese that they will give us all the assistance we need. The fighting has stopped. Everything is in order."

Phoem lighted a cigarette, took several quick puffs, inhaled, exhaled, and said nothing. An stared at Sewi as though he had never seen him before.

"Tell me, Sewi. The Japanese are occupying our country. You don't feel anything at all? You're not angry? Not sorry? Not even a little ashamed, or disappointed?"

"What are you talking about, An? We should all thank our lucky stars things have turned out this way. If we had stubbornly battled on we would have been annihilated. Think of the loss of lives, of devastated farmlands and cities going up in flame, and all for nothing. But we let them in as friends and now we are their respected ally, to be treated with consideration. In a global war, it's crucial for a country like ours to choose to be on the right side, the winning side. The wrong choice could mean utter ruin. So you might say we've turned defeat into victory, An."

"Wait, Pho Sewi," Phoem spoke up. "You're talking as though there were no *farang*s left. As Japan's ally, we'll have to fight the *farang*s who are Japan's enemies. Are you sure we can take them on?"

Khun Sewi was greatly amused. He laughed loudly and answered, "Your question doesn't surprise me, Khun Uncle. You stand in fear of the *farang*s because you were born and bred and spent your most impressionable years in the age of *farang* supremacy. That age has come to an end, Khun Uncle. Japan is ridding Asia of *farang* powers, driving them out of the Philippines and Malaya at this very moment, and going to drive them out of Burma, Java, Borneo, India. . . Even Australia might have to bow to Japan one of these days. When the smoke clears, Khun Uncle, Japan will be leading Asia, with us as their partner, because we've had the foresight to join with them from the start. Not to cooperate with them would amount to being unpatriotic."

An banged on the table. "You may do as you please, Sewi! You may cooperate with them to your heart's content, but it's not for you to call anybody unpatriotic. We all love our country, and there may be some to say it's you and people like you who have sold our country to the Japanese."

Glancing at Sewi, Phloi felt her flesh creep at the vicious anger in his eyes. But in the next instant it was gone, replaced by a bland expression, and when he spoke it was in a level voice. "Let's not stop being friends because we happen to hold different opinions. And by no means let us lapse into abusive language. I suggest you wait and see, An, before telling me I'm wrong. To go on arguing now will get us nowhere."

He yawned, then turned to Phloi with a smile. "I was up all night, Khun Mother. About time I got some sleep. Now, Khun Mother, I want you to relax and not worry about a thing. If problems should crop up and you need help, please don't hesitate to let me know. Our Japanese friends will be only too glad to lend a helping hand, I can assure you." Having thus spoken generously as a winner should, he made his exit.

An shook his head in consternation. How could he have been so completely mistaken about the man? Phoem consoled his nephew, saying he shouldn't waste time bothering about this kind of people.

And Phloi marvelled at how impersonal events could have the power to revive personal affections, or alienate them. What about blood ties, and relations through marriage? Should they not matter? She herself held them to be important and binding, but they did not seem to count very much with these men, not where their feel-ings were concerned.

FORTY-FOUR

STRANGE, Phloi thought, as she observed what was happening round her since the Japanese had come into *Muang Thai*. Strange how quickly the atmosphere had changed. Her son An had not been alone in his sadness: on that day, the eighth of December, the whole country (with Khun Sewi as the exception) had seemed to her to be in deep mourning, and at the same time trembling in the grip of fear, fear of invading devils. And then, not many days afterwards, both the fear and the sorrow had started to ebb, grow blurred, and soon disappeared altogether. Japanese soldiers constantly on the move had become a normal sight, hence inconspicuous, arousing little curiosity. A number of Japanese officers and civilians had since taken up residence here. They were not equated with the devils any more. They behaved well and got along well—some even intimately well—with the Thais. Important functions did not take place these days without being graced by the presence of a few Japanese dignitaries, and this, too, was considered normal. *Muang Thai* had signed the pact of alliance with Japan. The signing ceremony had taken place in the Temple of the Emerald Buddha. Japan's *farang* enemies had become *Muang Thai's* enemies, to be abominated or held in contempt. Japan was now the *Maha Mit*—the Great Friend.

Phloi herself had stopped feeling frightened of the war, now that the country was officially at war, formally one of the belligerent nations. The suspense was over, yet the situation had remained virtually the same as far as she could see. Her fellow Bangkokians were going about their daily routines with smiling faces, and the sun and the rain went on nourishing the earth and the birds went on chirping merrily in her garden. She had had visions of chaos, danger, disaster, and here she was listening to the birds sing. Strange. Prices were on the rise, true, but the same thing had happened in the last war and they had been able to manage all right, hadn't they? In fact, it was destined to turn out vastly different—not at all "the same thing"—but of course Phloi could not know that yet.

Some people were doing very well financially out of the war—Khun Sewi, for one. While remaining a high-ranking civil servant, he now figured importantly as a businessman in close association with some influential Japanese trading groups. Phloi was chatting with Praphai one day when An came to join them and in the course of the conversation brought up this subject.

"They say your husband has become very rich, Praphai. Tell us about it."

Praphai shook her head. "I can't, Phi An, I know nothing about it."

"How come? You're his wife. Doesn't he talk to you?"

"Not about where or how he makes his money, which suits me perfectly, because it's boring enough having him question me about Khun Mother's money, where it comes from and what's being done with it—and when I tell him I don't know and don't care to know he gets very annoyed and says I'll find myself a pauper one of these days. You can't imagine how tedious he can be on the subject of money."

"Well," An said. "He's making a lot of it these days. I've been told he's raking it in with the help of his Japanese friends. Makes me understand why he loves them so much."

And there An left the subject. The other two did not feel inclined to go on with it either. They had more amusing things to chat about. Afterwards, when Praphai had left, An asked after his younger brother.

"I've been thinking about Ot. How is he getting along, Mother? He never writes me."

"He's very busy," said Phloi. This was a fact, and a legitimate excuse. "His last letter came a few days ago. Not much news except that he's well and working away at his job."

An was silent for a minute, looking pensive. "I wish we could get him to come back and work in Bangkok. Things are fairly quiet now but there's no telling what may happen next. Ot should be here. I feel we ought to be together at a time like this."

"Oh, An!" Phloi cried joyfully. "It's wonderful to hear you say that! I'm *so* glad! But listen, you know as well as I do why he left home. You hurt him very much, An. You'll have to make your peace with him. Write him, An."

"I was hasty and unthoughtful that day and I've been feeling guilty about it ever since. I'll write him, Mother."

This he did without delay, and received a reply by return post. A pleasant brotherly letter in tone, but carrying a disappointing message: much as he would love to return to Bangkok, he could not possibly leave his job at this stage without seriously inconveniencing his boss-friend-benefactor.

"Perhaps he is still angry with me," An said, feeling guilty still.

Phloi assured him it was not so. "He's written to me, too. Here, read it yourself. He really feels he must show his gratitude to this good man by staying on."

Ot's letter to his mother read, in part: "He's been a true friend in need. When I first went to him I knew nothing about this business, yet he took me on, trained me, paid me, gave me all the comforts of home, treating me like a brother rather than an employee. To leave him at this juncture would be rank ingratitude on my part, and if we were Japanese I should cause all of you to suffer unspeakable shame and you would have to disembowel yourselves in order to salvage the family honour. . ."

In this letter Ot also sent news of Phi On. "He has been transferred to Turtle Island on the other side of the peninsula. It's too early to say with any certainty if he's going to be better or worse off than in Tarutao, so please wait for further news and don't let your imagination run riot, don't cry just yet, for you may be wasting tears. Be strong, as the radio announcer keeps exhorting us. Be strong. Our *Muang Thai* is now a Great Power, so we must all be strong. Therefore, be strong, do you hear?"

There was also a postscript to be passed on to Uncle Phoem: "Please tell Uncle I thought of him as I listened to the news of Mr.

Chamberlain resigning his premiership in England the day after we Thais overran *Muang* Kentung in Burma. Quite ingenious, we Thais!"

An chuckled at the letter. Then he remarked, "Come to think of it, maybe it's just as well Ot's not here. All this stuff about our being a great power side by side with our great ally will be difficult for Ot to stomach when he sees it in action right here in this house."

"What do you mean, An?"

"Surely, Mother, you must have seen him put on the lordly manner for our benefit lest we forget he's such a great man, being a great friend of Japan the Great Power. I mean *your* son-in-law, Mother."

"Well, I like that!" Phloi was all indignation. "You make it sound as though it was *I* who personally chose him for *my* son-in-law."

An laughed, at once amused and contrite. "I won't try to absolve myself from blame for having brought him here in the first place." He paused before adding matter-of-factly, "All is not well between Praphai and her husband, Mother."

"That's obvious enough, An, and it's been worrying me."

"Nothing you can do, Mother. Praphai's old enough to handle it herself. If she finds it unbearable to live with him she'll take steps to live apart from him. They'll go their separate ways and that will be that."

"Oh, An, I don't understand your modern ideas! Don't you believe it's worthwhile to try to stick together?"

"Why, of course! But not when it gets to be impossible, not to say unnatural, like trying to stick water to fire, or lime to turmeric. You need not be too concerned, Mother. Our Praphai is not the submissive long-suffering wife. She gets her own back."

He did not expand on the last statement but left it hanging in the air and went on to other matters less thought-provoking and more comprehensible to his mother.

THE war continued.

Malaya, the Philippines, Java, Sumatra, Borneo, Burma—all *farang* colonies from way back, all had now come under Japanese rule. It made Phloi wonder if this could really be the end of the *farang* power as her son-in-law had predicted right from the beginning. Khun Sewi gloried in Japan's conquests, and in his own prosperity. He kept saying, "You want more petrol, An? What do you need, Khun Mother? What about clothes or sugar? You only have to tell me." There was a shortage of these and other goods—it was wartime, after all—but Khun Sewi had no problems in getting them. An and Phloi politely but firmly declined these generous offers, the former perhaps on account of an obstinate streak, the latter from not wanting special privileges while her neighbours were being deprived, and also because she shied away from having to feel overly indebted to her son-in-law.

The war continued. Phoem dropped in to see his sister one day and they had the following war-related conversation:

"Mae Phloi, our *Muang Thai* nowadays seems to be acting as big as Japan, the Great Power."

"Isn't that as it should be, Khun Luang? When you have allied yourself to the Great Friend, wouldn't it be demeaning the Great Friendship to act small?"

"Ha! And now we're being told that *Muang Thai* cannot become a truly Great Power without *wathanatham*."

"What *wat*, Khun Luang?"

"It's not a *wat*, Mae Phloi, not a temple. It's a new word, freshly minted—haven't you heard? *Wathanatham* (culture)!"

"And what does it mean, Khun Luang?"

"Whatever the meaning, the government says we must acquire it for *Muang Thai* to get to be a real Great Power."

"And what do we have to do to acquire it?"

"We must wear hats, Mae Phloi."

"Are you playing one of your childish games with me? Hats and Great Power? Where's the connection?"

"But you just said it, Mae Phloi: hats and Great Power. *That's* the connection."

"But you've always worn a hat, Khun Luang, and so do the men of your generation. It's the young men of today who tend to go bare-headed."

"Never mind about us men, Mae Phloi. It's you women who are at the heart of this campaign. The government wants *you* to wear hats—young girls, spinsters, widows and others, each and every one of you. You must wear hats so that we can have the *wathanatham* so that our *Muang Thai* can become indisputably great. You have been entrusted with an enormous responsibility, Mae Phloi."

"Well, Khun Luang, all I can say is, the girls might go for it—a new fashion, you know—but it's not for me, thank you very much. In my young days hats were worn on rare occasions when you went out of town into the woods and fields. When I had to wear one in Bang Pa-in I felt like a clown!"

"Clown or no clown, you'll have to do it, my dear girl."

"And if I don't?"

"The police will get you."

"DON'T you find it cumbersome having to wear a hat all the time?" Phloi asked her daughter after the new cultural regulations had been in force for some weeks.

"Not at all, Mother. Hats are good fun, especially when I'm told I look good in them. What about you? But of course you haven't been out of the house all this time. We must do something about that—get you to go out and be seen in a hat."

"Don't be crazy, Praphai."

Praphai laughed. "You have no *wathanatham*, Khun Mother—that's the trouble with you. Beware, you might get arrested one of these days!"

That was the Era of the Hat. And when you turned on the radio you were apt to be reminded of its great symbolic importance by the announcer: *Mala nam Thai pai su Maha Amnat*—Hats lead Thais to Great Power.

The hat worn by Khun Choei, something broad-brimmed but otherwise indescribable, transformed her almost beyond recog-nition. She took it off, tossed it onto a chair, sat herself down on the floor, and laughed.

"Don't you like it, Phloi? You'd better, because it's the only one I have. A gift from my darling husband who could not stop laughing the first time I put it on. Now, Mae Phloi, I really don't mind looking absurd for the good of my country, but my dear, must I also stop chewing betel?" She was longingly eyeing Phloi's silver betel-nut tray. "May I help myself?" she said even as she did so. "Ummm, delicious! So very soul-satisfying! I've been dying for a good chew all morning."

Now that was also a prominent feature of the current cultural scene: betel-nut chewers going round dying for a good chew. They had been told to renounce the time-honoured custom and they obeyed the rule overtly but most went on doing their chewing illicitly, when the eye of the authorities was not fixed on them, as Khun Choei was doing now. When she first heard of the ban on betel, Phloi declared she had never thought she would live to witness such a strange happening in *Muang Thai*. Not that she minded the ban for herself, having given up the habit—except for an occasional chew after a meal—some twenty years ago. She had, however, all this time kept her silver betel-nut tray beautifully stocked, had never ceased applying the artistry she had acquired as an Inner Courtier in the carving of the nuts and the rolling of the *phlu* (betel) leaves for the pleasure of her betel-chewing visitors.

"Strange, yes," said Khun Choei, happily crunching her nut-and-leaf. "Quite fun, though, and makes you relish it more. Remind me to wash my mouth and teeth before I leave so the police won't suspect I've been misbehaving."

Quite fun, as Khun Choei said. Made it more flavourful. The vendors of areca nuts and betel leaves in the market also had fun concealing their now-precious, banned products under innocent-looking piles of fruit and vegetables and devising codewords and secret signs to alert their colleagues and customers. The operation had its risks, and its thrills. The hitherto merely routine commerce had been lifted into the realm of adventure.

CHOI enjoyed herself enormously in her fashion during this culture-conscious period. A sort of cultural demonstration was put on by Choi at Phloi's house one morning. When Phloi saw her starting to undress in broad daylight for no observable reason, she gasped: *Is my dear Choi going insane?* A moment later she caught on and burst into a laugh, and laughed on with tears streaming down her face. Choi had come marching up the driveway and Phloi from an open window could see she was all decked out in accordance with the *wathanatham* requirements, looking quaint enough in her hat and skirt (or would-be skirt, if truth be told), and then she had halted in front of the house at the foot of the stairs and proceeded to take them off—not only the hat, but the skirt, too! That was when Phloi thought she must be losing her mind. But no, the next instant did not reveal a naked Choi, thank goodness! Underneath the camouflage it was Choi draped as usual in her obsolescent counter-cultural *phanung*, who was now deftly folding up the discarded garment, then stuffing it into the big basket she had brought with her, then ascending the stairs.

"So you thought I must have gone mad," she said. "I thought the same of you. Khunying Phloi has taken leave of her senses, I thought, when I saw you going 'ha-ha-ha' like that all by yourself. Poor woman, I thought. Never mind, Phloi, it's not only you and I but the whole town has gone mad—isn't that wonderful?"

When they had sat down Choi brought out a parcel from her basket.

"I have a little gift for you, Phloi."

"What is it?"

"Hush, hush!" She unwrapped the parcel, disclosing rambutans and mangoes and, hidden under these and other fruit, the contraband areca nuts.

"Wait, Phloi, I'm not through yet." She rummaged in her capacious basket and produced another parcel. This one contained some very lovely betel leaves. "Don't they look invitingly chewable? Get some water quick, we must sprinkle them before they lose their freshness."

"Oh, Choi, you didn't have to turn into a smuggler for me!"

"My pleasure, Phloi. A bit of smuggling never hurt anybody. Who would have thought chewing betel could become so exciting, eh, Phloi? Do you suppose the opium-smokers feel it—the excitement of doing the forbidden thing? Or those women who prefer women?"

"Don't be naughty, Choi. But where have you been all this time? It's been ages. I thought you were dead."

"Not yet, as you can see. I've been busy making hats for sale. Lots of us in the Inner Court are doing it, some with more skill and ambition than others. I'm one of those who churn out the simplest things—like this one." She delved once again into the basket and came up with a sample. "Which I here and now present to you, Khunying Phloi. You may not win a prize in it but at least you will be following the leader and won't get arrested when you go out." (One of the wartime slogans was: *Tam phunam*, "Follow the leader.")

Holding it in front of her, Phloi gave the thing an objective appraisal, then she gave a smile. "It's a sweet little hat, Choi. What is the material?"

"You don't recognize it? Loofah—good old loofah. That's why it's so light. Half the time you forget it's sitting on your head, and that is real *wathanatham* for you. When I leave I'll show you how it should be worn when riding in the *samlo* with the wind blowing."

Some hours later, when Choi was ready to go back to the palace, a *samlo* was sent for. This three-wheeled vehicle, with the pedaller in front and the passenger-seat in the rear, was the popular form of transport in those years. Escorted by Phloi, Choi went down the stairs in her *phanung* and stepped into her quasi-skirt at the same spot she had taken it off earlier on. She then brought out her hat from the basket and now Phloi could see that it had two long strings hanging down from inside the crown. Choi put it on, the strings fluttering down to her skirt, and climbed up to her seat. How charmingly ridiculous she looked, Phloi thought, laughing delightedly out loud.

"Don't laugh but observe," Choi called out from the *samlo*. "Observe, Phloi, with my right hand I take hold of the strings which are long enough to enable me to keep down both the hat and the skirt at the same time—like this—so that they will follow the leader and not blow away in the breeze, while my left hand is free to wave to you—like this." Having executed the waving she stretched the arm forward and curved her hand upward in the manner of a dancer on stage, and in a commanding voice instructed the *samlo* pedaller to "Pedal away, my good man!"

FORTY-FIVE

HAPPY news came from the South: in about a month's time Ot would be able to take some leave and come home. "We'll be together soon, Mother. I'm counting the days."

Phloi read and reread the letter and went round with a big smile on her face telling everyone about it. To An she said, "And don't forget— if you really want him to stay on, get a job here in Bangkok and not return to the South, you must help me to persuade him."

"I will." An was all enthusiasm. "I will indeed! Even though I don't think you'll need my assistance. Ot will listen to you. If you ask him to stay, I'm sure he will. But you can count on me doing everything I can to keep him here. I do so want us to be together, Mother." And this made Phloi happier still. *This is a good omen,* she thought. *How blessed and thankful I feel. There's a war going on and all these strange rules and regulations and so many slogans aiming to change* Muang Thai *and* Khon Thai *into I don't know what, yet I feel so light-hearted—who knows, peace may be just around the corner and all will be well again. This is a good omen: Ot's coming home and An no longer disapproves of him but is concerned and affectionate as an older brother should be.*

So, one could easily understand how bitterly let down she felt when a couple of weeks later the flood came, the railway links were cut, and a telegram arrived from Ot: "Waiting for water to recede and train to run again."

That was the year of the big flood. When the tide began to swell Phoem said it would be like the one we had twenty-five years back—in 1917, a year of the small snake under the traditional twelve-year-cycle reckoning, but it turned out to be much higher and longer-lasting.

The roads and lanes in many parts of Bangkok were transformed into waterways and people went boating both for pleasure and business. In spite of the damage and the incon- venience, a holiday atmosphere prevailed. Even Phloi, after she had resigned herself to the inevitable, quite enjoyed the novelty of buying fish and vegetables from the vendors who came paddling their boats through the gate right up to her veranda. In the end she lost quite a few trees in her compound and in the old family place in Khlong Bang Luang. She regretted losing them, but this too she considered as something inevitable, and set about after the flood getting seeds and saplings to replenish her gardens.

"You can afford to take it calmly, Mae Phloi," Phoem said to her one day. "But think of those whose livelihood depends on the produce from their orchards. Some of them are facing ruin—their losses have been enormous. I only have potted plants—they're safe, they were moved up and out of harm's way—but it's heart-breaking to see rows and rows of dead trees even if they don't belong to you."

Phloi said, "Trees belong to the land. If the land is destined to be flooded, you and I have no power to keep it dry."

"No, but the powers that be of this land could extend sympathy and some practical help to the unlucky fruit-growers all the same. I don't seem to hear them talking about the plight of the fruit-growers, Mae Phloi. Or about anything else for that matter, except *kuaitieo*. Even in the silence of my room I seem to hear them telling me to eat *kuaitieo*, sell *kuaitieo*, love *kuaitieo*. It's funny to be told to eat something you've been eating all your life. Do you know how this really astonishing *kuaitieo* campaign got started, Mae Phloi?"

The word *kuaitieo*, meaning rice noodles (as distinguished from *bami,* or egg noodles), referred to a popular dish of Chinese origin whose main ingredients comprise boiling broth of pork bones (for cooking the noodles), pork, bean sprouts and dried shrimps, seasoned with fish sauce, lime juice, garlic, vinegar, dried and/or pickled chili, and for those who like them, garnished with chopped spring onions and/or coriander. *Kuaitieo* had been part of Thai society since time immemorial and there had been innumerable variations on the theme.

In the 1940s the sellers of *kuaitieo* were still mostly Chinese. In the present campaign the people were being urged not only to eat but set up booths and stalls selling this dish.

"Do you know how the campaign got started, Mae Phloi?" Phoem asked, and went on to say he could not vouch for the truth of what he'd heard, then proceeded to tell it anyway. "One day during the flood," so the story went, "someone thought it would be fun to bring a *kuaitieo* boat to Government House and have a kind of floating picnic for *than phu mi bun wasana* (personages possessing merit and merited glory). Well, Mae Phloi, *than phu mi bun wasana* enjoyed themselves hugely over the delicious *kuaitieo* and they all said to one another what first-class excellent fare this was! Then lo and behold! A policy was born then and there to promote it among the citizens of the land, Mae Phloi. So eat *kuaitieo*, love *kuaitieo*, think *kuaitieo*, and you'll be helping the economy of the country, Mae Phloi. I'm told all right-thinking officials are actively engaged in the campaign.What about your son-in-law? I'm sure he must be a keen *kuaitieo* man, Mae Phloi."

Very much so, Phloi told him. Khun Sewi has asked his wife to set up a stall selling *kuaitieo* at his department canteen, and Praphai had as good as passed the whole thing to Khun Mother—all the business of getting the ingredients and utensils and arranging for the servants to go and man the stall. Praphai had not thought much of her husband's wish to advertise his zeal for *kuaitieo* in this manner but had acquiesced to it for the sake of peace—an uneasy peace which she knew was preferred by Khun Mother to open hostility in any case.

AN had not been making many comments on the *kuaitieo* situation. He had been doing his work diligently (overdoing it, Phloi sometimes thought, seeing how tired he looked) and keeping reticent on matters having to do with official policies whether social, cultural, economic or political. But on one occasion, in the course of a rambling conversation, he suddenly asked his mother, "You do believe in the sacredness of oath-taking, don't you? And do you remember once you stopped me from uttering an oath some ten years ago?"

Phloi remembered quite well. She also thought she understood

what had been gnawing at his conscience, and she spoke to him soft
"I never questioned your integrity and your sincerity. I believed you
did what you did because you considered it to be right. I still do, my
son."

"I am grateful—you don't know how grateful I am to hear you say
that." Then he gave a deep sigh. "Nevertheless, when I hear people
talk about what's happening in *Muang Thai* it hurts as though a blade
was being driven through my ears. It's only right that I should suffer,
I have no doubt."

"Oh my son! You work too hard and you think to much. Don't.
Some results can be traced directly to our deeds good or bad, others
cannot, but that should not discourage us from getting on with our
good deeds. Don't despair, my son. You have your mother's blessing—
your mother who never doubts that your intentions have always been
honourable and your heart loyal and true."

An made a *krap* of gratitude with tears in his eyes.

An is perfectly capable of arranging his own life, Phloi reminded
herself. *But oh how stooped and forlorn he's looking. He needs a woman's
loving care. Why has he remained without a wife—it's been some ten
years now since Lucille went back to her country. Why don't you marry
again, my son? Get yourself a wife and make me a grandmother—I have
a longing to be grandmother, don't you know? My daughter Praphai has
made up her mind to be childless, my son On has no choice in the matter
at least for some time to come, and my son Ot . . .* Thinking of Ot, Phloi
shook her head with a smile, finding it almost impossible to picture
Ot as husband and father.

"YOU'RE just the same, Mother," Ot said. "I left you crying and
I come back to find you crying. It's wonderful how you haven't
changed."

Phloi laughingly blew her nose and dried her eyes. "Why didn't
you let me know you'd be arriving today, son? I've been waiting and
waiting for another telegram or a letter. I didn't expect you to suddenly
materialise like this. And that second telegram you sent when you
couldn't come because you weren't well—oh, that had me worried.

What was the matter with you?'

"Malaria, darling. Lots of us get it down there. Mine was the recurring type—the fever kept popping up without rhyme or reason, a real nuisance. But I'm all right now."

"You're slightly thinner, much darker, but you look very well I must say . . . You're going to stay long, aren't you, son?"

"Yes, Mother, I've come for a long stay."

"I'm so happy, son."

"So am I, Mother!"

He is happy, Phloi said to herself as she watched him at a family gathering with brother, sister and brother-in-law. *Happy in himself, happy with others. He's not being prickly and petulant with brother-in-law as I feared he might be. Perhaps it's having a job that has made him less sensitive to what others may think of him. He talks about his job most entertainingly—you can tell he loves it. Loves it for its own sake, though, not on account of the possible riches or advancement or honour it may bring him. Still the same unambitious Ot—though he has matured into a proper* phuyai. *It's so wonderful to have him back! I feel like bursting into song but had better not. . .*

Uncle Phoem, too, was happy to have Ot back. He had been missing him all this culturally exciting time. *Sanuk*—what fun, he said. It's good to laugh and better when I have Ot to do it with. He dropped in for a chat nearly every day, and on this particular afternoon it was a special chat he elected to conduct with Ot, special not in substance but in manner. He was experimenting, he was testing his proficiency in the New Thai Talk and Ot was helping him as best he could. This New Thai Talk was an official attempt to streamline our traditional speech style especially as regards its lavish profusion of personal pronouns (those of the first and the second person in particular), and polite endings. The official ruling would do away with the many *I*s and *you*s, leaving only *chan* and *than,* together with one lone polite ending: *cha.* It is impossible to explain how impossible it was for most people to refer (and feel natural when doing it) to themselves as *chan* indiscriminately (or uniformly) to all and sundry and to address all their interlocutors as *than,* having been in the life-long habit of identifying this self of theirs variously to various people, whom they likewise personalize variously according to the others' relationships with *them*—social relationship, sentimental relationship, spiritual relationship, hierarchical relationship, blood relationship; all this was taken into consideration. Uncle Phoem, for instance, called himself *phom* with most friends and acquaintances, *khraphom* with esteemed elders, *lung* with nephew Ot, *nua* with the children of his wife's elder's sister, *ua* or *kha* with some of his closest friends, and so on and so forth. So he and Ot got together this afternoon and went into their *chan*-and-*than* act, keeping the dialogue simple and "cultural" (such as *"sawaddi cha than, than sabai di ru cha, chan sabai di cha"*) and laughed at themselves with much enjoyment. An was also amused by their performance, but Phloi thought it ludicrous and said so. "I hope nobody's going to force *me* to talk like *that!*" she declared warmly.

"Mae Phloi," Phoem admonished her, "you are a 'flower of the nation,' and you must learn to talk properly."

The women of *Muang Thai* were being encouraged to think of themselves as *dok mai khong chat*—flowers of the nation—and the men to treasure and honour them as they deserved to be. A suggestion had also been put forward that husbands and wives should kiss or at least blow kisses to one another at appropriate moments—when the husband left the house in the morning, for example.

"This morning," Phoem related, "my very own 'flower of the nation' assaulted me as I was leaving the house. I sweetly told her to blow me a kiss and she gave me a blow instead. My poor 'f. of n.' has no *wathanatham*, but what can I do? I can't chuck her out—after all, we've been together since she was a fresh flower . . ."

He then asked Ot if he had mastered the new spelling, this being the most important part of the language betterment or simplification—or whatever—programme. Official papers were now written in accordance with the new system, under which a number of letters in the alphabet had been made redundant. Their disappearance from his life, Ot said, was difficult to adjust to, that losing them was like losing old friends. Very sad. Sentiment aside, Phoem said, in his humble opinion the denuded alphabet was bound to impoverish the Thai ᵍue besides rendering it chaotic and we would eventually have to ᵉvert to the old system so as to preserve our sanity and regain our wealth. Phoem was to reminisce in later years, "I'm not always accurate in my prognosis of events, but in this case I happened to be."

Before leaving that day, Phoem expressed again his delight at having Ot near at hand. He did not suggest that Ot should remain permanently in Bangkok—he seemed to take it for granted that he would be returning to his job in the South.

"I know that deep down you don't really want me to go back," Ot said to his mother after he had been home some weeks. "You haven't said anything but I know."

"Have you got to leave, my son?"

"Not right away, darling. I'll stay another month. I don't know how long I'll be gone this time, but when next I come home it will be for good, I promise."

He talked of the shortness of our existence, how very little time we had. "I want to be with you, yet I also have a lot more to do down there. I really must go back."

He talked about his life at the mines, about finding his feet, being on his own, doing something productive, feeling he was of some service to society. Phloi bestowed on him her maternal blessing, did not attempt to dissuade him, behaved rationally on the whole and did not let her disappointment show too plainly. While this conversation was in progress Phoem came in and, on learning of Ot's plan, heartily gave it his approval. To his sister he said, "Yes, Mae Phloi, let him go. At his age this is what he should be doing. And, who knows, he may even wind up with a rich Southern wife, and then he'll be able to take good care of his old uncle."

The mention of the possibility of a wife for her son worked like a charm. It wafted off disappointed feelings and conjured up visions of sweet little creatures dancing about the house. "I'd give anything," Phloi said, "to see my sons settled down with wives and children— my grandchildren! Tell me, Khun Luang, what bad deeds have I commited in my previous incarnations that I should now have three unmarried sons on my hands and not one grandchild?"

Phoem and Ot exchanged looks with twinkles in their eyes, but said nothing.

"What is it?" Phloi asked, "Why are you two smiling like that? Do you know something I don't?"

They quickly gave her a couple of meaningless answers before resuming their discussion of the state of the country's philological-cultural development. More than a month would pass before the facts behind those smiling glances of theirs were finally revealed to Phloi.

KNOWING she needed cheering up, An made it a point to devote as much time as possible to being with her, and it was during a leisurely chat they were having together one afternoon a week or so after Ot had left for the South that Phloi happened to remark once again on his singularly single status. "Why haven't you thought of marrying again, An? Don't you want a son to carry on the family name? Of course, apart from that, I just yearn for some grandchildren to brighten up this house."

An smiled. "So you only want a wife for me because you want grandchildren." Then his expression changed, and he said rather solemnly, "I made a mistake bringing Lucille into this house—made a lot of trouble for you. I don't want to repeat it."

"What do you mean, son? Your father and I got along all right with Lucille after the initial shock. No trouble at all."

An was silent for a few moments, then he asked, "You really want grandchildren?"

"Need you ask? It's the most natural thing in the world for a mother to want to be elevated to grandmother!" Suddenly she smiled at him—a hopeful smile. "Are you by any chance thinking of taking a wife, my son? You have someone in mind?"

"Khun Mother, oh Khun Mother! Don't be in such a rush ... We'll see, we'll see."

Phloi made no more mention of the subject but allowed herself to go on hoping, thinking, *Why not? It's not improbable that some girl may have attracted his attention and aroused his interest. We will see, we will see.*

And so, when on the following Sunday, after breakfast, An offered to take her out for a drive, she accepted with pleasure. *Perhaps we'll go past where this girl lives and he'll tell me all about it.*

The sky was a blue radianoe with fluffy clouds floating across it, the breeze freshly cooling and life in the streets smiling and peaceful as ever. They drove here, there, enjoying the lovely morning, chatting about this and that, having an altogether pleasant time. Phloi said perhaps they should not go too far—the petrol shortage being one of the realities of wartime. An smiled, continued in the same direction for a while, then turned into a lane and pulled to a stop along a corrugated fence with a small gate set in it. "Let's call on some friends, shall we?" he said. He ushered her in, up the staircase of the house to the narrow balcony. Before she had time to give any thought to what was happening he disappeared through a door and in no time at all re-emerged with a little boy in his arms and a little girl trailing a step behind.

He said to them, "Pay respects to your grandmother, children."

Phloi felt like laughing and crying, and indeed, she did a little of both while her thoughts flew straight to Khun Prem. *Oh my dear, are you here with me? You should be, to witness this scene with me. It's very much like the time you took me to the bungalow where you kept your secret, except that this time it's my son who's presenting me with his secrets—yes, two of them! And oh, Khun Prem, you should see how sweet they are! Now why do you suppose he's been hiding them from me?*

"Why didn't you tell me, An?"

She had her grandson in her lap and her granddaughter in her other arm. The boy was about a year old, the girl not yet five; his nickname was Aeo and hers was Aet.

"Why did you keep them from me for so long, An?"

"I didn't intend to make her my wife," An said. "But then—she was—but then Aet was born—and then Aeo came along." These incoherent phrases did not answer Phloi's question, but she decided to leave it for the time being.

She asked her next question, "Where is their mother?" with some apprehension, and felt relieved when An, turning his head towards a half-open door, called out, "Somchai! Somchai! Come and meet

Khun Mother." And she said to herself, "Good! The children have their mother to take care of them, unlike my poor little On."

She felt doubly relieved after meeting Somchai. She liked what she saw. Somchai, who was about Praphai's age, had a trim figure, an attractive face and a manner as polite and gentle as any mother could wish for in a son's wife. Her hair was permed, her eyebrows unplucked, her face lightly powdered but otherwise devoid of make-up, her *phasin* and blouse looked neat and suitable—there was nothing flashy or "daring" about the way she dressed, Phloi noted with satisfaction. She was shyly respectful with Phloi but not ill at ease. She had an air of genuineness and honesty which Phloi found most sympathetic.

They talked about the house and the children, with An (understandably somewhat nervous at first, but now quite relaxed) putting in a few words here and there. It was evident that he considered his wife an excellent mother and housekeeper, which pleased Phloi very much and earned grateful smiles from the girl.

"We must ask Khun Grandmother, to give Aet and Aeo their real names," An suggested at one point.

"Better than that," said Phloi. "I'll ask the abbot of our *wat* to do the naming. You write down their birthdates for him—the day of the week, the month, the exact hour, the year—so that he'll know what names to give that will be auspicious for them."

After a while Phloi, being by nature a quiet person, fell silent, though continuing to play with her grandchildren and exchanging smiles with their mother, and making plans in her mind. When An said it was time to leave, she said goodbye to Somchai, gave Aet and Aeo her grandmotherly kisses and blessing, then rather absently followed An back to the car.

The scene she had been a part of just now had a dreamlike quality about it—just as a dream could seem real, so this was the other way round. But she lost no time in coming to grips with it, and in coming to the point with An. "I'm not going to ask you how all this came about," she said. "But now that I know, you'll of course bring your wife and children to come and live with us as soon as I can get their rooms ready for them."

"There's no hurry, Mother." An spoke slowly, keeping his eyes on the road. "I'd like you to wait, take your time and think it out carefully first."

Phloi stared at his profile. "Oh, An, I don't understand you! I've been longing for grandchildren, and you've presented me with two—a boy and a girl. Made to order and just right for me!"

"And I don't understand you either," An replied. "I wasn't at all sure how you would take it—whether you'd be hurt, deceived, disappointed, furious, or what. But I certainly did not expect you to take it so calmly—as though I'd done nothing wrong."

"You're not the first person to have played this sort of trick on me," Phloi said, and as she uttered these words, the past once again momentarily blotted out the present. Then she went on with a smile, "Of course I was surprised—who wouldn't be? And I'm not being calm at all, An. I'm excited, and delighted, my son."

Mother and son remained mostly silent the rest of the way. An seemed to be concentrating hard on the steering wheel even though the traffic was sparse as ever, and Phloi was busy thinking of those rooms she would have fixed up to receive the new members of the family.

Back at the house, while An was putting the car in the garage, Phloi waited for him on the back veranda, feeling they had not quite finished discussing the situation.

It transpired that An's silence on the way home had not signified a ready consent to her plans. For when they got together again he tried to divert her from them and Phloi came very close to losing her temper once or twice during their exchange of views.

"I think I'll bring Aet here to live with you, and Aeo too when he's big enough. You'll have your grandchildren to take care of, Mother."

"And Somchai?"

"Oh, she won't mind."

"She won't mind what?"

"Giving you the children."

"An! Are you saying you'll leave Somchai there, that you want to separate the children from their mother? And you really think I'm heartless enough to let you do it?"

"Of course not, Mother. That's all right, then, Mother. I'm glad—I mean that we can go on like this, and when you want to see the children, I bring them here, or you go there to visit them. That's all right."

"No, that's all wrong! What's the matter—why don't you want Somchai to come and live here? Is it because you don't trust me? Are you afraid I'll treat her badly?"

"Of course not, Mother—what an idea!"

"I want to see you live openly with your wife and children, An. If you don't want to do it here, then set up your own household—but a proper one, open and aboveboard. I don't want you behaving in the sneaky fashion you've been behaving. That has gone on long enough and it's got to stop!"

"You know nothing about Somchai, Mother."

"Because you've kept us apart until today, An."

"Somchai came from nowhere, Mother. Her parents died when she was a small child and she had been living with some relatives when I met her. I had no intention of marrying her. I rented that house for her, thinking one day I'd find her a nice husband—someone suitable for her. Then Aed was born, I took pity on her and on my own child, and I made it legal. I seem to have blundered into it again, and that's why I didn't tell you, didn't want you to be burdened with it, even though Somchai is my registered wife and the children bear my name."

"I still don't see why you're reluctant about bringing her to live here with all of us. It's your house and since she's your wife it's also hers."

"I know you'll be kind to her, Mother. Very kind and loving. What I'm afraid of is that she might not turn out worthy of your loving kindness. What if she should make all kinds of mistakes and get on your nerves and make you unhappy and lose face with relatives and friends? She's uneducated, unaccustomed to the ways of people in high society—"

"Oh, stop it, An! You know I always respect your opinions, you with your book-learning and important position at the ministry and all that, but this time I think you've got dust in your eyes and can't see straight. If you went on like this, the children, when they're old enough, would believe that although you did marry their mother you were ashamed of her, considered her beneath you—for why else would you have kept her half-hidden in the background? They might not forgive you for treating their mother like that—or me, for permitting it. I wouldn't blame them either. Wait! I haven't finished. You say Somchai is uneducated. So why not educate her? She's young and capable of learning—she seemed an intelligent girl to me. She's well-mannered, well-spoken, in fact far more person-able than many society girls I've come across. In any case, son, you and I have not been brought up to reject people on account of their births but to treat all human beings as deserving our compassion."

"You have enough problems with your son-in-law, Mother. I just don't want to create more for you—"

"The problems are between Praphai and her husband, and the problems were between you and Lucille, remember? Of course I'm concerned when my children don't get along with their wife or husband, but that's another story."

"Some people will be scornful of her simply because she doesn't come from a good family. This will put you in a difficult position, Mother."

"They scorn me who scorn my daughter-in-law. I'll have nothing to do with them, that's all. But they'll treat her with respect if we do, you know."

"Do you think Ot and Praphai will accept Somchai?"

"I'm sure Ot will like his new sister and be like a brother to her— oh, how I wish he were here to help me reassure you! And Praphai? Praphai's no angel, but she is not petty-minded. Anyway, if she does anything silly, I'll deal with her myself."

An yielded in the end. "You win, Mother. I'll bring the three of them to live here as soon as you're ready to have them. I didn't know you could be quite so adamant about getting your own way, Mother."

"I didn't either," Phloi said, wiping the perspiration off her brow.

FORTY-SIX

LYING in bed with the moon shining outside the window, Phloi listened to her grandson Aeo making noises in the suite of rooms he shared with his parents and sister a few doors away. Smiling to herself, she listened to this normal expression of a healthy baby. *He sounds hungry*, she thought. *Or perhaps he's wet. How good to have noise in the house again—the innocent, heart-warming noise of children laughing, crying, playing. They've moved here only a few days ago, yet the atmosphere is entirely changed—the house more gay and lively than it has been for ages. I haven't had much time to get to know them, but then I have a whole lifetime to do it. Makes me feel a proper old woman having them here with me . . . Oh, Khun Prem, how I miss you—you would have been such a doting grandfather to them!*

Lying in her bed under blankets—for this was during "winter" and the weather happened to be seasonably cold that year—Phloi looked out the window at the glowing silvery sky, communing with her dead husband, thinking happy thoughts about her grand-children, and blissfully unaware of what was to unfold only a few minutes later.

Little Aeo's crying had stopped; Phloi was growing drowsy, when suddenly the serene night was shattered by the piercing shrieking wail of the air-raid warning. She sat up, clutching her heart, and for a brief wistful instant refused to believe it. The same warning had sounded once or twice soon after *Muang Thai* had declared war on the Allies, but nothing terrible had occurred and since then things had been quiet—not like citizens of so many other less fortunate parts of the world.

The alarm went on wailing. Throwing off the blankets, Phloi jumped out of bed and ran to the children's room, reaching it just as the door was opened by An. Inside the room a dazed-looking Somchai was sitting on the bed, hugging her two children who were both crying.

"Take Aet downstairs, Mae Somchai," Phloi said, trying to keep her voice steady. "Give Aeo to me. I'll carry him down."

An volunteered to do it but Phloi wouldn't let him, and with Aeo in her arms carefully walked down the steps, talking soothingly all the while. "Don't be frightened, Aeo. You're with your grand-mother. Now, now, don't cry, it's all right, little one. Father and Mother are coming with us, see? And Aet too . . . Don't cry . . . There's a good boy. . ."

They sat down on the floor in the hall downstairs, Phloi with Aeo in her lap, and they were soon joined by the servants and their families. The siren had died away; a hush prevailed, timidly broken by whispered phrases here and there. Nobody knew what to do, what to think, what to expect, but all drew some comfort and con-solation from one another's nearness. Praphai had come from her house—she must have run all the way. She was short of breath, nervous, giggly, and Phloi had to scold her.

"Pull yourself together, Praphai. And where's Khun Sewi?"

"Don't know, Mother. I think he went to dinner with some Japanese."

They sat waiting in the semi-darkness, watching the sky through the partly opened windows. They did not have to wait long. The planes arrived soon enough. A rumbling in the distance, then seemingly within seconds the heavens became one tremendous roar. Aeo screamed, and almost simultaneously the anti-aircraft guns situated not very far from Phloi's house burst into action with its own brand of furore. The sound of the bombs coming through the air was an eerie combination of whining, whistling and screeching; the sound of the bombs exploding made less of a din than the anti-aircraft guns but the impact made the room rock and sway. The people in the room held their breath or breathed heavily, or huddled down to the floor, or crept closer together. Phloi bent over her grandson, gently stroking him. She prayed for his safety, for everyone's safety—those in the room and elsewhere in the city, those behind the guns, even those in the planes up there, though knowing it to be a vain prayer. How can everyone be saved when the earth and the sky rage and storm against each other, unleash death and destruction on each other, and enemies unknown to you must kill or be killed by you, unknown to them, because it is war? At one moment she glanced up at the sky and saw one of the planes quite clearly. The searchlight was shining on it and it looked like a giant moth playing round a giant lamp. "Fly away please." she prayed. "Fly away, whoever you are." The men in the planes might well be the same age as her sons. Perhaps they were married, and with children. "Fly away please," she repeated, as another bomb hit the ground and the room shook, and somewhere, outside this room, in this city, some of her fellow citizens were being killed, or maimed, or made homeless.

Several spots in the city were on fire. Out there, bathed in the silvery light of the moon, the sky wavered in red and orange and in plumes of grey smoke. Phloi felt very cold, she wanted another shawl but rejected the idea of either going up the stairs herself or sending any of the servants to fetch it, feeling they must be just as reluctant to leave this room as she herself. She stopped shivering after a while. She waved her hands about to shoo away the mosquitoes, keeping them from attacking Aeo . . . Another outburst of sound and fury from the guns . . . Another tremor from the explosion. She covered Aeo's body with her own. Flimsy protection, but the best she could manage, and she thought, *Maybe Aeo and I are destined to die together in this room—who knows?*

Aeo had fallen asleep. Time passed and finally the planes went away. The mosquitoes had been feasting on Phloi's legs but she had been concentrating on sending up her prayers for everyone's safety and did not feel them. She had even grown immune to the uproar and was somewhat startled to hear An's voice saying, "It's over, Mother." It rang out so loud and unreal in the silence following the all-clear.

Phoem came by bright and early the following morning to make sure Phloi was all right, and to say to her in an excitedly vindicated tone of voice, "Didn't I tell you, Mae Phloi? The *farang*s are coming back—you saw it yourself last night."

"I saw nothing but what was terrible," Phloi said. "And be careful what you say, Khun Luang. I know you're not afraid of going to jail again, but I won't be able to visit you there if the bombs keep pelting down like last night. Oh Khun Luang, it was really terrible last night. I thought I'd die from fright if nothing else."

"Don't die just yet, Mae Phloi. Things have to get worse before they get better, so grin and bear it for a little while longer. Last night was the beginning of the end of the war, and when the war is over everything will be *riab-roi*—orderly, smooth, trouble-free—again."

Phoem, like so many of his fellow citizens, truly believed that all their present inconveniences and hardships had been imposed on their smiling land by the war and if it would only go away the situation would return to normal and everyone would live free and easy again. Phoem also looked forward to seeing some people he didn't like who had risen high these past few years (and whom he identified with the villainous war) to come crashing down in peacetime. "They'll get what's coming to them," he said with malicious glee.

His nephew An would have him abandon this simple optimism. "We will all get what's coming to us," he told him in a gloomy voice. "Our troubles will not end with the war, Uncle. Troubles for the whole country, from the high and mighty down to the little people like you and me."

"But that's not fair!" Phoem protested hotly. "I haven't done anything."

"All is fair in war and its aftermath, Uncle. Don't forget we will have lost the war, though in fact there will be plenty of troubles for both losers and winners. And the little people who 'haven't done anything' to bring about the war, or to feather their own nests during the war, will probably have the biggest share of troubles."

THERE was a lull of several days before the next air-raid, during which a bomb shelter had been built under An's direction near the front lawn of the house.

Now the bombers usually came when the moon was bright, and wherever you went the following morning you'd hear people talk about it—where the explosions had taken place, what buildings had been struck, who had miraculously escaped, who had been killed and in what sensational manner. Phoem had a large repertoire of bomb stories, some more sensational—not to say gruesome—than others, which he would relate with a zestfulness Phloi found deplorable even though sometimes he would make her laugh despite herself.

He dropped in one morning a few days after the Central Station at Hua Lamphong had been bombed in one of the fiercest raids they'd had from the Allies. "I'm happy to see you're all right," he said to Phloi. "I didn't come before because I've been very busy. Had to run round calling on my revered monks at various *wats*—and asking them to pour holy water on me to exorcise my rotten luck."

"What happened?" Phloi asked, preparing herself for yet another story.

"I'll tell you," he began. "I was there that night, Mae Phloi, right there at Hua Lamphong, having dinner with some friends at the Hotel Tunki—"

"Oh, Khun Luang!" Phloi interrupted. "Aren't you too old for that kind of place?"

"Oh, Mae Phloi, that's besides the point! Let me get on with my story . . . After dinner, we were just leaving the hotel when the siren sounded. Some of us wanted to find a shelter but I talked them out of it, so we were out there watching the planes when the sky burst and the bombs came showering down. We lay flat on the street by the pavement—there was nowhere else to go. I was praying hard but also thinking this could be my last night on this earth—but never mind, I thought. Couldn't hear myself think as a matter of fact. Hell was breaking loose, the noise was indescribable and parts and pieces of I don't know what were swirling about and dropping all round. I lay like that for a long time—didn't feel anything—didn't feel any pain. When it was over I congratulated myself and was about to get up when I heard a friend shout from behind, 'Hey, hey, keep calm! Looks like you've had it. Your inside is all outside, fellow! The whole bunch of it!' I turned my head—and sure enough—*the whole bunch of it* piled up on my back—and blood everywhere. Ugh! I flopped down again, composing myself to die as quietly as I could—with my innards dangling over my back. I couldn't understand why I felt no pain, but didn't worry too much about it, being preoccupied with dying. Then a policeman came by and I gave him my address and asked him to take my body to my poor wife. He looked long at me, then started to tap my back with a piece of wood or something—-and the next thing I saw was—yes, Mae Phloi, what I thought was my stomach and the rest of it had belonged to somebody else after all and the policeman was removing the debris from my back! Isn't that the worst, the most inauspicious thing that could happen to anyone? That's why I had to go to all the *wat*s and be sprinkled with holy water. Oh, what a night that was!"

BEFORE retiring each moonlit night Phloi would prepare her baskets to be taken to the bomb shelter in case of another raid—baskets containing smelling salts, mercurochrome, cotton wool, blankets, sweets and so forth. According to Phoem, the *farang*s wished to avoid dropping bombs on *wat*s and residential areas by mistake, hence their preference for the moon shining bright. Another reason (also according to Phoem) was that the planes would not be as conspicuous in the beams of the searchlights as in a dark sky.

But there was no moon that night and Phloi went to bed pleasureably anticipating an uninterrupted rest in her comfortable bed. When the siren woke her up not long after she had fallen asleep she rather felt more surprised than afraid but rose and went outside nonetheless. An had just come out of his room and he said, laughing lightly, "Someone must have blundered. I don't think they'll come tonight—it's so dark."

"And the children?" Phloi asked uncertainly.

"Sleeping soundly. Let's not wake them up."

Phloi's hand was on the doorknob when she heard the unmistakable rumble approaching from the distance.

"Must be Japanese planes, Mother," An said.

"No, son, I recognize the sound. I know it well. Let's get Somchai and the children."

They hurried across the lawn making for the shelter. Halfway there they all stopped suddenly and looked up. They could see nothing at first, but they stood transfixed listening to strange sounds they'd never heard before on previous raids. There was a lot of loud wheezing and whirring going on in the air and before they had time to think the sky erupted in explosions of noises and lights. And now there was light over the whole earth with the greens of the grass and of the leaves showing up more garishly than in the light of day.

"So now they're using flares," An murmured.

"All of you go down to the shelter," Phloi said jerkily. "I must stay out here a while. I want to see this if it kills me. I must watch this. I've never seen such fireworks in all my life."

An disappeared briefly into the shelter before rejoining his mother on one of the benches on the edge of the lawn. They sat in the glaring light listening to the planes which did not visit their neighbourhood that night and speculating about the sudden change in the pattern of the raids.

An mused, "I suppose from now on we may expect them on any night, in darkness or under a bright moon—it won't make any difference."

Phloi nodded. "So it means we'll have to keep awake every night and be ready for whatever may come."

As the bombing got worse those Bangkokians who had remained undaunted by the war until then grew properly apprehensive at last, even panicky. Quite a few took to evacuating. At first they only moved to other parts of the city as far away from their own as possible; thus one heard of residents of Khlong Toey migrating to Bangsue and residents of Bangsue flocking to Khlong Toey. But later on many families sent their women and children to remoter areas in the outlying provinces. An too would have liked his mother to go and live with some relatives in the country, but she refused. "No, An, I'd rather we stick together. I'm not going to leave all you people here."

"It's so tiring for you having to get up in the middle of the night like this."

"If I were somewhere else I wouldn't be able to sleep anyway, thinking of what might be happening to this house. We're old friends, ouse and I. If we should crumble together—well, why not?"

Phloem supported his sister's decision to stay put. His anti-evacuation rationale, such as it was, went something like this: "If a bomb should fall on your head in this house, people would say,'Oh, how sad.' But if after taking so much trouble to remove yourself somewhere and you got hit there anyway, people would laugh. What loss of face, eh?"

He trusted to her past good deeds—her accumulated merit—to keep her from harm, but to make doubly sure that no bad luck would come her way he took to providing her with every protective measure he could think of. He brought a red cloth inscribed with sacred signs which he hung in a corner of the house. He came bearing a bowl of lustral water which he sprinkled on Phloi and members of her household. He also brought a bag of sand and sprinkled it on the ground round the main building—after, he told Phloi, it had been invested with magical power to ward off danger. To each and everyone he distributed a handful of miniature Buddha images which he had obtained from the many *wat*s he frequented. One of the especially highly-prized amulets he insisted on giving Phloi was an old baht coin portraying King Chulalongkorn on the obverse side. Phloi loved the coin, and although her belief in amulets was not particularly strong she deferred to her brother's well-intentioned gestures and dutifully put all his good gifts in a bag to be carried down to the bomb shelter along with the medicines and the sweets.

SHE got up at dawn that day to make offerings to the monks at the *wat* near her house. It was Visakha Day—the day that com-memorates the birth, enlightenment and death of the Lord Buddha. Later in the morning she was back in the sitting room upstairs, reclining on the floor and having a pleasant chat with Khun Choei who had come to spend the day. Little Aeo was with them, playing with the new toys his great-aunt had brought him.

At that moment in time Phloi was in the middle of saying something to Khun Choei. She didn't finish it. She paused and listened intently. Was her ear playing tricks? It could not be the planes—not in broad daylight and without any warning!

"Do you hear it, Khun Choei?"

"Yes," Khun Choei answered calmly. "It's getting louder—and louder—coming our way, I think. Advance party surveying the ground—reconnaissance flight, you suppose? They're going to strike tonight, you think? Perhaps I'd better go home early."

No sooner had she stopped talking than the siren whined and the planes were upon them and the bombs went off somewhere in the vicinity—must be quite near because the windows were rattling crazily and the house shuddering as though overwhelmed by fear.

A few minutes afterwards saw all of them assembled in the shelter, all except An.

"Where is he?" Phloi asked.

"I don't know, Khun Mother." Somchai was on the brink of tears. "He went out this morning."

Phloi consoled her. "He'll know what to do, Somchai, and he'll come home as soon as he can, I'm sure. I wouldn't worry too much, Somchai." But of course both of them went on worrying.

Another thunderous bang went up outside, again somewhere nearby. Everyone in the shelter fell silent, not even a whimper from any of the children.

Then Khun Choei's voice broke the stillness. "Think of it, Phloi, when you and I had topknots and were running about by the *khlong*, aeroplanes weren't even heard of then. And now we flee them by running into holes. We've turned into cave creatures in the age of aeroplanes. Oh-oh, here it comes again—right above us!"

It came down almost right upon them this time. The world up there was being blown to smithereens, that's what it sounded like inside the shelter which was tossing like a boat in a turbulent sea. A beam fell from the ceiling but happily did not land on anybody. Phloi held her grandson tight in her arms, her mind a blank, her senses numb. The shock must have lasted some time. When she recovered from it she realized that the shelter had stopped rocking and the unimaginable noise had died down.

Khun Choei was the first one to make a move. "I'm going up now for some sun and air. I can't breathe in here."

She went, and after a while Phloi heard her call from the entrance of the shelter. "Come on up, Phloi. I think they've gone."

Khun Choei looked pale in the sunlight. She said, her voice shaking a little, "Let us be thankful we're alive, Phloi."

Phloi understood the meaning of those words as her eyes fell upon the sight across the lawn. The house was in ruins. The bombs had torn down its roof and walls, wrenched out its doors and windows, smashed and gashed and crushed its wood and bricks, and hurled the bits and pieces helter-skelter on the ground . . . Let us be thankful we're alive, Phloi. A house is only a material possession, extraneous to our being alive.

We can build another house . . . But it will never be the house I have known, the house I moved into as a bride, where I've loved and dreamed and laughed and wept. It's protected me, comforted me, rejoiced with me, grieved with me. It's known me as wife and mother and widow. Oh, Khun Prem, now it's gone! Look at it—poor broken ghost of a house. I've lost more than a material possession, Khun Prem. It's part of my life the bombs have destroyed.

Phloi had sat down on the grass without knowing it and someone had taken Aeo from her arms. People were bustling about pointing and talking among themselves round her as she sat there desolate and sick at heart. When An came back she was still there. He helped her up and settled her on a bench.

"Are you all right, Mother?"

Phloi nodded,

"What about the others? Is anyone hurt?"

Phloi had not inquired. How remiss of me, she rebuked herself, and called out, "Is everyone all right?"

"Every single one," Khun Choei answered from the other side of the lawn. "Not a bruise, not a scratch on anybody. Everyone is safe."

Yes, let us be thankful we're alive.

Phloi rose to her feet and started walking towards the crumbled house.

"Don't go too near, Mother," An warned. But she went anyway, and stood close to it, and looked round. Among the objects she saw lying

in the rubble was a framed picture, slashed by the splintered glass—
Khun Prem's picture, taken on the occasion of his promotion to the
rank of Phra. He was in his full-dress uniform and it was the picture
he had liked best of himself. Phloi retrieved it. It was the only thing
she took away from the dead house.

"I'll move to Khlong Bang Luang," she told An.

"Yes, Mother."

"With you and Somchai and the children."

"Yes, Mother. It should take four or five days to get the place ready."

"I'll sleep at Praphai's house tonight, and tomorrow I'll go and stay
with Choi in the Inner Court. You'll come and fetch me whenever
you're ready."

We're old friends, this house and I.

She looked at it once again, for the last time, silently paying her last
respects, then took her leave.

FORTY-SEVEN

"OH-HO—am I glad to see you! What brings you here so early, Phloi?"

"Can you put me up for a few days, Choi?"

"Of course! Wonderful! But can't you stay more than just a few days? I've been dying for a long chat with you. We'll stay together here in our old rooms, shall we? We don't want to open up other rooms and disturb the bats and the rats and the spiders, right? Actually, there are still some rooms containing human occupants, who flit in and out as they please. At the moment I'm the only one guarding Sadet's residence while her spirit watches over me. I'm used to being alone, but having you to be alone with is much, much better."

"Don't you want to know why I came seeking refuge, Choi?"

"I was so overjoyed I forgot to ask. So what happened? Did your children chase you out?. . ."

". . . I still can't get over it, Phloi. Why should this harsh punishment have been meted out to you of all people? You've committed no bad action in your life—not to my knowledge anyway."

"I don't think I have either. But perhaps I did in some former life, Choi."

"Now the course of karma is taking you back to Khlong Bang Luang. It's from Khlong Bang Luang that you came to live here in the Inner Court, so it's quite right that you should be stopping here for a while before returning there."

"Yes, retracing my steps back to where I was born, and where I shall live until I die. But Choi, you know, when we're together in this room

I might never have left the Inner Court at all. It has the same look, the same feel, the same lovely smell as on the day you and I first met—you with your topknot all askew, dear Choi."

"There are times, such as now, when it's so easy to forget I no longer have a topknot on my head. Yes, I have tried to protect this room from the onslaught of time as it were. I do it so that Khun Aunt's spirit should always feel at home here, and for my own pleasure too, of course-—this bit of continuity, this personal memorial to bygone years. You're smiling now, Phloi, I'm glad to see. You've had to swallow your tears now and then, these past few days, haven't you? Revisiting one's old haunts after a long absence often has this effect, my dear."

"Oh Choi, whenever I walk past those silent doors along those musty and mouldy passages I can't help remembering what this place was like once upon a time. Once there were lotus blooms in the courtyard but now the lotus jars lie broken and empty. Once, sitting outside at night, I would look up at the Upper Palace over there, at the lights twinkling at me from its windows. Now I look and shiver as the darkness and gloom stare back at me. And when we were upstairs wandering round Sadet's old rooms, how could I not cry, Choi?"

"I know, Phloi. I would have kept them fresh and fragrant and sparkling if I could. If I had the power and resources I would keep this residence in its once-upon-a-time condition. No, not only this residence but the whole Inner Court. As it is, I've got used to the ravaged landscape, Phloi. It doesn't pain me any more. I've become immune. You should come and visit me more often and build up your immunity."

"Upstairs in Sadet's sitting room, Choi, there's that screen decorated with photographs. I remember helping Sadet choose them. I can still hear her voice talking to me about them. They're smudged and faded now, those photographs. And that beautiful portrait of Sadet hanging on the wall has faded too. But her fine eyes look at me the same as when she was alive, and they smile, as caring and understanding as ever. She might be telling me to accept it again, the transient, the mutable. Accepting it is one thing, Choi. Accepting doesn't always make you feel any less sad."

"*Mai pen rai,* Phloi. Never mind. Sorrow doesn't last either. And tomorrow you're starting out on another journey. The journey back to your ancestral home, and that will be a happy reunion, a joyful occasion. In fact, I can't wait to come and see you. I'll give you a week or two to settle down, then I'll come."

"THIS is a joyful occasion, Mae Phloi, so I said to Khun Choei we must be here at the landing when you arrive. So here we are! Like that time—that first visit home of yours after you'd moved away to get turned into an Inner Courtier, remember? We must celebrate, Mae Phloi!"

"He's even more excited this time, Phloi. You'd have thought he was waiting to have you back so we could all play hide-and-go-seek or cops-and-robbers again. But of course, it's doubtful if he has ever stopped behaving like a little boy these intervening years. Really, Pho Phoem, you would have us still wearing our topknots! Celebrate, indeed! As though Phloi had not been bombed out—and in spite of all your magic formulae to ward off danger."

"Well, they have saved everybody, haven't they? Not one life was lost. What more can you ask? If this doesn't call for a celebration, I don't know what does!"

FORTY-EIGHT

NOT long after having resettled in the old house Phloi received a letter from Ot. He was going through another bout of malaria, not a severe one but troublesome enough to prevent him from travelling. And another nuisance, he wrote, was that the required medicine—an imported product in normal times—could not be found anywhere in the South. Perhaps it was still available in Bangkok, hence the enclosed doctor's prescription. "I'm rather impatient to get well," the letter said. "I'm anxious to come home and be with you."

Phloi showed the prescription to An, and he said, "Imported medicines are extremely difficult to track down, like searching for needles in the ocean, and they cost the earth when you do find them."

Phloi frowned at him. "Never mind the cost. Please find it and send it to him as quickly as possible."

An laughed. "You sound as though I would save money and let Ot die. No, Mother." He stopped laughing. "I'm only thinking of the situation in general, of the scarcity of imported pharmaceutical supplies, of the sharp businessmen who have cornered the market, of the astronomical price they charge, and of the fact that these days more deaths result from lack of medicine than enemy action."

And Khun Choei, as a physician's wife, had this to add: "My husband has never worked so hard in his life. You see, Phloi, now that *farang* medicines are impossible to get unless you're very well off, more and more people are reverting to traditional remedies, with the result that my poor Khun Luang has more patients than is good for his own health. He's accumulated a lot of merit, you may be sure of that. Merit, not profit."

The medicine for Ot was procured and dispatched, and after more than a week Phloi learned that he had received it. There were longer intervals between the next letters, for apart from his illness the lines of transport and communication between Bangkok and the South were often disrupted by enemy air attacks. His condition was improving in one of the letters; in another he felt he was strong enough to get about, but the doctor disagreed and ordered him to take it easy for another month or so. Phloi thought he sounded tired and irritable and wrote back telling him to heed the doctor's advice and not to tax his strength unnecessarily, and above all not to fret and fume over what could not be helped.

She herself these days was being told just that—not to fret and fume—by her brother, whose unfailing cheerfulness in the face of increasing difficulties and privations exasperated her at times. "Why fret and fume?" Phoem said. "Of course there is a shortage of everything, but it's not the end of the world." The shortage of everything—this was the ever-recurring topic of the moment. Shortage not only of medicine but of such everyday commodities as sugar and cloth and soap. That and the spiralling price. Phloi was not really fuming. She was doing her best to cope, to keep her extensive household reasonably fed and clothed and washed, but she felt she had the right to complain once in a while like most of us. Ironically enough, among the shortages she had to cope with was that of space. An had salvaged a mountain of impractical stuff from the bombed house ranging from ancient pots and pans and trays to huge beds and heavy tables all of which had long been hidden from sight, in storage. She must find room for them, but where?

"Sell them, Mae Phloi," Phoem advised, smiling that carefree smile of his.

"Oh, no, I can't, Khun Luang."

"Why not? Because you consider it beneath you, that it would be unbecoming, un-*phudi*-like? Afraid of losing face, are you? But my dear girl, lots of *phudi* folks are doing it—selling off their family heirlooms, bric-a-brac, odds and ends and what have you. It's become quite the fashionable practice; and they even brag about it, implying they are descendants of old aristocratic families to have so many old things to dispose of. I have a few Chinese friends in the antique business. I'll bring them here to rid you of what you have no room for. And Mae Phloi, prepare yourself to be amazed at the enormous amount of money you're going to get for it."

Phloi let him have his way and Phoem brought his friends and haggled with them in a most friendly way, with plenty of laughing and leg-pulling; and Phloi was amazed all right by the amount of money she received from the sale of "old things" (*khong kao*, a term conveniently embracing everything from Ming vases to second-hand junk)—amazed, astounded, and not a little disconcerted.

"You haven't robbed them," Phoem said cheerfully after the antique dealers had departed with the loot. "They'll get three, four, five times what they've paid you from the new rich. Easy come, easy go."

"I'm confused," Phloi said. "I don't know how much anything should cost any more."

"You're fretting again, Mae Phloi."

Phoem's cheerfulness rose to a new height when suddenly (that was how it seemed to Phloi) the government fell and a new government was formed. Phloi heard the new prime minister address the nation over the radio, and was very surprised to hear a traditional Thai love-song come on the air after the address instead of some "modern" composition with nationalistic flavour which had been in vogue these past years.

Well, well, she thought, *change of governments, change of songs.* In the following weeks she also learned that the people were now free to chew or not to chew betelnuts and to venture out of the house either hatted or bareheaded, shoeless or shod, and that the old mode of spelling and speaking had been officially re-installed. But if all those "cultural" regulations had faded away, the bombs, however, continued to fall, and prices continued to climb higher and higher.

One day An came home from the office to astonish his mother with this question. "Have you got any thousand-baht notes hidden away somewhere, Khun Mother?"

"Maybe one or two—why?"

"The government is recalling them from circulation."

"Oh?!"

"So you'd better give them to me and I'll get them registered and all that. It's all right, Mother, you'll get your money back eventually. It's a measure to combat inflation, you see. Not a bad policy actually. Let's hope it achieves its object, which is to keep the cost of living down."

He went on to expound some economic theory or other, quoting his economist friends. Phloi listened to him attentively at first, then dutifully and uncomprehendingly. It seemed to her the economists were enjoying themselves playing with thousand-baht notes mostly belonging to other people, but she could not see how the absence of these notes from our pockets was going to make it any cheaper for her to run her house.

Another measure launched by the government—Phloi wasn't sure if this, too, was designed to stem inflation—was legal gambling. This proved immensely popular with the citizenry and the casinos which had sprung up in nearly every street in Bangkok were all doing brisk business. They were, according to her brother Phoem, the liveliest spots in town. He came to her house one evening after a triumphant visit to one of them, bringing with him roast duck, chicken and pork and other dishes he had bought with his winnings. "Let's have a feast, Mae Phloi, to celebrate my good fortune and skill, for it's not all due to luck, you know. If these casinos go on operating, don't be surprised if you have a rich brother for a change."

"Gambling places were allowed at one time," Phloi said. "Then they were banned and if you got caught you could be sent to jail. Now they're back to being legal and respectable again. Why, Khun Luang? What's the reason for the change? Which government was right, or wrong?"

"The world turns and turns, Mae Phloi. The pendulum swings. Let us enjoy our roast duck."

The world kept on turning and a few days later there was our Mae Phloi thanking and blessing the government for doing what she deemed a very right thing indeed. At first, though, when she was informed by An of this very right and good governmental action she was so overcome with joy that she remained speechless for several minutes, and then all she could say, over and over again, was, "Is it true? Is it true? Can it be true?"

"Yes, Mother, it's true. The government has ordered the release of all political prisoners and Phi On will leave the island and be home in a couple of days!"

"Oh, An—An! How good and kind of the government. I can never thank them enough. May they continue to enjoy success and prosperity for a long time to come! But An, when and where did you hear this good news? Why didn't we have any inkling of it before?"

"Well, I did, Mother, but I wanted it absolutely confirmed before telling you."

"Tell me again, An. Say it again—such happy news!"

An laughed. "Phi On's coming home, Mother. It is wonderful news, isn't it?"

"And when is he arriving—you know the exact day?"

An gave her the date and she cried out, "I must start getting his rooms ready and his clothes made and—"

"Wait," An interrupted with another laugh. "Wait, Mother. I've already told Somchai about it and you are to let her and the servants do most of the work, please, and not exhaust yourself . . . Oh it will be great having Phi On back with us! You're not the only one who's missed him, you know."

An's affection for his long-lost and one-time estranged brother was plain to see. Phloi saw it; and now, as she had every right to, and as could be expected of her, she broke down and wept tears of thankfulness and joy.

Phoem said, "I'm not taking you with us, Mae Phloi. An and I can run fast enough if the *farang*s should feel like dropping a few more bombs on the station on this particular day. You would only be a burden to us if that happened."

"But Khun Luang, I never said I'd come to the station with you. No, I'll stay home and wait. After so many years of waiting, what's a few hours more? I want you to do something for me at the station, though. I want you to make it a happy meeting, Khun Luang. Those two haven't seen one another for a long time. If you sense any aloofness or awkwardness—"

"Say no more, Mae Phloi, I understand, though I don't think you have anything to worry about. I know how much An is looking forward to welcoming his brother, and I also know that On has no bitterness in his heart."

ON that particular day Phloi went down to the landing to see An and Phoem get into the ferry boat at the start of their journey to the station. After watching the boat glide out of sight she went back to the house, up the stairs to the rooms which had been fixed up for On, walked round and round glancing here and there and then with a smile of satisfaction made her way down again and proceeded to the kitchen. There were other servants in the kitchen besides the cook and they were all busy chopping and pounding away. Phloi gave them some last minute instructions which were more or less the same as those she had already repeated several times earlier on; this made them smile in a way which made Phloi suspect she had been overly fussy. Leaving them to carry on in peace she took a stroll round the garden; she was also seen, later on, pacing up and down the path between the garden and the house; after some minutes of this unwonted activity—she was not as a rule given to restless pacing—she returned to the landing pavilion to sit down and wait. It seemed the best place to be after all. Happy and excited, anxious too, yet oblivious of the passing time, she sat peering into the distance at the boats coming towards her from the mouth of the *khlong*. At long last appeared the boat she was waiting for—she could make out Phoem seated outside the awning and, smiling to herself, wished it had been On instead so that she would have a first glimpse of him. She rose, then sat down again and leaned over to get a better look at the approaching boat. . .Then she knew and went pale. *On was not in it. . .*

An and Phoem had brought back this brief note: "My dearest Khun Mother, I went to see Ot and was shocked to find him so ill. Seriously ill. I must postpone coming home, much as I long to see you. I'm going back to him as soon I've given this to a friend to take to Bangkok. I'll write more soon. Your loving son, On."

"Don't take it so hard, Mae Phloi," Phoem said. "Malaria is often like that. You're taken badly one day, the fever goes down the next and you're all right again. On had not known about Ot's illness before, that's why he was shocked, and of course he'd want to be near his brother and nurse him—they're very fond of each other. Look at the bright side, Mae Phloi—as soon as Ot is well enough to travel, On will bring him back and you'll have two sons coming home instead of one. Now go up to the house and lie down. You look all in."

Weeks passed. Letters and telegrams had been going back and forth between On and Khlong Bang Luang. Ot's condition had not improved. Everyone wanted to have him brought here for treatment but had to abandon the idea because the journey would have been too rough for him in his present state. On would bring him as soon as the doctors allowed him to be moved—they, the doctors, were doing everything they could to pull him through and we mustn't lose hope. *I must go on hoping and praying,* Phloi kept telling herself in desperation. She had turned into an ailing woman in a matter of days since receiving On's message. The very sight and smell of food made her feel ill, and sleepless nights had been giving her headaches and dizzy spells. Worn out, fatigued, she kept on praying and hoping while at the same time fearing the worst. Now she began to have premonitions that Ot would never come home again. She fought them off and clung to her hopes, but they kept creeping back to haunt her. There were times when she felt too ill and tired to go on fighting.

One night, totally exhausted, she dropped off to sleep, then woke up suddenly to find Ot beside her! She sat bolt upright. He grinned at her, he had recovered and was looking well and strong. "Darling Mother," he said, "you're always asking when am I coming home. Well, here I am! I've come home to be with you, and I'm not going to leave you ever again."

Then he was gone and this time Phloi really woke up. Happiness filled her heart for one fleeting second before flying away, vanishing as suddenly as Ot had.

On arrived home from the South four days after the dream had occurred. He paid respects at his mother's feet, sobbing his heart out. Phloi held him close to her and comforted him. "My son, my son, we are together again at last. You don't need to tell me about Ot. I've known it for days. He came to tell me himself."

"He talked of you—his thoughts were with you till the last moment, Mother."

"And mine were with him, On."

FORTY-NINE

IN the past Phloi had been able to do it—accept the death of her loved ones. Each time she had mourned her loss, then come to terms with it. But it had been many months now since Ot's cremation, held in the South without her presence because she had been too ill to travel, and she had yet to resign herself to the fact that he was gone from this world while she, his old ailing mother, was fated to go on living in it. Is this the course of karma? She kept putting the question to herself whereas on previous occasions she had more or less taken the course of karma for granted. What have I done to be so cruelly treated? What blundering unjust Power has snatched Ot from me? She ached for him; she repeated to herself those well-worn phrases about mortality and ached all the more. Their obvious truth failed to solace her and she was tired of hearing other people recite them at her. All of us were born to die. Rich or poor, young or old, death claims us all. So true, and so meaningless where Ot was concerned.

She had recovered from her physical illness, or at least that was her opinion. Luang Osot and Khun Choei considered her far from well and wanted to bring in a "modern" doctor. Phloi wouldn't hear of it, saying their time-honoured cure was good enough for her and would they please stop treating her like a patient. She was more worried about On's health than her own. His appearance distressed her. He had grown so thin and frail and looked much older than his age. He assured her he was perfectly all right but she kept urging him to eat more and sleep more as though he were still a growing boy. There was also the question of his resuming normal life in society. What kind of career would be suitable for him—or available for that matter? Her

…oncern for On did keep her from wholly submitting to the demands of her stubborn grief and that numbing sense of aimlessness and futility about her own existence. On needed her, and she was still able to give him the love and care he had been deprived of for so long. He didn't talk much about his experience on the islands, but he had said enough for Phloi to get a fair idea of what he must have gone through.

"I caught malaria on Tarutao," he said to her once, in answer to her question. "It got worse when we were moved to Turtle island. We had to work much harder there—roadbuilding, jungle-clearing. Sometimes I thought I wouldn't last another day. Then medicine arrived from Ot. I put it in a tin and hid it in the jungle—not only from the guards but from my friends, my fellow prisoners . . . I had no other thought but to survive. I told myself there was not enough medicine to be divided because so many of us were sick. A small dose would not cure anyone, so I might as well have the whole lot. I'm not of proud of what I did, Mother . . ."

It was On who made his mother feel joyful again after these many months. He did it one day by asking her to allow him to enter the monkhood.

"I need a transitional period, Mother. I can't go from those years on the islands straight into a new life. I'd like to ask your permission to become ordained."

"Oh I am delighted, my son! At last I shall see one of my sons in the yellow robe. This is a happy day for me! You have indeed my permission and my blessing."

"I thought you'd be glad. That's one of my reasons for wanting to become a monk—to give you some happiness. At the same time I do have this longing for peace and tranquility that only a *wat* can offer, and perhaps in order to cope with the world I must renounce it first. But the main reason is this—I want to do it for Ot, Mother. I'm not sure at all where we go when we're dead, and I don't know if the merit of my monkhood will reach him. But I believe that this one meritorious action of mine would please him if he had any way of knowing."

"I believe the merit will reach him, On. I ask you not to doubt it, though I can't prove it to you. If you ask for a logical explanation I have none to give. I only know that without this belief I would be utterly lost. When do you want to do it, my son?"

"I'm ready as soon as it can be arranged. And Mother, I have no wish to go to any of the famous *wat*s. Our small *wat* down the *khlong* would suit me very well."

Everyone in the family rejoiced in On's decision, Uncle Phoem most vociferously of all. Slapping this thigh and with a hearty laugh he proclaimed it "the most wonderful news I've heard in years," and immediately started making suggestions as to how the *tham khwan nak* should be conducted. This is a pre-ordination affair, a sort of blessing and farewell party for the *nak* or ordinand, the person about to leave ordinary life for the Sangha.

"We'll do it like in the old days," said Phoem, beaming with pleasurable anticipation. "We'll have the full-dress ceremony and it's going to be the merriest *tham khwan nak* in the history of Khlong Bang Luang."

"Please, Uncle," On protested gently. "That may be all right for a young person on the threshold of manhood, but I'm a little old now for that sort of thing. Besides, what with the high cost of living we ought to economize where we can. All things considered I'd like to do it as quietly as possible."

"But my dear boy," Uncle Phoem persisted, "You're going to be ordained a monk. You're entering the Sangha. It is a great occasion. Your rejoicing relatives and friends should be given the opportunity to celebrate it to their hearts' content."

On sent Phloi a look of appeal, saying in a small voice, "It's up to you, Mother."

"It will be as you wish, my son. Your becoming a *bhikkhu* is what 's important. It will not be less so if we don't hold a *tham khwan nak* prior to the ordination ceremony. After you're ordained the family can have another get together at the *wat* to make merit in honour of *Phra* On."

"Then what about the procession to the *wat*?" Phoem asked hopefully. "We are going to have the procession, aren't we? I'll take care of it—you can leave everything to me."

"Oh, Khun Luang!" Phloi sighed. "Didn't you hear your nephew say he'd like a quiet ordination?"

"Please, Uncle," said On earnestly. "All I want is to don the white robe of a *nak*, go into the chapel, ask permission to be ordained and, permission granted, go outside to put on the yellow robe then rejoin the congregation as a monk. That's all I want. I want no festivities, no procession, no parade. I really can't see myself in a gold-trimmed costume riding in a procession. The music, the dancing, the merry-making, all that wouldn't be right for me at all. It would be embarrassing. But in any case I'll go along with whatever Khun Mother thinks is the right thing to do."

"Don't worry, On," Phloi said. "I agree with you entirely. Your ordination will be a happy occasion—and a quiet one."

"Too quiet," Phoem muttered, shaking his head sadly. "Here I am, all set to lend my assistance, but nobody seems to want it. But, but—and you're not going to say no to this—I insist on throwing a feast on the eve of the ceremony, a family feast."

"Are you in the money again, Uncle?"

"I am or shall be. Money honestly won in a card game. Not money made from clever buying and selling the same old tins of soda ash—or whatever—over and over and over again. Not from exploiting the shortage and never mind if the price shoots up skyhigh and people suffer. Not from *sengli ho*, as they call it. 'Good business'—sounds better than 'profiteering,' doesn't it? This war has given greed another name—the respectable name of 'Good business.' If I were—"

"There you go again, Khun Luang," Phloi said, mildly cutting him short. "Shall we get back to On's ordination and listen to your sermon some other time?"

The subject of shortages and high prices kept returning throughout the following weeks. The word "unbelievable" was frequently exclaimed by Phloi and Khun Choei as they went from shop to shop making purchases for the coming ceremony and for equipping On with the articles he would need when taking up residence as a *bhikkhu* in the monastery down the *khlong*.

"A thousand baht for just one set of robes! Unbelievable!" Khun Choei cried. "Made of gold thread, you think?"

"Look at this mosquito netting," Phloi said, fingering the fabric in front of her and shaking her head incredulously. "Have you ever seen anything so coarse?"

"At this price, never in my life. You know, Phloi, with the money you're spending you could have sponsored the ordination of ten monks in the old days and have enough left to make offerings to them over the whole Lenten period."

"I know. But never mind, Khun Choei. Let's do the best we can."

"Yes, while we *still* can." Khun Choei sighed. "We're luckier than some, Phloi. I'm thinking of those friends of mine who have always been poor but not so poor as they are now. What will happen to them if they become too poor to afford merit-making?"

"But that's unthinkable, Khun Choei!"

"I pray it will never happen, Phloi. Merit-making is our way of life, but it seems to me the poor perform it with much more feeling than the rich, perhaps because when you're poor it involves greater sacrifice on your part or because the poorer you are the greater your hope for a better life in the next rebirth. In any case, you've been able to do it and it's become a habit with you—this act of giving, of merit-making. A beneficent habit. The sort that engenders kind-liness and generosity of the heart. It nourishes your sense of compas-sion towards others and helps keep you on the path of righteousness. So what would happen if you had to give up this habit of giving because you were simply too poor to do it?"

"Don't paint such a gloomy picture, Khun Choei."

"But rich or poor I think we, the Thai people as a whole, have changed for the worse these past few years. Don't you think so, Phloi? We're not so kind-hearted as we used to be. We've become harsher, more prone to greed, anger and ill-will, altogether more grasping and aggressive. You think it's because we live under greater pressure than before? Could circumstances drive us to be bad? Or make us morally blind, unable to distinguish between badness and goodness, right and wrong?"

"Why, you *are* feeling low today, Khun Choei!"

Khun Choei laughed. "Sorry, Phloi. Put it down to my garrulous old age—that and the shocking price of everything. By the way, have we got everything now? What about the offerings for the officiating monk and the tutorial monks? Have we done that?"

Phloi told her they had, and Khun Choei said, "Good! Oh, it will be a beautiful ordination, Phloi. Let me say once again how much I rejoice with you. And thanks to you I have a part in this merit-making."

"Thanks to On," Phloi corrected her with a proud smile.

ON the morning of the day before On's ordination the hall of the old house by the *khlong* looked like a flower shop. All over the floor stood baskets of jasmine buds, champaks, everlastings, etc., and the women, seated among them, chattered away as they plucked, threaded and shaped the flowers and leaves into various intricate lacy patterns for the different ceremonial articles and utensils. Choi had come early from the Inner Court. "What fun!" she kept remark-ing. She was plying her needle most skilfully and supervising everybody at the same time. These days she rarely got the chance to have this kind of fun inside or outside the palace, she said. "And why aren't you doing anything, Phloi?" she demanded. Phloi had been playing assistant to them all, handing them what they needed, clearing away the unwanted leaves and stems, serving them tea and titbits. She said that with age her hands and eyes had grown too stiff and dim for the exacting task of a flower artist.

"Affectation!" Choi mocked her. "Convenient excuses! Why don't you just admit you've been a lazy pampered Khunying for too long!"

They had a convivial meal that night, a real family gathering with only Khun Chit missing. Someone asked his wife Phuang if she had had any news. Yes, she said, he was living in Kanchanaburi, living the life of an invalid, half-paralyzed, but very well looked after by his other wife; and Phoem, who had no taste for tragedy, said with a chuckle, "Khun Chit will always have somebody to look after him. Of the two of us, I'd say he's by far the luckier brother."

They talked about Chao Khun Father and Khun Un, laughing together as they recalled how the latter had turned into a harmless old lady during the last years of her life. They refrained from talking about Ot, but Phloi did not need to hear his name mentioned in order to be reminded of him. She had difficulty swallowing her food, thinking how Ot would have enjoyed this gathering and made it more joyful still. She laughed with the others nonetheless and intended to stay with them to the end but Khun Choei ordered her to bed. Taking Phloi by the arm she walked her to her room and made her lie down, saying, "Don't you want to attend the ceremony tomorrow? Then do as you are told."

And Phloi did have a good rest, and woke up the next morning feeling better than she had ever felt since Ot's death.

Her first important task of the day was that of pouring water on On after he had had his head shaved. They talked of Ot during the ablution. Phloi had tears in her eyes though they were not altogether sad tears. Not today. On would be received into the Sangha today. It was the love he had for his brother which had inspired him to take this path. Phloi was glad about this, and glad also that she was doing her little bit in getting a son prepared for entrance into the holy life.

After the bathing On put on the white robe of a *nak*, then he and his family and friends got into the boats and went down the *khlong* to the small monastery where he would be spending his monkhood. On had wanted a quiet ordination, with no frills, no fanfare. He got his wish. His journey from home to *wat* was certainly a quiet one. No drums were beaten; no singers or dancers. Yet the plain undecorated boats did have the festive air of a procession, carrying as they did those trays of saffron robes and flowers and food and so many devotees with bright faces. The people of the *khlong* enjoyed the procession and paid their respects to the man in white.

Arriving at the *wat*, Phoem said they must now walk clockwise round the *bot* (chapel)—this part of the custom must be observed, he insisted—and proceeded to do so with the ordinand and most members of the party. Phloi, Choi and Khun Choei went inside. They first went to kneel in front of the Presiding Buddha Image and did the triple *krap*, paying reverence to the Buddha, the Dhamma and the Sangha. Then they got busy laying out and arranging the gift trays to be presented to the monks. Those who had been taking part in the circumambulation and other guests started to come in, sat down on the floor, and conversed among themselves the way people do while waiting for the start of a ceremony. Presently the monks entered and took their seats. On came in another door, escorted by his uncle.

"Isn't he a fine-looking *nak*?" Choi whispered rather loudly. "I hope he stays some time in the monkhood, so I'll have a chance of getting to heaven."

"How's that, Choi?" Khun Choei asked.

"Well, Mae Phloi here could hang on to the monk's robe of her son and ascend with him, right? So I'm planning to grab hold of the tail of Phloi's *phanung* and be hauled up with them."

"Don't forget me, Choi. I have no sons either. Won't you let me hold on to *your phanung* tail?"

"With pleasure, Khun Choei. We might startle those celestial beings but never mind—Oh look, Phloi, it's your turn now. Get ready to present the robe, my dear."

On came up and lowered his head and hands to the floor in homage to his mother; then he accepted from her hands the *trai*—the three pieces of a monk's robe—and took it with him to kneel before the officiating monk.

Taking a handkerchief from her purse, Phloi dabbed her eyes with it.

Choi whispered to Khun Choei, "Phloi's doing all right. It wouldn't be a proper ordination without some female relative shedding tears of happiness."

Khun Choei whispered back, "And why not? Wouldn't you?"

"Oh, I'd be sobbing out loud—or laughing like crazy—no telling what I might do. Lucky for the son I haven't got."

The ceremony had begun and was proceeding in accordance with the rules laid down over two thousand years ago. Having received instructions from the officiating monk (the *upacha*), the ordinand went out to change into the monk's robe, after which he rehearsed with his tutorial monks the *khu suat*—the answers to the enquiries regarding his fitness to enter the monkhood. While he stood outside the door reciting the Pali phrases Phloi watched him and marvelled. He looked transfigured, she thought. A most beautiful costume, the yellow robe. What it stood for had already bestowed on On an aura of peace and dignity. *"Sadhu!"* she prayed silently. "May he achieve what he is setting out to do. May he find what he has been searching for."

She watched him re-enter the hall and take his position before all the monks; she listened to the question and answer ritual in which he was found eligible to become a monk, and she saw him received into the Sangha. When the time came to make offerings to the new monk she moved forward on her knees, carrying the tray, followed by the others. Now it was she who prostrated herself before him to pay respects—those of a lay person to a *bhikkhu*.

As she did her *krap*, Phloi sent her thoughts to her husband. "Are you happy, Khun Prem? Are you here with me on this happy occasion? I'm very happy. Very happy though very, very tired," she added realistically.

The day after On's ordination, Phloi had a relapse. Her alarmed family, led by Luang Osot, sent for a "modern" doctor, who diagnosed a heart ailment, prescribed a course of treatment, and warned everyone that she must be kept absolutely quiet and free from the least emotional strains.

FIFTY

PHLOI accommodated herself to the family's ministrations without any positive desire to get well. She tried to be an easy patient and on the whole willingly deferred to their wishes, but as she could not bring herself to care whether she was going to live or die she would rather they didn't buy expensive medicine for her. She would prefer to have the money put by for her grandchildren.

One day while she and An were talking about this subject, Khun Sewi was ushered in.

"Just the man I want to see," An said to his brother-in-law, showing him a piece of paper with some lines in English written on it. "You know a lot of people in the pharmaceutical business, don't you? Can they help us get this for Mother? Imported, of course, and the supply has been dwindling steadily."

Sewi glanced at the paper and gave a confident smile. "Your worries are over, Khun Mother," he said. "I am at your service." He nodded at An. "Yes, you've come to the right person, my friend. I'm sure I can get it."

He returned the next day looking pleased with himself. "It was more difficult than I'd expected, but all is well. An obliging friend is willing to let us have it below market price."

"How much?"

"Forty-two hundred baht per ampule."

Phloi's astonishment on hearing this fantastic figure nearly finished off her weak heart. An himself was visibly taken aback. In a rather shaky voice he said, "Thank you, Sewi. I won't decide now because another friend has also been enquiring and I'd like to hear from him first. I'll let you know."

The other smiled understandingly. "Don't take too long, will you? The price may go up again."

An nodded, his face devoid of expression. Later, when alone with Phloi again, he said, "I've known for some time about him and his profiteering friends. They've been buying up all kinds of medical supplies, and I know for a fact they have this medicine in their stock. I could have told him this yesterday but I wanted to test him. I couldn't believe my ears when he named the price. Has the man lost all sense of decency to be doing this to us—to *you* especially? The answer is, yes!"

"In all fairness, " Phloi said, "if it was a business partnership he'd have to consider the others. He couldn't very well give it away free either to us or anybody else."

"He could at least offer it to his Khun Mother at cost, couldn't he? He's made enough money out of his despicable dealings. He's worse than a common thief who knows nothing about filial gratitude."

Phloi did not take it so personally. Her feelings were not hurt but she did feel saddened by the thought that perhaps there really was a general decline in loving compassion among people, that possibly it could be on its way to becoming extinct as a virtue.

As to this forty-two hundred baht stuff, why, it was ridiculous, she said to An. A series of injections would bring the expenditure up to tens of thousands of baht. All for nothing, for she had grave doubts as to its efficacy in so far as the nature of her disease was concerned. She would recover or she would not; either way it would depend on her karma—and the question of the disease taking its own course. So in her opinion, why not be practical and stick to the more common pills and liquid mixtures?

An did not argue with her. He simply went ahead and obtained the medicine, getting it not from his despised brother-in-law but through that other friend he had mentioned.

When he heard about it, Phoem was disgusted. He couldn't believe Sewi could have sunk so low. Then he said, "Never mind. They won't prosper for long, he and his friends. They're laughing now, but one day we'll see them weep—I hope soon."

An laughed mirthlessly. "I think you're going to be disappointed, Uncle. They'll go on prospering, and in the eyes of the world they will have done no wrong."

Phoem shook his head. "But in the eyes of the ghosts and the gods they have committed bad deeds. They will not be allowed to go on doing it with impunity."

"Why not, Uncle? The main thing is to prosper, to succeed. You can lie and cheat and stab people in the back as much as you like but as long as you do it expertly and succeed you can be sure of winning praise and admiration, Uncle. That's our society today."

Phoem stared at his nephew with a mixture of impatience and concern. "You're saying it causes no harm to commit bad deeds. But that can't be!"

"Oh, it causes harm, Uncle, but not to the perpetrators of those deeds, not to Sewi and Company. They don't suffer the conse-quences of what they do. The suffering is done by other people. And if you think you'll be all right because you're honest and sincere and kind, you'd better revise your thinking, Uncle."

"No, no!" Phoem waved his arms about. "You're being too cynical, my boy. Don't get so worked up. This is not a perfect world, I grant you, but I will not have you tell me that there's no justice left in it." He turned to his sister. "What do you say, Mae Phloi?" Phloi was thinking along slightly different lines. "It's dreadful," she said. "This not knowing who's going to suffer for the bad deeds you have committed. The 'me' in this life has no way of knowing who the 'me' in the next life is going to be. If I commit a bad deed and get away with it, who's that unknown innocent 'me' in some unknown future existence who'll have to pay for it?"

"I don't know either, Mae Phloi," Phoem grinned. "Sometimes I'm not even sure who this 'me' is in the present and known existence."

PHLOI'S condition in the ensuing months alternated between remaining virtually the same and taking a perceptible turn for the worse, with the result that she grew tired more easily and became more dependent on others in her movements. This annoyed her, but not to the extent of arousing her will to fight and conquer the lingering ailment. If anything, it made her feel more disheartened with this business of living on and on interminably.

Meanwhile the war was drawing to a close.

Phoem came to see her one day in a state of bubbling excitement. "It won't be long now, my dear girl," he said. A new kind of bomb possessing unheard-of power had been dropped on Japan by the United States, killing hundreds of thousands of people in a matter of minutes. Poor Japan could not be expected to hold out much longer.

"It's the very latest invention in weaponry. They call it the atomic bomb." Phoem spoke with pride, as though it were his own brainchild. "Think of it, Mae Phloi, what we read about in the Ramakien—the Supreme Prommas Arrow that can wipe out an entire army and many other magical weapons—it's come true in real life. What an astounding achievement!"

Phloi was not impressed. This latest man-made object only reminded her of the *fai-pralai-kalpa*, the Fire of Total Annihilation, which was supposed to blaze up and consume the whole universe at some vague date in the far, far future; but she felt more disspirited than ever on hearing Phoem's news.

"Why do we go on killing one another?" She couldn't help asking the unanswerable question. "Those people who fell under your bomb—old people and young children and wives and mothers who weren't doing any fighting—why did they have to be destroyed?"

"A way had to be found to end the war quickly," was Phoem's answer. "And they've found it. If the war continued, more lives would be lost and in the long run the devastation would have been far greater. Look at it that way, Mae Phloi. Now the war will soon end, and those who have survived will have a better world to live in."

"You make it sound so easy, Khun Luang. You tell me of death and destruction and then in the next breath you talk of a better world."

To most citizens of Bangkok the war ended as abruptly as it had started. They woke up one morning to learn that it was over. Just like that. Phloi received the news through her brother. Sporting a broad grin, Phoem strode up to her bedside that morning and announced in a sonorous voice, "No more war, Mae Phloi! The Japs have surrendered." Then he laughed with much amusement. "Actually, it is not quite over. Our *Muang Thai* has not surrendered yet, so we're the only nation left to fight the British and the Americans. What a big power we are!" He stopped laughing, resumed the grin and went on. "The war has ended. Peaceful days are here again. Gives you a marvelous feeling, doesn't it?"

"You must be very happy, Khun Luang," Phloi said, stating the obvious.

"Who wouldn't be, Mae Phloi? Things will get back to normal and we'll live in comfort again."

"Are you sure, Khun Luang?"

And Phoem reprimanded her, "Don't be such a pessimist, Mae Phloi."

In the ensuing months, however, he would remark that her attitude had been somewhat more realistic than his own.

"We're back in peacetime all right," he said to her one day. "But I must say it's different from what I used to dream about when the bombs were dropping." He even allowed himself a sigh or two.

Muang Thai had declared her Declaration of War to be null and void, and while this must have been good for the country in one political way or another it didn't seem to her people to have done much good for their everyday life. Prices continued to soar at an alarming rate. The Japanese troops had left and now the *farang* soldiers had come to replace them. Some people who had gloated at the departure of the former—the "occupying forces"—were now wondering if the latter intended to stay forever. Hailed as liberators in the early days of peace, the *farang*s in uniform had come to be regarded by many local citizens as too boisterous, not to say crude and coarse, for Thai taste. The youngsters along the *khlong*s and in the streets, however, remained neutrally uncritical as always, and went about shouting "Okay! Okay! Thank you! Thank you!" with the same spirit of fun that had generated their previous cries of "Bansai!" and "Arigato!"

"I don't know how to explain it," Phoem said on another occasion. "But after hating the Japs with a passion I started to pity them when the war was over—they looked so mournful, you know. And now that they're gone I even miss them. The truth of the matter is, I'm tired of looking at these *farang* soldiers."

An laughed. "You're not the only one, Uncle. Times have changed. During the war we used to sneak food to the *farang* soldiers. The whole trainload of Thais passing Ban Pong were always tossing fruit and sweets and cigarettes to the *farang*s working on the railroad, remember? Then the Japs became prisoners in their turn and we Thais without much ado promptly transferred our sympathies to them. It's the Thai compassion for the underdog, Uncle."

"Which is as it should be," Phloi remarked. "When misfortune befalls others, it's our duty to help them. In any case, the *farang*s weren't really our enemy, nor were the Japanese, when you come to think of it. The whole sad affair had nothing to do with us."

"Another declaration nulling and voiding everything!" Phoem exclaimed laughing. "We were at war these past years. Now she says it had nothing to do with us!"

The end of the war had also created new sets of winners and losers among those Thai personalities who had been jockeying for positions of power and glory. Phloi heard the latest stories about them from Phoem, who paid her a chatty visit nearly every day, but they did not interest her very much. She felt too old to care—and she had never been greatly concerned with either politics or the quest for power.

But one day Phoem came not to gossip about politicians but to give her the news that the king was to return home from Switzerland. He had correctly guessed that this was something to make her sit up and take notice. In fact it did much more than that. It made her come alive, and she delighted her brother by starting to talk with a great deal of excitement. The last time she had seen the king—how long ago was it? She could not remember the date, but the picture had remained vivid in her memory. A boy in short pants. Adorable! Only a boy, but oh so radiant, so full of poise and graceful beyond his years. She speculated on how tall and handsome he must be by now. She couldn't wait to get a good look at him. She hoped not to die before his arrival. And so on. Phoem went away that time quite satisfied with the result of his visit.

And from that day onwards she began to get better. Watching her progress towards recovery, her family all agreed it was quite miraculous; but even so, the week before the king was due to arrive, when she told An she wished to go out and welcome the king on the day of his return, he said no. There would be such crowds everywhere, he said, and it would be too tiring for her. She might have another relapse.

"No—no!" Phloi shook her head vigorously. "I've never felt so well, my son. Let me have my way just this once. Do me this favour and arrange for us to be somewhere where we can watch him go past and pay our homage. That's all I ask."

An yielded in the end. "All right, all right! I'd better see to it then . . . A friend of mine has a place in Ratchadamnoen. I can ask him. Yes, I think we can wait there quite comfortably. We'll take our own refreshments—and your medicine, of course . . . Well, Mother, you'll get to the see the king."

"Oh thank you, son! And we must have Choi with us. You'll fetch her from the palace, won't you? I know she'll have plenty of opportunity to see the king while he's here, but I'm sure she'll want to come out and join our party so that we can celebrate together!"

On the day of the king's return Phloi took a ferryboat to the Bangkok side, accompanied by An, Somchai, Phuang, the grandchildren and several members of her household staff, and fully equipped with food, drinks and medical supplies. The baskets containing these things made An laugh as he surveyed them.

"Ah, Mother, I see you're taking us on a trip lasting a whole week!"

Phloi laughed with him. "It does look like that, doesn't it? But there are so many of us, son. It's better to be well prepared."

They got to the shop belonging to An's friend on Ratchadamnoen Avenue well ahead of time but were by no means the only group to arrive early. The pavements were filling up fast everywhere. Phloi looked round, caught herself smiling at strangers as her eyes met theirs. But no, they're not strangers, she thought. They are Nai Luang's loyal subjects like me. We're here together to welcome him home. He belongs to us all—young, old, rich, poor—belongs to us as Nai Luang and as one of the family. He is both one of us and the one above us. We've been bereft for so long but now we'll have him back with us, with his Gracious Power to reign over us. We can take heart again. Those lost opportunities of the war years—we'll recover them with him. Those mistakes we made—we'll correct them with him. What a glorious day this is!

Some might say Phloi was making large demands on her Nai Luang. Too large. He was, after all a human being like the rest of us. Don't turn him into a Super Spirit, Phloi. This Gracious Power, this Phra Barami, is but another conventional phrase, as lovely as it may sound. But to Phloi there was no doubt about the reality of the goodness emanating from Phra Barami. She felt it in her heart as she saw it reflected in the faces of her fellow citizens shining with happiness and goodwill, washed clean of all malignity. What else but Phra Baramee has brought this about? she asked. It may be impossible to explain to people who have not experienced being touched by its glow, but to those who have, no explanation is necessary.

Now Phloi broke into another smile as she caught sight of the person to whom she certainly had no need to explain. Here came Choi, elbowing her way through the crowd. Choi came up panting and demanding a glass of ice-cold water.

"Oh, isn't this exciting!" she said after having taken a sip. "I've never seen such a big crowd—it's amazing! But are you sure you ought to be here, Phloi? I worry about you."

"Don't. I'm all right. But even if I weren't, I still would have come. Nothing could have kept me away."

"You and me both, Phloi! Oh, how I love him, this Nai Luang of mine—the first Nai Luang I ever dared love without feeling intimidated, overcome with awe—oh, you know what I mean—I've said it all before. I feel so close to him. Because of his youth, you think? Or could it be that I've gone democratic at long last? Hey, don't you laugh at me, An! What's so funny—you consider me too old for your new-fangled democracy?"

They went on chatting for a while, then were plunged into the general commotion. The moment the crowd had been waiting for was drawing near. No sign of the motorcade yet but it couldn't be too far away. People who had been seated were now standing. Some had run out to look and were now running back to reclaim their places. Others were pushing forward in the hope of squeezing into the front lines at the last minute. Phloi kept still. In front of her spread a sea of heads and shoulders but she had practiced standing on tiptoe and knew she would be able to see past them well enough. A few more minutes passed. The sound of "*Chaiyo!*" could be heard now, faintly at first, becoming gradually louder. Phloi stood up as tall as she could make herself. The cheering grew increasingly louder and then the royal car appeared, moving slowly, the royal standard fluttering in the breeze. Phloi's heart was racing and she placed her hands on it. Then she saw him, with his younger brother by his side. He waved and smiled, and was gone. He has such a gentle smile, Phloi thought. Our beloved Nai Luang. Long may he reign over us! She was crying, as were many women and men on the pavement in front of her.

She turned her head in search of Choi, wanting to share this moment with a kindred soul. But Choi was not there. In fact all her party had disappeared, with the lone exception of An who was eyeing her with some anxiety. Phloi asked about the others and was told they had all run out into the street.

"And Choi, where is she?"

An laughed. "She was the first to dash out . . . Look, over there! Can you see?"

Phloi could, and laughed at what she saw with affection and admiration. "Your Aunt Choi is indestructible," she said. "Eternal youth, that's what she has."

When the royal car had passed out of sight, Choi came back and announced that she was going to collapse. "Another glass of water, dearest Mae Phloi! Quick, quick, save my life and make merit."

Phloi handed her the glass, chuckling. "When are you going to start acting your age? You could have been trampled to death—you know that? What possessed you to go out and dance in the street anyway? We could see perfectly well from up here."

"Now stop scolding like an old woman, Khunying Phloi! Frankly,

I'll never know myself how I ever got out there. Oh, how beautiful he looked! If I were sixteen I would have galloped along with the car right up to the palace gate. But did you see those young girls, Phloi? They were jumping up and down and screaming—"

"I didn't see them but I saw you and you were jumping up and down and *chaiyo*-ing so loud that Nai Luang must have thought you were mad!"

"Was I—really? Imagine that! Well, Phloi, it's like that line in the old verse: 'Lovely lasses and grey-haired crones, he enchants them all!' Oh Phloi, how I wish you were still with us in the Inner Court. Nai Luang is going to reside at Borom Phiman Hall, you know. We could be watching out for him together, like we used to for his royal grandfather, remember? It's going to be marvellous, Phloi. We'll have life and colour again after these many drab years."

"But I hear he'll have to go back to Switzerland again. Now, I don't like that at all. I wish he'd stay here for good."

"Oh, we'll have fun celebrating his return once again. Phloi, do you remember the first royal return from Europe—the masked dance in Sanam Luang, the parties in the Grand Palace, the clothes we wore, how excited we were?"

"I'll never forget it, Choi. Never."

"So many, many years ago. Yet sometimes it does seem like yesterday. And do you remember the time when—?" The two women went on reminiscing until An said it was time to go home. Before bidding goodbye, Choi said rather smugly, "All in all, Phloi my dear, I think we've had a good life you and I."

SINCE that day Nai Luang became the main topic of Bangkok conversation. It was easy to see why. This or that other topic might cause tension, induce discord, or increase your worries, but when the theme was Nai Luang you could chat on and on in easy harmony. During the early weeks he was talked about because he was news; as time went on he continued to be talked about because he was good news—the best news the people had had since his last visit, in fact. He was their rediscovered source of hope and joy that had been in ort supply for so long. They felt hopeful when telling one another what they had heard and read about him, and if they had seen him in person they talked about it for days on end. They talked about his kingly virtues and his loveable qualities. We were full of confidence that his was destined to be a glorious reign.

Phloi said to Phoem she had never known anything like it. The Thai people had loved their king before, and loyalty to the throne had always been deep in their hearts and minds. But they had never revealed their feelings with so much openness and enthusiasm and in such jubilant spirit as they were doing now; and Phloi, who felt possessive towards her young Nai Luang even while she held him in great reverence, exulted in his triumph.

So despite her indifferent health those were happy months for Phloi. What did it matter if she would never recover completely? She was content not to be bedridden and to be able to move about and do small chores. With one son leading the good life of a monk and another a responsible family man holding an important position in government, what more could a mother wish for? True, Praphai was not getting along too well with Khun Sewi, but she seemed more mature these days and could be trusted not to do anything rash. If Ot had been alive . . . No, Phloi was still unable to think of him calmly, but she had learned to live with this sorrow as she had with her physical malady. Both had become part of her life.

Days went by, with no special event taking place to disturb the quiet rhythm of that life. Very soon now the king would be leaving. He was to return to Switzerland to complete his studies. Phloi still wished he could have stayed with his people but drew comfort from the fact that this time he would not be gone for very long.

That Sunday morning in June, Phloi was chatting with An and keeping an eye on her grandson when Phoem appeared in the doorway. She opened her mouth to ask what was the matter as he was looking so distraught, but he spoke first.

"Mae Phloi—An—" His voice shook and his lips were twitching. "Terrible news—the king is dead—"

"WHAT!?" Phloi shrieked. "What are you saying? Where did you pick up the rumour? You mustn't—"

"I was in the shop in front of the Grand Palace," Phoem spoke as if he had not heard her, "having a cup of coffee. Everybody was talking about it."

Ah—coffee shop rumours! Phloi breathed a sigh of relief. But she was furious with whoever had concocted and gone about spreading such an inauspicious story. How could they be so thoughtless and irreverent! And the most infuriating thing was that her own brother should be taking this idle talk to heart. She was upset, nonetheless, and was not sorry to have Phoem go away, taking An and the child with him. The two men would no doubt go off to trace this—this rumour.

"It's true, Mae Phloi," Phoem said in a tearful voice before leaving. But Phloi held on to her disbelief for as long as she could.

Choi came to her about one o'clock, a grieving figure in black, straight from the palace. She gave Phloi certain details about the king's death, details which were devastating beyond words.

They mourned him together. They wept quietly, but most of the time they sat in stunned silence. It was growing darker outside, and into the silent room came the sound of the wind and the birds, and of someone crying as though his heart would break. Then it was time for Choi to go back to the palace. There'd be a thousand things to do, she said, and she'd have to hurry. Choi the eternal Inner Courtier rushing back to her post. Dear, dear Choi—

When Choi was gone, Phloi rose to her feet. She felt deeply tired and went to lie down on her bed. She must rest. She had a great longing for rest and sleep. She would close her eyes and think of nothing. But before sleep finally came certain thoughts, confused and blurred, did flit through some part of her mind. Had it really happened? But how could it be? What gods or demons, what dark powers of the universe had allowed this to come to pass? What devious course of karma? Why did Nai Luang have to die? Why did Ot have to die? Dearest beloved son, and sovereign. Death could reach Ot easily—he had been nobody special. But how did death penetrate the thick walls and the royal guards to strike in the bed chamber? Where are you, Khun Prem? Help me to understand . . . It's all right, my love, never mind

... I begin to understand a little ... But I'm so tired. I've lived under four reigns—lived a long time—long enough ...

It was in the late afternoon of that Sunday, the ninth of June 1946, when the tide was low in Khlong Bang Luang, that Phloi's heart stopped beating and her transient joys and suffering in this life came to an end.

KINGS OF
THE CHAKRI DYNASTY

1. Phra Phutthayotfa (Rama I) 1782–1809
2. Phra Phuttaloetla (Rama II) 1809–1824
3. Phra Nangklao (Rama III) 1824–1851
4. Mongkut (Rama IV) 1851–1868
5. Chulalongkorn (Rama V) 1868–1910
6. Vajiravudh (Rama VI) 1910–1925
7. Prajadhipok (Rama VII) 1925–1935
8. Ananda Mahidol (Rama VIII) 1935–1946
9. Bhumibol Adulyadej 1946–

GLOSSARY

A

ai	familiar term of address for males, usually attached to a name
achan	teacher; professor
akusol	bad, sinful, malicious
apsara	nymph

B

bhikkhu	Theravada Buddhist monk

C

cha	affectionate particle placed after a name, title or kinship term to address someone
cha-em	sweet, edible plant in the family Leguminosae
chaiyo	bravo! hurrah!
champa	Magnoliaceae tree with orange or cream-colored flowers
chan	I, me
chan-ap	Chinese sweets
chang	old Thai monetary unit equivalent to 80 baht
chao chom	a lesser concubine of the king
chao kha	polite ending used by women
chao khun	a man with the conferred rank of *phraya* or *chao phraya*
Chao Phraya	river on which Bangkok is situated; also, an honorary title
chedi	stupa or pagoda
chongkraben	a lower garment of a wide strip of cloth with one end twisted and hitched between the legs, now rarely seen

D

dek   child

E

ee   familiar term of address for females, usually attached to a name

F

farang   foreign, Western; also, foreigner from the West

fuang   old Thai monetary unit equivalent to half a *satang*

G

godown   warehouse

K

kabot   revolt, rebellion, treason

kathin   annual festival after the rainy season during which new robes are presented to the monks

kha   polite

khamoi   thief, burglar

khanom chin   Thai rice noodles, eaten with various spicey sauces

khieo kratae   white, sweet-scented flower of the family Rubiaceae

khinari   mythical half-bird, half-man creature

khlon   female palace guard

khlong   canal

khon   people, person; Thai masked dance-drama

khon Thai   Thai people

khun   form of address roughly corresponding to Mr. or Ms.

khunying   title for the wife of a man conferred with the rank of Phraya

khwan   one's guardian spirit or psyche

khong wong   an instrument consisting of tuned gongs set in a circular frame

krathong   floats made of banana leaves carrying flowers, incense and candles that are sent out into the river during the *Loi Krathong* festival

krap   to prostrate oneself in obeisance

L

lakhon	drama
lamduan	flower of the family Annonaceae
liphao	a kind of grass used to weave baskets
Loi Krathong	full moon festival of thanksgiving to the water spirits
luang	second lowest conferred title for government officials
lung	uncle

M

mae	mother; formerly also used as a title in front of the first names of girls
maem	term for Caucasian women
mai pen rai	common phrase meaning "It doesn't matter."
mak	much, many, very
metta	kindness, mercifulness
muang	town, city, country, used before the proper name
muang nok	foreign country, usually outside Asia; abroad
Muang Thai	Thailand

N

naga	legendary serpent
Nai Luang	popular name for the king
nak	term for a man entering the priesthood
nam pla	fish sauce
nam phrik	chili sauce
nang	title placed before the first name of a married woman
niello	ornamental design incised in metal which is filled with a black metallic alloy
ngan	work; party

P

pa	aunt
phalai	flower-patterned cloth worn as a *phanung*
Pali	scriptural and liturgical language of Theravada Buddhism
phaendin	kingdom, reign

phakhaoma	a long strip of plaid cloth worn and used by men for various purposes
phanung	a lower garment of a wide strip of cloth with one end twisted and hitched between the legs, now rarely seen
phasin	a sarong-like lower garment worn by women
phi	term for older brother or sister
piphat	band
phleng yao	rhyming love poem
phlu	betel
pho	father; formerly also used as a title in front of the first names of boys and young men
Phra Abhidharma	chant
Phra Chao Yu Hua	king
Phra Ratchaya	royal consort
Phramen	Phra Meru, the grounds in Bangkok used for special ceremonies, including the cremation of members of the royal family
phraya	honorific title of nobility
phudi	person of nobility or wealth
phuyai	grownup or elder
pi	a wind instruments
plai	a kind of herbal medicine

R

Ramakien	Thai version of the Ramayana, the Hindu epic myth
ranat ek	traditional xylophone
rian nangsu	to go to school; to learn to read and write

S

sabai	easy, comfortable, without illness or difficulty
sabai di ru	How are you?
sadet	princess; also, to go, for royalty
sadhu	amen
sakkrawa	a type of witty, spoken verse, composed spontaneously

sala	pavilion used as a shelter, for rest and relaxation; a hall
salung	Thai monetary unit equivalent to twenty-five *satang* (1/4 of a baht)
samlo	three-wheeled vehicle, with pedaller in front and passenger seat in rear
Sanam Luang	See *Phramen*
sanuk	fun, entertaining, amusing
satang	Thai monetary unit, 100 of which equal one baht
sawaddi	term of greeting or farewell
sawanakhot	to go to heaven [used for royalty]
si	four
sinsae	Chinese term for respected teacher or doctor
sok	leaf
somdet	term used in certain royal titles
Songkran	Thai New Year (April 13–15)

T

tham khwan	to perform a ceremony in order to encourage or strengthen
tham khwan nak	ordination ceremony for Thai monks
tamlung	Thai monetary unit equivalent to four baht
than	you; polite title similar to Excellency
than phuying	highest ranking title for women

U

ubekkha	equanimity, one of the four states strived for in Buddhist practice

V

Vimanmek	palace in Bangkok

W

wai	placing the palms of the hands together and bowing the head slightly as a gesture of greeting or respect
wat	Buddhist temple
wathanatham	culture